The Tales of
HENRY JAMES

1875.

A

PASSIONATE PILGRIM,

AND OTHER TALES.

BY

HENRY JAMES, Jr.

BOSTON:
JAMES R. OSGOOD AND COMPANY,
Late Ticknor & Fields, and Fields, Osgood, & Co.
1875.

Title page of Henry James's first published book which was also his first collection of tales. Five of the tales gathered in the present volume first received book status in this collection.

The Tales of
HENRY JAMES

VOLUME TWO
1870–1874

EDITED BY
MAQBOOL AZIZ

CLARENDON PRESS
OXFORD
1978

Oxford University Press, Walton Street, Oxford OX2 6DP

OXFORD LONDON GLASGOW NEW YORK TORONTO MELBOURNE WELLINGTON
KUALA LUMPUR SINGAPORE JAKARTA HONG KONG TOKYO DELHI BOMBAY
CALCUTTA MADRAS KARACHI IBADAN NAIROBI DAR ES SALAAM CAPE TOWN

Oxford University Press 1978

British Library Cataloguing in Publication Data

James, Henry
    The tales of Henry James.
    Vol. 2: 1870–1874.
    I. Title II. Aziz, Maqbool
    813'.4   PS2110   78-40251

    ISBN 0-19-812572-0

*Printed in Great Britain by
Richard Clay (The Chaucer Press) Ltd
Bungay, Suffolk*

ACKNOWLEDGEMENTS

I HAVE HAD THE PLEASURE OF ACKNOWLEDGING MOST OF my many debts by name in the first volume of this edition. I am fortunate to say that the many friends and colleagues, as well as university libraries and similar other agencies, who helped me then have continued to show interest in the edition, for which I continue to be grateful to them.

I take this opportunity to thank, in particular, the University Library at Princeton for permission to use manuscript material in the Scribner Archive; the Houghton Library at Harvard for permission to use manuscript material in three of their collections: the James Family Papers, the Papers of W. D. Howells and the Papers of J. R. Lowell; the British Library for permission to quote from the Macmillan Archive; the Harvard University Press, Cambridge, Massachusetts, for permission to quote from the first volume of their edition of *Henry James Letters*, so excellently edited by Dr. Leon Edel.

Though no longer with the Oxford University Press, my friend Professor Jon Stallworthy's interest in the edition has been a source of encouragement to me. The distinguished James scholar, Mr. Simon Nowell-Smith's generous interest in my work has been, as ever, a source of strength and encouragement.

I am grateful to the Canada Council for a sabbatical award which made it possible for me to complete this volume and advance work on those to come. To my colleagues, Dr. Brian John, Dr. Michael Ross, and Dr. Graham Roebuck, I owe thanks for suggestions on some matters of detail, and for help of other kinds.

My very special thanks must once again go to Bushi, Ali, Deena, and Maya.

CONTENTS

REFERENCES AND ABBREVIATIONS

A Passionate Pilgrim	Henry James, *A Passionate Pilgrim and Other Tales* (Boston: James R. Osgood and Company, 1875).
The Madona of the Future	Henry James, *The Madonna of the Future and Other Tales*, 2 volumes (London: Macmillan and Company, 1879).
The Siege of London	Henry James, *The Siege of London; The Point of View; A Passionate Pilgrim* (Leipzig: Bernhard Tauchnitz, 1884).
Stories Revived	Henry James, *Stories Revived*, 3 volumes (London: Macmillan and Company, 1885).
Letters	*The Letters of Henry James*, 2 volumes, ed. Percy Lubbock (New York: Charles Scribner's Sons, 1920).
Life in Letters	*Life in Letters of William Dean Howells*, ed. Mildred Howells (New York: Doubleday, Doran, 1928; reprinted, 1968, by Russell and Russell). Quotations are from the edition of 1968.
The Art of the Novel	*The Art of the Novel*, Critical Prefaces by Henry James, with an Introduction by R. P. Blackmur (New York: Charles Scribner's Sons, 1934). Quotations are from the paperback edition of 1962.
Bibliography	Leon Edel and Dan H. Laurence, *A Bibliography of Henry James* (London: Rupert Hart-Davis, 1957; revised, 1961). References are to the edition of 1961.
Henry James Letters	*Henry James Letters*, vol. i, 1843–1875, ed. Leon Edel (Cambridge, Massachussetts: Harvard University Press, 1974).

Atlantic	The *Atlantic Monthly*.
Review	The *North American Review*.
Scribner's	The *Scribner's Monthly Magazine*.
MS. (Harvard).	(*a*) Collection of the James Family Papers in the Houghton Library, Harvard University;
	(*b*) Collection of the Papers of William Dean Howells;
	(*c*) Collection of the Papers of James Russell Lowell.
MS. (British Library).	The Macmillan Archive in the British Library (the British Museum).
MS. (Princeton).	The Scribner Archive in the Princeton University Library.

COLLECTED EDITIONS OF JAMES'S TALES AND NOVELS

Collective Edition	Collective Edition of 1883, 14 volumes (London: Macmillan and Company, 1883). 13 tales were included in their first revised state.
New York Edition	*The Novels and Tales of Henry James*, 'New York Edition', 24 volumes (New York: Charles Scribner's Sons, 1907–9). 55 tales were included in this 'definitive' edition, for which James heavily revised the tales for the last time.
	The Novels and Stories of Henry James, 35 volumes, ed. Percy Lubbock (London: Macmillan and Company, 1921–3). 95 tales were included in a variety of textual states.
	The Complete Tales of Henry James, 12 volumes, ed. Leon Edel (London: Rupert Hart-Davis, 1962–4). The text follows the first book editions.

[In bits and pieces, a few of the manuscript letters quoted in this volume have been published in various studies of James: since these are not regular collections of letters, I have referred the reader to the sources in manuscript collections.

The original, mildly incorrect form of the title of the tale, 'Mme. De Mauves', is preserved in all references to its magazine text; but the corrected 'Madame de Mauves' is used where the immediate point of reference is the revised text.]

THE COMPLETE TALES:
A CHRONOLOGICAL LIST

THE 112 TALES OF HENRY JAMES ARE LISTED BELOW IN order of their first publication. The original form of the titles is mentioned. The place and date of publication for each tale is given against the title. A brief parenthetical note identifies the works James did not serialize in magazines but first published in a collection or a book edition. The starred tales were included in the new York edition.

1. 'A Tragedy of Error'	*The Continental Monthly*	(1864)
2. 'The Story of a Year'	*The Atlantic Monthly*	(1865)
3. 'A Landscape Painter'	(1866)	
4. 'A Day of Days'	*The Galaxy*	(1866)
5. 'My Friend Bingham'	*The Atlantic Monthly*	(1867)
6. 'Poor Richard'	(1867)	
7. 'The Story of a Master-piece'	*The Galaxy*	(1868)
8. 'The Romance of Certain Old Clothes'	*The Atlantic Monthly*	(1868)
9. 'A Most Extraordinary Case'	(1868)	
10. 'A Problem'	*The Galaxy*	(1868)
11. 'De Grey: A Romance'	*The Atlantic Monthly*	(1868)
12. 'Osborne's Revenge'	*The Galaxy*	(1868)
13. 'A Light Man'	(1869)	
14. 'Gabrielle De Bergerac'	*The Atlantic Monthly*	(1869)
15. 'Travelling Companions'	(1870)	
*16. 'A Passionate Pilgrim'	(1871)	
17. 'At Isella'	*The Galaxy*	(1871)
18. 'Master Eustace'	(1871)	
19. 'Guest's Confession'	*The Atlantic Monthly*	(1872)
*20. 'The Madonna of the Future'	(1873)	
21. 'The Sweetheart of M. Briseux'	*The Galaxy*	(1873)
22. 'The Last of the Valerii'	*The Atlantic Monthly*	(1874)

INTRODUCTION

1.

DURING HIS LONG AND RICHLY VARIED CAREER HENRY
James published 112 works of short fiction varying in length between
seven and fifty thousand words. All were called 'tales' by James. It
was with one of these that he launched himself as a writer in 1864;
and it was with a collection of these that, a decade later, he made his
first book, *A Passionate Pilgrim*. More than five decades after his first
published tale, the work which closed his career as a writer of fiction
was also a collection of reprinted short stories, *The Uniform Tales of
Henry James*.[1] The first volume of this work appeared in 1915, less
than a year before his death. There are only eight years in the forty-
six years of his story-telling when he did not publish any tale. More
than two dozen of the many volumes of fiction published by James
are selections or collections of tales. The 'shorter form', then, 'the
beautiful and blest *nouvelle*', the 'small circular frame',[2] was no
diversion from novel writing: 'to write a series of good little tales'
was, young James once told C. E. Norton, 'ample work for a lifetime.'[3]

All but nine of the 112 tales were originally published in thirty-
four different periodicals on both sides of the Atlantic. Most were
given book status by James himself, some receiving the honour more
than once, in the collections which he issued from time to time. Only
fifty-five stories, however, found their way into the 'definitive' New
York Edition. Many—but not all—of the pieces 'rejected' were re-
surrected by Percy Lubbock in his edition of *The Novels and Stories
of Henry James*. The tales included there number ninety-five. The

---

[1] (London: Martin Secker, 1915-20.) The New York Edition text of thirteen,
and one newly revised tale, are reproduced in this collection in fourteen separate volumes.

[2] These and several other terms are used by James to describe his fictions
which do not qualify as novels. But within 'the shorter form' there are other
finer distinctions; these are explored and stated in the Prefaces to the volumes
of tales in the New York Edition. The Prefaces are also available in a separate
volume, *The Art of the Novel*.

[3] Letter of 16 January 1871, to C. E. Norton. *Henry James Letters*, p. 253.
In a letter to R. L. Stevenson, dated 31 July 1888, James reiterated his faith
in the shorter form. He told Stevenson that after *The Tragic Muse*, which he
was then writing for the *Atlantic*, 'with God's help, I propose, for a longish
period, to do nothing but short lengths. I want to leave a multitude of pictures
of my time, projecting my small circular frame upon as many different spots
as possible and going in for number as well as quality, so that the number
may constitute a total having a certain value as observation and testimony.'
Letters, i, p. 138.

stories first appeared in their entirety in *The Complete Tales of Henry James*, edited by Leon Edel.

It was James's lifelong practice to revise his magazine writings for book publication and, not infrequently, the book texts for subsequent reprintings. As a result, most of the tales, as well as many novels and other prose writings, now exist in multiple versions.[4] This textual multiplicity is an aspect which no serious student of James can afford to ignore.[5] In the existing state of the texts, when the multiple versions are scattered in old periodicals and early collections of the stories, it is not easy to assemble different versions of a work together for comparison and examination. This new edition of the tales is designed to meet this difficulty. Its principal aim is to provide the reader with a chronologically consistent text of the tales, together with a complete record of substantive textual variants for the stories revised.

The copy-text for the present edition is the original, serial text of the tales. For those James did not serialize the edition will reprint *their* original form in the book editions. The decision to reprint the original versions has been influenced by a variety of factors which I shall now try to explain. But I should first like to attempt a brief survey of the present state of the texts, and of the problems that are likely to confront an editor looking for a suitable basic text for a complete chronological edition.

The texts of James's tales are available in the following forms:

A. Manuscripts and typescripts—only seven tales appear to have survived in this form.[6]

B. The serial versions—all but nine tales are available in this state.

C. Manuscript revisions—one complete manuscript revision of a tale and a half-finished revision appear to have survived.[7]

D. The first authorized book versions—eighty-seven tales are available in this state. Most are revised forms of the serial versions.

E. Revised reprints (excluding the New York Edition) of the first

---

[4] It is difficult to decide when a new edition of a text becomes a separate version. For the purpose of this essay, however, any new edition of a tale showing substantive variants introduced by James constitutes a new version.

[5] See 'Henry James Reprints' [by Simon Nowell-Smith], the *Times Literary Supplement*, 5 February 1949, p. 96; and my paper ' "Four Meetings": A Caveat for James Critics' in *Essays in Criticism*, xviii (July 1968), pp. 258–74.

[6] See the *Bibliography*, pp. 390–3.

[7] The only complete manuscript revision of a tale to have survived is that of 'A Light Man'. The incomplete manuscript revision which has been preserved is that of 'At Isella'. This item is not mentioned in the *Bibliography*, but I found six heavily revised magazine pages of the tale in the Houghton Library. One of the pages is reproduced in the first volume of this edition as an illustration.

book versions—over two dozen tales are available in this state.

F. The New York Edition—fifty-five tales were included in this definitive edition.

If we disregard categories A and C, which are of no relevance to the present purpose, we are left with four categories to choose from. All carry James's authority. As three of the four (D, E, and F) do not represent all the tales, they may be considered only as *possible bases* for a copy-text.

Viewed from the author's own point of view, the question as to which of the four has the greater authority poses no serious difficulty. In the New York Edition James has given us a 'definitive' edition of his fiction: if his own wishes are to be respected, then the text of the tales in that edition is the one which the editor is obliged to reprint. In other words, if the New York Edition texts are being used as the basis, a new edition of the tales would reprint fifty-five works in that text and the remaining fifty-seven in *their* final form. On the face of it this seems a perfectly sensible approach. But there is an inherent contradiction in it. If the principle behind such a policy is to respect the author's own final plan, then common sense would demand that it be accepted in full—in all its detail. The New York Edition is what it is because of three closely interrelated factors: its particular thematic design, the exclusions and rejections which are an integral part of that design, and the extensive revisions specially carried out to give the whole an overall unity of style and structure.[8] The editor cannot claim superior authority for the definitive text without also accepting the principles of exclusion and revision which give the definitive text that authority. In practical terms, he cannot, without violating James's intention, give the rejected tales the status the author himself wished to deny them.

It could be argued that James excluded many of his stories not because he thought they were of inferior quality, but because he did not have space for them, or they did not seem to belong in the grand design he had in mind. For some tales not included this might well have been the case. However, we do know that the number of volumes for the edition was decided upon by James himself, and he was quite perturbed when his original choice of twenty-three came to be twenty-four.[9] It is difficult to believe that James was not aware of the implications of the limit he so insistently wanted to impose upon

[8] See Leon Edel, 'The Architecture of Henry James's "New York Edition" ', the *New England Quarterly*, xxiv (June 1951), pp. 169–78; as well as the note on the New York Edition below.

[9] Ibid., pp. 177–8. (On this matter, see also the Scribner letter to James below.)

the final edition. The limit was, indeed, partly dictated by the fact that he simply could not reread some of his early works.[10] Therefore, it cannot be denied that critical judgement—'the whole growth of one's "taste" ', as James put it[11]—played a large role in his decision to limit the number of stories to be included to fifty-five.

The selections made, James proceeded to consolidate the exclusive design of his plan by giving the selected works a uniform style. The stories and novels, especially of the early and middle periods, were so drastically revised for the edition that, in matters of detail, their 'definitive' form bears little relation to their original, in which many had first seen the light several decades before the New York Edition. The final revision is thus a case of 'renewals of vision', the 'exploring tread' taking the author, not back over 'the original tracks', but forcing him to 'break the surface in other places'.[12]

In short, the form in which the fifty-five tales have been revised and arranged in the definitive edition places them in a class by itself from which, if the wishes of the designer of the edition are to be respected, they may not be disengaged. In any case, the problem of textual and chronological inconsistency is not resolved if we decide to reprint one tale in the high manner of the final phase, one in the 'middle style', and one in its early unrevised state—which is precisely the form the new edition would take with the definitive texts as its textual basis.

This latter difficulty stays with us when we turn to an alternative possibility: an edition based on the final versions of the revised tales —categories E and D—but excluding the New York Edition. As the number of tales to have undergone two separate revisions prior to the definitive edition is rather small, such an edition would once again end up with a text in three different states. Some stories will appear in their unrevised state, some in their first (and only) revised form, and some in their second revised form. The stylistic difference, however, will not be as great now as it might be with the New York Edition joining in. The one advantage of this approach is that it strikes a good compromise: while allowing the definitive edition its special status, it offers the tales in a text which would have been their final had James not embarked upon a definitive edition of his writings. The major drawback of this approach, as we have said, is that it too cannot cope with the chronological problem. Also, like the definitive texts, the second revised versions, as well as the first, of some tales are far removed from their originals.

For a revised copy-text, the first book versions—category D—seem

---

[10] Ibid., p. 172.   [12] Ibid., p. 336.
[11] *The Art of the Novel*, p. 340.

to offer a more satisfactory alternative. The arguments in favour of this text are the obvious ones. Other than the serial form, this is the text in which *most* tales are available in a theoretically uniform state. And in this state the revised works have had the benefit of a revision. An edition based on the first book versions would, therefore, be a much simpler, and, in a sense, more logical affair. A great many of the tales would appear in it in their first (and only) revised form, and some in their unrevised form—only two different texts. But this apparently simple policy is not without its problems, which begin to crop up when we examine the character of the first revision in particular cases. To take one example, James revised and reprinted 'The Romance of Certain Old Clothes' (1868) in his first collection of tales, *A Passionate Pilgrim* (1875). Some years later he revised the 1875 text and reprinted the story in *Stories Revived* (1885).[13] Now, if our reason for reprinting the text of 1875 is that in that form the tale has had the benefit of revision then we must be using the term in a very restricted sense, to mean 'mild alteration'. For the text of 1875 is far more a case of small alterations in several places than of revision proper; it is the text of 1885 which gives us a revised text in any significant sense of the term. If, however, we argue that 'mild alteration' is precisely the sense in which we are applying the term, then what are we to do with tales like 'A Light Man', or 'Poor Richard', the first revised form of which, appearing more than a decade after first publication, is radically different from their original? So it is only in theory that this textual policy promises to offer the whole corpus in two different textual states. In actual fact, because of the varying scale of the first revisions, the final design of an edition based on the first book versions would not be any different from the possibilities considered above.

We may now turn to the last of the four possibilities—category B—the first published versions. This is the only form in which *all* of James's writings are available in an historically, chronologically, and textually uniform state—in which, that is, the texts of the tales are simply there in their right, original order. From a strictly historical point of view, this is the only entirely satisfactory alternative for a complete edition of the tales. Yet, obviously, if we apply the authorial point of view here, as we did while considering the New York Edition texts, it is not. For we cannot now decide to go against James's wishes and select the original form of a work which has been revised by him.

The moral to be drawn from the foregoing is that, if we are look-

---

[13] See the first volume of this edition.

ing for a copy-text which does not present any chronological difficulties, has been revised and re-revised to the author's complete satisfaction, does no violence to any other of his plans and intentions,
conveys a sense of development, etc., is, in short, satisfactory on all
counts, then we are not likely to find one in the maze of James's
texts. James revised some of his tales only once, some twice, some
three times, and some never at all. The gaps of time, moreover, between different classes of revision, and between the original and revised form, or forms, of individual works range from a month or so
to thirty-five years. The result of this process of 'fingering' has been
a state of textual multiplicity in James to which order can now be
given only by an outside hand.[14]

There are, in the final analysis, three courses open to the editor
of James—or, for that matter, of any constantly revising author—
who wants to make a single-text edition of the tales. All involve the
editor's own judgement, choice, and decision. He can either approach the question from the author's point of view and, disregard-
ing the demands of history and chronology, prepare an edition based
on the final texts; or he can take a purely critical view and, dis-
regarding not only the historical principle but also James's final
revisions, base his edition on the versions he considers (from his
particular point of view) the best; or he can take the historical approach and, completely ignoring the revisions, make an edition based
on the original texts. There is one other solution—and it seems
the ideal possibility. The editor can combine the three approaches
in a 'variant edition' of the works: an edition based on any one
version but providing, within the single framework, all the other
available textual evidence.

It is this last course which I have chosen for this edition. The
decision to use the serial versions of the tales as the basic text for
the edition is based on the theory that the *first published* form, in
manuscript or print, of a multiple-version work is the only one which
may be said to have the 'right' authority. The manuscript, when it
exists, which is not the case with the tales, cannot claim this
authority simply because, essentially, it is the author's message to the
printer, and remains a private document until it is translated into
print and thus allowed to become public. If, however, the author

---

[14] The image comes from James himself. Dencombe, the writer in the tale
'The Middle Years' (1893), 'was a passionate corrector, a fingerer of style; the
last thing he ever arrived at was a form final for himself. His ideal would have
been to publish secretly, and then, on the published text, treat himself to
the terrified revise, sacrificing always a first edition and beginning for posterity
and even for the collectors, poor dears, with a second.'

allows the manuscript to circulate in public in that form then the manuscript would obviously have definite priority.

The revised versions cannot make such a claim for different reasons. The creative activity which originates with the inception of a new idea culminates when, having been realized in the finished artefact, the idea is given to the public. Any authorial alterations or revisions which may appear in a future version of the artefact, following the original event, cannot be considered as anything but the author's second thoughts, his comment and gloss upon the published work. No revision of a published work is ever an integral part of the chain of events which makes up the original creative sequence. All published revisions are, therefore, afterthoughts and represent a consciousness other than the one which created the original work. This last remark is of special significance in a consideration of multiple-version works by James, who carried out his major revisions years after their first publication.

In making these observations, it is of course not my intention to suggest that the revised versions of the tales are in any way inferior in quality, or are less authoritative and representative. The distinction I am proposing is that, while most instances of revision in James make for better literary effects, in his case—as well as in that of any other 'revisionist'—a revised version can be said to possess representative authority only in so far as it represents a new phase of his developing consciousness—'the growth', as James put it, 'of the immense array of terms, perceptional and expressional'.[15] The alterations in the third text of 'The Madonna of the Future', for instance, which came in 1879, small though they are, cannot claim to represent the writer who first issued the tale in 1873. The authority likewise of the text of 1879 is fixed in time. In other words, when an editor is confronted with a multiple-version work, he cannot afford to think of textual authority in any absolute terms—even the so-called final version is a tentative final with a compulsive revisionist. The only textual authority that he can single out and establish is the 'right' authority of the first published version.

In view of all these considerations, and because an historical principle seems to me to be inherent in the idea of a variant edition, I have decided to reprint the serial texts of the tales. It is, for this edition, a happy coincidence that in their original form—the form in which they were known to contemporary readers[16]—most of the tales have never been reprinted before.

---

[15] *The Art of the Novel*, p. 339.
[16] In the first decade of his career, James did not publish any volume and

The serial text is here reprinted without any major editorial inter-ference. All misprints found in the text have been silently corrected. Similarly, missing punctuation marks—for the most part involving commas, hyphens for compound words, quotation marks, etc.—have been supplied where the text appeared to need them. Words and phrases appearing in different spelling, at different places, have been normalized according to current English usage. Full stops after the titles have been deleted. Spaced contractions—*had n't, could n't*, etc., —which, incidentally, disappear in most early book versions but come back in the New York Edition, have also been normalized. Where applicable, the notes about the division of texts into parts, which may have had James's tacit approval but may not have been a feature of the manuscripts, have been preserved. In order to preserve some flavour of James's early treatment of foreign expressions and foreign place-names, no attempt is made to normalize these—or impose consistency where James is inconsistent—according to current usage; however, obvious printing errors in this category have been corrected. English spellings have been substituted for American, and single quotation marks for double. All illustrations accompanying the serial texts will be reproduced.

Since it is difficult to determine the dates of composition for many of the tales, I have decided to follow throughout the chronology of publication. The twelve tales in the present volumes are arranged in the order in which they were first published in magazines. Each tale carries a brief headnote which provides its complete publishing his-tory during James's lifetime. Textual variants for the revised tales in this volume will be found in the textual section. The present volume covers the second phase of James's apprenticeship: it opens with his first 'international' tale and closes with his first major novel.

2.

As a writer James came of age in 1875, with the publication that year of his first two books, *A Passionate Pilgrim* and *Transatlantic Sketches*,[17] and the serialization of his first major novel, *Roderick Hudson*. The magazine writing he had been doing through the

---

was known to his contemporaries as a writer of magazine stories and novels. He continued to reach a wider audience through magazines even after his work began to be reprinted in book editions simply because the magazines had a much larger circulation than any of his collections or book editions.

[17] All items included in these two collections had prior magazine publication in America.

previous decade may be seen as a preparation for the confidence demonstrated in 1875.

The decade neatly divides itself into two phases. During the first of these, 1864-9,[18] James taught himself the craft of writing and, by offering his small 'wares'—book reviews and experimental tales—to magazine editors, made his name known to literary circles of Boston and New York. This accomplished, he decided to go out into the wider, international world to look for a suitable 'subject' for his art. Quite appropriately, he spent the first phase in his native New England, close to the magazines; and the second, 1869-74, largely in England and on the continent of Europe. (No less than nine out of the twelve tales in the present volume are a direct result of the European experience.)

The European harvest of this decade was also gathered in two separate phases. James's first chance to see the Old World as an adult came in February 1869, and his tour lasted until April of the year following. He visited England, France, Switzerland, and Italy, treating himself to a feast of impressions, the most interesting record of which is to be found in the lengthy letters he wrote to his family in New England. Evidently, he did no literary work during these months of travel. It was when he returned to Cambridge that he began to realize the full significance of his recent European experience, and also produced three of his earliest 'international' tales.

However, as it turned out, for James, the significance of Europe was more complex than his quick discovery that the European world, especially in its relation to the American, held an incomparably richer soil for his art than the 'extraordinary cases' of small-town America. In the lively Cambridge letters of 1870-1 to the Nortons, with whom the previous year James had spent some time in England, there emerges a triangular conflict between the rival claims of the 'dear detestable common Cambridge', the 'sylvan seclusion' of the 'untrodden hills and woods' of America (any neglect of which might 'haunt' and 'wrack' the imagination in exile) and, of course, once confronted, the constant presence of Florence 'within'. For James, the problem now was to bring about a happy reconciliation between these warring elements and to make such a reconciliation work as well as pay. By the end of 1871, when he had reflected enough on the relative merits of Europe and America, James was left in no doubt that in one sense or another his literary future lay elsewhere than in America—that, in short, the reconciliation had to be effected. Yet, he also felt that 'the European orange', as well as the American, needed

[18] See the Introduction to the first volume of this edition.

some more squeezing before he would be ready to make the final commitment—which he eventually made in 1875, when he moved permanently to Europe.

So, before too long, he was back in Europe. Together with his sister, Alice, and Aunt Kate, James sailed for England in May 1872. He was supposed to escort the ladies on their tour of Europe; however, while the ladies returned to Cambridge later in the year, James stayed on until the autumn of 1874. He had now come determined to 'squeeze the European orange' in order to see its literary and practical relation to his future as a writer. During this visit, therefore, his eye was keener and more penetrating than had been the case during 1869–70, and his pen was quick to turn to the all-important test. Now he not only observed the European scene but instantly turned his impressions into some memorable portraits of places, and a set of international tales some of which compare favourably with his best productions in the genre. Indeed, packages of his 'wares' would arrive in America with such frequency and regularity that the editors of the Nation, the Galaxy, and the Atlantic could not keep pace with their transatlantic contributor—the Atlantic particularly was 'chronically choked' with them—and his ever-loyal literary agent at home, Henry James Senior, had to find new avenues to place his son's work. When James returned to Cambridge in 1874, his initial impression had been confirmed: the writer in him was at home in Europe than in America. Moreover, as the flow of revenue from his writings could testify, the mode of reconciliation devised in the 'international theme' was not without financial rewards.

For the historian of James's writings, the most remarkable feature of the second phase of his apprenticeship is that, in spite of his transatlantic comings and goings, he managed to produce an astonishingly large body of work. From the day he left Cambridge in 1869 to the end of his second tour in the summer of 1874, he wrote and published one short novel, twelve long tales, forty travel notes, thirty-six book reviews, two short plays, and had completed a large part of Roderick Hudson. All this was accomplished in the short working-time of less than three years. Unfortunately, largely because of the peculiar circumstances in which most of these works were composed by their constantly travelling author, and often dispatched to their destinations in America from across the Atlantic, it is extremely difficult, if not altogether impossible, to give the writings any definite dates of composition. What can be claimed with certainty is that the chronology of their publication as currently known to us does not bear much relation to the actual intervals between the works and the order in which they may have been composed. This alone is

justification enough for the (often conjectural) exercise in dating—
intended to give the twelve tales in the present volume a more probable chronology of composition—which must now follow. We may
begin where this account in the first volume of this edition ends—the
publication of 'Gabrielle De Bergerac' in 1869.

3.

We have already seen how 'Gabrielle De Bergerac', which may be
said to close the first phase of James's apprenticeship, was a great
success. The editor of the *Atlantic*, W. D. Howells, wrote to James
(who was then in Europe) about its popularity;[19] so did Alice, followed by Mrs. James:

what an enthusiasm there is about your last story. I have taken more
pleasure in it than in anything you have ever written. The last part,
darling Harry, was exquisite—Mr. Boott is one of your ardent admirers—
he predicts for you a great future.[20]

While there was, indeed, a prophetic touch to Mr. Boott's enthusiasm, James himself, who had not contributed anything to the
magazines since his departure, took a more critical view of his latest
achievement. He 'groaned and moaned and howled' when he saw the
work in print; he thought his treatment of the past in it was 'amus-
ingly thin and watery';[21] more revealingly, the tale struck him 'as the
product of a former state of being'.[22] Through another remark on the
same work, this state is defined as being one in which the artist is not
in full possession of the 'facts' with which he wants to feed his imagination. For the time being, therefore, James had no desire—and little
time—to capitalize on his first popular success.

Even Howells could not make him change his mind. A few months
after the publication of 'Gabrielle De Bergerac', he wrote to James
about the sorry state of 'Literature' in Boston and asked for a contribution:

Now, you think I've been keeping you from literature [there is other talk
in the opening parts of the letter] long enough. Well there isn't as much
to tell about literature as one at your distance would believe. A new

[19] See the Introduction to the first volume of this edition.

[20] MS. letter (Harvard), 24 July 1869. Mrs. James is referring to a section of
the second part of the tale, and not to the last instalment, for September,
which came late in August: it was common with periodicals to appear on the
stalls a week or so before the due date. Mr. Boott is Francis Boott, an old
friend of the family, whose daughter, Elizabeth, was a friend of James.

[21] Letter to Alice James, 31 August 1869, *Henry James Letters*, pp. 127, 132.

[22] Letter to Mrs. James, 28 June 1869. Ibid., p. 126.

magazine has been started under the editorship of Rev. E. E. Hale, by Hurd and Houghton, called *Old and New*, which has not been enviably good. But it has a chance to grow much better, which isn't the case with A. M. [the *Atlantic*] unless you will write for it. And by the way, why don't you? As the matter goes you're in great danger of having your private letters stolen and published. 'What we want,' says Mr. Fields [the *Atlantic*'s chief editor], with perfect truth, 'is short, cheerful stories'; and our experience of you is quite in that way of fiction. In all seriousness ... I wish you could send us something. Any sketch of what you see or do would be welcome—I'd almost print any art criticism from you ...

In the second part of the letter, added at a later date, Howells goes on to say:

I believe there is little or nothing to tell you about literature. I believe we grow more poverty stricken in that direction every day. Editorially, I have a pretty good survey of the whole field, and the prospect is a discouraging one. The signs of growth are very small and feeble, while there are some striking instances of dwindling. There is no sort of freshness in the things that are sent to us at least.[23]

James must have been amused and flattered to receive this appeal from his admiring friend and publisher in New England. American literature, however, had to wait another few months before the talented writer of tales, who was then feasting upon the glories of European art, would be ready to return and resume the rescue operation.

Equipped with new ideas and impressions, having cultivated, as it were, a new state of being, James returned to Cambridge in May 1870. The first fictional fruit of his new awareness, 'Travelling Companions', saw the light of day within six months after his arrival. There is, thus, a gap of a year between the last tale of his first phase of apprenticeship and the first of the second. What this year of creative abstinence taught James may be seen as a wholly new mode of acquiring material for his fiction. The title itself of the new tale serves as an appropriate metaphor and signpost for this mode. With few exceptions, all his tales and novels of the seventies deal with situations in which, in one sense or another, the central characters are travellers and, disguised or not, the observing eye is often that of the author himself. Needless to say, this set-up has a close parallel in James's own life and preoccupations at the time.[24] He had begun to

[23] MS. letter (Harvard). Howells began this letter on 2 January 1870, and completed it on 6 March.
[24] There is, indeed, a close correspondence between the documentary and the imaginative concerns of James during these years. In many instances, the stories, the letters, and the travel notes complement each other. See also below.

realize that there was only one way he could demonstrate complete command over the subject of his fictions: he must draw upon first-hand experience and observation. The authenticity of feeling, as well as the documentary authenticity, so much in evidence in 'Travelling Companions' and related 'international' tales, but lacking in the stories of 1864-9, is owing entirely to this awareness.

'Travelling Companions' was published in the *Atlantic* in November–December 1870. It was James's last publication for the year and was preceded by a relatively small body of writing—four travel notes on American places which he wrote for the *Nation* and two book reviews. On the face of it, for one like young James, this meagre output would seem to confirm his constant complaint to Grace Norton that 'the dear detestable common Cambridge' had little to stimulate his creative imagination. Such, however, was not the case. Contrary to the impression given by the chronology of his published works, and contrary also to the sentiments conveyed to Grace Norton, James wrote a good deal more than he was able to publish in 1870; and, though it was the last of his pieces to be published that year, 'Travelling Companions' was the first to be written, and submitted for publication, upon his return to Cambridge.

Evidence for these assertions comes from the letters. While no title is mentioned, a letter of 24 September 1870, to James T. Fields, indicates that a story by James was accepted by the *Atlantic* as early as June or July. James wrote to ask for payment:

The *Atlantic* was so good, *a couple of months ago* [italics added], as to accept the m.s. of a story from my pen. May I take the liberty of suggesting through you, that Messrs. F. and F. should send me a cheque in payment at their earliest convenience, instead of awaiting the publication of the story? I should be much obliged to you for your intercession.[25]

Since 'Travelling Companions' is the only fiction by James to be published that year, we can confidently assume the reference is to this work which, in view of James's vague allusion to the date, must have been offered for publication some time in June or July—certainly within two months following his arrival. If we now look at James's activities and movements during the summer, we should be able to give the tale a probable date of composition.

James arrived in the second week of May. Early in June, he left for Saratoga where he stayed for a month; he then went to Pomfret for a fortnight, visited Lake George for a week and spent another

---

[25] *Henry James Letters*, pp. 241-2. This letter is quite definitely of the September of 1870: it could not have originated in any other September.

fortnight at Newport, returning to Cambridge in September. One of
the reasons James undertook this tour was to write short articles on
these places for the *Nation*. We have evidence that James spent the
better part of July and August writing these articles as well as sections of his first novel, *Watch and Ward*.

In fact, he had three of the five instalments of the novel completed
by the end of October—if not before. In its unfinished form, the novel
was accepted by the *Atlantic*. James wanted publication to begin with
the January (1871) number of the magazine, but Fields was against
this. In a letter of 15 November 1870, James told Fields that he would
accept the latter's decision provided he could ' "realize" upon [the
three parts] without delay'.[26] He was, in fact, relieved to find he had
more time to complete the novel than would have been the case with
the January publication. The first instalment of *Watch and Ward*
appeared in the *Atlantic* in August 1871, nine months after these
negotiations and a year after its inception and partial completion.

As James was busy writing these other things in July, August, and
September, we are left with the half of May and June in which to
place 'Travelling Companions': the tale must have been composed
during this period of six or eight weeks. Italy being very much on his
mind then, it was quite natural for him to set his first 'international'
tale in that country.

In a letter of 16 January 1871 James told C. E. Norton that he had
been 'scribbling some little tales which in the course of time [Norton]
will have a chance to read'.[27] The date of the letter is interesting: unless James had some unpublished pieces in the bag, he had no real
reason to speak of 'tales' in that January when in actual fact he had
published only one, 'Travelling Companions', since his last meeting
with the Nortons in England. The reference cannot be said to embrace *Watch and Ward*—hardly a 'little tale'. What other works,
then, are the point of reference in this letter? The obvious candidates
are his next two published tales, 'A Passionate Pilgrim' and 'At Isella',
both 'international' pieces and in many ways similar to 'Travelling
Companions'. 'A Passionate Pilgrim' was published in the *Atlantic* in
the numbers for March and April 1871; and 'At Isella' in the August
issue of the *Galaxy*.

The technical and thematic similarity between the tales would
indicate that all three belong to a single phase of inspiration; that,
in other words, all three could be a product of the period of 'Travelling Companions'. While this certainly is the case with 'A Passionate

26 Ibid., p. 248.
27 Ibid., p. 253.

Pilgrim' which, James himself tells us, was 'written in the year 1870',[28] even young James could not have produced three long tales, more than half of a novel, several travel sketches, and some book reviews, all within a period of a little over four months. It is more likely that he wrote his first two 'international' tales shortly after his arrival, and returned to the theme with 'At Isella' when he took a short break from work on *Watch and Ward*—that is, he wrote 'At Isella' in the autumn of 1870. Such an hypothesis makes the gap between that tale's composition and publication look more normal with the *Galaxy* than would be the case otherwise. Since the *Atlantic* was already beginning to 'choke' with James's 'wares', 'At Isella', as well as 'Master Eustace', which followed it, went to the *Galaxy*.

These observations lead us to one important conclusion of bibliographical and critical significance: that the dates of publication of these tales, or for that matter of James's other writings, cannot be taken as a wholly reliable evidence for any critical assessment of his *development*; that, for instance, 'A Passionate Pilgrim', which appeared in print six months *before Watch and Ward,* was written *after* the completion of a large part of that novel. The same is true of 'At Isella'.

Those of young James's admirers who had a keener sense of the cultural issues involved in the complex fate of Clement Searle—Euro-Americans such as the Nortons and the Bootts—received 'A Passionate Pilgrim' with great enthusiasm. Apparently, this was the kind of reader James had in mind when he made his early forays into the 'international' theme. In a letter to Grace Norton, he asks her to 'thank [Charles] in especial, until I do so directly, for his generous estimate of my *Passionate Pilgrim.* I wrote it, in truth, for him and him more than for anyone, and I am glad to find it going so straight to its address.'[29] Of 'At Isella', James told Grace that it was

the fruit of a vague desire to reproduce a remembered impression and mood of mine. The lady herself [the central character in the tale] is a gross fit. At the time, I wanted something to happen; I have improved on vulgar experience by supposing that something *did*. It is not much as you'll see, and such as it is, not perhaps an improvement.[30]

[28] See Appendix II below.
[29] Letter of 16 July 1871. *Henry James Letters*, p. 257.
[30] Ibid., p. 259. The actual experience on which the tale is based is described in detail in a letter of 31 August 1869, to Alice James (ibid., pp. 127–30). The letter and the tale in particular, but also a travel sketch of a later date, carry intriguing verbal echoes. The same is true of the Oxford passages in 'A Passionate Pilgrim' and a letter to William James of 26 April 1869 (ibid., pp. 108–13), in which James describes his own first glimpse of Oxford. To William, James wrote: 'As I walked along the river I saw hundreds of mighty lads of

James's next tale, 'Master Eustace', with which he brought his explorations of the 'international' theme to a temporary halt, appeared in the *Galaxy* of November 1871. A surviving letter to the editor shows that the work is quite definitely of a much earlier date. The manuscript was in the hands of the editor even before the publication of 'At Isella'. James did not like the way the magazine had treated that tale, printing it on pages divided into columns of small print. On 21 July 1871, he wrote to say that he hoped his new tale for the magazine would receive different treatment: 'Many thanks for your cheque [payment for 'At Isella']: it reached me this morning. May I express the hope that you will be able to print *Master Eustace* in the *larger type*—undivided pages—of the magazine? As the text is little broken up by paragraphs of talk, there will be little waste of space in doing so'.[31] The letter clearly shows that 'Master Eustace' was not only in existence but had arrived in the office of its first publisher by the middle of July. While this information does not help us give the tale a definite date of composition, it excludes the possibility of a date later than the early summer of 1871. It also goes on to confirm that, repeating his experience of the previous year—when James had visited some American places to write travel notes for the *Nation*—the four travel sketches of Canadian places which he published in the same magazine in the autumn of 1871,[32] were written after 'Master Eustace', though all four preceded the tale in print.

There is a gap of a year between 'Master Eustace' and 'Guest's Confession', which came next and appeared in the *Atlantic* in October–November 1872—when James was back in Europe on his second trip (see below). However, a mysterious allusion in a letter by Mrs. James suggests that the two works may have been composed in close succession, some time in the first half of 1871—'Guest's Confession' even

---

England, clad in white flannel and blue, immense, fair-haired, magnificent in their youth, lounging down the stream in their punts or pulling in straining crews and rejoicing in their godlike strength. When along with this you think of their haunts in the grey-green quadrangles, you esteem them as elect among men.' In the original version of 'A Passionate Pilgrim', the relevant passage reads: 'Here, of course, we encountered in hundreds the mighty lads of England, clad in white flannel and blue, immense, fair-haired, magnificent in their youth, lounging down the current in their idle punts, in friendly couples, or in solitude possibly pregnant of scholastic honours; or pulling in straining crews and hoarsely exhorted from the near bank.'

[31] MS. letter in the W.C. Church Collection in the New York Public Library.

[32] The articles on Quebec appeared in the issues of 28 September and 5 October; and those on Niagara in the issues of 12 and 19 October.

preceding 'Master Eustace'! The letter is of 26 July 1872, and is
addressed to her two children then in Europe. Mrs. James is delighted to see her son's European travel notes in the *Nation* but
wonders: 'why doesn't the *Atlantic Monthly* publish what he [James]
gave them a year ago.'[33] Although no title is mentioned in the letter,
the process of elimination leaves us in no doubt that 'Guest's Confession' must be that work, the publication of which the *Atlantic*
had deffered for an unusually long time: no other work by James,
published after 'Master Eustace', can have originated in the period
vaguely indicated by Mrs. James.

There may even be a certain connection between Mrs. James's
annoyance in July and the appearance of a proof of the tale some
weeks later; for, on 6 August, Henry James Senior told the same
correspondents that Howells had 'promised' him 'Harry's proof in a
day or two, and said he likes the story very much.'[34] The reference
here is to 'Guest's Confession'—published towards the end of 1872,
but written perhaps early in 1871.

Howells did like the story—so did Mrs. Howells. Their appreciation
was conveyed to James by Howells himself:

Your 'Guest's Confession' has on the whole been received with more
favour than anything else you've printed in the *Atlantic*; and though I
don't give up my early favourites, I see many reasons why G's.C. should
be generally liked. Mrs. Howells, who is not a "genial critic"—of her
husband's writings, at any rate—praises it very highly; says your people
both speak and act from motives of their own; and the different scenes
are intense, and the whole plot nice and good. Whereupon I enviously
point out that somehow the end does not come with a click, and that
there's a certain obscurity in Mrs. Beck's fate, so that your brother and I
disputed as to whom she marries. I think you don't make your young
man generous enough to merit that good girl. Nevertheless I admire the
story greatly.[35]

William wrote separately to say that he admired the tale

though not loving it exactly. I noted at the time a couple of blemishes,
one of the French phrase *les indifférents* at the end of one of her [Laura's]
sentences which suddenly chills one's very marrow. The other the expression 'to whom I had dedicated a sentiment,' earlier in the story.... Of
the people who experience a personal dislike, so to speak, of your stories,
the most I think will be repelled by the element which gets expression in
these two phrases, something cold, thin blooded and priggish suddenly

[33] MS. letter (Harvard).
[34] MS. letter (Harvard).
[35] Letter of 28 October 1872. MS. (Harvard).

popping in and freezing the genial current. And I think that is the principal defect you have now to guard against.[36]

4.

It was about the time that 'Master Eustace' appeared in print that James intimated to Grace Norton his 'fantastic dream ... of another visitation of England and Italy'.[37] Europe had constantly been on his mind since his experience of it the year before; also, lately, he had been translating that experience into works of fiction with remarkable success. This in itself was reason enough for him to start thinking in terms of a return visit for a further 'squeezing' of the 'European orange'. By the end of January 1872, the 'dream' began to take the form of a vague determination. On 24 January, James told Elizabeth Boott that he had 'a certain absurdly vague hope ... of getting to Europe by hook or by crook, in the late summer or early autumn next.'[38] Within months of this letter, events so transpired that he found himself telling Charles Norton that '[his] departure for England with [his] aunt and sister [was] now but five days off (May 11th)'.[39] He had been asked to escort Alice and Aunt Kate on their tour of Europe; and he had managed to obtain a commission from the *Nation*, where he had been trying his hand at travel writing, to write similar notes for them, this time on European places. By 20 May 1872, he was writing letters home from S.S. *Algeria*.

The itinerary of this trip is of some interest to us as seven of the twelve tales of the second phase were written during this tour, which, for James, lasted for two years, and during which he was often on the move and constantly writing. The three travellers spent about two months in England, James commencing his 'letters' for the *Nation* with sketches of places the three had a chance to visit. In July they crossed the Channel and visited selected places in France, Switzerland, Austria, and Italy. In Italy, they visited, in that order, Milan, Venice, and Verona—but not Florence. The whole tour lasted until the middle of October when the two ladies returned to Cambridge, and James, after seeing them off in England, went back to Paris early in November 'to try [his] luck at remaining abroad'.[40] He stayed in Paris for about two months, then moved to Italy (trying Rome at first, then Florence) towards the end of 1872. He lived mostly

---

[36] Letter of 24 November 1872. Ms. (Harvard).

[37] Letter of 27 November 1871. *Henry James Letters*, p. 266.

[38] Ibid., p. 270.

[39] Letter of 6 May 1872. Ibid., p. 276.

[40] Letter of 22 September 1872, to William James. Ibid., p. 300.

in Italy until the summer of 1874 when he began his journey back to Cambridge.

James's next tale, 'The Madonna of the Future', was published in the *Atlantic* in March, 1873. It is set in Florence and, through a first-person narrator, tells of the narrator's encounter with an American artist trying to paint a masterpiece in Europe. That it is not a by-product of James's second visit to Florence should be obvious from the fact that the work was in print about two months before James returned to that city. However, it can be argued that the Florentine setting is not the result of any immediate experience of the place, but of James's renewed vision of the general Italian scene with Alice and Aunt Kate, which, interestingly enough, did include an actual encounter with an American painter in Venice. Naturally, such a argument would have to presuppose that the tale was written *after* the brief Italian tour. (As we are told by James himself, the Italian part of their trip took place in the last week of August and the first week of September 1872; the Venetian encounter with the American artist coming during the second leg of the tour.)

James's biographer, Dr. Leon Edel, seems to take precisely this view when he tells us that 'The Madonna of the Future' was written during James's 'stopover' in Paris in November 1872. He also points out that the encounter with the American artist, recounted in a sketch for the *Nation*, 'foreshadows the opening scene of "The Madonna of the Future" ...'[41]

While Dr. Edel's dating of the story makes good critical and historical sense, two surviving letters from Howells to James show that the tale was in existence, and the manuscript evidently already with Howells, in fact prior to James's Italian jaunt with his sister and aunt—that is, two months before the November in which Dr.

---

[41] Leon Edel, *Henry James: The Conquest of London, 1870–1881* (Philadelphia, New York: J. B. Lippincott & Company, 1962), pp. 74–5.

It was towards the end of August 1872 that the Jameses arrived in Italy from Switzerland. They spent a week travelling and sightseeing in the region of Milan and then repaired to Venice where, on the morning of their arrival, James met in the Piazza 'a young American painter who told me that he had been spending the summer just where I found him, I could have assaulted him for very envy. He was painting forsooth the interior of St. Mark's. To be a young American painter unperplexed by the mocking, elusive soul of things and satisfied with their wholesome light-bathed surface and shape; keen of eye; fond of colour, of sea and sky and anything that may chance between them ... this, I consider, is to be as happy as is consistent with the preservation of reason.' ('Venice: An Early Impression', *Italian Hours*, New York: Grove Press, Inc., 1959, p. 54; originally published in the *Nation*, xvi, 6 March 1873, pp. 163–5.)

Edel places the tale. On 1 September 1872, Howells told James that he was going to print 'Guest's Confession' in the October issue of the magazine and went on to add: 'I think I shall put the Florentine story into January.'[42] Howells does not mention any title but there is little doubt he is referring to 'The Madonna of the Future', the only 'Florentine story' of the whole period. However, he could not print the tale in the January number but was willing to arrange payment for it in lieu of publication later. On 28 October, he told James that he had 'asked [the accounts section of the magazine] to send you the cheque some time ago, so that by now I hope you have it. The story I am going to print in February.'[43] Again, there is no mention of a title; though again the process of elimination clearly points to 'The Madonna' as 'the story' of the letter.

Thus, the tale is not a work of November 1872; nor can the sketch of Venice be seen to 'foreshadow' its opening scene: the fiction was in existence before the documentary account of Venice. A more likely date, then, of its composition might be the months of June and July —the renewed encounter of Europe acting as a spur to James's 'international' imagination; it is another matter that this first fruit of the new 'international' phase draws entirely upon his memories of the trip of 1869. This last point gains further strength from a curious footnote in the three revised versions of the text, which points to 1869 as the date of a particular Florentine prospect described in the tale.

The textual history of this work is no less complicated. The story James originally wrote has been lost; the extant text is James's work drastically altered by his family and Howells. The original work appears to have been much longer and was to appear in two issues of the magazine; the alterations and excisions were made on the galleys. The most detailed and interesting account of the whole extraordinary affair is given by Henry James Senior in a letter to his son. The letter is of 14 January 1873:

We had a sitting last evening, and the evening before in the library, at which were present mother, Alice and Willy to whom I read the proof of your *Madonna of the Future* which I had from Howells; and which is to appear in the March *Atlantic*. We were all charmed with the story. A great many eulogiums were passed upon it as I proceeded and when I finished both evenings (for its length was 25 pages), Willy pronounced it very *distingué*, mother charming, Alice exquisite. I was very much struck with it as a whole, and admired it greatly also in parts. But I have a story to tell. Mr Howells could not agree to give 25 pages of one number of the

---

[42] *Life in Letters*, pp. 171–2.
[43] MS. letter (Harvard).

magazine to it; that was positive. And then besides he had a decided shrinking from one episode—that in which Theobald tells of his love for, and his visit from the Titian-ic beauty, and his subsequent disgust of her worthlessness—as being risky for the magazine; and then moreover he objected to the interview at the end between the writer and the old English neighbour, as rubbing into the reader what was sufficiently evident without it. On both the first and second points, we all thought that while Howells *in general* is too timid, there was good ground for his timidity in the present case. Both mother and Alice shrank from both the episodes as not helping the understanding of the story along, and as being scary rather in themselves. Willy thought the second quite unnecessary, superfluous, and thought the first, if it had not been so much detailed but had been condensed into half a column, would perhaps do. But I thought they were both utterly uncalled for by the actual necessities of the table, while they would both alike confer upon it a disagreeable murky odour strikingly at war with its unworldly beauty. I went to Howells accordingly this morning and told him that if he could consent to publish the whole tale in one piece, I would take upon me the responsibility of striking out the two episodes. He agreed and he has made the connection of the parts perfect, so that no one would ever dream of anything stricken out. He promises me also to save the excluded pieces and I will send them to you or keep them for you so that you may publish them, if you like, in your volume—which Howells says ought to be published forthwith. I ought to say also that Howells admires the story very much, thinks it very beautiful, and only objects to these episodes as being too much fashioned upon French literature. He thought also that the first one was very well done except for the details.[44]

William, too, wrote about the matter, but after the tale had appeared in print:

Today *Advertiser* and *Tribune* are out with notices of your tale, which I clip out and enclose. Father decided to squeeze it into one number by docking its two episodes, I think, with advantage, though the first one might have had its sense preserved, with the loss of its somewhat cold and repulsive details had anyone here had the art to abridge it into a short and poetically vague statement that he [Theobald] had once broken with an inconoclastic love. On a third reading I quite agreed with Howells that the story was transparent enough without the second episode, which then became excrescence. Altogether the story is a masterpiece.[45]

[44] MS. letter (Harvard).
[45] Letter of 13–14 February 1873. MS. (Harvard). Under its column 'Current Literature', the *Boston Daily Advertiser*'s notice said: 'Mr Henry James, jr., contributes an exceptionally good story of Italian life, entitled "The Madonna of the Future". The pathos of the story of the artist-hero has its counterpart in every profession and every land.' Vol. 121, no. 38; 13 February 1873 (page number missing in this copy).

And, characteristically, Howells was 'burning' to tell James what he thought of 'The Madonna',

and to report the undissenting voice of acclaim with which it has been hailed. Ever so many people have spoken of it, the Delphic Dennett alone remaining mum. Truly it has been a success, and justly, for it is a bravely solid and excellent piece of work. All like the well-managed pathos of it, the dissertations on pictures, the tragic, most poetical central fact, and I hope that many feel with me its unity and completeness. Every figure in it is a real character, and has some business there. The sole blemish on it to my mind is the insistence on the cats and monkeys philosophy. I don't think you ought to have let that *artista* appear a second time, and, I confess, to have the cats and monkeys for a refrain at the close, marred the fine harmony of what went before, till I managed to forget them.[46]

Naturally, James did not like the treatment his work had to undergo before it could be published, though he was grateful for his father's part in it. In reply to the latter's detailed account of the affair, James wrote on 1 February 1873:

I have just received your long and most satisfactory letter about the proof of my story and Howells's restrictions, invitations [Howells had invited James to write a short piece for the *Atlantic* on a monthly basis], etc. The former I regret, and as far as I can remember the 'immoral' episodes don't artistically affront. With such a standard of propriety, it makes a bad look-out ahead for imaginative writing. For what class of minds is it that such very timorous scruples are thought necessary?—But of course you were quite right to make all convenient concessions, and I am obliged to you for your trouble. Evidently, too, Howells has a better notion of the allowances of the common public than I have, and I am much obliged to him for performing the excision personally, for of course he will have done it neatly.[47]

---

[46] Letter of 10 March 1873, *Life in Letters*, pp. 175–6. The 'Delphic Dennett' of Howells's letter is John Richard Dennett of the editorial staff of the *Nation*, who wrote a monthly commentary on the current magazines. Most early critical notices of James's tales appearing in the *Nation* (see Appendix III below) were from his pen. He was not a 'genial' critic; rather, he was often genuinely critical in his judgements, which earned him a reputation as a man to be feared. Also, he came to play an unfortunate part in the '*Middlemarch* Affair' between James and the *Nation*: for a mysterious reason, the magazine refused to accept James's review of the novel by George Eliot, although it had given him the impression that his notice would be welcome. On one occasion, Mrs. James was so incensed with a remark of Dennett's that she wrote her son: 'You will not be half as indignant as your friends and admirers here are, when you see the *Nation*; the meanness of Dennett in his notice of your article and his sarcasm are beneath contempt, and a disgrace to the paper for which he writes.' Letter of 27 April 1873. MS. (Harvard).

[47] *Henry James Letters*, pp. 333–4.

Unfortunately, we have no knowledge of the whereabouts of the excised pages which Henry James Senior was going to save for his son. However, when James himself came to revise the tale—and he had the opportunity on three different occasions—he did not think it necessary to restore the missing parts. He introduced many verbal alterations but otherwise left the tale as he found it in the first printed version.

While 'The Madonna' was definitely not the story James wrote during his stay in Paris, he did write a tale in those weeks and set it in France. After a rather complicated passage, 'The Sweetheart of M. Briseux', James's next tale, appeared in the *Galaxy* in June 1873. The tale is one of a few of the period which can be dated with any certainty. According to James himself, it was written in the second half of November in 1872. On November 31, he wrote to his brother: 'I have been busy the last fortnight writing a little story, which now that it is finished I hardly know what to do with—having other designs on the *Atlantic* I shall probably send it to the magazine (*Wood's Household*—degrading connection!) for which Gail Hamilton lately appealed to me.'[48] A few weeks before James wrote this letter, a tale by him had appeared in the *Atlantic*, while two more of his writings were awaiting their turn with the same magazine. Moreover, as the reference to 'other designs' vaguely indicates, James was beginning to think in terms of a serial for the *Atlantic*. That avenue, therefore, was not available for 'The Sweetheart of M. Briseux'. The *Galaxy* was the obvious alternative, but the new venture, *Wood's Household*, seemed to James a more lucrative possibility. Its founder, Gail Hamilton (whose real name was Mary Abigail Dodge), was a writer of casual essays and had co-edited a periodical in the sixties. She knew the James family and, through the young novelist's mother, asked for a contribution from her son for the first issue of her magazine.

James sent 'The Sweetheart of M. Briseux' to Gail Hamilton some time in December. But the magazine never saw the light of day. In dismay, he wrote to his father in February 1873:

I sent six weeks since a short MS. story to Miss Dodge, according to her invitation (which I thought seemed to promise remuneration) for *Wood's Magazine*. I yesterday hear from her that she has had bilious fever, *Wood's Magazine* is exploded, and what shall she do with the precious packet? I have written her to send it you; and would like you to forward it (marked visibly outside with my initials—or even name) to F. P. Church, Editor *Galaxy*, whose address you will find in the corner of the magazine and to whom I enclose a note for you to post. I don't offer the story to

---

[48] Ibid., p. 312.

Howells, because, like the *Madonna of the Future*, it hinges on a picture, and because I am on the point of sending him something else.[49]

On 4 March, Henry James Senior wrote back to say that, since he had not heard from her, he had 'written to Gail Hamilton to send me your tale; but she does it not as yet. I will renew my invitation to her in a day or two if necessary.'[50] The manuscript arrived at Quincy Street shortly after this letter; on 18 March, the father reported to his son that the *Galaxy* had been forwarded the story originally

sent to Gail Hamilton who returned it to me with these words: 'Here is a manuscript belonging to that lovely boy of yours which he bids me send you—I part from it with regret. I only wish I had a magazine to launch, because I am sure such freight would make its future.' I will tell Church [one of the editors of the *Galaxy*] to send me a proof and a cheque.[51]

The editors of the *Galaxy* did not acknowledge receipt of the manuscript, causing Mrs. James some annoyance, who wrote to her son complaining that 'the *Galaxy* people make no sign of acceptance of your story but send tardily $30 for *Middlemarch* [James's review of the novel by George Eliot]—I presume it is only bad manners.'[52] When at last the tale appeared in the June number of the magazine, it added little to the growing admiration for James's writings. Writing to his brother on 25 May 1873, William was quick to confess that he had read 'The Sweetheart of M. Briseux' but 'without, I must say, the delight I have so often got from your things'.[53] On his part, James was sorry that such was the case; he had hoped the tale 'was sufficiently pleasing. But one can't know.'[54]

The first mention of 'The Last of the Valerii', James's next published tale, occurs in a letter written shortly after his move from Paris to Rome at the end of 1872. Thus, the actual gap between 'The Sweetheart of M. Briseux' and 'The Last of the Valerii' is not, as indicated by their dates of publication, of six months or so, but only of a few weeks. Evidently, James started writing the tale in the first week of January 1873, and was, by the end of the month, 'on the point of sending' it to the *Atlantic*. He mailed the manuscript to Howells on 17 February[55]—when 'The Sweetheart of M. Briseux' was

[49] Letter of 1 February 1873. Ibid., p. 334. There is no evidence that Howells objected to the presence of 'a picture' in 'The Madonna of the Future'.
[50] MS. letter (Harvard).
[51] MS. letter (Harvard).
[52] Letter of 1 April 1873. MS. (Harvard).
[53] MS. letter (Harvard).
[54] Letter of 18 June 1873. *Henry James Letters*, p. 394.
[55] This is announced by James—of course, without naming the title—in a letter of this date. Ibid., p. 343.

still making its 'rounds'. Barely three weeks later, in a letter of 10
March, also quoted above, Howells acknowledged receipt of the
manuscript: 'I have your Roman Romance, and I shall print it very
soon. I like it but I shall tell you more about it when I get it in print.'[56]
However, largely because of James himself, who was constantly
ahead of his publishers, Howells could not print the tale as 'soon' as
he had hoped he would. Once again it was left to Mrs. James to
report to her son, on the 1st of July, that there was to be a delay;
that Howells had told her and Henry James Senior that 'he will
work in ['The Last of the Valerii'] when he can do so.'[57] The tale
was published in the *Atlantic* in January, 1874—about a year after its
composition. Shortly before its publication, on 5 December 1873,
Howells again wrote to James about it—and a related matter of
interest to both:

I have your *Last of the Valerii* in the January number, and I like it very
much. It did not strike me so favourably in manuscript as it does in print;
but now I think it excellent. By the way, I hope you won't send any of
your stories to *Scribner's* [the *Scribner's Monthly*]. We have of course
no claim upon you, but we have hitherto been able to print all the
stories you have sent, and so it shall be hereafter. Scribner [Charles
Scribner, whose firm will bring out The New York Edition forty years
later] is trying to lure away all our contributors, with the siren song of
Doctor Holland, [one of the founders of the magazine] and my professional pride is touched.[58]

James's response to the concern expressed in Howell's letter explains the situation from *his* point of view. He thanked Howells for
'speaking well of ['The Last of the Valerii']; it reads agreeably
enough though I suppose that, to many readers, it will seem rather
idle.' He was 'obliged' to Howells

for the esteem implied in [his reference to James's relations with the
Atlantic]; but it remains true, in a general way, that I *can't* really get on
without extracting tribute from [the *Scribner's Monthly*]. It's a mere
money question. The *Atlantic* can't publish as many stories as I ought
and expect to be writing. At home, it could, for then I needed scantier
revenues. But now, with all the francs it takes to live in these lovely
climes, I need more strings to my bow and more irons always on the fire.
But I heartily promise you that the *Atlantic* shall have the best things I
do . . .[59]

---

[56] *Life in Letters*, p. 176.
[57] MS. letter (Harvard).
[58] *Life in Letters*, p. 181.
[59] *Henry James Letters*, p. 424.

James had, indeed, become so prolific that the four magazines to
which he had been contributing since he began publishing in the
early sixties simply could not keep pace with him. (Earlier, Mrs.
James had wisely put the matter thus to Alice: 'Let Harry's wares be
ever so good; unless he can find a brisker market than the *Atlantic
Monthly* and the *Nation* afford, they will neither add to his reputation nor fill his purse.'[60]) As a result, there were frequent and long
delays in publication which irritated James and did not help his
already sensitive relations with at least two of the four, the *Galaxy*
and the *Nation*. There was then the question of money, of which
James now expected and demanded more from his old publishers. On
one occasion he had tried to persuade the *Galaxy* to pay him more for
one of his tales—probably 'The Sweetheart of M. Briseux'—than he
would have got otherwise from that magazine. The result of his
appeal was reported to him by Mrs. James. A letter, she said, had
arrived

from the *Galaxy* people saying that some days after your piece for them
was in print, they received from Mr. Church an announcement of your
having asked $150 for it. They go on to say that they *never* give more
than $100 for any piece however long unless it is previously agreed upon,
and that Mr. Church who knew perfectly this arrangement, must be held
responsible for the difference. This seems a strange way of doing business
—but Father [Henry James Senior] will write at once and make Church,
if possible, pay up.[61]

The situation was further complicated by the fact that James himself was not available to negotiate with his editors. Quite often decisions of a practical nature had to be taken by his father, in con-
sultation with William James, when he was available, and even
Howells. (It is interesting that, although James had been writing
now for almost a decade, and had several literary contacts in England, he did not think his work was good enough for English magazines: the few allusions he makes to such a possibility show that, at
this point in his career, he was afraid of English readers.) The following letter from Mrs. James to her son gives us a good glimpse of
the state of affairs. The letter is of 8 December 1873:

Father received from Perry [an old friend of James's who had lately
joined the *Review* as its Assistant Editor] your notice of Howells's poems,
saying that he had already another in the press.... at Howells's suggestion ... Father sent it to the *Independent*. H [Howells] said he thought
they would be glad to have it with your name, that they paid well and

[60] Letter of 26 July 1872. MS. (Harvard).
[61] Letter of 25 May 1873. MS. (Harvard).

that it would be a good vehicle for some of your things. Father is awaiting their answer, and will send the notes of travel, returned by *Scribner*, to *Lippincott*, he thinks. The N.A. [the *Review*] sends $25 for *Meta Holdenis* [James's review of the novel by Cherbuliez]—the Albano paper [a travel sketch] will be paid for in a few days—we have nothing of late from the *Nation*, but some of your returns will soon be flowing in. . . .[62]

However, although James continued to prefer the *Atlantic* for his fiction, and the *Nation* and the *Review* for his occasional pieces, he was now beginning to spread his wings: in fact, what he did not tell his friend, he had mailed a tale to the *Scribner's Monthly* shortly before he wrote the letter to Howells quoted above. But the work that went to the *Scribner's* was not the story which came next: James's next tale, 'Mme. De Mauves'—his first small masterpiece—went to the *Galaxy* and appeared there in the numbers for February and March 1874.

A few weeks before James had dispatched 'The Last of the Valerii' to Howells, he had received a letter from his father carrying a message from Howells that it was time James brought out a volume of his tales. James responded through a letter to his mother, dated 24 March 1873. He told her he was planning a collection of tales 'on the theme of American adventurers in Europe, leading off with the *Passionate Pilgrim*. I have three or four more to write: one I have lately sent to Howells ['The Last of the Valerii'] and have *half finished* another [italic added].'[63] Not surprisingly, the identity of the 'half finished' work is not revealed by James. However, the context in which the mention is made points straight to 'Mme. De Mauves' as the work in question. Of the six tales included in the collection 'on the theme of American adventurers in Europe'—*A Passionate Pilgrim*—four had already been written or published when James wrote this letter, while one was written much later; this leaves 'Mme. De Mauves', the sixth item in the collection, to be identified as the 'half finished' tale of the letter. (James rarely, if ever at all, left his literary projects unfinished.) There is, thus, reason to suppose that James started work on 'Mme. De Mauves' early in 1873; also, that his own dating of the tale in the Preface to the New York Edition of the work is only partially true.

There, he recalls 'the tolerably wide court of an old inn at Bad-Homburg in the Taunus hills—a dejected and forlorn little place ...' where, 'in the summer of 1873', he wrote the tale.[64] He indeed did

---

[62] MS. (Harvard).

[63] *Henry James Letters*, p. 357. See also the note on Revisions in the first volume of this edition.

[64] See Appendix II below.

complete the story then. By May 1873 he had moved his residence from Rome to Florence. About a month later, in order to escape the heat of Florence, he went on a leisurely tour of Switzerland which ended in a ten-week long stay in Germany. As he told his parents in a letter of 14 August—again, without mentioning the title—it was during these weeks that he completed 'Mme. De Mauves' and mailed the manuscript to the *Galaxy*: 'I yesterday despatched a tale in three parts to the *Galaxy*—with regret, as it is the best written thing I have done. But it was the only thing I could do.'[65] James goes on to imply that he had considered the possibility of sending the story to an English magazine but did not, because he wanted to 'approach English organs on some other basis than American subjects—usually they are very "racy" ...'[66] That the work in question is 'Mme. De Mauves', we are assured by the simple process of elimination: no other tale of the period, appearing in the *Galaxy*, fits the description.

The note of 'regret' in the letter is briefly explained in a letter written two months later. James was annoyed by the fact that the *Galaxy* had, once again, not bothered to acknowledge receipt of the manuscript; as late as the fourth week of October, he had no word from them. On 26 October 1873, he wrote to his father:

[The *Galaxy* has] two M.S. of mine—one a piece on Rome and one a story in three parts of which I can obtain no tidings whatever. I will write to them immediately either to let me hear something about them or of their intentions concerning them or else to enclose them to you. You in that case will please send them to Lippincott. I lately sent a M.S. to Scribner and am on the point of sending them another—a story in two parts: so that they are for the moment choked with my wares. Poor Howells is chronically; besides, he would not publish the *Galaxy* story on account of the subject, I'm afraid. (It's needless to say that *I* think the subject all right—in fact very fine!)[67]

No doubt James would have liked his 'best written thing' to appear in a reputed journal such as the *Atlantic*; but I have not seen any evidence that he ever showed the manuscript to Howells. Rather, what seems more likely, knowing that the length of the work would delay its publication in the *Atlantic*, and fearing, perhaps wrongly, that the mildly erotic overtones of its subject would not appeal to Howells, James sent the tale to the *Galaxy*.

However, begun early in the spring of 1873, and completed late that summer in three parts, 'Mme. De Mauves' appeared in print in two parts in the beginning of 1874. As could be expected, Mrs. James

[65] MS. (Harvard).
[66] Ibid.
[67] *Henry James Letters*, pp. 405-6.

was quick to convey to her son her enthusiasm over his latest tale. On 23 January 1874, soon after the appearance of the first instalment, she wrote to William—who had joined his brother in Italy in the last week of the previous October—to 'tell Harry that the first number of "Madame de Mauves" has just appeared, and promises to make a mark.'[68] When William returned to Cambridge some weeks later, he discovered that the tale had, indeed, made 'a mark': 'your "Madame de Mauves"', he told his brother, 'gets great praise from all quarters. I think it is one of your best things.'[69]

Next came 'Adina': it was this tale which went to the *Scribner's*, and thus became the first work of fiction by James, in almost nine years of his story-telling, not to appear in the *Atlantic* or the *Galaxy*. An allusion in James's letter of 26 October 1873 (to his parents), quoted above, indicates that he first attempted to appear in the *Scribner's* in that October. The manuscript he offered the magazine was a travel sketch, but it was rejected by the editor. He sent 'Adina' in November and it was accepted. James was pleased to learn from his mother that his fiction had made a very good impression with the *Scribner's*: the payment had been prompt and handsome.[70] As William reported to his brother, a proof of the tale was taken in the following March, and was corrected by Henry James Senior; the tale appeared in the *Scribner's* for May and June 1874. On the fragmentary evidence available, it seems quite likely that, like its predecessor as well as 'Eugene Pickering' to come, 'Adina' was written some time in the summer or autumn of 1873.

The vagaries of magazine publication appear to have reversed the chronology of James's next two tales, 'Professor Fargo' and 'Eugene Pickering'. 'Professor Fargo'—a curious oddity in the present sequence of 'international' studies—followed 'Adina', and was published in the *Galaxy* for August 1874; while 'Eugene Pickering' appeared two months later in the *Atlantic* for October and November. In actual fact, however, 'Eugene Pickering' was completed and submitted for publication several months *before* 'Professor Fargo'.

In a letter of 22 December 1873, James told his father that he had 'lately sent [the *Scribner's*] a tale in two parts ['Adina'] and [was] sending it another of the same dimensions'.[71] This 'other' tale is 'Eugene Pickering' which, the manner of the reference here would seem to suggest, James had already completed. But this does not

---

[68] MS. letter (Harvard).

[69] Letter of 22 March 1874. MS. (Harvard).

[70] A letter of Mrs. James to her son, dated 23 January 1874, contains this information: James was paid $150 for 'Adina'. MS. (Harvard).

[71] *Henry James Letters*, p. 420.

appear to have been quite the case; for, a few weeks later, on 9 January 1874, James mailed a package, not to the *Scribner's* but to Howells, which throws a different light on the matter:

Let me explain without further delay the nature of the package which will go with this, in another cover. It is the first one half of a tale in two parts, for use at your convenience. I have been reading it to my brother who pronounces it 'quite brilliant'. I was on the point of sending it to Scribner, but your words in deprecation of this course made me face about.[72]

Evidently, the second part, completed later, was dispatched early in February, and the tale never went to the *Scribner's*. In a letter of 10 March to Howells, dealing with another matter, James added a note inquiring about the fate of 'Eugene Pickering': 'I sent you lately, at three or four weeks' interval, the two parts of a tale. You have them, I hope.'[73] Still no word came from Howells; however, on the 22nd of the month, William wrote to say that 'Howells says he will print your last story about the ingenuous youth in Baden and the Coquette in one number. He says it is your best thing.'[74] James was pleased to know the manuscript had safely reached its destination and the tale was to appear in a single number; he also hoped it would not have to undergo too lengthy a period of waiting. But its publication did go through a delay which, as ever before, Mrs. James came to report to her son. 'Your story,' she told her son on 6 July 1874, 'will not appear in the *Atlantic* until October'[75]—which is indeed when it appeared, not in one number, but in the original two parts. Thus, conceived probably in the summer of 1873, when James was staying in Germany (the setting of the tale), 'Eugene Pickering' saw the light of day a year later.[76]

There is only one brief and casual allusion to 'Professor Fargo' in the letters; however, the date of the allusion leaves us in no doubt

[72] Ibid., p. 424. In a similar connection, another part of this letter is quoted above.

[73] Ibid., p. 437.

[74] MS. letter (Harvard).

[75] MS. letter (Harvard).

[76] Three of James's tales from this period—'A Passionate Pilgrim', 'The Last of the Valerii' and 'Eugene Pickering'—were translated into French by Lucien Biart and published in *Revue des Deux Mondes*. 'Eugene Pickering' appeared in the number for 1 January 1876: it is quite likely that J. R. Lowell was referring to this work when he praised a James tale appearing in French in a letter of 4 March 1876, to James: 'I read one of your stories over again in the Revue des D. M. the other day and found it even cleverer in French than in American. I am proud to be the correspondent of a contributor to that august periodical.' MS. (Harvard).

that the work must have originated several months after 'Eugene Pickering', even though it managed to precede the latter in publication. The letter is of 3 May 1874, and is addressed to William:

I have fairly settled down to work upon my long story for the *Atlantic* and hope to bring it home finished or nearly so. Except therefore for two or three more Italian sketches (if opportunity offers) I shall send home no short things before I leave, and shall have to draw in more money than, for the present, I cause to flow in. But if I am paid down, even in part, for my M.S. [the long story for the *Atlantic*] I shall be able to offer full reimbursement. I lately sent a tale to the *Galaxy* and a couple more reviews to the *Nation*.[77]

The tale 'lately sent . . . to the Galaxy' is, of course, 'Professor Fargo'. Little else is known about its history: one even wonders why James wrote this curious piece at this juncture in his career.

5.

The 'long story for the *Atlantic*' of the letter just quoted is *Roderick Hudson*—James's first major novel, begun in Florence not long after 'Eugene Pickering', and serialized in the *Atlantic* from January to December 1875. James's introduction to the *Scribner's Monthly*, and William's few months with his brother in Italy—the two events coincided—had a decisive influence on his plans. Although the idea of starting a serial novel had been put into his head by Howells back in 1872, and all along James had been thinking about it, it was Dr. Holland, the editor of the *Scribner's* who, in February 1874, even before 'Adina' appeared in print in his magazine, put forward a *definite* proposal of a serial by James to start appearing in the *Scribner's* towards the end of 1874. James, who was now beginning to feel lonely and isolated in Europe—William's brief appearance did not help the feeling—and not a little frustrated by the kind of reviewing and travel writing he had been doing lately, was greatly excited by the new prospect. But he felt morally obliged to make such a contract first with the *Atlantic*. Therefore, shortly after the invitation from Dr. Holland, James wrote to Howells about it and added that he would gladly offer the projected serial to the *Atlantic* on the same terms as he had in mind for Dr. Holland. Howells, motivated partly by feelings of rivalry with the *Scribner's*, accepted James's terms without any delay.[78] In this way, *Roderick*

---

[77] *Henry James Letters*, p. 443.
[78] Howells's note of acceptance was contained in a letter Henry James Senior sent to his son. James commented on the exciting news to his sister: 'I wrote

Hudson, though not even started yet, had its 'practical' foundation laid by the end of March 1874.[79]

Back in Quincy Street, there was an air of delight and fond expectation. Barely a week following the new agreement with Howells, Mrs. James wrote to her son:

Will [William] wrote to you at once about the success of your application to Howells; and by the time this reaches you, you will be mentally launched upon the largest enterprise you have undertaken. The things you have sent out of late are evidently making a mark, and preparing a way for a favourable reception of what may come after. The *Daily Advertiser* says this morning, speaking of your article in N.A.R. [the *Review*, which had just published James's notice of some tales by Turgenev]: 'Mr. James is always fascinating, whether he writes a story, a sketch of travel, or a criticism'—every one is delighted with 'Mme. de Mauves', so you must be sure not to fall below that.[80]

In the spring of 1874, when James 'launched' himself 'upon the largest enterprise' so far of his career, he was thirty-one years of age. By a nice coincidence, the 'launching' also marked, almost to date, the tenth anniversary of his literary career. For ten years he had been publishing tales, book reviews, and travel sketches, but could not as yet claim authorship of even a single volume. He had, indeed, often thought of making a collection of his tales and another of his travel sketches, but had yet to give any practical shape to these plans. The writing of the major novel now under way, more than ever before he felt it was time for him to gather some of his other writings into volumes. This in turn meant that he should arrange to be, as he told his mother, 'on the premises' when and where his books would be printed. William too, during his stay in Italy, had suggested that, having fruitfully squeezed the 'European orange' for over two years, James should consider returning to America.

---

about a week ago from Leghorn to mother, in answer to her letter of March 24th. Since then (yesterday) has come father's of the 31st enclosing Howells's acceptance of my story for the *Atlantic*. With this I am very content: especially as it gives me a longer time to write. I shall immortalize myself: *vous allez voir*.' Ibid., pp. 437–8. In an annotation at the end of this letter, Dr. Edel identifies 'my story for the *Atlantic*' as being 'Eugene Pickering'—which is clearly not the case. In his letter, James is alluding to his story *to come*, the serial novel. This is made abundantly clear by James's letter to Howells himself which appears a few pages later (p. 443) in Dr. Edel's edition.

[79] While it is always difficult to date such matters, James's letters indicate that he started work on the early chapters of *Roderick Hudson* sometime in the middle of April 1874.

[80] Letter of 3 April 1874. MS. (Harvard).

With mixed feelings and mixed motives, James sailed for America in August 1874. The literary outcome of his two years in Europe had left him in no doubt that, in some fundamental way, his creative future was bound up with a permanent European connection. Yet, for the feeling young man in him, Europe had been quite lonely—and therefore, paradoxically, more American than America. In all those months in France, Italy, and Germany, James had failed to strike up any living relationship with a Frenchman, or a German, or an Italian: his social life was confined to a round of visits with the other passionate pilgrims. There was, thus, in him now a hankering for the domestic hearth, for its, as he himself admitted, 'tomatoes, ice cream, corn, melons, cranberries, and other indigenous victuals';[81] while there was also present a clear sense that, in order to establish any permanent connection with Europe in the future, he must first establish his status as an author of 'books' rather than just magazine pieces, and give America another chance.

Before James actually started his journey back, Mrs. James, who had been watching her son's coming of age with the deepest interest, and had lately heard a first-hand account of his European life from William, had some advice for her returning son:

Although I have not written to you so much of late, I believe I have never thought so much about you as since Willy came home. I feel so often that I want to throw around you the mantle of the family affection, and fold you in my own tenderest embrace. It seems to me, darling Harry, that your life must need this succulent, fattening element more than you know yourself. That notwithstanding the charm and beauty that surrounds you, and that so inspires and vivifies your intellectual and aesthetic life,—your social life, the life of your affections, must need the moisture and sunshine, which only home, or the intercourse of a circle of familar friends can give. I know only one thing that would solve the difficulty, and harmonize the discordant elements in your life. You would make, dear Harry, according to my estimate, the most loving and lovable and happiest of husbands. I wish I could see you in a favourable attitude of heart towards the divine institution of marriage. In the atmosphere of a happy home of your own, you would thrive in every way, especially if your own tent were pitched in Europe; but even in your own less favoured land, it would be a blessing to you. You will doubtless exclaim, after getting thus far, what on earth has got into mother! The dear old soul is getting childish, what does it all mean! It means simply that I see so much in favour of your staying abroad, and I *feel* so much in favour of your coming home, that I am blindly feeling about, for some easy way of reconciling the difficulty—that is all it means, and we will say no more about it.[82]

[81] Letter of 28 July 1874, to Mrs. James. *Henry James Letters*, p. 459.
[82] Letter of 18 May 1874. MS. (Harvard).

6.

The Madonna of the Future, The Collective Edition of 1883, The
New York Edition: The Revisions

Seven of the twelve tales, the dates of composition of which we
have been trying to ascertain, were later revised and, with one exception—'At Isella'[83]—reprinted by James in one or more of the following collections and selections of his fiction: *A Passionate Pilgrim*,
The Madonna of the Future, the Collective Edition of 1883, *The
Siege of London* (continental edition), *Stories Revived* and the New
York Edition. A brief account of the making of *A Passionate Pilgrim*
and *Stories Revived*, two collections where the first or second revised
forms of some of the tales in the present volume saw the light of
day, is given in the first volume of this edition. I take this opportunity
to say a few words about three of the remaining four titles: unfortunately, I have no account to give of the continental edition of
The Siege of London.

It was not until long after his permanent move to England that
James was able, in the summer of 1877, to find an English publisher
for his works. Evidently, it was the success of *The American* in
America that first aroused the curiosity of the house of Macmillan
about the novel's author. James was delighted to discover that the
firm had been trying to find his whereabouts 'with some apparent
intention of making a proposal ... with regard to the simultaneous
issue here of a novel [by him—*The American*] lately published in
Boston'.[84] At the time, however, he could not give the novel, but
offered instead a collection of his critical reviews. The offer was
accepted by Macmillan, and James made his debut in England, not
as a novelist but as a critic, as the author of *French Poets and
Novelists* (1878). But he did not have to wait long before his novels
and tales too began to appear in England: in fact, within two years
of this first encounter, Macmillan had brought out two novels by
James and two collections of his tales.

It appears that the proposal for *The Madonna of the Future* came
from Macmillan in the summer of 1879, shortly after James contributed his first tale to the firm's monthly, *Macmillan's Magazine*.
By the middle of July 1879, copy for a two-volume collection was already with the printer. James visited Frederick Macmillan on the
morning of the fourteenth when they talked about the new collec-

[83] See headnote to 'At Isella'.
[84] Letter of 7 August 1877, to Macmillan. MS. (British Library).

tion; that evening he wrote to Macmillan to say that 'if copy for "M. of the F." should prove scanty for two volumes, I have one or two tales which I could easily add.'[85] As the six items of the published edition do not seem scanty for two volumes, it is quite likely the original copy contained fewer tales. For three of the six tales—'The Madonna', 'Mme. De Mauves' and 'Eugene Pickering'—the copy consisted of their revised texts in *A Passionate Pilgrim*; for the other three James went to their only appearance to date, the magazine text. However, all six were further revised, or re-revised, for the new collection: whether these changes were made on the copy, or on proofs, is not easy to determine.

James had hoped the book would come out in August. On 14 August, he wrote to Macmillan from Paris: 'When the "Madonna of the Future" appears as I suppose she is liable to do just now at any time—will you please send me a single copy by book-post to the above address, without sending any, as you have usually done, to my London address? When the book is out, I will send you a list of a few people to whom I shall like it despatched.'[86] The book, however, did not arrive until the middle of October; but James was pleased to see it when it came: 'I received yesterday the copy of the "Madonna" which you sent me by post, and which makes a very comely appearance. I wish the book all possible success—more than that of its scantily prosperous predecessors.'[87]

The first Collective Edition of James's novel and tales, in fourteen volumes, was also initiated by Macmillan. James received the proposal for it in the spring of 1883 in America, where he had gone to be at his father's deathbed. His response was quick and enthusiastic:

Let me immediately answer your inquiry about my view of the projected new edition of my stories. I like the idea very much, and only make the condition that these books be as pretty as possible. Can you make them really pretty for 18 pence a volume? I should like them to be *charming*, and beg you to spare no effort to make them so. Your specimen page will enlighten me as to this, and I will, after receiving it, lay out the arrangement into volumes as you suggest. ... I hope fortune will favour the enterprise.[88]

Although for a short while James had toyed with the idea of using the 'grouping' of tales as in his two collections already published by Macmillan, on 8 May 1883, he wrote to Macmillan, proposing a new

[85] Letter of 14 July 1879, to Macmillan. MS. (British Library).
[86] Letter of 14 August 1879, to Macmillan. MS. (British Library).
[87] Letter of 19 October 1879, to Macmillan. MS. (British Library).
[88] Letter of 19 April 1883, to Macmillan. MS. (British Library).

arrangement for the tales to be included in his first collected edition. It appears the new grouping was determined by considerations of size, rather than by those of structural or thematic unity. James wanted the volumes carrying the tales to be four in number, each consisting of 250 pages.[89] While the published edition does contain four volumes of short fiction, these do not conform to the number of pages specified, though all are well within the limit preferred by James. For the first collected edition of his writings, James completely ignored all his American tales of the sixties, and chose from the international tales of the seventies. In all cases, the text selected came from recent, revised reprintings, for the most part those published by Macmillan.

Limitations of space do not allow for any adequate, let alone comprehensive, account of the making of the New York Edition: the long and complicated story is preserved in a massive correspondence, carried out over several years, between James; his agent, J. B. Pinker; the publisher of the edition in America, the Scribner's; and some other publishers. I hope I shall have occasion to tell the whole story on some other occasion. Meanwhile, it should suffice to say that the idea of preparing a definitive edition of his writings for posterity was present in James's mind long before the first practical step was taken towards it in the first week of April 1900.

It was then that Pinker had a lengthy discussion with E. L. Burlinghame of Scribner on the possibility of 'some collected form of James's books'.[90] The 'books' at this stage included his fictional as well as non-fictional prose. In the months that followed there was some more discussion, but the matter appears to have been dropped later in the year. In the summer of 1904, when James was planning what was to be his last American tour, Pinker returned to the matter of the Collected Edition in a letter to Burlinghame of 3 August 1904:

I recollect our conversation about the collected edition of Mr. Henry James' books, and I thought you would like to know that Mr. James thinks the time for that has come. Of course you are aware he is crossing to America this year. He sails on the 24th. inst., and according to present arrangements he will stay about six months in the States. He goes first to visit his brother in New Hampshire, and will, I think, return to New York in the autumn. Either then or later, as his convenience determines, I am going over to America to arrange for the Collected edition and various other projects which Mr. James has in view, and perhaps before that time you will have discussed matters with Mr. Scribner, as I think when you

[89] James wrote to Macmillan about this matter on 8 May 1883. MS. (British Library).

[90] A detailed account of the discussion is contained in a set of notes made by Burlinghame following his meeting with Pinker. MS. (Princeton).

spoke to me you had not done so. Mr. James' idea is to write for each
volume a preface of a rather intimate, personal character, and there is no
doubt that such a preface would add greatly to the interest of the books.
Mr. James has received various proposals regarding this collected edition,
but nothing will be done until we arrive, and I think he will certainly
wish me to discuss the matter with Mr. Scribner and yourself before
making any definite arrangements.[91]

Thus, negotiations and preparations for the edition began in earnest
in the autumn of 1904. These took yet another almost two years
before James was able to sign a firm contract in February 1906. Most
problems and difficulties at this stage in the making of the edition
had to do with questions of copyright. However, by 8 March 1906,
minutely revised copy of *Roderick Hudson*, the first to go to the
printer, was on its way.

The most interesting single fact that the correspondence reveals
is that the design of the New York Edition *evolved* as work progressed on it: the particular grouping of the tales in the volumes of
short fiction, as well as the chronological scheme of the novels, both
were worked out while some of the works had already gone into
print, or were in the process of being revised. There were, of course,
on these and other matters, several misunderstandings between James
and his publisher, and several changes of heart and mind. While
Scribner, for instance, welcomed James's decision to provide 'intimate' Prefaces, his extensive revisions created a small crisis. On the
whole, however, all important literary and aesthetic decisions for the
edition were taken by James himself: the decision to limit the
edition to twenty-three volumes (volume twenty-four *became* a
necessity later), to revise all works selected for inclusion, to punctuate
the text in a particular way, to write the Prefaces, to appoint a particular photographer to take images of particular views to go as
frontispieces, all these and such other decisions originated with
James.

But, as I have suggested above, he did not always get his way:
purely mechanical factors too had a part in shaping the New York
Edition. The precise nature of the difficulties the edition got into
may be gleaned from the following appeal from James's publisher:

We have been much chagrined to find ourselves confronted with a serious
complication in the issue of The New York Edition, with regard to which
we must lose no time in conferring with you and soliciting your assistance.
In brief, we find that the volumes of tales reach proportions destructive of
almost all expectation of profitable publication, and we are forced to ask

[91] MS. (Princeton).

your consideration of the possibility of redistributing them in such a way as to make an additional volume,—the set thus numbering twenty-four instead of the determined twenty-three. So smoothly had everything proceeded, thanks to your prevision and scrupulous attention to every forwarding detail, that our awakening to the real state of the case is as sudden as it is uncomfortable, and our attention having but just been called to the existing situation we write you at once with regard to it in the hope, as we say, that you may be able to make some advantageous re-distribution of these stories. Had we had the entire 'copy' for any one volume in hand before beginning the composition of it, we should have appreciated the fact that it was outrunning practicable limits. But your considerateness itself in sending the 'copy' to us in instalments, and thus cooperating so effectively to avoid delay, has ironically contributed to our failure to realize the condition of things sooner. ... You will not think us unmindful of the great difficulties you have successfully surmounted in the arrangement of these volumes of short stories, or unappreciative of the value, interest and importance of their present grouping. We fear that any other would lose in both art and logic, as well as involve a disconcert-ing and nearly tragic recasting of the carefully considered and con-catenated prefaces, which are such a vital feature of the edition. But we must lay the matter before you and ask most seriously if you cannot consider the possibility of relieving this congestion by some new in-spiration of distribution and the increase of the number of volumes in the set to twenty-four.[92]

The first two volumes of the edition, *Roderick Hudson* and *The American*, came out towards the end of 1907—James was delighted with his 'Christmas present'. The remaining volumes, two at a time, continued to appear at regular intervals until the end of 1909. The edition follows an overall chronological *principle* which is interrupted in the middle to accommodate volumes of short novels and tales. The chronology is then resumed with the final novels. In this way, with-out doing too much damage to the chronological principle, the edition divides itself into three neat segments: the novels up to the so-called major phase, the shorter fiction—James repeatedly refers to this, in terms which suggest that he saw this whole part as a separate edition, as the *Shorter Novels and Tales*—and the last novels.

While it is true that, as James told Howells during the progress of the edition, if he could persuade himself to abandon the limit of twenty-three volumes, he would have included more of his novels and tales in the definitive edition, it is clear these would not have come from his first decade. The decision to select from his early work only 'A Passionate Pilgrim', 'The Madonna' and 'Mme. De

[92] Letter of 2 December 1908, from W. C. Burlinghame to James. MS. (Prince-ton).

Mauves', but nothing else, appears to have been definite and final: James did not think any other very early fiction deserved a place in the New York Edition.

The original plan for the volume in which the lucky three were to make their appearance in the New York Edition—volume xiii, *The Reverberator, Etc.*—consisted of six items, instead of the present five in the published edition. 'The Author of Beltraffio', which now heads volume xvi of the New York Edition, came to occupy that place of distinction as a result of a change of heart: it was a part, originally, of volume xiii. The copy for volume xiii went to the printer in the spring of 1908, when the process of revising had been in full swing for some time. It is quite likely that the three tales with which we are immediately concerned were revised—heavily—for the last time shortly before they found their way to America; that is, either in the winter of 1907, or in the early months of 1908.

Even those who are highly critical of James's decision to subject his writings to a process of rigorous selection and revision would readily admit that the task James set himself was of heroic proportions. In the three years in which the New York Edition was in the making, James simply rewrote, and with the utmost care, no less than twenty-four volumes of his narrative prose. He had hoped the edition would justify his labours by bringing him a substantial reward. But such, alas, was not the case. Quite early in the progress of the edition it became apparent that the venture was heading for a financial disaster. In October 1908, the royalty James received was so small that he was in a state of shock. When 'the hour of the shock' had passed, he wrote to Pinker about the 'vast smothering boa-constrictor':

I am afraid my anti-climax has come from the fact that since the publication of the series began no dimmest light or 'lead' as to its actualities or possibilities of profit has reached me—whereby, in the absence of special warning, I found myself concluding in the sense of some probable fair return—beguiled thereto also by the measure, known only to myself, of the treasures of ingenuity and labour I have lavished on the amelioration of every page of the thing, and as to which I felt that they couldn't *not* somehow 'tell'. . . . However, I am now, as it were, prepared for the worst, and as soon as I can get my desk *absolutely* clear (for like the convolutions of a vast smothering boa-constrictor, such voluminosities of proof—of the Edition—to be carefully read—still keep rolling in) that mere fact will by itself considerably relieve me. And I have such visions and arrears of inspiration——![93]

[93] Letter of 23 October 1908. *Letters,* ii, pp. 106–7.

7.

The exegetical pressures of the modern university department of English, together with our age's perverse lust for the wildly obscure and esoteric in art and literature, have so confused our response to James's work—and to the work of many other writers—and so blurred the focus of this response, that the very human and humane, and for the most part very accessible, writings of James appear to a majority of readers a particularly difficult puzzle, meant only for the initiated. The scandalous reputation of *The Ambassadors,* and of some other late works, as one of the many (unread!) classics of our time, a direct consequence of the tendencies mentioned above as it is, has sent more readers away from James than it has brought to him.

This uncritical celebration of the so-called 'major phase', in the thesis-oriented studies of his work at any rate, has had two particularly unfortunate, interrelated effects: while it has tended to force upon us an image of James's mind and art which is only, if at all, partially true, this image has in turn relegated a sizeable gathering of his fine *early* works into critical oblivion. Thus, we have all kinds of theories about *The Sacred Fount,* and countless explicatory exercises on many of the late tales, but few of even James's informed readers are familiar with such carefully modulated early tales as 'A Passionate Pilgrim', 'The Madonna of the Future', 'Four Meetings', 'The Pension Beaurepas', etc., or such marvellously executed early short novels as 'Mme. De Mauves' and 'An International Episode'.

'Mme. De Mauves' is indeed quintessential James. Almost all of James's most important thematic preoccupations as a critic of life receive their first clear recognition and statement in this work. There are a few portraits of women in his fiction the literary lineage of which could not be traced back to the peculiar fate of Euphemia Clive. She is Daisy Miller, Caroline Spencer, Isabel Archer, Milly Theale, Maggie Verver, to name but a few, all rolled into one.

What is more significant, however, is that it is in this work that we first get a completely satisfactory articulation of the twin themes of dispossession and crisis of identity which so occupied James's literary career, and which were the crucial discovery of the second phase of his apprenticeship. While in a limited way the themes are explored in the very first 'international' tale, 'Travelling Companions', and are examined in greater detail in tales such as 'A Passionate Pilgrim' and 'The Madonna of the Future', 'Mme. De Mauves' tackles them with maturer concern, sympathy and seriousness.

Because of the maturity of outlook, not only are the novella's inhabitants more immediately believable, but also the effects created nicely coalesce with the prevailing rhythm and mood of the work. Even the prose, languorous and lyrical, is in complete concert with the gentle pathos of the situation. There is, moreover, remarkable ease in the different modes of irony which control the portraits of Richard de Mauves and Madame Clairin, and the imaginative understanding which informs the brief appearance of the old Madame de Mauves.

James's vision of Euphemia's (and Longmore's) response to the former's predicament—he returns to the matter in *The Portrait of a Lady* with a clearly intended reference to the novella—reveals the real source of the work's own strength, and that of James as a poetic novelist—his 'sentimentality'. (The word as well as the attribute are in disrepute these days, which is a pity.) Here, as elsewhere in James, it is a definite virtue, very much in the same way as it is a virtue in Shakespeare, or in Wordsworth, or Dickens, or George Eliot, or Hardy, or, for that matter, in any instance of heroic or tragic art (and action). It is this quality which in turn initiates the repeated ritual of renunciation in James, inaugurated by Euphemia in 'Mme. De Mauves', and, in a different way, concluded by Maggie Verver in *The Golden Bowl*.

In short, 'Mme. De Mauves'—as also three or four other pieces of the period—is quite unlike anything James had produced in the Cambridge years of his first phase. That the discovery of the 'international' theme, fictionalized in the five years under scrutiny, should so suddenly transform James's art and sensibility need not surprise us: after all, it is not internationalism *per se* which is at issue, but its fearful concomitants— the perils of dispossession, disinheritance, alienation, the moving away from one's spiritual and cultural orbit. Needless to add, these were precisely the matters James had been discussing too much with *himself* during the five years; the decision to turn his narrative art upon such discussions simply meant that from now on the subject of his fiction would be able to claim the right kind of 'emotional sanction' from its author. Just that is the case with the international tales of the period.

Travelling Companions

[First appeared in the *Atlantic Monthly*, vol. xxvi (November–December 1870), pp. 600–14, 684–97. Not reprinted during James's lifetime.]

I.

THE MOST STRICTLY IMPRESSIVE PICTURE IN ITALY IS incontestably the Last Supper of Leonardo at Milan. A part of its immense solemnity is doubtless due to its being one of the first of the great Italian masterworks that you encounter in coming down from the North. Another secondary source of interest resides in the very completeness of its decay. The mind finds a rare delight in filling each of its vacant spaces, effacing its rank defilement, and repairing, as far as possible, its sad disorder. Of the essential power and beauty of the work there can be no better evidence than this fact that, having lost so much, it has yet retained so much. An unquenchable elegance lingers in those vague outlines and incurable scars; enough remains to place you in sympathy with the unfathomable wisdom of the painter. The fresco covers a wall, the reader will remember, at the end of the former refectory of a monastery now suppressed, the precinct of which is occupied by a regiment of cavalry. Horses stamp, soldiers rattle their oaths, in the cloisters which once echoed to the sober tread of monastic sandals and the pious greetings of meek-voiced friars.

It was the middle of August, and summer sat brooding fiercely over the streets of Milan. The great brick-wrought dome of the church of St. Mary of the Graces rose black with the heat against the brazen sky. As my *fiacre* drew up in front of the church, I found another vehicle in possession of the little square of shade which carpeted the glaring pavement before the adjoining convent. I left the two drivers to share this advantage as they could, and made haste to enter the cooler presence of the Cenacolo. Here I found the occupants of the *fiacre* without, a young lady and an elderly man. Here also, besides the official who takes your tributary franc, sat a long-haired copyist, wooing back the silent secrets of the great fresco into the cheerfullest commonplaces of yellow and blue. The gentleman was earnestly watching this ingenious operation; the young lady sat with her eyes fixed on the picture, from which she failed to move them when I took my place on a line with her. I too, however, speedily became as unconscious of her presence as she of mine, and lost myself in the study of the work before us. A single glance had assured me that she was an American.

Since that day, I have seen all the great art treasures of Italy: I have seen Tintoretto at Venice, Michael Angelo at Florence and Rome, Correggio at Parma; but I have looked at no other picture with an emotion equal to that which rose within me as this great creation of Leonardo slowly began to dawn upon my intelligence from the tragical twilight of its ruin. A work so nobly conceived can never utterly die, so long as the half-dozen main lines of its design remain. Neglect and malice are less cunning than the genius of the great painter. It has stored away with masterly skill such a wealth of beauty as only perfect love and sympathy can fully detect. So, under my eyes, the restless ghost of the dead fresco returned to its mortal abode. From the beautiful central image of Christ I perceived its radiation right and left along the sadly broken line of the disciples. One by one, out of the depths of their grim dismemberment, the figures trembled into meaning and life, and the vast, serious beauty of the work stood revealed. What is the ruling force of this magnificent design? Is it art? is it science? is it sentiment? is it knowledge? I am sure I can't say; but in moments of doubt and depression I find it of excellent use to recall the great picture with all possible distinctness. Of all the works of man's hands it is the least superficial.

The young lady's companion finished his survey of the copyist's work and came and stood behind his chair. The reader will remember that a door has been rudely cut in the wall, a part of it entering the fresco.

'He hasn't got in that door,' said the old gentleman, speaking apparently of the copyist.

The young lady was silent. 'Well, my dear,' he continued. 'What do you think of it?'

The young girl gave a sigh. 'I see it,' she said.

'You see it, eh? Well, I suppose there is nothing more to be done.'

The young lady rose slowly, drawing on her glove. As her eyes were still on the fresco, I was able to observe her. Beyond doubt she was American. Her age I fancied to be twenty-two. She was of middle stature, with a charming slender figure. Her hair was brown, her complexion fresh and clear. She wore a white piqué dress and a black lace shawl, and on her thick dark braids a hat with a purple feather. She was largely characterized by that physical delicacy and that personal elegance (each of them sometimes excessive) which seldom fail to betray my young countrywomen in Europe. The

gentleman, who was obviously her father, bore the national stamp
as plainly as she. A shrewd, firm, generous face, which told of many
dealings with many men, of stocks and shares and current prices,—a
face, moreover, in which there lingered the mellow afterglow of a
sense of excellent claret. He was bald and grizzled, this perfect
American, and he wore a short-bristled white moustache between
the two hard wrinkles forming the sides of a triangle of which his
mouth was the base and the ridge of his nose, where his eye-glass sat,
the apex. In deference perhaps to this exotic growth, he was better
dressed than is common with the typical American citizen, in a blue
necktie, a white waistcoat, and a pair of grey trousers. As his daughter still lingered, he looked at me with an eye of sagacious conjecture.

'Ah, that beautiful, beautiful, beautiful Christ,' said the young
lady, in a tone which betrayed her words in spite of its softness. 'O
father, what a picture!'

'Hum!' said her father, 'I don't see it.'

'I must get a photograph,' the young girl rejoined. She turned
away and walked to the farther end of the hall, where the custodian
presides at a table of photographs and prints. Meanwhile her father
had perceived my Murray.

'English, sir?' he demanded.

'No, I'm an American, like yourself, I fancy.'

'Glad to make your acquaintance, sir. From New York?'

'From New York. I have been absent from home, however, for a
number of years.'

'Residing in this part of the world?'

'No. I have been living in Germany. I have only just come into
Italy.'

'Ah, so have we. The young lady is my daughter. She is crazy
about Italy. We were very nicely fixed at Interlaken, when suddenly
she read in some confounded book or other that Italy should be seen
in summer. So she dragged me over the mountains into this fiery
furnace. I'm actually melting away. I have lost five pounds in three
days.'

I replied that the heat was indeed intense, but that I agreed with
his daughter that Italy should be seen in summer. What could be
pleasanter than the temperature of that vast cool hall?

'Ah, yes,' said my friend; 'I suppose we shall have plenty of this
kind of thing. It makes no odds to me, so long as my poor girl has
a good time.'

'She seems,' I remarked, 'to be having a pretty good time with the
photographs.' In fact, she was comparing photographs with a great
deal of apparent energy, while the salesman lauded his wares in the

Italian manner. We strolled over to the table. The young girl was seemingly in treaty for a large photograph of the head of Christ, in which the blurred and fragmentary character of the original was largely intensified, though much of its exquisite pathetic beauty was also preserved. 'They'll not think much of that at home,' said the old gentleman.

'So much the worse for them,' said his daughter, with an accent of delicate pity. With the photograph in her hand, she walked back to the fresco. Her father engaged in an English dialogue with the custodian. In the course of five minutes, wishing likewise to compare the copy and the original, I returned to the great picture. As I drew near it the young lady turned away. Her eyes then for the first time met my own. They were deep and dark and luminous,—I fancied streaming with tears. I watched her as she returned to the table. Her walk seemed to me peculiarly graceful; light, and rapid, and yet full of decision and dignity. A thrill of delight passed through my heart as I guessed at her moistened lids.

'Sweet fellow-countrywoman,' I cried in silence, 'you have the divine gift of feeling.' And I returned to the fresco with a deepened sense of its virtue. When I turned around, my companions had left the room.

In spite of the great heat, I was prepared thoroughly to 'do' Milan. In fact, I rather enjoyed the heat; it seemed to my Northern senses to deepen the Italian, the Southern, the local character of things. On that blazing afternoon, I have not forgotten, I went to the church of St. Ambrose, to the Ambrosian Library, to a dozen minor churches. Every step distilled a richer drop into the wholesome cup of pleasure. From my earliest manhood, beneath a German sky, I had dreamed of this Italian pilgrimage, and, after much waiting and working and planning, I had at last undertaken it in a spirit of fervent devotion. There had been moments in Germany when I fancied myself a clever man; but it now seemed to me that for the first time I really *felt* my intellect. Imagination, panting and exhausted, withdrew from the game; and Observation stepped into her place, trembling and glowing with open-eyed desire.

I had alrealy been twice to the Cathedral, and had wandered through the clustering inner darkness of the high arcades which support those light-defying pinnacles and spires. Towards the close of the afternoon I found myself strolling once more over the great column-planted, altar-studded pavement, with the view of ascending to the roof. On presenting myself at the little door in the right transept, through which you gain admission to the upper regions, I perceived my late fellow-visitors of the fresco preparing apparently for an upward movement, but not without some reluctance on the paternal side. The poor gentleman had been accommodated with a chair, on which he sat fanning himself with his hat and looking painfully apoplectic. The sacristan meanwhile held open the door with an air of invitation. But my corpulent friend, with his thumb in his Murray, balked at the ascent. Recognizing me, his face expressed a sudden sense of vague relief.

'Have you been up, sir?' he inquired, groaningly.

I answered that I was about to ascend; and recalling then the fact, which I possessed rather as information than experience, that young American ladies may not improperly detach themselves on occasion from the parental side, I ventured to declare that, if my friend was unwilling to encounter the fatigue of mounting to the roof in person, I should be most happy, as a fellow-countryman, qualified already perhaps to claim a traveller's acquaintance, to accompany and assist his daughter.

'You're very good, sir,' said the poor man; 'I confess that I'm about played out. I'd far rather sit here and watch these pretty Italian ladies saying their prayers. Charlotte, what do you say?'

'Of course if you're tired I should be sorry to have you make the effort,' said Charlotte. 'But I believe the great thing is to see the view from the roof. I'm much obliged to the gentleman.'

It was arranged accordingly that we should ascend together. 'Good luck to you,' cried my friend, 'and mind you take good care of her.'

Those who have rambled among the marble immensities of the summit of Milan Cathedral will hardly expect me to describe them. It is only when they have been seen as a complete concentric whole that they can be properly appreciated. It was not as a whole that I saw them; a week in Italy had assured me that I have not the architectural *coup d'œil*. In looking back on the scene into which we emerged from the stifling spiral of the ascent, I have chiefly a confused sense of an immense skyward elevation and a fierce blind efflorescence of fantastic forms of marble. There, reared for the action of the sun, you find a vast marble world. The solid whiteness lies in mighty slabs along the iridescent slopes of nave and transept, like the lonely snow-fields of the higher Alps. It leaps and climbs and shoots and attacks the unsheltered blue with a keen and joyous incision. It meets the pitiless sun with a more than equal glow; the day falters, declines, expires, but the marble shines for ever, unmelted and unintermittent. You will know what I mean if you have looked upward from the Piazza at midnight. With confounding frequency too, on some uttermost point of a pinnacle, its plastic force explodes into satisfied rest in some perfect flower of a figure. A myriad carven

statues, known only to the circling air, are poised and niched beyond reach of human vision, the loss of which to mortal eyes is, I
suppose, the gain of the Church and the Lord. Among all the
jewelled shrines and overwrought tabernacles of Italy, I have seen
no such magnificent waste of labour, no such glorious synthesis of
cunning secrets. As you wander, sweating and blinking, over the
changing levels of the edifice, your eye catches at a hundred points
the little profile of a little saint, looking out into the dizzy air, a
pair of folded hands praying to the bright immediate heavens, a
sandalled monkish foot planted on the edge of the white abyss. And
then, besides this mighty world of the great Cathedral itself, you
possess the view of all green Lombardy,—vast, lazy Lombardy, resting from its Alpine upheavals.

My companion carried a little white umbrella, with a violet lining.
Thus protected from the sun, she climbed and gazed with abundant
courage and spirit. Her movements, her glance, her voice, were full
of intelligent pleasure. Now that I could observe her closely, I saw
that, though perhaps without regular beauty, she was yet, for youth,
summer, and Italy, more than pretty enough. Owing to my residence
in Germany, among Germans, in a small university town, Americans
had come to have for me, in a large degree, the interest of novelty
and remoteness. Of the charm of American women, in especial, I
had formed a very high estimate, and I was more than ready to be
led captive by the far-famed graces of their frankness and freedom.
I already felt that in the young girl beside me there was a different
quality of womanhood from any that I had recently known; a keenness, a maturity, a conscience, which deeply stirred my curiosity. It
was positive, not negative maidenhood.

'You're an American,' I said, as we stepped to look at the distance.

'Yes; and you?' In her voice alone the charm faltered. It was high,
thin, and nervous.

'Oh, happily, I'm also one.'

'I shouldn't have thought so. I should have taken you for a
German.'

'By education I am a German. I knew you were an American the
moment I looked at you.'

'I suppose so. It seems that American women are easily recognized.
But don't talk about America.' She paused and swept her dark eye
over the whole immensity of prospect. 'This is Italy,' she cried,
'Italy, Italy!'

'Italy indeed. What do you think of the Leonardo.'

'I fancy there can be only one feeling about it. It must be the
saddest and finest of all pictures. But I know nothing of art. I have

seen nothing yet but that lovely Raphael in the Brera.'
'You have a vast deal before you. You're going southward, I suppose.'
'Yes, we are going directly to Venice. There I shall see Titian.'
'Titian and Paul Veronese.'
'Yes, I can hardly believe it. Have you ever been in a gondola?'
'No; this is my first visit to Italy.'
'Ah, this is all new, then, to you as well.'
'Divinely new,' said I, with fervour.
She glanced at me, with a smile,—a ray of friendly pleasure in my pleasure. 'And you are not disappointed!'
'Not a jot. I'm too good a German.'
'I'm too good an American. I live at Araminta, New Jersey!'
We thoroughly 'did' the high places of the church, concluding with an ascent into the little gallery of the central spire. The view from this spot is beyond all words, especially the view towards the long mountain line which shuts out the North. The sun was sinking: clear and serene upon their blue foundations, the snow-peaks sat clustered and scattered, and shrouded in silence and light. To the south the long shadows fused and multiplied, and the bosky Lombard flats melted away into perfect Italy. This prospect offers a great emotion to the Northern traveller. A vague, delicious impulse of conquest stirs in his heart. From his dizzy vantage-point, as he looks down at her, beautiful, historic, exposed, he embraces the whole land in the far-reaching range of his desire. 'That is Monte Rosa,' I said; 'that is the Simplon pass; there is the triple glitter of those lovely lakes.'
'Poor Monte Rosa,' said my companion.
'I'm sure I never thought of Monte Rosa as an object of pity.'
'You don't know what she represents. She represents the genius of the North. There she stands, frozen and fixed, resting her head upon that mountain wall, looking over at this lovely southern world and yearning towards it for ever in vain.'
'It is very well she can't come over. She would melt.'
'Very true. She is beautiful, too, in her own way. I mean to fancy that I am her chosen envoy, and that I have come up here to receive her blessing.'
I made an attempt to point out a few localities. 'Yonder lies Venice, out of sight. In the interval are a dozen divine little towns. I hope to visit them all. I shall ramble all day in their streets and churches, their little museums, and their great palaces. In the evening I shall sit at the door of a café in the little piazza, scanning some lovely civic edifice in the moonlight, and saying, "Ah! this is Italy!"'

'You gentlemen are certainly very happy. I'm afraid we must go straight to Venice.'

'Your father insists upon it?'

'He wishes it. Poor father! in early life he formed the habit of being in a hurry, and he can't break it even now, when, being out of business, he has nothing on earth to do.'

'But in America I thought daughters insisted as well as fathers.'

The young girl looked at me, half serious, half smiling. 'Have you a mother?' she asked; and then, blushing the least bit at her directness and without waiting for an answer, 'This is not America,' she said. 'I should like to think I might become for a while a creature of Italy.'

Somehow I felt a certain contagion in her momentary flash of frankness. 'I strongly suspect,' I said, 'that you are American to the depths of your soul, and that you'll never be anything else; I hope not.'

In this hope of mine there was perhaps a little impertinence; but my companion looked at me with a gentle smile, which seemed to hint that she forgave it. 'You, on the other hand,' she said, 'are a perfect German, I fancy; and you'll never be anything else.'

'I am sure I wish with all my heart,' I answered, 'to be a good American. I'm open to conversion. Try me.'

'Thank you; I haven't the ardour; I'll make you over to my father. We mustn't forget, by the way, that he is waiting for us.'

We did forget it, however, awhile longer. We came down from the tower and made our way to the balustrade which edges the front of the edifice, and looked down on the city and the piazza below. Milan had, to my sense, a peculiar charm of temperate gaiety,—the softness of the South without its laxity; and I felt as if I could gladly spend a month there. The common life of the streets was beginning to stir and murmur again, with the subsiding heat and the approaching night. There came up into our faces a delicious emanation as from the sweetness of Transalpine life. At the little balconies of the windows, beneath the sloping awnings, with their feet among the crowded flower-pots and their plump bare arms on the iron rails, lazy, dowdy Italian beauties would appear, still drowsy with the broken *siesta*. Beautiful, slim young officers had begun to dot the pavement, glorious with their clanking swords, their brown moustaches, and their legs of azure. In gentle harmony with these, various ladies of Milan were issuing forth to enjoy the cool; elegant, romantic, provoking, in short black dresses and lace mantillas depending from their *chignons*, with a little cloud of powder artfully enhancing the darkness of their hair and eyes. How it all wasn't Germany!

how it couldn't have been Araminta, New Jersey! 'It's the South, the South,' I kept repeating,—'the South in nature, in man, in manners.' It was a brighter world. 'It's the South,' I said to my companion. 'Don't you feel it in all your nerves?'

'O, it's very pleasant,' she said.

'We must forget all our cares and duties and sorrows. We must go in for the beautiful. Think of this great trap for the sunbeams, in this city of yellows and russets and crimsons, of liquid vowels and glancing smiles being, like one of our Northern cathedrals, a temple to Morality and Conscience. It doesn't belong to heaven, but to earth, —to love and light and pleasure.'

My friend was silent a moment. 'I'm glad I'm not a Catholic,' she said at last. 'Come, we must go down.'

We found the interior of the Cathedral delightfully cool and shadowy. The young lady's father was not at our place of ingress, and we began to walk through the church in search of him. We met a number of Milanese ladies, who charmed us with their sombre elegance and the Spanish romance of their veils. With these pale penitents and postulants my companion had a lingering sisterly sympathy.

'Don't you wish you were a Catholic now?' I asked. 'It would be so pleasant to wear one of those lovely mantillas.'

'The mantillas are certainly becoming,' she said. 'But who knows what horrible old-world sorrows and fears and remorses they cover? Look at this person.' We were standing near the great altar. As she spoke, a woman rose from her knees, and as she drew the folds of her lace mantle across her bosom, fixed her large dark eyes on us with a peculiar significant intensity. She was of less than middle age, with a pale, haggard face, a certain tarnished elegance of dress, and a remarkable nobleness of gesture and carriage. She came towards us, with an odd mixture, in her whole expression, of decency and defiance. 'Are you English?' she said in Italian. 'You are very pretty. Is he a brother or a lover?'

'He is neither,' said I, affecting a tone of rebuke.

'Neither? only a friend! You are very happy to have a friend, Signorina. Ah, you are pretty! You were watching me at my prayers just now; you thought me very curious, apparently. I don't care. You may see me here any day. But I devoutly hope you may never have to pray such bitter, bitter prayers as mine. A thousand excuses.' And she went her way.

'What in the world does she mean?' said my companion.

'Monte Rosa,' said I, 'was the genius of the North. This poor woman is the genius of the Picturesque. She shows us the essential misery that lies behind it. It's not an unwholesome lesson to receive at the outset. Look at her sweeping down the aisle. What a poise of the head! The picturesque is handsome, all the same.'

'I do wonder what is her trouble,' murmured the young girl. 'She has swept away an illusion in the folds of those black garments.'

'Well,' said I, 'here is a solid fact to replace it.' My eyes had just lighted upon the object of our search. He sat in a chair, half tilted back against a pillar. His chin rested on his shirt-bosom, and his hands were folded together over his waistcoat, where it most protruded. Shirt and waistcoat rose and fell with visible, audible regularity. I wandered apart and left his daughter to deal with him. When she had fairly aroused him, he thanked me heartily for my care of the young lady, and expressed the wish that we might meet again. 'We start tomorrow for Venice,' he said. 'I want awfully to get a whiff of the sea-breeze and to see if there is anything to be got out of a gondola.'

As I expected also to be in Venice before many days, I had little doubt of our meeting. In consideration of this circumstance, my friend proposed that we should exchange cards; which we accordingly did, then and there, before the high altar, above the gorgeous chapel which enshrines the relics of St. Charles Borromeus. It was thus that I learned his name to be Mr. Mark Evans.

'Take a few notes for us!' said Miss Evans, as I shook her hand in farewell.

I spent the evening, after dinner, strolling among the crowded streets of the city, tasting of Milanese humanity. At the door of a café I perceived Mr. Evans seated at a little round table. He seemed to have discovered the merits of absinthe. I wondered where he had left his daughter. She was in her room, I fancied, writing her journal.

The fortnight which followed my departure from Milan was in all respects memorable and delightful. With an interest that hourly deepened as I read, I turned the early pages of the enchanting romance of Italy. I carried out in detail the programme which I had sketched for Miss Evans. Those few brief days, as I look back on them, seem to me the sweetest, fullest, calmest of my life. All personal passions, all restless egotism, all worldly hopes, regrets, and fears were stilled and absorbed in the steady perception of the material present. It exhaled the pure essence of romance. What words can reproduce the picture which these Northern Italian towns project upon a sympathetic retina? They are shabby, deserted, dreary, decayed, unclean. In those August days the southern sun poured into them with a fierceness which might have seemed fatal to any lurking shadow of picturesque mystery. But taking them as cruel time had made them and left them, I found in them an immeasurable instruction and charm. My perception seemed for the first time to live a sturdy creative life of its own. How it fed upon the mouldy crumbs of the festal past! I have always thought the observant faculty a windy impostor, so long as it refuses to pocket pride and doff its bravery and crawl on all-fours, if need be, into the unillumined corners and crannies of life. In these dead cities of Verona, Mantua, Padua, how life had revelled and postured in its strength! How sentiment and passion had blossomed and flowered! How much of history had been performed! What a wealth of mortality had ripened and decayed! I have never elsewhere got so deep an impression of the social secrets of mankind. In England, even, in those verdure-stifled haunts of domestic peace which muffle the sounding chords of British civilization, one has a fainter sense of the possible movement and fruition of individual character. Beyond a certain point you fancy it merged in the general medium of duty, business, and politics. In Italy, in spite of your knowledge of the strenuous public conscience which once inflamed these compact little states, the unapplied, spontaneous moral life of society seems to have been more active and more subtle. I walked about with a volume of Stendhal in my pocket; at every step I gathered some lingering testimony to the exquisite vanity of ambition.

But the great emotion, after all, was to feel myself among scenes in which art had ranged so freely. It had often enough been bad, but it had never ceased to be art. An invincible instinct of beauty had presided at life,—an instinct often ludicrously crude and primitive. Wherever I turned I found a vital principle of grace,—from the smile of a chambermaid to the curve of an arch. My memory reverts with an especial tenderness to certain hours in the dusky, faded saloons of those vacant, ruinous palaces which boast of 'collections'. The pictures are frequently poor, but the visitor's impression is generally rich. The brick-tiled floors are bare; the doors lack paint; the great windows, curtains; the chairs and tables have lost their gilding and their damask drapery; but the ghost of a graceful aristocracy treads at your side and does the melancholy honours of the abode with a dignity that brooks no sarcasm. You feel that art and piety here have been blind, generous instincts. You are reminded in persuasive accents of the old personal regimen in human affairs. Certain pictures are veiled and curtained *virginibus puerisque*. Through these tarnished halls lean and patient abbés led their youthful virginal pupils. Have you read Stendhal's *Chartreuse de Parme*? There was such a gallery in the palace of the Duchess of San Severino. After a long day of strolling, lounging, and staring, I found a singularly

perfect pleasure in sitting at the door of a café in the warm starlight, eating an ice and making an occasional experiment in the way
of talk with my neighbours. I recall with peculiar fondness and
delight three sweet sessions in the delicious Piazza dei Signori at
Verona. The Piazza is small, compact, private almost, accessible only
to pedestrians, paved with great slabs which have known none but
a gentle human tread. On one side of it rises in elaborate elegance
and grace, above its light arched *loggia*, the image-bordered mass of
the ancient palace of the Council; facing this stand two sterner,
heavier buildings, dedicated to municipal offices and to the lodgement of soldiers. Step through the archway which leads out of the
Piazza and you will find a vast quadrangle with a staircase climbing
sunward, along the wall, a row of gendarmes sitting in the shade,
a group of soldiers cleaning their muskets, a dozen persons of either
sex leaning downward from the open windows. At one end of the
little square rose into the pale darkness the high slender shaft of a
brick campanile; in the centre glittered steadily a colossal white
statue of Dante. Behind this statue was the Caffè Dante, where on
three successive days I sat till midnight, feeling the scene, learning
its sovereign 'distinction'. But of Verona I shall not pretend to speak.
As I drew near Venice I began to feel a soft impatience, an expectant
tremor of the heart. The day before reaching it I spent at Vicenza.
I wandered all day through the streets, of course, looking at Pal-
ladio's palaces and enjoying them in defiance of reason and Ruskin.
They seemed to me essentially rich and palatial. In the evening I
resorted, as usual, to the city's generous heart, the decayed ex-
glorious Piazza. This spot at Vicenza affords you a really soul-stirring
premonition of Venice. There is no Byzantine Basilica and no Ducal
Palace; but there is an immense impressive hall of council, and a
soaring campanile, and there are two discrowned columns telling of
defeated Venetian dominion. Here I seated myself before a café
door, in a group of gossiping votaries of the Southern night. The
tables being mostly occupied, I had some difficulty in finding one.
In a short time I perceived a young man walking through the crowd,
seeking where he might bestow himself. Passing near me, he stopped
and asked me with irresistible grace if he might share my table. I
cordially assented: he sat down and ordered a glass of sugar and
water. He was of about my own age, apparently, and full of the
opulent beauty of the greater number of young Italians. His dress
was simple even to shabbiness: he might have been a young prince
in disguise, a Haroun-al-Raschid. With small delay we engaged in
conversation. My companion was boyish, modest, and gracious; he
nevertheless discoursed freely on the things of Vicenza. He was so

good as to regret that we had not met earlier in the day; it would have given him such pleasure to accompany me on my tour of the city. He was passionately fond of art: he was in fact an artist. Was I fond of pictures? Was I inclined to purchase? I answered that I had no desire to purchase modern pictures, that in fact I had small means to purchase any. He informed me that he had a beautiful ancient work which, to his great regret, he found himself compelled to sell; a most divine little Correggio. Would I do him the favour to look at it? I had small belief in the value of this unrenowned masterpiece; but I felt a kindness for the young painter. I consented to have him call for me the next morning and take me to his house, where for two hundred years, he assured me, the work had been jealously preserved.

He came punctually, beautiful, smiling, shabby, as before. After a ten minutes' walk we stopped before a gaudy half-palazzo which rejoiced in a vague Palladian air. In the basement, looking on the court, lived my friend; with his mother, he informed me, and his sister. He ushered me in, through a dark antechamber, into which, through a gaping kitchen door, there gushed a sudden aroma of onions. I found myself in a high, half-darkened saloon. One of the windows was open into the court, from which the light entered verdantly through a row of flowering plants. In an armchair near the window sat a young girl in a dressing-gown, empty-handed, pale, with wonderful eyes, apparently an invalid. At her side stood a large elderly woman in a rusty black silk gown, with an agreeable face, flushed a little, apparently with the expectation of seeing me. The young man introduced them as his mother and his sister. On a table near the window, propped upright in such a way as to catch the light, was a small picture in a heavy frame. I proceeded to examine it. It represented in simple composition a Madonna and Child; the mother facing you, pressing the infant to her bosom, faintly smiling, and looking out of the picture with a solemn sweetness. It was pretty, it was good; but it was not Correggio. There was indeed a certain suggestion of his exquisite touch; but it was a likeness merely, and not the precious reality. One fact, however, struck swiftly home to my consciousness: the face of the Madonna bore a singular resemblance to that of Miss Evans. The lines, the character, the expression, were the same; the faint half-thoughtful smile was hers, the feminine frankness and gentle confidence of the brow, from which the dark hair waved back with the same even abundance. All this, in the Madonna's face, was meant for heaven; and on Miss Evans's in a fair degree, probably, for earth. But the mutual likeness was, nevertheless, perfect, and it quickened my interest in the picture to a point which the intrinsic merit of the work would doubtless have failed to justify; although I confess that I was now not slow to discover a great deal of agreeable painting in it.

'But I doubt of its being a Correggio,' said I.

'A Correggio, I give you my word of honour, sir!' cried my young man.

'*Ecco*! my son's word of honour,' cried his mother.

'I don't deny,' I said, 'that it is a very pretty work. It is perhaps Parmigianino.'

'O no, sir,' the elder insisted, 'a true Correggio! We have had it two hundred years! Try another light; you will see. A true Correggio! Isn't it so, my daughter?'

The young man put his arm in mine, played his fingers airily over the picture, and whispered of a dozen beauties.

'O, I grant you,' said I, 'it's a very pretty picture.' As I looked at it I felt the dark eyes of the young girl in the arm-chair fixed upon me with almost unpleasant intensity. I met her gaze for a moment: I found in it a strange union of defiant pride and sad despondent urgency.

'What do you ask for the picture?' I said.

There was a silence.

'Speak, *madre mia*,' said the young man.

'*La senta*!' and the lady played with her broken fan. 'We should like you to name a price.'

'O, if I named a price, it would not be as for a Correggio. I can't afford to buy Correggios. If this were a real Correggio, you would be rich. You should go to a duke, a prince, not to me.'

'We would be rich! Do you hear, my children? We are very poor, sir. You have only to look at us. Look at my poor daughter. She was once beautiful, fresh, gay. A year ago she fell ill; a long story, sir, and a sad one. We have had doctors; they have ordered five thousand things. My daughter gets no better. There it is, sir. We are very poor.'

The young girl's look confirmed her mother's story. That she had been beautiful I could easily believe; that she was ill was equally apparent. She was still remarkable indeed for a touching, hungry, unsatisfied grace. She remained silent and motionless, with her eyes fastened upon my face. I again examined the pretended Correggio. It was wonderfully like Miss Evans. The young American rose up in my mind with irresistible vividness and grace. How she seemed to glow with strength, freedom, and joy, besides this sombre, fading, Southern sister! It was a happy thought that, under the benediction of her image, I might cause a ray of healing sunshine to fall at this poor girl's feet.

'Have you ever tried to sell the picture before?'

'Never!' said the old lady, proudly. 'My husband had it from his father. If we have made up our minds to part with it now,—most blessed little Madonna!—it is because we have had an intimation from heaven.'

'From heaven?'

'From heaven, Signore. My daughter had a dream. She dreamed that a young stranger came to Vicenza, and that he wandered about the streets saying, "Where, ah where, is my blessed Lady?" Some told him in one church, and some told him in another. He went into all the churches and lifted all the curtains, giving great fees to the sacristans! But he always came out shaking his head and repeating his question, "Where is my blessed Lady? I have come from over the sea, I have come to Italy to find her!"' The woman delivered herself of this recital with a noble florid unction and a vast redundancy, to my Northern ear, of delightful liquid sounds. As she paused momentarily, her daughter spoke for the first time.

'And then I fancied,' said the young girl, 'that I heard his voice pausing under my window at night. "His blessed Lady is here," I said, "we must not let him lose her." So I called my brother and bade him go forth in search of you. I dreamed that he brought you back. We made an altar with candles and lace and flowers, and on it we placed the little picture. The stranger had light hair, light eyes, a flowing beard like you. He knelt down before the little Madonna and worshipped her. We left him at his devotions and went away. When we came back the candles on the altar were out: the Madonna was gone, too; but in its place there burned a bright pure light. It was a purse of gold!'

'What a very pretty story!' said I. 'How many pieces were there in the purse?'

The young man burst into a laugh. 'Twenty thousand!' he said.

I made my offer for the picture. It was esteemed generous apparently; I was cordially thanked. As it was inconvenient, however, to take possession of the work at that moment, I agreed to pay down but half the sum, reserving the other half to the time of delivery. When I prepared to take my departure the young girl rose from her chair and enabled me to measure at once her weakness and her beauty. 'Will you come back for the picture yourself?' she asked.

'Possibly. I should like to see you again. You must get better.'

'O, I shall never get better.'

'I can't believe that. I shall perhaps have a dream to tell you!'

'I shall soon be in heaven. I shall send you one.'

'Listen to her!' cried the mother. 'But she is already an angel.'

With a farewell glance at my pictured Madonna I departed. My visit to this little Vicenza household had filled me with a painful, indefinable sadness. So beautiful they all were, so civil, so charming, and yet so mendacious and miserable! As I hurried along in the train towards the briny cincture of Venice, my heart was heavy with the image of that sombre, dying Italian maiden. Her face haunted me. What fatal wrong had she suffered? What hidden sorrow had blasted the freshness of her youth? As I began to smell the nearing Adriatic, my fancy bounded forward to claim asylum in the calmer presence of my bright American friend. I have no space to tell the story of my arrival in Venice and my first impressions. Mr. Evans had not mentioned his hotel. He was not at the Hotel de l'Europe, whither I myself repaired. If he was still in Venice, however, I foresaw that we should not fail to meet. The day succeeding my arrival I spent in a restless fever of curiosity and delight, now lost in the sensuous ease of my gondola, now lingering in charmed devotion before a canvas of Tintoretto or Paul Veronese. I exhausted three gondoliers and saw all Venice in a passionate fury and haste. I wished to probe its fullness and learn at once the best—or the worst. Late in the afternoon I disembarked at the Piazzetta and took my way haltingly and gazingly to the many-domed Basilica,—that shell of silver with a lining of marble. It was that enchanting Venetian hour when the ocean-touching sun sits melting to death, and the whole still air seems to glow with the soft effusion of his golden substance. Within the church, the deep brown shadow-masses, the heavy, thick-tinted air, the gorgeous composite darkness, reigned in richer, quainter, more fantastic gloom than my feeble pen can reproduce the likeness of. From those rude concavities of dome and semi-dome, where the multitudinous facets of pictorial mosaic shimmer and twinkle in their own dull brightness; from the vast antiquity of innumerable marbles, incrusting the walls in roughly mated slabs, cracked and polished and triple-tinted with eternal service; from the wavy carpet of compacted stone, where a thousand once-bright fragments glimmer through the long attrition of idle feet and devoted knees; from sombre gold and mellow alabaster, from porphyry and malachite, from long dead crystal and the sparkle of undying lamps,—there proceeds a dense rich atmosphere of splendour and sanctity which transports the half-stupefied traveller to the age of a simpler and more awful faith. I wandered for half an hour beneath those reverted cups of scintillating darkness, stumbling on the great stony swells of the pavement as I gazed upward at the long mosaic saints who curve gigantically with the curves of dome and ceiling. I had left Europe; I was in the East. An overwhelming sense of the sadness of man's spiritual history took possession of my heart. The clustering picturesque shadows about me seemed to represent the darkness of a past from which he had slowly and painfully struggled. The great mosaic images, hideous, grotesque, inhuman, glimmered like the cruel spectres of early superstitions and terrors. There came over me, too, a poignant conviction of the ludicrous folly of the idle spirit of travel. How with Murray and an opera-glass it strolls and stares where omniscient angels stand diffident and sad! How blunted and stupid are its senses! How trivial and superficial its imaginings! To this builded sepulchre of trembling hope and dread, this monument of mighty passions, I had wandered in search of pictorial effects. O vulgarity! Of course I remained, nevertheless, still curious of effects. Suddenly I perceived a very agreeable one. Kneeling on a low *prie-dieu*, with her hands clasped, a lady was gazing upward at the great mosaic Christ in the dome of the choir. She wore a black lace shawl and a purple hat. She was Miss Evans. Her attitude slightly puzzled me. Was she really at her devotions, or was she only playing at prayer? I walked to a distance, so that she might have time to move before I addressed her. Five minutes afterwards, however, she was in the same position. I walked slowly towards her, and, as I approached her, attracted her attention. She immediately recognized me and smiled and bowed, without moving from her place.

'I saw you five minutes ago,' I said, 'but I was afraid of interrupting your prayers.'

'O, they were only half-prayers,' she said.

'Half-prayers are pretty well for one who only the other day was thanking Heaven that she was not a Catholic.'

'Half-prayers are no prayers. I'm not a Catholic yet.'

Her father, she told me, had brought her to the church, but had returned on foot to the hotel for his pocket-book. They were to dine at one of the restaurants in the Piazza. Mr. Evans was vastly contented with Venice, and spent his days and nights in gondolas. Awaiting his return, we wandered over the church. Yes, incontestably, Miss Evans resembled my little Vicenza picture. She looked a little pale with the heat and the constant nervous tension of sight-seeing; but she pleased me now as effectually as she had pleased me before. There was an even deeper sweetness in the freedom and breadth of her utterance and carriage. I felt more even than before that she was an example of woman active, not of woman passive. We strolled through the great Basilica in serious, charmed silence. Miss Evans told me that she had been there much: she seemed to know it well. We went into the dark Baptistery and sat down on a bench against the wall, trying to discriminate in the vaulted dimness the harsh mediaeval reliefs behind the altar and the mosaic Crucifixion above it.

'Well,' said I, 'what has Venice done for you?'

'Many things. Tired me a little, saddened me, charmed me.'

'How have you spent your time?'

'As people spend it. After breakfast we get into our gondola and remain in it pretty well till bedtime. I believe I know every canal, every canaletto, in Venice. You must have learned already how sweet it is to lean back under the awning, to feel beneath you that steady, liquid lapse, to look out at all this bright, sad elegance of ruin. I have been reading two or three of George Sand's novels. Do you know *La Dernière Aldini*? I fancy a romance in every palace.'

'The reality of Venice seems to me to exceed all romance. It's romance enough simply to be here.'

'Yes; but how brief and transient a romance!'

'Well,' said I, 'we shall certainly cease to be here, but we shall never cease to have been here. You are not to leave directly, I hope.'

'In the course of ten days or a fortnight we go to Florence.'

'And then to Rome?'

'To Rome and Naples, and then by sea, probably, to Genoa, and thence to Nice and Paris. We must be at home by the new year. And you?'

'I hope to spend the winter in Italy.'

'Are you never coming home again?'

'By no means. I shall probably return in the spring. But I wish you, too, were going to remain.'

'You are very good. My father pronounces it impossible. I have only to make the most of it while I'm here.'

'Are you going back to Araminta?'

Miss Evans was silent a moment. 'O, don't ask!' she said.

'What kind of a place is Araminta?' I asked, maliciously.

Again she was silent. 'That is John the Baptist on the cover of the basin,' she said, at last, rising to her feet, with a light laugh.

On emerging from the Baptistery we found Mr. Evans, who greeted me cordially and insisted on my coming to dine with them. I think most fondly of our little dinner. We went to the Caffè Quadri and occupied a table beside an open window, looking out into the Piazza, which was beginning to fill with the evening loungers and listeners to the great band of music in the centre. Miss Evans took off her hat and sat facing me in friendly silence. Her father sustained the larger burden of conversation. He seemed to feel its weight, however, as the dinner proceeded and when he had

attacked his second bottle of wine. Miss Evans then questioned me
about my journey from Milan. I told her the whole story, and felt
that I infused into it a great deal of colour and heat. She sat charming me forward with her steady, listening smile. For the first time in
my life I felt the magic of sympathy. After dinner we went down into
the Piazza and established ourselves at one of Florian's tables. Night
had become perfect; the music was magnificent. At a neighbouring
table was a group of young Venetian gentlemen, splendid in dress,
after the manner of their kind, and glorious with the wondrous
physical glory of the Italian race.

'They only need velvet and satin and plumes,' I said, 'to be subjects for Titian and Paul Veronese.'

They sat rolling their dark eyes and kissing their white hands at
passing friends, with smiles that were like the moon-flashes on the
Adriatic.

'They are beautiful exceedingly,' said Miss Evans; 'the most
beautiful creatures in the world, except——'

'Except, you mean, this other gentleman.'

She assented. The person of whom I had spoken was a young man
who was just preparing to seat himself at a vacant table. A lady and
gentleman, elderly persons, had passed near him and recognized
him, and he had uncovered himself and now stood smiling and talking. They were all genuine Anglo-Saxons. The young man was rather
short of stature, but firm and compact. His hair was light and crisp,
his eye a clear blue, his face and neck violently tanned by exposure
to the sun. He wore a pair of small blonde whiskers.

'Do you call him beautiful?' demanded Mr. Evans. 'He reminds
me of myself when I was his age. Indeed, he looks like you, sir.'

'He's not beautiful,' said Miss Evans, 'but he is handsome.'

The young man's face was full of decision and spirit; his whole
figure had been moulded by action, tempered by effort. He looked
simple and keen, upright, downright.

'Is he English?' asked Miss Evans, 'or American?'

'He is both,' I said, 'or either. He is made of that precious clay
that is common to the whole English-speaking race.'

'He's American.'

'Very possibly,' said I; and indeed we never learned. I repeat the
incident because I think it has a certain value in my recital. Before
we separated I expressed the hope that we might meet again on the
morrow.

'It's very kind of you to propose it,' said Miss Evans; 'but you'll
thank us for refusing. Take my advice, as for an old Venetian, and
spend the coming three days alone. How can you enjoy Tintoretto

and Bellini, when you are racking your brains for small talk for me?'

'With you, Miss Evans, I shouldn't talk small. But you shape my programme with a liberal hand. At the end of three days, pray, where will you be?'

They would still be in Venice, Mr. Evans declared. It was a capital hotel, and then those jolly gondolas! I was unable to impeach the wisdom of the young girl's proposition. To be so wise, it seemed to me, was to be extremely charming.

For three days, accordingly, I wandered about alone. I often thought of Miss Evans and I often fancied I should enjoy certain great pictures none the less for that deep associated contemplation and those fine emanations of assent and dissent which I should have known in her society. I wandered far; I penetrated deep, it seemed to me, into the heart of Venetian power. I shook myself free of the sad and sordid present, and embarked on that silent contemplative sea whose irresistible tides expire at the base of the mighty canvases in the Scuola di San Rocco. But on my return to the hither shore, I always found my sweet young countrywoman waiting to receive me. If Miss Evans had been an immense coquette, she could not have proceeded more cunningly than by this injunction of a three days' absence. During this period, in my imagination, she increased tenfold in value. I don't mean to say that there were not hours together when I quite forgot her, and when I had no heart but for Venice and the lessons of Venice, for the sea and sky and the great painters and builders. But when my mind had executed one of these great passages of appreciation, it turned with a sudden sense of solitude and lassitude to those gentle hopes, those fragrant hints of intimacy, which clustered about the person of my friend. She remained modestly uneclipsed by the women of Titian. She was as deeply a woman as they, and yet so much more of a person; as fit as the broadest and blondest to be loved for herself, yet full of serene superiority as an active friend. To the old, old sentiment what an exquisite modern turn she might give! I so far overruled her advice as that, with her father, we made a trio every evening, after the day's labours, at one of Florian's tables. Mr. Evans drank absinthe and discoursed upon the glories of our common country, of which he declared it was high time I should make the acquaintance. He was not the least of a bore: I relished him vastly. He was in many ways an excellent, representative American. Without taste, without culture or polish, he nevertheless produced an impression of substance in character, keenness in perception, and intensity in will, which effectually redeemed him from vulgarity. It often seemed to me, in fact, that his good-humoured tolerance and easy morality, his rank self-confidence, his nervous decision and vivacity, his fearlessness of either gods or men, combined in proportions of which the union might have been very fairly termed aristocratic. His voice, I admit, was of the nose, nasal; but possibly, in the matter of utterance, one eccentricity is as good as another. At all events, with his clear, cold grey eye, with that just faintly impudent, more than level poise of his ample chin, with those two hard lines which flanked the bristling wings of his grey moustache, with his general expression of un-challenged security and practical aptitude and incurious scorn of tradition, he impressed the sensitive beholder as a man of incon-testable force. He was entertaining, too, partly by wit and partly by position. He was weak only in his love of absinthe. After his first glass he left his chair and strolled about the piazza, looking for pos-sible friends and superbly unconscious of possible enemies. His daughter sat back in her chair, her arms folded, her ungloved hands sustaining them, her prettiness half defined, her voice enhanced and subdued by the gas-tempered starlight. We had infinite talk. Without question, she had an admirable feminine taste: she was worthy to know Venice. I remember telling her so in a sudden ex-plosion of homage. 'You are really worthy to know Venice, Miss Evans. We must learn to know it together. Who knows what hidden treasures we may help each other to find?'

II.

At the end of my three days' probation, I spent a week constantly with my friends. Our mornings were, of course, devoted to churches and galleries, and in the late afternoon we passed and repassed along the Grand Canal or betook ourselves to the Lido. By this time Miss Evans and I had become thoroughly intimate; we had learned to know Venice together, and the knowledge had helped us to know each other. In my own mind, Charlotte Evans and Venice had played the game most effectively into each other's hands. If my fancy had been called upon to paint her portrait, my fancy would have sketched her with a background of sunset-flushed palace wall, with a faint reflected light from the green lagoon playing up into her face. And if I had wished to sketch a Venetian scene, I should have painted it from an open window, with a woman leaning against the casement,—as I had often seen her lean from a window in her hotel. At the end of a week we went one afternoon to the Lido, timing our departure so as to allow us to return at sunset. We went over in silence, Mr. Evans sitting with reverted head, blowing his cigar-smoke against the dazzling sky, which told so fiercely of sea and summer; his daughter motionless and thickly veiled; I facing them, feeling the broken swerve of our gondola, and watching Venice grow level and rosy beyond the liquid interval. Near the landing-place on the hither side of the Lido is a small *trattoria* for the refreshment of visitors. An arbour outside the door, a horizontal vine checkering still further a dirty table-cloth, a pungent odour of *frittata*, an admiring circle of gondoliers and beggars, are the chief attractions of this suburban house of entertainment,—attractions sufficient, however, to have arrested the inquisitive steps of an elderly American gentleman, in whom Mr. Evans speedily recognized a friend of early years, a comrade in affairs. A hearty greeting ensued. This worthy man had ordered dinner: he besought Mr. Evans at least to sit down and partake of a bottle of wine. My friend vacillated between his duties as a father and the prospect of a rich old-boyish revival of the delectable interests of home; but his daughter graci-ously came to his assistance. 'Sit down with Mr. Munson, talk till you are tired, and then walk over to the beach and find us. We shall not wander beyond call.'

She and I accordingly started slowly for a stroll along the barren strand which averts its shining side from Venice and takes the tides of the Adriatic. The Lido has for me a peculiar melancholy charm, and I have often wondered that I should have felt the presence of beauty in a spot so destitute of any exceptional elements of beauty. For beyond the fact that it knows the changing moods and hues of the Adriatic, this narrow strip of sand-stifled verdure has no very rare distinction. In my own country I know many a sandy beach, and many a stunted copse, and many a tremulous ocean line of little less purity and breadth of composition, with far less magi-cal interest. The secret of the Lido is simply your sense of adjacent Venice. It is the salt-sown garden of the city of the sea. Hither came short-paced Venetians for a meagre taste of *terra firma*, or for a wider glimpse of their parent ocean. Along a narrow line in the middle of the island are market-gardens and breeze-twisted orchards, and a hint of hedges and lanes and inland greenery. At one end is a series of low fortifications duly embanked and moated and sentinelled. Still beyond these, half over-drifted with sand and over-clambered with rank grasses and coarse thick shrubbery, are certain quaintly lettered funeral slabs, tombs of former Jews of Venice. Towards these we slowly wandered and sat down in the grass. Between the sand-heaps, which shut out the beach, we saw in a dozen places the blue agitation of the sea. Over all the scene there brooded the deep bright sadness of early autumn.

I lay at my companion's feet and wondered whether I was in love. It seemed to me that I had never been so happy in my life. They say, I know, that to be in love is not pure happiness; that in the mood of the unconfessed, unaccepted lover there is an element of poignant doubt and pain. Should I at once confess myself and taste of the perfection of bliss? It seemed to me that I cared very little for the meaning of her reply. I only wanted to talk of love; I wanted in some manner to enjoy in that atmosphere of romance the woman who was so blessedly fair and wise. It seemed to me that all the agitation of fancy, the excited sense of beauty, the fervour and joy and sadness begotten by my Italian wanderings, had suddenly resolved themselves into a potent demand for expression. Miss Evans was sitting on one of the Hebrew tombs, her chin on her hand, her elbow on her knee, watching the broken horizon. I was stretched on the grass on my side, leaning on my elbow and on my hand, with my eyes on her face. She bent her own eyes and encountered mine; we neither of us spoke or moved, but exchanged a long steady regard; after which her eyes returned to the distance. What was her feeling towards me? Had she any sense of my emotion or of any answering trouble in her own wonderful heart? Suppose she should deny me: should I suffer, would I persist? At any rate, I should have struck a blow for love. Suppose she were to accept me; would my joy be any greater than in the mere translation of my heartbeats? Did I in truth long merely for a bliss which should be of that hour and that hour alone? I was conscious of an immense respect for the woman beside me. I was unconscious of the least desire even to touch the hem of her garment as it lay on the grass, touching my own. After all, it was but ten days that I had known her. How little I really knew of her! how little else than her beauty and her wit! How little she knew of me, of my vast outlying, unsentimental, spiritual self! We knew hardly more of each other than had appeared in this narrow circle of our common impressions of Venice. And yet if into such a circle Love had forced his way, let him take his way! Let him widen the circle! Transcendent Venice! I rose to my feet with a violent movement, and walked ten steps away. I came back and flung myself again on the grass.

'The other day at Vicenza,' I said, 'I bought a picture.'

'Ah? an "original"?'

'No, a copy.'

'From whom?'

'From you!'

She blushed. 'What do you mean?'

'It was a little pretended Correggio; a Madonna and Child.'

'Is it good?'

'No, it's rather poor.'

'Why, then, did you buy it?'

'Because the Madonna looked singularly like you.'

'I'm sorry, Mr. Brooke, you hadn't a better reason. I hope the picture was cheap.'

'It was quite reason enough. I admire you more than any woman in the world.'

She looked at me a moment, blushing again. 'You don't know me.'

'I have a suspicion of you. It's ground enough for admiration.'

'Oh, don't talk about admiration. I'm tired of it all beforehand.'

'Well, then,' said I, 'I'm in love.'

'Not with me, I hope.'

'With you, of course. With whom else?'

'Has it only just now occurred to you?'

'It has just occurred to me to say it.'

Her blush had deepened a little; but a genuine smile came to its relief. 'Poor Mr. Brooke!' she said.

'Poor Mr. Brooke indeed, if you take it in that way.'

'You must forgive me if I doubt of your love.'

'Why should you doubt?'

'Love, I fancy, doesn't come in just this way.'

'It comes as it can. This is surely a very good way.'

'I know it's a very pretty way, Mr. Brooke; Venice behind us, the Adriatic before us, these old Hebrew tombs! Its very prettiness makes me distrust it.'

'Do you believe only in the love that is born in darkness and pain? Poor love! it has trouble enough, first and last. Allow it a little ease.'

'Listen,' said Miss Evans, after a pause. 'It's not with me you're in love, but with that painted picture. All this Italian beauty and delight has thrown you into a romantic state of mind. You wish to make it perfect. I happen to be at hand, so you say, "Go to, I'll fall in love." And you fancy me, for the purpose, a dozen fine things that I'm not.'

'I fancy you beautiful and good. I'm sorry to find you so dogmatic.'

'You mustn't abuse me, or we shall be getting serious.'

'Well,' said I, 'you can't prevent me from adoring you.'

'I should be very sorry to. So long as you "adore" me, we're safe! I can tell you better things than that I'm in love with you.'

I looked at her impatiently. 'For instance?'

She held out her hand. 'I like you immensely. As for love, I'm in love with Venice.'

'Well, I like Venice immensely, but I'm in love with you.'

'In that way I am willing to leave it. Pray don't speak of it again today. But my poor father is probably wandering up to his knees in the sand.'

I had been happy before, but I think I was still happier for the words I had spoken. I had cast them abroad at all events; my heart was richer by a sense of their possible fruition. We walked far along the beach. Mr. Evans was still with his friend.

'What is beyond that horizon?' said my companion.

'Greece, among other things.'

'Greece! only think of it! Shall you never go there?'

I stopped short. 'If you will believe what I say, Miss Evans, we may both go there.' But for all answer she repeated her request that I should forbear. Before long, retracing our steps, we met Mr. Evans, who had parted with his friend, the latter having returned to Venice. He had arranged to start the next morning for Milan. We went back over the lagoon in the glow of the sunset, in a golden silence which suffered us to hear the far-off ripple in the wake of other gondolas, a golden clearness so perfect that the rosy flush on the marble palaces seemed as light and pure as the life-blood on the forehead of a sleeping child. There is no Venice like the Venice of that magical hour. For that brief period her ancient glory returns. The sky arches over her like a vast imperial canopy crowded with its clustering mysteries of light. Her whole aspect is one of unspotted splendour. No other city takes the crimson evanescence of day with such magnificient effect. The lagoon is sheeted with a carpet of fire. All torpid, pallid hues of marble are transmuted to a golden glow. The dead Venetian tone brightens and quickens into life and lustre, and the spectator's enchanted vision seems to rest on an embodied dream of the great painter who wrought his immortal reveries into the ceilings of the Ducal Palace.

It was not till the second day after this that I again saw Miss Evans. I went to the little church of San Cassiano, to see a famous Tintoretto, to which I had already made several vain attempts to obtain access. At the door in the little bustling *campo* which adjoins the church I found her standing expectant. A little boy, she told me, had gone for the sacristan and his key. Her father, she proceeded to explain, had suddenly been summoned to Milan by a telegram from Mr. Munson, the friend whom he had met at the Lido, who had suddenly been taken ill.

'And so you're going about alone? Do you think that's altogether proper? Why didn't you send for me?' I stood lost in wonder and admiration at the exquisite dignity of her self-support. I had heard of American girls doing such things; but I had yet to see them done.

'Do you think it less proper for me to go about alone than to send for you? Venice has seen so many worse improprieties that she'll forgive me mine.'

The little boy arrived with the sacristan and his key, and we were ushered into the presence of Tintoretto's Crucifixion. This great picture is one of the greatest of the Venetian school. Tintoretto, the travelled reader will remember, has painted two masterpieces on this tremendous theme. The larger and more complex work is at the Scuola di San Rocco; the one of which I speak is small, simple, and sublime. It occupies the left side of the narrow choir of the shabby little church which we had entered, and is remarkable as being, with two or three exceptions, the best preserved work of its incomparable author. Never, in the whole range of art, I imagine, has so powerful an effect been produced by means so simple and select; never has the intelligent choice of means to an effect been pursued with such a refinement of perception. The picture offers to our sight the very central essence of the great tragedy which it depicts. There is no swooning Madonna, no consoling Magdalen, no mockery of contrast, no cruelty of an assembled host. We behold the silent summit of Calvary. To the right are the three crosses, that of the Saviour foremost. A ladder pitched against it supports a turbaned executioner, who bends downward to receive the sponge offered him by a comrade. Above the crest of the hill the helmets and spears of a line of soldiery complete the grimness of the scene. The reality of the picture is beyond all words: it is hard to say which is more impressive, the naked horror of the fact represented, or the sensible power of the artist. You breathe a silent prayer of thanks that you, for your part, are without the terrible clairvoyance of genius. We sat and looked at the picture in silence. The sacristan loitered about; but finally, weary of waiting, he retired to the *campo* without. I observed my companion: pale, motionless, oppressed, she evidently felt with poignant sympathy the commanding force of the work. At last I spoke to her; receiving no answer, I repeated my question. She rose to her feet and turned her face upon me, illumined with a vivid ecstasy of pity. Then passing me rapidly, she descended into the aisle of the church, dropped into a chair, and, burying her face in her hands, burst into an agony of sobs. Having allowed time for her feeling to expend itself, I went to her and recommended her not to let the day close on this painful emotion. 'Come with me to the Ducal Palace,' I said; 'let us look at the Rape of Europa.' But before departing we went back to our Tintoretto, and gave it another solemn half-hour. Miss Evans repeated aloud a dozen verses from St. Mark's Gospel.

'What is it here,' I asked, 'that has moved you most, the painter or the subject?'

'I suppose it's the subject. And you?'

'I'm afraid it's the painter.'

We went to the Ducal Palace, and immediately made our way to that transcendent shrine of light and grace, the room which contains the masterpiece of Paul Veronese, and the Bacchus and Ariadne of his solemn comrade. I steeped myself with unprotesting joy in the gorgeous glow and salubrity of that radiant scene, wherein, against her bosky screen of immortal verdure, the rosy-footed, pearl-circled, nymph-flattered victim of a divine delusion rustles her lustrous satin against the ambrosial hide of bovine Jove. 'It makes one think more agreeably of life,' I said to my friend, 'that such visions have blessed the eyes of men of mortal mould. What has been may be again. We may yet dream as brightly, and some few of us translate our dreams as freely.'

'This, I think, is the brighter dream of the two,' she answered, indicating the Bacchus and Ariadne. Miss Evans, on the whole, was perhaps right. In Tintoretto's picture there is no shimmer of drapery, no splendour of flowers and gems; nothing but the broad, bright glory of deep-toned sea and sky, and the shining purity and symmetry of deified human flesh. 'What do you think,' asked my companion, 'of the painter of that tragedy at San Cassiano being also the painter of this dazzling idyl; of the great painter of darkness being also the great painter of light?'

'He was a colourist! Let us thank the great man, and be colourists too. To understand this Bacchus and Ariadne we ought to spend a long day on the lagoon, beyond sight of Venice. Will you come tomorrow to Torcello?' The proposition seemed to me audacious; I was conscious of blushing a little as I made it. Miss Evans looked at me and pondered. She then replied with great calmness that she preferred to wait for her father, the excursion being one that he would probably enjoy. 'Will you come, then,—somewhere?' I asked.

Again she pondered. Suddenly her face brightened. 'I should very much like to go to Padua. It would bore my poor father to go. I fancy he would thank you for taking me. I should be almost willing,' she said with a smile, 'to go alone.'

It was easily arranged that on the morrow we should go for the day to Padua. Miss Evans was certainly an American to perfection. Nothing remained for me, as the good American which I aspired to be, but implicitly to respect her confidence. To Padua, by an early train, we accordingly went. The day stands out in my memory delightfully curious and rich. Padua is a wonderful little city. Miss Evans was an excellent walker, and, thanks to the broad arcades which cover the footways in the streets, we rambled for hours in perpetual shade. We spent an hour at the famous church of St. Anthony, which boasts one of the richest and holiest shrines in all church-burden Italy. The whole edifice is nobly and darkly ornate and picturesque, but the chapel of its patron saint—a wondrous combination of chiselled gold and silver and alabaster and perpetual flame—splendidly outshines and outshadows the rest. In all Italy, I think, the idea of palpable, material sanctity is nowhere more potently enforced.

'O, the Church, the Church!' murmured Miss Evans, as we stood contemplating.

'What a real pity', I said, 'that we are not Catholics; that that dazzling monument is not something more to us than a mere splendid show! What a different thing this visiting of churches would be for us, if we occasionally felt the prompting to fall on our knees. I begin to grow ashamed of this perpetual attitude of bald curiosity. What a pleasant thing it must be, in such a church as this, for two good friends to say their prayers together!'

'*Ecco!*' said Miss Evans. Two persons had approached the glittering shrine,—a young woman of the middle class and a man of her own rank, some ten years older, dressed with a good deal of cheap elegance. The woman dropped on her knees; her companion fell back a few steps, and stood gazing idly at the chapel. 'Poor girl!' said my friend, 'she believes; he doubts.'

'He doesn't look like a doubter. He's a vulgar fellow. They're a betrothed pair, I imagine. She is very pretty.' She had turned round and flung at her companion a liquid glance of entreaty. He appeared not to observe it; but in a few moments he slowly approached her, and bent a single knee at her side. When presently they rose to their feet, she passed her arm into his with a beautiful, unsuppressed lovingness. As they passed us, looking at us from the clear darkness of their Italian brows, I keenly envied them. 'They are better off than we,' I said. 'Be they husband and wife, or lovers, or simply friends, we, I think, are rather vulgar beside them.'

'My dear Mr. Brooke,' said Miss Evans, 'go by all means and say your prayers.' And she walked away to the other side of the church. Whether I obeyed her injunction or not, I feel under no obligation to report. I rejoined her at the beautiful frescoed chapel in the opposite transept. She was sitting listlessly turning over the leaves of her Murray. 'I suppose,' she said, after a few moments, 'that nothing is more vulgar than to make a noise about having been called vulgar. But really, Mr. Brooke, don't call me so again. I have been of late so fondly fancying I am not vulgar.'

'My dear Miss Evans, you are——'

'Come, nothing vulgar!'

'You're divine!'

'*A la bonne heure!* Divinities needn't pray. They are prayed to.'

I have no space and little power to enumerate and describe the various curiosities of Padua. I think we saw them all. We left the best, however, for the last, and repaired in the late afternoon, after dining fraternally at a restaurant, to the Chapel of Giotto. This little empty church, standing unshaded and forlorn in the homely market-garden which was once a Roman arena, offers one of the deepest lessons of Italian travel. Its four walls are covered, almost from base to ceiling, with that wonderful series of dramatic paintings which usher in the golden prime of Italian art. I had been so ill-informed as to fancy that to talk about Giotto was to make more or less of a fool of one's self, and that he was the especial property of the mere sentimentalists of criticism. But you no sooner cross the threshold of that little ruinous temple—a mere empty shell, but coated as with the priceless substance of fine pearls and vocal with a murmured eloquence as from the infinite of art—than you perceive with whom you have to deal: a complete painter of the very strongest sort. In one respect, assuredly, Giotto has never been surpassed,—in the art of presenting a story. The amount of dramatic expression compressed into those quaint little scenic squares would equip a thousand later masters. How, beside him, they seem to fumble and grope and trifle! And he, beside them, how direct he seems, how essential, how masculine! What a solid simplicity, what an immediate purity and grace! The exhibition suggested to my friend and me more wise reflections than we had the skill to utter. 'Happy, happy art,' we said, as we seemed to see it beneath Giotto's hand tremble and thrill and sparkle, almost, with a presentiment of its immense career, 'for the next two hundred years what a glorious felicity will be yours!' The chapel door stood open into the sunny corn-field, and the lazy litter of verdure enclosed by the crumbling oval of Roman masonry. A loutish boy who had come with the key lounged on a bench, awaiting tribute, and gazing at us as we gazed. The ample light flooded the inner precinct, and lay hot upon the coarse, pale surface of the painted wall. There seemed an irresistible pathos in such a combination of shabbiness and beauty. I thought of this subsequently at the beautiful Museum at Bologna, where mediocrity is so richly enshrined. Nothing that we had yet seen together had filled us with so deep a sense of enjoyment. We stared, we laughed, we wept almost, we raved with a decent delight. We went over the little compartments one by one: we lingered and returned and compared; we studied; we melted together in unanimous homage. At last the light began to fade and the little saintly figures to grow quaint and terrible in the gathering dusk. The loutish boy had transferred himself significantly to the door-post: we lingered for a farewell glance.

'Mr. Brooke,' said my companion, 'we ought to learn from all this to be *real*; real even as Giotto is real; to discriminate between genuine and factitious sentiment; between the substantial and the trivial; between the essential and the superfluous; sentiment and sentimentality.'

'You speak,' said I, 'with appalling wisdom and truth. You strike a chill to my heart of hearts.'

She spoke unsmiling, with a slightly contracted brow and an apparent sense of effort. She blushed as I gazed at her.

'Well,' she said, 'I'm extremely glad to have been here. Good, wise Giotto! I should have liked to know you.—Nay, let me pay the boy.' I saw the piece she put into his hand; he was stupefied by its magnitude.

'We shall not have done Padua,' I said, as we left the garden, 'unless we have been to the Caffè Pedrocchi. Come to the Caffè Pedrocchi. We have more than an hour before our train,—time to eat an ice.' So we drove to the Caffè Pedrocchi, the most respectable *café* in the world; a *café* monumental, scholastic, classical.

We sat down at one of the tables on the cheerful external platform, which is washed by the gentle tide of Paduan life. When we had finished our ices, Miss Evans graciously allowed me a cigar. How it came about I hardly remember, but, prompted by some happy accident of talk, and gently encouraged perhaps by my smoke-wreathed quietude, she lapsed, with an exquisite feminine reserve, into a delicate autobiographical strain. For a moment she became egotistical; but with a modesty, a dignity, a lightness of touch which filled my eyes with admiring tears. She spoke of her home, her family, and the few events of her life. She had lost her mother in her early years; her two sisters had married young; she and her father were equally united by affection and habit. Upon one theme she touched, in regard to which I should be at loss to say whether her treatment told more, by its frankness, of our friendship, or, by its reticence, of her modesty. She spoke of having been engaged, and of having lost her betrothed in the Civil War. She made no story of it; but I felt from her words that she had tasted of sorrow. Having finished my cigar, I was proceeding to light another. She drew out her watch. Our train was to leave at eight o'clock. It was now a quarter past. There was no later evening train.

The reader will understand that I tell the simple truth when I say that our situation was most disagreeable and that we were deeply annoyed. 'Of course,' said I, 'you are utterly disgusted.'

She was silent. 'I am extremely sorry,' she said, at last, just vanquishing a slight tremor in her voice.

'Murray says the hotel is good,' I suggested.

She made no answer. Then, rising to her feet, 'Let us go immediately,' she said. We drove to the principal inn and bespoke our rooms. Our want of luggage provoked, of course, a certain amount of visible surprise. This, however, I fancy, was speedily merged in a more flattering emotion, when my companion, having communed with the chambermaid, sent her forth with a list of purchases.

We separated early. 'I hope,' said I, as I bade her good night, 'that you will be fairly comfortable.'

She had recovered her equanimity. 'I have no doubt of it.'

'Good night.'

'Good night.' Thank God, I silently added, for the dignity of American women. Knowing to what suffering a similar accident would have subjected a young girl of the orthodox European training, I felt devoutly grateful that among my own people a woman and her reputation are more indissolubly one. And yet I was unable to detach myself from my Old-World associations effectually enough not to wonder whether, after all, Miss Evans's calmness might not be the simple calmness of despair. The miserable words rose to my lips, 'Is she Compromised?' If she were, of course, as far as I was concerned, there was but one possible sequel to our situation.

We met the next morning at breakfast. She assured me that she had slept, but I doubted it. I myself had not closed my eyes,—not from the excitement of vanity. Owing partly, I suppose, to a natural reaction against our continuous talk on the foregoing day, our return to Venice was attended with a good deal of silence. I wondered whether it was a mere fancy that Miss Evans was pensive, appealing, sombre. As we entered the gondola to go from the railway station to the Hotel Danieli, she asked me to request the gondoliers to pass along the Canalezzo rather than through the short cuts of the smaller canals. 'I feel as if I were coming home,' she said, as we floated beneath the lovely façade of the Ca' Doro. Suddenly she laid her hand on my arm. 'It seems to me,' she said, 'that I should like to stop for Mrs. L——,' and she mentioned the wife of the American Consul. 'I have promised to show her some jewellery.

This is a particularly good time. I shall ask her to come home with me.' We stopped accordingly at the American Consulate. Here we found, on inquiry, to my great regret, that the Consul and his wife had gone for a week to the Lake of Como. For a moment my companion meditated. Then, 'To the hotel,' she said with decision. Our arrival attracted apparently little notice. I went with Miss Evans to the door of her father's sitting-room, where we met a servant, who informed us with inscrutable gravity that Monsieur had returned the evening before, but that he had gone out after breakfast and had not reappeared.

'Poor father,' she said. 'It was very stupid of me not to have left a note for him.' I urged that our absence for the night was not to have been foreseen, and that Mr. Evans had in all likelihood very plausibly explained it. I withdrew with a handshake and permission to return in the evening.

I went to my hotel and slept, a long, sound, dreamless sleep. In the afternoon I called my gondola, and went over to the Lido. I crossed to the outer shore and sought the spot where a few days before I had lain at the feet of Charlotte Evans. I stretched myself on the grass and fancied her present. To say that I *thought* would be to say at once more and less than the literal truth. I was in a tremulous glow of feeling. I listened to the muffled rupture of the tide, vaguely conscious of my beating heart. Was I or was I not in love? I was able to settle nothing. I wandered musingly further and further from the point. Every now and then, with a deeper pulsation of the heart, I would return to it, but only to start afresh and follow some wire-drawn thread of fancy to a nebulous goal of doubt. That she was a most lovely woman seemed to me of all truths the truest, but it was a hard-featured fact of the senses rather than a radiant mystery of faith. I felt that I was not possessed by a passion; perhaps I was incapable of passion. At last, weary of self-bewilderment, I left the spot and wandered beside the sea. It seemed to speak more musingly than ever of the rapture of motion and freedom. Beyond the horizon was Greece, beyond and below was the wondrous Southern world which blooms about the margin of the Midland Sea. To marry, somehow, meant to abjure all this, and in the prime of youth and manhood to sink into obscurity and care. For a moment there stirred in my heart a feeling of anger and pain. Perhaps, after all, I *was* in love!

I went straight across the lagoon to the Hotel Danieli, and as I approached it I became singularly calm and collected. From below I saw Miss Evans alone on her balcony, watching the sunset. She received me with perfect friendly composure. Her father had again gone out, but she had told him of my coming, and he was soon to return. He had not been painfully alarmed at her absence, having learned through a chambermaid, to whom she had happened to mention her intention, that she had gone for the day to Padua.

'And what have you been doing all day?' I asked.

'Writing letters,—long, tiresome, descriptive letters. I have also found a volume of Hawthorne, and have been reading "Rappacini's Daughter". You know the scene is laid in Padua.' And what had I been doing?

Whether I was in a passion of love or not, I was enough in love to be very illogical. I was disappointed, Heaven knows why! that she should have been able to spend her time in this wholesome fashion. 'I have been at the Lido, at the Hebrew tombs, where we sat the other day, thinking of what you told me there.'

'What I told you?'

'That you liked me immensely.'

She smiled; but now that she smiled, I fancied I saw in the movement of her face an undercurrent of pain. Had the peace of her heart been troubled? 'You needn't have gone so far away to think of it.'

'It's very possible,' I said, 'that I shall have to think of it, in days to come, farther away still.'

'Other places, Mr. Brooke, will bring other thoughts.'

'Possibly. This place has brought that one.' At what prompting it was that I continued I hardly know; I *would* tell her that I loved her. 'I value it beyond all other thoughts.'

'I do like you, Mr. Brooke. Let it rest there.'

'It may rest there for you. It can't for me. It begins there! Don't refuse to understand me.'

She was silent. Then, bending her eyes on me, 'Perhaps,' she said, 'I understand you too well.'

'O, in Heaven's name, don't play at coldness and scepticism!'

She dropped her eyes gravely on a bracelet which she locked and unlocked on her wrist. 'I think,' she said, without raising them, 'you had better leave Venice.' I was about to reply, but the door opened and Mr. Evans came in. From his hard, grizzled brow he looked at us in turn; then, greeting me with an extended hand, he spoke to his daughter.

'I have forgotten my cigar-case. Be so good as to fetch it from my dressing-table.'

For a moment Miss Evans hesitated and cast upon him a faint protesting glance. Then she lightly left the room. He stood holding my hand, with a very sensible firmness, with his eyes on mine. Then, laying his other hand heavily on my shoulder, 'Mr. Brooke,' he said, 'I believe you are an honest man.'

'I hope so,' I answered.

He paused, and I felt his steady grey eyes. 'How the devil,' he said, 'came you to be left at Padua?'

'The explanation is a very simple one. Your daughter must have told you.'

'I have thought best to talk very little to my daughter about it.'

'Do you regard it, Mr. Evans,' I asked, 'as a very serious calamity?'

'I regard it as an infernally disagreeable thing. It seems that the whole hotel is talking about it. There is a little beast of an Italian downstairs——'

'Your daughter, I think, was not seriously discomposed.'

'My daughter is a d—d proud woman!'

'I can assure you that my esteem for her is quite equal to your own.'

'What does that mean, Mr. Brooke?' I was about to answer, but Miss Evans reappeared. Her father, as he took his cigar-case from her, looked at her intently, as if he were on the point of speaking, but the words remained on his lips, and, declaring that he would be back in half an hour, he left the room.

His departure was followed by a long silence.

'Miss Evans,' I said, at last, 'will you be my wife?'

She looked at me with a certain firm resignation. 'Do you *feel* that, Mr. Brooke? Do you know what you ask?'

'Most assuredly.'

'Will you rest content with my answer?'

'It depends on what your answer is.'

She was silent.

'I should like to know what my father said to you in my absence.'

'You had better learn from himself.'

'I think I know. Poor father!'

'But you give me no answer,' I rejoined, after a pause.

She frowned a little. 'Mr. Brooke,' she said, 'you disappoint me.'

'Well, I'm sorry. Don't revenge yourself by disappointing me.'

'I fancied that I had answered your proposal; that I had, at least, anticipated it, the other day at the Lido.'

'Oh, that was very good for the other day; but do give me something different now.'

'I doubt of your being more in earnest today than then.'

'It seems to suit you wonderfully well to doubt!'

'I thank you for the honour of your proposal: but I can't be your wife, Mr. Brooke.'

'That's the answer with which you ask me to remain satisfied!'

'Let me repeat what I said just now. You had better leave Venice, otherwise we must leave it.'

'Ah, that's easy to say!'

'You mustn't think me unkind or cynical. You have done your duty.'

'My duty,—what duty?'

'Come,' she said, with a beautiful blush and the least attempt at a smile, 'you imagine that I have suffered an injury by my being left with you at Padua. I don't believe in such injuries.'

'No more do I.'

'Then there is even less wisdom than before in your proposal. But I strongly suspect that if we had not missed the train at Padua, you would not have made it. There is an idea of reparation in it.—O Sir!' And she shook her head with a deepening smile.

'If I had flattered myself that it lay in my power to do you an injury,' I replied, 'I should now be rarely disenchanted. As little almost as to do you a benefit!'

'You have loaded me with benefits. I thank you from the bottom of my heart. I may be very unreasonable, but if I had doubted of my having to decline your offer three days ago, I should have quite ceased to doubt this evening.'

'You are an excessively proud woman. I can tell you that.'

'Possibly. But I'm not as proud as you think. I believe in my common sense.'

'I wish that for five minutes you had a grain of imagination!'

'If only for the same five minutes you were without it. You have too much, Mr. Brooke. You imagine you love me.'

'Poor fool that I am!'

'You imagine that I'm charming. I assure you I'm not in the least. Here in Venice I have not been myself at all. You should see me at home.'

'Upon my word, Miss Evans, you remind me of a German philosopher. I have not the least objection to seeing you at home.'

'Don't fancy that I think lightly of your offer. But we have been living, Mr. Brooke, in poetry. Marriage is stern prose. Do let me bid you farewell!'

I took up my hat. 'I shall go from here to Rome and Naples,' I said. 'I must leave Florence for the last. I shall write you from Rome and of course see you there.'

'I hope not. I had rather not meet you again in Italy. It perverts our dear good old American truth!'

'Do you really propose to bid me a final farewell?'

She hesitated a moment. 'When do you return home?'

'Some time in the spring.'

'Very well. If a year hence, in America, you are still of your present mind, I shall not decline to see you. I feel very safe! If you are not of your present mind, of course I shall be still more happy. Farewell.' She put out her hand; I took it.

'Beautiful, wonderful woman!' I murmured.

'That's rank poetry! Farewell!'

I raised her hand to my lips and released it in silence. At this point Mr. Evans reappeared, considering apparently that his half-hour was up. 'Are you going?' he asked.

'Yes. I start tomorrow for Rome.'

'The deuce! Daughter, when are we to go?'

She moved her hand over her forehead, and a sort of nervous tremor seemed to pass through her limbs. 'O, you must take me home!' she said. 'I'm horribly home-sick!' She flung her arms round his neck and buried her head on his shoulder. Mr. Evans with a movement of his head dismissed me.

At the top of the staircase, however, he overtook me. 'You made your offer!' And he passed his arm into mine.

'Yes!'

'And she refused you?' I nodded. He looked at me, squeezing my arm. 'By Jove, sir, if she had accepted——'

'Well!' said I, stopping.

'Why, it wouldn't in the least have suited me! Not that I don't esteem you. The whole house shall see it.' With his arm in mine we passed down stairs, through the hall, to the landing-place, where he called his own gondola and requested me to use it. He bade me farewell with a kindly hand-shake, and the assurance that I was too 'nice a fellow not to keep as a friend'.

I think, on the whole, that my uppermost feeling was a sense of freedom and relief. It seemed to me on my journey to Florence that I had started afresh, and was regarding things with less of nervous rapture than before, but more of sober insight. Of Miss Evans I forbade myself to think. In my deepest heart I admitted the truth, the partial truth at least, of her assertion of the unreality of my love. The reality I believed would come. The way to hasten its approach was, meanwhile, to study, to watch, to observe,—doubtless even to enjoy. I certainly enjoyed Florence and the three days I spent there. But I shall not attempt to deal with Florence in a parenthesis. I subsequently saw that divine little city under circumstances which peculiarly coloured and shaped it. In Rome, to begin with, I spent a week and went down to Naples, dragging the heavy Roman chain which she rivets about your limbs for ever. In Naples I discovered the real South—the Southern South,—in art, in nature, in man, and the least bit in woman. A German lady, an old kind friend, had given me a letter to a Neapolitan lady whom she assured me she held in high esteem. The Signora B— was at Sorrento, where I presented my letter. It seemed to me that 'esteem' was not exactly the word; but the Signora B— was charming. She assured me on my first visit that she was a 'true Neapolitan', and I think, on the whole, she was right. She told me that I was a true German, but in this she was altogether wrong. I spent four days in her house; on one of them we went to Capri, where the Signora had an infant—her only one—at nurse. We saw the Blue Grotto, the Tiberian ruins, the tarantella and the infant, and returned late in the evening by moonlight. The Signora sang on the water in a magnificent contralto. As I looked upward at Northern Italy, it seemed, in contrast, a cold, dark hyperborean clime, a land of order, conscience, and virtue. How my heart went out to that brave, rich, compact little Verona! How there Nature seemed to have mixed her colours with potent oil, instead of, as here, with crystalline water, drawn though it was from the Neapolitan Bay! But in Naples, too, I pursued my plan of vigilance and study. I spent long mornings at the Museum and learned to know Pompeii; I wrote once to Miss Evans, about the statues in the Museum, without a word of wooing, but received no answer. It seemed to me that I returned to Rome a wiser man. It was the middle of October when I reached it. Unless Mr. Evans had altered his programme, he would at this moment be passing down to Naples.

A fortnight elapsed without my hearing of him, during which I was in the full fever of initiation into Roman wonders. I had been introduced to an old German archaeologist, with whom I spent a series of memorable days in the exploration of ruins and the study of the classical topography. I thought, I lived, I ate, and drank, in Latin, and German Latin at that. But I remember with especial delight certain long lonely rides on the Campagna. The weather was perfect. Nature seemed only to slumber, ready to wake far on the hither side of wintry death. From time to time, after a passionate gallop, I would pull up my horse on the slope of some pregnant mound and embrace with the ecstasy of quickened senses the tragical beauty of the scene; strain my ear to the soft low silence, pity the dark dishonoured plain, watch the heavens come rolling down in tides of light, and breaking in waves of fire against the massive stillness of temples and tombs. The aspect of all this sunny solitude and haunted vacancy used to fill me with a mingled sense of exaltation and dread. There were moments when my fancy swept that vast funereal desert with passionate curiosity and desire, moments when it felt only its potent sweetness and its high historic charm. But there were other times when the air seemed so heavy with the exhalation of unburied death, so bright with sheeted ghosts, that I turned short about and galloped back to the city. One afternoon after I had indulged in one of these super-sensitive flights on the Campagna, I betook myself to St. Peter's. It was shortly before the opening of the recent Council, and the city was filled with foreign ecclesiastics, the increase being of course especially noticeable in the churches. At St. Peter's they were present in vast numbers; great armies encamped in prayer on the marble plains of its pavement: an inexhaustible physiognomical study. Scattered among them were squads of little tonsured neophytes, clad in scarlet, marching and counter-marching, and ducking and flapping, like poor little raw recruits for the heavenly host. I had never before, I think, received an equal impression of the greatness of this church of churches, or, standing beneath the dome, beheld such a vision of erected altitude,—of the builded sublime. I lingered awhile near the brazen image of St. Peter, observing the steady procession of his devotees. Near me stood a lady in mourning, watching with a weary droop of the head the grotesque deposition of kisses. A peasant-woman advanced with the file of the faithful and lifted up her little girl to the well-worn toe. With a sudden movement of impatience the lady turned away, so that I saw her face to face. She was strikingly pale, but as her eyes met mine the blood rushed into her cheeks. This lonely mourner was Miss Evans. I advanced to her with an outstretched hand. Before she spoke I had guessed at the truth.

'You're in sorrow and trouble!'

She nodded, with a look of simple gravity.

'Why in the world haven't you written to me?'

'There was no use. I seem to have sufficed to myself.'

'Indeed, you have not sufficed to yourself. You are pale and worn; you look wretchedly.' She stood silent, looking about her with an air of vague unrest. 'I have as yet heard nothing,' I said. 'Can you speak of it?'

'O Mr. Brooke!' she said with a simple sadness that went to my heart. I drew her hand through my arm and led her to the extremity of the left transept of the church. We sat down together, and she told me of her father's death. It had happened ten days before, in consequence of a severe apoplectic stroke. He had been ill but a single day, and had remained unconscious from first to last. The American

physician had been extremely kind, and had relieved her of all care
and responsibility. His wife had strongly urged her to come and
stay in their house, until she should have determined what to do;
but she had preferred to remain at her hotel. She had immediately
furnished herself with an attendant in the person of a French maid,
who had gone with her to the church and was now at confession. At
first she had wished greatly to leave Rome, but now that the first
shock of grief had passed away she found it suited her mood to
linger on from day to day. 'On the whole,' she said, with a sober
smile, 'I have got through it all rather easily than otherwise. The
common cares and necessities of life operate strongly to interrupt
and dissipate one's grief. I shall feel my loss more when I get home
again.' Looking at her while she talked, I found a pitiful difference
between her words and her aspect. Her pale face, her wilful smile,
her spiritless gestures, spoke most forcibly of loneliness and weakness. Over this gentle weakness and dependence I secretly rejoiced;
I felt in my heart an immense uprising of pity,—of the pity that
goes hand in hand with love. At its bidding I hastily, vaguely
sketched a magnificent scheme of devotion and protection.

'When I think of what you have been through,' I said, 'my heart
stands still for very tenderness. Have you made any plans?' She
shook her head with such a perfection of helplessness that I broke
into a sort of rage of compassion: 'One of the last things your father
said to me was that you are a very proud woman.'

She coloured faintly. 'I may have been! But there is not among
the most abject peasants who stand kissing St. Peter's foot a creature
more bowed in humility than I.'

'How did you expect to make that weary journey home?'

She was silent a moment and her eyes filled with tears. 'O, don't
cross-question me, Mr. Brooke!' she softly cried; 'I expected nothing.
I was waiting for my stronger self.'

'Perhaps your stronger self has come.' She rose to her feet as if
she had not heard me, and went forward to meet her maid. This
was a decent, capable-looking person, with a great deal of apparent
deference of manner. As I rejoined them, Miss Evans prepared to
bid me farewell. 'You haven't yet asked me to come and see you,'
I said.

'Come, but not too soon!'

'What do you call too soon? This evening?'

'Come tomorrow.' She refused to allow me to go with her to her
carriage. I followed her, however, at a short interval, and went as
usual to my restaurant to dine. I remember that my dinner cost me

ten francs,—it usually cost me five. Afterwards, as usual, I adjourned
to the Caffè Greco, where I met my German archaeologist. He discoursed with even more than his wonted sagacity and eloquence; but
at the end of half an hour he rapped his fist on the table and asked
me what the deuce was the matter; he would wager I hadn't heard
a word of what he said.

I went forth the next morning into the Roman streets, doubting
heavily of my being able to exist until evening without seeing Miss
Evans. I felt, however, that it was due to her to make the effort. To
help myself through the morning, I went into the Borghese Gallery.
The great treasure of this collection is a certain masterpiece of
Titian. I entered the room in which it hangs by the door facing the
picture. The room was empty, save that before the great Titian,
beside the easel of an absent copyist, stood a young woman in mourning. This time, in spite of her averted head, I immediately knew her
and noiselessly approached her. The picture is one of the finest of
its admirable author,—rich and simple and brilliant with the true
Venetian fire. It unites the charm of an air of latent symbolism with
a steadfast splendour and solid perfection of design. Beside a low
sculptured well sit two young and beautiful women: one richly
clad, and full of mild dignity and repose; the other with unbound
hair, naked, ungirdled by a great reverted mantle of Venetian purple,
and radiant with the frankest physical sweetness and grace. Between
them a little winged cherub bends forward and thrusts his chubby
arm into the well. The picture glows with the inscrutable chemistry
of the prince of colourists.

'Does it remind you of Venice?' I said, breaking a long silence,
during which she had not noticed me.

She turned and her face seemed bright with reflected colour. We
spoke awhile of common things; she had come alone. 'What an
emotion, for one who has loved Venice,' she said, 'to meet a Titian
in other lands.'

'They call it,' I answered,—and as I spoke my heart was in my
throat,—'a representation of Sacred and Profane Love. The name
perhaps roughly expresses its meaning. The serious, stately woman
is the likeness, one may say, of love as an experience,—the gracious,
impudent goddess of love as a sentiment; this of the passion that
fancies, the other of the passion that knows.' And as I spoke I passed
my arm, in its strength, around her waist. She let her head sink on
my shoulders and looked up into my eyes.

'One may stand for the love I denied,' she said; 'and the other——'

'The other,' I murmured, 'for the love which, with this kiss, you
accept.' I drew her arm into mine, and before the envious eyes that

watched us from gilded casements we passed through the gallery and left the palace. We went that afternoon to the Pamfili-Doria Villa. Saying just now that my stay in Florence was peculiarly coloured by circumstances, I meant that I was there with my wife.

A Passionate Pilgrim
IN TWO PARTS

[First appeared in the *Atlantic Monthly*, vol. xxvii (March–April 1871), pp. 352–71, 478–99. The tale was revised and reprinted in *A Passionate Pilgrim* (1875). The 1875 text was heavily revised and reprinted in the Continental edition of the collection, *The Siege of London* (1884). A note in this volume, on the text of 'A Passionate Pilgrim', reads: 'It is proper to state that the last of the three tales contained in this volume, a story originally published in Boston in 1872 [*sic*], has been, in the matter of language, much altered and amended for reproduction here.' Less than a year later, this newly revised text was further retouched and the tale reprinted in volume ii of *Stories Revived* (1885).* James *rewrote* the tale for inclusion in the New York Edition where it appears in volume xiii (*The Reverberator, Etc.*, 1908).]

PART I

INTENDING TO SAIL FOR AMERICA IN THE EARLY PART OF June, I determined to spend the interval of six weeks in England, of which I had dreamed much but as yet knew nothing. I had formed in Italy and France a resolute preference for old inns, deeming that what they sometimes cost the ungratified body they repay the delighted mind. On my arrival in London, therefore, I lodged at a certain antique hostelry far to the east of Temple Bar, deep in what I used to denominate the Johnsonian city. Here, on the first evening of my stay, I descended to the little coffee-room and bespoke my dinner of the very genius of decorum, in the person of the solitary waiter. No sooner had I crossed the threshold of this apartment than I felt I had mown the first swath in my golden-ripe crop of British 'impressions'. The coffee-room of the Red-Lion, like so many other places and things I was destined to see in England, seemed to have been waiting for long years, with just that sturdy sufferance of time written on its visage, for me to come and gaze, ravished but unamazed.

The latent preparedness of the American mind for even the most delectable features of English life is a fact which I never fairly probed to the depths. The roots of it are so deeply buried in the virgin soil of our primary culture, that, without some great upheaval of ex-

---

* The *Bibliography* (see pp. 57–58, 72) gives an incorrect account of this textual state.

perience, it would be hard to say exactly when and where and how it begins. It makes an American's enjoyment of England an emotion more fatal and sacred than his enjoyment, say, of Italy or Spain. I had seen the coffee-room of the Red-Lion years ago, at home,—at Saragossa, Illinois,—in books, in visions, in dreams, in Dickens, in Smollett, and Boswell. It was small, and subdivided into six small compartments by a series of perpendicular screens of mahogany, something higher than a man's stature, furnished each on either side with a narrow, uncushioned ledge, esteemed in ancient Britain a seat. In each of the little dining-boxes thus immutably constituted was a small table, which in crowded seasons was expected to accommodate the several agents of a fourfold British hungriness. But crowded seasons had passed away from the Red-Lion for ever. It was crowded only with memories and ghosts and atmosphere. Round the room there marched, breast-high, a magnificent panelling of mahogany, so dark with time and so polished with unremitted friction, that by gazing awhile into its lucid blackness I fancied I could discern the lingering images of a party of gentlemen in periwigs and short-clothes, just arrived from York by the coach. On the dark yellow walls, coated by the fumes of English coal, of English mutton, of Scotch whisky, were a dozen melancholy prints, sallow-toned with age,—the Derby favourite of the year 1807, the Bank of England, her Majesty the Queen. On the floor was a Turkey carpet,—as old as the mahogany, almost, as the Bank of England, as the Queen,—into which the waiter in his lonely revolutions had trodden so many massive sootflakes and drops of overflowing beer, that the glowing looms of Smyrna would certainly not have recognized it. To say that I ordered my dinner of this superior being would be altogether to misrepresent the process, owing to which, having dreamed of lamb and spinach and a rhubarb tart, I sat down in penitence to a mutton-chop and a rice pudding. Bracing my feet against the cross-beam of my little oaken table, I opposed to the mahogany partition behind me that vigorous dorsal resistance which expresses the old-English idea of repose. The sturdy screen refused even to creak; but my poor Yankee joints made up the deficiency. While I was waiting for my chop there came into the room a person whom I took to be my sole fellow-lodger. He seemed, like myself, to have submitted to proposals for dinner; the table on the other side of my partition had been prepared to receive him. He walked up to the fire, exposed his back to it, consulted his watch, and looked apparently out of the window, but really at me. He was a man of something less than middle age and more than middle stature, though indeed you would have called him neither young nor tall. He was chiefly remarkable for his exaggerated leanness. His hair, very thin on the summit of his head, was dark, short, and fine. His eye was of a pale, turbid grey, unsuited, perhaps, to his dark hair and brow, but not altogether out of harmony with his colourless, bilious complexion. His nose was aquiline and delicate; beneath it hung a thin, comely, black moustache. His mouth and chin were meagre and uncertain of outline; not vulgar, perhaps, but weak. A cold, fatal, gentlemanly weakness, indeed, seemed expressed in his elegant person. His eye was restless and deprecating; his whole physiognomy, his manner of shifting his weight from foot to foot, the spiritless forward droop of his head, told of exhausted purpose, of a will relaxed. His dress was neat and careful, with an air of half-mourning. I made up my mind on three points: he was unmarried, he was ill, he was not an Englishman. The waiter approached him, and they murmured momentarily in barely audible tones. I heard the words, 'claret', 'sherry', with a tentative inflection, and finally 'beer', with a gentle affirmitive. Perhaps he was a Russian in reduced circumstances; he reminded me of a certain type of Russian which I had met on the Continent. While I was weighing this hypothesis,—for you see I was interested,—there appeared a short, brisk man with reddish-brown hair, a vulgar nose, a sharp blue eye, and a red beard, confined to his lower jaw and chin. My possible Russian was still standing on the rug; with his mild gaze bent on vacancy; the other marched up to him, and with his umbrella gave him a playful poke in the concave frontage of his melancholy waistcoat. 'A penny-ha'penny for your thoughts!' said the newcomer.

His companion uttered an exclamation, stared, then laid his two hands on the other's shoulders. The latter looked round at me keenly, compassing me in a momentary glance. I read in its own high light that this was an American eyebeam; and with such confidence that I hardly needed to see its owner, as he prepared, with his friend, to seat himself at the table adjoining my own, take from his overcoat-pocket three New York papers and lay them beside his plate. As my neighbours proceeded to dine, I became conscious that, through no indiscretion of my own, a large portion of their conversation made its way over the top of our dividing partition and mingled its flavours with those of my simple repast. Occasionally their tone was lowered, as with the intention of secrecy; but I heard a phrase here and a phrase there distinctly enough to grow very curious as to the burden of the whole, and, in fact, to succeed at last in guessing at it. The two voices were pitched in an unforgotten key, and equally native to our Cisatlantic air, they seemed to fall upon the muffled medium of surrounding parlance as the rattle of peas on the face of a drum. They

were American, however, with a difference; and I had no hesitation
in assigning the lighter and softer of the two to the pale, thin gentleman, whom I decidedly preferred to his comrade. The latter began
to question him about his voyage.

'Horrible, horrible! I was deadly sick from the hour we left New
York.'

'Well, you *do* look considereably reduced,' his friend affirmed.

'Reduced! I've been on the verge of the grave. I haven't slept six
hours in three weeks.' This was said with great gravity. 'Well, I have
made the voyage for the last time.'

'The deuce you have! You mean to stay here for ever?'

'Here, or somewhere! It's likely to be a short for ever.'

There was a pause; after which: 'You're the same old boy, Searle.
Going to die tomorrow, eh?'

'I almost wish I were.'

'You're not in love with England, then? I've heard people say at
home that you dressed and talked and acted like an Englishman.
But I know Englishmen, and I know you. You're not one of them,
Searle, not you. You'll go under here, sir; you'll go under as sure as
my name is Simmons.'

Following this, I heard a sudden clatter, as of the dropping of a
knife and fork. 'Well, you're a delicate sort of man, Simmons! I have
been wandering about all day in this accursed city, ready to cry
with homesickness and heartsickness and every possible sort of
sickness, and thinking, in the absence of anything better, of meeting
you here this evening, and of your uttering some syllable of cheer
and comfort and giving me some feeble ray of hope. Go under? Am
I not under now? I can't sink lower, except to sink into my grave!'

Mr. Simmons seems to have staggered a moment under this outbreak of passion. But the next, 'Don't cry, Searle,' I heard him say.
'Remember the waiter. I've grown Englishman enough for that. For
heaven's sake don't let us have any feelings. Feelings will do nothing
for you here. It's best to come to the point. Tell me in three words
what you expect of me.'

I heard another movement, as if poor Searle had collapsed in his
chair. 'Upon my word, Simmons, you are inconceivable. You got
my letter?'

'Yes, I got your letter. I was never sorrier to get anything in my
life.'

At this declaration Mr. Searle rattled out an oath, which it was well
perhaps that I but partially heard. 'John Simmons,' he cried, 'what
devil possesses you? Are you going to betray me here in a foreign
land, to turn out a false friend, a heartless scamp?'

'Go on, sir,' said stout Simmons. 'Pour it all out. I'll wait till you have done.—Your beer is very bad,' to the waiter. 'I'll have some more.'

'For God's sake, explain yourself!' cried Searle.

There was a pause, at the end of which I heard Mr. Simmons set down his empty tankard with emphasis. 'You poor morbid man,' he resumed, 'I don't want to say anything to make you feel sore. I pity you. But you must allow me to say that you have acted like a blasted fool!'

Mr. Searle seemed to have made an effort to compose himself. 'Be so good as to tell me what was the meaning of your letter.'

'I was a fool, myself, to have written that letter. It came of my infernal meddlesome benevolence. I had much better have let you alone. To tell you the plain truth, I never was so horrified in my life as when I found that on the strength of that letter you had come out here to seek your fortune.'

'What did you expect me to do?'

'I expected you to wait patiently till I had made further inquiries and had written to you again.'

'You have made further inquiries now.'

'Inquiries! I have made assaults.'

'And you find I have no claim?'

'No claim to call a claim. It looked at first as if you had a very pretty one. I confess the idea took hold of me——'

'Thanks to your preposterous benevolence!'

Mr. Simmons seemed for a moment to experience a difficulty in swallowing. 'Your beer is undrinkable,' he said to the waiter. 'I'll have some sherry.—Come, Searle,' he resumed, 'don't challenge me to the arts of debate, or I'll settle right down on you. Benevolence, as I say, was part of it. The reflection that if I put the thing through it would be a very pretty feather in my cap, and a very pretty penny in my purse, was part of it. And the satisfaction of seeing a poor nobody of a Yankee walk right into an old English estate was a good deal of it. Upon my word, Searle, when I think of it, I wish with all my heart that, erratic genius as you are, you had a claim, for the very beauty of it. I should hardly care what you did with the confounded property when you got it. I could leave you alone to turn it into Yankee notions,—into ducks and drakes, as they call it here. I should like to see you stamping over it and kicking up its sacred dust in their faces!'

'You don't know me, Simmons!' said Searle, for all response to this untender benediction.

'I should be very glad to think I didn't, Searle. I have been to no

small amount of trouble for you. I have consulted by main force
three first-rate men. They smile at the idea. I should like you to see
the smile negative of one of these London big-wigs. If your title were
written in letters of fire, it would expire in that baleful emanation!
I sounded in person the solicitor of your distinguished kinsman. He
seemed to have been in a manner forewarned and forearmed. It
seems your brother George, some twenty years ago, put forth a feeler.
So you are not to have the glory of even frightening them.'

'I never frightened anyone,' said Searle. 'I shouldn't begin at this
time of day. I should approach the subject like a gentleman.'

'Well, if you want very much to do something like a gentleman,
you've got a capital chance. Take your disappointment like a gentleman.'

I had finished my dinner, and I had become keenly interested in
poor Mr. Searle's mysterious claim; so interested that it was vexatious
to hear his emotions reflected in his voice without noting them in
his face. I left my place, went over to the fire, took up the evening
paper, and established a post of observation behind it.

Lawyer Simmons was in the act of choosing a soft chop from the
dish,—an act accompanied by a great deal of prying and poking
with his own personal fork. My disillusioned compatriot had pushed
away his plate; he sat with his elbows on the table, gloomily nursing
his head with his hands. His companion stared at him a moment,
I fancied, half tenderly; I am not sure whether it was pity or whether
it was beer and sherry. 'I say, Searle,'—and for my benefit, I think,
taking me for some unnoticeable native, he attuned his voice to
something of a pompous pitch,—'in this country it is the inestimable
privilege of a loyal citizen, under whatsoever stress of pleasure or of
pain, to make a point of eating his dinner.'

Searle disgustedly gave his plate another push. 'Anything may
happen, now!' he said. 'I don't care a straw.'

'You ought to care. Have another chop, and you *will* care. Have
some sherry. Take my advice!'

Searle from behind his two hands looked at him. 'I have had
enough of your advice!' he said.

'A little more,' said Simmons, mildly; 'I shan't trouble you again.
What do you mean to do?'

'Nothing.'

'O, come!'

'Nothing, nothing, nothing!'

'Nothing but starve. How about your money?'

'Why do you ask? You don't care.'

'My dear fellow, if you want to make me offer you twenty pounds, you set most clumsily about it. You said just now I don't know you. Possibly! There is, perhaps, no such enormous difference between knowing you and not knowing you. At any rate, you don't know me. I expect you to go home.'

'I won't go home! I have crossed the ocean for the last time.'

'What's the matter? Are you afraid?'

'Yes, I'm afraid! "I thank thee, Jew, for teaching me that word!"'

'You're more afraid to go than to stay?'

'I shan't stay. I shall die.'

'O, are you sure of that?'

'One can always be sure of that.'

Mr. Simmons started and stared: his mild cynic had turned a grim stoic. 'Upon my soul,' he said, 'one would think that Death had named the day!'

'We have named it, between us.'

This was too much for Mr. Simmons's as yet uncorrupted piety. 'I say, Searle,' he cried, 'I'm not more of a stickler than the next man, but if you are going to blaspheme, I shall wash my hands of you. If you'll consent to return home with me by the steamer of the 23rd, I'll pay your passage down. More than that, I'll pay your wine bill.'

Searle meditated. 'I believe I never willed anything in my life,' he said; 'but I feel sure that I have willed this, that I stay here till I take my leave for a newer world than that poor old New World of ours. It's an odd feeling,—I rather like it! What should I do at home?'

'You said just now you were homesick.'

'So I was—for a morning. But haven't I been all my life long sick for Europe? And now that I've got it, am I to cast it off again? I'm much obliged to you for your offer. I have enough for the present. I have about my person some forty pounds' worth of British gold and the same amount, say, of Yankee vitality. They'll last me out together! After they are gone, I shall lay my head in some English churchyard, beside some ivied tower, beneath an English yew.'

I had thus far distinctly followed the dialogue; but at this point the landlord came in, and, begging my pardon, would suggest that No. 12, a most superior apartment, having now been vacated, it would give him pleasure, etc. The fate of No. 12 having been decreed, I transferred my attention back to my friends. They had risen to their feet; Simmons had put on his overcoat; he stood polishing his rusty black hat with his napkin. 'Do you mean to go down to the place?' he asked.

'Possibly. I have dreamed of it so much I should like to see it.'

'Shall you call on Mr. Searle?'

'Heaven forbid!'

'Something has just occurred to me,' Simmons pursued, with an unhandsome grin, as if Mephistopheles were playing at malice. 'There's a Miss Searle, the old man's sister.'

'Well?' said the other, frowning.

'Well, sir! suppose, instead of dying, you should marry!'

Mr. Searle frowned in silence. Simmons gave him a tap on the stomach. 'Line those ribs a bit first!' The poor gentleman blushed crimson and his eyes filled with tears. 'You *are* a coarse brute,' he said. The scene was pathetic. I was prevented from seeing the conclusion of it by the reappearance of the landlord, on behalf of No. 12. He insisted on my coming to inspect the premises. Half an hour afterwards I was rattling along in a Hansom towards Convent Garden, where I heard Adelina Patti in the Barber of Seville. On my return from the opera I went into the coffee-room, vaguely fancying I might catch another glimpse of Mr. Searle. I was not disappointed. I found him sitting before the fire, with his head fallen on his breast, sunk in the merciful stupor of sleep long delayed. I looked at him for some moments. His face, pale and refined in the dim lamplight, impressed me with an air of helpless, ineffective delicacy. They say fortune comes while we sleep. Standing there I felt benignant enough to be poor Mr. Searle's fortune. As I walked away, I perceived amid the shadows of one of the little refectory boxes which I have described, the lonely ever-dressed waiter dozing attendance on my friend, and shifting aside for a while the burden of waiterhood. I lingered a moment beside the old inn-yard, in which, upon a time, the coaches and post-chaises found space to turn and disgorge. Above the upward vista of the enclosing galleries, from which lounging lodgers and crumpled chambermaids and all the picturesque domesticity of an antique tavern must have watched the great entrances and exits of the posting and coaching drama, I descried the distant lurid twinkle of the London constellations. At the foot of the stairs, enshrined in the glittering niche of her well-appointed bar, the landlady sat napping like some solemn idol amid votive brass and plate.

The next morning, not finding the innocent object of my benevolent curiosity in the coffee-room, I learned from the waiter that he had ordered breakfast in bed. Into this asylum I was not yet prepared to pursue him. I spent the morning running about London, chiefly on business, but snatching by the way many a vivid impression of its huge metropolitan interest. Beneath the sullen black and grey of that hoary civic world the hungry American mind detects the magic colours of association. As the afternoon approached, however, my impatient heart began to babble of green fields; it was of English meadows I had chiefly dreamed. Thinking over the suburban lions,

I fixed upon Hampton Court. The day was the more propitious that it yielded just that dim, subaqueous light which sleeps so fondly upon the English landscape.

At the end of an hour I found myself wandering through the multitudinous rooms of the great palace. They follow each other in infinite succession, with no great variety of interest or aspect, but with a grand sort of regal monotony, and a fine specific flavour. They are most exactly of their various times. You pass from great painted and panelled bedchambers and closets, anterooms, drawing-rooms, council-rooms, through king's suite, queen's suite, and prince's suite, until you feel as if you were strolling through the appointed hours and stages of some decorous monarchical day. On one side are the old monumental upholsteries, the vast cold tarnished beds and canopies, with the circumference of disapparelled royalty attested by a gilded balustrade, the great carved and yawning chimney-places, where dukes-in-waiting may have warmed their weary heels: on the other side, in deep recesses, the immense windows, the framed and draped embrasures where the sovereign whispered and favourites smiled, looking out on the terraced gardens and the misty glades of Bushey Park. The dark walls are grandly decorated by innumerable dark portraits of persons attached to Court and State, more especially with various members of the Dutch-looking *entourage* of William of Orange, the restorer of the palace; with good store, too, of the lily-bosomed models of Lely and Kneller. The whole tone of this long-drawn interior is immensely sombre, prosaic, and sad. The tints of all things have sunk to a cold and melancholy brown, and the great palatial void seems to hold no stouter tenantry than a sort of pungent odorous chill. I seemed to be the only visitor. I held ungrudged communion with the formal genius of the spot. Poor mortalized kings! ineffective lure of royalty! This, or something like it, was the murmured burden of my musings. They were interrupted suddenly by my coming upon a person standing in apparently devout contemplation before a simpering countess of Sir Peter Lely's creation. On hearing my footstep this person turned his head, and I recognized my fellow-lodger at the Red-Lion. I was apparently recognized as well; I detected a sort of overture in his glance. In a few moments, seeing I had a catalogue, he asked the name of the portrait. On my ascertaining it, he inquired, timidly, how I liked the lady.

'Well,' said I, not quite timidly enough, perhaps, 'I confess she seems to me rather a light piece of work.'

He remained silent, and a little abashed, I think. As we strolled away he stole a sidelong glance of farewell at his leering shepherdess.

To speak with him face to face was to feel keenly that he was weak and interesting. We talked of our inn, of London, of the palace; he uttered his mind freely, but he seemed to struggle with a weight of depression. It was a simple mind enough, with no great culture, I fancied, but with a certain appealing native grace. I foresaw that I should find him a true American, full of that perplexing interfusion of refinement and crudity which marks the American mind. His perceptions, I divined, were delicate; his opinions, possibly, gross. On my telling him that I too was an American, he stopped short and seemed overcome with emotion: then silently passing his arm into my own, he suffered me to lead him through the rest of the palace and down into the gardens. A vast gravelled platform stretches itself before the basement of the palace, taking the afternoon sun. A portion of the edifice is reserved as a series of private apartments, occupied by state pensioners, reduced gentlewomen in receipt of the Queen's bounty, and other deserving persons. Many of these apartments have their little private gardens; and here and there, between their verdure-coated walls, you catch a glimpse of these dim horticultural closets. My companion and I took many a turn up and down this spacious level, looking down on the antique geometry of the lower garden and on the stout-fibred tapestry of compacted bloom which clothes the sunny fruit-walls and muffles the brick substructures of the huge red pile. I thought of the various images of Old-World gentility which, early and late, must have strolled upon that ancient terrace and felt the great protecting quietude of the solemn palace. We looked through an antique grating of hammered and twisted iron into one of the little private gardens, and saw an old lady with a black mantilla on her head, a decanter of water in one hand and a crutch in the other, come forth, followed by three little dogs and a cat, to sprinkle a plant. She had an opinion, I fancied, on the merits of Queen Caroline. There are few sensations so exquisite in life as to stand with a companion in a foreign land and inhale to the depths of your consciousness the alien burden of the air and the tonic picturesqueness of things. This common perception of a local mystery solders friend to friend with a closeness unfelt at home. My companion seemed oppressed with vague amazement. He stared and lingered and wooed the scene with a gentle scowl. His enjoyment appeared to give him pain. I proposed, at last, that we should dine in the neighbourhood and take a late train to town. We made our way out of the gardens into the adjoining village, where we found an excellent inn. Mr. Searle sat down to table with small apparent interest in the repast, but gradually warming to his work, he declared at the end of half an hour that for the first time in a month he felt an appetite.

'You're an invalid?' I said.

'Yes,' he answered. 'A hopeless one!'

The little village of Hampton Court stands clustered about the broad entrance of Bushey Park. After we had dined we lounged along into the huge central avenue. As far as the eye can follow it, between the double borders of its great horse-chestnuts, broad of base and round of summit, it prolongs the turfy hollow of its mist-shrouded vista. Fallen from its ancient privacy, common, open to idle starers, the great park is yet delightfully noble and English. We followed the retreating mist along its grassy channel, as if, within some curtained shrine in the deep greenwood, we should find some plaintive genius of the past. There is a rare emotion, familiar to every intelligent traveller, in which the mind, with a great passionate throb, asserts a magical synthesis of its impressions. You feel England: you feel Italy! The sensation for the moment stirs the innermost depths of your being. I had known it from time to time in Italy, and had opened my soul to it as to the spirit of the Lord. Since my arrival in England I had been waiting for it to come. A bottle of excellent Burgundy at dinner had perhaps unlocked to it the gates of sense; it came now with a conquering tread. Just the scene around me was the England of my visions. Over against us, amid the deep-hued bloom of its ordered gardens, the dark red palace, with its formal copings and its vacant windows, seemed to tell of a proud and splendid past; the little village nestling between park and palace, around a patch of turfy common, with its tavern of gentility, its ivy-towered church, its parsonage, retained to my modernized fancy the lurking semblance of a feudal hamlet; the great degenerate privacy of the antique chase seemed to make it an excellent hiding-place for patrician ghosts. It was in this dark composite light that I had read all English prose; it was this mild moist air that had blown from the verses of English poets; beneath these broad acres of rain-deepened greenness a thousand honoured dead lay buried.

'Well,' I said to my friend, 'I think there is no mistake about this being England. We may like it or not, it's positive! No more dense and stubborn fact ever settled down on an expectant tourist. It brings my heart into my throat.'

Searle was silent. I looked at him; he was looking up at the sky, as if he were watching some visible descent of the elements. 'On me too,' he said, 'it's settling down!' Then with a forced smile: 'Heaven give me strength to bear it!'

'O mighty world,' I cried, 'to hold at once so rare an Italy and so brave an England!'

'To say nothing of America,' added Searle.

'O,' I answered, 'America has a world to herself.'

'You have the advantage over me,' my companion resumed, after a pause, 'in coming to all this with an educated eye. You already know the old. I have never known it but by report. I have always fancied I should like it. In a small way at home, you know, I have tried to stick to the old. I must be a conservative by nature. People at home—a few people—used to call me a snob.'

'I don't believe you were a snob,' I cried. 'You look too amiable.'

He smiled sadly. 'There it is,' he said. 'It's the old story! I'm amiable! I know what that means! I was too great a fool to be even a snob! If I had been I should probably have come abroad earlier in life—before—before——' He paused and his head dropped sadly on his breast.

The bottle of Burgundy had loosened his tongue. I felt that my learning his story was merely a question of time. Something told me that I had gained his confidence and he would impart himself. 'Before you lost your health,' I said.

'Before I lost my health,' he answered. 'And my property,—the little I had. And my ambition. And my self-esteem.'

'Come!' I said. 'You shall get them all back. This tonic English climate will wind you up in a month. And with the return of health, all the rest will return.'

He sat musing, with his eyes fixed on the distant palace. 'They are too far gone,—self-esteem especially! I should like to be an old genteel pensioner, lodged over there in the palace, and spending my days in maundering about these classic haunts. I should go every morning, at the hour when it gets the sun, into that long gallery where all those pretty women of Lely's are hung,—I know you despise them!—and stroll up and down and pay them compliments. Poor, precious forsaken creatures! So flattered and courted in their day, so neglected now! Offering up their shoulders and ringlets and smiles to that inexorable solitude!'

I patted my friend on the shoulder. 'You shall be yourself again yet,' I said.

Just at this moment there came cantering down the shallow glade of the avenue a young girl on a fine black horse,—one of those lovely budding gentlewomen, perfectly mounted and equipped, who form to American eyes the sweetest incident of English scenery. She had distanced her servant, and, as she came abreast of us, turned slightly in her saddle and looked back at him. In the movement she dropped her whip. Drawing in her horse, she cast upon the ground a glance of maidenly alarm. 'This is something better than a Lely,' I said. Searle hastened forward, picked up the whip, and removing his hat with an air of great devotion, presented it to the young girl. Fluttered and blushing, she reached forward, took it with a whispered 'Thanks!' and the next moment was bounding over the elastic turf. Searle stood watching her; the servant, as he passed us, touched his hat. When Searle turned towards me again, I saw that his face was glowing with a violent blush. 'I doubt of your having come abroad too late,' I said, laughing.

A short distance from where we had stopped was an old stone bench. We went and sat down on it and watched the light mist turning to sullen gold in the rays of the evening sun. 'We ought to be thinking of the train back to London, I suppose,' I said at last.

'O, hang the train!' said Searle.

'Willingly! There could be no better spot than this to feel the magic of an English twilight.' So we lingered, and the twilight lingered around us,—a light and not a darkness. As we sat, there came trudging along the road an indivdual whom, from afar, I recognized as a member of the genus 'tramp'. I had read of the British tramp, but I had never yet encountered him, and I brought to bear upon the present specimen the utmost keenness of my tourist-gaze. As he approached us he slackened pace and finally halted, touching his cap. He was a man of middle age, clad in a greasy cap, with greasy ear-locks depending from its sides. Round his neck was a grimy red scarf, tucked into his waistcoat; his coat and trousers had a remote affinity with those of a reduced hostler. In one hand he had a stick; on his arm he bore a tattered basket, with a handful of withered green stuff in the bottom. His face was pale, haggard, and degraded beyond description,—a singular mixture of brutality and *finesse*. He had a history. From what height had he fallen, from what depth had he risen? Never was a form of rascally beggarhood more complete. There was a merciless fixedness of outline about him which filled me with a kind of awe. I felt as if I were in the presence of a personage,—an artist in vagrancy.

'For God's sake, gentlemen,' he said, in that raucous tone of weather-beaten poverty suggestive of chronic sore-throat exacerbated by perpetual gin,—'for God's sake, gentlemen, have pity on a poor fern-collector!'—turning up his stale dandelions. 'Food hasn't passed my lips, gentlemen, in the last three days.'

We gaped responsive, in the precious pity of guileless Yankeeism. 'I wonder,' thought I, 'if half a crown would be enough.' And our fasting botanist went limping away through the park with a mystery of satirical gratitude superadded to his general mystery.

'I feel as if I had seen my *Doppelgänger*,' said Searle. 'He reminds me of myself. What am I but a tramp?'

Upon this hint I spoke. 'What are you, my friend?' I asked. 'Who are you?'

A sudden blush rose to his pale face, so that I feared I had offended him. He poked a moment at the sod with the point of his umbrella, before answering. 'Who am I?' he said at last. 'My name is Clement Searle. I was born in New York and in New York I have always lived. What am I? That's easily told. Nothing! I assure you, nothing.'

'A very good fellow, apparently,' I protested.

'A very good fellow! Ah, there it is! You've said more than you mean. It's by having been a very good fellow all my days that I've come to this. I have drifted through life. I'm a failure, sir,—a failure as hopeless and helpless as any that ever swallowed up the slender investments of the widow and the orphan. I don't pay five cents on the dollar. Of what I was to begin with, no memory remains. I have been ebbing away, from the start, in a fatal tide which, at forty, has left this arid sand-bank behind. To begin with, certainly, I was not a fountain of wisdom. All the more reason for a definite channel,—for will and purpose and direction. I walked by chance and sympathy and sentiment. Take a turn through New York and you'll find my tattered sympathies and sentiments dangling on every bush and fluttering in every breeze; the men to whom I lent money, the women to whom I made love, the friends I trusted, the dreams I cherished, the poisonous fumes of pleasure, amid which nothing was sweet or precious but the manhood they stifled! It was my fault that I believed in pleasure here below. I believe in it still, but as I believe in God and not in man. I believed in eating your cake and having it. I respected Pleasure, and she made a fool of me. Other men, treating her like the arrant strumpet she is, enjoyed her for the hour, but kept their good manners for plain-faced Business, with the larger dowry, to whom they are now lawfully married. My taste was to be delicate: well, perhaps I was so. I had a little money: it went the way of my little wit. Here in my pocket I have forty pounds of it left. The only thing I have to show for my money and my wit is a little volume of verses, printed at my own expense, in which fifteen years ago I made bold to sing the charms of love and idleness. Six months since I got hold of the volume; it reads like the poetry of fifty years ago. The form is incredible. I hadn't seen Hampton Court then. When I was thirty I married. It was a sad mistake, but a generous one. The young girl was poor and obscure, but beautiful and proud. I fancied she would make an elegant woman. It was a sad mistake! She died at the end of three years, leaving no children. Since then I have idled along. I have had bad habits. To this impalpable thread of existence the current of my life has shrunk. Tomorrow I shall be dry. Was I meant to come to this? Upon my soul I wasn't! If I say what I feel, you'll fancy my vanity quite equal to my folly, and set me down as one of those theorizers after the fact who draw any moral from their misfortunes but the damning moral that vice is vice and that's an end of it. Take it for what it's worth: I have always fancied that I was meant for a gentler world. Before heaven, sir,—whoever you are,—I'm in practice so absurdly tender-hearted that I can afford to say it, I came into the world an aristocrat. I was born with a soul for the picturesque. It condemns me, I confess; but in a measure, too, it absolves me. I found it nowhere. I found a world all hard lines and harsh lights, without shade, without composition, as they say of pictures, without the lovely mystery of colour. To furnish colour, I melted down the very substance of my own soul. I went about with my brush, touching up and toning down; a very pretty chiaroscuro you'll find in my track! Sitting here, in this old park, in this old land, I feel—I feel that I hover on the misty verge of what might have been. I should have been born here and not there; here my vulgar idleness would have been—don't laugh now!— would have been elegant leisure. How it was that I never came abroad is more than I can say. It might have cut the knot; but the knot was too tight. I was always unwell or in debt or entangled. Besides, I had a horror of the sea,—with reason, as heaven knows! A year ago I was reminded of the existence of an old claim to a portion of an English estate, cherished off and on by various members of my family for the past eighty years. It's undeniably slender and desperately hard to define. I am by no means sure that to this hour I have mastered it. You look as if you had a clear head. Some other time, if you'll consent, we'll puzzle it out, such as it is, together. Poverty was staring me in the face; I sat down and got my claim by heart, as I used to get nine times nine as a boy. I dreamed about it for six months, half expecting to wake up some fine morning to hear through a latticed casement the cawing of an English rookery. A couple of months since there came out here on business of his own a sort of half-friend of mine, a sharp New Yorker lawyer, an extremely common fellow, but a man with an eye for the weak point and the strong point. It was with him yesterday that you saw me dining. He undertook, as he expressed it, to "nose round" and see if anything could be made of this pretended right. The matter had never seriously been taken up. A month later I got a letter from Simmons, assuring me that things looked mighty well, that he should be vastly amazed if I hadn't a case. I took fire in a humid sort of way; I acted, for the first time in my life; I sailed for England. I have been here three days: it seems three months. After keeping me waiting for thirty-six hours, last evening my precious Simmons makes his appearance and informs me, with his mouth full of mutton, that I was a blasted fool to have taken him at his word; that he had been precipitate; that I had been precipitate; that my claim was moonshine; and that I must do pennance and take a ticket for another fortnight of sea-sickness in his agreeable society. My friend, my friend! Shall I say I was disappointed? I'm already resigned. I doubted the practicability of my claim. I felt in my deeper consciousness that it was the crowning illusion of a life of illusions. Well, it was a pretty one. Poor Simmons! I forgive him with all my heart. But for him I shouldn't be sitting in this place, in this air, with these thoughts. This is a world I could have loved. There's a great fitness in its having been kept for the last. After this nothing would have been tolerable. I shall now have a month of it, I hope, and I shall not have a chance to be disenchanted. There's one thing!'—and here pausing, he laid his hand on mine; I rose and stood before him,— 'I wish it were possible you should be with me to the end.'

'I promise you,' I said, 'to leave you only at your own request. But it must be on condition of your omitting from your conversation this intolerable flavour of mortality. The end! Perhaps it's the beginning.'

He shook his head. 'You don't know me. It's a long story. I'm incurably ill.'

'I know you a little. I have a strong suspicion that your illness is in great measure a matter of mind and spirits. All that you've told me is but another way of saying that you have lived hitherto in yourself. The tenement's haunted! Live abroad! Take an interest!'

He looked at me for a moment with his sad weak eyes. Then with a faint smile: 'Don't cut down a man you find hanging. He has had a reason for it. I'm bankrupt.'

'O, health is money!' I said. 'Get well, and the rest will take care of itself. I'm interested in your claim.'

'Don't ask me to expound it now! It's a sad muddle. Let it alone. I know nothing of business. If I myself were to take the matter in hand, I should break short off the poor little silken thread of my expectancy. In a better world than this I think I should be listened to. But in this hard world there's small bestowal of ideal justice. There is no doubt, I fancy, that, a hundred years ago, we suffered a palpable wrong. But we made no appeal at the time, and the dust of a century now lies heaped upon our silence. Let it rest!'

'What is the estimated value of your interest?'

'We were instructed from the first to accept a compromise. Compared with the whole property, our utmost right is extremely small. Simmons talked of eighty-five thousand dollars. Why eighty-five I'm sure I don't know. Don't beguile me into figures.'

'Allow me one more question. Who is actually in possession?'

'A certain Mr. Richard Searle. I know nothing about him.'

'He is in some way related to you?'

'Our great-grandfathers were half-brothers. What does that make?'

'Twentieth cousins, say. And where does your twentieth cousin live?'

'At Lockley Park, Herefordshire.'

I pondered awhile, 'I'm interested in you, Mr. Searle,' I said. 'In your story, in your title, such as it is, and in this Lockley Park, Herefordshire. Suppose we go down and see it.'

He rose to his feet with a certain alertness. 'I shall make a sound man of him, yet,' I said to myself.

'I shouldn't have the heart,' he said, 'to accomplish the melancholy pilgrimage alone. But with you, I'll go anywhere.'

On our return to London we determined to spend three days there together, and then to go into the country. We felt to excellent purpose the sombre charm of London, the mighty mother-city of our mighty race, the great distributing heart of our traditional life. There are places in London, monuments, seasons, hints of history, local moods, and memories, more impressive to an American soul than aught else that Europe holds. With an equal attentive piety my friend and I glanced at these things. Their influence on Searle was deep and singular. His observation I soon perceived to be extremely acute. His almost passionate relish for the old, the artificial, and social, wellnigh extinct from its long inanition, began now to tremble and thrill with a tardy vitality. I watched in silent wonderment this new metaphysical birth. Between the fair boundaries of the counties of Hereford and Worcester rise in a long undulation the sloping pastures of the Malvern Hills. Consulting a select publication on the castles and manors of England, we found Lockley Park to be seated near the base of this grassy range, just within the confines of Hertfordshire. In the pages of this genial volume, Lockley Park and its appurtenances made a very pretty figure. We took up our abode at a certain little wayside inn, at which in the days of leisure the coach must have stopped for lunch, and burnished pewters of rustic ale been tenderly exalted to 'outsides' athirst with breezy progression. Here we stopped for the very Englishness of its steep-thatched roof, its latticed windows, and its decent porch. We allowed a couple of days to elapse in vague, undirected strolls and sweet sentimental observance of the land, before we prepared to execute the especial purpose of our journey. In this most admirable region the general sense of England was enjoined upon us with persuasive force. The noble friendliness of the scenery, its subtle old-friendliness, the magical familiarity of its multitudinous details, appealed to us at every glance. Deep in our souls a simple sentiment of love replied. The whole land, in the full, warm rains of the last of April, had burst into sudden perfect spring. The dark walls of the hedgerows had turned into blooming screens; the sodden verdure of lawn and meadow was streaked with a ranker freshness; the coated twigs of the black trees were multiplied a thousand-fold. We went forth without loss of time for a long walk on the hills. Reaching their summits, you find half England unrolled at your feet. A dozen broad counties, within the vast range of your vision, commingle their green exhalations. Closely beneath us lay the dark, rich flats of hedgy Worcestershire and the copse-checkered slopes of rolling Hereford, white with the blossom of apples. From their meadows and orchards and farmsteads and parks, from that dense and definite detail which makes even the landscape of Italy seem vacant and vague, there rises a magnificent emanation of composite colour. At widely opposite points of the large expanse two great cathedral towers rise sharply, taking the light, from the settled shadow of their circling towns,—the light, the ineffable English light! 'Out of England,' cried Searle, 'it's but a garish world!' The whole vast sweep of our surrounding prospect lay answering in a myriad fleeting shades the cloudy process of the tremendous sky. The English heaven is a fit antithesis to the English earth,—as rich, as highly wrought, as densely peopled with effects. We possess in America the infinite beauty of the blue; England possesses the splendour of combined and animated clouds. Over against us, from our station on the hills, we saw them piled and dissolved, compacted and shifted, in innumerable phases of power. Here they blot the great brightness with sullen purposes of rain; here they stretch, breeze-fretted, into dappled fields of grey; at a dozen points the confined and arrested sun bursts out in a storm of light or escapes in a drizzle of silver. We made our way along the rounded summits of these well-grazed heights,—mild, breezy inland downs, and descended through long-drawn slopes of fields, green to cottage doors, to where a rural village beckoned us from its seat among the meadows. Close beside it, I admit, the railway shoots fiercely from its tunnel in the hills; and yet there broods upon this charming hamlet an old-time quietude and privacy, which seems to make it a violation of confidence to tell its name so far away. We struck through a narrow lane, a 'green lane', dim with its height of hedges; it led us to a superb old farm-house, now jostled by the multiplied lanes and roads which have curtailed its ancient appanage. It stands in stubborn picturesqueness, at the receipt of sad-eyed contemplation and the sufferance of 'sketches'. I doubt whether out of Nuremberg—or Pompeii!—you may find so forcible an image of the domiciliary genius of the past. It is cruelly complete. Poor sacred superannuated home! Its bended beams and joists, beneath the great burden of its many gables, seem to ache and groan with memories and regrets. The short, low windows, where lead and glass combine in equal proportions to hint to the wondering stranger of the mediaeval gloom within, still prefer their darksome office to the grace of modern day. Such an old house fills an American with an indefinable feeling of respect. So propped and patched and tinkered with clumsy tenderness, clustered so richly about its central English sturdiness, its oaken vertebrations, so humanized with ages of use and touches of beneficent affection, and above all so densely and cunningly ornate, with its close-wrought vestment of detail,—the mildew of climate, the deposit of history,—it seemed to offer to our grateful eyes a small, rude synthesis of the great English social order. Passing out upon the highroad, we came to the common browsing-patch, the 'village green' of the tales of our youth. Nothing was wanting; the shaggy, mouse-coloured donkey, nosing the turf with his mild and huge proboscis, the geese, the old woman,—*the* old woman, in person, with her red cloak and her black bonnet, frilled about the face and double-frilled beside her decent, placid cheeks,—the towering ploughman with his white smock-frock, puckered on chest and back, his short corduroys, his mighty calves, his big, red, rural face. We greeted these things as children greet the loved pictures in a story-book, lost and mourned and found again. It was marvellous how well we knew them. Beside the road we saw a ploughboy straddle, whistling, on a stile. Mulready might have painted him. Beyond the stile, across the level velvet of a meadow, a footpath lay, like a thread of darker woof. We followed it from field to field and from stile to stile. It was the way to church. At the church we finally arrived, lost in its rook-haunted churchyard, hidden from the work-day world by the broad stillness of pastures,—a grey, grey tower, a huge black yew, a cluster of village graves, with crooked headstones, in grassy low relief. The whole scene was deeply ecclesiastical. My companion was overcome.

'You must bury me here,' he cried. 'It's the first church I have seen in my life. How it makes a Sunday where it stands!'

The next day we saw a church of a larger kind. We walked over to

Worcester, through a region so thick-sown with native features and incidents that I felt like one of Smollett's pedestrian heroes, faring tavernward for a night of adventures. As we neared the provincial city, we saw the steepled mass of the cathedral, long and high, rise far into the cloud-freckled blue. And as we came nearer still, we stopped on the bridge and viewed the calm minster reflected in the yellow Severn. And going further yet, we entered the town,—where surely Miss Austen's heroines, in chariots and phaetons, must often have come a-shopping for swansdown boas and lace mittens;—we lounged about the gentle Close and gazed insatiably at that most soul-soothing sight, the waning, wasting afternoon light, the visible ether which feels the voices of the chimes, far aloft on the broad perpendicular field of the cathedral tower; saw it linger and nestle and abide, as it loves to do on all bold architectural spaces, converting them graciously into registers and witnesses of nature; tasted, too, as deeply of the peculiar stillness of this clerical precinct; saw a rosy English lad come forth and lock the door of the old foundation school, which marries its hoary basement to the soaring Gothic of the church, and carry his big responsible key into one of the quiet canonical houses; and then stood musing together on the effect on one's mind of having in one's boyhood haunted such cathedral shades as a King's scholar, and yet kept ruddy with much cricket in misty meadows by the Severn. On the third morning we betook ourselves to Lockley Park, having learned that the greater part of it was open to visitors, and that, indeed, on application, the house was occasionally shown.

Within its vast enclosure many a declining spur of the great hills melted into park-like slopes and dells. A long avenue wound and circled from the outermost gate through an untrimmed woodland, whence you glanced at further slopes and glades and copses and bosky recesses,—at everything except the limits of the place. It was as free and wild and untended as the villa of an Italian prince; and I have never seen the stern English fact of property wear such an abandon of welcome. The weather had just become perfect; it was one of the dozen exquisite days of the English year,—days stamped with a refinement of purity unknown in more liberal climes. It was as if the mellow brightness, as tender as that of the primroses which starred the dark waysides like petals wind-scattered over beds of moss, had been meted out to us by the cubic foot; tempered, refined, recorded, islanded in months of gloom, inestimably precious and rare. From this external region we passed into the very heart of the park, through a second lodge-gate, with weather-worn gilding on its twisted bars, to the smooth slopes where the great trees stood singly and the tame deer browsed along the bed of a woodland stream. Hence, before us, we perceived the dark Elizabethan manor among its blooming parterres and terraces.

'Here you can wander all day,' I said to Searle, 'like a proscribed and exiled prince, hovering about the dominion of the usurper.'

'To think,' he answered, 'of people having enjoyed this all these years! I know what I am,—what might I have been? What does all this make of you?'

'That it makes you happy,' I said, 'I should hesitate to believe. But it's hard to believe that such a place hasn't some beneficent action of its own.'

'What a perfect scene and background it forms!' Searle went on. 'What legends, what histories it knows! My heart is breaking with unutterable visions. There's Tennyson's Talking Oak. What summer days one could spend here! How I could lounge my bit of life away on this shady stretch of turf! Haven't I some maiden-cousin in yon moated grange who would give me kind leave?' And then turning almost fiercely upon me: 'Why did you bring me here? Why did you drag me into this torment of vain regrets?'

At this moment there passed near us a servant who had emerged from the gardens of the great house. I hailed him and inquired whether we should be likely to gain admittance. He answered that Mr. Searle was away from home and that he thought it probable the housekeeper would consent to do the honours of the mansion. I passed my arm into Searle's. 'Come!' I said. 'Drain the cup, bitter-sweet though it be. We shall go in.' We passed a third lodge-gate and entered the gardens. The house was an admirable specimen of complete Elizabethan, a huge brick pile, in which the picturesque irregularities of the style, the gables and porches, the oriels and turrets, the screens of ivy and the pinnacles of slate, were clustered and multiplied in delightful fulness. Two broad terraces commanded the great wooded horizon of the adjacent domain. Our summons was answered by the butler in person, solemn and *tout de noir habillé*. He repeated the statement that Mr. Searle was away from home, and that he would present our petition to the housekeeper. We would be so good, however, as to give him our cards. This request, following directly upon the assertion that Mr. Searle was absent, seemed to my companion not distinctly pertinent. 'Surely not for the housekeeper,' he said.

The butler gave a deferential cough. 'Miss Searle is at home.'

'Yours alone will suffice,' said Searle. I took out a card and pencil, and wrote beneath my name, *New York*. Standing with the pencil in my hand I felt a sudden impulse. Without in the least weighing proprieties or results, I yielded to it. I added above my name, *Mr. Clement Searle*. What would come of it?

Before many minutes the housekeeper attended us,—a fresh rosy little old woman in a dowdy clean cap and a scanty calico gown; an exquisite specimen of refined and venerable servility. She had the accent of the country, but the manners of the house. Under her guidance we passed through a dozen apartments, duly stocked with old pictures, old tapestry, old carvings, old armour, with all the constituent properties of an English manor. The pictures were especially valuable. The two Vandykes, the trio of rosy Rubenses, the sole and sombre Rembrandt, glowed with conscious authenticity. A Claude, a Murillo, a Greuze, and a Gainsborough hung gracious in their chosen places. The great intervals were peopled with various breadths of mellow gloom,—landscapes of late Italian fabric, poorish as masterpieces, but admirable as furniture. Searle strolled about silent, pale and grave, with bloodshot eyes and lips compressed. He uttered no comment and asked no question. Missing him at a certain moment from my side, I retraced my steps and found him in a room we had just left, on a tarnished silken divan, with his face buried in his hands. Before him, ranged on an antique buffet, was a magnificent collection of old Italian majolica; huge platters radiant with their steady colours, jugs and vases nobly bellied and embossed. There came to me, as I looked, a sudden vision of the young English gentleman, who, eighty years ago, had travelled by slow stages to Italy and had bargained with a pale, persuasive Roman for these treasures of his musty shop, or had taken the bright things in payment for a gaming debt from some debased inheritor of a ransacked Venetian palace. 'What is it, Searle?' I asked. 'Are you unwell?'

He uncovered his haggard face and showed a burning blush. Then smiling in hot irony : 'A memory of the past! I was thinking of a china vase that used to stand on the parlour mantelshelf while I was a boy, with the portrait of General Jackson painted on one side and a bunch of flowers on the other. How long do you suppose that majolica-ware has been in the family?'

'A long time probably. It was brought hither in the last century, into old, old England, out of old, old Italy, by some old young buck of this excellent house with a taste for *chinoiseries*. Here it has stood for a hundred years, keeping its clear, firm hues in this aristocratic *demi-jour*.'

Searle sprang to his feet. 'I say,' he cried, 'in heaven's name take me away! I can't stand this. Before I know it I shall do something I shall be ashamed of. I shall steal one of their d—d majolicas. I shall proclaim my identity and assert my rights! I shall go blubbering to Miss Searle and ask her in pity's name to keep me here for a month!'

If poor Searle could ever have been said to look 'dangerous', he looked so now. I began to regret my officious presentation of his name, and prepared without delay to lead him out of the house. We overtook the housekeeper in the last room of the suite, a small, unused boudoir, over the chimney-piece of which hung a noble portrait of a young man in a powdered wig and a brocaded waistcoat. I was immediately struck with his resemblance to my companion.

'This is Mr. Clement Searle, Mr. Searle's great-uncle, by Sir Joshua Reynolds,' quoth the housekeeper. 'He died young, poor gentleman. He perished at sea, going to America.'

'He's the young buck,' I said, 'who brought the majolica-ware out of Italy.'

'Indeed, sir, I believe he did,' said the housekeeper, staring.

'He's the image of you, Searle,' I murmured.

'He's wonderfully like the gentleman, saving his presence,' said the housekeeper.

My friend stood gazing. 'Clement Searle—at sea—going to America——' he muttered. Then harshly, to the housekeeper, 'Why the deuce did he go to America?'

'Why, indeed, sir? You may well ask. I believe he had kinsfolk there. It was for them to come to him.'

Searle broke into a laugh. 'It was for them to have come to him! Well, well,' he said, fixing his eyes on the little old woman, 'they have come to him at last!'

She blushed like a wrinkled roseleaf. 'Indeed, sir,' she said, 'I verily believe that you are one of *us*!'

'My name is the name of that lovely youth,' Searle went on. 'Kinsman, I salute you! Attend!' and he grasped me by the arm. 'I have an idea! He perished at sea. His spirit came ashore and wandered forlorn till it got lodgement again in my poor body. In my poor body it has lived, homesick, these forty years, racking its wretched casing, urging me, stupid, to carry it back to the scenes of its youth. And I never knew what was the matter with me! Let me exhale my spirit here!'

The housekeeper essayed a timorous smile. The scene was embarrassing. My confusion was not allayed when I suddenly perceived in the doorway the figure of a lady. 'Miss Searle!' whispered the housekeeper. My first impression of Miss Searle was that she was neither young nor beautiful. She stood with a timid air on the threshold, pale, trying to smile, and twirling my card in her fingers. I immediately bowed; Searle, I think, gazed marvelling.

'If I am not mistaken,' said the lady, 'one of you gentlemen is Mr. Clement Searle.'

'My friend is Mr. Clement Searle,' I replied. 'Allow me to add that I alone am responsible for your having received his name.'

'I should have been sorry not to receive it,' said Miss Searle, beginning to blush. 'Your being from America has led me to—to interrupt you.'

'The interruption, madam, has been on our part. And with just that excuse,—that we are from America.'

Miss Searle, while I spoke, had fixed her eyes on my friend, as he stood silent beneath Sir Joshua's portrait. The housekeeper, amazed and mystified, took a liberty. 'Heaven preserve us, Miss! It's your great-uncle's picture come to life.'

'I'm not mistaken, then,' said Miss Searle. 'We are distantly related.' She had the aspect of an extremely modest woman. She was evidently embarrassed at having to proceed unassisted in her overture. Searle eyed her with gentle wonder from head to foot. I fancied I read his thoughts. This, then, was Miss Searle, his maiden-cousin, prospective heiress of these manorial acres and treasures. She was a person of about thirty-three years of age, taller than most women, with health and strength in the rounded amplitude of her shape. She had a small blue eye, a massive chignon of yellow hair, and a mouth at once broad and comely. She was dressed in a lustre-less black satin gown, with a short train. Around her neck she wore a blue silk handkerchief, and over this handkerchief, in many convolutions, a string of amber beads. Her appearance was singular; she was large, yet not imposing; girlish, yet mature. Her glance and accent, in addressing us, were simple, too simple. Searle, I think, had been fancying some proud cold beauty of five-and-twenty; he was relieved at finding the lady timid and plain. His person was suddenly illumined by the grace of an old disused gallantry.

'We are distant cousins, I believe. I am happy to avow a relationship which you are so good as to remember. I hadn't in the least counted on your doing so.'

'Perhaps I have done wrong,' and Miss Searle blushed anew and smiled. 'But I have always known of there being people of our blood in America, and I have often wondered and asked about them; without learning much, though. Today, when this card was brought me, and I knew of a Clement Searle wandering about the house like a stranger, I felt as if I ought to do something. I hardly knew what! My brother is in London. I have done what I think he would have done. Welcome, as a cousin.' And with a gesture at once frank and shy, she put out her hand.

'I'm welcome indeed,' said Searle, taking it, 'if he would have done it half as graciously.'

'You've seen the show,' Miss Searle went on. 'Perhaps now you'll have some lunch.' We followed her into a small breakfast-room, where a deep bay-window opened on the mossy flags of the great terrace. Here, for some moments, she remained silent and shy, in the manner of a person resting from a great effort. Searle, too, was formal and reticent, so that I had to busy myself with providing small-talk. It was of course easy to descant on the beauties of park and mansion. Meanwhile I observed our hostess. She had small beauty and scanty grace; her dress was out of taste and out of season; yet she pleased me well. There was about her a sturdy sweetness, a homely flavour of the sequestered *châtelaine* of feudal days. To be so simple amid this massive luxury, so mellow and yet so fresh, so modest and yet so placid, told of just the spacious leisure in which I had fancied human life to be steeped in many a park-circled home. Miss Searle was to the *Belle au Bois Dormant* what a fact is to a fairy-tale, an interpretation to a myth. We, on our side, were to our hostess objects of no light scrutiny. The best possible English breeding still marvels visibly at the native American. Miss Searle's wonderment was guileless enough to have been more overt and yet inoffensive; there was no taint of offence indeed in her utterance of the unvarying *gracieuseté* that she had met an American family on the Lake of Como, whom she would have almost taken to be English.

'If I lived here,' I said, 'I think I should hardly need to go away, even to the Lake of Como.'

'You might perhaps get tired of it. And then the Lake of Como! If I could only go abroad again!'

'You have been but once?'

'Only once. Three years ago my brother took me to Switzerland. We thought it extremely beautiful. Except for this journey, I have always lived here. Here I was born. It's a dear old place, indeed, and I know it well. Sometimes I fancy I'm a little tired.' And on my asking her how she spent her time and what society she saw, 'It's extremely quiet,' she went on, proceeding by short steps and simple statements in the manner of a person summoned for the first time to define her situation and enumerate the elements of her life. 'We see very few people. I don't think there are many nice people hereabouts. At least we don't know them. Our own family is very small. My brother cares for little else but riding and books. He had a great sorrow ten years ago. He lost his wife and his only son, a dear little boy, who would have succeeded him in the estates. Do you know that I'm likely to have them now? Poor me! Since his loss my brother has preferred to be quite alone. I'm sorry he's away. But you must wait till he comes back. I expect him in a day or two.' She talked more and more, with a rambling earnest vapidity, about her circumstances, her solitude, her bad eyes, so that she couldn't read, her flowers, her ferns, her dogs, and the curate, recently inducted by her brother and warranted sound orthodox, who had lately begun to light his altar candles; pausing every now and then to blush in self-surprise, and yet moving steadily from point to point in the deepening excitement of temptation and occasion. Of all the old things I had seen in England, this mind of Miss Searle's seemed to me the oldest, the quaintest, the most ripely verdant; so fenced and protected by convention and precedent and usage; so passive and mild and docile. I felt as if I were talking with a potential heroine of Miss Burney. As she talked, she rested her dull, kind eyes upon her kinsman with a sort of fascinated stare. At last, 'Did you mean to go away,' she demanded, 'without asking for us?'

'I had thought it over, Miss Searle, and had determined not to trouble you. You have shown me how unfriendly I should have been.'

'But you knew of the place being ours and of our relationship?'

'Just so. It was because of these things that I came down here,— because of them, almost, that I came to England. I have always liked to think of them.'

'You merely wished to look, then? We don't pretend to be much to look at.'

'You don't know what you are, Miss Searle,' said my friend, gravely.

'You like the old place, then?'

Searle looked at her in silence. 'If I could only tell you,' he said at last.

'Do tell me! You must come and stay with us.'

Searle began to laugh. 'Take care, take care,' he cried. 'I should surprise you. At least I should bore you. I should never leave you.'

'O, you'd get homesick for America.'

At this Searle laughed the more. 'By the way,' he cried to me, 'tell Miss Searle about America!' And he stepped through the window out upon the terrace, followed by two beautiful dogs, a pointer and a young stag-hound, who from the moment we came in had established the fondest relation with him. Miss Searle looked at him as he went, with a certain tender wonder in her eye. I read in her glance, methought, that she was interested. I suddenly recalled the last words I had heard spoken by my friend's adviser in London. 'Instead of dying you'd better marry.' If Miss Searle could be gently manipulated. O for a certain divine tact! Something assured me that her heart was virgin soil; that sentiment had never bloomed there. If I could but sow the seed! There lurked within her the perfect image of one of the patient wives of old.

'He has lost his heart to England,' I said. 'He ought to have been born here.'

'And yet,' said Miss Searle, 'he's not in the least an Englishman.'

'How do you know that?'

'I hardly know how. I never talked with a foreigner before; but he looks and talks as I have fancied foreigners.'

'Yes, he's foreign enough!'

'Is he married?'

'He's a widower,—without children.'

'Has he property?'

'Very little.'

'But enough to travel on?'

I meditated. 'He has not expected to travel far,' I said, at last. 'You know he's in poor health.'

'Poor gentleman! So I fancied.'

'He's better, though, than he thinks. He came here because he wanted to see your place before he dies.'

'Poor fellow!' And I fancied I perceived in her eye the lustre of a rising tear. 'And he was going off without my seeing him?'

'He's a modest man, you see.'

'He's very much of a gentleman.'

'Assuredly!'

At this moment we heard on the terrace a loud, harsh cry. 'It's the great peacock!' said Miss Searle, stepping to the window and passing out. I followed her. Below us on the terrace, leaning on the parapet, stood our friend, with his arm round the neck of the pointer. Before him, on the grand walk, strutted a splendid peacock, with ruffled neck and expanded tail. The other dog had apparently indulged in a momentary attempt to abash him; but at Searle's voice he had bounded back to the terrace and leaped upon the parapet, where he now stood licking his new friend's face. The scene had a beautiful old-time air: the peacock flaunting in the foreground, like the very genius of antique gardenry; the broad terrace, which tickled so cunningly an innate taste of mine for all deserted promenades and esplanades to which people may have adjourned from formal dinners, to drink coffee in old Sèvres, and where the stiff brocade of women's dresses may have rustled autumnal leaves; and far around us, with one leafy circle melting into another, the timbered acres of the park. 'The very beasts have made him welcome,' I said, as we rejoined our companion.

'The peacock has done for you, Mr. Searle,' said his cousin, 'what he

does only for very great people. A year ago there came here a duchess
to see my brother. I don't think that since then he has spread his tail
as wide for any one else by a dozen feathers.'

'It's not alone the peacock,' said Searle. 'Just now there came slipping across my path a little green lizard, the first I ever saw, the lizard
of literature! And if you have a ghost, broad daylight though it be, I
expect to see him here. Do you know the annals of your house, Miss
Searle?'

'O dear, no! You must ask my brother for all those things.'

'You ought to have a book full of legends and traditions. You
ought to have loves and murders and mysteries by the roomful. I
count upon it.'

'O Mr. Searle! We have always been a very well-behaved family.
Nothing out of the way has ever happened, I think.'

'Nothing out of the way? O horrors! We have done better than
that in America. Why, I myself!'—and he gazed at her a moment
with a gleam of malice, and then broke into a laugh,—'suppose I
should turn out a better Searle than you? Better than you, nursed
here in romance and luxury. Come, don't disappoint me. You have
some history among you all, you have some poetry. I have been
famished all my days for these things. Do you understand? Ah, you
can't understand! Tell me something! When I think of what must
have happened here! when I think of the lovers who must have
strolled on this terrace and wandered through those glades! of all the
figures and passions and purposes that must have haunted these walls!
of the births and deaths, the joys and sufferings, the young hopes and
the old regrets, the immortal picturesqueness——' And here he
faltered a moment, with the increase of his vehemence. The gleam
in his eye, which I have called a gleam of malice, had settled into a
deep, unnatural light. I began to fear that he had become over-
excited. But he went on with redoubled passion: 'To see it all evoked
before me,' he cried, 'if the devil alone could do it, I'd make a bargain
with the devil. O Miss Searle, I'm a most unhappy man!'

'O dear, O dear!' said Miss Searle.

'Look at that window, that blessed oriel!' And he pointed to a
small, protruding casement above us, relieved against the purple
brick-work, framed cunningly in chiselled stone, and curtained with
ivy.

'It's my room,' said Miss Searle.

'Of course it's a maiden's room. Think of the forgotten loveliness
which has peeped from that window; think of the old-time women's
lives which have known chiefly that outlook on this bosky world. O
gentle cousins! And you, Miss Searle, you're one of them yet.' And

he marched towards her and took her great white hand. She surrendered it, blushing to her eyes, and pressing her other hand to
her breast. 'You're a woman of the past. You're nobly simple. It has
been a romance to see you. It doesn't matter what I say to you. You
didn't know me yesterday, you'll not know me tomorrow. Let me today do a mad, sweet thing. Let me fancy you the soul of all the
dead women who have trod these terrace-flags, which lie here like
sepulchral tablets in the pavement of a church. Let me say I worship you.' And he raised her hand to his lips. She gently withdrew it,
and for a moment averted her face. Meeting her eyes the next moment, I saw that they were filled with tears. The *Belle au Bois Dormant* was awake.

There followed an embarrassed pause. An issue was suddenly presented by the appearance of the butler bearing a letter. 'A telegram,
Miss,' he said.

'Dear me!' cried Miss Searle, 'I can't open a telegram. Cousin, help
me.'

Searle took the missive, opened it, and read aloud: '*I shall be home
to dinner. Keep the American.*'

PART II

'Keep the American!' Miss Searle, in compliance with the injunction conveyed in her brother's telegram (with something certainly of
telegraphic curtness) lost no time in expressing the pleasure it would
give her to have my companion remain. 'Really you must,' she said;
and forthwith repaired to the housekeeper, to give orders for the
preparation of a room.

'How in the world,' asked Searle, 'did he know of my being here?'

'He learned, probably,' I expounded, 'from his solicitor of the visit
of your friend Simmons. Simmons and the solicitor must have had
another interview since your arrival in England. Simmons, for reasons
of his own, has communicated to the solicitor your journey to this
neighbourhood, and Mr. Searle, learning this, has immediately taken
for granted that you have formally presented yourself to his sister.
He's hospitably inclined, and he wishes her to do the proper thing
by you. More, perhaps! I have my little theory that he is the very
Phoenix of usurpers, that his nobler sense has been captivated by
the exposition of these men of law, and that he means gracefully to
surrender you your fractional interest in the estate.'

'*Je m'y perds!*' said my friend, musing. 'Come what, come will!'

'You of course,' said Miss Searle, reappearing and turning to me, 'are included in my brother's invitation. I have bespoken your lodging as well. Your luggage shall immediately be sent for.'

It was arranged that I in person should be driven over to our little inn, and that I should return with our effects in time to meet Mr. Searle at dinner. On my arrival, several hours later, I was immediately conducted to my room. The servant pointed out to me that it communicated by a door and a private passage with that of my companion. I made my way along this passage,—a most antique and picturesque little corridor, with a long horizontal latticed casement, through which there streamed, upon a series of grotesquely sculptured oaken closets and cupboards, the lurid animating glow of the western sun, —knocked at his door, and, getting no answer, opened it. In an armchair by the open window sat my friend, sleeping, with arms and legs relaxed and head placidly reverted. It was a great relief to find him resting from his early excitement. I watched him for some moments before waking him. There was a faint glow of colour in his cheek and a light parting of his lips, as in a smile; something nearer to brightness and peace than I had yet seen in him. It was almost happiness, it was almost health. I laid my hand on his arm and gently shook it. He opened his eyes, gazed at me a moment, vaguely recognized me, then closed them again, 'Let me dream, let me dream!' he said.

'What are you dreaming about?'

A moment passed before his answer came. 'About a tall woman in a quaint black dress, with yellow hair, and a sweet, sweet smile, and a soft, low, delicious voice! I'm in love with her.'

'It's better to see her,' I said, 'than to dream about her. Get up and dress, and we shall go down to dinner and meet her.'

'Dinner—dinner——' And he gradually opened his eyes again. 'Yes, upon my word, I shall dine!'

'You're a well man!' I said, as he rose to his feet. 'You'll live to bury Mr. Simmons.' He had spent the hours of my absence, he told me, with Miss Searle. They had strolled together over the park and through the gardens and green-houses. 'You must already be intimate!' I said, smiling.

'She is intimate with me,' he answered. 'Heaven knows what rigmarole I've treated her to!' They had parted an hour ago, since when, he believed, her brother had arrived.

The slow-fading twilight still abode in the great drawing-room as we entered it. The housekeeper had told us that this apartment was rarely used, there being a smaller and more convenient one for the same needs. It seemed now, however, to be occupied in my comrade's honour. At the farther end of it, rising to the roof, like a ducal tomb in a cathedral, was the great chimney-piece of chiselled alabaster, in which a light fire was crackling. Before the fire stood a small short man with his hands behind him; near him stood Miss Searle, so transformed by her dress that at first I knew her not. There was in our entrance and reception something profoundly chilling and solemn. We moved in silence up the long room. Mr. Searle advanced slowly a dozen steps to meet us. His sister stood motionless. I was conscious of her masking her visage with a large white tinselled fan, and of her eyes, grave and expanded, watching us intently over the top of it. The master of Lockley Park grasped in silence the proffered hand of his kinsman, and eyed him from head to foot, suppressing, I think, a start of surprise at his resemblance to Sir Joshua's portrait. 'This is a happy day,' he said. And then turning to me with a bow, 'My cousin's friend is my friend.' Miss Searle lowered her fan.

The first thing that struck me in Mr. Searle's appearance was his short and meagre stature, less by half a head than that of his sister. The second was the flaming redness of his hair and beard. The former, fine as silk apparently in texture, scarlet almost in hue, and densely abundant, surrounded his head like a huge lurid nimbus. His beard sprang fanlike from lips and cheek and chin, as like to his amazing locks as if it had been the downward image of them reflected in water. His face was pale and attenuated, like the face of a scholar, a dilettante, a man who lives in a library, bending over books and prints and medals. At a distance it had an oddly innocent and youthful look; but on a nearer view it revealed a number of finely etched and scratched wrinkles of a singularly aged and cunning effect. The complexion was that of a man of fifty. His nose was arched and delicate, identical almost with the nose of my friend. In harmony with the effect of his hair was that of his eyes, which were large and deep-set, with a sort of vulpine keenness and redness, but full of temper and spirit. Imagine this physiognomy—grave and solemn in tone, grotesquely solemn, almost, in spite of the bushy brightness in which it was encased—set in motion by a smile which seemed to whisper terribly, 'I am *the* smile, the sole and single, the grin to command,' and you will have an imperfect notion of the remarkable presence of our host; something better worth seeing and knowing, I fancied as I covertly scrutinized him, than anything our excursion had yet revealed to us. Of how thoroughly I had entered into sympathy with my companion and how effactually I had associated my sensibilities with his, I had small suspicion until, within the short five minutes which preceded the announcement of dinner, I distinctly perceived him stiffen himself into a posture (morally speaking) of indefinable protest and mistrust. To neither of us was Mr.

Searle, as the Italians would say, *simpatico*. I might have fancied from her attitude that Miss Searle apprehended our thoughts. A signal change had been wrought in her since the morning; during the hour, indeed (as I read in the light of the wondering glance he cast at her), that had elapsed since her parting with her cousin. She had not yet recovered from some great agitation. Her face was pale and her eyes red with weeping. These tragic signs and tokens gave an unexpected dignity to her aspect, which was further enhanced by the rare picturesqueness of her dress. Whether it was taste or whether it was accident, I know not; but Miss Searle, as she stood there, half in the cool twilight, half in the arrested glow of the fire as it spent itself in the vastness of its marble cave, was a figure for a cunning painter. She was dressed in the faded splendour of a beautiful tissue of combined and blended silk and crepe of a tender sea-green colour, festooned and garnished and puffed into a massive *bouillonnement;* a piece of millinery which, though it must have witnessed a number of stately dinners, preserved still the grand air of a noble fashion. Over her white shoulders she wore an ancient web of the most precious and venerable lace, and about her heavy throat a necklace of heavy pearls. I went with her into dinner, and Mr. Searle, following with my friend, took his arm (as the latter afterwards told me) and pretended sportively to conduct him. As dinner proceeded, the feeling grew within me that a drama had begun to be played in which the three persons before me were actors, each of a most exacting part. The part of my friend, however, seemed the most heavily charged, and I was filled with a strong desire that he should acquit himself with honour. I seemed to see him summon his shadowy faculties to obey his shadowy will, poor fellow, playing solemnly at self-esteem. With Miss Searle, credulous, passive, and pitying, he had finally flung aside all vanity and pretence, and had unpacked his fantastic heart with words. But with our host there might be no talking of nonsense nor taking of liberties; there and then, if ever, sat a double-distilled conservative, breathing the flattering fumes of hereditary privilege and peace. For an hour, then, I saw my poor friend turn painfully about to speak graciously of barren things. He was to assert himself at heart a sound American, so that his relish of this elder world might seem purely disinterested. What his kinsman had expected to find him, I know not; but, with all his poised and projected amenity, he was unable to repress a shade of annoyance at finding him likely to speak graciously at all. Mr. Searle was not the man to show his hand, but I think his best card had been a certain implicit confidence that this exotic parasite would hardly have good manners. Mr. Searle, with great decency, led the conversation to America, talking of it rather as if it were some fabled planet, alien to the British orbit, lately proclaimed indeed to have the proportion of atmospheric gases required to support animal life, but not, save under cover of a liberal afterthought, to be admitted into one's regular conception of things. I felt nothing but regret that the spheric smoothness of his universe should be strained to cracking by the intrusion of our square shoulders.

'I knew in a general way,' said our host, 'of my having relations in America; but you know one hardly realizes those things. I could hardly more have imagined people of our blood there, than I could have imagined being there myself. There was a man I knew at college, a very odd fellow, a nice fellow too; he and I were rather cronies; I think he afterwards went to America; to the Argentine Republic, I believe. Do you know the Argentine Republic? What an extraordinary name, by the way! And then, you know, there was that great-uncle of mine whom Sir Joshua painted. He went to America, but he never got there. He was lost at sea. You look enough like him to have one fancy he did *get* there, and that he has lived along till now. If you *are* he, you've not done a nice thing to show yourself here. He left a bad name behind him. There's a ghost who comes sobbing about the house every now and then, the ghost of one against whom he wrought a great evil!'

'O brother!' cried Miss Searle, in simple horror.

'Of course you know nothing of such things,' said Mr. Searle. 'You're too sound a sleeper to hear the sobbing of ghosts.'

'I'm sure I should like immensely to hear the sobbing of a ghost!' said my friend, with the light of his previous eagerness playing up into his eyes. 'Why does it sob? Unfold the wondrous tale.'

Mr. Searle eyed his audience for a moment gaugingly; and then, as the French say, *se recueillit*, as if he were measuring his own imaginative force.

He wished to do justice to his theme. With the five finger-nails of his left hand nervously playing against the tinkling crystal of his wineglass, and his bright eye telling of a gleeful sense that, small and grotesque as he sat there, he was for the moment profoundly impressive, he distilled into our untutored minds the sombre legend of his house. 'Mr. Clement Searle, from all I gather, was a young man of great talents but a weak disposition. His mother was left a widow early in life, with two sons, of whom he was the older and the more promising. She educated him with the utmost fondness and care. Of course, when he came to manhood, she wished him to marry well. His means were quite sufficient to enable him to overlook the want of means in his wife; and Mrs. Searle selected a young lady who possessed, as she conceived, every good gift save a fortune,—a fine, proud, handsome girl, the daughter of an old friend,—an old lover, I fancy, of her own. Clement, however, as it appeared, had either chosen otherwise or was as yet unprepared to choose. The young lady discharged upon him in vain the battery of her attractions; in vain his mother urged her cause. Clement remained cold, insensible, inflexible. Mrs. Searle possessed a native force of which in its feminine branch the family seems to have lost the trick. A proud, passionate, imperious woman, she had had great cares and a number of lawsuits; they had given her a great will. She suspected that her son's affections were lodged elsewhere, and lodged amiss. Irritated by his stubborn defiance of her wishes, she persisted in her importunities. The more she watched him the more she believed that he loved in secret and beneath him. He went about sombre, sullen, and preoccupied. At last, with the fatal indiscretion of an angry woman, she threatened to bring the young lady of her choice—who, by the way, seems to have been no shrinking blossom—to stay in the house. A stormy scene was the result. He threatened that if she did he would leave the country and sail for America. She probably disbelieved him: she knew him to be weak, but she overrated his weakness. At all events, the fair rejected arrived and Clement departed. On a dark December day he took ship at Southampton. The two women, desperate with rage and sorrow, sat alone in this great house, mingling their tears and imprecations. A fortnight later, on Christmas eve, in the midst of a great snow-storm long famous in the country, there came to them a mighty quickening of their bitterness. A young woman, soaked and chilled by the storm, gained entrance to the house and made her way into the presence of the mistress and her guest. She poured out her tale. She was a poor curate's daughter of Hereford. Clement Searle had loved her,—loved her all too well. She had been turned out in wrath from her father's house; his mother, at least, might pity her,—if not for herself, then for the child she was soon to bring forth. The poor girl had reckoned too fondly. The women, in scorn, in horror, with blows, possibly, turned her forth again into the storm. In the storm she wandered, and in the deep snow she died. Her lover, as you know, perished in that hard winter weather at sea; the news came to his mother late, but soon enough. We are haunted by the curate's daughter.'

There was a pause of some moments. 'Ah, well we may be!' said Miss Searle, with a great pity.

Searle blazed up into enthusiasm. 'Of course, you know,'—and suddenly he began to blush violently,—'I should be sorry to claim any identity with my faithless namesake, poor fellow. But I shall be hugely tickled if this poor ghost should be deceived by my resemblance and mistake me for her cruel lover. She's welcome to the comfort of it. What one *can* do in the case I shall be glad to do. But can a ghost haunt a ghost? I *am* a ghost!'

Mr. Searle stared a moment, and then smiling superbly: 'I could almost believe you are!' he said.

'O brother—cousin,' cried Miss Searle, with the gentlest yet most appealing dignity, 'how can you talk so horribly?'

This horrible talk, however, evidently possessed a potent magic for my friend; and his imagination, chilled for a while by the frigid contact of his kinsman, began to glow again with its earlier fire. From this moment he ceased to mind his *p*'s and *q*'s, to care what he said or how he said it, so long as he expressed the passionate satisfaction which the scene about him infused into his heart. As he talked I ceased even mentally to protest. I have wondered since that I should not have resented the exhibition of so rank and florid an egotism. But a great frankness for the time makes its own law, and a great passion its own channel. There was, moreover, an immense sweetness in the manner of my friend's speech. Free alike from either adulation or envy, the very soul of it was a divine apprehension, an imaginative mastery, free as the flight of Ariel, of the rich facts beneath whose earthly shadow our entertainers sat darkened and at loss, unable, as the saying goes, to see the forest on account of the trees.

'How does the look of age come?' he demanded, at dessert. 'Does it come of itself, unobserved, unrecorded, unmeasured? Or do you woo it and set baits and traps for it, and watch it like the dawning brownness of a meerschaum pipe, and nail it down when it appears, just where it peeps out, and light a votive taper beneath it and give thanks to it daily? Or do you forbid it and fight it and resist it, and yet feel it settling and deepening about you, as irresistible as fate?'

'What the deuce is the man talking about?' said the smile of our host.

'I found a grey hair this morning,' said Miss Searle.

'Good heavens! I hope you respected it,' cried Searle.

'I looked at it for a long time in my little glass,' said his cousin, simply.

'Miss Searle, for ten years to come, can afford to be amused at grey hairs,' I said.

'Ten years hence I shall be forty-three.'

'That's my age,' said Searle. 'If I had only come here ten years ago! I should have had more time to enjoy the feast, but I should have had less of an appetite. I needed to get famished for it!'

'Why did you wait for the starving-point?' asked Mr. Searle. 'To think of these ten years that we might have been enjoying you!' And at the thought of these wasted ten years Mr. Searle broke into a violent nervous laugh.

'I always had a notion,—a stupid, vulgar notion, if there ever was one,—that to come abroad properly one ought to have a pot of money. My pot was too nearly empty. At last I came with my empty pot!'

Mr. Searle coughed with an air of hesitation. 'You're a—you're in "limited circumstances"?'

My friend apparently was vastly tickled to have his bleak situation called by so soft a name. 'Limited circumstances!' he cried with a long, light laugh: 'I'm in no circumstances at all!'

'Upon my word!' murmured Mr Searle, with an air of being divided between his sense of the indecency and his sense of the rarity of a gentleman taking just that tone about his affairs. 'Well—well—well!' he added, in a voice which might have meant everything or nothing; and proceeded, with a twinkle in his eye, to finish a glass of wine. His sparkling eye, as he drank, encountered mine over the top of his glass, and, for a moment, we exchanged a long deep glance,— a glance so keen as to leave a slight embarrassment on the face of each. 'And you,' said Mr. Searle, by way of carrying it off, 'how about your circumstances?'

'O, his,' said my friend, 'his are unlimited! He could buy up Lockley Park!' He had drunk, I think, a rather greater number of glasses of port—I admit that the port was infinitely drinkable—than was to have been desired in the interest of perfect self-control. He was rapidly drifting beyond any tacit dissuasion of mine. A certain feverish harshness in his glance and voice warned me that to attempt to direct him would simply irritate him. As we rose from table he caught my troubled look. Passing his arm for a moment into mine, 'This is the great night!' he whispered. 'The night of experience, the night of destiny!'

Mr. Searle had caused the whole lower region of the house to be thrown open and a multitude of lights to be placed in convenient and effective positions. Such a marshalled wealth of ancient candlesticks and flambeaux I had never beheld. Niched against the dark panellings, casting great luminous circles upon the pendent stiffness of sombre tapestries, enhancing and completing with admirable effect the vastness and mystery of the ancient house, they seemed to people the great rooms, as our little group passed slowly from one to another, with a dim, expectant presence. We had a delightful hour of it. Mr. Searle at once assumed the part of *cicerone,* and—I had not hitherto done him justice—Mr. Searle became agreeable. While I lingered behind with Miss Searle, he walked in advance with his kinsman. It was as if he had said, 'Well, if you want the old place, you shall have it, metaphysically, at least!' To speak vulgarly, he rubbed it in. Carrying a great silver candlestick in his left hand, he raised it and lowered it and cast the light hither and thither, upon pictures and hangings and bits of carving and a hundred lurking architectural treasures. Mr. Searle knew his house. He hinted at innumerable traditions and memories, and evoked with a very pretty wit the figures of its earlier occupants. He told a dozen anecdotes with an almost reverential gravity and neatness. His companion attended, with a sort of brooding intelligence. Miss Searle and I, meanwhile, were not wholly silent.

'I suppose that by this time,' I said, 'you and your cousin are almost old friends.'

She trifled a moment with her fan, and then raising her homely candid gaze: 'Old friends, and at the same time strangely new! My cousin—my cousin,'—and her voice lingered on the word,—'it seems so strange to call him my cousin; after thinking these many years that I had no cousin! He's a most singular man.'

'It's not so much he as his circumstanecs that are singular,' I ventured to say.

'I'm so sorry for his circumstances. I wish I could help him in some way. He interests me so much.' And here Miss Searle gave a rich, mellow sigh. 'I wish I had known him a long time ago. He told me that he is but the shadow of what he was.'

I wondered whether Searle had been consciously playing upon the fancy of this gentle creature. If he had, I believed he had gained his point. But in fact, his position had become to my sense so charged with opposing forces, that I hardly ventured wholly to rejoice. 'His better self just now,' I said, 'seems again to be taking shape. It will have been a good deed on your part, Miss Searle, if you help to restore him to soundness and serenity.'

'Ah, what can I do?'

'Be a friend to him. Let him like you, let him love you! You see in him now, doubtless, much to pity and to wonder at. But let him simply enjoy awhile the grateful sense of your nearness and dearness. He will be a better and stronger man for it, and then you can love him, you can respect him without restriction.'

Miss Searle listened with a puzzled tenderness of gaze. 'It's a hard part for poor me to play!'

Her almost infantine gentleness left me no choice but to be absolutely frank. 'Did you ever play any part, at all?' I asked.

Her eyes met mine, wonderingly; she blushed, as with a sudden sense of my meaning. 'Never! I think I have hardly lived.'

'You've begun now, perhaps. You have begun to care for something outside the narrow circle of habit and duty. (Excuse me if I am rather too outspoken: you know I'm a foreigner.) It's a great moment: I wish you joy!'

'I could almost fancy you are laughing at me. I feel more trouble than joy.'

'Why do you feel trouble?'

She paused, with her eyes fixed on our two companions. 'My cousin's arrival,' she said at last, 'is a great disturbance.'

'You mean that you did wrong in recognizing him? In that case, the fault is mine. He had no intention of giving you the opportunity.'

'I did wrong, after a fashion! But I can't find it in my heart to regret it. I never shall regret it! I did what I thought proper. Heaven forgive me!'

'Heaven bless you, Miss Searle! Is any harm to come of it? I did the evil; let me bear the brunt!'

She shook her head gravely. 'You don't know my brother!'

'The sooner I *do* know him, then, the better!' And hereupon I felt a dull irritation which had been gathering force for more than an hour explode into sudden wrath. 'What on earth *is* your brother?' I demanded. She turned away. 'Are you afraid of him?' I asked.

She gave me a tearful sidelong glance. 'He's looking at me!' she murmured.

I looked at him. He was standing with his back to us, holding a large Venetian hand-mirror, framed in *rococo* silver, which he had taken from a shelf of antiquities, in just such a position that he caught the reflection of his sister's person. Shall I confess it? Something in this performance so tickled my sense of the picturesque, that it was with a sort of blunted anger that I muttered, 'The villain!' Yet I felt passion enough to urge me forward. It seemed to me that by implication I, too, was being covertly watched. I should not be watched for nothing! 'Miss Searle,' I said, insisting upon her attention, 'promise me something.'

She turned upon me with a start and the glance of one appealing from some great pain. 'O, don't ask me!' she cried. It was as if she were standing on the verge of some sudden lapse of familiar ground and had been summoned to make a leap. I felt that retreat was impossible, and that it was the greater kindness to beckon her forward.

'Promise me!' I repeated.

Still with her eyes she protested. 'O, dreadful day!' she cried, at last.

'Promise me to let him speak to you, if he should ask you, any wish you may suspect on your brother's part notwithstanding.'

She coloured deeply. 'You mean,' she said,—'you mean that he—has something particular to say.'

'Something most particular!'

'Poor cousin!'

I gave her a deeply questioning look. 'Well, poor cousin! But promise me.'

'I promise,' she said, and moved away across the long room and out of the door.

'You're in time to hear the most delightful story!' said my friend, as I rejoined the two gentlemen. They were standing before an old sombre portrait of a lady in the dress of Queen Anne's time, with her ill-painted flesh tints showing livid in the candlelight against her dark drapery and background. 'This is Mistress Margaret Searle,—a sort of Beatrix Esmond,—who did as she pleased. She married a paltry Frenchman, a penniless fiddler, in the teeth of her whole family. Fair Margaret, I honour you! Upon my soul, she looks like Miss Searle! Pray go on. What came of it all?'

Mr. Searle looked at his kinsman for a moment with an air of distaste for his boisterous homage and of pity for his crude imagination. Then resuming, with a very effective dryness of tone: 'I found a year ago, in a box of very old papers, a letter from Mistress Margaret to Cynthia Searle, her elder sister. It was dated from Paris and dreadfully ill-spelled. It contained a most passionate appeal for—a —for pecuniary assistance. She had just been confined, she was starving and neglected by her husband; she cursed the day she left England. It was a most dismal effusion. I never heard that she found means to return.'

'So much for marrying a Frenchman!' I said, sententiously.

Mr. Searle was silent for some moments. 'This was the first,' he said, finally, 'and the last of the family who has been so d—d un-English!'

'Does Miss Searle know her history?' asked my friend, staring at the rounded whiteness of the lady's heavy cheek.

'Miss Searle knows nothing!' said our host, with zeal.

This utterance seemed to kindle in my friend a generous opposing zeal. 'She shall know at least the tale of Mistress Margaret,' he cried, and walked rapidly away in search of her.

Mr. Searle and I pursued our march through the lighted rooms. 'You've found a cousin,' I said, 'with a vengeance.'

'Ah, a vengeance?' said my host, stiffly.

'I mean that he takes as keen an interest in your annals and possessions as yourself.'

'O, exactly so!' and Mr. Searle burst into resounding laughter.
'He tells me,' he resumed, in a moment, 'that he is an invalid. I
should never have fancied it.'

'Within the past few hours,' I said, 'he's a changed man. Your
place and your kindness have refreshed him immensely.'

Mr. Searle uttered the little shapeless ejaculation with which
many an Englishman is apt to announce the concussion of any
especial courtesy of speech. He bent his eyes on the floor frowningly,
and then, to my surprise, he suddenly stopped and looked at me with
a penetrating eye. 'I'm an honest man!' he said. I was quite prepared
to assent; but he went on, with a sort of fury of frankness, as if it
was the first time in his life he had been prompted to expound himself, as if the process was mightily unpleasant to him and he was
hurrying through it as a task. 'An honest man, mind you! I know
nothing about Mr. Clement Searle! I never expected to see him. He
has been to me a—a——' And here Mr. Searle paused to select a
word which should vividly enough express what, for good or for ill,
his kinsman had been to him. 'He has been to me an *amazement*!
I have no doubt he is a most amiable man! You'll not deny, however, that he's a very odd style of person. I'm sorry he's ill! I'm
sorry he's poor! He's my fiftieth cousin! Well and good! I'm an honest
man. He shall not have it to say that he was not received at my
house.'

'He, too, thank Heaven! is an honest man!' I said, smiling.

'Why the deuce, then,' cried Mr. Searle, turning almost fiercely
upon me, 'has he established this underhand claim to my property?'

This startling utterance flashed backward a gleam of light upon the
demeanour of our host and the suppressed agitation of his sister.
In an instant the jealous soul of the unhappy gentleman revealed
itself. For a moment I was so amazed and scandalized at the directness of his attack that I lacked words to respond. As soon as he had
spoken, Mr. Searle appeared to feel that he had struck too hard a
blow. 'Excuse me, sir,' he hurried on, 'if I speak of this matter with
heat. But I have seldom suffered so grievous a shock as on learning,
as I learned this morning from my solicitor, the monstrous proceedings of Mr. Clement Searle. Great Heaven, sir, for what does the
man take me? He pretends to the Lord-knows-what fantastic passion for my place. Let him respect it then. Let him, with his tawdry
parade of imagination, imagine a tithe of what I feel. I love my estate;
it's my passion, my life, myself! Am I to concede a round fraction
of it to a beggarly foreigner, a man without means, without proof,

a stranger an adventurer, a Bohemian? I thought America boasted that she had land for all men! Upon my soul, sir, I have never been so shocked in my life.'

I paused for some moments before speaking, to allow his passion fully to expend itself and to flicker up again if it chose; for on my own part it seemed well that I should answer him once for all. 'Your really absurd apprehensions, Mr. Searle,' I said, at last,—'your terrors, I may call them,—have fairly overmastered your common sense. You are attacking a man of straw, a creature of base illusion; though I'm sadly afraid you have wounded a man of spirit and of conscience. Either my friend has no valid claim on your estate, in which case your agitation is superfluous; or he has a valid claim——'

Mr. Searle seized my arm and glared at me, as I may say; his pale face paler still with the horror of my suggestion, his great keen eyes flashing, and his radiant hair erect and quivering with the force of sensation.

'A valid claim!' he whispered. 'Let him try it!'

We had emerged into the great hall of the mansion and stood facing the main doorway. The door stood open into the noble porch, through whose stone archway I saw the garden glittering in the blue light of a full moon. As Mr. Searle uttered the words I have just repeated, I beheld my companion come slowly up into the porch from without, bareheaded, bright in the outer moonlight, dark then in the shadow of the archway, and bright again in the lamplight on the threshold of the hall. As he crossed the threshold the butler made his appearance at the head of the staircase on our left, faltered visibly a moment on seeing Mr. Searle; but then, perceiving my friend, he gravely descended. He bore in his hand a small plated salver. On the salver, gleaming in the light of the suspended lamp, lay a folded note. Clement Searle came forward, staring a little and startled, I think, by some fine sense of a near explosion. The butler applied the match. He advanced towards my friend, extending salver and note. Mr. Searle made a movement as if to spring forward, but controlled himself. 'Tottenham!' he shouted in a strident voice.

'Yes, sir!' said Tottenham, halting.

'Stand where you are. For whom is that note?'

'For Mr. Clement Searle,' said the butler, staring straight before him as if to discredit a suspicion of his having read the direction.

'Who gave it to you?'

'Mrs. Horridge, sir.' (The housekeeper.)

'Who gave it Mrs. Horridge?'

There was on Tottenham's part just an infinitesimal pause before replying.

'My dear sir,' broke in Searle, completely sobered by a scene of violated courtesy, 'isn't that rather my business?'

'What happens in my house is my business; and mighty strange things seem to be happening.' Mr. Searle had become exasperated to that point that, a rare thing for an Englishman, he compromised himself before a servant.

'Bring me that note!' he cried. The butler obeyed.

'Really, this is too much!' cried my companion, affronted and helpless.

I was disgusted. Before Mr. Searle had time to take the note, I possessed myself of it. 'If you have no regard for your sister,' I said, 'let a stranger, at least, act for her.' And I tore the disputed thing into a dozen pieces.

'In Heaven's name,' cried Searle, 'what does this horrid business mean?'

Mr. Searle was about to break out upon him; but at this moment his sister appeared on the staircase, summoned evidently by our high-pitched and angry voices. She had exchanged her dinner-dress for a dark dressing-gown, removed her ornaments, and begun to disarrange her hair, a heavy tress of which escaped from the comb. She hurried downward, with a pale, questioning face. Feeling distinctly that, for ourselves, immediate departure was in the air, and divining Mr. Tottenham to be a butler of infinite intuitions and extreme celerity, I seized the opportunity to request him, *sotto voce*, to send a carriage to the door without delay. 'And put up our things,' I added.

Our host rushed at his sister and seized the white wrist which escaped from the loose sleeve of her dress. 'What was in that note?' he demanded.

Miss Searle looked first at its scattered fragments and then at her cousin. 'Did you read it?' she asked.

'No, but I thank you for it!' said Searle.

Her eyes for an instant communed brightly with his own; then she transferred them to her brother's face, where the light went out of them and left a dull, sad patience. An inexorable patience he seemed to find it: he flushed crimson with rage and the sense of his unhandsomeness, and flung her away. 'You're a child!' he cried. 'Go to bed.'

In poor Searle's face as well the gathered serenity was twisted into a sickened frown and the reflected brightness of his happy day turned to blank confusion. 'Have I been dealing these three hours with a madman?' he asked, plaintively.

'A madman, yes, if you will! A man mad with the love of his home and the sense of its rounded integrity! I have held my tongue till now, but you have been too much for me. Who are you, what are you? From what paradise of fools do you come, that you fancy I shall cut off a piece of my land, my home, my heart, to toss to you? Forsooth, I shall break my diamond! Prove your infernal claim! There isn't *that* in it!' And he kicked one of the bits of paper on the floor.

Searle received this broadside gaping. Then turning away, he went and seated himself on a bench against the wall and rubbed his forehead amazedly. I looked at my watch, and listened for the wheels of our carriage.

Mr. Searle went on. 'Wasn't it enough that you should have practised against my property? Need you have come into my very house to practise against my sister?'

Searle put his two hands to his face. 'Oh, oh, oh!' he softly roared. Miss Searle crossed rapidly and dropped on her knees at his side.

'Go to bed, you fool!' shrieked her brother.

'Dear cousin,' said Miss Searle, 'it's cruel that you are to have thus to think of us!'

'O, I shall think of you!' he said. And he laid a hand on her head.

'I believe you have done nothing wrong!' she murmured.

'I've done what I could,' her brother pursued. 'But it's arrant folly to pretend to friendship when this abomination lies between us. You were welcome to my meat and my wine, but I wonder you could swallow them. The sight spoiled my appetite!' cried the furious little man, with a laugh. 'Proceed with your case! My people in London are instructed and prepared.'

'I have a fancy,' I said to Searle, 'that your case has vastly improved since you gave it up.'

'Oho! you don't feign ignorance then!' and he shook his flaming *chevelure* at me. 'It is very kind of you to give it up!' And he laughed resoundingly. 'Perhaps you will also give up my sister!'

Searle sat in his chair in a species of collapse, staring at his adversary. 'O miserable man!' he moaned at last. 'I fancied we had become such friends!'

'Boh! you imbecile!' cried our host.

Searle seemed not to hear him. 'Am I seriously expected,' he pursued, slowly and painfully,—'am I seriously expected—to—to sit here and defend myself—to prove I have done nothing wrong? Think what you please.' And he rose, with an effort, to his feet. 'I know what *you* think!' he added, to Miss Searle.

The carriage wheels resounded on the gravel, and at the same moment the footman descended with our two portmanteaus. Mr.

Tottenham followed him with our hats and coats.

'Good God!' cried Mr. Searle; 'you are not going away!' This ejaculation, under the circumstances, had a grand comicality which prompted me to violent laughter. 'Bless my soul!' he added; 'of course, you're going.'

'It's perhaps well,' said Miss Searle, with a great effort, inexpressibly touching in one for whom great efforts were visibly new and strange, 'that I should tell you what my poor little note contained.'

'That matter of your note, madam,' said her brother, 'you and I will settle together!'

'Let me imagine its contents,' said Searle.

'Ah! they have been too much imagined!' she answered simply. 'It was a word of warning. I knew something painful was coming.'

Searle took his hat. 'The pains and the pleasures of this day,' he said to his kinsman, 'I shall equally never forget. Knowing you,' and he offered his hand to Miss Searle, 'has been the pleasure of pleasures. I hoped something more was to come of it.'

'A deal too much has come of it!' said our host, irrepressibly.

Searle looked at him mildly, almost benignantly, from head to foot; and then closing his eyes with an air of sudden physical distress : 'I'm afraid so! I can't stand more of this.' I gave him my arm and crossed the threshold. As we passed out I heard Miss Searle burst into a torrent of sobs.

'We shall hear from each other yet, I take it!' cried our host, harassing our retreat.

Searle stopped and turned round on him sharply, almost fiercely. 'O foolish man!' he cried.

'Do you mean to say you shall not prosecute?' screamed the other. 'I shall force you to prosecute! I shall drag you into court, and you shall be beaten—beaten—beaten!' And this gentle verb continued to ring in our ears as we drove away.

We drove, of course, to the little wayside inn whence we had departed in the morning so free, in all broad England, of either enemies or friends. My companion, as the carriage rolled along, seemed utterly overwhelmed and exhausted. 'What a dream!' he murmured stupidly. 'What an awakening! What a long, long day! What a hideous scene! Poor me! Poor woman!' When we had resumed possession of our two little neighbouring rooms, I asked him if Miss Searle's note had been the result of anything that had passed between them on his going to rejoin her. 'I found her on the terrace,' he said, 'walking a restless walk in the moonlight. I was greatly excited; I hardly know what I said. I asked her, I think, if she knew the story of Margaret Searle. She seemed frightened and troubled, and she used just the words her brother had used, "I know nothing." For the moment, somehow, I felt as a man drunk. I stood before her and told her, with great emphasis, how sweet Margaret Searle had married a beggarly foreigner, in obedience to her heart and in defiance of her family. As I talked the sheeted moonlight seemed to close about us, and we stood in a dream, in a solitude, in a romance. She grew younger, fairer, more gracious. I trembled with a divine loquacity. Before I knew it I had gone far. I was taking her hand and calling her "Margaret!" She had said that it was impossible; that she could do nothing; that she was a fool, a child, a slave. Then, with a sudden huge conviction, I spoke of my claim against the estate. "It exists, then?" she said. "It exists," I answered, "but I have forgone it. Be generous! Pay it from your heart!" For an instant her face was radiant. "If I marry you," she cried, "it will solve the trouble." "In our marriage," I affirmed, "the trouble will melt away like a raindrop in the ocean." "Our marriage!" she repeated, wonderingly; and the deep, deep ring of her voice seemed to shatter the crystal walls of our illusion. "I must think, I must think!" she said; and she hurried away with her face in her hands. I walked up and down the terrace for some moments, and then came in and met you. This is the only witchcraft I have used!'

The poor fellow was at once so excited and so exhausted by the day's events, that I fancied he would get little sleep. Conscious, on my own part, of a stubborn wakefulness, I but partly undressed, set my fire a-blazing, and sat down to do some writing. I heard the great clock in the little parlour below strike twelve, one, half past one. Just as the vibration of this last stroke was dying on the air the door of communication into Searle's room was flung open, and my companion stood on the threshold, pale as a corpse, in his nightshirt, standing like a phantom against the darkness behind him. 'Look at me!' he said, in a low voice, 'touch me, embrace me, revere me! You see a man who has seen a ghost!'

'Great Heaven, what do you mean?'

'Write it down!' he went on. 'There, take your pen. Put it into dreadful words. Make it of all ghost-stories the ghostliest, the truest! How do I look? Am I human? Am I pale? Am I red? Am I speaking English? A woman! A ghost! What was I born for? What have I lived for? To see a ghost!'

I confess there came upon me, by contact, a great supernatural shock. I shall always feel that I, too, have seen a ghost. My first movement—I can't smile at it even now—was to spring to the door, close it with a great blow, and then turn the key upon the gaping blackness from which Searle had emerged. I seized his two hands; they were

wet with perspiration. I pushed my chair to the fire and forced him to
sit down in it. I kneeled down before him and held his hands as firmly
as possible. They trembled and quivered; his eyes were fixed, save
that the pupil dilated and contracted with extraordinary force. I
asked no questions, but waited with my heart in my throat. At last
he spoke. 'I'm not frightened, but I'm—O, EXCITED! This is life! This
is living! My nerves—my heart—my brain! They are throbbing with
the wildness of a myriad lives! Do you feel it? Do you tingle? Are
you hot? Are you cold? Hold me tight—tight—tight! I shall tremble
away into waves—waves—waves, and know the universe and approach my Maker!' He paused a moment and then went on: 'A
woman—as clear as that candle—far clearer! In a blue dress, with a
black mantle on her head, and a little black muff. Young, dreadfully
pretty, pale and ill, with the sadness of all the women who ever loved
and suffered, pleading and accusing in her dead dark eyes. God
knows, I never did any such thing! But she took me for my elder,
for the other Clement. She came to me here as she would have come
to me there. She wrung her hands and spoke to me. "Marry me!" she
moaned; "marry me and right me!" I sat up in bed just as I sit here,
looked at her, heard her,—heard her voice melt away, watched her
figure fade away. Heaven and earth! Here I am!'
  I make no attempt either to explain my friend's vision or to discredit it. It is enough that I felt for the hour the irresistible contagion of his immense sensation. On the whole, I think my own
vision was the more interesting of the two. He beheld but the transient, irresponsible spectre; I beheld the human subject, hot from the
spectral presence. Nevertheless, I soon recovered my wits sufficiently
to feel the necessity of guarding my friend's health against the bad
results of excitement and exposure. It was tacitly established that,
for the night, he was not to return to his room; and I soon made him
fairly comfortable in his place by the fire. Wishing especially to
obviate a chill, I removed my bedding and wrapped him hugely about
with multitudinous blankets and counterpanes. I had no nerves left
either for writing or sleep; so I put out my lights, renewed the fire
and sat down on the opposite side of the hearth. I found a kind of
solemn entertainment in watching my friend. Silent, swathed and
muffled to his chin, he sat rigid and erect with the dignity of his
great adventure. For the most part his eyes were closed; though
from time to time he would open them with a vast steady expansion and gaze unblinking into the firelight, as if he again beheld,
without terror, the image of that blighted maid. With his cadaverous,
emaciated face, his tragic wrinkles, intensified by the upward glow
from the hearth, his drooping black moustache, his transcendent

gravity, and a certain high fantastical air in the flickering alternations of his brow, he looked like the vision-haunted knight of La Mancha, nursed by the Duke and Duchess. The night passed wholly without speech. Towards its close I slept for half an hour. When I awoke the birds had begun to twitter of another day. Searle sat unperturbed, staring at me. We exchanged a long look; I felt with a pang that his glittering eyes had tasted their last of natural sleep. 'How is it? are you comfortable?' I asked.

He gazed for some time without replying. Then he spoke with a strange, innocent grandiloquence and with pauses between his words, as if an inner voice were slowly prompting him. 'You asked me, when you first knew me, what I was. "Nothing," I said, —"nothing". Nothing I have always deemed myself. But I have wronged myself. I'm a personage! I'm rare among men! I'm a haunted man!'

Sleep had passed out of his eyes: I felt with a deeper pang that perfect sanity had passed out of his voice. From this moment I prepared myself for the worst. There was in my friend, however, such an essential gentleness and conservative patience that to persons surrounding him the worst was likely to come without hurry or violence. He had so confirmed a habit of good manners that, at the core of reason, the process of disorder might have been long at work, without finding a faithless servant to transmit its messages or subverting these serried and investing sentinels. As morning began fully to dawn upon us, I brought our grotesque vigil to an end. Searle appeared so weak that I gave him my hands to help him to rise from his chair; he retained them for some moments after rising to his feet, from an apparent inability to keep his balance. 'Well,' he said, 'I've seen one ghost, but I doubt of my living to see another. I shall soon be myself as brave a ghost as the best of them. I shall haunt Mr. Searle! It can only mean one thing,—my near, dear death.'

On my proposing breakfast, 'This shall be my breakfast!' he said; and he drew from his travelling-sack a phial of some habitual narcotic. He took a strong dose and went to bed. At noon I found him on foot again, dressed, shaved, and apparently refreshed. 'Poor fellow!' he said, 'you have got more than you bargained for,—a ghost-encumbered comrade. But it won't be for long.' It immediately became a question, of course, whither we should now direct our steps. 'As I have so little time,' said Searle, 'I should like to see the best, the best alone.' I answered that, either for time or eternity, I had imagined Oxford to be the best thing in England; and for Oxford in the course of an hour we accordingly departed.

Of Oxford I feel small vocation to speak in detail. It must long remain for an American one of the supreme gratifications of travel.

The impression it produces, the thoughts it generates, in an American mind, are too large and various to be compassed by words. It seems to embody with an undreamed completeness and overwhelming massiveness a dim and sacred ideal of the Western intellect,— a scholastic city, an appointed home of contemplation. Truly, no other spot in Europe, I imagine, extorts from our barbarous hearts so passionate an admiration. A braver pen than mine must enumerate the splendid devices by which it performs this great office. I can bear testimony only to the dominant tone of its effect. Passing through the streets innumerable in which the obverse longitude of the hoary college walls seems to maintain an antique stillness, a mediaeval vacancy, you feel this to be the most dignified of towns. Over all, through all, the great corporate fact of the University prevails and penetrates, like some steady bass in a symphony of lighter chords, like the mediaeval and mystical presence of the Empire in the linked dispersion of lesser states. The plain Gothic of the long street-fronts of the colleges—blessed seraglios of culture and leisure —irritate the fancy like the blank harem-walls of Eastern towns. Within their arching portals, however, you perceive more sacred and sunless courts and the dark verdure grateful and restful to bookish eyes. The grey-green quadrangles stand for ever open with a noble and trustful hospitality. The seat of the humanities is stronger in the admonitory shadow of her great name than in a marshalled host of wardens and beadles. Directly after our arrival my friend and I strolled vaguely forth in the luminous early dusk. We reached the bridge which passes beneath the walls of Magdalen and saw the eight-spired tower, embossed with its slender shaftings, rise in temperate beauty—the perfect prose of Gothic—wooing the eyes to the sky, as it was slowly drained of day. We entered the little monkish doorway and stood in that dim, fantastic outer court, made narrow by the dominant presence of the great tower, in which the heart beats faster and the swallows niche more lovingly in the tangled ivy, I fancied, than elsewhere in Oxford. We passed thence into the great cloister, and studied the gaunt stone images along the entablature of the arcade, which transmit to the smiling present the grim conceits of the founders. I was pleased to see that Searle became extremely interested; but I very soon began to fear that the influence of the place would prove too potent for his unbalanced imagination. I may say that from this time forward, with my unhappy friend, I found it hard to distinguish between the play of fancy and the labour of thought, and to fix the balance between perception and illusion. He had already taken a fancy to confound his identity with that of the earlier Clement Searle; he now began to speak almost wholly as from the imagined consciousness of his Old-World kinsman.

'This was my college, you know,' he said; 'the noblest in all Oxford. How often I have paced this gentle cloister, side by side with a friend of the hour! My friends are all dead, but many a young fellow as we meet him, dark or fair, tall or short, reminds me of them. Even Oxford, they say, feels about its massive base the murmurs of the tide of time; there are things eliminated, things insinuated! Mine was ancient Oxford,—the fine old haunt of rank abuses, of precedent and privilege. What cared I, who was a perfect gentleman, with my pockets full of money? I had an allowance of two thousand a year.'

It became evident to me, on the following day, that his strength had begun to ebb, and that he was unequal to the labour of any large exploration. He read my apprehension in my eyes, and took pains to assure me that I was right. 'I am going down hill. Thank Heaven it's an easy slope, coated with English turf and with an English churchyard at the foot.' The almost hysterical emotion produced by our adventure at Lockley Park had given place to a broad, calm satisfaction, in which the scene around us was reflected as in the depths of a lucid lake. We took an afternoon walk through Christ-Church Meadow,—worthy of its sounding name!—and at the river-bank procured a boat, which I pulled up the stream to Iffley, to 'Iffley church, the church that crowns the hill', and to the slanting woods of Nuneham,—the sweetest, flattest, reediest stream-side landscape that the heart need demand. Here, of course, we encountered in hundreds the mighty lads of England, clad in white flannel and blue, immense, fair-haired, magnificent in their youth, lounging down the current in their idle punts, in friendly couples, or in solitude possibly pregnant of scholastic honours; or pulling in straining crews and hoarsely exhorted from the near bank. When with this freighted channel of masculine motion, you think of the verdant quietude and the blooming sanctities of the college gardens, you can't but esteem that the youth of England have their porridge well salted. As my companion found himself less and less able to walk, we repaired on three successive days to these various gardens and spent long hours sitting in their greenest places. The perfect weather continued, securely transmitted from hour to hour, hushing them each into a golden silence of gratitude, fitfully broken by a breezy murmur of disbelief. These scholastic domains seemed to us the fairest possible things in England and the ripest and sweetest fruits of the English system. Locked in their antique verdure, guarded (as in the case of New College) by gentle battlements of silver grey, outshouldering the matted leafage of centenary vines, filled with perfumes and pri-

vacy and memories, with students lounging bookishly on the turf (as
if tenderly to spare it the pressure of their bootheels), and with the
great conservative presence of the college front appealing gravely
from the restless outer world, they seem places to lie down on the
grass in for ever, in the happy faith that life is all a vast old English
garden and time an endless English afternoon. This charmed seclusion was especially grateful to my friend, and his sense of it reached
its climax, I remember, on the last afternoon of our three, as we sat
worshipping in the spacious garden of St. John's. The long college
façade here broods over the lawn with a more effective air of property
than elsewhere. Searle fell into unceasing talk and exhaled his
swarming impressions with a tender felicity and an odd union of
wisdom and folly which I can but partly reproduce. Every student
who passed us was the subject of an extemporized romance, and
every feature of the place the theme of a lyric rhapsody. My friend's
whole being, indeed, seemed now more and more to tremble with
the racking act of vision; and if I had been asked on what sole condition his life might be prolonged, I would have said on that of
sudden blindness.

'Isn't it all,' he demanded, 'a delightful lie? Mightn't one fancy this
the very central point of the world's heart, where all the echoes of
the world's life arrive only to falter and die? Listen! The air is thick
with arrested voices. It is well there should be such places, shaped in
the interest of factitious needs; framed to minister to the book-begotten longing for a medium in which one may dream unwaked, and
believe unconfuted; to foster the sweet illusion that all is well in this
weary world, all perfect and rounded, mellow and complete in this
sphere of the pitiful unachieved and the dreadful uncommenced.
The world's made! work's over! Now for leisure! England's safe!
Now for Theocritus and Horace, for lawn and sky! What a sense it
all gives one of the composite life of England, and how essential a
factor of the educated British consciousness one omits in not thinking of Oxford! Thank Heaven they had the wit to send me here in
the other time. I'm not much with it, perhaps; but what should I
have been without it? The misty spires and towers of Oxford, seen
far off on the level, have been all these years one of the constant
things of memory. Seriously, what does Oxford do for these people?
Are they wiser, gentler, richer, deeper? At moments, when its massive influence surges into my mind like a tidal wave, I feel a certain
injury in the shock; I beseech the waters with a passionate voice. My
soul reverts to the naked background of our own education, the
dead white wall before which we played our parts. I assent to it all
with a sort of desperate calmness; I bow to it with a dogged pride.

We are nursed at the opposite pole. Naked come we into a naked world. There is a certain grandeur in the absence of a *mise en scène*, a certain heroic strain in those young imaginations of the West, which find nothing made to their hands, which have to concoct their own mysteries and raise high into our morning air, with a ringing hammer and nails, the castles in which they dwell. *Noblesse oblige:* Oxford obliges. What a horrible thing not to respond to the obligations here contracted! If you pay the pious debt to the last farthing of interest, you bear upon your forehead her great benediction; but if you let it stand unhonoured, you are far more blankly unaccredited, I deem, than the most unschooled and unstamped of Americans. But for better or worse, in a myriad private hearts, think how she must be loved! How the youthful sentiment of mankind seems visibly to brood upon her! Think of the young lives now taking colour in her corridors and cloisters. Think of the centuries' tale of dead lads,—dead alike with the close of the young days to which these haunts were a present world and the ending of the larger lives which a sterner mother-scene has gathered into her massive history. What are those two young fellows kicking their heels over on the grass, there? One of them has the Saturday Review; the other—upon my soul, the other has Artemus Ward! Where do they live, how do they live, to what end do they live? Miserable boys! How can they read Artemus Ward under those windows of Elizabeth? What do you think loveliest in all Oxford? The poetry of certain windows. Do you see that one yonder, the second of those lesser bays, with the broken mullion and open casement? That used to be the window of a Pylades of mine, a hundred years ago. Remind me to tell you the story of that broken mullion. Don't tell me it's not a common thing to have one's Pylades at another college. Pray, was I pledged to common things? He was a charming fellow. By the way, he was a good deal like you. Of course his cocked hat, his long hair in a black ribbon, his cinnamon velvet suit, and his flowered waistcoat, made a difference! We gentlemen used to wear swords.'

There was something surprising and impressive in my friend's gushing magniloquence. The poor disheartened *flâneur* had turned rhapsodist and seer. I was particularly struck with his having laid aside the diffidence and shy self-consciousness, which had marked him during the first days of our acquaintance. He was becoming more and more a disembodied observer and critic; the shell of sense, growing daily more transparent and tenuous, transmitted unallayed the tremor of his quickened spirit. He revealed an unexpected faculty for becoming acquainted with the lounging gownsmen whom we met in our vague peregrinations. If I left him for ten minutes, I was sure to find him, on my return, in earnest conversation with some affable wandering scholar. Several young men with whom he had thus established relations invited him to their rooms and entertained him, as I gathered, with boisterous hospitality. For myself, I chose not to be present on these occasions; I shrunk partly from being held in any degree responsible for his vagaries, and partly from witnessing that painful aggravation of them which I feared might be induced by champagne and youthful society. He reported these adventures with less elequence than I had fancied he might use; but, on the whole, I suspect that a certain method in his madness, a certain firmness in his most melting *bonhomie*, had ensured him perfect respect. Two things, however, became evident,—that he drank more champagne than was good for him, and that the boyish grossness of his entertainers tended rather, on reflection, to disturb in his mind the pure image of Oxford. At the same time it completed his knowledge of the place. He dined in Hall in half a dozen colleges, and alluded afterwards to these banquets with a sort of religious brevity and relish. One evening, at the close of one of these entertainments, he came back to the hotel in a cab, accompanied by a friendly student and a physician, and looking deadly pale and exhausted. He had swooned away on leaving table, and had remained so stubbornly unconscious as to excite great alarm among his companions. The following twenty-four hours, of course, he spent in bed; but on the third day he declared himself strong enough to go out. On reaching the street his strength again forsook him, and I insisted upon his returning to his room. He besought me with tears in his eyes not to shut him up. 'It's my last chance,' he said. 'I want to go back for an hour to that garden of St. John's. Let me look and feel; tomorrow I die.' It seemed to me possible that with a Bath-chair the expedition might be accomplished. The hotel, it appeared, possessed such an article: it was immediately produced. It became necessary hereupon that we should have a person to propel the chair. As there was no one available on the spot, I prepared to perform the office; but just as Searle had got seated and wrapped (he had come to suffer acutely from cold), an elderly man emerged from a lurking-place near the door, and, with a formal salute, offered to wait upon the gentleman. We assented, and he proceeded solemnly to trundle the chair before him. I recognized him as an individual whom I had seen lounging shyly about the hotel doors, at intervals during our stay, with a depressed air of wanting employment and a hopeless doubt of finding any. He had once, indeed, in a half-hearted way, proposed himself as an amateur *cicerone* for a tour through the colleges; and I now, as I looked at him, remembered with a pang that I had declined his services with untender curtness. Since then, his shyness, apparently, had grown less or his misery greater; for it was with a strange, grim avidity that he now attached himself to our service. He was a pitiful image of shabby gentility and the dinginess of 'reduced circumstances'. He imparted an original force to the term 'seedy'. He was, I suppose, some fifty years of age; but his pale, haggard, unwholesome visage, his plaintive, drooping carriage, and the irremediable decay of his apparel, seemed to add to the burden of his days and experience. His eyes were bloodshot and weak-looking, his handsome nose had turned to purple, and his sandy beard, largely streaked with grey, bristled with a month's desperate indifference to the razor. In all this rusty forlornness there lurked a visible assurance of our friend's having known better days. Obviously, he was the victim of some fatal depreciation in the market value of pure gentility. There had been something terribly pathetic in the way he fiercely merged the attempt to touch the greasy rim of his antiquated hat into a rounded and sweeping bow, as from jaunty equal to equal. Exchanging a few words with him as we went along, I was struck with the perfect refinement of his tone and manner of speech.

'Take me by some long roundabout way,' said Searle; 'so that I may see as many college walls as possible.'

'You can wander without losing your way?' I said to our attendant.

'I ought to be able to, sir,' he said, after a moment, with pregnant gravity. And as we were passing Wadham College, 'that's my college, sir,' he added.

At these words Searle commanded him to stop and come and stand in front of him. 'You say that is *your* college?' he demanded.

'Wadham might deny me, sir; but Heaven forbid I should deny Wadham. If you'll allow me to take you into the quad, I'll show you my windows, thirty years ago!'

Searle sat staring, with his huge, pale eyes, which now had come to usurp the greatest place in his wasted visage, filled with wonder and pity. 'If you'll be so kind,' he said, with immense politeness. But just as this degenerate son of Wadham was about to propel him across the threshold of the court, he turned about, disengaged his hands, with his own hand, from the back of the chair, drew him alongside of him and turned to me. 'While we are here, my dear fellow,' he said, 'be so good as to perform this service. You understand?' I smiled sufferance at our companion, and we resumed our way. The latter showed us his window of thirty years ago, where now a rosy youth in a scarlet smoking-fez was puffing a cigarette in the open lattice. Thence we proceeded into the little garden, the smallest, I believe, and certainly the sweetest of all the bosky resorts in Oxford. I pushed the chair along to a bench on the lawn, wheeled it about towards the façade of the college, and sat down on the grass. Our attendant shifted himself mournfully from one foot to the other. Searle eyed him open-mouthed. At length he broke out: 'God bless my soul, sir, you don't suppose that I expect you to stand! There's an empty bench.'

'Thank you,' said our friend, bending his joints to sit.

'You English,' said Searle, 'are—*impayables*! I don't know whether I most admire you or protest against you! Now tell me: who are you? what are you? what brought you to this?'

The poor fellow blushed up to his eyes, took off his hat and wiped his forehead with a ragged handkerchief. 'My name is Rawson, sir. Beyond that, it's a long story.'

'I ask out of sympathy,' said Searle. 'I have a fellow-feeling! You're a poor devil; I'm a poor devil, too.'

'I'm the poorer devil of the two,' said the stranger, with a little emphatic nod of the head.

'Possibly. I suppose an English poor devil is the poorest of all poor devils. And then you have fallen from a height. From Wadham College as a gentleman commoner (is that what they called you?) to Wadham College as a Bath-chair man! Good heavens, man, the fall's enough to kill you!'

'I didn't take it all at once, sir. I dropped a bit one time and a bit another.'

'That's me, that's me!' cried Searle, clapping his hands.

'And now,' said our friend. 'I believe I can't drop further.'

'My dear fellow,' and Searle clasped his hand and shook it, 'there's a perfect similarity in our lot.'

Mr. Rawson lifted his eyebrows. 'Save for the difference of sitting in a Bath-chair and walking behind it!'

'O, I'm at my last gasp, Mr. Rawson.'

'I'm at my last penny, sir.'

'Literally, Mr. Rawson?'

Mr. Rawson shook his head, with a world of vague bitterness. 'I have almost come to the point,' he said, 'of drinking my beer, and buttoning my coat figuratively; but I don't talk in figures.'

Fearing that the conversation had taken a turn which might seem to cast a rather fantastic light upon Mr. Rawson's troubles, I took the liberty of asking him with great gravity how he made a living.

'I don't make a living,' he answered, with tearful eyes, 'I can't make a living. I have a wife and three children, starving, sir. You wouldn't believe what I have come to. I sent my wife to her mother's, who can ill-afford to keep her, and came to Oxford a week ago, thinking I might pick up a few half-crowns by showing people about the colleges. But it's no use. I haven't the assurance. I don't look decent. They want a nice little old man with black gloves, and a clean shirt, and a silver-headed stick. What do I look as if I knew about Oxford, sir?'

'Dear me,' cried Searle, 'why didn't you speak to us before?'

'I wanted to; half a dozen times I have been on the point of it. I knew you were Americans.'

'And Americans are rich!' cried Searle, laughing. 'My dear Mr. Rawson, American as I am, I'm living on charity.'

'And I'm not, sir! There it is. I'm dying for the want of charity. You say you're a pauper; it takes an American pauper to go bowling about in a Bath-chair. America's an easy country.'

'Ah me!' groaned Searle. 'Have I come to Wadham gardens to hear the praise of America?'

'Wadham gardens are very well!' said Mr. Rawson; 'but one may sit here hungry and shabby, so long as one isn't too shabby, as well as elsewhere. You'll not persuade me that it's not an easier thing to keep afloat yonder than here. I wish I were there, that's all!' added Mr. Rawson, with a sort of feeble-minded energy. Then brooding for a moment on his wrongs: 'Have you a brother? or you, sir? It matters little to you. But it has mattered to me with a vengeance! Shabby as I sit here, I have a brother with his five thousand a year. Being a couple of years my senior, he gorges while I starve. There's England for you! A very pretty place for *him*!'

'Poor England!' said Searle, softly.

'Has your brother never helped you?' I asked.

'A twenty-pound note now and then! I don't say that there have not been times when I have sorely tried his generosity. I have not been what I should. I married dreadfully amiss. But the devil of it is that he started fair and I started foul; with the tastes, the desires, the needs, the sensibilities of a gentleman,—and nothing else! I can't afford to live in England.'

'This poor gentleman,' said I, 'fancied a couple of months ago that he couldn't afford to live in America.'

'I'd change chances with him!' And Mr. Rawson gave a passionate slap to his knee.

Searle reclined in his chair with his eyes closed and his face twitching with violent emotion. Suddenly he opened his eyes with a look of awful gravity. 'My friend,' he said, 'you're a failure! Be judged! Don't talk about chances. Don't talk about fair starts and foul starts. I'm at that point myself that I have a right to speak. It lies neither in one's chance nor one's start to make one a success; nor in anything one's brother can do or can undo. It lies in one's will! You and I, sir, have had none; that's very plain! We have been weak, sir; as weak as water. Here we are, sitting staring in each other's faces and reading our weakness in each other's eyes. We are of no account!'

Mr. Rawson received this address with a countenance in which heartfelt conviction was oddly mingled with a vague suspicion that a proper self-respect required him to resent its unflattering candour. In the course of a minute a proper self-respect yielded to the warm, comfortable sense of his being understood, even to his light dishonour. 'Go on, sir, go on,' he said. 'It's wholesome truth.' And he wiped his eyes with his dingy handkerchief.

'Dear me!' cried Searle. 'I've made you cry. Well! we speak as from man to man. I should be glad to think that you had felt for a moment the side-light of that great undarkening of the spirit which precedes—which precedes the grand illumination of death.'

Mr. Rawson sat silent for a moment, with his eyes fixed on the ground and his well-cut nose more deeply tinged by the force of emotion. Then at last, looking up: 'You're a very good-natured man, sir; and you'll not persuade me that you don't come of a good-natured race. Say what you please about a chance, when a man's fifty—degraded, penniless, a husband and father—a chance to get on his legs again is not to be despised. Something tells me that my chance is in your country,—that great home of chances. I can starve here, of course; but I don't want to starve. Hang it, sir, I want to live. I see thirty years of life before me yet. If only, by God's help, I could spend them there! It's a fixed idea of mine. I've had it for the last ten years. It's not that I'm a radical. I've no ideas! Old England's good enough for me, but I'm not good enough for England. I'm a shabby man that wants to get out of a room full of staring gentle-folks. I'm for ever put to the blush. It's a perfect agony of spirit. Everything reminds me of my younger and better self. O, for a cooling, cleansing plunge into the unknowing and the unknown! I lie awake thinking of it.'

Searle closed his eyes and shivered with a long-drawn tremor which I hardly knew whether to take for an expression of physical or of mental pain. In a moment I perceived it was neither. 'O my country, my country, my country,' he murmured in a broken voice; and then sat for some time abstracted and depressed. I intimated to our companion that it was time we should bring our *séance* to a close, and he, without hesitating, possessed himself of the little hand-rail of the Bath-chair and pushed it before him. We had got half-way home before Searle spoke or moved. Suddenly in the High Street, as we were passing in front of a chophouse, from whose open doors there proceeded a potent suggestion of juicy joints and suet puddings, he motioned us to halt. 'This is my last five pounds,' he said, drawing a note from his pocket-book. 'Do me the favour, Mr. Rawson, to accept it. Go in there and order a colossal dinner. Order a bottle of Burgundy and drink it to my immortal health!' Mr. Rawson stiffened himself up and received the gift with momentarily irresponsive fingers. But Mr. Rawson had the nerves of a gentleman. I saw the titillation of his pointed finger-tips as they closed upon the crisp paper; I noted the fine tremor in his empurpled nostril as it became more deeply conscious of the succulent flavour of the spot. He crushed the crackling note in his palm with a convulsive pressure.

'It shall be Chambertin!' he said, jerking a spasmodic bow. The next moment the door swung behind him.

Searle relapsed into his feeble stupor, and on reaching the hotel I helped him to get to bed. For the rest of the day he lay in a half-somnolent state, without motion or speech. The doctor, whom I had constantly in attendance, declared that his end was near. He expressed great surprise that he should have lasted so long: he must have been living for a month on a cruelly extorted strength. Towards evening, as I sat by his bedside in the deepening dusk, he aroused himself with a purpose which I had vaguely felt gathering beneath his quietude. 'My cousin, my cousin,' he said, confusedly. 'Is she here?' It was the first time he had spoken of Miss Searle since our exit from her brother's house. 'I was to have married her,' he went on. 'What a dream! That day was like a string of verses, rhymed hours. But the last verse is bad measure. What's the rhyme to "love"? *Above*. Was she a simple person, a sweet person? Or have I dreamed it? She had the healing gift; her touch would have cured my madness. I want you to do something. Write three lines, three words: "Good bye; remember me; be happy."' And then after a long pause: 'It's strange a man in my condition should have a wish. Need a man eat his breakfast before his hanging? What a creature is man! what a farce is life! Here I lie, worn down to a mere throbbing fever-point; I breathe and nothing more, and yet I *desire*! My desire lives. If I could see her! Release it and let me die.'

Half an hour later, at a venture, I despatched a note to Miss Searle: '*Your cousin is rapidly dying. He asks to see you.*' I was conscious of a certain unkindness in doing so. It would bring a great trouble, and no power to face the trouble. But out of her distress, I fondly hoped a sufficient energy might be born. On the following day my friend's weakness became so complete that I began to fear that his intelligence was altogether gone. But towards evening he rallied awhile, and talked in a maundering way about many things, confounding the memories of the past weeks and those of bygone years in a ghastly monotonous jumble. 'By the way,' he said suddenly, 'I have made no will. I haven't much to bequeath. Yet I've something.' He had been playing listlessly with a large signet ring on his left hand, which he now tried to draw off. 'I leave you this,' working it round and round vainly, 'if you can get it off. What mighty knuckles! There must be such knuckles in the mummies of the Pharaohs. Well, when I'm gone! Nay, I leave you something more precious than gold, —the sense of a great kindness. But I have a little gold left. Bring me those trinkets.' I placed on the bed before him several articles of jewellery, relics of early elegance: his watch and chain, of great value, a locket and seal, some shirt-buttons and scarf-pins. He trifled with them feebly for some moments, murmuring various names and dates associated with them. At last, looking up with a sudden energy, 'What's become of Mr. Rawson?'

'You want to see him?'

'How much are these things worth?' he asked, without heeding me. 'How much would they bring?' And he held them up in his weak hands. 'They have a great weight. Two hundred pounds? I am richer than I thought! Rawson—Rawson—you want to get out of this awful England?'

I stepped to the door and requested the servant, whom I kept in constant attendance in the adjoining sitting-room, to descend and ascertain if Mr. Rawson was on the premises. He returned in a few moments, introducing our shabby friend. Mr. Rawson was pale, even to his nose, and with his grave agitation had an air of great distinction. I led him up to the bed. In Searle's eyes, as they fell on him, there shone for a moment the light of a high fraternal greeting.

'Great God!' said Mr. Rawson, fervently.

'My friend,' said Searle, 'there is to be one American the less. Let there be one the more. At the worst, you'll be as good a one as I. Foolish me! Take these trinkets; let them help you on your way. They are gifts and memories, but this is a better use. Heaven speed you! May America be kind to you. Be kind, at the last, to your own country!'

'Really, this is too much; I can't,' our friend protested in a tremulous voice. 'Do get well, and I'll stop here!'

'Nay; I'm booked for my journey, you for yours. I hope you don't suffer at sea.'

Mr. Rawson exhaled a groan of helpless gratitude, appealing piteously from so awful a good fortune. 'It's like the angel of the Lord,' he said, 'who bids people in the Bible to rise and flee!'

Searle had sunk back upon his pillow, exhausted: I led Mr. Rawson back into the sitting-room, where in three words I proposed to him a broad valuation of our friend's trinkets. He assented with perfect good-breeding; they passed into my possession and a second bank-note into his.

From the collapse into which this beneficent interview had plunged him, Searle gave few signs of being likely to emerge. He breathed, as he had said, and nothing more. The twilight deepened: I lit the night-lamp. The doctor sat silent and official at the foot of the bed; I resumed my constant place near the head. Suddenly Searle opened his eyes widely. 'She'll not come,' he murmured. 'Amen! she's an English sister.' Five minutes passed. He started forward. 'She has come, she is here!' he whispered. His words conveyed to my mind so absolute an assurance, that I lightly rose and passed into the sitting-room. At the same moment, through the opposite door, the servant introduced a lady. A lady, I say; for an instant she was simply such; tall, pale, dressed in deep mourning. The next moment I had uttered her name—'Miss Searle!' She looked ten years older.

She met me, with both hands extended, and an immense question in her face. 'He has just spoken your name,' I said. And then, with a fuller consciousness of the change in her dress and countenance: 'What has happened?'

'O death, death!' said Miss Searle. 'You and I are left.'

There came to me with her words a sort of sickening shock, the sense of some grim *escamotage* of poetic justice. 'Your brother?' I demanded.

She laid her hand on my arm, and I felt its pressure deepen as she spoke. 'He was thrown from his horse in the park. He died on the spot. Six days have passed.—Six months!'

She took my arm. A moment later we had entered the room and approached the bedside. The doctor withdrew. Searle opened his eyes and looked at her from head to foot. Suddenly he seemed to perceive her mourning. 'Already!' he cried, audibly; with a smile, as I believe, of pleasure.

She dropped on her knees and took his hand. 'Not for you, cousin,' she whispered. 'For my poor brother.'

He started in all his deathly longitude as with a galvanic shock. 'Dead! *he* dead! Life itself!' And then, after a moment, with a slight rising inflection: 'You are free?'

'Free, cousin. Sadly free. And now—*now*—with what use for freedom?'

He looked steadily a moment into her eyes, dark in the heavy shadow of her musty mourning veil. 'For me,' he said, 'wear colours!'

In a moment more, death had come, the doctor had silently attested it and Miss Searle had burst into sobs.

We buried him in the little churchyard in which he had expressed the wish to lie; beneath one of the mightiest of English yews and the little tower than which none in all England has a softer and older grey. A year has passed. Miss Searle, I believe, has begun to wear colours.

At Isella

[First appeared in the *Galaxy*, vol. xii (August 1871), pp. 241–55. Not reprinted during James's lifetime.

In 1885, while preparing *Stories Revived* for Macmillan (see my Introduction to the first volume of this edition, pp. xlv–xlvi), James told his publisher that he could 'without difficulty supply plenty of copy for 3 volumes' (MS. letter, dated 7 January, in the Macmillan Archive in the British Library). Apparently, James had selected, and partially revised, more tales than the fourteen printed in the three volumes of *Stories Revived*. Although not included in that gathering, 'At Isella' appears to have been one of the tales originally considered for inclusion. This seems to be the only plausible explanation of the existence of a copy of the magazine text, with numerous textual alterations in James's hand on the opening six pages. The copy is preserved in the Houghton Library: a page from it is reproduced in the first volume of this edition. The quality and quantity of the revisions suggests that the version in the making was not intended for any other collection of revised tales.]

MY STORY BEGINS PROPERLY, I SUPPOSE, WITH MY journey, and my journey began properly at Lucerne. It had been on the point of beginning a number of times before. About the middle of August I actually started. I had been putting it off from day to day in deference to the opinion of several discreet friends, who solemnly assured me that a man of my make would never out-weather the rage of an Italian August. But ever since deciding to winter in Italy, instead of subsiding unimaginatively upon Paris, I had had a standing quarrel with Switzerland. What was Switzerland after all? Little else but brute Nature surely, of which at home we have enough and to spare. What we seek in Europe is Nature refined and transmuted to art. In Switzerland, what a pale historic colouring; what a penury of relics and monuments! I pined for a cathedral or a gallery. Instead of dutifully conning my Swiss Bädeker, I had fretfully deflowered my Murray's North Italy. Lucerne indeed is a charming little city, and I had learned to know it well. I had watched the tumbling Reuss, blue from the melting pinnacles which know the blue of heaven, come rushing and swirling beneath those quaintly-timbered bridges, vaulted with mystical paintings in the manner of Holbein, and through the severed mass of the white, compact town. I had frequented the great, bald, half-handsome, half-hideous church of the Jesuits, and listened in the twilight to the seraphic choir which breathes through its mighty organ-tubes. I had taken the most reckless pleasure in the fact that this was

Catholic Switzerland. I had strolled and restrolled across the narrow market-place at Altorf, and kept my countenance in the presence of that ludicrous plaster-cast of the *genius loci* and his cross-bow. I had peregrinated further to the little hamlet of Bürglen, and peeped into the frescoed chapel which commemorates the hero's natal scene. I had also investigated that sordid lake-side sanctuary, with its threshold lapped by the waves and its walls defiled by cockneys, which consecrates the spot at which the great mountaineer, leaping from among his custodians in Gesler's boat, spurned the stout skiff with his invincible heel. I had contemplated from the deck of the steamer the images of the immortal trio, authors of the oath of liberation, which adorn the pier at Brunnen. I had sojourned at that compact little State of Gersau, sandwiched between the lake and the great wall of the Righi, and securely niched somewhere in history as the smallest and most perpetual of republics. The traveller's impatience hereabouts is quickened by his nearness to one of the greatest of the Alpine highways. Here he may catch a balmy side-wind, stirred from the ranks of southward-trooping pilgrims. The Saint Gothard route begins at Lucerne, where you take your place in the diligence and register your luggage. I used to fancy that a great wave of Southern life rolled down this mighty channel to expire visibly in the blue lake, and ripple to its green shores. I used to imagine great gusts of warm wind hovering about the coach office at Fluelen, scented with oleander and myrtle. I used to buy at Fluelen, to the great peril of my digestion, certain villainous peaches and plums, offered by little girls at the steamboat landing, and of which it was currently whispered that they had ripened on those further Italian slopes.

One fine morning I marked my luggage *Milan*! with a great imaginitive flourish which may have had something to do with my subsequent difficulty in recovering it in the Lombard capital, banished it for a fortnight from sight and mind, and embarked on the steamboat at Lucerne with the interval's equipment in a knapsack. It is noteworthy how readily, on leaving Switzerland, I made my peace with it. What a pleasure-giving land it is, in truth! Besides the massive glory of its mountains, how it heaps up the measure of delight with the unbargained grace of town and tower, of remembered name and deed! As we passed away from Lucerne, my eyes lingered with a fresher fondness than before upon an admirable bit of the civic picturesque—a great line of mellow-stuccoed dwellings, with verdurous water-steps and grated basements, rising squarely from the rushing cobalt of the Reuss. It was a palpable foretaste of Venice. I am not ashamed to say how soon I began to look out for premonitions of Italy. It was better to begin too soon than too late; so, to miss nothing, I began to note 'sensations' at Altorf, the historic heart of Helvetia. I remembered here certain formal burgher mansions, standing back from the dusty highroad beyond spacious, well-swept courts, into which the wayfarer glances through immense gates of antique wrought iron. I had a notion that deserted Italian palazzos took the lingering sunbeams at somewhat such an angle, with just that coarse glare. I wondered of course who lived in them, and how they lived, and what was society in Altorf; longing plaintively, in the manner of roaming Americans, for a few stray crumbs from the native social board; with my fancy vainly beating its wings against the great blank wall, behind which, in travel-haunted Europe, all gentle private interests nestle away from intrusion. Here, as everywhere, I was struck with the mere surface-relation of the Western tourist to the soil he treads. He filters and trickles through the dense social body in every possible direction, and issues forth at last the same virginal water-drop. 'Go your way,' these antique houses seemed to say, from their quiet courts and gardens; 'the road is yours and welcome, but the land is ours. You may pass and stare and wonder, but you may never know us.' The Western tourist consoles himself, of course, by the reflection that the gentry of Altorf and other ancient burghs gain more from the imagination possibly than they might bestow upon it.

I confess that so long as I remained in the land, as I did for the rest of the afternoon—a pure afternoon of late summer, charged with mellow shadows from the teeming verdure of the narrow lowland, beyond which tomorrow and Italy seemed merged in a vague bright identity—I felt that I was not fairly under way. The land terminates at Amstaeg, where I lay that night. Early the next morning I attacked the mighty slopes. Just beyond Amstaeg, if I am not mistaken, a narrow granite bridge spans the last mountain-plunge of the Reuss; and just here the great white road begins the long toil of its ascent. To my sense, these mighty Alpine highways have a grand poetry of their own. I lack, doubtless, that stout stomach for pure loneliness which leads your genuine mountaineer to pronounce them a desecration of the mountain stillness. As if the mountain stillness were not inviolable! Gleaming here and there against the dark sides of the gorges, unrolling their measured bands further and higher, doubling and stretching and spanning, but always climbing, they break it only to the anxious eye. The Saint Gothard road is immensely long-drawn, and, if the truth be told, somewhat monotonous. As you follow it to its uppermost reaches, the landscape takes on a darker local colour. Far below the wayside, the yellow Reuss tumbles and leaps and foams over a perfect torture-bed of broken rock. The higher slopes lie naked and raw, or coated with slabs of grey. The valley lifts and narrows and darkens into the scenic mountain-pass of the fancy. I was haunted as I walked by an old steel plate in a French book that I used to look at as a child, lying on my stomach on the parlour-floor. Under it was written 'Saint Gothard.' I remembered distinctly the cold, grey mood which this picture used to generate; the same tone of feeling is produced by the actual scene. Coming at last to the Devil's Bridge, I recognized the source of the steel plate of my infancy. You have no impulse here to linger fondly. You hurry away after a moment's halt, with an impression fierce and chaotic as the place itself. A great torrent of wind, sweeping from a sudden outlet and snatching uproar and spray from the mad torrent of water leaping in liquid thunderbolts beneath; a giddy, deafened, deluged stare, with my two hands to my hat, and a rapid shuddering retreat— these are my chief impressions of the Devil's Bridge. If, on leaving Amstaeg in the morning, I had been asked whither I was bending my steps, 'To Italy!' I would have answered, with a grand absence of detail. The radiance of this broad fact had quenched the possible side-lights of reflection. As I approached the summit of the pass, it became a profoundly solemn thought that I might, by pushing on with energy, lay my weary limbs on an Italian bed. There was something so delightful in the mere protracted, suspended sense of approach, that it seemed a pity to bring it to so abrupt a close. And then suppose, metaphysical soul of mine, that Italy should not, in vulgar parlance, altogether come up to time? Why not prolong awhile the possible bliss of ignorance—of illusion? Something short of the summit of the Saint Gothard pass, the great road of the Furca diverges to the right, passes the Rhône Glacier, enters the Rhône Valley, and conducts you to Brig and the foot of the Simplon. Reaching in due course this divergence of the Furca road, I tarried awhile beneath the mountain sky, debating whether or not delay would add to pleasure. I opened my Bädeker and read that within a couple of hours' walk from my halting-place was the *Albergo di San Gothardo, vaste et sombre auberge italienne.* To think of being at that distance from a vast, sombre Italian inn! On the other hand, there were some very pretty things said of the Simplon. I tossed up a napoleon; the head fell uppermost. I trudged away to the right. The road to the Furca lies across one of those high desolate plateaux which represent the hard prose of mountain-scenery. Naked and stern it lay before me, rock and grass, without a shrub, without a tree, without a grace— like the dry bed of some gigantic river of prehistoric times.

The stunted hamlet of Realp, beside the road, dwarfed by the huge scale of things, seemed little more than a cluster of naked, sun-blackened boulders. It contained an inn, however, and the inn contained the usual Alpine larder of cold veal and cheese, and as I remember, a very affable maid-servant, who spoke excellent lowland French, and confessed in the course of an after-dinner conversation that the winters in Realp were *un peu tristes*. This conversation took place as I sat resting outside the door in the late afternoon, watching the bright, hard light of the scene grow grey and cold beneath a clear sky, and wondering to find humanity lodged in such an exaltation of desolation.

The road to the Furca, as I discovered the next morning, is a road and little else. Its massive bareness, however, gives it an incontestable grandeur. The broad, serpentine terrace uncoils its slanting *cordons* with a multiplicity of curves and angles and patient reaches of circumvention, which give it the air of some wanton revelry of engineering genius. Finally, after a brief level of repose, it plunges down to the Rhône Glacier. I had the good fortune to see this great spectacle on the finest day of the year. Its perfect beauty is best revealed beneath the scorching glare of an untempered sun. The sky was without a cloud—the air incredibly lucid. The glacier dropped its billowy sheet—a soundless tumult of whiteness, a torrent of rolling marble—straight from the blue of heaven to the grassy margin of the road. It seems to gather into its bosom the whole diffused light of the world, so that round about it all objects lose their colour. The rocks and hills stand sullen and neutral; the lustre of the sky is turned to blackness. At the little hotel near the glacier I waited for the coach to Brig, and started thitherward in the early afternoon, sole occupant of the *coupé*.

Let me not, however, forget to commemorate the French priest whom we took in at one of the squalid villages of the dreary Haut-Valais, through which on that bright afternoon we rattled so superbly. It was a Sunday, and throughout this long dark chain of wayside hamlets the peasants were straddling stolidly about the little central *place* in the hideous festal accoutrements of the rustic Swiss. He came forth from the tavern, gently cleaving the staring crowd, accompanied by two brother ecclesiastics. These were portly, elderly men; he was young and pale and priestly in the last degree. They had a little scene of adieux at the coach door. They whispered gently, gently holding each other's hands and looking lovingly into each other's eyes, and then the two elders saluted their comrade on each cheek, and, as we departed, blew after him just the least little sacramental kiss. It was all, dramatically speaking, delightfully low in tone. Before we reached Brig the young priest had gained a friend to console him for those he had lost. He proved to be a most amiable person; full of homely frankness and appealing innocence of mundane things; and invested withal with a most pathetic air of sitting there as a mere passive object of transmission—a simple priestly particle in the great ecclesiastical body, transposed by the logic of an inscrutable *thither!* and *thus!* On learning that I was an American, he treated me so implicitly as a travelled man of the world, that he almost persuaded me for the time I was one. He was on pins and needles with his sense of the possible hazards of travel. He asked questions the most innocently *saugrenues.* He was convinced on general grounds that our driver was drunk, and that he would surely overturn us into the Rhône. He seemed possessed at the same time with a sort of school-boy relish for the profane humour of things. Whenever the coach made a lurch towards the river-bank or swung too broadly round a turn, he would grasp my arm and whisper that our hour had come; and then, before our pace was quite readjusted, he would fall to nursing his elbows and snickering gently to himself. It seemed altogether a larger possibility than any he had been prepared for that on his complaining of the cold I should offer him the use of my overcoat. Of this and of other personal belongings he ventured to inquire the price, and indeed seemed oppressed with the sudden expensiveness of the world. But now that he was fairly launched he was moving in earnest. He was to reach Brig, if possible, in time for the night-diligence over the Simplon, which was to deposit him at the Hospice on the summit.

By a very early hour the next morning I had climbed apace with the sun. Brig was far below me in the valley. I had measured an endless number of the giant elbows of the road, and from the bosky flank of the mountain I looked down at nestling gulfs of greenness, cool with shade; at surging billows of forest crested with the early brightness; at slopes in light and cliffs in shadow; at all the heaving mountain-zone which belongs to the verdant nearness of earth; and then straight across to the sacred pinnacles which take their tone from heaven.

If weather could bless an enterprise, mine was blessed beyond words. It seemed to me that Nature had taken an interest in my little project and was determined to do the thing handsomely. As I mounted higher, the light flung its dazzling presence on all things. The air stood still to take it; the green glittered within the green, the blue burned beyond it; the dew on the forests gathered to dry into massive crystals, and beyond the brilliant void of space the clear snow-fields stood out like planes of marble inserted in a field of lapis-lazuli. The Swiss side of the Simplon has the beauty of a boundless luxury of green; the view remains gentle even in its immensity. The ascent is gradual and slow, and only when you reach the summit do you get a sense of proper mountain grimness. On this favouring day of mine the snowy horrors of the opposite Aletsch Glacier seemed fairly to twinkle with serenity. It seemed to me when I reached the Hospice that I had been winding for hours along the inner hollow of some mighty cup of verdure towards a rim of chiselled silver crowned with topaz. At the Hospice I made bold to ask leave to rest. It stands on the bare topmost plateau of the pass, bare itself as the spot it consecrates, and stern as the courage of the pious brothers who administer its charities. It broods upon the scene with the true, bald, convent look, with rugged yellow walls and grated windows, striving to close in human weakness from blast and avalanche, as in valleys and cities to close it in from temptation and pollution. A few St. Bernard dogs were dozing outside in the chilly sunshine. I climbed the great stone steps which lift the threshold above the snowland, and tinkled the bell of appeal. Here for a couple of hours I was made welcome to the cold, hard fare of the convent. There was to my mind a solemn and pleasant fitness in my thus entering church-burdened Italy through the portal of the church, for from the convent door to the plain of Lombardy it was all to be downhill work. I seemed to feel on my head the hands of especial benediction, and to hear in my ears the premonition of countless future hours to be passed in the light of altar-candles. The inner face of the Hospice is well-nigh as cold and bare as the face it turns defiant to the Alpine snows. Huge stone corridors and ungarnished rooms, in which poor unacclimatized friars must sit aching and itching with chilblains in high midsummer; everywhere that peculiar perfume of churchiness—the *odeur de sacristie* and essence of incense—which impart throughout the world an especial pungency to Catholicism. Having the good fortune, as it happened, to be invited to dine with the Prior, I found myself in fine priestly company. A dozen of us sat about the board in the greasy, brick-paved refectory, lined with sombre cupboards of ponderous crockery, all in stole and cassock but myself. Several of the brothers were *in transitu* from below. Among them I had the pleasure of greeting my companion in the *coupé* to Brig, slightly sobered perhaps by his relapse into the clerical ranks, but still timidly gracious and joyous. The Prior himself, however, especially interested me, so every inch was he a prior—a priest dominant and militant. He was still young, and familiar, I should say, with the passions of youth; tall and powerful in frame, stout-necked and small-headed, with a brave beak of a nose and closely-placed, fine, but sinister eyes. The simple, childish cut of his black cassock, with its little linen band across his great pectoral expanse as he sat at meat, seemed to denote a fantastical, ironical humility. Was it a mere fancy of a romantic Yankee tourist that he was more evil than gentle? Heaven grant, I mused as I glanced at him, that his fierce and massive manhood be guided by the Lord's example. What was such a man as that doing up there on a lonely mountain top, watching the snow clouds from closed windows and doling out restorative cognac to frost-bitten wagoners? He ought to be down in the hard, dense world, fighting and sinning for his mother Church. But he was one who could bide his time. Unless I'm scribbling nonsense, it will come. In deference probably to the esoteric character of a portion of the company, our conversation at dinner was not rigidly clerical. In fact, when my attention wandered back to its theme, I found the good brothers were talking of Alexandre Dumas with a delightful air of protest and hearsay, and a spice of priestly malice. The great romancer, I believe, had among his many fictions somewhere promulgated an inordinate fiction touching the manners and customs of the Hospice. The game being started, each of them said his say and cast his pebble, weighted always with an 'on dit', and I was amazed to find they were so well qualified to reprobate the author of 'Monte Cristo'. When we had dined my young Frenchman came up and took me by the arm and led me in great triumph over the whole convent, delighted to have something to show me—me who had come from America and had lent him my overcoat. When at last I had under his auspices made my farewell obeisance to the Prior, and started on my downward course, he bore me company along the road. But before we lost sight of the Hospice he gave me his fraternal blessing. 'Allons!' he was pleased to say, 'the next time I shall know an American;' and he gathered up his gentle petticoat, and, as I looked behind, I saw his black stockings frolicking back over the stones by a short cut to the monastery.

I should like to be able to tell the veracious tale of that divine afternoon. I should like to be able to trace the soft stages by which those rugged heights melt over into a Southern difference. Now at last in good earnest I began to watch for the *symptoms* of Italy. Now that the long slope began to tend downward unbroken, it was not absurd to fancy a few adventurous tendrils of Southern growth might have crept and clambered upward. At a short distance beyond the Hospice stands the little village of Simplon, where I believe the coach stops for dinner; the uttermost outpost, I deemed it, of the lower world, perched there like an empty shell, with its murmur not yet quenched, tossed upward and stranded by some climbing Southern wave. The little inn at the Italian end of the street, painted in a bright Italian medley of pink and blue, must have been decor-

ated by a hand which had learned its cunning in the land of the
fresco. The Italian slope of the Simplon road commands a range of
scenery wholly different from the Swiss. The latter winds like a
thread through the blue immensity; the former bores its way beneath
crag and cliff, through gorge and mountain crevice. But though its
channel narrows and darkens, Italy nears and nears none the less.
You suspect it first in—what shall I say?—the growing warmth of the
air, a fancied elegance of leaf and twig; a little while yet, and they
will curl and wanton to your heart's content. The famous Gorge of
Gondo, at this stage of the road, renews the sombre horrors of the
Via Mala. The hills close together above your head, and the daylight
filters down their corrugated sides from three inches of blue. The
mad torrent of the Doveria, roaring through the straitened vale, fills
it for ever with a sounding din, as—to compare poetry to prose—a
railway train a tunnel. Emerging from the Gorge of Gondo, you fairly
breathe the Italian air. The gusts of a mild climate come wandering
along the road to meet you. Lo! suddenly, by the still wayside, I
came upon a sensation: a little house painted a hot salmon colour,
with a withered pine-twig over the door in token of entertainment,
and above this inscribed in square chirography—literally in Italics—
Osteria! I stopped devotedly to quaff a glass of sour wine to Italy
gained. The place seemed wrapped in a desolation of stillness, save
that as I stood and thumped the doorpost, the piping cry of a baby
rose from the loft above and tickled the mountain echoes. Anon
came clattering down the stairs a nursing mother of peasants; she
gave me her only wine, out of her own bottle, out of her only glass.
While she stood to wait on me, the terrible cry of her infant became
so painful that I bade her go and fetch him before he strangled;
and in a moment she reappeared, holding him in her arms, pacified
and utterly naked. Standing there with the little unswaddled child on
her breast, and smiling simply from her glowing brow, she made a
picture which, in coming weeks, I saw imitated more or less vividly
over many an altar and in many a place. Onward still, through its
long-drawn evolutions, the valley keeps darkly together, as if to hold
its own to the last against the glittering breadth of level Lombardy.
In truth, I had gained my desire. If Italy meant stifling heat, this was
the essence of Italy. The afternoon was waning, and the early
shadows of the valley deepening into a dead summer night. But the
hotter the better, and the more Italian! At last, at a turn in the road,
glimpsed the first houses of a shallow village, pressed against the
mountain wall. It was Italy—the Dogana Isella! so I quickened my
jaded steps. I met a young officer strolling along the road in sky-blue
trousers, with a moustache *à la* Victor Emmanuel, puffing a cigarette,

and yawning with the sensuous *ennui* of Isella—the first of that swarming company of warriors whose cerulean presence, in many a rich street-scene, in later hours touched up so brightly the foreground of the picture. A few steps more brought me to the Dogana, and to my first glimpse of those massive and shadowy arcades so delightfully native to the South. Here it was my privilege to hear for the first time the music of an Italian throat vibrate upon Italian air. 'Nothing to declare—*niente*?' asked the dark-eyed functionary, emerging from the arcade. *'Niente'* seemed to me delicious; I would have told a fib for the sake of repeating the word. Just beyond stood the inn, which seemed to me somehow not as the inns of Switzerland. Perched something aloft against the hillside, a vague, light tendency to break out into balconies and terraces and trellises seemed to enhance its simple façade. Its open windows had an air of being familiar with Southern nights; with balmy dialogues, possibly, passing between languid ladies leaning on the iron rails, and lounging gentlemen, star-gazing from the road beneath at their mistresses' eyes. Heaven grant it should not be fastidiously neat, scrubbed and furbished and *frotté* like those prosy taverns on the Swiss lakes! Heaven was generous. I was ushered into a room whereof the ceiling was frescoed with flowers and gems and cherubs, but whose brick-tiled floor would have been vastly amended by the touch of a wet cloth and broom. After repairing my toilet within the limits of my resources, I proceeded to order supper. The host, I remember, I decreed to have been the *chef de cuisine* of some princely house of Lombardy. He wore a grizzled moustache and a red velvet cap, with little gold ear-rings. I could see him, under proper inspiration, whip a towel round his waist, turn back his sleeves, and elaborate a masterly pasticcio. 'I shall take the liberty,' he said, 'of causing monsieur to be served at the same time with a lady.'

'With a lady—an English lady?' I asked.

'An Italian lady. She arrived an hour ago.' And mine host paused a moment and honoured me with a genial smile. 'She is alone—she is young—she is pretty.'

Stolid child of the North that I was, surely my smile of response was no match for his! But, nevertheless, in my heart I felt that fortune was kind. I went forth to stroll down the road while my repast was being served, and while daylight still lingered, to reach forward as far as possible into the beckoning land beyond. Opposite the inn the mountain stream, still untamed, murmured and tumbled between the stout parapet which edged the road and the wall of rock which enclosed the gorge. I felt indefinably curious, expectant, impatient. Here was Italy at last; but what next? Was I to eat my supper and go contentedly to bed? Was there nothing I could see, or do, or feel? I had been deeply moved, but I was primed for a deeper emotion still. Would it come? Along the road towards Domo d'Ossola the evening shadows deepened and settled, and filled the future with mystery. The future would take care of itself; but ah, for an intenser present! I stopped and gazed wistfully along the broad dim highway. At this moment I perceived beyond me, leaning against the parapet, the figure of a woman, alone and in meditation. Her two elbows rested on the stone coping, her two hands were laid against her ears to deaden the din of the stream, and her face, between them, was bent over upon the waters. She seemed young and comely. She was bare-headed; a black organdy shawl was gathered round her shoulders; her dress, of a light black material, was covered with a multitude of little puffs and flounces, trimmed and adorned with crimson silk. There was an air of intense meditation in her attitude; I passed near her without her perceiving me. I observed her black-brown tresses, braided by a cunning hand, but slightly disarranged by travel, and the crumpled disorder of her half-fantastic dress. She was a lady and an Italian; she was alone, young, and pretty; was she possibly my destined companion? A few yards beyond the spot at which she stood, I retraced my steps; she had now turned round. As I approached her she looked at me from a pair of dark expressive eyes. Just a hint of suspicion and defiance I fancied that at this moment they expressed. 'Who are you, what are you, roaming so close to me?' they seemed to murmur. We were alone in this narrow pass, I a newcomer, she a daughter of the land; moreover, her glance had almost audibly challenged me; instinctively, therefore, and with all the deference I was master of, I bowed. She continued to gaze for an instant; then suddenly she perceived, I think, that I was utterly a foreigner and presumably a gentleman, and hereupon, briefly but graciously, she returned my salute. I went my way and reached the hotel. As I passed in, I saw the fair stranger come slowly along the road as if also to enter the inn. In the little dining-room I found mine host of the velvet cap bestowing the finishing touches upon a small table set *en tête-à-tête* for two. I had heard, I had read, of the gracious loquacity of the Italian race and their sweet familiarities of discourse. Here was a chance to test the quality of the matter. The landlord, having poised two fantastically folded napkins directly *vis-à-vis*, glanced at me with a twinkle in his eye which seemed to bespeak recognition of this cunning arrangement.

'*A propos*,' I said, 'this lady with whom I am to dine? Does she wear a black dress with red flounces?'

'Precisely, Signore. You have already had a glimpse of her? A pretty woman, isn't it so?'

'Extremely pretty. Who is the lady?'

'Ah!' And the landlord turned back his head and thrust out his chin, with just the least play of his shoulders. 'That's the question! A lady of that age, with that face and those red flounces, who travels alone——not even a maid—you may well ask who she is! She arrived here an hour ago in a carriage from Domo d'Ossola, where, her vetturino told me, she had arrived only just before by the common coach from Arona. But though she travels by the common vehicle, she is not a common person; one may see that with half an eye. She comes in great haste, but ignorant of the ways and means. She wishes to go by the diligence to Brig. She ought to have waited at Domo, where she could have found a good seat. She didn't even take the precaution of engaging one at the office there. When the diligence stops here, she will have to fare as she can. She is pretty enough indeed to fare very well—or very ill; isn't it so, Signore?' demanded the worthy Bonifazio, as I believe he was named. 'Ah, but behold her strolling along the road, bare-headed, in those red flounces! What is one to say? After dusk, with the dozen officers in garrison here watching the frontier! Watching the ladies who come and go, *per Dio*! Many of them, saving your presence, Signore, are your own compatriots. You'll not deny that some of them are a little free—a little bold. What will you have? Out of their own country! What else were the use of travel? But this one; eh! she's not out of her own country yet. Italians are Italians, Signore, up to the frontier—eh! eh!' And the Signor Bonifazio indulged in a laugh the most *goguenard*. 'Nevertheless, I have not kept an inn these twenty years without learning to know the sheep from the goats. This is an honourable lady, Signore; it is for that reason that I have offered to you to sup with her. The other sort! one can always sup with them!'

It seemed to me that my host's fluent commentary was no meagre foretaste of Italian frankness. I approached the window. The fair object of our conversation stood at the foot of the stone staircase which ascended to the inn-door, with the toe of her shoe resting upon the first step. She was looking fixedly and pensively up the road towards Switzerland. Her hand clasped the knob of the iron balustrade and her slight fingers played an impatient measure. She had begun to interest me. Her dark eyes, intent upon the distant turn of the road, seemed to expand with a vague expectancy. Whom was she looking for? Of what romance of Italy was she the heroine? The *maître d'hôtel* appeared at the head of the steps, and with a flourish of his napkin announced that the Signora was served. She started a little, then lightly shrugged her shoulders. At the same moment I caught her eye as I stood gazing from the window. With a just visible deepening of her colour, she slowly ascended the steps. I was suddenly seized with a sense of being dingy, travel-stained, unpresentable to a woman so charming. I hastily retreated to my room, and, surveying myself in my dressing-glass, objurgated fortune that I lacked the wherewithal to amend my attire. But I could at least change my cravat. I had no sooner replaced my black neck-tie by a blue one than it occurred to me that the Signora would observe the difference; but what then? It would hardly offend her. With a timid hope that it might faintly gratify her as my only feasible tribute to the honour of her presence, I returned to the dining-room. She was seated and had languidly addressed herself to the contents of her soup-plate. The worthy Bonifazio had adorned our little table with four lighted candles and a centre-piece of Alpine flowers. As I installed myself opposite my companion, after having greeted her and received a murmured response, it seemed to me that I was sitting down to one of those factitious repasts which are served upon the French stage, when the table has been moved close to the footlights, and the ravishing young widow and the romantic young artist begin to manipulate the very *nodus* of the comedy. Was the Signora a widow? Our attendant, with his crimson cap, his well-salted discourse, his right-handed gestures, and his smile from behind the scenes, might have passed for a classic *valet de théâtre*. I had the appetite of a man who had been walking since sunrise, but I found ample occasion, while I plied my knife and fork, to inspect the Signora. She merely pretended to eat; and to appeal, perhaps, from the overflattering intentness of my vision, she opened an idle conversation with Bonifazio. I listened admiringly, while the glancing shuttle of Italian speech passed rapidly from lip to lip. It was evident, frequently, that she remained quite heedless of what he said, losing herself for ever in a kind of fretful intensity of thought. The repast was long and multifarious, and as he time and again removed her plate with its contents untouched, mine host would catch my eye and roll up his own with an air of mock commiseration, turning back his thumb at the same moment towards the region of his heart. '*Un coup de tête*,' he took occasion to murmur as he reached over me to put down a dish. But the more I looked at the fair unknown, the more I came to suspect that the source of her unrest lay deeper than in the petulance of wounded vanity. Her face wore to my eye the dignity of a deep resolution—a resolution taken in tears and ecstasy. She was some twenty-eight years of age, I imagined; though at moments a painful gravity resting upon her brow gave her the air of a woman who in youth has anticipated old age. How beautiful she was by natural gift I am unable to say; for at this especial hour of her destiny, her face was too serious to be fair and too interesting to be plain. She was pale, worn, and weary-looking; but in the midst of her weariness there flickered a fierce impatience of delay and forced repose. She was a gentle creature, turned brave and adventurous by the stress of fate. It burned bright in her soft, grave eyes, this longing for the larger freedom of the tarrying morrow. A dozen chance gestures indicated the torment of her spirit—the constant rapping of her knife against the table, her bread crumbed to pieces but uneaten, the frequent change from posture to posture of her full and flexible figure, shifting through that broad range of attitude—the very gamut of gracefulness—familiar to Italian women.

The repast advanced without my finding a voice to address her. Her secret puzzled me, whatever it was, but I confess that I was afraid of it. A *coup de tête*! Heaven only knew how direful a *coup*! My mind was flooded by the memory of the rich capacity of the historic womanhood of Italy. I thought of Lucrezia Borgia, of Bianca Capello, of the heroines of Stendhal. My fair friend seemed invested with an atmosphere of candid passion, which placed her quite apart from the ladies of my own land. The gallant soul of the Signor Bonifazio, however, had little sufferance for this pedantic view of things. Shocked by my apparent indifference to the privilege of my rare position, he thrust me by the shoulders into the conversation. The Signora eyed me for a moment not ungraciously, and then, 'Do you understand Italian?' she asked.

I had come to Italy with an ear quite unattuned, of course, to the spoken tongue; but the mellow cadence of the Signora's voice rang in upon my senses like music. 'I understand *you*,' I said.

She looked at me gravely, with the air of a woman used to receive compliments without any great flutter of vanity. 'Are you English?' she abruptly asked.

'English is my tongue.'

'Have you come from Switzerland?'

'He has walked from Brig!' proclaimed our host.

'Ah, you happy men, who can walk—who can run—who needn't wait for coaches and conductors!' The Signora uttered these words with a smile of acute though transient irony. They were followed by a silence. Bonifazio, seeing the ice was broken, retired with a flourish of his napkin and a contraction of his eyelids as much in the nature of a wink as his respect for me, for the Signora, and for himself allowed. What was the motive of the Signora's impatience? I had a presentiment that I should learn. The Italians are confidential; of this I had already received sufficient assurance; and my companion, with her lucid eye and her fine pliable lips, was a bright example of the eloquent genius of her race. She sat idly pressing with her fork the crimson substance out of a plateful of figs, without raising them to her lips.

'You are going over into Switzerland,' I said, 'and you are in haste.' She eyed me a minute suspiciously. 'Yes, I'm in haste!'

'I, who have just begun to feel the charm of Italy,' I rejoined, 'can hardly understand being in haste to leave it.'

'The charm of Italy!' cried the Signora, with a slightly cynical laugh. 'Foreigners have a great deal to say about it.'

'But you, a good Italian, certainly know what we mean.'

She shrugged her shoulders—an operation she performed more gracefully than any I ever saw, unless it be Mlle. Madeleine Brohan of the Théâtre Français. 'For me it has no charm! I have been unhappy here. Happiness for me is *there*!' And with a superb nod of her head she indicated the Transalpine world. Then, as if she had spoken a thought too freely, she rose suddenly from her chair and walked away to the window. She stepped out on the narrow balcony, looked intently for an instant up and down the road and at the band of sky above it, and then turned back into the room. I sat in my place, divided between my sense of the supreme sweetness of figs and my wonder at my companion's mystery. 'It's a fine night!' she said. And with a little jerk of impatience she flung herself into an arm-chair near the table. She leaned back, with her skirt making a great wave around her and her arms folded. I went on eating figs. There was a long silence. 'You've eaten at least a dozen figs. You'll be ill!' said the Signora at last.

This was friendly in its frankness. 'Ah, if you only knew how I enjoy them!' I cried, laughing. 'They are the first I ever tasted. And this the first Asti wine. We don't have either in the North. If figs and Asti wine are for anything in your happiness, Signora,' I added, 'you had better not cross the Alps. See, the figs are all gone. Do you think it would hurt me to have any more?'

'Truly,' cried the Signora, 'I don't know what you English are made of!'

'You think us very coarse, and given up altogether to eating and drinking?' She gave another shrug tempered by a smile. 'To begin with, I am not an Englishman. And in the second place, you'd not call me coarse if you knew—if you only knew what I feel this evening. Eh! such thick-coming fancies!'

'What are your fancies?' she demanded, with a certain curiosity gleaming in her dark eye.

'I *must* finish this Asti!' This I proceeded to do. I am very glad I did, moreover, as I borrowed from its mild and luscious force something of the courage with which I came to express myself. 'I don't know how it is that I'm talking Italian at such a rate. Somehow the words come to me. I know it only from books. I have never talked it.'

'You speak as well,' the Signora graciously affirmed, 'as if you had lived six months in the country.'

'Half an hour in your society,' said I, 'is as profitable as six months elsewhere.'

'Bravo!' she responded. 'An Italian himself couldn't say it better.'

Sitting before me in the vague candlelight, beautiful, pale, dark-browed, sad, the Signora seemed to me an incorporate image of her native land. I had come to pay it my devotions. Why not perform them at her feet? 'I have come on a pilgrimage,' I said. 'To understand what I mean, you must have lived, as I have lived, in a land beyond the seas, barren of romance and grace. This Italy of yours, on whose threshold I stand, is the home of history, of beauty, of the arts —of all that makes life splendid and sweet. Italy, for us dull strangers, is a magic word. We cross ourselves when we pronounce it. We are brought up to think that when we have earned leisure and rest—at some bright hour, when fortune smiles—we may go forth and cross oceans and mountains and see on Italian soil the primal substance—the Platonic "idea"—of our consoling dreams and our richest fancies. I have been brought up in these thoughts. The happy hour has come to me—Heaven be praised!—while I am still young and strong and sensitive. Here I sit for the first time in the enchanted air in which love and faith and art and knowledge are warranted to become deeper passions than in my own chilly clime. I begin to behold the promise of my dreams. It's Italy. How can I tell you what that means to one of us? Only see already how fluent and tender of speech I've become. The air has a perfume; everything that enters my soul, at every sense, is a suggstion, a promise, a performance. But the best thing of all is that I have met you, *bella-donna*! If I were to tell you how you seem to me, you would think me either insincere or impertinent. *Ecco!*'

She listened to me without changing her attitude or without removing her fathomless eyes from my own. Their blue-black depths, indeed, seemed to me the two wells of poetic unity, from which I drew my somewhat transcendental allocution. She was puzzled, I think, and a little amused, but not offended. Anything from an Inglese! But it was doubtless grateful to feel these rolling waves of sentiment break softly at her feet, chained as she was, like Andromeda, to the rock of a lonely passion. With an admirable absence of *minauderie*, 'How is it that I seem to you, Signore?' she asked.

I left my place and came round and stood in front of her. 'Ever since I could use my wits,' I said, 'I have done little else than fancy dramas and romances and love-tales, and lodge them in Italy. You seem to me as the heroine of all my stories.'

There was perhaps a slight movement of coquetry in her reply: 'Your stories must have been very dull, Signore,' and she gave a sad smile.

'Nay, in future', I said, 'my heroines shall be more like you than ever. Where do you come from?' I seated myself in the chair she had quitted. 'But it's none of my business,' I added. 'From anywhere. In Milan or Venice, in Bologna or Florence, Rome or Naples, every grave old palazzo I pass, I shall fancy your home. I'm going the whole length of Italy. My soul, what things I shall see!'

'You please me, Signore. I say to you what I wouldn't say to another. I came from Florence. Shall you surely go there?'

'I have reasons,' I said, 'for going there more than elsewhere. In Florence'—and I hesitated, with a momentary horror at my perfect unreserve—'in Florence I am to meet my—my *promessa sposa*.'

The Signora's face was instantly irradiated by a generous smile. 'Ah!' she said, as if now for the first time she really understood me.

'As I say, she has been spending the summer at the Baths of Lucca. She comes to Florence with her mother in the middle of September.'

'Do you love her?'

'Passionately.'

'Is she pretty?'

'Extremely. But not like you. Very fair, with blue eyes.'

'How long since you have seen her?'

'A year.'

'And when are you to be married?'

'In November, probably, in Rome.' She covered me for a moment with a glance of the largest sympathy. 'Ah, what happiness!' she cried abruptly.

'After our marriage,' I said, 'we shall go down to Naples. Do you know Naples?'

Instead of answering, she simply gazed at me, and her beautiful eyes seemed to grow larger and more liquid. Suddenly, while I sat in the benignant shadow of her vision, I saw the tears rise to her lids. Her face was convulsed and she burst into sobs. I remember that in my amazement and regret I suddenly lost my Italian. 'Dearest lady,' I cried in my mother tongue, 'forgive me that I have troubled you. Share with me at least the sorrow that I have aroused.' In an instant, however, she had brushed away her tears and her face had recovered its pale composure. She tried even to smile.

'What will you think of me?' she asked. 'What do you think of me already?'

'I think you are an extremely interesting woman. You are in trouble. If there is anything I can do for you, pray say the word.'

She gave me her hand. I was on the point of raising it to my lips. 'No—*à l'anglaise*,' she said, and she lightly shook my own. 'I like you —you're an honest man—you don't try to make love to me. I should like to write a note to your *promessa sposa* to tell her she may trust you. You can't help me. I have committed myself to God and the Holy Virgin. They will help me. Besides, it's only a little longer. Eh, it's a long story, Signore! What is said in your country of a woman who travels alone at night without even a servant?'

'Nothing is said. It's very common.'

'Ah! women must be very happy there, or very unhappy! Is it never supposed of a woman that she has a lover? That is worst of all.'

'Fewer things are "supposed" of women there than here. They live more in the broad daylight of life. They make their own law.'

'They must be very good then—or very bad. So that a man of fancy like you, with a taste for romance, has to come to poor Italy, where he can suppose at leisure! But we are not all romance, I assure you. With me, I promise you, it's no light-minded *coup de tête*.' And the Signora enforced her candid assurance with an almost imperious nod. 'I know what I'm doing. Eh! I'm an old woman. I've waited and waited. But now my hour has come! Ah, the heavenly freedom of it! Ah, the peace—the joy! Just God, I thank thee!' And sitting back in her chair, she folded her hands on her bosom and closed her eyes in a kind of ecstasy. Opening them suddenly, she perceived, I suppose, my somewhat intent and dilated countenance. Breaking then into a loud, excited laugh, 'How you stare at me!' she cried. 'You think I've at least poisoned my husband. No, he's safe and sound and strong! On the contrary, I've forgiven him. I forgive him with all my heart, with all my soul; there! I call upon you to witness it. I bear him no rancour. I wish never to think of him again; only let me never see him—never hear of him! Let him never come near me: I shall never trouble him! Hark!' She had interrupted herself and pressed her hand with a startled air upon my arm. I listened, and in a moment my ear caught the sound of rolling wheels on the hard highroad. With a great effort at self-composure, apparently, she laid her finger on her lips. 'If it should be he—if it should be he!' she murmured. 'Heaven preserve me! Do go to the window and see.'

I complied, and perceived a two-horse vehicle advancing rapidly from the Italian quarter. 'It's a carriage of some sort from Italy,' I said. 'But what—whom do you fear?'

She rose to her feet. 'That my husband should overtake me,' and she gave a half-frantic glance round the room, like a hunted stag at bay. 'If it should be he, protect me! Do something, say something—anything! Say I'm not fit to go back to him. He wants me because he thinks me good. Say I'm not good—to your knowledge. Oh, Signore—Holy Virgin!' Recovering herself, she sank into a chair, and sat stiff and superb, listening to the deepening sound of the wheels. The vehicle approached, reached the inn, passed it, and went on to the Dogana.

'You're safe,' I said. 'It's not a posting-chaise, but a common wagon with merchandise.'

With a hushed sigh of relief she passed her hand over her brow, and then looking at me: 'I have lived these three days in constant terror. I believe in my soul he has come in pursuit of me; my hope is in my having gained time through his being absent when I started. My nerves are broken. I have neither slept nor eaten, nor till now have I spoken. But I *must* speak! I'm frank; it's good to take a friend when you find one.'

I confess that to have been thus freely admitted by the fair fugitive into the whirling circle of her destiny was one of the keenest emotions of my life. 'I know neither the motive of your flight nor the goal of your journey,' I answered; 'but if I may help you and speed you, I will joyfully turn back from the threshold of Italy and give you whatever furtherance my company may yield. To go with you,' I added, smiling, 'will be to remain in Italy, I assure you.'

She acknowledged my offer with a glance more potent than words. 'I'm going to a friend,' she said, after a silence. 'To accept your offer would be to make friendship cheap. He is lying ill at Geneva; otherwise I shouldn't be *thus*! But my head is on fire. This room is close; it smells of supper. Do me the favour to accompany me into the air.'

She gathered her shawl about her shoulders, I offered her my arm, and we passed into the entry towards the door. In the doorway stood mine host, with his napkin under his arm. He drew himself up as we approached, and, as if to deprecate a possible imputation of scandal, honoured us with a bow of the most ceremonious homage. We descended the steps and strolled along the road towards the Swiss frontier. A vague remnant of daylight seemed to linger imprisoned in the narrow gorge. We passed the Dogana and left the village behind us. My thoughts reverted, as we went, to the aching blank of my fancy as I entered Isella an hour before. It seemed to palpitate now with a month's experience. Beyond the village a narrow bridge spans the stream and leads to a path which climbs the opposite hill-side. We diverged from the road and lingered on the bridge while the sounding torrent gushed beneath us, flashing in the light of the few stars which sparkled in our narrow strip of sky, like diamonds tacked upon a band of velvet. I remained silent, thinking a passive silence the most graceful tribute to the Signora's generous intentions. 'I will tell you all!' she said at last. 'Do you think me pretty? But you needn't answer. The less you think so, the more you'll say it. I *was* pretty! I don't pretend to be so now. I have suffered too much. I have a miserable fear that when *he* sees me, after these three years, he'll notice the loss of my beauty. But, *poverino!* he is perhaps too ill to notice anything. He is young—a year younger than I—twenty-seven. He is a painter; he has a most beautiful talent. He loved me four years ago, before my marriage. He was a friend of my poor brother, who was fatally wounded at the battle of Mentana, where he fought with Garibaldi. My brother, Giuseppino, was brought home with his wound; he died in a week. Ernesto came to make a drawing of his face before we lost it for ever. It was not the first time I had seen him, but it was the first time we understood each other. I was sitting by poor Giuseppino's bedside, crying—crying! He, too, cried while he drew and made great blisters on the paper. I know where to look for them still. They loved each other devotedly. I, too, had loved my brother! for my mother was dead, and my father was not a mother—not even a father! Judge for yourself! We placed together the love which each of us had borne for Giuseppino, and it made a great love for each other. It was a misfortune; but how could we help it? He had nothing but his talent, which as yet was immature. I had nothing at all but the poor little glory of my father's being a Marchese, without a *soldo*, and my prettiness! But you see what has become of that! My father was furious to have given his only son to that scoundrel of a Garibaldi, for he is of that way of thinking. You should have heard the scene he made me when poor Ernesto in despair asked leave to marry me. My husband, whom I had never seen or at least never noticed, was at that time in treaty for my hand. By his origin he was little better than a peasant, but he had made a fortune in trade, and he was very well pleased to marry a *marchesina*. It's not every man who is willing to take a penniless girl; it was the first chance and perhaps the best. So I was given over blindfold, bound hand and foot, to that brute. Eh! what I hadn't brought in cash I had to pay down in patience. If I were to tell you what I've suffered these three years, it would bring tears to your eyes—Inglese as you are. But they are things which can't be told. He is a peasant, with the soul of a peasant—the taste, the manners, the vices of a peasant. It was my great crime that I was proud. I had much to be proud of. If I had only been a woman of his own sort! to pay him in his own coin! Ernesto, of course, had been altogether suppressed. He proposed to me to escape with him before my marriage, and I confess to you that I would have done it if I could. I tried in vain; I was too well watched. I implored him then to go away till better days; and he at last consented to go to Paris and pursue his studies. A week after my marriage he came to bid me farewell. My husband had taken me to Naples, to make me believe I was not wretched. Ernesto followed me, and I contrived to see him. It lasted three minutes by the clock: I have not seen him since. In three years I have had five letters from him; they are here in my dress. I am sure of his love; I don't need to have him write, to tell me. I have answered him twice. These letters—seven in all, in three years!—are all my husband has to reproach me with. He is furious at not having more. He knows of course that I love another; he knows that to bear such things a woman must borrow strength somewhere. I have had faith, but it has not been all faith! My husband has none; nothing is sacred to him, not the Blessed Virgin herself. If you were to hear the things he says about the Holy Father! I have waited and waited. I confess it, I have hoped at times that my husband would die. But he has the health of a peasant. He used to strike me—to starve me—to lock me up without light or fire. I appealed to my father, but, I'm sorry to say it, my father is a coward! Heaven forgive me! I'm saying dreadful things here! But, ah, Signore, let me breathe at last! I've waited and waited, as I say, for this hour! Heaven knows I have been good. Though I stand here now, I have not trifled with my duties. It's not coquetry! I determined to endure as long as I could, and then to break—to break for ever! A month ago strength and courage left me; or rather, they came to me! I wrote to Ernesto that I would come to him. He answered that he would come down to meet me—if possible at Milan. Just afterwards he wrote me in a little scrawl in pencil that he had been taken ill in Geneva, and that if I could I must come alone, before he got worse. Here I am then, alone, pursued, frantic with ignorance and dread. Heaven only keep him till I come. I shall do the rest! Exactly how I left home, I can't tell you. It has been like a dream! My husband—God be praised!—was obliged to make a short absence on business, of which I took advantage. My great trouble was getting a little money. I never have any. I sold a few trinkets for a few francs—hardly enough! The people saw I was too frightened to make a stand, so that they cheated me. But if I can only come to the end! I'm certain that my husband has pursued me. Once I get to Switzerland, we can hide. Meanwhile I'm in a fever.

I've lost my head. I began very well, but all this delay has so vexed and confused me. I hadn't even the wit to secure a place in the coach at Domo d'Ossola. But I shall go, if I have to sit on the roof—to crouch upon the doorstep. If I had only a little more money, so that I needn't wait for coaches. To overtake me my husband, for once in his life, won't count his *lire!*'

I listened with a kind of awe to this torrent of passionate confidence. I had got more even than I had bargained for. The current of her utterance seemed to gather volume as it came, and she poured out her tragic story with a sort of rapturous freedom. She had unburdened at last her heavy heart. As she spoke, the hot breath of her eloquence seemed to pass far beyond my single attentive sense, and mingle joyously with the free air of the night. Her tale, in a measure, might be untrue or imperfect; but her passion, her haste, her sincerity, were imperiously real. I felt, as I had never felt it, the truth of the poet's claim for his touch of nature. I became conscious of a hurrying share in my companion's dread. I seemed to hear in the trembling torrent the sound of rapid wheels. I expected every moment to see the glare of lights along the road, before the inn, then a strong arm locked about her waist, and, in the ray of a lantern from the carriage window, to catch the mute agony of her solemn eyes. My heart beat fast; I was part and parcel of a romance! Come! the *dénouement* shouldn't fail by any prosy fault of mine.

'How I've talked!' cried the Signora, after a brief pause. 'And how you stare at me! Eh! don't be afraid. I've said all, and it has done me good. You'll laugh with your *promessa sposa* about that crazy creature who was flying from her husband. The idea of people not being happy in marriage, you'll say to her!'

'I thank you with all my heart,' I said, 'for having trusted me as you have. But I'm almost sorry you have taken the time. You oughtn't to be lingering here while your husband is making the dust fly.'

'That's easy to say, Signore; but I can't walk to Brig, like you. A carriage costs a hundred and fifty francs. I have only just enough to pay my place in the coach.'

I drew out my portemonnaie and emptied it in my hand; it contained a hundred and seventy francs. '*Ecco!*' I said, holding them out to her.

She glanced at them an instant, and then, with a movement which effectually rounded and completed my impression of her simple and passionate sincerity, seized with both her hands my own hands as it held them. 'Ah, the Blessed Virgin be praised!' she cried. 'Ah, you're an angel from heaven! Quick, quick! A carriage, a carriage!'

She thrust the money into her pocket, and, without waiting for an answer, hurried back to the road, and moved swiftly towards the inn. I overtook her as she reached the doorstep, where our host was enjoying a pipe in the cool. 'A carriage!' she cried. 'I must be off. Quick, without delay! I have the money; you shall be well paid. Don't tell me you haven't one. There must be one here. Find one, prepare it, lose not a moment. Do you think I can lie tossing here all night? I shall put together my things, and give you ten minutes! You, sir, see that they hurry!' And she rapidly entered the house.

Bonifazio stared, somewhat aghast at the suddenness and the energy of her requisition. Fearing that he might not be equal to the occasion, I determined to take him by his gallantry. 'Come, my friend,' I said, 'don't stand scratching your head, but *act*. I know *you* admire the Signora. You don't want to see so charming a woman in trouble. You don't wish to have a scandal in your inn. It is of the first importance that she should leave in ten minutes. Stir up your hostler.'

A wise grin illumined his face. 'Ah,' said he, 'it's as bad as that. I had my notions. I'll do what I can.' He exerted himself to such good purpose that in the incredibly short period of twenty minutes a small closed carriage was drawn by a couple of stout horses to the door. Going in to summon the fair fugitive, I found her in the dining-room, where, fretting with impatience, and hooded and shawled, she had suffered a rather bungling chambermaid to attempt the insertion of a couple of necessary pins. She swept past me on her exit as if she had equally forgotten my face and her obligations, and entered the carriage with passionate adjurations of haste. I followed her and watched her take her place; but she seemed not even to see me. My hour was over. I had added an impulse to her straining purpose; its hurrying current had left me alone on the brink. I could not resist the influence of a poignant regret at having dropped from her consciousness. Learning from a peasant who was lounging near at hand that an easy footpath wound along the side of the mountain and struck the highroad at the end of half an hour's walk, I immediately discovered and followed it. I saw beneath me in the dimness as I went the white highroad, with the carriage slowly beginning its ascent. Descending at last from the slope, I met the vehicle well on its way up the mountain, and motioned to the driver to stop. The poor Signora, haunted with the fear of interruption, thrust her pale face from the window. Seeing me, she stared an instant almost vacantly, and then passing her hand over her face broke into a glorious smile. Flinging open the carriage door from within, she held out her two hands in farewell.

'Give me your blessing,' she cried, 'and take mine! I had almost forgotten you. Love is selfish, Signore. But I should have remembered you later and cried with gratitude. My Ernesto will write to you. Give me your card—write me your address, there in the carriage lamp. No? As you please, then. Think of me kindly. And the young girl you marry—use her well—love her if only a little—it will be enough. We ask but a little, but we need that. Addio!' and she raised her two hands to her lips, seemed for an instant to exhale her whole soul upon her finger tips, and flung into the air a magnificent Italian kiss.

I returned along the winding footpath more slowly, a wiser, possibly a sadder man than a couple of hours before. I had entered Italy, I had tasted a sentiment, I had assisted at a drama. It was a good beginning. I found Bonifazio finishing his pipe before the inn. 'Well, well, Signore,' he cried, 'what does it all mean?'

'Aren't you enough of an Italian to guess?' I asked.

'Eh, eh, it's better to be an Inglese and to be told,' cried Bonifazio with a twinkle.

'You must sleep tonight with an ear open,' I said. 'A personage will arrive post-haste from Domo. Stop him if you can.'

Bonifazio scratched his head. 'If a late supper or an early breakfast will stop him!' he murmured. I looked deep into his little round eye, expecting to read there the recipe for the infusion of a sleeping potion into *café au lait*.

My room that night was close and hot, and my bed none of the best. I tossed about in a broken sleep. I dreamed that I was lying ill in a poor tavern at Naples, waiting, waiting with an aching heart, for the arrival from the Baths of Lucca of a certain young lady, who had been forced by her mother, Mrs. B. of Philadelphia, into a cruel marriage with a wealthy Tuscan *contadino*. At last I seemed to hear a great noise without and a step on the stairs; through the opened door rushed in my *promessa sposa*. Her blue eyes were bright with tears, and she wore a flounced black dress trimmed with crimson silk. The next moment she was kneeling at my bedside crying, 'Ernesto, Ernesto!' At this point I awoke into the early morning. The noise of horses and wheels and voices came up from outside. I sprang from my bed and stepped to my open window. The huge, high-piled, yellow diligence from Domo d'Ossola had halted before the inn. The door of the *coupé* was open; from the aperture half emerged the Personage. 'A peasant,' she had called him, but he was well *dicrotti*, though he *had* counted his *lire* and taken the diligence. He struck me as of an odd type for an Italian: dark sandy hair, a little sandy moustache, waxed at the ends, and sandy whiskers *à l'anglaise*. He had a broad face, a large nose, and a small keen eye, without any visible brows. He wore a yellow silk handkerchief tied as a nightcap about his head, and in spite of the heat he was very much muffled. On the steps stood Bonifazio, cap in hand, smiling and obsequious.

'Is there a lady here?' demanded the gentleman from the *coupé*. 'A lady alone—good-looking—with little luggage?'

'No lady, Signore,' said Bonifazio. 'Alas! I have an empty house. If *eccellenza* would like to descend——'

'Have you had a lady—yesterday, last night? Don't lie.'

'We had three, *eccellenza*, a week ago—three Scotch ladies going to Baveno. Nay, three days since we had a *prima donna* on her way to Milan.'

'Damn your Scotch *prima donna*!' said the other. 'Have you had my wife?'

'The wife of *eccellenza*? Save the ladies I mention, we have had neither wife nor maid. Would *eccellenza* like a cup of coffee?'

'*Sangue di Dio!*' was *eccellenza*'s sole response. The *coupé* door closed with a slam, the conductor mounted, the six horses started, and the great mountain coach rolled away.

Master Eustace

[First appeared in the *Galaxy*, vol. xii (November 1871), pp. 595–612. The tale was revised and reprinted in volume iii of *Stories Revived* (1885).]

HAVING HANDED ME MY CUP OF TEA, SHE PROCEEDED TO make her own; an operation she performed with a delicate old-maidish precision I delighted to observe.

The story is not my own—she then began—but that of persons with whom for a time I was intimately connected. I have led a quiet life. This is my only romance—and it's the romance of others. When I was a young woman of twenty-two my poor mother died, after a long, weary illness, and I found myself obliged to seek a new home. Making a home requires time and money. I had neither to spare, so I advertised for a 'situation', rating my accomplishments modestly, and asking rather for kind treatment than high wages. Mrs. Garnyer immediately answered my advertisement. She offered me a fair salary and a peaceful asylum. I was to teach her little boy the rudiments of my slender stock of sciences and to make myself generally useful. Something in her tone and manner assured me that in accepting this latter condition I was pledging myself to no very onerous servitude, and I never found reason to repent of my bargain. I had always valued my freedom before all things, and it seemed to me that in trading it away even partially I was surrendering a priceless treasure; but Mrs. Garnyer made service easy. I liked her from the first, and I doubt that she ever fairly measured my fidelity and affection. She knew that she could trust me, and she always spoke of me as 'a good creature'; but she never estimated the trouble I saved her, or the little burdens I lifted from her pretty, feeble shoulders. Both in her position and her person there was something singularly appealing. She was in those days—indeed she always remained—a very pretty little woman. But she had grace even more than beauty. She was young, and looked even younger than her years; slight, light of tread and of gesture, though not at all rapid (for in all her movements there was a kind of pathetic morbid languor), and fairer, whiter, purer in complexion than any woman I have seen. She reminded me of a sketch from which the 'shading' has been omitted. She had her shadows indeed, as well as her lights; but they were all turned inward. She might have seemed compounded of the airy substance of lights and shadows. Nature in making her had left out that wholesome leaden ballast of will, of logic, of worldly zeal, with which we are all more or less weighted. Experience, however, had given her a burden to carry; she was evidently sorrow-laden. She shifted the cruel weight from shoulder to shoulder, she ached and sighed under it, and in the depths of her sweet natural smile you saw it pressing the tears from her soul. Mrs. Garnyer's trouble, I confess, was in my eyes an added charm. I was desperately fond of a bit of romance, and as I was plainly never to have one of my own, I made the most of my neighbour's. This secret sadness of hers would have covered more sins than I ever had to forgive her. At first, naturally, I connected her unavowed sorrow with the death of her husband; but as time went on, I found reason to believe that there had been little love between the pair. She had married against her will. Mr. Garnyer was fifteen years her senior, and, as she frankly intimated, coarsely and cruelly dissipated. Their married life had lasted but three years, and had come to an end to her great and obvious relief. Had he done her while it lasted some irreparable wrong? I fancied so; she was like a garden rose with half its petals plucked. He had left her with diminished means, though her property (mostly her own) was still ample for her needs. These, with those of her son, were extremely simple. To certain little luxuries she was obstinately attached; but her manner of life was so monotonous and frugal that she must have spent but a fraction of her income. It was her single son—the heir of her hopes, the apple of her eye—that she entrusted to my care. He was five years old, and she had taught him his letters—a great feat, she seemed to think; she was as proud of it as if she had invented the alphabet for the occasion. She had called him Eustace, for she meant that he should have the best of everything—the prettiest clothes, the prettiest playthings, and the prettiest name. He was himself as pretty as his name, though but little like his mother. He was slight like her, but far more nervous and decided, and he had neither her features nor her colouring. Least of all had he her expression. Mrs. Garnyer's attitude was one of tender, pensive sufferance modified by hopes— a certain half-mystical hope which seemed akin to religion, but which was not all religion, for the heaven she dreamed of was lodged here below. The boy from his early childhood wore an air of defiance and authority. He was not one to wait for things, good or evil, but to snatch boldly at the one sort and snap his fingers at the other. He had a pale, dark skin, not altogether healthy in tone; a mass of fine brown hair, which seemed given him just to emphasize by its dancing sweep the petulant little nods and shakes of his head; and a deep, wilful, malicious eye. His eyes told me from the first that I should have no easy work with him; and in spite of a vast expense of tact and tenderness, no easy work it turned out to be. His wits were so quick, however, and his imagination so lively, that I gradually managed to fill out his mother's meagre little programme of study. This had been drawn up with a sparing hand; her only fear was of his being overworked. The poor lady had but a dim conception of what a man of the world is expected to know. She thought, I believe, that with his handsome face, his handsome property, and his doting mother, he would need to know little more than how to sign that pretty name of Eustace to replies to invitations to dinners. I wonder now that with her constant interference I contrived to set the child intellectually on his legs. Later, when he had a tutor, I received a compliment for my perseverance.

The truth is, I became fond of him; his very imperfections fascinated me. He would soon enough have to take his chance of the world's tolerance, and society would cease to consist for him of a couple of coaxing women. I told Mrs. Garnyer that there was never an easier child to spoil, and that those caressing hands of hers would sow a crop of formidable problems for future years. But Mrs. Garnyer was utterly incapable of taking a rational view of matters, or of sacrificing today to tomorrow; and her folly was the more incurable as it was founded on a strange, moonshiny little principle—a crude, passionate theory that love, love, pure love is the sum and substance of maternal duty; and that the love which reasons and exacts and denies is cruel and wicked and hideous. 'I know you think I'm a silly goose,' she said, 'and not fit to have a child at all. But you're wrong—I promise you you're wrong. I'm very reasonable, I'm very patient; I have a great deal to bear—more than you know—and I bear it very well. But one can't be always on the stretch—always hard and wise and good. In some things one must break down and be one's poor, natural, lonely self. Eustace can't turn out wrong; it's impossible; it would be too cruel. You mustn't say it nor hint it. I shall do with him as my heart bids me; he's all I have; he consoles me.'

My notions perhaps were a little old-fashioned; but surely it will never altogether go out of fashion to teach a child that he is not to have the moon by crying for it. Now Eustace had a particular fancy for the moon—for everything bright and inaccessible and absurd. His will was as sharp as a steel spring, and it was vain to attempt to bend it or break it. He had an indefeasible conviction that he was number one among men; and if he had been born in the purple, as they say, of some far-off Eastern court, or the last consummate fruit of a shadowy line of despots, he couldn't have been more closely curtained in this superb illusion. I pierced it here and there as roughly as I dared; but his mother's light fingers speedily repaired my punctures. The poor child had no sense of justice. He had the graceful virtues, but not the legal ones. He could condescend, he could forgive, he could permit this, that, and the other, with due leave asked; but he couldn't endure the hint of conflicting right. Poor puny little mortal, sitting there wrapped in his golden mist, listening to the petty trickle of his conscious favour and damming it—a swelling fountain of privileges! He could love, love passionately; but he was so jealous and exacting that his love cost you very much more than it was worth. I found it no sinecure to possess the confidence I had striven so cunningly to obtain. He fancied it a very great honour that he should care to harness me up as his horse, to throw me his ball by the hour, to have me joggle with him (sitting close to the middle) on the see-saw till my poor bones ached. Nevertheless, in this frank, childish arrogance there was an almost irresistible charm, and I was absurdly flattered by enjoying his favour. Poor me! at twenty-three I was his first 'conquest'—the first in a long list, as I believe it came to be. If he demanded great licence, he used it with a peculiar grace of his own, and he admitted the corresponding obligation of being clever and brilliant. As a child even, he seemed to be in a sort of occult sympathy with the picturesque. His talents were excellent, and teaching him, whatever it may have been, was at least not dull work. It was indeed less to things really needful than to the luxuries of learning that he took most kindly. He had an excellent ear for music, and though he never fairly practised, he turned off an air as neatly as you could have wished. In this he resembled his mother, who was a natural musician. She, however, was always at the piano, and whenever I think of her in those early years, I see her sitting before it musingly, half sadly, with her pretty head on one side, her fair braids thrust behind her ears— ears from which a couple of small but admirable diamonds were never absent—and her white hands wandering over the notes, seeking vaguely for an air which they seemed hardly to dare to remember. Eustace had an insatiable appetite for stories, though he was one of the coolest and most merciless of critics. I can fancy him now at my knee with his big, superbly-expectant eyes fastened on my lips, demanding more wonders and more, till my poor little short-winded invention had to cry mercy for its impotence. Do my best, I could never startle him; my giants were never big enough and my fairies never small enough, and my enchanters, my prisoners, my castles never on the really grand scale of his own imaginative needs. I felt pitifully prosaic. At last he would always open his wilful little mouth and gape in my face with a dreadfully dry want of conviction. I felt flattered when by chance I had pleased him, for, by a precocious instinct, he knew tinsel from gold. 'Look here,' he would say, 'you're dreadfully ugly; what makes you so ugly? Your nose is so big at the end.' (You needn't protest; I *was* ugly. Like most very plain women, I have improved with time.) Of course I used to rebuke him for his rudeness, though I secretly thanked it, for it taught me a number of things. Once he said something, I forget what, which made me burst into tears. It was the first time, and the last; for I found that, instead of stirring his pity, tears only moved his contempt, and apparently a kind of cynical, physical disgust. The best way was to turn the tables on him by pretending to be cool and indifferent and superior. In that case he himself would condescend to tears—bitter, wrathful tears. Then you had perhaps gained nothing, but you had lost nothing. In every other case you had.

Of course these close relations lasted but a couple of years. I had made him very much wiser than myself; he was growing tall and boyish and terribly inquisitive. My poor little stories ceased to have any illusion for him; and he would spend hours lying on his face on the carpet, kicking up his neat little legs and poring over the 'Arabian Nights', the 'Fairy Queen', the dozen prime enchanters of childhood. My advice would have been to pack him off to school; but I might as well have asked his mother to send him to the penitentiary. He was to be educated *en prince*; he was to have a teacher to himself. I thought sympathetically of the worthy pedagogue who was to enjoy Eustace without concurrence. But such a one was easily found—in fact, he was found three times over. Three private tutors came and went successively. They fell in love, categorically, with Mrs. Garnyer. Their love indeed she might have put up with; but unhappily, unlike Viola, they told their love—by letter—with an offer of their respective hands. Their letters were different, but to Mrs. Garnyer their hands were all alike, and alike distasteful. 'The horrid creatures!' was her invariable commentary. 'I wouldn't speak to them for the world. My dear, you must do it.' And I, who had never declined an offer on my own account, went to work in this wholesale fashion for my friend! You will say that young as she was, pretty, independent, lonely, Mrs. Garnyer would have looked none the worse for a spice of coquetry. Nay, in her own eyes, she would have been hideous. Her greatest charm for me was a brave little passion of scorn for this sort of levity, and indeed a general contempt for cheap sentimental effects. It was as if, from having drunk at the crystal head-spring, she had lost her taste for standing water. She was absolutely indifferent to attention; in fact, she seemed to shrink from it. She hadn't a trace of personal vanity; she was even without visible desire to please. Unfortunately, as you see, she pleased in spite of herself. As regards love, she had an imposing array of principles; on this one point her floating imagination found anchorage. 'It's either a passion,' she said, 'or it's nothing. You can know it by being willing to give up everything for it—name and fame, past and future, this world and the next. Do you keep back a feather's weight of tenderness or trust? Then you're not in love. You must risk everything, for you get everything—if you're happy. I can't understand a woman trifling with love. They talk about the unpardonable sin; that's it, it seems to me. Do you know the word in the language I most detest? *Flirtation.* Poh! it makes me ill.' When Mrs. Garnyer uttered this hint of an esoteric doctrine, her clear blue eyes would become clouded with the gathered mists of memory. In this matter she understood herself and meant what she said.

Defiant as she was of admiration, she saw little of the world. She met her few friends but two or three times a year, and was without a single intimate. As time went on, she came to care more for me than for any one. When Eustace had outgrown my teaching, she insisted on my remaining in any capacity I chose—as housekeeper, companion, seamstress, guest; I might make my own terms. I became a little of each of these, and with the increasing freedom of our intercourse grew to regard her as a younger and weaker sister. I gave her, for what it was worth, my frankest judgment on all things. Her own confidence always stopped short of a certain point. A little curtain of reticence seemed always to hang between us. Sometimes I fancied it growing thinner and thinner, becoming almost transparent and revealing the figures behind it. Sometimes it seemed to move and flutter in the murmur of our talk, so that in a moment it might drop or melt away into air. But it was a magical web; it played a hundred tormenting tricks, and year after year it hung in its place. Of course this inviolate mystery stirred my curiosity, but I can't say more for the disinterested tenderness I felt for Mrs. Garnyer than that it never unduly irritated it. I lingered near the door of her Blue-Beard's chamber, but I never peeped through the keyhole. She was a poor lady with a secret; I took her into my heart, secret and all. She proclaimed that her isolation was her own choice, and pretended to be vastly content that society let her so well alone. She made her widowhood serve as a motive for her lonesome days, and declared that her boy's education amply filled them. She was a widow, however, who never of her own accord mentioned her husband's name, and she wore her weeds very lightly. She was very fond of white, and for six months of the year was rarely seen in a dark dress. Occasionally, on certain fixed days, she would flame forth in some old-fashioned piece of finery from a store which she religiously preserved, and would flash about the house in rose-colour or blue. One day, her boy's birthday, she kept with fantastic solemnity. It fell in the middle of September. On this occasion she would put on a faded ball-dress, overload herself with jewels and trinkets, and dress her hair with flowers. Eustace, too, she would trick out in a suit of crimson velvet, and in this singular guise the pair would walk with prodigious gravity about the garden and up and down the avenue. Every now and then she would stoop and give him a convulsive hug. The child himself seemed to feel the magnitude of this festival, and played his part with precocious discretion. He would appear at dusk with the curl still in his hair, his velvet trousers unstained, his ruffles uncrumpled. In the evening the coachman let off rockets in the garden; we feasted on ice-cream, and a bottle of champagne was sent to the kitchen. No wonder Master Eustace took on the graces of an heir-apparent! Once, I remember, the mother and son were overtaken in their festal promenade by some people who had come to live in the neighbourhood, and who drove up rather officiously to leave their cards. They stared in amazement from the carriage window, and were told Mrs. Garnyer was not at home. A few days later we heard that Mrs. Garnyer was out of her mind; she had been found masquerading in her grounds with her little boy, in the most indecent costume. From time to time she received an invitation, and occasionally she accepted one. When she went out she deepened her mourning, but she always came home in a fret. 'It is the last house I will go to,' she declared, as I helped her to undress. 'People's neglect I can bear, and thank them for it; but Heaven deliver me from their kindness! I won't be patronized—I won't, I won't! Shall I, my boy? We'll wait till you grow up, shan't we, my darling? Then his poor little mother shan't be patronized, shall she, my brave little man?' The child was constantly dangling at his mother's skirts, and was seldom beyond the reach of some such passionate invocation.

A preceptor had at last been found of a less inflammable composition than the others—a worthy, elderly German of fair attainments, with a stout, sentimental wife—she gave music lessons in town—who monopolized his ardour. He was a mild, patient man—a nose of wax, as the saying is. A pretty nose it grew to be in Eustace's supple fingers! I'll answer for it that in all those years he never carried a point. I believe that, like me, he had begun with tears; but finding this an altogether losing game, he was content now to take off his spectacles, drop his head on one side, look imploringly at his pupil with his weak blue eyes, and then exhale his renunciation in a plaintive *Lieber Gott!* Under this discipline the boy bloomed like a flower. But it was to my sense a kind of hothouse growth. His tastes were sedentary, and he lived largely within doors. He kept a horse and took long lonely rides; but most of the time he spent lounging over a book, trifling at the piano, or fretting over a water-colour sketch, which he was sure to throw aside in disgust. One amusement he pursued with unwearying constancy; it was a sign of especial good humour, and I never knew it to fail him. He would sit for hours lounging in a chair, with his head thrown back and his legs extended, staring at vacancy, or what seemed to us so, but a vacancy filled with the silent revel of his fancy and the images it evoked. What was the substance of these beatific visions? The broad, happy life before him, the great world whose far-off murmur caressed his ear—the joys of consummate manhood—pleasure, suc-cess, prosperity—a kind of triumphant and transfigured egotism. His reveries swarmed with ideal shapes and transcendent delights; his handsome young face, his idle, insolent smile wore the cold re-flection of their brightness. His mother, after watching him for a while in these moods, would steal up behind him and kiss him softly on the forehead, as if to marry his sweet illusions to sweet reality. For my part, I wanted to divorce them. It was a sad pity, I thought, that desire and occasion in the lad's life played so deftly into each other's hands. I longed to spoil the game, to shuffle the cards afresh and give him a taste of bad luck. I felt as if between them—she by her measureless concessions, he by his consuming arrogance—they were sowing a crop of dragon's teeth. This sultry summer of youth couldn't last for ever, and I knew that the poor lady would be the first to suffer by a change of weather. He would turn some day in his passionate vanity and rend the gentle creature who had fed it with the delusive wine of her love. And yet he had a better angel as well as a worse. It was a marvel to see how this sturdy seraph tussled with the fiend, and, in spite of bruises and ruffled pinions, returned again and again to the onset. There were days when his generous, boyish gaiety—the natural sunshine of youth and intelligence—warmed our women's hearts to their depths and kindled our most trusting smiles. Me, as he grew older, he treated as a licenced old-time friend. I was the prince's jester. I used to tell him his truths, as the French say. He believed them just enough to feel an agreeable irritation in listening; for the rest, doubtless, they seemed as vague and remote as a croaking good-wife's gossip. There were moments, I think, when the eternal blue sky of his mother's temper wearied his capricious brain. At such times he would come and sprawl on the sofa near my little work-table, clipping my threads, mixing my spools, mislaying my various utensils, and criticising my work without reserve—chattering, gossip-

ing, complaining, boasting. With all his faults Eustace had one
sovereign merit—that merit without which even the virtues he lacked
lose half their charm : he was superbly frank. He was only too transparent. The light of truth played through his rank pretensions, and
against it they stood relieved in their hard tenacity, like young trees
against a sunset. He uttered his passions, and uttered them only too
loudly; you received ample notice of his vengeance. It came as a
matter of course; he never took it out in talk; but you were warned.

If these intense meditations of which I have spoken followed exclusively the vista of his personal fortunes, his conversation was
hardly more disinterested. It was altogether about himself—his
ambitions, his ailments, his dreams, his needs, his intentions. He
talked a great deal of his property, and, though he had a great aversion to figures, he knew the amount of his expectations before he
was out of jackets. He had a shrewd relish for luxury—and indeed,
as he respected pretty things and used them with a degree of tenderness which he by no means lavished upon animated objects, saving,
sparing, and preserving them, this seemed to me one of his most
human traits, though, I admit, an expensive virtue—and he promised
to spend his fortune in books and pictures, in art and travel. His
mother was imperiously appealed to to do the honours of his castles
in the air. She would look at him always with her doting smile, and
with a little glow of melancholy in her eyes—a faint tribute to some
shadowy chance that even her Eustace might reckon without his
host. She would shake her head tenderly, or lean it on his shoulder
and murmur, 'Who knows, who knows? It's perhaps as foolish, my
son, to try and forecast happiness as to attempt to take the measure
of misery. We know them each when they come. Whatever comes
to us, at all events, we shall meet it together.' Resting in this delicious
contact, with her arm round his neck and her cheek on his hair, she
would close her eyes in a kind of tremor of ecstasy. As I have never
had a son myself, I can speak of maternity but by hearsay; but I
feel as if I knew some of its secrets, as if I had gained from Mrs.
Garnyer a revelation of maternal passion. The perfect humility of
her devotion, indeed, seemed to me to point to some motive deeper
than vulgar motherhood. It looked like a kind of penance, a kind
of pledge. Had she done him some early wrong? Did she meditate
some wrong to come? Did she wish to purchase pardon for the past
or impunity for the future? One might have fancied from the lad's
calm relish of her incense—as if it were the fumes of some perfumed
chibouque palpitating lazily through his own lips—that he had a
comfortable sense of something to forgive. In fact, he had something
to forgive us all—our dullness, our vulgarity, our not guessing his

unuttered desires—the want of a supercelestial harmony between our wills and his. I fancied, however, that there were even moments when he turned dizzy on the cope of this awful gulf of his mother's self-sacrifice. Fixing his eyes, then, an instant to steady himself, he took comfort in the thought that she had ceased to suffer—her personal ambitions lay dead at the bottom. He could vaguely see them —distant, dim, motionless. It was to be hoped that no adventurous ghost of these shuffled passions would climb upwards to the light.

A frequent source of complaint with Eustace, when he had no more immediate displeasure, was that he had not known his father. He had formed a mental image of the late Mr. Garnyer which I am afraid hardly tallied at all points with the original. He knew that his father had been a man of pleasure, and he had painted his portrait in ideal hues. What a charming father—a man of pleasure! the boy thought, fancying that gentlemen of this stamp take their pleasure in the nursery. What pleasure they might have shared; what rides, what talks, what games, what adventures—what far other hours hours than those he passed in the deserted billiard-room (this had been one of Mr. Garnyer's pleasures) clicking the idle balls in the stillness. He learned to talk very early of (shaping his life on his father's.) What he had done his son would do. A dozen odds and ends which had belonged to Mr. Garnyer he carried to his room, where he arranged them on his mantel-shelf like relics on a high altar. When he had turned seventeen he began to smoke an old silver-mounted pipe which had his father's initials embossed on the bowl. 'It would be a great blessing,' he said as he puffed this pipe— it made him dismally sick, for he hated tobacco—'to have some man in the house. It's so fearfully womanish here. No one but you two and Hauff, and what's he but an old woman? Mother, why have you always lived in this way? What's the matter with you? You've got no *savoir vivre*. What are you blushing about? That comes of moping here all your days—that you blush for nothing. I don't want my mother to blush for anything or any one, not even for me. But I give you notice, I can stand it no longer. Now I'm seventeen, it's time I should see the world. I'm going to travel. My father travelled; he went all over Europe. There's a little French book upstairs, the poems of Parny—it's awfully French, too—with "Henry Garnyer, Paris, 1802", on the fly-leaf. I must go to Paris. I shan't go to college. I've never been to school. I want to be complete—privately educated altogether. Very few people are, here; it's quite a distinction. Besides, I know all I want to know. Hauff brought me out some college catalogues. They're absurd; he laughs at them. We did all that three years ago. I know more about books than most young fellows; what

I want is knowledge of the world. My father had it, and you haven't, mother. But he had plenty of taste, too. Hauff says that little edition of Parny is very rare. I shall bring home lots of such things. You'll see!' Mrs. Garnyer listened to such effusions of filial emulation in sad, distracted silence. I couldn't but pity her. She knew that her husband was no proper model for her child; yet she couldn't in decency turn his heart against his father's memory. She took refuge in that attitude of tremulous contemplation which committed her neither to condemnation of her husband nor to approval with her son.

She had recourse at this period, as I had known her to do before, to a friend attached to a mercantile house in India—an old friend, she had told me; 'in fact,' she had added, 'my only friend, a man to whom I am under immense obligations.' Once in six months there came to her from this distant benefactor a large square letter, heavily sealed and covered with foreign post-marks. I used to fancy it a kind of bulletin of advice for the coming half year. Advice about what? Her cares were so few, her habits so simple, that they offered scanty matter for discussion. But now, of course, came a packet of counsel as to Eustace's absence. I knew that she dreaded it; but since her oracle had spoken, she wore a brave face. She was certainly a devout postulant. She concealed from Eustace the extent of her dependence on this far-away adviser, for the boy would have resented such interference, even though it favoured his own schemes. She had always read her friend's letters in secret; this was the only practice of her life she failed to share with her son. Me she now for the first time admitted into her confidence. 'Mr. Cope strongly recommends my letting him go,' she said. 'He says it will make a man of him. He needs to rub against other men. I suppose at least,' she cried with her usual sweet fatuity, 'it will do other men no harm! Perhaps I don't love him as I ought, and that I must lose him awhile to learn to prize him. If I only get him back again! It would be monstrous that I shouldn't! But why are we cursed with these frantic woes and fears? It's a weary life!' She would have said more if she had known that it was not his departure but his return that was to be cruel.

The excellent Mr. Hauff was deemed too mild and infirm to cope with the hazards of travel; but a companion was secured in the person of his nephew, an amiable young German who claimed to possess erudition and discretion in equal manner. For a week before he left us Eustace was so serene and joyous of humour as to double his mother's sense of loss. 'I give her into your care,' he said to me. 'If anything happens to her, I shall hold you responsible. She is very woe-begone just now, but she'll cheer up yet. But, mother, you're not to be too cheerful, mind. You're not to forget me an instant. If you do, I'll never forgive you. I insist on being missed. There's little enough merit in loving me when I'm here; I wish to be loved in my absence.' For many weeks after he left, he might have been satisfied. His mother wandered about like a churchyard ghost keeping watch near a buried treasure. When his letters began to come, she read them over a dozen times, and sat for hours with her eyes closed holding them in her hand. They were wretchedly meagre and hurried; but their very brevity gratified her. He was prosperous and happy, and could snatch but odd moments from his pleasure-taking.

One morning, after he had been away some three months, there came two letters, one from Eustace, the other from India, the latter very much in advance of its time. Mrs. Garnyer opened the Indian letter first. I was pouring out tea; I observed her from behind the urn. As her eyes ran over the pages she turned deadly pale; then raising her glance she met mine. Immediately her paleness turned to crimson. She rose to her feet and hurried out of the room, leaving Eustace's letter untouched on the table. This little fact was eloquent, and my curiosity was aroused. Later in the day it was partially satisfied. She came to me with a singular conscious look—the look of a sort of oppression of happiness—and announced that Mr. Cope was coming home. He had obtained release from his engagements in India, and would arrive in a fortnight. She uttered herewith no words of rejoicing, but I fancied her joy was of the unutterable sort. As the days elapsed, however, her emotion betrayed itself in a restless, aimless flutter of movement, so intense as to seem to me almost painful. She roamed about the house singing to herself, gazing out of the windows, shifting the chairs and tables, smoothing the curtains, trying vaguely to brighten the faded look of things. Before every mirror she paused and inspected herself, with that frank audacity of pretty women which I have always envied, tucking up a curl of her blonde hair or smoothing a crease in those muslins which she always kept so fresh. Of Eustace for the moment she rarely spoke; the boy's prediction had not been so very much amiss. Who was this wonderful Mr. Cope, this mighty magician?

I very soon learned. He arrived on the day he had fixed, and took up his lodging in the house. From the moment I looked at him, I felt that here was a man I should like. My poor unflattered soul, I suppose, was won by the kindness of his greeting. He had often heard of me, he said; he knew how good a friend I had been to Mrs. Garnyer; he begged to bespeak a proportionate friendship for himself. I felt as if I were amply thanked for my years of household zeal. But in spite of this pleasant assurance, I had a sense of being for the moment altogether *de trop*. He was united to his friend by a closer bond than I had suspected. I left them alone with their mutual secrets and effusions, and confined myself to my own room; though indeed I had noticed between them a sort of sentimental intelligence, so deep and perfect that many words were exchanged without audible speech. Mrs. Garnyer underwent a singular change; I seemed to know her now for the first time. It was as if she had flung aside a veil which muffled her tones and blurred her features. There was a new decision in her tread, a deeper meaning in her smile. So, at thirty-eight her girlhood had come back to her! She was as full of blushes and random prattle and foolish falterings for very pleasure as a young bride. Upon Mr. Cope the years had set a more ineffaceable seal. He was a man of forty-five, but you would have given him ten years more. He had that look which I have always liked of people who have lived in hot climates, a bronzed complexion, and a cool deliberate gait, as if he had learned to think twice before moving. He was tall and lean, yet extremely massive in shape, like a stout man emaciated by circumstances. His hair was thin and perfectly white, and he wore a grizzled moustache. He dressed in loose light-coloured garments of those fine Eastern stuffs. I had a singular impression of having seen him before, but I could never say when or where. He was extremely deaf—so deaf that I had to force my voice; though I observed that Mrs. Garnyer easily made him hear by speaking slowly and looking at him. He had peculiarly that patient appealing air which you find in very deaf persons less frequently than in the blind, but which has with them an even deeper eloquence, enforced as it is by the normal pathos of the eye. It has an especially mild dignity where, as in Mr. Cope, it overlies a truly masculine mind. He had been obliged to make good company of himself, and the glimpses that one got of this blessed fellowship in stillness were of a kind to make one long to share it. But with others, too, he was a charming talker, though he was obliged to keep the talk in his own hands. He took your response for granted with a kind of conciliating *bonhomie*, guessed with a glance at your opinion, and phrased it usually more wittily than you would have done.

For ten years I had been pitying Mrs. Garnyer; it was odd to find myself envying her. Patient waiting is no loss; at last her day had come. I had always rather wondered at her patience; it was spiced with a logic all its own. But she had lived by precept and example, by chapter and verse; for *his* sake it was easy to be wise. I say for 'his' sake, because as a matter of course I now connected her visitor with that undefined secret which had been one of my earliest impressions of Mrs. Garnyer. Mr. Cope's presence renewed my memory of it. I fitted the key to the lock, but on coming to open the casket I was disappointed to find that the best of the mystery had evaporated. Mr. Cope, I imagined, had been her first and only love. Her parents had frowned on him and forced her into a marriage with poor dissolute Mr. Garnyer—a course the more untender as he had already spent half his own property and was likely to make sad havoc with his wife's. He had a high social value, which the girl's own family, who were plain enough people to have had certain primitive scruples in larger measure, deemed a compensation for his vices. The discarded lover, thinking she had not resisted as firmly as she might, embarked for India, and there, half in spite, half in despair, married as sadly amiss as herself. He had trifled with his happiness; he lived to repent. His wife lived as well to perpetuate his misery; it was my belief that she had only recently died, and that this event was the occasion of his return. When he arrived he wore a weed on his hat; the next day it had disappeared. Reunion had come to them in the afternoon of life, when the tricks and graces of passion are no longer becoming; but when these have spent themselves something of passion still is left, and this they were free to enjoy. They had begun to enjoy it with the chastened zeal of which I caught the aroma. Such was my reading of the riddle. Right or not, at least it made sense.

I had promised Eustace to write to him, and one afternoon as I sat alone, well pleased to have a theme, I despatched him a long letter full of the praises of Mr. Cope, and by implication of the echo of his mother's happiness. I wished to anticipate his possible suspicions and reconcile him with the altered situation. But after I had posted my letter, it seemed to me that I had spoken too frankly. I doubted whether, even amid the wholesome novelty of travel, he had unlearned the old trick of jealousy. Jealousy surely would have been quite misplaced, for Mr. Cope's affection for his hostess embraced her boy in its ample scope. He regretted the lad's absence; he manifested the kindliest interest in everything that spoke of him; he turned over his books, he looked at his sketches, he examined and compared the half dozen portraits which the fond mother had caused to be executed at various stages of his growth. One hot day, when poor old Mr. Hauff travelled out from town for news of his pupil, he made a point of being introduced and of shaking his hand. The old man stayed to dinner, and on Mr. Cope's proposition we drank the boy's health in brimming glasses. The old German of course wept profusely; it was Eustace's mission to make people cry. I fancied too I saw a tear on Mr. Cope's lid. The cup of his contentment was full; at a touch it overflowed. On the whole, however, he took this bliss of reunion more quietly than his friend. He was a melancholy man. He had the air of one for whom the moral of this fable of life has greater charms than the plot, and who has made up his mind to ask no favours of destiny. When he met me, he used to smile gently, frankly, saying little; but I had a vast relish for his smile. It seemed to say much—to murmur, 'Receive my compliments. You and I are a couple of tested souls; we understand each other. We are not agog with the privilege of existence, like charity children on a picnic. We have had, each of us, to live for years without the thing we once fancied gave life its only value. We have tasted of bondage, and patience, taken up as a means, has grown grateful as an end. It has cured us of eagerness.' So easily it gossiped, the smile of our guest. No wonder I liked it.

One evening, a month after his advent, Mrs. Garnyer came to me with a strange, embarrassed smile. 'I have something to tell you,' she said; 'something that will surprise you. Do you consider me a very old woman? I am old enough to be wiser, you'll say. But I've never been so wise as today. I'm engaged to Mr. Cope. There! make the best of it. I have no apologies to make to any one,' she went on with a kind of defiant manner. 'It's between ourselves. If we suit each other, it's no one's business. I know what I'm about. He means to remain in this country; we should be constantly together and extremely intimate. As he says, I'm young enough to be—what do they call it?—compromised. Of course, therefore, I'm young enough to marry. It wil make no difference with you; you'll stay with me all the same. Who cares, after all, what I do? No one but Eustace, and he will thank me for giving him such a father. Ah, I shall do well by my boy!' she cried, clasping her hands with ecstasy. 'I shall do better than he knows. My property, it appears, is dreadfully entangled. Mr. Garnyer did as he pleased with it; I was given to him with my hands tied. Mr. Cope has been looking into it, and he tells me that it will be a long labour to restore order. I have been living all these years at the mercy of unprincipled strangers. But now I have given up everything to Mr. Cope. He'll drive the money-changers from the temple! It's a small reward to marry him. Eustace has no head for money matters; he only knows how to spend. For years now he needn't think of them. Mr. Cope is our providence. Don't be afraid; Eustace won't blaspheme! and at last he'll have a companion—the best, the wisest, the kindest. You know how he used to long for one—how tired he was of me and you. It will be a new life. Oh, I'm a happy mother—at last—at last! Don't look at me so hard; I'm a blushing bride, remember. Smile, laugh, kiss me. There! You're a good creature. I shall make my boy a present—the handsomest that ever was made! Poor Mr. Cope! I'm happier than he. I have had my boy all these years, and he has had none. He has the heart of a father. He has longed for a son. Do you know,' she added with a strange deepening of her smile, 'that I think he marries me as much for my son's sake as for my own? He marries me at all events, boy and all!' This speech was uttered with a forced and hurried animation which betrayed the effort to cheat herself into pure enthusiasm. The matter was not quite so simple as she tried to believe. Nevertheless, I was deeply pleased, and I kissed her in genuine sympathy. The more I thought of it the better I liked the marriage. It relieved me personally of a burdensome sense of ineffectual care, and it filled out solidly a kind of defenceless breach which had always existed on the worldly face of Mrs. Garnyer's position. Moreover, it promised to be full of wholesome profit for Eustace. It was a pity that Eustace had but a slender relish for wholesome profit. I ventured to hope, however, that his high esteem for his father's memory had been, at bottom, the expression of a need for counsel and support, and of a capacity to grant respect if there should be something of inspiration in it. Yet I took the liberty of suggesting to Mrs. Garnyer that she perhaps counted too implicitly on her son's concurrence; that he was always in opposition; that a margin should be left for his possible jealousy. Of course I was called a suspicious wretch for my pains.

'For what do you take him?' she cried. 'He'll thank me on his knees. I shall place them face to face. Eustace has instinct! A word to the wise, says the proverb. I know what I'm about.'

She knew it, I think, hardly as well as she declared. I had deemed it my duty to make a modest little speech of congratulation to the bridegroom elect. He blushed—somewhat to my surprise—but he answered me with a grave, grateful bow. He was preoccupied; Mrs. Garnyer was of a dozen different minds about her wedding-day. I had taken for granted that they would wait for Eustace's return; but I was somewhat startled on learning that Mr. Cope disapproved of further delay. They had waited twenty years! Mrs. Garnyer told me that she had not announced the news to Eustace. She wished it to be a 'surprise'. She seemed, however, not altogether to believe in her surprise. Poor lady! she had made herself a restless couch. One evening, coming into the library, I found Mr. Cope pleading his cause. For the first time I saw him excited. This hint of autumnal ardour was very becoming. He turned appealingly to me. 'You have great authority with this lady,' he said. 'Plead my case. Are we people to care for Mrs. Grundy? Has she been so very civil to us? We don't marry to please her; I don't see why she should arrange the wedding. Mrs. Garnyer has no *trousseau* to buy, no cards to send. Indeed, I think any more airs and graces are rather ridiculous. They don't belong to our years. There's little Master Grundy, I know,' he went on, smiling—'a most honourable youth! But I'll take charge of him. I should like vastly, of course, to have him at the wedding; but one of these days I shall make up for the breach of ceremony by punctually attending his own.' It was only an hour before this, as it happened, that I had received Eustace's answer to my letter. It was brief and hasty, but he had found time to insert some such words as this: 'I don't at all thank you for your news of Mr. Cope. I knew that my mother only wanted a chance to forget me and console herself, as they say in France. Demonstrative mothers always do. I'm like Hamlet—I don't approve of mothers consoling themselves. Mr. Cope may be an excellent fellow—I've no doubt he is; but I do hope he will have made his visit by the time I get back. The house isn't large enough for both of us. You'll find me a bigger man than when I left home. I give you warning. I've got a roaring black moustache, and I'm proportionately fiercer.' I said nothing about this letter. A week later they were married. The time will always be memorable to me, apart from this matter of my story, from the intense and overwhelming heat which then prevailed. It had lasted several days when the wedding took place; it bade fair to continue unbroken. The ceremony was performed by the little old Episcopal clergyman whose ministrations Mrs. Garnyer had regularly attended, and who had always given her a vague parochial countenance. His sister, a mature spinster who wore her hair cut short, and called herself 'strong-minded', and, thus qualified, had made overtures to Mrs. Garnyer—this lady and myself were the only witnesses. The marriage had nothing of a festive air; it seemed a grave sacrifice to the unknown god. Mrs. Garnyer was very much oppressed by the heat; in the vestibule, on leaving the church, she fainted. They had arranged to go for a week to the seaside, to a place they had known of old. When she had revived we placed her in the carriage, and they immediately started. I, of course, remained in charge of the empty house, vastly envying them their seaside breezes.

On the morning after the wedding, sitting alone in the darkened library, I heard a rapid tread in the hall. My first thought of course was burglars—my second of Eustace. In a moment he came striding into the room. His step, his glance, his whole outline foretold trouble. He was amazingly changed, and all for the better. He seemed taller, older, manlier. He was bronzed by travel and dressed with great splendour. The moustache he had mentioned, though but a slender thing as yet, gave him, to my eye, a formidable foreign look. He gave me no greeting.

'Where's my mother?' he cried.

My heart rose to my throat; his tone seemed to put us horribly in the wrong. 'She's away—for a day,' I said. 'But you'—and I took his hand—'pray where have you dropped from?'

'From New York, from shipboard, from Southampton. Is this the way my mother receives me?'

'Why, she never dreamed you were coming.'

'She got no letter? I wrote from New York.'

'Your letter never came. She left town yesterday, for a week.'

He looked at me hard. 'How comes it you're not with her?'

'I am not needed. She has—she has——' But I faltered.

'Say it—say it!' he cried; and he stamped his foot. 'She has a companion.'

'Mr. Cope went with her,' I said, in a still small voice. I was ashamed of my tremor, I was outraged by his imperious manner, but the thought of worse to come unnerved me.

'Mr. Cope—ah!' he answered, with an indefinable accent. He looked about the room with a kind of hungry desire to detect some invidious difference as a trace of Mr. Cope's passage. Then flinging himself into a chair, 'What infernal heat!' he went on. 'What a hideous climate you've got here! Do bring me a glass of water.'

I brought him his glass, and stood before him as he quickly drank it. 'Don't think you're not welcome,' I ventured to say, 'if I ask what has brought you home so suddenly.'

He gave me another hard look over the top of his glass. 'A suspicion. It's none too soon. Tell me what is going on between my mother and Mr. Cope.'

'Eustace,' I said, 'before I answer you, let me remind you of the respect which under all circumstances you owe your mother.'

He sprang from his chair. 'Respect! I'm right then. They mean to marry! Speak!' And as I hesitated, 'You needn't speak,' he cried. 'I see it in your face. Thank God I'm here!'

His violence roused me. 'If you have a will to enforce in the matter,' I said, 'you are indeed none too soon. You're too late. Your mother is married.' I spoke passionately, but in a moment I repented of my words.

'MARRIED!' the poor boy shouted. 'Married, you say!' He turned deadly pale and stood staring at me with his mouth wide open. Then, trembling in all his limbs, he dropped into a chair. For some moments he was silent, gazing at me with fierce stupefaction, overwhelmed by the treachery of fate. 'Married!' he went on. 'When,

where, how? Without me—without notice—without shame! And
you stood and watched it, as you stand and tell me now! I called
you friend!' he cried, with the bitterest reproach. 'But if my mother
betrays me, what can I expect of *you*? Married!' he repeated. 'Is the
devil in it? I'll unmarry her! When—when—when?' And he seized
me by the arm.

'Yesterday, Eustace. I entreat you to be calm.'

'Calm? Is it a case for calmness? *She* was calm enough—that she
couldn't wait for her son!' He flung aside the hand I had laid upon
his to soothe him, and began a furious march about the room. 'What
has come to her? Is she mad? Has she lost her head, her heart, her
memory—all that made her mine? You're joking—come, it's a
horrible dream?' And he stopped before me, glaring through fiery
tears. 'Did she hope to keep it a secret? Did she hope to hide away
her husband in a cupboard? Her husband! And I—I—I what has she
done with me? Where am I in this devil's game? Standing here crying like a schoolboy for a cut finger—for the bitterest of disappoint-
ments! She has blighted my life—she has blasted my rights. She
has insulted me—dishonoured me. Am I a man to treat in that
fashion? Am I a man to be made light of? Brought up as a
flower and trampled as a weed! Bound in cotton and steeped in
vitriol! You needn't speak'—I had tried, for pity, to remonstrate.
'You can say nothing but bald folly. There's nothing to be said but
this—that I'm *insulted*. Do you understand?' He uttered the word
with a concentrated agony of vanity. 'I guessed it from the first. I
knew it was coming. Mr. Cope—Mr. Cope—always Mr. Cope. It
poisoned my journey—it poisoned my pleasure—it poisoned Italy.
You don't know what that means. But what matter, so long as it
has poisoned my home? I held my tongue—I swallowed my rage; I
was patient, I was gentle, I forbore. And for this! I could have
damned him with a word! At the seaside, hey? Enjoying the breezes
—splashing in the surf—picking up shells. It's idyllic, it's ideal—great
heavens, it's fabulous, it's monstrous! It's well she's not here. I don't
answer for myself. Yes, madam, stare, stare, wring your hands! You
see an angry man, an outraged man, but a man, mind you! He
means to act as one.'

This sweeping torrent of unreason I had vainly endeavoured to
arrest. He pushed me aside, strode out of the room, and went bounding up stairs to his own chamber, where I heard him close the door
with a terrible bang and turn the key. My hope was that his passion
would expend itself in this first explosion; I was glad to bear the
brunt of it. But I deemed it my duty to communicate with his
mother. I wrote her a hurried line: 'Eustace is back—very ill. Come

home.' This I entrusted to the coachman, with injunctions to carry it in person to the place of her sojourn. I believed that if she started immediately on the receipt of it, she might reach home late at night. Those were days of private conveyances. Meanwhile I did my best to pacify the poor young man. There was something terrible and portentous in his rage; he seemed absolutely rabid. This was the sweet compliance, the fond assent, on which his mother had counted; this was the 'surprise'! I went repeatedly to his chamber door with soft speeches and urgent prayers and offers of luncheon, of wine, of vague womanly comfort. But there came no answer but shouts and imprecations, and finally a sullen silence. Late in the day I heard him from the window order the gardener to saddle his horse; and in a short time he came stamping down stairs, booted and spurred, pale, dishevelled, with bloodshot eyes. 'Where are you going,' I said, 'in this awful heat?'

'To ride—ride—ride myself cool!' he cried. 'There's nothing so hot as my rage!' And in a moment he was in the saddle and bounding out of the gate. I went up to his room. Its wild disorder bore vivid evidence of the tumult of his temper. A dozen things were strewn broken on the floor; old letters were lying crumpled and torn; I was sickened by the sight of a pearl necklace, snatched from his gaping valise, and evidently purchased as a present to his mother, ground into fragments on the carpet as if by his boot-heels. His father's relics were standing in a row untouched on the mantel-shelf, save for a couple of pistols mounted with his initials in silver, which were tossed upon the table. I made a brave effort to thrust them into a drawer and turn the key, but to my eternal regret I was afraid to touch them. Evening descended and wore away; but neither Eustace nor his mother returned. I sat gloomily enough on the verandah, listening for wheels or hoofs. Towards midnight a carriage rattled over the gravel; my friend descended with her husband at the door. She fluttered into my arms with a kind of shrinking yet impetuous dread. 'Where is he—how is he?' she cried.

I was spared the pain of answering, for at the same moment I heard Eustace's horse clatter into the stable-yard. He had rapidly dismounted and passed into the house by one of the side windows, which opened from the piazza into the drawing-room. There the lamps were lighted. I led in my companions. Eustace had crossed the threshold of the window; the lamp-light fell upon him, relieving him against the darkness. His mother with a shriek flung herself towards him, but in an instant with a deeper cry she stopped short, pressing her hand to her heart. He had raised his hand, and, with a gesture which had all the spiritual force of a blow, he had cast her off. 'Ah,

my son, my son!' she cried with a piteous moan, and looking round
at us in wild bewilderment.

'I'm not your son!' said the boy in a voice half stifled with passion.
'I give you up! You're not my mother! Don't touch me! You've
cheated me—you've betrayed me—you've *insulted* me!' In this mad
peal of imprecations, it was still the note of vanity which rang
clearest.

I looked at Mr. Cope. He was deadly pale. He had seen the lad's
gesture; he was unable to hear his words. He sat down in the nearest
chair and eyed him wonderingly. I hurried to his poor wife's relief.
She seemed smitten with a sudden tremor, a deadly chill. She clasped
her hands, but she could barely find her voice. 'Eustace—my boy—
my darling—my own—do you know what you say? Listen, listen,
Eustace. It's all for you—that you should love me more. I've done
my best. I seem to have been hasty, but hasty to do for you—to do
for you——' Her strength deserted her; she burst into tears. 'He
curses me—he denies me!' she cried. 'He has killed me!'

'Cry, cry!' Eustace retorted; 'cry as I've been crying! But don't be
falser than you have been. That you couldn't even wait! And you
prate of my happiness! Is my happiness in a broken home—in a
disputed heart—in a bullying stepfather! You've chosen him big
and strong! Cry your eyes out—you're no mother of mine.'

'He's killing me—he's killing me,' groaned his mother. 'O
Heaven! if I dared to speak, I should kill *him*!' She turned to her
husband. 'Go to him—go to him!' she cried. 'He's ill, he's mad—
he doesn't know what he says. Take his hand in yours—look at him,
soothe him, heal him. It's the hot weather,' she rambled on. 'Let him
feel your touch! Eustace, Eustace, be healed!'

Poor Mr. Cope had risen to his feet, passing his handkerchief over
his forehead, on which the perspiration stood in great drops. He went
slowly towards the young man, bending his eyes on him half in
entreaty, half in command. Before him he stopped and frankly
held out his hand. Eustace eyed him defiantly from head to foot—
him and his proffered friendship, enforced as it was by a gaze of the
most benignant authority. Then pushing his hand savagely down,
'Hypocrite!' he roared close to his face—'can you hear that?' and
marched bravely out of the room. Mr. Cope shook his head with a
world of tragic meaning, and for an instant exchanged with his wife
a long look brimming with anguish. She fell upon his neck shaken
with resounding sobs. But soon recovering herself; 'Go to him,' she
urged, 'follow him; say everything, spare nothing. No matter for
me; I've got *my* blow.'

I helped her up to her room. Her strength had completely left her;

she but half undressed and let me lay her on her bed. She was in a state of the intensest excitement. Every nerve in her body was thrilling and ringing. She kept murmuring to herself, with a kind of heart-breaking incoherency. 'Nothing can hurt me now; I needn't be spared. Nothing can disgrace me— or grace me. I've got my blow. It's my fault—all, all, all! I heaped up folly on folly and weakness on weakness. My heart's broken; it will never serve again. You have been right, my dear—I perverted him, I taught him to strike. Oh, what a blow! He's hard—he's hard. He's cruel. He has no heart. He's blind with vanity and egotism. But it matters little now; I shan't live to suffer. I've suffered enough. I'm dying, my friend, I'm dying.'

In this broken strain the poor lady poured out the bitterness of her grief. I used every art to soothe and console her, but I felt that the tenderest spot in her gentle heart had received an irreparable bruise. 'I don't want to live,' she murmured. 'I'm disillusioned. It could never be patched up; we should never be the same. He has shown the bottom of his soul. It's bad.'

In spite of my efforts to restore her to calmness, she became—not more excited, for her strength seemed to be ebbing and her voice was low—but more painfully and incoherently garrulous. Nevertheless, from her distressing murmur I gathered the glimmer of a meaning. She seemed to wish to make a kind of supreme confession. I sat on the cope of her bed, with her hand in mine. From time to time, above her loud whispers, I heard the sound of the two gentlemen's voices. Adjoining her chamber was a large dressing-room; beyond this was Eustace's apartment. The three rooms opened upon a long uncovered balcony.

Mr. Cope had followed the young man to his own chamber, and was addressing him in a low, steady voice. Eustace apparently was silent; but there was something sullen and portentous to my ear in this unnatural absence of response.

'What have you thought of me, my friend, all these years?' his mother asked. 'Have I seemed to you like other women? I haven't been like others. I have tried to be so—and you see—you see! Let me tell you. It doesn't matter whether you despise me—I shan't know it. These are my last words; let them be frank.'

They were not, however, so frank as she intended. She seemed to lose herself in a dim wilderness of memories; her faculty wandered, faltered, stumbled. Not from her words—they were ambiguous—but from her silence and from the rebound of my own impassioned sympathy, as it were, I guessed the truth. It blossomed into being vivid and distinct; it exhaled a long illuminating glow upon the past—a lurid light upon the present. Strange it seemed now that my suspicions had been so late to bear fruit; but our imagination is always too timid. Now all things were clear! Heaven knows that in this un-pitying light I felt no contempt for the poor woman who lay before me, panting from her violated soul.

Poor victims of destiny! If I could only bring them to terms! For the moment, however, the unhappy mother and wife demanded all my attention. I left her and passed along the balcony, intending to summon her husband. The light in Eustace's room showed me the young man and his companion. They sat facing each other in mo-mentary silence. Mr. Cope's two hands were on his knees, his eyes were fixed on the carpet, his teeth were set—as if, baffled, irate, desperate, he were preparing to play his last card. Eustace was look-ing at him hard, with a terribly untender gaze. It made me sick. I was on the point of rushing in and adjuring Eustace by the truth. But suddenly Mr. Cope raised his eyes and exchanged with the boy a look with which he seemed to read his very soul. He waved his hand in the air as if to dismiss fond patience.

'If you were to see yourself as I see you,' he said, 'you would be vastly amazed; you would know your absurd appearance. Young as you are, you are rotten with arrogance and pride. What would you say if I were to tell you that, least of men, you have reason to be proud? Your stable boy there has more. There's a leak in your vanity; there's a blot on your escutcheon! You force me to strong measures. Let me tell you, in the teeth of your monstrous egotism, what you are. You're a——'

I knew what was coming, but I hadn't the heart to hear it. The word, ringing out, overtook my ear as I hurried back to Mrs. Cope. It was followed by a loud, incoherent cry, the sound, prolonged for some moments, of a scuffle, and then the report of a pistol. This was lost in the noise of crashing glass. Mrs. Cope rose erect in bed and shrieked aloud, 'He has killed him—and me.' I caught her in my arms; she breathed her last. I laid her gently on the bed and made my trembling way, by the balcony, to Eustace's room. The first glance reassured me. Neither of the men was visibly injured; the pistol lay smoking on the floor. Eustace had sunk into a chair with his head buried in his hands. I saw his face crimson through his fingers.

'It's not murder,' Mr. Cope said to me as I crossed the threshold, 'but it has just missed being suicide. It has been fatal only to the looking-glass.' The mirror was shivered.

'It *is* murder,' I answered, seizing Eustace by the arm and forcing him to rise. 'You have killed your mother. This is your father!'

*

My friend paused and looked at me with a triumphant air, as if she was very proud of her effect. Of course I had foreseen it half an hour ago. 'What a dismal tale,' I said. 'But it's interesting. Of course Mrs. Cope recovered.'

She was silent an instant. 'You're like me,' she answered. 'Your imagination is timid.'

'I confess,' I rejoined, 'I am rather at a loss how to dispose of our friend Eustace. I don't see how the two could very well shake hands —nor yet how they couldn't.'

'They did once—and but once. They were for years, each in his way, lonely men. They were never reconciled. The trench had been dug too deep. Even the poor lady buried there didn't avail to fill it up. Yet the son was forgiven—the father never!'

Guest's Confession

IN TWO PARTS

[First appeared in the *Atlantic Monthly,* vol. xxx (October–November 1872), pp. 385–403, 566–83. Not reprinted during James's lifetime.]

PART I

I.

'ARRIVE HALF PAST EIGHT. SICK. MEET ME.'

The telegrammatic brevity of my stepbrother's missive gave that melancholy turn to my thoughts which was the usual result of his communications. He was to have come on the Friday; what had made him start off on Wednesday? The terms on which we stood were a perpetual source of irritation. We were utterly unlike in temper and taste and opinions, and yet, having a number of common interests, we were obliged, after a fashion, to compromise with each other's idiosyncrasies. In fact, the concessions were all on my side. He was altogether too much my superior in all that makes the man who counts in the world for me not to feel it, and it cost me less to let him take his way than to make a stand for my dignity. What I did through indolence and in some degree, I confess, through pusillanimity, I had a fancy to make it appear (by dint of much whistling, as it were, and easy thrusting of my hands into my pockets) that I did through a sort of generous condescension. Edgar cared little enough upon what recipe I compounded a salve for my vanity, so long as he held his own course; and I am afraid I played the slumbering giant to altogether empty benches. There had been, indeed, a vague tacit understanding that he was to treat me, in form, as a man with a mind of my own, and there was occasionally something most incisively sarcastic in his observance of the treaty. What made matters the worse for me, and the better for him, was an absurd physical disparity; for Musgrave was like nothing so much as Falstaff's description of Shallow,—a man made after supper of a cheese-paring. He was a miserable invalid, and was perpetually concerned with his stomach, his lungs, and his liver, and as he was both doctor and patient in one, they kept him very busy. His head was grotesquely large for his diminutive figure, his eye fixed and salient, and his complexion liable to flush with an air of indignation and suspicion. He practised a most resolute little strut on a most attenuated pair of little legs. For myself, I was tall, happily; for I was broad enough, if I had been shorter, to have perhaps incurred that invidious mono-syllabic epithet which haunted Lord Byron. As compared with Edgar, I was at least fairly good-looking; a stoutish, blondish, indolent, amiable, rather gorgeous young fellow might have served as my personal formula. My patrimony, being double that of my step-brother (for we were related by my mother), was largely lavished on the adornment of this fine person. I dressed in fact, as I recollect, with a sort of barbaric splendour, and I may very well have passed for one of the social pillars of a small watering-place.

L— was in those days just struggling into fame, and but that it savoured overmuch of the fresh paint lately lavished upon the various wooden barracks in which visitors were to be accommodated, it yielded a pleasant mixture of rurality and society. The vile taste and the soverign virtue of the spring were fairly established, and Edgar was not the man to forego the chance of trying the waters and abusing them. Having heard that the hotel was crowded, he wished to secure a room at least a week beforehand; the upshot of which was, that I came down on the 19th of July with the mission to retain and occupy his apartment till the 26th. I passed, with people in general, and with Edgar in particular, for so very idle a person that it seemed almost a duty to saddle me with some wholesome errand. Edgar had, first and always, his health to attend to, and then that neat little property and those everlasting accounts, which he was never weary of contemplating, verifying, and overhauling. I had made up my mind to make over his room to him, remain a day or two for civility's sake and then leave him to his cups. Meanwhile, on the 24th, it occurred to me that I ought really to see something of the place. The weather had been too hot for going about, and, as yet, I had hardly left the piazza of the hotel. Towards afternoon the clouds gathered, the sun was obscured, and it seemed possible even for a large, lazy man to take a walk. I went along beside the river, under the trees, rejoicing much in the midsummer prettiness of all the land and in the sultry afternoon stillness. I was discomposed and irritated, and all for no better reason than that Edgar was coming. What was Edgar that his comings and goings should affect me? Was I, after all, so excessively his younger brother? I would turn over a new leaf! I almost wished things would come to a crisis between us, and that in the glow of exasperation I might say or do something unpardonable. But there was small chance of my quarrelling with Edgar for vanity's sake. Somehow, I didn't believe in my own egotism, but I had an indefeasible respect for his. I was fatally good-natured, and I should continue to do his desire until I began to do that of someone else. If I might only fall in love and exchange my master for a mistress, for some charming goddess of unreason who would declare that Mr. Musgrave was simply intolerable and that was an end of it!

So, meditating vaguely, I arrived at the little Episcopal chapel, which stands on the margin of the village where the latter begins to melt away into the large river-side landscape. The door was slightly ajar: there came through it into the hot outer stillness the low sound of an organ,—the rehearsal, evidently, of the organist or of some gentle amateur. I was warm with walking, and this glimpse of the cool musical dimness within prompted me to enter and rest and listen. The body of the church was empty; but a feeble glow of colour was diffused through the little yellow and crimson windows upon the pews and the cushioned pulpit. The organ was erected in a small gallery facing the chancel, into which the ascent was by a short stairway directly from the church. The sound of my tread was apparently covered by the music, for the player continued without heeding me, hidden as she was behind a little blue silk curtain on the edge of the gallery. Yes, that gentle, tentative, unprofessional touch came from a feminine hand. Uncertain as it was, however, it wrought upon my musical sensibilities with a sort of provoking force. The air was familiar, and, before I knew it, I had begun to furnish the vocal accompaniment,—first gently, then boldly. Standing with my face to the organ, I awaited the effect of my venture. The only perceptible result was that, for a moment, the music faltered and the curtains were stirred. I saw nothing, but I had been seen, and, reassured apparently by my aspect, the organist resumed the chant. Slightly mystified, I felt urged to sing my best, the more so that, as I continued, the player seemed to borrow confidence and emulation from my voice. The notes rolled out bravely, and the little vault re-sounded. Suddenly there seemed to come to the musician, in the ardour of success, a full accession of vigour and skill. The last chords were struck with a kind of triumphant intensity, and their cadence was marked by a clear soprano voice. Just at the close, however, voice and music were swallowed up in the roll of a huge thunder-clap. At the same instant, the storm-drops began to strike the chapel-windows, and we were sheeted in a summer rain. The rain was a bore; but, at least, I should have a look at the organist, concerning whom my curiosity had suddenly grown great. The thunder-claps followed each other with such violence that it was vain to continue to play. I waited, in the confident belief that that charming voice—

half a dozen notes had betrayed it—denoted a charming woman. After the lapse of some moments, which seemed to indicate a graceful and appealing hesitancy, a female figure appeared at the top of the little stairway and began to descend. I walked slowly down the aisle. The stormy darkness had rapidly increased, and at this moment, with a huge burst of thunder, following a blinding flash, a momentary midnight fell upon our refuge. When things had become visible again, I beheld the fair musician at the foot of the steps, gazing at me with all the frankness of agitation. The little chapel was rattling to its foundations.

'Do you think there is any danger?' asked my companion.

I made haste to assure her there was none. 'The chapel has nothing in the nature of a spire, and even if it had, the fact of our being in a holy place ought to insure us against injury.'

She looked at me wonderingly, as if to see whether I was in jest. To satisfy her, I smiled as graciously as I might. Whereupon, gathering confidence, 'I think we have each of us,' she said, 'so little right to be here that we can hardly claim the benefit of sanctuary.'

'Are you too an interloper?' I asked.

She hesitated a moment. 'I'm not an Episcopalian,' she replied; 'I'm a good Unitarian.'

'Well, I'm a poor Episcopalian. It's six of one and half a dozen of the other.' There came another long, many-sheeted flash and an immediate wild reverberation. My companion, as she stood before me, was vividly illumined from head to foot. It was as if some fierce natural power had designed to interpose her image on my soul forever, in this merciless electric glare. As I saw her then, I have never ceased to see her since. I have called her fair, but the word needs explanation. Singularly pleasing as she was, it was with a charm that was all her own. Not the charm of beauty, but of a certain intense expressiveness, which seems to have given beauty the go-by in the very interest of grace. Slender, meagre, without redundancy of outline or brilliancy of colour, she was a person you might never have noticed, but would certainly never forget. What there was was so charming, what there might be so interesting! There was none of the idleness of conscious beauty in her clear grey eyes; they seemed charged with the impatience of a restless mind. Her glance and smile, her step and gesture, were as light and distinct as a whispered secret. She was nervous, curious, zealous, slightly imperious, and delicately elegant withal; without which, possibly, she might have seemed a trifle too positive. There is a certain sweet unreason in a picturesque toilet. She was dressed in a modish adjustment of muslins and lace, which denoted the woman who may have fancied that

even less beauty might yet please. While I drew my conclusions,—
they were eminently flattering,—my companion was buttoning her
gloves and looking anxiously at the dripping windows. Wishing, as
far as I might, to beguile her impatience, I proceeded to apologize for
the liberty I had taken in singing to her music. 'My best excuse,' I
said, 'is your admirable playing, and my own most sensitive ear!'

'You might have frightened me away,' she answered. 'But you sang
too well for that, better than I played. In fact, I was afraid to stop,
I thought you might be one of the—the hierarchy.'

'A bishop!'

'A bishop,—a dean,—a deacon,—or something of that sort.'

'The sexton, perhaps.'

'Before the sexton I should have succumbed. I take it his business
would have been to eject me as a meddlesome heretic. I came in for
no better reason than that the church door was ajar.'

'As a church door ought always to be.'

She looked at me a moment. 'No; see what comes of it.'

'No great harm, it seems to me.'

'O, that's very well for us! But a church shouldn't be made a place
of convenience.'

I wished, in the interest of our growing intimacy, to make a point.
'If it is not a place of convenience,' I ventured to propound, deprecating offence with a smile, 'what is it?'

It was an observation I afterwards made, that in cases when many
women drop their eyes and look prettily silly or prudishly alarmed,
this young lady's lucid glance would become more unaffectedly
direct and searching. 'Indeed,' she answered, 'you *are* but an indifferent Episcopalian! I came in because the door was open, because
I was warm with my walk, and because, I confess, I have an especial
fondness for going into churches on week-days. One does it in
Europe, you know; and it reminds me of Europe.'

I cast a glance over the naked tabernacle, with the counterfeit
graining scarcely dry on its beams and planks, and a strong aroma
of turpentine and putty representing the odour of sanctity. She followed my glance; our eyes met, and we laughed. From this moment
we talked with a freedom tempered less by the sanctity of the spot
than by a certain luxury of deference with which I felt prompted
to anticipate possible mistrust. The rain continued to descend with
such steady good-will that it seemed needful to accept our situation
frankly and conjure away the spirit of awkwardness. We spoke of
L—, of the people there, of the hot weather, of music. She had as
yet seen little of the place, having been confined to her apartments
by domestic reasons. I wondered what her domestic reasons were.

She had come forth at last to call upon a friend at one of the boarding-houses which adorned this suburb of the village. Her friend being out, but likely soon to return, she had sought entertainment in a stroll along the road, and so had wandered into the chapel. Our interview lasted half an hour. As it drew to a close, I fancied there had grown up between us some delicate bond, begotten of our mutual urbanity. I might have been indiscreet; as it was, I took my pleasure in tracing the gradual evanescence of my companion's sense of peril. As the moments elapsed, she sat down on the bench with an air of perfect equanimity, and looked patiently at the trickling windows. The still small voice of some familiar spirit of the Lord, haunting the dedicated vault, seemed to have audibly blessed our meeting. At last the rain abated and suddenly stopped, and through a great rift in the clouds there leaped a giant sunbeam and smote the trickling windows. Through little gaudy lozenges the chapel was flooded with prismatic light. 'The storm is over,' said my companion. She spoke without rising, as if she had been cheated of the sense of haste. Was it calculated civility, or was it momentary self-oblivion? Whatever it was, it lasted but a moment. We were on our feet and moving towards the door. As we stood in the porch, honest gallantry demanded its rights.

'I never knew before,' I said, 'the possible blessings of a summer rain.'

She proceeded a few steps before she answered. Then glancing at the shining sky, already blue and free, 'In ten minutes,' she said, 'there will be no trace of it!'

'Does that mean,' I frankly demanded, 'that we are not to meet again as friends?'

'Are we to meet again at all?'

'I count upon it.'

'Certainly, then, not as enemies!' As she walked away, I imprecated those restrictions of modern civilization which forbade me to stand and gaze at her.

Who was she? What was she?—questions the more intense as, in the absence of any further evidence than my rapid personal impression, they were so provokingly vain. They occupied me, however, during the couple of hours which were to elapse before my step-brother's arrival. When his train became due, I went through the form, as usual, of feeling desperately like treating myself to the luxury of neglecting his summons and leaving him to shift for himself; as if I had not the most distinct prevision of the inevitable event,—of my being at the station half an hour too early, of my calling his hack and making his bargain and taking charge of his precious little handbag, full of medicine-bottles, and his ridiculous bundle of umbrellas and canes. Somehow, this evening, I felt un-wontedly loath and indocile; but I contented myself with this bold flight of the imagination.

It is hard to describe fairly my poor step-brother's peculiar turn of mind, to give an adequate impression of his want of social charm, to put it mildly, without accusing him of wilful malevolence. He was simply the most consistent and incorruptible of egotists. He was per-petually affirming and defining and insuring himself, insisting upon a personal right or righting a personal wrong. And above all, he was a man of conscience. He asked no odds, and he gave none. He made honesty something unlovely, but he was rigidly honest. He de-manded simply his dues, and he collected them to the last farthing. These things gave him a portentous solemnity. He smiled perhaps once a month, and made a joke once in six. There are jokes of his making which, to this day, give me a shiver when I think of them. But I soon perceived, as he descended from the train, that there would be no joke that evening. Something had happened. His face was hard and sombre, and his eye bright and fierce. 'A carriage,' he said, giving me his hand stiffly. And when we were seated and driv-ing away, 'First of all,' he demanded, 'are there any mosquitoes? A single mosquito would finish me. And is my room habitable, on the shady side, away from the stairs, with a view, with a hair-mattress?' I assured him that mosquitoes were unknown, and that his room was the best, and his mattress the softest in the house. Was he tired? how had he been?

'Don't ask me. I'm in an extremely critical state. Tired? Tired is a word for well people! When I'm tired I shall go to bed and die. Thank God, so long as I have any work to do, I can hold up my head! I haven't slept in a week. It's singular, but I'm never so well disposed for my duties as when I haven't slept! But be so good, for the present, as to ask me no questions. I shall immediately take a bath and drink some arrow-root; I have brought a package in my bag, I suppose I can get them to make it. I'll speak about it at the office. No, I think, on the whole, I'll make it in my room; I have a little machine for boiling water. I think I shall drink half a glass of the spring tonight, just to make a beginning.'

All this was said with as profound a gravity as if he were dictating his will. But I saw that he was at a sort of white-heat exasperation, and I knew that in time I should learn where the shoe pinched. Meanwhile, I attempted to say something cheerful and frivolous, and offered some information as to who was at the hotel and who was expected; 'No one you know or care about, I think.'

'Very likely not. I'm in no mood for gossip.'

'You seem nervous,' I ventured to say.

'Nervous? Call it frantic! I'm not blessed with your apathetic temperament, nor with your elegant indifference to money-matters. Do you know what's the matter with me? I've lost twenty thousand dollars.'

I, of course, demanded particulars; but, for the present, I had to content myself with the naked fact. 'It's a mighty serious matter,' said Edgar. 'I can't talk of it further till I have bathed and changed my linen. The thermometer has been at ninety-one in my rooms in town. I've had this pretty piece of news to keep me cool.'

I left him to his bath, his toilet, and his arrow-root and strolled about pondering the mystery of his disaster. Truly, if Edgar had lost money, shrewdness was out of tune. Destiny must have got up early to outwit my step-brother. And yet his misfortune gave him a sort of unwonted grace, and I believe I wondered for five minutes whether there was a chance of his being relaxed and softened by it. I had, indeed, a momentary vision of lending him money, and taking a handsome revenge as a good-natured creditor. But Edgar would never borrow. He would either recover his money or grimly do without it. On going back to his room I found him dressed and re-freshed, screwing a little portable kettle upon his gas-burner.

'You can never get them to bring you water that really boils,' he said. 'They don't know what it means. You're altogether wrong about the mosquitoes; I'm sure I heard one, and by the sound, he's a mon-ster. But I have a net folded up in my trunk, and a hook and ring which I mean to drive into the ceiling.'

'I'll put up your net. Meanwhile, tell me about your twenty thou-sand dollars.'

He was silent awhile, but at last he spoke in a voice forcibly at-tuned to composure. 'You're immensely tickled, I suppose, to find me losing money! That comes of worrying too much and handling my funds too often. Yes, I *have* worried too much.' He paused, and then, suddenly, he broke out into a kind of fury. 'I hate waste, I hate shiftlessness, I hate nasty mismanagement! I hate to see money bring in less than it may. My imagination loves a good investment. I respect my property, I respect other people's. But your own honesty is all you'll find in this world, and it will go no farther than you're there to carry it. You've always thought me hard and suspicious and grasping. No, you never said so; should I have cared if you had? With your means, it's all very well to be a fine gentleman, to skip the items and glance at the total. But, being poor and sick, I have to be close. I wasn't close enough. What do you think of my having been cheated?—cheated under my very nose? I hope I'm genteel enough now!'

'I should like to see the man!' I cried.

'You shall see him. All the world shall see him. I've been looking into the matter. It has been beautifully done. If I were to be a rascal, I should like to be just such a one.'

'Who is your rascal?'

'His name is John Guest.'

I had heard the name, but had never seen the man.

'No, you don't know him,' Edgar went on. 'No one knows him but I. But I know him well. He had things in his hands for a week, while I was debating a transfer of my New Jersey property. In a week—this is how he mixed matters.'

'Perhaps, if you had given him time,' I suggested, 'he meant to get them straight again.'

'O, I shall give him time. I mean he shall get 'em straight, or I shall twist him so crooked his best friend won't know him.'

'Did you never suspect his honesty?'

'Do you suspect mine?'

'But you have legal redress?'

'It's no thanks to him. He had fixed things to a charm, he had done his best to cut me off and cover his escape. But I've got him, and he shall disgorge!'

I hardly know why it was; but the implacable firmness of my brother's position produced in my mind a sort of fantastic reaction in favour of Mr. John Guest. I felt a sudden gush of the most inconsequent pity. 'Poor man!' I exclaimed. But to repair my weakness, I plunged into a series of sympathetic questions and listened attentively to Edgar's statement of his wrongs. As he set forth the case, I found myself taking a whimsical interest in Mr. Guest's own side of it, wondering whether he suspected suspicion, whether he dreaded conviction, whether he had an easy conscience, and how he was getting through the hot weather. I asked Edgar how lately he had discovered his loss and whether he had since communicated with the criminal.

'Three days ago, three nights ago, rather; for I haven't slept a wink since. I have spoken of the matter to no one; for the present I need no one's help, I can help myself. I haven't seen the man more than three of four times; our dealings have generally been by letter. The last person you'd suspect. He's as great a dandy as you yourself, and in better taste, too. I was told ten days ago, at his office, that he had gone out of town. I suppose I'm paying for his champagne at Newport.'

II.

On my proposing, half an hour later, to relieve him of my society and allow him to prepare for rest, Edgar declared that our talk had put an end to sleep and that he must take a turn in the open air. On descending to the piazza, we found it in the deserted condition into which it usually lapsed about ten o'clock, either from a wholesome desire on the part of our fellow-lodgers to keep classic country hours, or from the soporific influences of excessive leisure. Here and there the warm darkness was relieved by the red tip of a cigar in suggestive proximity to a light corsage. I observed, as we strolled along, a lady of striking appearance, seated in the zone of light projected from a window, in conversation with a gentleman. 'Really, I'm afraid you'll take cold,' I heard her say as we passed. 'Let me tie my handkerchief round your neck.' And she gave it a playful twist. She was a pretty woman, of middle age, with great freshness of toilet and complexion, and a picturesque abundance of blonde hair, upon which was coquettishly poised a fantastic little hat, decorated with an immense pink rose. Her companion was a seemingly affable man, with a bald head, a white waistcoat, and a rather florid air of distinction. When we passed them a second time, they had risen and the lady was preparing to enter the house. Her companion went with her to the door; she left him with a great deal of coquettish by-play, and he turned back to the piazza. At this moment his glance fell upon my step-brother. He started, I thought, and then, replacing his hat with an odd, nervous decision, came towards him with a smile. 'Mr. Musgrave!' he said.

Edgar stopped short, and for a moment seemed to lack words to reply. At last he uttered a deep, harsh note: 'Mr. Guest!'

In an instant I felt that I was in the presence of a 'situation'. Edgar's words had the sound of the 'click' upon the limb of the entrapped fox. A scene was imminent; the actors were only awaiting their cues. Mr. Guest made a half-offer of his hand, but, perceiving no response in Edgar's, he gracefully dipped it into his pocket. 'You must have just come!' he murmured.

'A couple of hours ago.'

Mr. Guest glanced at me, as if to include me in the operation of his urbanity, and his glance stirred in my soul an impulse of that kindness which we feel for a man about to be executed. It's no more than human to wish to shake hands with him. 'Introduce me, Edgar,' I said.

'My step-brother,' said Edgar, curtly. 'This is Mr. Guest, of whom we have been talking.'

I put out my hand; he took it with cordiality. 'Really,' he declared, 'this is a most unexpected—a—circumstance.'

'Altogether so to me,' said Edgar.

'You've come for the waters, I suppose,' our friend went on. 'I'm sorry your health continues—a—unsatisfactory.'

Edgar, I perceived, was in a state of extreme nervous exacerbation, the result partly of mere surprise and partly of keen disappointment. His plans had been checked. He had determined to do thus and so, and he must now extemporize a policy. Well, as poor, pompous Mr. Guest wished it, so he should have it! 'I shall never be strong,' said Edgar.

'Well, well,' responded Mr. Guest, 'a man of your parts may make a little strength serve a great purpose.'

My step-brother was silent a moment, relishing secretly, I think, the beautiful pertinence of this observation. 'I suppose I can defend my rights,' he rejoined.

'Exactly! What more does a man need?' and he appealed to me with an insinuating smile. His smile was singularly frank and agreeable, and his glance full of a sort of conciliating gallantry. I noted in his face, however, by the gaslight, a haggard, jaded look which lent force to what he went on to say. 'I have been feeling lately as if I hadn't even strength for that. The hot weather, an overdose of this abominable water, one thing and another, the inevitable premonitions of—a—mortality, have quite pulled me down. Since my arrival here, ten days ago, I have really been quite—a—the invalid. I've actually been in bed. A most unprecedented occurrence!'

'I hope you're better,' I ventured to say.

'Yes, I think I'm myself again,—thanks to capital nursing. I think I'm myself again!' He repeated his words mechanically, with a sort of exaggerated gaiety, and began to wipe his forehead with his handkerchief. Edgar was watching him narrowly, with an eye whose keenness it was impossible to veil; and I think Edgar's eye partly caused his disquiet. 'The last thing I did, by the way, before my indisposition, was to write you ten lines, Mr. Musgrave, on—a little matter of business.'

'I got your letter,' said Edgar, grimly.

Mr. Guest was silent a moment. 'And I hope my arrangements have met your approval?'

'We shall talk of that,' said Edgar.

At this point, I confess, my interest in the situation had become painful. I felt sick. I'm not a man of ready-made resolution, as my story will abundantly prove. I am discountenanced and bullied by disagreeable things. Poor Mr. Guest was so infallibly booked for exposure that I instinctively retreated. Taking advantage of his allusion to business, I turned away and walked to the other end of the piazza. This genial gentleman, then, was embodied fraud! this sayer of civil things was a doer of monstrously shabby ones! that irreproachable white waistcoat carried so sadly spotted a conscience! Whom had he involved in his dishonour? Had he a wife, children, friends? Who was that so prosperously pretty woman, with her flattering solicitude for his health? I stood for some time reflecting how guilt is not the vulgar bugaboo we fancy it,—that it has organs, senses, affections, passions, for all the world like those of innocence. Indeed, from my cursory observation of my friend, I had rarely seen innocence so handsomely featured. Where, then, was the line which severed rectitude from error? Was manhood a baser thing than I had fancied, or was sin a thing less base? As I mused this, my disgust ebbed away, and the return of the wave brought an immense curiosity to see what it had come to betwixt guilt and justice. Had Edgar launched his thunder? I retraced my steps and rejoined my companions. Edgar's thunder was apparently still in the clouds; but there had been a premonitory flash of lightning. Guest stood before him, paler than before, staring defiantly, and stammering out some fierce denial. 'I don't understand you,' he said. 'If you mean what you seem to mean, you mean rank insult.'

'I mean the truth,' said Edgar. 'It's a pity the truth should be insulting.'

Guest glared a moment, like a man intently taking thought for self-defence. But he was piteously unmasked. His genial smile had taken flight and left mere vulgar confusion. 'This is between ourselves, sir,' he cried, angrily turning to me.

'A thousand pardons,' I said, and passed along. I began to be doubtful as to the issue of the quarrel. Edgar had right on his side, but, under the circumstances, he might not have force. Guest was altogether a stouter, bigger, weightier person. I turned and observed them from a distance. Edgar's thunderbolt had fallen and his victim stood stunned. He was leaning against the balustrade of the piazza, with his chin on his breast and his eyes sullenly fixed on his adversary, demoralized and convicted. His hat had dropped upon the floor. Edgar seemed to have made a proposal; with a passionate gesture he repeated it. Guest slowly stooped and picked up his hat, and Edgar led the way towards the house. A series of small sitting-rooms opened by long windows upon the piazza. These were for the most part lighted and empty. Edgar selected one of them, and, stop-

ping before the window, beckoned to me to come to him. Guest, as
I advanced, bestowed upon me a scowl of concentrated protest. I felt,
for my own part, as if I were horribly indelicate. Between Edgar and
him it was a question of morals, but between him and myself it was,
of course, but one of manners. 'Be so good as to walk in,' said Edgar,
turning to me with a smile of unprecedented suavity. I might have
resisted his dictation; I couldn't his petition.

'In God's name, what do you mean to do?' demanded Guest.

'My duty!' said Edgar. 'Go in.'

We passed into the room. The door of the corridor was open; Guest
closed it with a passionate kick. Edgar shut the long window and
dropped the curtain. In the same fury of mortification, Guest turned
out one of the two burners of the chandelier. There was still light
enough, however, for me to see him more distinctly than on the
piazza. He was tallish and stoutish, and yet sleek and jaunty. His
fine blue eye was a trifle weak, perhaps, and his handsome grizzled
beard was something too foppishly trimmed; but, on the whole, he
was a most comely man. He was dressed with the punctilious elegance of a man who loved luxury and appreciated his own good
points. A little moss-rosebud figured in the lappet of his dark-blue
coat. His whole person seemed redolent of what are called the 'feelings of a gentleman.' Confronted and contrasted with him under the
lamp, my step-brother seemed woefully mean and grotesque; though
for a conflict of forces that lay beneath the surface, he was visibly
the better equipped of the two. He seemed to tremble and quiver
with inexorable purpose. I felt that he would heed no admonitory
word of mine, that I could not in the least hope to blunt the edge of
his resentment, and that I must on the instant decide either to stand
by him or leave him. But while I stood thus ungraciously gazing at
poor Guest, the instant passed. Curiosity and a mingled sympathy
with each—to say nothing of a touch of that relish for a fight inherent in the truly masculine bosom—sealed my lips and arrested
my steps. And yet my heart paid this graceful culprit the compliment of beating very violently on his behalf.

'I wish you to repeat before my brother,' said Edgar, 'the three
succinct denials to which you have just treated me.'

Guest looked at the ceiling with a trembling lip. Then dropping
upon the sofa, he began to inspect his handsome finger-nails
mechanically, in the manner of one who hears in some horrible hush
of all nature the nearing footsteps of doom. 'Come, repeat them!'
cried Edgar. 'It's really delicious. You never wrote to Stevens that
you had my assent in writing to the sale of the bonds. You never
showed Stevens my telegram from Boston, and assured him that my

"Do as you think best" was a permission to raise money on them. If it's not forgery, sir, it's next door to it, and a very flimsy partition between.'

Guest leaned back on the sofa, with his hands grasping his knees. 'You might have let things stand a week or so,' he said, with unnatural mildness 'You might have had common patience. Good God, there's a gentlemanly way of doing things! A man doesn't begin to roar for a pinch. I would have got things square again.'

'O, it would have been a pity to spoil them! It was such a pretty piece of knavery! Give the devil his due!'

'I would have rearranged matters,' Guest went on. 'It was just a temporary convenience. I supposed I was dealing with a man of common courtesy. But what are you to say to a gentleman who says, "Sir, I trust you," and then looks through the keyhole?'

'Upon my word, when I hear you scuttling through the window,' cried Edgar, 'I think it's time I should break down the door. For God's sake, don't nauseate me with any more lies! You know as well as you sit there, that you had neither chance nor means nor desire to redeem your fraud. You'd cut the bridge behind you! You thought you'd been knowing enough to eat your cake and have it, to lose your virtue and keep your reputation, to sink half my property through a trap-door and then stand whistling and looking t'other way while I scratched my head and wondered what the devil was in it! Sit down there and write me your note for twenty thousand dollars at twenty days.'

Guest was silent a moment. 'Propose something reasonable,' he said, with the same tragic gentleness.

'I shall let the law reason about it.'

Guest gave a little start and fixed his eyes on the ground. 'The law wouldn't help you,' he answered, without looking up.

'Indeed! do you think it would help *you*? Stoddard and Hale will help me. I spoke to them this morning.'

Guest sprang to his feet. 'Good heavens! I hope you mentioned no names.'

'Only one!' said Edgar.

Guest wiped his forehead and actually tried to smile. 'That was your own, of course! Well, sir, I hope they advised you to—a—temper justice with mercy.'

'They are not parsons, Mr. Guest; they are lawyers. They accept the case.'

Guest dropped on the sofa, buried his face in his hands, and burst into tears. 'O my soul!' he cried. His soul, poor man, was a rough term for name and fame and comfort and all that made his universe. It was a pitiful sight.

'Look here, Edgar,' I said. 'Don't press things too hard. I'm not a parson either——'

'No, you've not that excuse for your sentimentality!' Edgar broke out. 'Here it is, of course! Here come folly and fear and ignorance maundering against the primary laws of life! Is rascality alone of all things in the world to be handled without gloves? Didn't he press me hard? He's danced his dance,—let him pay the piper! Am I a child, a woman, a fool, to stand and haggle with a swindler? Am I to go to the wall to make room for impudent fraud? Not while I have eyes to know black from white! I'm a decent man. I'm this or I'm nothing. For twenty years I've done my best for order and thrift and honesty. I've never yielded an inch to the detestable sharp practice that meets one nowadays at every turn. I've hated fraud as I hate all bad economy; I've no more patience with it than a bull with a red rag. Fraud is fraud; it's waste, it's wantonness, it's chaos; and I shall never give it the go-by. When I catch it, I shall hold it fast, and call all honest men to see how vile and drivelling a thing it is!'

Guest sat rigidly fixed, with his eyes on the carpet. 'Do you expect to get your money?' he finally demanded.

'My money be hanged! I expect to let people know how they may be served if they entrust their affairs to you! A man's property, sir, is a man's person. It's as if you had given me a blow in the chest!'

Guest came towards him and took him by the button-hole. 'Now see here,' he said, with the same desperate calmness. 'You call yourself a practical man. Don't go on like one of those d—d long-haired reformers. You're off the track. Don't attempt too much. Don't make me confoundedly uncomfortable out of pure fantasticality. Come, sir, you're a man of the world.' And he patted him gently on the shoulder. 'Give me a chance. I confess to not having been quite square. There! My very dear sir, let me get on my legs again.'

'O, you confess!' cried Edgar. 'That's a vast comfort. You'll never do it again! Not if I know it. But other people, eh? Suppose I had been a decent widow with six children, and not a penny but that! You'd confess again, I suppose. Would your confession butter their bread! Let your confession be public!'

'My confession *is* public!' and Guest, with averted eyes, jerked his head towards me.

'O, my step-brother! Why, he's the most private creature in the world. Cheat him and he'll thank you! David, I retain you as a witness that Mr. Guest has confessed.'

'Nothing will serve you then? You mean to prosecute?'

'I mean to prosecute.'

The poor man's face flushed crimson, and the great sweat-drops trickled from his temples. 'O you blundering brute!' he cried. 'Do you know what you mean when you say that? Do we live in a civilized world?'

'Not altogether,' said Edgar. 'But I shall help it along.'

'Have you lived among decent people? Have you known women whom it was an honour to please? Have you cared for name and fame and love? Have you had a dear daughter?'

'If I had a dear daughter,' cried Edgar, flinching the least bit at this outbreak, 'I trust my dear daughter would have kept me honest! Not the sin, then, but the detection unfits a man for ladies' society! —Did you kiss your daughter the day you juggled away my bonds?'

'If it will avail with you, I didn't. Consider her feelings. My fault has been that I have been too tender a father,—that I have loved the poor girl better than my own literal integrity. I became embarrassed because I hadn't the heart to tell her that she must spend less money. As if to the wisest, sweetest girl in the world a whisper wouldn't have sufficed! As if five minutes of her divine advice wouldn't have set me straight again! But the stress of my embarrassment was such——'

'Embarrassment!' Edgar broke in. 'That may mean anything. In the case of an honest man it may be a motive for leniency; in that of a knave it's a ground for increased suspicion.'

Guest, I felt, was a good-natured sinner. Just as he lacked rectitude of purpose, he lacked rigidity of temper, and he found in the mysteries of his own heart no clue to my step-brother's monstrous implacability. Looking at him from head to foot with a certain dignity,—a reminiscence of his former pomposity,—'I do you the honour, sir,' he said, 'to believe you are insane.'

'Stuff and nonsense! you believe nothing of the sort,' cried Edgar.

I saw that Guest's opposition was acting upon him as a lively irritant. 'Isn't it possible,' I asked, 'to adopt some compromise? You're not as forgiving a man under the circumstances as I should be.'

'In these things,' retorted Edgar, without ceremony, 'a forgiving man is a fool.'

'Well, take a fool's suggestion. You can perhaps get satisfaction without taking your victim into court.—Let Mr. Guest write his confession.'

Guest had not directly looked at me since we entered the room. At these words he slowly turned and gave me a sombre stare by which the brilliancy of my suggestion seemed somewhat obscured. But my interference was kindly meant, and his reception of it seemed rather ungrateful. At best, however, I could be but a thorn in his side. I had done nothing to earn my sport. Edgar hereupon flourished his hand as if to indicate the superfluity of my advice. 'All in good time, if you please. If I'm insane, there's a method in my madness!' He paused, and his eyes glittered with an intensity which might indeed, for the moment, have seemed to be that of a disordered brain. I wondered what was coming. 'Do me the favour to get down on your knees.' Guest jerked himself up as if he had received a galvanic shock. 'Yes, I know what I say,—on your knees. Did you never say your prayers? You can't get out of a tight place without being squeezed. I won't take less. I shan't feel like an honest man till I've seen you there at my feet.'

There was in the contrast between the inflated self-complacency of Edgar's face as he made this speech, and the blank horror of the other's as he received it, something so poignantly grotesque that it acted upon my nerves like a mistimed joke, and I burst into irrepressible laughter. Guest walked away to the window with some muttered imprecation, pushed aside the curtain, and stood looking out. Then, with a sudden turn, he marched back and stood before my brother. He was drenched with perspiration. 'A moment,' said Edgar. 'You're very hot. Take off your coat.' Guest, to my amazement, took it off and flung it upon the floor. 'Your shirt-sleeves will serve as a kind of sackcloth and ashes. Fold your hands, so. Now, beg my pardon.'

It was a revolting sight,—this man of ripe maturity and massive comeliness on his two knees, his pale face bent upon his breast, his body trembling with the effort to keep his shameful balance; and above him Edgar, with his hands behind his back, solemn and ugly as a miniature idol, with his glittering eyes fixed in a sort of rapture on the opposite wall. I walked away to the window. There was a perfect stillness, broken only by Guest's hard breathing. I have no notion how long it lasted; when I turned back into the room he was still speechless and fixed, as if he were ashamed to rise. Edgar pointed to a blotting-book and inkstand which stood on a small table against the wall. 'See if there is pen and paper!' I obeyed and made a clatter at the table, to cover our companion's retreat. When I had laid out a sheet of paper he was on his feet again. 'Sit down and write,' Edgar went on. Guest picked up his coat and busied himself mechanically with brushing off the particles of dust. Then he put it on and sat down at the table.

'I dictate,' Edgar began. 'I hereby, at the command of Edgar Musgrave, Esq., whom I have grossly wronged, declare myself a swindler.' At these words, Guest laid down the pen and sank back in his chair, emitting long groans, like a man with a violent toothache. But he had taken that first step which costs, and after a moment's rest he started afresh. 'I have on my bended knees, in the presence of Mr. Musgrave and his step-brother, expressed my contrition; in consideration of which Mr. Musgrave forfeits his incontestable right to publish his injury in a court of justice. Furthermore, I solemnly declare myself his debtor in the sum of twenty thousand dollars; which, on his remission of the interest, and under pain of exposure in a contrary event, I pledge myself to repay at the earliest possible moment. I thank Mr. Musgrave for his generosity.'

Edgar spoke very slowly, and the scratching of Guest's pen kept pact with his words. 'Now sign and date,' he said; and the other, with a great heroic dash, consummated this amazing document. He then pushed it away, and rose and bestowed upon us a look which I long remembered. An outraged human soul was abroad in the world, with which henceforth I felt I should have somehow to reckon.

Edgar possessed himself of the paper and read it coolly to the end, without blushing. Happy Edgar! Guest watched him fold it and put it into his great morocco pocket-book. 'I suppose,' said Guest, 'that this is the end of your generosity.'

'I have nothing further to remark,' said Edgar.

'Have *you*, by chance, anything to remark, Mr. Step-brother?' Guest demanded, turning to me, with a fierceness which showed how my presence galled him.

I had been, to my own sense, so abjectly passive during the whole scene that, to reinstate myself as a responsible creature, I attempted to utter an original sentiment. 'I pity you,' I said.

But I had not been happy in my choice. 'Faugh, you great hulking brute!' Guest roared, for an answer.

The scene at this point might have passed into another phase, had it not been interrupted by the opening of the door from the corridor. 'A lady!' announced a servant, flinging it back.

The lady revealed herself as the friend with whom Guest had been in conversation on the piazza. She was apparently, of her nature, not a person to mind the trifle of her friend's being accompanied by two unknown gentlemen, and she advanced, shawled as if for departure, and smiling reproachfully. 'Ah, you ungrateful creature,' she cried, 'you've lost my rosebud!'

Guest came up smiling, as they say. 'Your own hands fastened it!— Where is my daughter?'

'She's coming. We've been looking for you, high and low. What on earth have you been doing here? Business? You've no business with business. You came here to rest. Excuse me, gentlemen! My carriage has been waiting this ten minutes. Give me your arm.'

It seemed to me time we should disembarrass the poor man of our presence. I opened the window and stepped out upon the piazza. Just as Edgar had followed me, a young lady hastily entered the room.

'My dearest father!' she exclaimed.

Looking at her unseen from without, I recognized with amazement my charming friend of the Episcopal chapel, the woman to whom—I felt it now with a sort of convulsion—I had dedicated a sentiment.

III.

My discovery gave me that night much to think of, and I thought of it more than I slept. My foremost feeling was one of blank dismay as if Misfortune, whom I had been used to regard as a good-natured sort of goddess, who came on with an easy stride, letting off signals of warning to those who stood in her path, should have blinded her lantern and muffled her steps in order to steal a march on poor me,— of all men in the world! It seemed a hideous practical joke. 'If I had known,—if I had only known!' I kept restlessly repeating. But towards morning, 'Say I had known,' I asked myself, 'could I have acted otherwise? I might have protested by my absence; but would I not thus have surrendered poor Guest to the vengeance of a very Shylock? Had not that suggestion of mine divested the current of Edgar's wrath and saved his adversary from the last dishonour? Without it, Edgar would have held his course and demanded his pound of flesh!' Say what I would, however, I stood confronted with this acutely uncomfortable fact, that by lending a hand at that revolting interview, I had struck a roundabout blow at the woman to whom I owed a signally sweet impression. Well, my blow would never reach her, and I would devise some kindness that should! So I consoled myself, and in the midst of my regret I found a still further compensation in the thought that chance, rough-handed though it had been, had forged between us a stouter bond that any I had ventured to dream of as I walked sentimental a few hours before. Her father's being a rascal threw her image into more eloquent relief. If she suspected it, she had all the interest of sorrow; if not, she wore the tender grace of danger.

The result of my meditations was that I determined to defer indefinitely my departure from L—. Edgar informed me, in the course of the following day, that Guest had gone by the early train to New York, and that his daughter had left the hotel (where my not having met her before was apparently the result of her constant attendance on her father during his illness) and taken up her residence with the lady in whose company we had seen her. Mrs. Beck, Edgar had learned this lady's name to be; and I fancied it was upon her that Miss Guest had made her morning call. To begin with, therefore, I knew where to look for her. 'That's the charming girl,' I said to Edgar, 'whom you might have plunged into disgrace.'

'How do you know she's charming?' he asked.

'I judge by her face.'

'Humph! Judge her father by his face and *he*'s charming.'

I was on the point of assuring my step-brother that no such thing could be said of him; but in fact he had suddenly assumed a singularly fresh and jovial air. 'I don't know what it is,' he said, 'but I feel like a trump; I haven't stood so firm on my legs in a twelvemonth. I wonder whether the waters have already begun to act. Really, I'm elated. Suppose, in the afternoon of my life, I were to turn out a sound man. It winds me up, sir. I shall take another glass before dinner.'

To do Miss Guest a kindness, I reflected, I must see her again. How to compass an interview and irradiate my benevolence, it was not easy to determine. Sooner or later, of course, the chances of watering-place life would serve me. Meanwhile, I felt most agreeably that here was something more finely romantic than that feverish dream of my youth, treating Edgar some fine day to the snub direct. Assuredly, I was not in love; I had cherished a youthful passion, and I knew the signs and symptoms; but I was in a state of mind that really gave something of the same zest to consciousness. For a couple of days I watched and waited for my friend in those few public resorts in which the little world of L— used most to congregate,—the drive, the walk, the post-office, and the vicinage of the spring. At last, as she was nowhere visible, I betook myself to the little Episcopal chapel, and strolled along the road, past a scattered cluster of decent boarding-houses, in one of which I imagined her hidden. But most of them had a shady strip of garden stretching towards the river, and thitherward, of course, rather than upon the public road, their inmates were likely to turn their faces. A happy accident at last came to my aid. After three or four days at the hotel, Edgar began to complain that the music in the evening kept him awake and to wonder whether he might find tolerable private lodgings. He was more and more interested in the waters. I offered, with alacrity, to make inquiries for him, and as a first step, I returned to the little colony of riverside boarding-houses. I began with one I had made especial note of,—the smallest, neatest, and most secluded. The mistress of the establishment was at a neighbour's, and I was requested to await her return. I stepped out of the long parlour window, and began hopefully to explore the garden. My hopes were brightly rewarded. In a shady summer-house, on a sort of rustic embankment, overlooking the stream, I encountered Miss Guest and her coquettish duenna. She looked at me for a moment with a dubious air, as if to satisfy herself that she was distinctly expected to recognize me, and then, as I stood proclaiming my hopes in an appealing smile, she bade me a frank good-morning. We talked, I lingered, and at last, when the proper moment came for my going my way again, I sat down and paid a call in form.

'I see you know my name,' Miss Guest said, with the peculiar—the almost boyish—directness which seemed to be her most striking feature; 'I can't imagine how you learned it, but if you'll be so good as to tell me your own, I'll introduce you to Mrs. Beck. You must learn that she's my deputed chaperon, my she-dragon, and that I'm not to know you unless she knows you first and approves.'

Mrs. Beck poised a gold eye-glass upon her pretty *retroussé* nose,—not sorry, I think, to hold it there a moment with a plump white hand and acquit herself of one of her most effective manoeuvres,—and glanced at me with mock severity. 'He's a harmless-looking young man, my dear,' she declared, 'and I don't think your father would object.' And with this odd sanction I became intimate with Miss Guest,—intimate as, by the soft operation of summer and rural juxtaposition, an American youth is free to become with an American maid. I had told my friends, of course, the purpose of my visit, and learned, with complete satisfaction, that there was no chance for Mr. Musgrave, as they occupied the only three comfortable rooms in the house,—two as bedrooms, the third as a common parlour. Heaven forbid that I should introduce Edgar *dans cette galère*. I inquired elsewhere, but saw nothing I could recommend, and, on making my report to him, found him quite out of conceit of his project. A lady had just been telling him horrors of the local dietary and making him feel that he was vastly well off with the heavy bread and cold gravy of the hotel. It was then too, I think, he first mentioned the symptoms of that relapse which subsequently occurred. He would run no risks.

I had prepared Miss Guest, I fancy, to regard another visit as a matter of course. I paid several in rapid succession; for, under the circumstances, it would have been a pity to be shy. Her father, she told me, expected to be occupied for three or four weeks in New York, so that for the present I was at ease on that score. If I was to please, I must go bravely to work. So I burned my ships behind me, and blundered into gallantry with an ardour over which, in my absence, the two ladies must have mingled their smiles. I don't sup-

posc I passed for an especially knowing fellow; but I kept my friends
from wearying of each other (for such other chance acquaintances as
the place afforded they seemed to have little inclination), and by my
services as a retailer of the local gossip, a reader of light literature,
an explorer and suggester of drives and strolls, and, more particularly, as an oarsman in certain happy rowing-parties on the placid
river whose slow, safe current made such a pretty affectation of Mrs.
Beck's little shrieks and shudders, I very fairly earned my welcome.
That detestable scene at the hotel used to seem a sort of horrid fable
as I sat in the sacred rural stillness, in that peaceful streamside nook,
learning what a divinely honest girl she was, this daughter of the
man whose dishonesty I had so complacently attested. I wasted many
an hour in wondering on what terms she stood with her father's
rankling secret, with his poor pompous peccability in general, if not
with Edgar's particular grievance. I used to fancy that certain
momentary snatches of revery in the midst of our gaiety, and even
more, certain effusions of wilful and excessive gaiety at our duller
moments, portended some vague torment in her filial heart. She
would quit her place and wander apart for a while, leaving me to
gossip it out with Mrs. Beck, as if she were oppressed by the constant
need of seeming interested in us. But she would come back with a
face that told so few tales that I always ended by keeping my compassion in the case for myself, and being reminded afresh, by my
lively indisposition to be thus grossly lumped, as it were, with the
duenna, of how much I was interested in the damsel. In truth, the
romance of the matter apart, Miss Guest was a lovely girl. I had read
her dimly in the little chapel, but I had read her aright. Felicity in
freedom, that was her great charm. I have never known a woman
so simply and sincerely original, so finely framed to enlist the
imagination and hold expectation in suspense, and yet leave the
judgment in such blissful quietude. She had a genius for frankness;
this was her only coquetry and her only cleverness, and a woman
could not have acquitted herself more naturally of the trying and
ungracious rôle of being expected to be startling. It was the pure
personal accent of Miss Guest's walk and conversation that gave
them this charm; everything she did and said was gilded by a ray of
conviction; and to a respectful admirer who had not penetrated to
the sources of spiritual motive in her being, this sweet, natural, various emphasis of conduct was ineffably provoking. Her creed, as I
guessed it, might have been resumed in the simple notion that a
man should do his best; and nature had treated her, I fancied, to
some brighter vision of uttermost manhood than illumined most
honest fellows' consciences. Frank as she was, I imagined she had a

remote reserve of holiest contempt. She made me feel deplorably ignorant and idle and unambitious, a foolish, boyish spendthrift of time and strength and means; and I speedily came to believe that to win her perfect favour was a matter of something more than undoing a stupid wrong,—doing, namely, some very pretty piece of right. And she was poor Mr. Guest's daughter, withal! Truly, fate was a master of irony.

I ought in justice to say that I had Mrs. Beck more particularly to thank for my welcome, and for the easy terms on which I had become an *habitué* of the little summer-house by the river. How could I know how much or how little the younger lady meant by her smiles and hand-shakes, by laughing at my jokes and consenting to be rowed about in my boat? Mrs. Beck made no secret of her relish for the society of a decently agreeable man, or of her deeming some such pastime the indispensable spice of life; and in Mr. Guest's absence, I was graciously admitted to competition. The precise nature of their mutual sentiments—Mr. Guest's and hers—I was slightly puzzled to divine, and in so far as my conjectures seemed plausible, I confess they served as but a scanty offset to my knowledge of the gentleman's foibles. This lady was, to my sense, a very artificial charmer, and I think that a goodly portion of my admiration for Miss Guest rested upon a little private theory that for her father's sake she thus heroically accepted a companion whom she must have relished but little. Mrs. Beck's great point was her 'preservation'. It was rather too great a point for my taste, and partook too much of the nature of a physiological curiosity. Her age really mattered little, for with as many years as you pleased one way or the other, she was still a triumph of juvenility. Plump, rosy, dimpled, frizzled, with rings on her fingers and rosettes on her toes, she used to seem to me a sort of fantastic vagary or humorous experiment of time. Or, she might have been fancied a strayed shepherdess from some rococo Arcadia, which had melted into tradition during some profane excursion of her own, so that she found herself saddled in our prosy modern world with this absurdly perpetual prime. All this was true, at least of her pretty face and figure; but there was another Mrs. Beck, visible chiefly to the moral eye, who seemed to me excessively wrinkled and faded and world-wise, and whom I used to fancy I could hear shaking about in this enamelled envelope, like a dried nut in its shell. Mrs. Beck's morality was not Arcadian; or if it was, it was that of a shepherdess with a keen eye to the state of the wool and the mutton market, and a lively perception of the possible advantages of judicious partnership. She had no design, I suppose, of proposing to me a consolidation of our sentimental and pecuniary interests,

but she performed her duties of duenna with such conscientious precision that she shared my society most impartially with Miss Guest.
I never had the good fortune of finding myself alone with this young
lady. She might have managed it, I fancied, if she had wished, and
the little care she took about it was a sign of that indifference which
stirs the susceptible heart to effort. 'It's really detestable', I at last
ventured to seize the chance to declare, 'that you and I should never
be alone.'

Miss Guest looked at me with an air of surprise. 'Your remark is
startling,' she said, 'unless you have some excellent reason for demanding this interesting seclusion.'

My reason was not ready just yet, but it speedily ripened. A happy
incident combined at once to bring it to maturity and to operate a
diversion for Mrs. Beck. One morning there appeared a certain Mr.
Crawford out of the West, a worthy bachelor who introduced himself to Mrs. Beck and claimed cousinship. I was present at the
moment, and I could not but admire the skill with which the lady
gauged her aspiring kinsman before saying yea or nay to his claims.
I think the large diamond in his shirt-front decided her; what he may
have lacked in elegant culture was supplied by this massive ornament. Better and brighter than his diamond, however, was his frank
Western *bonhomie*, his simple friendliness, and a certain half-boyish
modesty which made him give a humorous twist to any expression
of the finer sentiments. He was a tall, lean gentleman, on the right
side of forty, yellow-haired, with a somewhat arid complexion, an
irrepressible tendency to cock back his hat and chew his toothpick,
and a spasmodic liability, spasmodically repressed when in a sedentary posture, to a centrifugal movement of the heels. He had a clear
blue eye, in which simplicity and shrewdness contended and
mingled in so lively a fashion that his glance was the oddest dramatic
twinkle. He was a genial sceptic. If he disbelieved much that he saw,
he believed everything he fancied, and for a man who had seen much
of the rougher and baser side of life, he was able to fancy some very
gracious things of men, to say nothing of women. He took his place
as a very convenient fourth in our little party, and without obtrud-
ing his eccentricities, or being too often reminded of a story, like
many cooler humourists, he treated us to a hundred anecdotes of
his adventurous ascent of the ladder of fortune. The upshot of his
history was that he was now owner of a silver mine in Arizona, and
that he proposed in his own words to 'lay off and choose'. Of the
nature of his choice he modestly waived specification; it of course
had reference to the sex of which Mrs. Beck was an ornament. He
lounged about meanwhile with his hands in his pockets, watching

the flies buzz with that air of ecstatically suspended resolve proper to a man who has sunk a shaft deep into the very stuff that dreams are made of. But in spite of shyness he exhaled an atmosphere of regretful celibacy which might have relaxed the conjugal piety of a more tenderly mourning widow than Mrs. Beck. His bachelor days were evidently numbered, and unless I was vastly mistaken, it lay in this lady's discretion to determine the residuary figure. The two were just nearly enough akin to save a deal of time in courtship.

Crawford had never beheld so finished a piece of ladyhood, and it pleased and puzzled him and quickened his honest grin very much as a remarkably neat mechanical toy might have done. Plain people who have lived close to frank nature often think more of a fine crisp muslin rose than a group of dewy petals of garden growth. Before ten days were past, he had begun to fumble tenderly with the stem of this unfading flower. Mr. Crawford's *petits soins* had something too much of the ring of the small change of the Arizona silver-mine, consisting largely as they did of rather rudimentary nosegays compounded by amateur florists from the local front-yards, of huge bundles of 'New York candy' from the village store, and of an infinite variety of birch-bark and bead-work trinkets. He was no simpleton, and it occurred to me, indeed, that if these offerings were not the tokens and pledges of a sentiment, they were the offset and substitute of a sentiment; but if they were profuse for that, they were scanty for this. Mrs. Beck, for her part, seemed minded to spin the thread of decision excessively fine. A silver-mine was all very well, but a lover fresh from the diggings was to be put on probation. Crawford lodged at the hotel, and our comings and goings were often made together. He indulged in many a dry compliment to his cousin, and, indeed, declared that she was a magnificent little woman. It was with surprise, therefore, that I learned that his admiration was divided. 'I've never seen one just like her,' he said; 'one so out and out a woman,—smiles and tears and everything else! But Clara comes out with her notions, and a man may know what to expect. I guess I can afford a wife with a notion or so! Short of the moon, I can give her what she wants.' And I seemed to hear his hands producing in his pockets that Arizonian tinkle which served with him as the prelude to renewed utterance. He went on, 'And tells me I mustn't make love to my grandmother. That's a very pretty way of confessing to thirty-five. She's a bit of coquette, is Clara!' I handled the honest fellow's illusions as tenderly as I could, and at last he eyed me askance with a knowing air. 'You praise my cousin,' he said, 'because you think I want you to. On the contrary, I want you to say something against her. If there is anything, I want to know it.' I declared I knew nothing in the world; whereupon Crawford, after a silence, heaved an impatient sigh.

'Really,' said I, laughing, 'one would think you were disappointed.'

'I wanted to draw you out,' he cried; 'but you're too confoundedly polite. I suppose Mrs. Beck's to be my fate; it's borne in on me. I'm being roped in fast. But I only want a little backing to hang off awhile. Look here,' he added suddenly, 'let's be frank!' and he stopped and laid his hand on my arm. 'That other young lady isn't so pretty as Mrs. Beck, but it seems to me I'd kind of trust her further. You didn't know I'd noticed her. Well, I've taken her in little by little, just as she gives herself out. Jerusalem! there's a woman. But you know it, sir, if I'm not mistaken; and that's where the shoe pinches. First come, first served. I want to act on the square. Before I settle down to Mrs. Beck, I want to know distinctly whether you put in a claim to Miss Guest.'

The question was unexpected and found me but half prepared. 'A claim?' I said. 'Well, yes, call it a claim!'

'Anyway,' he rejoined, 'I've no chance. She'd never look at me. But I want to have her put out of my own head, so that I can concentrate on Mrs. B. If you're not in love with her, my boy, let me tell you you ought to be! If you are, I've nothing to do but to wish you success. If you're not, upon my word, I don't know but what I would go in! She could but refuse me. Modesty is all very well; but after all, it's the handsomest thing you can do by a woman to offer yourself. As a compliment alone, it would serve. And really, a compliment with a round million isn't so bad as gallantry goes hereabouts. You're young and smart and good-looking, and Mrs. Beck tells me you're rich. If you succeed, you'll have more than your share of good things. But Fortune has her favourites, and they're not always such nice young men. If you're in love, well and good! If you're not,—by Jove, I am!'

This admonition was peremptory. My companion's face in the clear starlight betrayed his sagacious sincerity. I felt a sudden satisfaction in being summoned to take my stand. I performed a rapid operation in sentimental arithmetic, combined my factors, and established my total. It exceeded expectation. 'Your frankness does you honour,' I said, 'and I'm sorry I can't make a kinder return. But— I'm madly in love!'

PART II

IV.

My situation, as I defined it to Crawford, was not purely delightful. Close upon my perception of the state of my heart followed an oppressive sense of the vanity of my pretensions. I had cut the ground from under my feet; to offer myself to Miss Guest would be to add insult to injury. I may truly say, therefore, that, for a couple of days, this manifest passion of mine rather saddened than exalted me. For a dismal forty-eight hours I left the two ladies unvisited. I even thought of paying a supreme tribute to delicacy and taking a summary departure. Some day, possibly, Miss Guest would learn with grief and scorn what her father had to thank me for; and then later, as resentment melted into milder conjecture, she would read the riddle of my present conduct and do me justice,—guess that I had loved her, and that, to punish myself, I had renounced her for ever. This fantastic magnanimity was followed by a wholesome reaction. I was punished enough, surely, in my regret and shame; and I wished now not to suffer, but to act. Viewing the matter reasonably, she need never learn my secret; if by some cruel accident she should, the favour I had earned would cover that I had forfeited. I stayed, then, and tried to earn this precious favour; but I encountered an obstacle more serious, I fancied, than even her passionate contempt would have been,—her serene and benevolent indifference. Looking back at these momentous days, I get an impression of a period of vague sentimental fervent and trouble, rather than of definite utterance and action; though I believe that by a singular law governing human conduct in certain cases, the very modesty and humility of my passion expressed itself in a sort of florid and hyperbolical gallantry; so that, in so far as my claims were inadmissible, they might pass, partly as a kind of compensatory homage, and partly as a jest. Miss Guest refused to pay me the compliment of even being discomposed, and pretended to accept my addresses as an elaborate device for her amusement. There was a perpetual assurance in her tone of her not regarding me as a serious, much less as a dangerous, man. She could not have contrived a more effective irritant to my resolution; and I confess there were certain impatient moods when I took a brutal glee in the thought that it was not so very long since, on a notable occasion, my presence had told. In so far as I *was* serious, Miss Guest frankly offered to accept me as a friend, and laughingly intimated, indeed, that with a little matronly tuition of her dispensing, I might put myself into condition to please some simple maiden in her flower. I was an excellent, honest fellow; but I was excessively young and—as she really wished to befriend me, she would risk the admonition—I was decidedly frivolous. I lacked 'character'. I was fairly clever, but I was more clever than wise. I liked overmuch to listen to my own tongue. I had done nothing; I was idle; I had, by my own confession, never made an effort; I was too rich and too indolent; in my very good-nature there was nothing moral, no hint of principle; in short, I was—boyish. I must forgive a woman upon whom life had forced the fatal habit of discrimination. I suffered this genial scepticism to expend itself freely, for her candour was an enchantment. It was all true enough. I had been indolent and unambitious; I had made no effort; I had lived in vulgar ignorance and ease; I had in a certain frivolous fashion tried life at first hand, but my shallow gains had been in proportion to my small hazards. But I was neither so young nor so idle as she chose to fancy, and I could at any rate prove I was constant. Like a legendary suitor of old, I might even slay my dragon. A monstrous accident stood between us, and to dissipate its evil influence would be a fairly heroic feat.

Mr. Guest's absence was prolonged from day to day, and Laura's tone of allusion to her father tended indeed to make a sort of invincible chimera of her possible discovery of the truth. This fond filial reference only brought out the more brightly her unlikeness to him. I could as little fancy her doing an act she would need to conceal as I could fancy her arresting exposure by a concession to dishonour. If I was a friend, I insisted on being a familiar one; and while Mrs. Beck and her cousin floated away on perilous waters, we dabbled in the placid shallows of disinterested sentiment. For myself, I sent many a longing glance towards the open sea, but Laura remained firm in her preference for the shore. I encouraged her to speak to her father, for I wished to hear all the good that could be told of him. It sometimes seemed to me that she talked of him with a kind of vehement tenderness designed to obscure, as it were, her inner vision. Better—had she said to herself?—that she should talk fond nonsense about him than that she should harbour untender suspicions. I could easily believe that the poor man was a most lovable fellow, and could imagine how, as Laura judged him in spite of herself, the sweet allowances of a mother had grown up within the daughter. One afternoon Mrs. Beck brought forth her photograph-book, to show to her cousin. Suddenly, as he was turning it over, she stayed his hand and snatched one of the pictures from its place. He tried to recover it and a little tussle followed, in the course of which she escaped, ran to Miss Guest, and thrust the photograph into her hand. 'You keep it,' she cried; 'he's not to see it.' There was a great crying out from Crawford about Mrs. Beck's inconstancy and his *right* to see the picture, which was cut short by Laura's saying with some gravity that it was too childish a romp for a man of forty and a woman of—thirty! Mrs. Beck allowed us no time to relish the irony of this attributive figure; she caused herself to be pursued to the other end of the garden, where the amorous frolic was resumed over the following pages of the album. 'Who is it?' I asked. Miss Guest, after a pause, handed me the card.

'Your father!' I cried precipitately.

'Ah, you've seen him?' she asked.

'I know him by his likeness to you.'

'You prevent my asking you, as I meant, if he doesn't look like a dear good man. I do wish he'd drop his stupid business and come back.'

I took occasion hereupon to ascertain whether she suspected his embarrassments. She confessed to a painful impression that something was wrong. He had been out of spirits for many days before his return to town; nothing indeed but mental distress could have affected his health, for he had a perfect constitution. 'If it comes to that,' she went on, after a long silence, and looking at me with an almost intimate confidence, 'I wish he would give up business altogether. All the business in the world, for a man of his open, joyous temper, doesn't pay for an hour's depression. I can't bear to sit by and see him embittered and spoiled by this muddle of stocks and shares. Nature made him a happy man; I insist on keeping him so. We are quite rich enough, and we need nothing more. He tries to persuade me that I have expensive tastes, but I've never spent money but to please him. I have a lovely little dream which I mean to lay before him when he comes back; it's very cheap, like all dreams, and more practicable than most. He's to give up business and take me abroad. We're to settle down quietly somewhere in Germany, in Italy, I don't care where, and I'm to study music seriously. I'm never to marry; but as he grows to be an old man, he's to sit by a window, with his cigar, looking out on the Arno or the Rhine, while I play Beethoven and Rossini.'

'It's a very pretty programme,' I answered, 'though I can't subscribe to certain details. But do you know,' I added, touched by a forcible appeal to sympathy in her tone, 'although you refuse to believe me anything better than an ingenuous fool, this liberal concession to my interest in your situation is almost a proof of respect.'

She blushed a little, to my great satisfaction. 'I surely respect you,' she said, 'if you come to that! Otherwise we should hardly be sitting here so simply. And I think, too,' she went on, 'that I speak to you of my father with peculiar freedom, because—because, somehow, you remind me of him.' She looked at me as she spoke with such penetrating candour that it was my turn to blush. 'You are genial, and gentle, and essentially honest, like him; and like him,' she added with a half-smile, 'you're addicted to saying a little more than it would be fair to expect you to stand to. You ought to be very good friends. You'll find he has your own *jeunesse de coeur*.'

I murmured what I might about the happiness of making his acquaintance; and then, to give the conversation a turn, and really to test the force of this sympathetic movement of hers, I boldly mentioned my fancy that he was an admirer of Mrs. Beck. She gave me a silent glance, almost of gratitude, as if she needed to unburden her heart. But she did so in a few words. 'He does admire her,' she said. 'It's my duty, it's my pleasure, to respect his illusions. But I confess to you that I hope this one will fade.' She rose from her seat and we joined our companions; but I fancied, for a week afterwards, that she treated me with a certain gracious implication of deference. Had I ceased to seem boyish? I struck a truce with urgency and almost relished the idea of being patient.

A day or two later, Mr. Guest's 'illusions' were put before me in a pathetic light. It was a Sunday; the ladies were at church, and Crawford and I sat smoking on the piazza. 'I don't know how things are going with you,' he said; 'you're either perfectly successful or desperately resigned. But unless it's rather plainer sailing than in my case, I don't envy you. I don't know where I am, anyway! She will and she won't. She may take back her word once too often, I can tell her that! You see, she has two strings to her bow. She likes my money, but she doesn't like *me*. Now, it's all very well for a woman to relish a fortune, but I'm not prepared to have my wife despise— my *person*!' said Crawford with feeling. 'The alternative, you know, is Mr. Guest, that girl's father. I suppose he's handsome, and a wit, and a dandy; though I must say an old dandy, to my taste, is an old fool. She tells me a dozen times an hour that he's a fascinating man. I suppose if I were to leave her alone for a week, I might seem a fascinating man. I wish to heaven she wasn't so confoundedly taking. I can't give her up; she amuses me too much. There was once a little actress in Galveston, but Clara beats that girl! If I could only have gone in for some simple wholesome girl who doesn't need to count on her fingers to know the state of her heart!'

That evening as we were gathered in the garden, poor Crawford approached Laura Guest with an air of desperate gallantry, as if from a desire to rest from the petty torment of Mrs. Beck's sentimental mutations. Laura liked him, and her manner to him had always been admirable in its almost sisterly frankness and absence of provoking arts; yet I found myself almost wondering, as they now strolled about the garden together, whether there was any danger of this sturdy architect of his own fortunes putting out my pipe. Mrs. Beck, however, left me no chance for selfish meditation. Her artless and pointless prattle never lacked a purpose; before you knew it she was, in vulgar parlance, 'pumping' you, trying to pick your pocket of your poor little receipt for prosperity. She took an intense delight in imaginatively bettering her condition, and one was forced to carry bricks for her castles in the air.

'You needn't be afraid of my cousin,' she said, laughing, as I followed his red cigar-tip along the garden-paths. 'He admires Laura altogether too much to make love to her. There's modesty! Don't you think it's rather touching in a man with a million of dollars? I don't mind telling you that he has made love to me, that being no case for modesty. I suppose you'll say that my speaking of it is. But what's the use of being an aged widow, if one can't tell the truth?'

'There's comfort in being an aged widow,' I answered gallantly, 'when one has two offers a month.'

'I don't know what you know about my offers; but even two swallows don't make a summer! However, since you've mentioned the subject, tell me frankly what you think of poor Crawford. Is he at all presentable? You see I like him, I esteem him, and I'm afraid of being blinded by my feelings. Is he so dreadfully rough? You see I like downright simple manliness and all that; but a little polish does no harm, even on fine gold. I do wish you'd take hold of my poor cousin and teach him a few of the amenities of life. I'm very fond of the amenities of life; it's very frivolous and wicked, I suppose, but I can't help it. I have the misfortune to be sensitive to ugly things. Can one really accept a man who wears a green cravat? Of course you can make him take it off; but you'll be knowing all the while that he pines for it, that he would put it on if he could. Now that's a symbol of that dear, kind, simple fellow,—a heart of gold, but a green cravat! I've never heard a word of wisdom about that matter yet. People talk about the sympathy of souls being the foundation of happiness in marriage. It's pure nonsense. It's not the great things, but the little, that we dispute about, and the chances are terribly against the people who have a different taste in colours.'

It seemed to me that, thus ardently invoked, I might hazard the observation, 'Mr. Guest would never wear a green cravat.'

'What do you know about Mr. Guest's cravats?'

'I've seen his photograph, you know.'

'Well, you do him justice. You should see him in the life. He looks like a duke. I never saw a duke, but that's my notion of a duke. Distinction, you know; perfect manners and tact and wit. If I'm right about it's being perfection in small things that assures one's happiness, I might—well, in two words, I might be very happy with Mr. Guest!'

'It's Crawford and soul, then,' I proposed, smiling, 'or Guest and manners!'

She looked at me a moment, and then with a toss of her head and a tap of her fan, 'You wretch!' she cried, 'you want to make me say something very ridiculous. I'll not pretend I'm not worldly. I'm excessively worldly. I always make a point of letting people know it. Of course I know very well my cousin's rich, and that so long as he's good he's none the worse for that. But in my quiet little way I'm a critic, and I look at things from a high ground. I compare a rich man who is simply a good fellow to a perfect gentleman who has simply a nice little fortune. Mr. Guest has a nice property, a very nice property. I shouldn't have to make over my old bonnets. You may ask me if I'm not afraid of Laura. But you'll marry Laura and carry her off!'

I found nothing to reply for some moments to this little essay in 'criticism'; and suddenly Mrs. Beck, fancying perhaps that she was indiscreetly committing herself, put an end to our interview. 'I'm really very kind,' she cried, 'to be talking so graciously about a lover who leaves me alone for a month and never even drops me a line. It's not such good manners after all. If you're not jealous of Mr. Crawford, I am of Miss Guest. We'll go down and separate them.'

Miss Guest's repose and dignity were decidedly overshadowed. I brought her the next afternoon a letter from the post-office, super-scribed in a hand I knew, and wandered away while she sat in the garden and read it. When I came back she looked strangely sad. I sat down near her and drew figures in the ground with the end of her parasol, hoping that she would do me the honour to communi-cate her trouble. At last she rose in silence, as if to return to the house. I begged her to remain. 'You're in distress,' I said, speaking as calmly and coldly as I could, 'and I hoped it might occur to you that there is infinite sympathy close at hand. Instead of going to your own room to cry, why not stay here and talk of it with me?'

She gave me a brilliant, searching gaze; I met it steadily and felt that I was turning pale with the effort not to obey the passionate impulse of self-denunciation. She began slowly to walk away from the house, and I felt that a point was gained. 'It's your father, of course,' I said. It was all I could say. She silently handed me his un-folded letter. It ran as follows: —

MY DEAREST DAUGHTER: —I have sold the house and everything in it, except your piano and books, of course at a painful sacrifice. But I needed ready money. Forgive your poor blundering, cruel father. My old luck has left me; but only *trust me*, and we shall be happy again.'

Her eyes, fortunately, were wandering while I read; for I felt myself blushing to my ears.

'It's not the loss of the house,' she said at last; 'though of course we were fond of it. I grew up there,—my mother died there. It's the trouble it indicates. Poor dear father! Why does he talk of "luck"? I detest the word! Why does he talk of forgiving him and trusting him? There's a wretched tone about it all. If he would only come back and let me look at him!'

'Nothing is more common in business,' I answered, 'than a temporary embarrassment demanding ready money. Of course it must be met at a sacrifice. One throws a little something overboard to lighten the ship, and the ship sails ahead. As for the loss of the house, nothing could be better for going to Italy, you know. You've no excuse left for staying here. If your father will forgive me the interest I take in his affairs, I strongly recommend his leaving business and its sordid cares. Let him go abroad and forget it all.'

Laura walked along in silence, and I led the way out of the garden into the road. We followed it slowly till we reached the little chapel. The sexton was just leaving it, shouldering the broom with which he had been sweeping it for the morrow's services. I hailed him and gained his permission to go in and try the organ, assuring him that we were experts. Laura said that she felt in no mood for music; but she entered and sat down in one of the pews. I climbed into the gallery and attacked the little instrument. We had had no music since our first meeting, and I felt an irresistible need to recall the circumstances of that meeting. I played in a simple fashion, respectably enough, and fancied, at all events, that by my harmonious fingers I could best express myself. I played for an hour, in silence, choosing what I would, without comment or response from my companion. The summer twilight overtook us; when it was getting too dark to see the keys, I rejoined Miss Guest. She rose and came into the aisle. 'You play very well,' she said, simply; 'better than I supposed.'

Her praise was sweet; but sweeter still was a fancy of mine that I perceived in the light gloom just the glimmer of a tear. 'In this place,'

I said, 'your playing once moved me greatly. Try and remember the scene distinctly.'

'It's easily remembered,' she answered, with an air of surprise.

'Believe, then, that when we parted, I was already in love with you.'

She turned away abruptly. 'Ah, my poor music!'

The next day, on my arrival, I was met by Mrs. Beck, whose pretty forehead seemed clouded with annoyance. With her own fair hand she buttonholed me. 'You apparently,' she said, 'have the happiness to be in Miss Guest's confidence. What on earth is going on in New York? Laura received an hour ago a letter from her father. I found her sitting with it in her hand as cheerful as a Quakeress in meeting. "Something's wrong, my dear," I said; "I don't know what. In any case, be assured of my sympathy." She gave me the most extraordinary stare. "You'll be interested to know," she said, "that my father has lost half his property." Interested to know! I verily believe the child meant an impertinence. What is Mr. Guest's property to me? Has he been speculating? Stupid man!' she cried, with vehemence.

I made a brief answer. I discovered Miss Guest sitting by the river, in pale contemplation of household disaster. I asked no questions. She told me of her own accord that her father was to return immediately, 'to make up a month's sleep,' she added, glancing at his letter. We spoke of other matters, but before I left her, I returned to this one. 'I wish you to tell your father this,' I said. 'That there is a certain gentleman here, who is idle, indolent, ignorant, frivolous, selfish. That he has certain funds for which he is without present use. That he places them at Mr. Guest's absolute disposal in the hope that they may partially relieve his embarrassment.' I looked at Laura as I spoke and watched her startled blush deepen to crimson. She was about to reply; but before she could speak, 'Don't forget to add,' I went on, 'that he hopes his personal faults will not prejudice Mr. Guest's acceptance of his offer, for it is prompted by the love he bears his daughter.'

'You must excuse me,' Laura said, after a pause. 'I had rather not tell him this. He would not accept your offer.'

'Are you sure of that?'

'I shouldn't allow him.'

'And why not, pray? Don't you, after all, like me well enough to suffer me to do you so small a service?'

She hesitated; then gave me her hand with magnificent frankness. 'I like you too well to suffer you to do me just that service. We take that from les indifférents.'

v.

Before the month was out, Edgar had quarrelled with the healing waters of L—. His improvement had been most illusory; his old symptoms had returned in force, and though he now railed bitterly at the perfidious spring and roundly denounced the place, he was too ill to be moved away. He was altogether confined to his room. I made a conscience of offering him my company and assistance, but he would accept no nursing of mine. He would be tended by no one whom he could not pay for his trouble and enjoy a legal right to grumble at. 'I expect a nurse to *be* a nurse,' he said, 'and not a fine gentleman, waiting on me in gloves. It would be fine work for me, lying here, to have to think twice whether I might bid you not to breathe so hard.' Nothing had passed between us about John Guest, though the motive for silence was different on each side. For Edgar, I fancied, our interview with him was a matter too solemn for frequent allusion; for me it was a detestable thought. But wishing now to assure myself that, as I supposed, he had paid his ugly debt, I asked Edgar, on the evening I had extorted from Miss Guest those last recorded words of happy omen, whether he had heard from our friend in New York. It was a very hot night; poor Edgar lay sweltering under a sheet, with open windows. He looked pitifully ill, and yet somehow more intensely himself than ever. He drew a letter from under his pillow. 'This came today,' he said. 'Stevens writes me that Guest yesterday paid down the twenty thousand dollars in full. It's quick work. I hope he's not robbed Peter to pay Paul.'

'Mr. Guest has a conscience,' I said; and I thought bitterly of the reverse of the picture. 'I'm afraid he has half ruined himself to do it.'

'Well, ruin for ruin, I prefer his. I've no doubt his affairs have gone to the dogs. The affairs of such a man must, sooner or later! I believe, by the. way, you've been cultivating the young lady. What does the papa say to that?'

'Of course,' I said, without heeding his question, 'you've already enclosed him the—the little paper.'

Edgar turned in his bed. 'Of course I've done no such thing!'

'You mean to keep it?' I cried.

'Of course I mean to keep it. Where else would be his punishment?'

There was something vastly grotesque in the sight of this sickly little mortal erecting himself among his pillows as a dispenser of justice, an appraiser of the wages of sin; but I confess that his attitude struck me as more cruel even than ludicrous. I was disappointed. I had certainly not expected Edgar to be generous, but I had ex-

pected him to be just, and in the heat of his present irritation he was
neither. He was angry with Guest for his excessive promptitude,
which had given a sinister twist to his own conduct. 'Upon my word,'
I cried, 'you're a veritable Shylock!'

'And you're a veritable fool! Is it set down in the bond that I'm
to give it up to him? The thing's mine, to have and to hold forever.
The scoundrel would be easily let off indeed! This bit of paper in my
hands is to keep him in order and prevent his being too happy. The
thought will be wholesome company,—a *memento mori* to his
vanity.'

'He's to go through life, then, with possible exposure staring him
in the face?'

Edgar's great protuberant eyes expanded without blinking. 'He
has committed his fate to Providence.'

I was revolted. 'You may have the providential qualities, but you
have not the gentlemanly ones, I formally protest. But, after a decent
delay, he'll of course demand the document.'

'Demand it? He shall have it then, with a vengeance!'

'Well, I wash my hands of further complicity! I shall inform Mr.
Guest that I count for nothing in this base negation of his right.'

Edgar paused for a moment to stare at me in my unprecedented
wrath. Then making me a little ironical gesture of congratulation,
'Inform him of what you please. I hope you'll have a pleasant talk
over it! You made rather a bad beginning, but who knows, if you
put your heads together to abuse me, you may end as bosom friends!
I've watched you, sir!' he suddenly added, propping himself forward
among his pillows; 'you're in love!' I may wrong the poor fellow,
but it seemed to me that in these words he discharged the bitterness
of a lifetime. He too would have hoped to please, and he had lived
in acrid assent to the instinct which told him such hope was vain.
In one way or another a man pays his tax to manhood. 'Yes, sir,
you're grossly in love! What do I know about love, you ask? I know
a drivelling lover when I see him. You've made a clever choice. Do
you expect John Guest to give the girl away? He's a good-natured
man, I know; but really, considering your high standard of gentlemanly conduct, you ask a good deal.'

Edgar had been guilty on this occasion of a kind of reckless moral
self-exposure, which seemed to betray a sense that he should never
need his reputation again. I felt as if I were standing by something
very like a death-bed, and forbearingly, without rejoinder, I withdrew. He had simply expressed more brutally, however, my own
oppressive belief that the father's aversion stood darkly massed in
the rear of the daughter's indifference. I had, indeed, for the present,

the consolation of believing that with Laura the day of pure indifference was over; and I tried hard to flatter myself that my position was tenable in spite of Mr. Guest. The next day as I was wandering on the hotel piazza, communing thus sadly with my hopes, I met Crawford, who, with his hands in his pockets and his hat on the bridge of his nose, seemed equally a sullen probationer of fate.

'I'm going down to join our friends,' I said; 'I expected to find you with them.'

He gave a gloomy grin. 'My nose is out of joint,' he said; 'Mr. Guest has come back.' I turned pale, but he was too much engaged with his own trouble to observe it. 'What do you suppose my cousin is up to? She had agreed to drive with me and I had determined to come home, once for all, engaged or rejected. As soon as she heard of Guest's arrival, she threw me overboard and tripped off to her room, to touch up her curls. Go down there now and you'll find her shaking them at Mr. Guest. By the Lord, sir, she can whistle for me now! If there was a decently good-looking woman in this house, I'd march straight up to her and offer myself. You're a happy man, my boy, not to have a d—d fool to interfere with you, and not to be in love with a d—d fool either.'

I had no present leisure to smooth the turbid waters of poor Crawford's passion; but I remembered a clever remark in a French book, to the effect that even the best men—and Crawford was one of the best—are subject to a momentary need not to respect what they love. I repaired alone to the house by the river, and found Laura in the little parlour which she shared with Mrs. Beck. The room was flooded with the glow of a crimson sunset, and she was looking out of the long window at two persons in the garden. In my great desire to obtain some firm assurance from her before her father's interference should become a certainty, I lost no time. 'I've been able to think of nothing,' I said, 'but your reply to that poor offer of mine. I've been flattering myself that it really means something,—means, possibly, that if I were to speak—here—now—all that I long to speak, you would listen to me more kindly. Laura,' I cried, passionately, 'I repent of all my follies and I love you!'

She looked at me from head to foot with a gaze almost strange in its intensity. It betrayed trouble, but, I fancied, a grateful trouble. Then, with a smile, 'My father has come,' she said. The words set my heart a-beating, and I had a horrible fancy that they were maliciously uttered. But as she went on I was reassured. 'I want him to see you, though he knows nothing of your offer.'

Somehow, by her tone, my mind was suddenly illumined with a

delicious apprehension of her motive. She had heard the early murmur of that sentiment whose tender essence resents compulsion. 'Let me feel then,' I said, 'that I am not to stand or fall by *his* choice.'

'He's sure to like you,' she answered; 'don't you remember my telling you so? He judges better of men than of women,' she added sadly, turning away from the window.

Mr. Guest had been advancing towards the house, side by side with Mrs. Beck. Before they reached it the latter was met by two ladies who had been ushered into the garden from the front gate, and with whom, with an air of smothered petulance, perceptible even at a distance, she retraced her steps towards the summer-house. Her companion entered our little parlour alone from the piazza. He stepped jauntily and looked surprisingly little altered by his month's ordeal. Mrs. Beck might still have taken him for a duke, or, at least, for an earl. His daughter immediately introduced me. 'Happy to make your acquaintance, sir,' he exclaimed, in a voice which I was almost shocked to find how well I knew. He offered his hand. I met it with my own, and the next moment we were fairly face to face. I was prepared for anything. Recognition faltered for a mere instant in his eyes; then I felt it suddenly leap forth in the tremendous wrench of his hand, 'Ah, you—*you*—you!'

'Why, you know him!' exclaimed Laura.

Guest continued to wring my hand, and I felt to my cost that he was shocked. He panted a moment for breath, and then burst into a monstrous laugh. I looked askance at Laura; her eyes were filled with wonder. I felt that for the moment anger had made her father reckless, and anything was better than that between us the edge of our secret should peep out. 'We have been introduced,' I said, trying to smile. Guest dropped my hand as if it burned him, and walked the length of the room.

'You should have told me!' Laura added, in a tone of almost familiar reproach.

'Miss Guest,' I answered, hardly knowing what I said, 'the world is so wide——'

'Upon my soul, I think it's damnably narrow!' cried Guest, who had turned very pale.

I determined then that he should know the worst. 'I'm here with a purpose, Mr. Guest,' I said; 'I love your daughter.'

He stopped short, fairly glaring at me. Laura stepped towards him and laid her two hands on his arm. 'Something is wrong,' she said, 'very wrong! It's your horrible money-matters! Weren't you really then so generous?,' and she turned to me.

Guest laid his other hand on hers as they rested on his arm and

patted them gently. 'My daughter,' he said solemnly, 'do your poor
father a favour. Dismiss him forever. Turn him out of the house,'
he added, fiercely.

'You wrong your daughter,' I cried, 'by asking her to act so
blindly and cruelly.'

'My child,' Guest went on, 'I expect you to obey!'

There was a silence. At last Laura turned to me, excessively pale.
'Will you do me the very great favour,' she said, with a trembling
voice, 'to leave us?'

I reflected a moment. 'I appreciate your generosity; but in the
interest of your own happiness, I beg you not to listen to your father
until I have had a word with him alone.'

She hesitated and looked, as if for assent, at her father. 'Great
heavens, girl!' he cried, 'you don't mean you love him!' She blushed
to her hair and rapidly left the room.

Guest took up his hat and removed a speck of dust from the ribbon
by a fillip of his finger-nail. 'Young man,' he said, 'you waste words!'

'Not, I hope, when, with my hand on my heart, I beg your pardon.'

'Now that you have something to gain. If you respect me, you
should have protested before. If you don't, you've nothing to do with
me or mine.'

'I allow for your natural resentment, but you might keep it within
bounds. I religiously forget, ignore, efface the past. Meet me half-
way! When we met a month ago, I already loved your daughter. If
I had dreamed of your being ever so remotely connected with her, I
would have arrested that detestable scene even by force, brother of
mine though your adversary was!'

Guest put on his hat with a gesture of implacable contempt. 'That's
all very well! You don't know me, sir, or you'd not waste your breath
on *ifs*! The thing's done. Such as I stand here, I've been *dishonoured*!' And two hot tears sprang into his eyes. 'Such as I stand
here, I carry in my poor, sore heart the vision of your great, brutal,
staring, cruel presence. And now you ask me to accept that presence
as perpetual! Upon my soul, I'm a precious fool to talk about it.'

I made an immense effort to remain calm and courteous. 'Is there
nothing I can do to secure your good-will? I'll make any sacrifice.'

'Nothing but to leave me at once and for ever. Fancy my living
with you for an hour! Fancy, whenever I met your eyes, my seeing
in them the reflection of—of that piece of business! And your walking about looking wise and chuckling! My precious young man,'
he went on with a scorching smile, 'if you knew how I hated you,
you'd give me a wide berth.'

I was silent for some moments, teaching myself the great patience

which I foresaw I should need. 'This is after all but the question of
our personal relations, which we might fairly leave to time. Not only
am I willing to pledge myself to the most explicit respect——'

'Explicit respect!' he broke out. 'I should relish that vastly!
Heaven deliver me from your explicit respect!'

'I can quite believe,' I quietly continued, 'that I should get to like
you. Your daughter has done me the honour to say that she believed
you would like me.'

'Perfect! You've talked it all over with her?'

'At any rate,' I declared roundly, 'I love her, and I have reason to
hope that I may render myself acceptable to her. I can only add,
Mr. Guest, that much as I should value your approval of my suit, if
you withhold it I shall try my fortune without it!'

'Gently, impetuous youth!' And Guest laid his hand on my arm
and lowered his voice. 'Do you dream that if my daughter ever so
faintly suspected the truth, she would even look at you again?'

'The truth? Heaven forbid she should dream of it! I wonder that
in your position you should allude to it so freely.'

'I was prudent once; I shall treat myself to a little freedom now.
Give it up, I advise you. She may have thought you a pretty young
fellow; I took you for one myself at first; but she'll keep her affection
for a man with the bowels of compassion. She'll never love a coward,
sir. Upon my soul, I'd sooner she married your beautiful brother. *He*,
at least, had a grievance. Don't talk to me about my own child. She
and I have an older love than yours; and if she were to learn that
I've been weak—Heaven help me!—she would only love me the more.
She would feel only that I've been outraged.'

I confess that privately I flinched, but I stood to it bravely. 'Miss
Guest, doubtless, is as perfect a daughter as she would be a wife.
But allow me to say that a woman's heart is not so simple a mechanism. Your daughter is a person of a very fine sense of honour, and I
can imagine nothing that would give her greater pain than to be
reduced to an attitude of mere compassion for her father. She likes
to believe that men are strong. The sense of respect is necessary to
her happiness. We both wish to assure that happiness. Let us join
hands to preserve her illusions.'

I saw in his eye no concession except to angry perplexity. 'I don't
know what you mean,' he cried, 'and I don't want to know. If you
wish to intimate that my daughter is so very superior a person that
she'll despise me, you're mistaken! She's beyond any compliment
you can pay her. You can't frighten me now; I don't care for things.'
He walked away a moment and then turned about with flushed face
and trembling lip. 'I'm broken, I'm ruined! I don't want my

daughter's respect, nor any other woman's. It's a burden, a mockery, a snare! What's a woman worth who can be kind only while she believes? Ah, ah!' and he began to rub his hands with a sudden air of helpless senility, 'I should never be so kissed and coddled and nursed. I can tell her what I please; I shan't mind what I say now. I've ceased to care,—all in a month! Reputation's a farce; a pair of tight boots, worn for vanity. I used to have a good foot, but I shall end my days in my slippers. I don't care for anything!'

This mood was piteous, but it was also formidable, for I was scantily disposed to face the imputation of having reduced an amiable gentleman, in however strictly just a cause, to this state of plaintive cynicism. I could only hope that time would repair both his vanity and his charity, seriously damaged as they were. 'Well,' I said, taking my hat, 'a man in love, you know, is obstinate. Confess yourself that you'd not think the better of me for accepting dismissal philosophically. A single word of caution, keep cool; don't lose your head; don't speak recklessly to Laura. I protest that, for myself, I'd rather my mistress shouldn't doubt of her father.'

Guest had seated himself on the sofa with his hat on, and remained staring absently at the carpet, as if he were deaf to my words. As I turned away, Mrs. Beck crossed the piazza and stood on the threshold of the long window. Her shadow fell at Mr. Guest's feet; she sent a searching glance from his face to mine. He started, stared, rose, stiffened himself up, and removed his hat. Suddenly he coloured to the temples, and after a second's delay there issued from behind this ruby curtain a wondrous imitation of a smile. I turned away, reassured. 'My case is not hopeless,' I said to myself. 'You *do* care for something, yet.' Even had I deemed it hopeless, I might have made my farewell. Laura met me near the gate, and I remember thinking that trouble was vastly becoming to her.

'Is your quarrel too bad to speak of?' she asked.

'Allow me to make an urgent request. Your father forbids me to think of you, and you, of course, to think of me. You see,' I said, mustering a smile, 'we're in a delightfully romantic position, persecuted by a stern parent. He will say hard things of me; I say nothing about your believing them, I leave that to your own discretion. But don't contradict them. Let him call me cruel, pusillanimous, false, whatever he will. Ask no questions; they will bring you no comfort. Be patient, be a good daughter, and—wait!'

Her brow contracted painfully over her intensely lucid eyes, and she shook her head impatiently. 'Let me understand. Have you really done wrong?'

I felt that it was but a slender sacrifice to generosity to say Yes, and to add that I had repented. I even felt gratefully that whatever it might be to have a crime to confess to, it was not 'boyish'.

For a moment, I think, Laura was on the point of asking me a supreme question about her father, but she suppressed it and abruptly left me.

My step-brother's feeble remnant of health was now so cruelly reduced that the end of his troubles seemed near. He was in constant pain, and was kept alive only by stupefying drugs. As his last hour might strike at any moment, I was careful to remain within call, and for several days saw nothing of father or daughter. I learned from Crawford that they had determined to prolong their stay into the autumn, for Mr. Guest's 'health'. 'I don't know what's the matter with his health,' Crawford grumbled. 'For a sick man he seems uncommonly hearty, able to sit out of doors till midnight with Mrs. B., and always as spick and span as a bridegroom. I'm the invalid of the lot,' he declared; 'the climate don't agree with me.' Mrs. Beck, it appeared, was too fickle for patience; he would be made a fool of no more. If she wanted him, she must come and fetch him; and if she valued her chance, she must do it without delay. He departed for New York to try the virtue of missing and being missed.

On the evening he left us, the doctor told me that Edgar could not outlast the night. At midnight, I relieved the watcher and took my place by his bed. Edgar's soundless and motionless sleep was horribly like death. Sitting watchful by his pillow, I passed an oppressively solemn night. It seemed to me that a part of myself was dying, and that I was sitting in cold survival of youthful innocence and of the lavish self-surrender of youth. There is a certain comfort in an ancient grievance, and as I thought of having heard for the last time the strenuous quaver of Edgar's voice, I could have wept as for the effacement of some revered horizon-line of life. I heard his voice again, however; he was not even to die without approving the matter. With the first flash of dawn and the earliest broken bird-note, he opened his eyes and began to murmur disconnectedly. At length he recognized me, and, with me, his situation. 'Don't go on tiptoe, and hold your breath, and pull a long face,' he said; 'speak up like a man. I'm doing the biggest job I ever did yet, you'll not interrupt me; I'm dying. One—two, three—four; I can almost count the ebbing waves. And to think that all these years they've been breaking on the strand of the universe! It's only when the world's din is shut out, at the last, that we hear them. I'll not pretend to say I'm not sorry; I've been a man of this world. It's a great one; there's a vast deal to do in it, for a man of sense. I've not been a fool, either. Write that for my epitaph, *He was no fool!*—except when he went to L. I'm not satisfied yet. I might have got better, and richer. I wanted to try galvanism, and to transfer that Pennsylvania stock. Well, I'm to be transferred myself. If dying's the end of it all, it's as well to die worse as to die better. At any rate, while time was mine, I didn't waste it. I went over my will, pen in hand, for the last time, only a week ago, crossed the *t*'s and dotted the *i*'s. I've left you—nothing. You need nothing for comfort, and of course you expect nothing for sentiment. I've left twenty thousand dollars to found an infirmary for twenty indigent persons suffering from tumour in the stomach. *There*'s sentiment! There will be no trouble about it, for my affairs are in perfect shape. Twenty snug little beds in my own little house in Philadelphia. They can get five into the dining-room.' He was silent awhile, as if with a kind of ecstatic vision of the five little beds in a row. 'I don't know that there is anything else,' he said, at last, 'except a few old papers to be burned. I hate leaving rubbish behind me; it's enough to leave one's mouldering carcass!'

At his direction I brought a large tin box from a closet and placed it on a chair by the bedside, where I drew from it a dozen useless papers and burned them one by one in the candle. At last, when but three or four were left, I laid my hand on a small sealed document labelled *Guest's Confession*. My hand trembled as I held it up to him, and as he recognized it a faint flush overspread his cadaverous pallor. He frowned, as if painfully confused. 'How did it come there? I sent it back, I sent it back,' he said. Then suddenly with a strangely erroneous recollection of our recent dispute, 'I told you so the other day, you remember; and you said I was too generous. And what did you tell me about the daughter? You're in love with her? Ah yes! What a muddle!'

I respected his confusion. 'You say you've left me nothing,' I answered. 'Leave me this.'

For all reply, he turned over with a groan, and relapsed into stupor. The nurse shortly afterwards came to relieve me; but though I lay down, I was unable to sleep. The personal possession of that little scrap of paper acted altogether too potently on my nerves and my imagination. In due contravention of the doctor, Edgar outlasted the night and lived into another day. But as high noon was clashing out from the village church, and I stood with the doctor by his bedside, the latter, who had lifted his wrist a little to test his pulse, released it, not with the tenderness we render to suffering, but with a more summary reverence. Suffering was over.

By the close of the day I had finished my preparations for attending my step-brother's remains to burial in Philadelphia, among those of his own people; but before my departure, I measured once more that well-trodden road to the house by the river, and requested a moment's conversation with Mr. Guest. In spite of my attention being otherwise engaged, I had felt strangely all day that I carried a sort of magic talisman, a mystic key to fortune. I was constantly fumbling in my waistcoat-pocket to see whether the talisman was really there. I wondered that, as yet, Guest should not have demanded a surrender of his note; but I attributed his silence to shame, scorn, and defiance, and promised myself a sort of golden advantage by anticipating his claim with the cogent frankness of justice. But as soon as he entered the room I foresaw that Justice must show her sword as well as her scales. His resentment had deepened into a kind of preposterous arrogance, of a temper quite insensible to logic. He had more than recovered his native buoyancy and splendour; there was an air of feverish impudence in his stare, his light swagger, in the very hue and fashion of his crimson necktie. He had an evil genius with blonde curls and innumerable flounces.

'I feel it to be a sort of duty,' I said, 'to inform you that my brother died this morning.'

'Your brother? What's your brother to me? He's been dead to me these three days. Is that all you have to say?'

I was irritated by the man's stupid implacability, and my purpose received a check. 'No,' I answered, 'I've several things more to touch upon.'

'In so far as they concern my daughter, you may leave them unsaid. She tells me of your offer to—to *buy off* my opposition. Am I to understand that it was seriously made? You're a coarser young man than I fancied!'

'She told you of my offer?' I cried.

'O, you needn't build upon that! She hasn't mentioned your name since.'

I was silent, thinking my own thoughts. I won't answer for it that, in spite of his caution, I did *not* lay an immaterial brick or two. 'You're still irreconcilable?' I contented myself with asking.

He assumed an expression of absolutely jovial contempt. 'My dear sir, I detest the sight of you!'

'Have you no question to ask, no demand to make?'

He looked at me a moment in silence, with just the least little twitch and tremour of mouth and eye. His vanity, I guessed on the instant, was determined stoutly to ignore that I held him at an advantage and to refuse me the satisfaction of extorting from him the least allusion to the evidence of his disgrace. He had known bitter compulsion once; he would not do it the honour to concede that it had not spent itself. 'No demand but that you will excuse my further attendance.'

My own vanity took a hand in the game. Justice herself was bound to go no more than half-way. If he was not afraid of his little paper, he might try a week or two more of bravery. I bowed to him in silence and let him depart. As I turned to go I found myself face to face with Mrs. Beck, whose pretty visage was flushed with curiosity. 'You and Mr. Guest have quarrelled,' she said roundly.

'As you see, madam.'

'As I see, madam! But what is it all about?'

'About—his daughter.'

'His daughter and his ducats! You're a very deep young man, in spite of those boyish looks of yours. Why did you never tell me you knew him? You've quarrelled about money matters.'

'As you say,' I answered, 'I'm very deep. Don't tempt me to further subterfuge.'

'He has lost money, I know. Is it much? Tell me that.'

'It's an enormous sum!' I said with mock solemnity.

'Provoking man!' And she gave a little stamp of disgust.

'He's in trouble,' I said. 'To a woman of your tender sympathies he ought to be more interesting than ever.'

She mused a moment, fixing me with her keen blue eye. 'It's a sad responsibility to have a heart!' she murmured.

'In that,' I said, 'we perfectly agree.'

VI.

It was a singular fact that Edgar's affairs turned out to be in by no means the exemplary order in which he had flattered himself he placed them. They were very much at sixes and sevens. The discovery, to me, was almost a shock. I might have drawn from it a pertinent lesson on the fallacy of human pretensions. The gentleman whom Edgar had supremely honoured (as he seemed to assume in his will) by appointing his executor, responded to my innocent surprise by tapping his forehead with a peculiar smile. It was partly from curiosity as to the value of this explanation, that I helped him to look into the dense confusion which prevailed in my step-brother's estate. It revealed certainly an odd compound of madness and method. I learned with real regret that the twenty eleemosynary beds at Philadelphia must remain a superb conception. I was horrified at every step by the broad license with which his will had to be interpreted. All profitless as I was in the case, when I thought of the comfortable credit in which he had died, I felt like some greedy kinsman of tragedy making impious havoc with a sacred bequest. There matters detained me for a week in New York, where I had joined my brother's executor. At my earliest moment of leisure, I called upon Crawford at the office of a friend to whom he had addressed me, and learned that after three or four dismally restless days in town, he had taken a summary departure for L. A couple of days later, I was struck with a certain dramatic connection between his return and the following note from Mr. Guest, which I give verbally, in its pregnant brevity: —

SIR: —I possess a claim on your late brother's estate which it is needless to specify. You will either satisfy it by return of mail or forfeit for ever the common respect of gentlemen.   J. G.

Things had happened with the poor man rather as I hoped than as I expected. He had borrowed his recent exaggerated defiance from the transient smiles of Mrs. Beck. They had gone to his head like the fumes of wine, and he had dreamed for a day that he could afford to snap his fingers at the past. What he really desired and hoped of Mrs. Beck I was puzzled to say. In this woeful disrepair of his fortunes he could hardly have meant to hold her to a pledge of matrimony extorted in brighter hours. He was infatuated, I believed, partly by a weak, spasmodic optimism which represented his troubles as momentary, and enjoined him to hold firm till something turned up, and partly by a reckless and frivolous susceptibility to the lady's unscrupulous blandishments. While they prevailed, he lost all notion of the wholesome truth of things, and would have been capable of any egregious folly. Mrs. Beck was in love with him, in so far as she was capable of being in love; his gallantry, of all gallantries, suited her to a charm; but she reproached herself angrily with this amiable weakness, and prudence every day won back an inch of ground. Poor Guest indeed had clumsily snuffed out his candle. He had slept in the arms of Delilah, and he had waked to find that Delilah had guessed, if not his secret, something uncomfortably like it. Crawford's return had found Mrs. Beck with but a scanty remnant of sentiment and a large accession of prudence, which was graciously placed at his service. Guest, hereupon, as I conjectured, utterly disillusioned by the cynical frankness of her defection, had seen his horizon grow ominously dark, and begun to fancy, as I remained silent, that there was thunder in the air. His pompous waiving, in his note, of allusion both to our last meeting and to my own present claim, seemed to me equally characteristic of his weakness and of his distress. The bitter after-taste of Mrs.

Beck's coquetry had, at all events, brought him back to reality. For myself, the real fact in the matter was the image of Laura Guest, sitting pensive, like an exiled princess.

I sent him nothing by return of mail. On my arrival in New York, I had enclosed the precious document in an envelope, addressed it, and stamped it, and put it back in my pocket. I could not rid myself of a belief that by that sign I should conquer. Several times I drew it forth and laid it on the table before me, reflecting that I had but a word to say to have it dropped into the post. Cowardly, was it, to keep it? But what was it to give up one's mistress without a battle? Which was the uglier, my harshness or Guest's? In a holy cause,— and holy, you may be sure, I had dubbed mine,—were not all arms sanctified? Possession meant peril, and peril to a manly sense, of soul and conscience, as much as of person and fortune. Mine, at any rate, should share the danger. It was a sinister-looking talisman certainly; but when it had failed, it would be time enough to give it up.

In these thoughts I went back to L. I had taken the morning train; I arrived at noon, and with small delay proceeded to the quiet little house which harboured such world-vexed spirits. It was one of the first days of September, and the breath of autumn was in the air. Summer still met the casual glance; but the infinite light of summer had found its term; it was as if there were a leak in the crystal vault of the firmament through which the luminous ether of June was slowly stealing away.

Mr. Guest, I learned from the servant, had started on a walk,— to the mill, she thought, three miles away. I sent in my card to Laura, and went into the garden to await her appearance—or her answer. At the end of five minutes, I saw her descend from the piazza and advance down the long path. Her light black dress swept the little box-borders, and over her head she balanced a white parasol. I met her, and she stopped, silent and grave. 'I've come to learn,' I said, 'that absence has not been fatal to me.'

'You've hardly been absent. You left a—an influence behind,—a very painful one. In Heaven's name!' she cried, with vehemence, 'what horrible wrong have you done?'

'I have done no horrible wrong. Do you believe me?' She scanned my face searchingly for a moment; then she gave a long, gentle, irrepressible sigh of relief. 'Do you fancy that if I had, I could meet your eyes, feel the folds of your dress? I've done that which I have bitterly wished undone; I did it in ignorance, weakness, and folly; I've repented in passion and truth. Can a man do more?'

'I never was afraid of the truth,' she answered slowly; 'I don't see that I need fear it now. I'm not a child. Tell me the absolute truth!'

'The absolute truth,' I said, 'is that your father once saw me in a very undignified position. It made such an impression on him that he's unable to think of me in any other. You see I was rather cynically indifferent to his observation, for I didn't know him then as your father.'

She gazed at me with the same adventurous candour, and blushed a little as I became silent, then turned away and strolled along the path. 'It seems a miserable thing,' she said, 'that two gentle spirits like yours should have an irreparable difference. When good men hate each other, what are they to do to the bad men? You must excuse my want of romance, but I cannot listen to a suitor of whom my father complains. Make peace!'

'Shall peace with him be peace with you?'

'Let me see you frankly shake hands,' she said, not directly answering. 'Be very kind! You don't know what he has suffered here lately.' She paused, as if to conceal a tremor in her voice.

Had she read between the lines of that brilliant improvisation of mine, or was she moved chiefly with pity for his recent sentimental tribulation,—pitying them the more that she respected them the less? 'He has walked to the mill,' I said; 'I shall meet him, and we'll come back arm in arm.' I turned away, so that I might not see her face pleading for a clemency which would make me too delicate. I went down beside the river and followed the old towing-path, now grassy with disuse. Reaching the shabby wooden bridge below the mill, I stopped midway across it and leaned against the railing. Below, the yellow water swirled past the crooked piers. I took my little sealed paper out of my pocket-book and held it over the stream, almost courting the temptation to drop it; but the temptation never came. I had just put it back in my pocket when I heard a footstep on the planks behind me. Turning round, I beheld Mr. Guest. He looked tired and dusty with his walk, and had the air of a man who had been trying by violent exercise to shake off a moral incubus. Judging by his haggard brow and heavy eyes, he had hardly succeeded. As he recognized me, he started just perceptibly, as if he were too weary to be irritated. He was about to pass on without speaking, but I intercepted him. My movement provoked a flash in his sullen pupil. 'I came on purpose to meet you,' I said. 'I have just left your daughter, and I feel more than ever how passionately I love her. Once more, I demand that you withdraw your opposition.'

'Is that your answer to my letter?' he asked, eyeing me from under his brows.

'Your letter put me in a position to make my demand with force. I refuse to submit to this absurd verdict of accident. I have just seen your daughter, and I have authority to bring you to reason.'

'My daughter has received you?' he cried, flushing.

'Most kindly.'

'You scoundrel!'

'Gently, gently. Shake hands with me here where we stand, and let me keep my promise to Laura of our coming back to her arm in arm, at peace, reconciled, mutually forgiving and forgetting, or I walk straight back and put a certain little paper into her hands.'

He turned deadly pale, and a fierce oath broke from his lips. He had been beguiled, I think, by my neglect of his letter, into the belief that Edgar had not died without destroying his signature,— a belief rendered possible by an indefeasible faith he must have had in my step-brother's probity. 'You've kept that thing!' he cried. 'The Lord be praised! I'm as honest a man as either of you!'

'Say but two words,—"Take her!"—and we shall be honest together again. The paper's yours.' He turned away and leaned against the railing of the bridge, with his head in his hands, watching the river.

'Take your time,' I continued; 'I give you two hours. Go home, look at your daughter, and choose. An hour hence I'll join you. If I find you've removed your veto, I undertake to make you forget you ever offered it: if I find you've maintained it, I expose you.'

'In either case you lose your mistress. Whatever Laura may think of me, there can be no doubt as to what she will think of you.'

'I shall be forgiven. Leave that to me! That's my last word. In a couple of hours I shall take the liberty of coming to learn yours.'

'O Laura, Laura!' cried the poor man in his bitter trouble. But I left him and walked away. I turned as I reached the farther end of the bridge, and saw him slowly resume his course. I marched along the road to the mill, so excited with having uttered this brave *ultimatum* that I hardly knew whither I went. But at last I bethought me of a certain shady streamside nook just hereabouts, which a little exploration soon discovered. A shallow cove, screened from the road by dense clumps of willows, stayed the current a moment in its grassy bend. I had noted it while boating, as a spot where a couple of lovers might aptly disembark and moor their idle skiff; and I was now tempted to try its influence in ardent solitude. I flung myself on the ground, and as I listened to the light gurgle of the tarrying stream and to the softer rustle of the cool grey leafage around me, I suddenly felt that I was exhausted and sickened. I lay motionless, watching the sky and resting from my anger. Little by little it melted away and left me horribly ashamed. How long I lay there I know not, nor what was the logic of my meditations, but an ineffable change stole over my spirit. There are fathomless depths in spiritual mood and motive. Opposite me, on the farther side of the stream, winding along a path through the bushes, three or four cows had come down to drink. I sat up and watched them. A young man followed them, in a red shirt, with his trousers in his boots. While they were comfortably nosing the water into ripples, he sat down on a stone and began to light his pipe. In a moment I fancied I saw the little blue thread of smoke curl up from the bowl. From beyond, just droning through the air, came the liquid rumble of the mill. There seemed to me something in this vision ineffably pastoral, peaceful, and innocent; it smote me to my heart of hearts. I felt a nameless wave of impulse start somewhere in the innermost vitals of conscience and fill me with passionate shame. I fell back on the grass and burst into tears.

The sun was low and the breeze had risen when I rose to my feet. I scrambled back to the road, crossed the bridge, and hurried home by the towing-path. My heart, however, beat faster than my footfalls. I passed into the garden and advanced to the house; as I stepped upon the piazza, I was met by Mrs. Beck. 'Answer me a simple question,' she cried, laying her hand on my arm.

'I should like to hear you ask one!' I retorted, impatiently.

'Has Mr. Guest lost his mind?'

'For an hour! I've brought it back to him.'

'You've a pretty quarrel between you. He comes up an hour ago, as I was sitting in the garden with—with Mr. Crawford, requests a moment's interview, leads me apart and—offers himself. "If you'll have me, take me now; you won't an hour hence," he cried. "Neither now nor an hour hence, thank you," said I. "My affections are fixed—elsewhere."'

'You've not lost your head, at any rate,' said I; and, releasing myself, I went into the parlour. I had a horrible fear of being too late. The candles stood lighted on the piano, and tea had been brought in, but the kettle was singing unheeded. On the divan facing the window sat Guest, lounging back on the cushions, his hat and stick flung down beside him, his hands grasping his knees, his head thrown back, and his eyes closed. That he should have remained so for an hour, unbrushed and unfurbished, spoke volumes as to his mental state. Near him sat Laura, looking at him askance in mute anxiety. What had passed between them? Laura's urgent glance as I entered was full of trouble, but I fancied without reproach. He had apparently chosen neither way; he had simply fallen there, weary, desperate, and dumb.

'I'm disappointed!' Laura said to me gravely.

Her father opened his eyes, stared at me a moment, and then closed them. I answered nothing; but after a moment's hesitation went and took my seat beside Guest. I laid my hand on his own with a grasp of which he felt, first the force, then, I think, the kindness; for, after a momentary spasm of repulsion, he remained coldly passive. He must have begun to wonder. 'Be so good,' I said to Laura, 'as to bring me one of the candles.' She looked surprised; but she complied and came towards me, holding the taper, like some pale priestess expecting a portent. I drew out the note and held it to the flame. 'Your father and I have had a secret,' I said, 'which has been a burden to both of us. Here it goes.' Laura's hand trembled as she held the candle, and mine as I held the paper; but between us the vile thing blazed and was consumed. I glanced askance at Guest; he was staring wide-eyed at the dropping cinders. When the last had dropped, I took the candle, rose, and carried it back to the piano. Laura dropped on her knees before her father, and, while my back was turned, something passed between them with which I was concerned only in its consequences.

When I looked round, Guest had risen and was passing his fingers through his hair. 'Daughter,' he said, 'when I came in, what was it I said to you?'

She stood for an instant with her eyes on the floor. Then, 'I've forgotten!' she said, simply.

Mrs. Beck had passed in by the window in time to hear these last words. 'Do you know what you said to me when you came in?' she cried, mirthfully shaking a finger at Guest. He laughed nervously, picked up his hat, and stood looking, with an air of odd solemnity, at his boots. Suddenly it seemed to occur to him that he was dusty and dishevelled. He settled his shirt-collar and levelled a glance at the mirror, in which he caught my eye. He tried hard to look insensible; but it was the glance of a man who felt more comfortable than he had done in a month. He marched stiffly to the door.

'Are you going to dress?' said Mrs. Beck.

'From head to foot!' he cried, with violence.

'Be so good, then, if you see Mr. Crawford in the hall, as to ask him to come in and have a cup of tea.'

Laura had passed out to the piazza, where I immediately joined her. 'Your father accepts me,' I said; 'there is nothing left but for you——'

Five minutes later, I looked back through the window to see if we were being observed. But Mrs. Beck was busy adding another lump of sugar to Crawford's cup of tea. His eye met mine, however, and I fancied he looked sheepish.

The Madonna of the Future

[First appeared in the *Atlantic Monthly*, vol. xxxi (March 1873), pp. 276–97. The tale was revised and reprinted in *A Passionate Pilgrim* (1875). The 1875 text was revised and reprinted in volume i of *The Madonna of the Future* (1879). This text was later reproduced in volume xiv of James's first 'Collective Edition' (1883). James finally revised the tale for the New York Edition where it appears in volume xiii (*The Reverberator, Etc.*, 1908).]

WE HAD BEEN TALKING ABOUT THE MASTERS WHO HAD achieved but a single masterpiece,—the artists and poets who but once in their lives had known the divine afflatus, and touched the high level of the best. Our host had been showing us a charming little cabinet picture by a painter whose name we had never heard, and who, after this one spasmodic bid for fame, had apparently relapsed into fatal mediocrity. There was some discussion as to the frequency of this phenomenon; during which, I observed, H—— sat silent, finishing his cigar with a meditative air, and looking at the picture, which was being handed round the table. 'I don't know how common a case it is,' he said at last, 'but I've seen it. I've known a poor fellow who painted his one masterpiece, and'—he added with a smile—'he didn't even paint that. He made his bid for fame, and missed it.' We all knew H— for a clever man who had seen much of men and manners, and had a great stock of reminiscences. Someone immediately questioned him further, and, while I was engrossed with the raptures of my neighbour over the little picture, he was induced to tell his tale. If I were to doubt whether it would bear repeating, I should only have to remember how that charming woman, our hostess, who had left the table, ventured back in rustling rose-colour, to pronounce our lingering a want of gallantry, and, finding us a listening circle, had sunk into her chair in spite of our cigars, and heard the story out so graciously, that when the catastrophe was reached she glanced across at me, and showed me a tender tear in each of her beautiful eyes.

It relates to my youth, and to Italy: two fine things! (H— began.) I had arrived late in the evening at Florence, and while I finished my bottle of wine at supper, had fancied that, tired traveller though I was, I might pay the city a finer compliment than by going vulgarly to bed. A narrow passage wandered darkly away out of the little

square before my hotel, and looked as if it bored into the heart of
Florence. I followed it, and at the end of ten minutes emerged upon
a great piazza, filled only with the mild autumn moonlight. Opposite
rose the Palazzo Vecchio like some huge civic fortress, with the
great bell-tower springing from its embattled verge like a mountain-
pine from the edge of a cliff. At its base, in its projected shadow,
gleamed certain dim sculptures which I wonderingly approached.
One of the images, on the left of the palace door, was a magnificent
colossus shining through the dusky air like some young god of Defiance. In a moment I recognized him as Michael Angelo's David. I
turned with a certain relief from his sinister strength to a slender
figure in bronze, stationed beneath the high, light *loggia*, which
opposes the free and elegant span of its arches to the dead masonry
of the palace; a figure supremely shapely and graceful; gentle, almost, in spite of his holding out with his light nervous arm the snaky
head of the slaughtered Gorgon. His name is Perseus, and you may
read his story, not in the Greek mythology, but in the memoirs of
Benvenuto Cellini. Glancing from one of these fine fellows to the
other, I probably uttered some irrepressible commonplace of praise,
for, as if provoked by my voice, a man rose from the steps of the
Loggia, where he had been sitting in the shadow, and addressed me
in good English,—a small, slim personage, clad in a sort of black
velvet tunic (as it seemed), and with a mass of auburn hair, which
gleamed in the moonlight escaping from a little mediaeval *berretta*.
In a tone of the most insinuating deference, he asked me for my 'impressions'. He seemed picturesque, fantastic, slightly unreal. Hovering there in this consecrated neighbourhood, he might have passed
for the genius of aesthetic hospitality,—if the genius of aesthetic
hospitality were not commonly some shabby little *custode*, flourish-
ing a calico pocket-handkerchief, and openly resentful of the divided
franc. This fantasy was made none the less plausible by the fine
tirade with which he greeted my embarrassed silence.

'I've known Florence long, sir, but I've never known her so lovely
as tonight. It's as if the ghosts of her past were abroad in the empty
streets. The present is sleeping; the past hovers about us like a
dream made visible. Fancy the old Florentines strolling up in couples
to pass judgment on the last performance of Michael, of Benvenuto!
We should come in for a precious lesson if we might overhear what
they say. The plainest burgher of them, in his cap and gown, had a
taste in the matter! That was the prime of art, sir. The sun stood
high in heaven, and his broad and equal blaze made the darkest
places bright and the dullest eyes clear. We live in the evening of
time! We grope in the grey dusk, carrying each our poor little

taper of selfish and painful wisdom, holding it up to the great models and to the dim idea, and seeing nothing but overwhelming greatness and dimness. The days of illumination are gone! But do you know I fancy—I fancy,'—and he grew suddenly almost familiar in this visionary fervour,—'I fancy the light of that time rests upon us here for an hour! I have never seen the David so grand, the Perseus so fair! Even the inferior productions of John of Bologna and of Baccio Bandinelli seem to realize the artist's dream. I feel as if the moonlight air were charged with the secrets of the masters, and as if, standing here in religious contemplation, we might—we might witness a revelation!' Perceiving at this moment, I suppose, my halting comprehension reflected in my puzzled face, this interesting rhapsodist paused and blushed. Then with a melancholy smile, 'You think me a moonstruck charlatan, I suppose. It's not my habit to hang about the piazza and pounce upon innocent tourists. But to-night, I confess, I'm under the charm. And then, somehow, I fancied you, too, were an artist!'

'I'm not an artist, I'm sorry to say, as you must understand the term. But pray make no apologies. I am also under the charm; your eloquent reflections have only deepened it.'

'If you're not an artist, you're worthy to be one!' he rejoined, with a bow. 'A young man who arrives at Florence late in the evening, and, instead of going prosaically to bed, or hanging over the travellers' book at his hotel, walks forth without loss of time to pay his *devoir*s to the Beautiful, is a young man after my own heart!'

The mystery was suddenly solved; my friend was an American! He must have been, to take the picturesque so prodigiously to heart. 'None the less so, I trust,' I answered, 'if the young man is a sordid New-Yorker.'

'New-Yorkers,' he solemnly proclaimed, 'have been munificent patrons of art!'

For a moment I was alarmed. Was this midnight reverie mere Yankee enterprise, and was he simply a desperate brother of the brush who had posted himself here to extort an 'order' from a sauntering tourist? But I was not called to defend myself. A great brazen note broke suddenly from the far-off summit of the bell-tower above us and sounded the first stroke of midnight. My companion started, apologized for detaining me, and prepared to retire. But he seemed to offer so lively a promise of further entertainment, that I was indisposed to part with him, and suggested that we should stroll homeward together. He cordially assented, so we turned out of the Piazza, passed down before the statued arcade of the Uffizi, and came out upon the Arno. What course we took I hardly remember, but we roamed slowly about for an hour, my companion delivering by snatches a sort of moon-touched aesthetic lecture. I listened in puzzled fascination, and wondered who the deuce he was. He confessed with a melancholy but all-respectful head-shake to his American origin. 'We are the disinherited of Art!' he cried. 'We are condemned to be superficial! We are excluded from the magic circle. The soil of American perception is a poor little barren, artificial deposit. Yes! we are wedded to imperfection. An American, to excel, has just ten times as much to learn as a European. We lack the deeper sense. We have neither taste nor tact nor force. How should we have them? Our crude and garish climate, our silent past, our deafening present, the constant pressure about us of unlovely circumstance, are as void of all that nourishes and prompts and inspires the artist, as my sad heart is void of bitterness in saying so! We poor aspirants must live in perpetual exile.'

'You seem fairly at home in exile,' I answered, 'and Florence seems to me a very pretty Siberia. But do you know my own thought? Nothing is so idle as to talk about our want of a nutritive soil, of opportunity, of inspiration, and all the rest of it. The worthy part is to do something fine! There's no law in our glorious Constitution against that. Invent, create, achieve! No matter if you've to study fifty times as much as one of these! What else are you an artist for? Be you our Moses,' I added, laughing and laying my hand on his shoulder, 'and lead us out of the house of bondage!'

'Golden words,—golden words, young man!' he cried, with a tender smile. '"Invent, create, achieve!" Yes, that's our business: I know it well. Don't take me, in Heaven's name, for one of your barren complainers,—querulous cynics who have neither talent nor faith. I'm at work!'—and he glanced about him and lowered his voice as if this were a quite peculiar secret,—'I'm at work night and day. I've undertaken a *creation*! I'm no Moses; I'm only a poor, patient artist; but it would be a fine thing if I were to cause some slender stream of beauty to flow in our thirsty land! Don't think me a monster of conceit,' he went on, as he saw me smile at the avidity with which he adopted my fantasy; 'I confess that I'm in one of those moods when great things seem possible! This is one of my nervous nights,—I dream waking! When the south-wind blows over Florence at midnight, it seems to coax the soul from all the fair things locked away in her churches and galleries; it comes into my own little studio with the moonlight, and sets my heart beating too deeply for rest. You see I am always adding a thought to my conception! This evening I felt that I couldn't sleep unless I had communed with the genius of Michael!'

He seemed deeply versed in local history and tradition, and he expatiated *con amore* on the charms of Florence. I gathered that he was an old resident, and that he had taken the lovely city into his heart. 'I owe her everything,' he declared. 'It's only since I came here that I have really lived, intellectually. One by one, all profane desires, all mere worldly aims, have dropped away from me, and left me nothing but my pencil, my little note-book' (and he tapped his breast-pocket), 'and the worship of the pure masters,—those who were pure because they were innocent and those who were pure because they were strong!'

'And have you been very productive all this time?' I asked, with amenity.

He was silent awhile before replying. 'Not in the vulgar sense!' he said, at last. 'I have chosen never to manifest myself by imperfection. The good in every performance I have reabsorbed into the generative force of new creations; the bad—there's always plenty of that —I have religiously destroyed. I may say, with some satisfaction, that I have not added a mite to the rubbish of the world. As a proof of my conscientiousness,'—and he stopped short, and eyed me with extraordinary candour, as if the proof were to be overwhelming,—'I've never sold a picture! "At least no merchant traffics in my heart!" Do you remember the line in Browning? My little studio has never been profaned by superficial, feverish, mercenary work. It's a temple of labour, but of leisure! Art is long. If we work for ourselves, of course we must hurry. If we work for her, we must often pause. She can wait!'

This had brought us to my hotel door, somewhat to my relief, I confess, for I had begun to feel unequal to the society of a genius of this heroic strain. I left him, however, not without expressing a friendly hope that we should meet again. The next morning my curiosity had not abated; I was anxious to see him by common daylight. I counted upon meeting him in one of the many aesthetic haunts of Florence, and I was gratified without delay. I found him in the course of the morning in the Tribune of the Uffizi,—that little treasure-chamber of perfect works. He had turned his back on the Venus di Medici, and with his two arms resting on the railing which protects the pictures, and his head buried in his hands, he was lost in the contemplation of that superb triptych of Andrea Mantegna,— a work which has neither the material splendour nor the commanding force of some of its neighbours, but which, glowing there with the loveliness of patient labour, suits possibly a more constant need of the soul. I looked at the picture for some time over his shoulder; at last, with a heavy sigh, he turned away and our eyes met. As he

recognized me a deep blush rose to his face; he fancied, perhaps, that
he had made a fool of himself overnight. But I offered him my hand
with a frankness which assured him I was not a scoffer. I knew him
by his ardent *chevelure*; otherwise he was much altered. His midnight mood was over, and he looked as haggard as an actor by daylight. He was far older than I had supposed, and he had less bravery
of costume and gesture. He seemed the quite poor, patient artist he
had proclaimed himself, and the fact that he had never sold a
picture was more obvious than glorious. His velvet coat was thread-
bare, and his short slouched hat, of an antique pattern, revealed a
rustiness which marked it an 'original', and not one of the picturesque reproductions which brethren of his craft affect. His eye was
mild and heavy, and his expression singularly gentle and ac-
quiescent; the more so for a certain pallid leanness of visage which I
hardly knew whether to refer to the consuming fire of genius or to
a meagre diet. A very little talk, however, cleared his brow and
brought back his eloquence.

'And this is your first visit to these enchanted halls?' he cried.
'Happy, thrice happy youth!' And taking me by the arm, he prepared to lead me to each of the pre-eminent works in turn and show
me the cream of the gallery. But before we left the Mantegna, he
pressed my arm and gave it a loving look. '*He* was not in a hurry,' he
murmured. 'He knew nothing of "raw Haste, half-sister to Delay"!'
How sound a critic my friend was I am unable to say, but he was an
extremely amusing one; overflowing with opinions, theories, and
sympathies, with disquisition and gossip and anecdote. He was a
shade too sentimental for my own sympathies, and I fancied he
was rather too fond of superfine discriminations and of discovering subtle intentions in the shallow felicities of chance. At
moments, too, he plunged into the sea of metaphysics and floundered
awhile in waters too deep for intellectual security. But his abound-
ing knowledge and happy judgment told a touching story of long
attentive hours in this worshipful company; there was a reproach
to my wasteful saunterings in so devoted a culture of opportunity.
'There are two moods,' I remember his saying, 'in which we may
walk through galleries, the critical and the ideal. They seize us
at their pleasure, and we can never tell which is to take its turn.
The critical mood, oddly, is the genial one; the friendly, the condescending. It relishes the pretty trivialities of art, its vulgar clever-
nesses, its conscious graces. It has a kindly greeting for anything
which looks as if, according to his light, the painter had enjoyed
doing it,—for the little Dutch cabbages and kettles, for the taper
fingers and breezy mantles of late-coming Madonnas, for the little

blue-hilled pastoral, sceptical Italian landscapes. Then there are
the days of fierce, fastidious longing,—solemn church-feasts of the
intellect,—when all vulgar effort and all petty success is a weariness, and everything but the best—the best of the best—disgusts. In
these hours we are relentless aristocrats of taste. We'll not take
Michael for granted, we'll not swallow Raphael whole!'

The gallery of the Uffizi is not only rich in its possessions, but
peculiarly fortunate in that fine architectural accident, as one may
call it, which unites it—with the breadth of river and city between
them—to those princely chambers of the Pitti Palace. The Louvre
and the Vatican hardly give you such a sense of sustained enclosure
as those long passages projected over street and stream to establish
a sort of inviolate transition between the two palaces of art. We
passed along the gallery in which those precious drawings by emi-
ment hands hang chaste and grey above the swirl and murmur of
the yellow Arno, and reached the ducal saloons of the Pitti. Ducal
as they are, it must be confessed that they are imperfect as show-
rooms, and that, with their deep-set windows and their massive
mouldings, it is rather a broken light that reaches the pictured walls.
But here the masterpieces hang thick, and you seem to see them in
a luminous atmosphere of their own. And the great saloons, with
their superb dim ceilings, their outer wall in splendid shadow, and
the sombre opposite glow of mellow canvas and dusky gilding, make
themselves almost as fine a picture as the Titians and Raphaels they
imperfectly reveal. We lingered briefly before many a Raphael and
Titian; but I saw my friend was impatient, and I suffered him at last
to lead me directly to the goal of our journey,—the most tenderly
fair of Raphael's Virgins, the Madonna in the Chair. Of all the fine
pictures of the world, it seemed to me this is the one with which
criticism has least to do. None betrays less effort, less of the mechanism of effect and of the irrepressible discord between conception
and result, which shows dimly in so many consummate works. Graceful, human, near to our sympathies as it is, it has nothing of manner,
of method, nothing, almost, of style; it blooms there in rounded softness, as instinct with harmony as if it were an immediate exhalation
of genius. The figure melts away the spectator's mind into a sort of
passionate tenderness which he knows not whether he has given to
heavenly purity or to earthly charm. He is intoxicated with the
fragrance of the tenderest blossom of maternity that ever bloomed
on earth.

'That's what I call a fine picture,' said my companion, after we had
gazed awhile in silence. 'I have a right to say so, for I've copied it so
often and so carefully that I could repeat it now with my eyes shut.

Other works are of Raphael: this *is* Raphael himself. Others you can praise, you can qualify, you can measure, explain, account for: this you can only love and admire. I don't know in what seeming he walked among men, while this divine mood was upon him; but after it, surely, he could do nothing but die; this world had nothing more to teach him. Think of it awhile, my friend, and you'll admit that I'm not raving. Think of his seeing that spotless image, not for a moment, for a day, in a happy dream, or a restless fever-fit, not as a poet in a five minutes' frenzy, time to snatch his phrase and scribble his immortal stanza, but for days together, while the slow labour of the brush went on, while the foul vapours of life interposed, and the fancy ached with tension, fixed, radiant, distinct, as we see it now! What a master, certainly! But ah, what a seer!'

'Don't you imagine,' I answered, 'that he had a model, and that some pretty young woman——'

'As pretty a young woman as you please! It doesn't diminish the miracle! He took his hint, of course, and the young woman, possibly, sat smiling before his canvas. But, meanwhile, the painter's idea had taken wings. No lovely human outline could charm it to vulgar fact. He saw the fair form made perfect; he rose to the vision without tremor, without effort of wing; he communed with it face to face, and resolved into finer and lovelier truth the purity which completes it as the perfume completes the rose. That's what they call idealism; the word's vastly abused, but the thing is good. It's my own creed, at any rate. Lovely Madonna, model at once and muse, I call you to witness that I too am an idealist!'

'An idealist, then,' I said, half-jocosely, wishing to provoke him to further utterance, 'is a gentleman who says to Nature in the person of a beautiful girl, "Go to, you're all wrong! Your fine is coarse, your bright is dim, your grace is *gaucherie*. This is the way you should have done it!" Isn't the chance against him?'

He turned upon me almost angrily, but perceiving the genial flavour of my sarcasm, he smiled gravely. 'Look at that picture,' he said, 'and cease your irreverent mockery! Idealism is *that*! There's no explaining it; one must feel the flame! It says nothing to Nature, or to any beautiful girl, that they'll not both forgive! It says to the fair woman, "Accept me as your artist-friend, lend me your beautiful face, trust me, help me, and your eyes shall be half my master-piece!" No one so loves and respects the rich realities of nature as the artist whose imagination caresses and flatters them. He knows what a fact may hold; (whether Raphael knew, you may judge by his portrait behind us there, of Tommaso Inghirami;) but his fancy hovers above it, as Ariel above the sleeping prince. There is only one

Raphael, but an artist may still be an artist. As I said last night, the days of illumination are gone; visions are rare; we have to look long to see them. But in meditation we may still woo the ideal; round it, smooth it, perfect it. The result—the result' (here his voice faltered suddenly, and he fixed his eyes for a moment on the picture; when they met my own again they were full of tears)—'the result may be less than this; but still it may be good, it may be *great!*' he cried with vehemence. 'It may hang somewhere, in after years, in goodly company, and keep the artist's memory warm. Think of being known to mankind after some such fashion as this! of hanging here through the slow centuries in the gaze of an altered world, living on and on in the cunning of an eye and hand that are part of the dust of ages, a delight and a law to remote generations; making beauty a force and purity an example!'

'Heaven forbid,' I said, smiling, 'that I should take the wind out of your sails; but doesn't it occur to you that beside strong in his genius, Raphael was happy in a certain good faith of which we have lost the trick? There are people, I know, who deny that his spotless Madonnas are anything more than pretty blondes of that period, enhanced by the Raphaelesque touch, which they declare is a profane touch. Be that as it may, people's religious and aesthetic needs went hand in hand, and there was, as I may say, a demand for the Blessed Virgin, visible and adorable, which must have given firmness to the artist's hand. I'm afraid there is no demand now.'

My companion seemed painfully puzzled; he shivered, as it were, in this chilling blast of scepticism. Then shaking his head with sublime confidence: 'There is always a demand!' he cried; 'that ineffable type is one of the eternal needs of man's heart; but pious souls long for it in silence, almost in shame; let it appear, and this faith grows brave. How *should* it appear in this corrupt generation? It can't be made to order. It could, indeed, when the order came, trumpet-toned, from the lips of the Church herself, and was addressed to genius panting with inspiration. But it can spring now only from the soil of passionate labour and culture. Do you really fancy that while, from time to time, a man of complete artistic vision is born into the world, that image can perish? The man who paints it has painted everything. The subject admits of every perfection,—form, colour, expression, composition. It can be as simple as you please, and yet as rich, as broad and pure, and yet as full of delicate detail. Think of the chance for flesh in the little naked, nestling child, irradiating divinity; of the chance for drapery in the chaste and ample garment of the mother! Think of the great story you compress into that simple theme! Think, above all, of the mother's face and its ineffable suggestiveness, of the mingled burden of joy and trouble, the tenderness turned to worship, and the worship turned to far-seeing pity! Then look at it all in perfect line and lovely colour, breathing truth and beauty and mastery!'

'*Anch' io son pittore!*' I cried. 'Unless I'm mistaken, you've a masterpiece on the stocks. If you put all that in, you'll do more than Raphael himself did. Let me know when your picture is finished, and wherever in the wide world I may be, I'll post back to Florence and salute—the *Madonna of the future!*'

He blushed vividly and gave a heavy sigh, half of protest, half of resignation. 'I don't often mention my picture, in so many words. I detest this modern custom of premature publicity. A great work needs silence, privacy, mystery even. And then, do you know, people are so cruel, so frivolous, so unable to imagine a man's wishing to paint a Madonna at this time of day, that I've been laughed at,— laughed at, sir!' And his blush deepened to crimson. 'I don't know what has prompted me to be so frank and trustful with you. You look as if you wouldn't laugh at me. My dear young man,'—and he laid his hand on my arm,—'I'm worthy of respect. Whatever my talents may be, I'm honest. There's nothing grotesque in a pure ambition, or in a life devoted to it!'

There was something so sternly sincere in his look and tone, that further questions seemed impertinent. I had repeated opportunity to ask them, however; for after this we spent much time together. Daily, for a fortnight, we met by appointment, to see the sights. He knew the city well, he had strolled and lounged so often through its streets and churches and galleries, he was so deeply versed in its greater and lesser memories, so imbued with the local genius, that he was an altogether ideal *valet de place*, and I was glad enough to leave my Murray at home, and gather facts and opinions alike from his gossiping commentary. He talked of Florence like a lover, and admitted that it was a very old affair; he had lost his heart to her at first sight. 'It's the fashion to talk of all cities as feminine,' he said, 'but, as a rule, it's a monstrous mistake. Is Florence of the same sex as New York, as Chicago? She's the sole true woman of them all; one feels towards her as a lad in his teens feels to some beautiful older woman with a "history". It's a sort of aspiring gallantry she creates.' This disinterested passion seemed to stand my friend in stead of the common social ties; he led a lonely life, apparently, and cared for nothing but his work. I was duly flattered by his having taken my frivolous self into his favour, and by his generous sacrifice of precious hours, as they must have been, to my society. We spent many of these hours among those early paintings in which Florence is so rich, returning ever and anon with restless sympathies to wonder whether these tender blossoms of art had not a vital fragrance and savour more precious than the full-fruited knowledge of the later works. We lingered often in the sepulchral chapel of San Lorenzo, and watched Michael Angelo's dim-visaged warrior sitting there like some awful Genius of Doubt and brooding behind his eternal mask upon the mysteries of life. We stood more than once in the little convent chambers where Fra Angelico wrought, as if an angel indeed had held his hand, and gathered that sense of scattered dews and early birdnotes which makes an hour among his relics seem like a morning stroll in some monkish garden. We did all this and much more, wandered into dark chapels, damp courts, and dusty palace-rooms, in quest of lingering hints of fresco and lurking treasures of carving. I was more and more impressed with my companion's prodigious singleness of purpose. Everything was a pretext for some wild aesthetic rhapsody or reverie. Nothing could be seen or said that didn't end sooner or later in a glowing discourse on the true, the beautiful, and the good. If my friend was not a genius, he was certainly a monomaniac; and I found as great a fascination in watching the odd lights and shades of his character as if he had been a creature from another planet. He seemed, indeed, to know very little of this one, and lived and moved altogether in his own little province of art. A creature more unsullied by the world it is impossible to conceive, and I often thought it a flaw in his artistic character that he hadn't a harmless vice or two. It amused me vastly at times to think that he was of our shrewd Yankee race; but, after all, there could be no better token of his American origin than this same fantastic fever. The very heat of his devotion was a sign of conversion; those born to European opportunity manage better to reconcile enthusiasm with comfort. He had, moreover, all our native mistrust for intellectual discretion and our native relish for sonorous superlatives. As a critic he was vastly more generous than just, and his mildest terms of approbation were 'glorious', 'superb', and 'magnificent'. The small change of admiration seemed to him no coin for a gentleman to handle; and yet, frank as he was intellectually, he was, personally, altogether a mystery. His professions, somehow, were all half-professions, and his allusions to his work and circumstances left something dimly ambiguous in the background. He was modest and proud, and never spoke of his domestic matters. He was evidently poor; yet he must have had some slender independence, since he could afford to make so merry over the fact that his culture of ideal beauty had never brought him a penny. His poverty, I supposed, was his motive for neither inviting me to his lodging nor mentioning its whereabouts. We met either in some public place or at my hotel, where I entertained him as freely as I might without appearing to be moved by charity. He seemed always hungry, which was his nearest approach to a 'redeeming vice'. I made a point of asking no impertinent questions, but, each time we met, I ventured to make some respectful allusion to the *magnum opus*, to inquire, as it were, as to its health and progress. 'We're getting on, with the Lord's help,' he would say with a grave smile. 'We're doing well. You see I have the grand advantage that I lose no time. These hours I spend with you are pure profit. They're *suggestive*! Just as the truly religious soul is always at worship, the genuine artist is always in labour. He takes his property wherever he finds it, and learns some precious secret from every object that stands up in the light. If you but knew the rapture of observation! I gather with every glance some hint for light, for colour or relief! When I get home, I pour out my treasures into the lap of my Madonna. O, I'm not idle! *Nulla dies sine linea.*'

I was introduced in Florence to an American lady whose drawing-room had long formed an attractive place of reunion for the foreign residents. She lived on the fourth floor, and she was not rich; but she offered her visitors very good tea, little cakes at option, and conversation not quite to match. Her conversation had mainly an aesthetic flavour, for Mrs. Coventry was famously 'artistic'. Her apartment was a sort of Pitti Palace *au petit pied*. She possessed 'early masters' by the dozen,—a cluster of Peruginos in her dining-room, a Giotto in her boudoir, an Andrea del Sarto over her parlour chimney-piece. Backed by these treasures, and by innumerable bronzes, mosaics, majolica dishes, and little worm-eaten diptychs showing angular saints on gilded panels, our hostess enjoyed the dignity of a sort of high-priestess of the arts. She always wore on her bosom a huge miniature copy of the Madonna della Seggiola. Gaining her ear quietly one evening, I asked her whether she knew that remarkable man, Mr. Theobald.

'Know him!' she exclaimed; 'know poor Theobald! All Florence knows him, his flame-coloured locks, his black velvet coat, his interminable harangues on the beautiful, and his wondrous Madonna that mortal eye has never seen, and that mortal patience has quite given up expecting.'

'Really,' I cried, 'you don't believe in his Madonna?'

'My dear ingenuous youth,' rejoined my shrewd friend, 'has he made a convert of you? Well, we all believed in him once; he came down upon Florence and took us by storm. Another Raphael, at the very least, had been born among men, and poor, dear America was to have the credit of him. Hadn't he the very hair of Raphael flowing down on his shoulders? The hair, alas, but not the head! We swallowed him whole, however; we hung upon his lips and proclaimed his genius on the house-tops. The women were all dying to sit to him for their portraits and be made immortal, like Leonardo's Joconde. We decided that his manner was a good deal like Leonardo's,— mysterious and inscrutable and fascinating. Mysterious it certainly was; mystery was the beginning and the end of it. The months passed by, and the miracle hung fire; our master never produced his masterpiece. He passed hours in the galleries and churches, posturing, musing, and gazing; he talked more than ever about the beautiful, but he never put brush to canvas. We had all subscribed, as it were, to the great performance; but as it never came off, people began to ask for their money again. I was one of the last of the faithful; I carried devotion so far as to sit to him for my head. If you could have seen the horrible creature he made of me, you would admit that even a woman with no more vanity than will tie her bonnet straight must have cooled off then. The man didn't know the very alphabet of drawing. His strong point, he intimated, was his sentiment; but is it a consolation, when one has been painted a fright, to know it has been done with peculiar gusto? One by one, I confess, we fell away from the faith, and Mr. Theobald didn't lift his little finger to preserve us. At the first hint that we were tired of waiting and that we should like the show to begin, he was off in a huff. "Great work requires time, contemplation, privacy, mystery! O ye of little faith!" We answered that we didn't insist on a great work; that the five-act tragedy might come at his convenience; that we merely asked for something to keep us from yawning, some inexpensive little *lever de rideau*. Hereupon the poor man took his stand as a genius misconceived and persecuted, an *âme méconnue*, and washed his hands of us from that hour! No, I believe he does me the honour to consider me the head and front of the conspiracy formed to nip his glory in the bud,—a bud that has taken twenty years to blossom. Ask him if he knows me, and he'd tell you I'm a horribly ugly old woman who has vowed his destruction because he wouldn't paint her portrait as a *pendant* to Titian's Flora. I fancy that since then he has had none but chance followers, innocent strangers like yourself, who have taken him at his word. The mountain's still in labour; I've not heard that the mouse has been born. I pass him once in a while in the galleries, and he fixes his great dark eyes on me with a sublimity of indifference, as if I were a bad copy of a Sassoferrato. It is a long time ago now that I heard that he was making studies for a Madonna who was to be a *résumé* of all the other Madonnas of the

Italian school, like that antique Venus who borrowed a nose from one great image and an ankle from another. It's certainly a masterly idea. The parts may be fine, but when I think of my unhappy portrait I tremble for the whole. He has communicated this fine idea under the pledge of solemn secrecy to fifty chosen spirits, to every one he has ever been able to button-hole for five minutes. I suppose he wants to get an order for it, and he's not to blame; for heaven knows how he lives. I see by your blush,' my hostess frankly continued, 'that you have been honoured with his confidence. You needn't be ashamed, my dear young man; a man of your age is none the worse for a certain generous credulity, only allow me to give you a word of advice: keep your credulity out of your pockets. Don't pay for the picture till it's delivered. You've not been treated to a peep at it, I imagine. No more have your fifty predecessors in the faith. There are people who doubt whether there is any picture to be seen. I fancy, myself, that if one were to get into his studio, one would find something very like the picture in that tale of Balzac's, —a mere mass of incoherent scratches and daubs, a jumble of dead paint!'

I listened to this pungent recital in silent wonder. It had a painfully plausible sound, and was not inconsistent with certain shy suspicions of my own. My hostess was a clever woman, and presumably a generous one. I determined to let my judgment wait upon events. Possibly she was right; but if she was wrong, she was cruelly wrong! Her version of my friend's eccentricities made me impatient to see him again and examine him in the light of public opinion. On our next meeting, I immediately asked him if he knew Mrs. Coventry. He laid his hand on my arm and gave me a sad smile. 'Has she taxed *your* gallantry at last?' he asked. 'She's a foolish woman. She's frivolous and heartless, and she pretends to be serious and kind. She prattles about Giotto's second manner and Vittoria Colonna's *liaison* with "Michael",—one would think that Michael lived across the way and was expected in to take a hand at whist,—but she knows as little about art, and about the conditions of production, as I know about Buddhism. She profanes sacred words,' he added more vehemently, after a pause. 'She cares for you only as someone to hand teacups in that horrible mendacious little *parlour* of hers, with its trumpery Peruginos! If you can't dash off a new picture every three days, to show to her guests, she tells them in plain English you're an impostor!'

This attempt of mine to test Mrs. Coventry's accuracy was made in the course of a late afternoon walk to the quiet old church of San Miniato, on one of the hill-tops which directly overlook the city, from whose gate you are guided to it by a stony and cypress-bordered walk, which seems a most fitting avenue to a shrine. No spot is more propitious to lingering repose than the broad terrace in front of the church, where, lounging against the parapet, you may glance in slow alternation from the black and yellow marbles of the church façade, seamed and crackled with time and wind-sown with a tender flora of its own, down to the full domes and slender towers of Florence and over to the blue sweep of the wide-mouthed cup of mountains into whose hollow the little treasure-city has been dropped. I had proposed, as a diversion from the painful memories evoked by Mrs. Coventry's name, that Theobald should go with me the next evening to the opera, where some rarely played work was to be given. He declined, as I had half expected, for I had observed that he regularly kept his evenings in reserve, and never alluded to his manner of passing them. 'You have reminded me before,' I said, smiling, 'of that charming speech of the Florentine painter in Alfred de Musset's "Lorenzaccio": *"I do no harm to any one. I pass my days in my studio. On Sunday, I go to the Annunziata or to Santa Maria; the monks think I have a voice; they dress me in a white gown and a red cap, and I take a share in the choruses, sometimes I do a little solo: these are the only times I go into public. In the evening, I visit my sweetheart; when the night is fine, we pass it on her balcony."* I don't know whether you have a sweetheart, or whether she has a balcony. But if you're so happy, it's certainly better than trying to find a charm in a third-rate *prima donna*.'

He made no immediate response, but at last he turned to me solemnly. 'Can you look upon a beautiful woman with reverent eyes?'

'Really,' I said, 'I don't pretend to be sheepish, but I should be sorry to think I was impudent.' And I asked him what in the world he meant. When at last I had assured him that I could undertake to temper admiration with respect, he informed me, with an air of religious mystery, that it was in his power to introduce me to the most beautiful woman in Italy. 'A beauty with a soul!'

'Upon my word,' I cried, 'you're extremely fortunate. And I shall rejoice to witness the conjunction.'

'This woman's beauty,' he answered, 'is a lesson, a morality, a poem! It's my daily study.'

Of course, after this, I lost no time in reminding him of what, before we parted, had taken the shape of a promise. 'I feel somehow,' he had said, 'as if it were a sort of violation of that privacy in which I have always contemplated her beauty. This is friendship, my friend. No hint of her existence has ever fallen from my lips. But with too great a familiarity, we are apt to lose a sense of the real value of things, and you perhaps will throw some new light upon it and offer a fresher interpretation.' We went accordingly by appointment to a certain ancient house in the heart of Florence,—the precinct of the Mercato Vecchio,—and climbed a dark, steep staircase to the very summit of the edifice. Theobald's beauty seemed as jealously exalted above the line of common vision as the Belle aux Cheveux d'Or in her tower-top. He passed without knocking into the dark vestibule of a small apartment and, flinging open an inner door, ushered me into a small saloon. The room seemed mean and sombre, though I caught a glimpse of white curtains swaying gently at an open window. At a table, near a lamp, sat a woman dressed in black, working at a piece of embroidery. As Theobald entered, she looked up calmly, with a smile; but seeing me, she made a movement of surprise, and rose with a kind of stately grace. Theobald stepped forward, took her hand and kissed it, with an indescribable air of immemorial usage. As he bent his head, she looked at me askance, and I thought she blushed.

'*Ecco la Serafina!*' said Theobald, frankly, waving me forward. 'This is a friend, and a lover of the arts,' he added, introducing me. I received a smile, a courtesy, and a request to be seated.

The most beautiful woman in Italy was a person of a generous Italian type and of great simplicity of demeanour. Seated again at her lamp with her embroidery, she seemed to have nothing whatever to say. Theobald, bending towards her in a sort of Platonic ecstasy, asked her a dozen paternally tender questions as to her health, her state of mind, her occupations, and the progress of her embroidery, which he examined minutely and summoned me to admire. It was some portion of an ecclesiastical vestment,—yellow satin wrought with an elaborate design of silver and gold. She made answer in a full, rich voice, but with a brevity which I hesitated whether to attribute to native reserve or to profane constraint of my presence. She had been that morning to confession; she had also been to market, and had bought a chicken for dinner. She felt very happy; she had nothing to complain of, except that the people for whom she was making her vestment, and who furnished her materials, should be willing to put such rotten silver thread into the garment, as one might say, of the Lord. From time to time, as she took her slow stitches, she raised her eyes and covered me with a glance which seemed at first to denote a placid curiosity, but in which, as I saw it repeated, I thought I perceived the dim glimmer of an attempt to establish an understanding with me at the expense of our companion. Meanwhile, as mindful as possible of Theobald's injunction of reverence, I considered the lady's personal claims to the fine compliment he had paid her.

That she was indeed a beautiful woman I perceived, after recovering from the surprise of finding her without the freshness of youth. Her beauty was of a sort which, in losing youth, loses little of its essential charm, expressed for the most part as it was in form and structure, and, as Theobald would have said, in 'composition'. She was broad and ample, low-browed and large-eyed, dark and pale. Her thick brown hair hung low beside her cheek and ear, and seemed to drape her head with a covering as chaste and formal as the veil of a nun. The poise and carriage of her head was admirably free and noble, and the more effective that their freedom was at moments discreetly corrected by a little sanctimonious droop, which harmonized admirably with the level gaze of her dark and quiet eye. A strong, serene physical nature and the placid temper which comes of no nerves and no troubles seemed this lady's comfortable portion. She was dressed in plain dull black, save for a sort of dark blue kerchief which was folded across her bosom and exposed a glimpse of her massive throat. Over this kerchief was suspended a little silver cross. I admired her greatly, and yet with a large reserve. A certain mild intellectual apathy belonged properly to her type of beauty, and had always seemed to round and enrich it; but this *bourgeoise* Egeria, if I viewed her right, betrayed a rather vulgar stagnation of mind. There might have been once a dim, spiritual light in her face; but it had long since begun to wane. And furthermore, in plain prose, she was growing stout. My disappointment amounted very nearly to complete disenchantment when Theobald, as if to facilitate my covert inspection, declaring that the lamp was very dim and that she would ruin her eyes without more light, rose and fetched a couple of candles from the mantel-piece, which he placed, lighted, on the table. In this brighter illumination I perceived that our hostess was decidedly an elderly woman. She was neither haggard nor worn nor grey: she was simply coarse. The 'soul' which Theobald had promised seemed scarcely worth making such a point of; it was no deeper mystery than a sort of matronly mildness of lip and brow. I would have been ready even to declare that that sanctified bend of the head was nothing more than the trick of a person constantly working at embroidery. It occurred to me even that it was a trick of a less innocent sort; for, in spite of the mellow quietude of her wits, this stately needlewoman dropped a hint that she took the situation rather less *au sérieux* than her friend. When he rose to light the candles, she looked across at me with a quick, intelligent smile and tapped her forehead with her forefinger; then, as, from a sudden feeling of compassionate loyalty to poor Theobald, I preserved a blank face, she gave a little shrug and resumed her work.

What was the relation of this singular couple? Was he the most ardent of friends or the most respectful of lovers? Did she regard him as an eccentric youth whose benevolent admiration of her beauty she was not ill-pleased to humour at this small cost of having him climb into her little parlour and gossip of summer nights? With her decent and sombre dress, her simple gravity, and that fine piece of priestly needlework, she looked like some pious lay-member of a sisterhood, living by special permission outside her convent walls. Or was she maintained here aloft by her friend in comfortable leisure, so that he might have before him the perfect, eternal type, uncorrupted and untarnished by the struggle for existence? Her shapely hands, I observed, were very fair and white; they lacked the traces of what is called 'honest toil'.

'And the pictures, how do they come on?' she asked of Theobald, after a long pause.

'Finely, finely! I have here a friend whose sympathy and encouragement give me new faith and ardour.'

Our hostess turned to me, gazed at me a moment rather inscrutably, and then tapping her forehead with the gesture she had used a minute before, 'He has a magnificent genius!' she said, with perfect gravity.

'I'm inclined to think so,' I answered, with a smile.

'Eh, why do you smile?' she cried. 'If you doubt it, you must see the *bambino*!' And she took the lamp and conducted me to the other side of the room, where on the wall, in a plain black frame, hung a large drawing in red chalk. Beneath it was festooned a little bowl for holy-water. The drawing represented a very young child, entirely naked, half nestling back against his mother's gown, but with his two little arms outstretched, as if in the act of benediction. It was executed with singular freedom and power, and yet seemed vivid with the sacred bloom of infancy. A sort of dimpled elegance and grace, in the midst of its boldness, recalled the touch of Correggio. 'That's what he can do!' said my hostess. 'It's the blessed little boy whom I lost. It's his very image, and the Signor Teobaldo gave it me as a gift. He has given me many things beside!'

I looked at the picture for some time and admired it vastly. Turning back to Theobald, I assured him that if it were hung among the drawings in the Uffizi and labelled with a glorious name, it would hold its own. My praise seemed to give him extreme pleasure; he pressed my hands, and his eyes filled with tears. It moved him apparently with the desire to expatiate on the history of the drawing, for he rose and made his adieux to our companion, kissing her hand with the same mild ardour as before. It occurred to me that the offer of a similar piece of gallantry on my own part might help me to know what manner of woman she was. When she perceived my intion, she withdrew her hand, dropped her eyes solemnly, and made me a severe courtesy. Theobald took my arm and led me rapidly into the street.

'And what do you think of the divine Serafina?' he cried with fervour.

'It's certainly good solid beauty!'

He eyed me an instant askance, and then seemed hurried along by the current of remembrance. 'You should have seen the mother and the child together, seen them as I first saw them,—the mother with her head draped in a shawl, a divine trouble in her face, and the bambino pressed to her bosom. You would have said, I think, that Raphael had found his match in common chance. I was coming in, one summer night, from a long walk in the country, when I met this apparition at the city gate. The woman held out her hand. I hardly knew whether to say, "What do you want?" or to fall down and worship. She asked for a little money. I saw that she was beautiful and pale. She might have stepped out of the stable of Bethlehem! I gave her money and helped her on her way into the town. I had guessed her story. She, too, was a maiden mother, and she had been turned out into the world in her shame. I felt in all my pulses that here was my subject marvellously realized. I felt like one of the old convent artists who had had a vision. I rescued them, cherished them, watched them as I would have done some precious work of art, some lovely fragment of fresco discovered in a mouldering cloister. In a month,—as if to deepen and consecrate the pathos of it all,—the poor little child died. When she felt that he was going, she held him up to me for ten minutes, and I made that sketch. You saw a feverish haste in it, I suppose; I wanted to spare the poor little mortal the pain of his position. After that, I doubly valued the mother. She is the simplest, sweetest, most natural creature that ever bloomed in this brave old land of Italy. She lives in the memory of her child, in her gratitude for the scanty kindness I have been able to show her, and in her simple religion! She's not even conscious of her beauty; my admiration has never made her vain. Heaven knows I've made no secret of it. You must have observed the singular transparency of her expression, the lovely modesty of her glance. And was there ever such a truly virginal brow, such a natural classic elegance in the wave of the hair and the arch of the forehead? I've studied her; I may say I know her. I've absorbed her little by little;

my mind is stamped and imbued, and I have determined now to clinch the impression; I shall at last invite her to sit for me!'

'"At last,—at last"?' I repeated, in much amazement. 'Do you mean that she has never done so yet?'

'I've not really had—a—a sitting,' said Theobald, speaking very slowly. 'I've taken notes, you know; I've got my grand fundamental impression. That's the great thing! But I've not actually had her as a model, posed and draped and lighted, before my easel.'

What had become for the moment of my perception and my tact I am at a loss to say; in their absence, I was unable to repress a piece of *brusquerie* which I was destined to regret. We had stopped at a turning, beneath a lamp. 'My poor friend,' I exclaimed, laying my hand on his shoulder, 'you've *dawdled*! She's an old, old woman— for a Madonna!'

It was as if I had brutally struck him; I shall never forget the long, slow, almost ghastly look of pain with which he answered me. 'Dawdled—old, old!' he stammered. 'Are you joking?'

'Why, my dear fellow, I suppose you don't take the woman for twenty?'

He drew a long breath and leaned against a house, looking at me with questioning, protesting, reproachful eyes. At last, starting forward, and grasping my arm: 'Answer me solemnly: does she seem to you truly old? Is she wrinkled, is she faded, am I blind?'

Then at last I understood the immensity of his illusion; how, one by one, the noiseless years had ebbed away, and left him brooding in charmed inaction, forever preparing for a work forever deferred. It seemed to me almost a kindness now to tell him the plain truth. 'I should be sorry to say you're blind,' I answered, 'but I think you're deceived. You've lost time in effortless contemplation. Your friend was once young and fresh and virginal; but, I protest, that was some years ago. Still, she has *beaux restes*. By all means make her sit for you!' I broke down; his face was too horribly reproachful.

He took off his hat and stood passing his handkerchief mechanically over his forehead. '*De beaux restes?* I thank you for sparing me the plain English. I must make up my Madonna out of *beaux restes*! What a masterpiece she'll be! Old—old! Old—old!' he murmured.

'Never mind her age,' I cried, revolted at what I had done, 'never mind my impression of her! You have your memory, your notes, your genius. Finish your picture in a month. I proclaim it before-hand a masterpiece, and I hereby offer you for it any sum you may choose to ask.'

He stared, but he seemed scarcely to understand me. 'Old—old!' he kept stupidly repeating. 'If she is old, what am I? If her beauty has faded, where—where is my strength? Has life been a dream? Have I worshipped too long,—have I loved too well?' The charm, in truth, was broken. That the chord of illusion should have snapped at my light, accidental touch showed how it had been weakened by excessive tension. The poor fellow's sense of wasted time, of vanished opportunity, seemed to roll in upon his soul in waves of darkness. He suddenly dropped his head and burst into tears.

I led him homeward with all possible tenderness, but I attempted neither to check his grief, to restore his equanimity, nor to unsay the hard truth. When we reached my hotel I tried to induce him to come in. 'We'll drink a glass of wine,' I said, smiling, 'to the completion of the Madonna!'

With a violent effort he held up his head, mused for a moment with a formidably sombre frown, and then giving me his hand, 'I'll finish it,' he cried, 'in a month! No, in a fortnight! After all, I have it *here*!' and he tapped his forehead. 'Of course she's old! She can afford to have it said of her,—a woman who has made twenty years pass like a twelvemonth! Old—old! Why, sir, she shall be eternal!'

I wished to see him safely to his own door, but he waved me back and walked away with an air of resolution, whistling, and swinging his cane. I waited a moment, and then followed him at a distance and saw him proceed to cross the Santa Trinità Bridge. When he reached the middle, he suddenly paused, as if his strength had deserted him, and leaned upon the parapet gazing over into the river. I was careful to keep him in sight; I confess that I passed ten very nervous minutes. He recovered himself at last, and went his way, slowly and with hanging head.

That I should really have startled poor Theobald into a bolder use of his long-garnered stores of knowledge and taste, into the vulgar effort and hazard of production, seemed at first reason enough for his continued silence and absence; but as day followed day without his either calling or sending me a line, and without my meeting him in his customary haunts, in the galleries, in the chapel at San Lorenzo, or strolling between the Arno-side and the great hedge-screen of verdure which, along the drive of the Cascine, throws the fair occupants of barouche and phaeton into such becoming relief, —as for more than a week I got neither tidings nor sight of him, I began to fear that I had fatally offended him, and that, instead of giving a wholesome impetus to his talent, I had brutally paralysed it. I had a wretched suspicion that I had made him ill. My stay at Florence was drawing to a close, and it was important that, before resuming my journey, I should assure myself of the truth. Theobald to the last had kept his lodging a mystery, and I was altogether at a loss where to look for him. The simplest course was to make inquiry of the beauty of the Mercato Vecchio, and I confess that unsatisfied curiosity as to the lady herself counselled it as well. Perhaps I had done her injustice, and she was as immortally fresh and fair as he conceived her. I was, at any rate, anxious to behold once more the ripe enchantress who had made twenty years pass for a twelvemonth. I repaired accordingly, one morning, to her abode, climbed the interminable staircase, and reached her door. It stood ajar, and as I hesitated whether to enter, a little serving-maid came clattering out with an empty kettle, as if she had just performed some savoury errand. The inner door, too, was open; so I crossed the little vestibule and entered the room in which I had formerly been received. It had not its evening aspect. The table, or one end of it, was spread for a late breakfast, and before it sat a gentleman,—an individual, at least, of the male sex,—dealing justice upon a beefsteak and onions and a bottle of wine. At his elbow, in friendly proximity, was placed the lady of the house. Her attitude, as I entered, was not that of an enchantress. With one hand she held in her lap a plate of smoking maccaroni; with the other she had lifted high in air one of the pendulous filaments of this succulent compound, and was in the act of slipping it gently down her throat. On the uncovered end of the table, facing her companion, were ranged half a dozen small statuettes, of some snuff-coloured substance resembling terra-cotta. He, brandishing his knife with ardour, was apparently descanting on their merits.

Evidently, I darkened the door. My hostess dropped her maccaroni —into her mouth, and rose hastily with a harsh exclamation and a flushed face. I immediately perceived that the Signora Serafina's secret was even better worth knowing than I had supposed, and that the way to learn it was to take it for granted. I summoned my best Italian, I smiled and bowed and apologized for my intrusion; and in a moment, whether or no I had dispelled the lady's irritation, I had, at least, recalled her prudence. I was welcome, she said; I must take a seat; this was another friend of hers, also an artist, she declared with a smile which was almost amiable. Her companion wiped his moustache and bowed with great civility. I saw at a glance that he was equal to the situation. He was presumably the author of the statuettes on the table, and he knew a money-spending *forestiere* when he saw one. He was a small, wiry man, with a clever, impudent, *retroussé* nose, a sharp little black eye, and waxed ends to his moustache. On the side of his head he wore jauntily a little crimson velvet smoking-cap, and I observed that his feet were encased in brilliant slippers. On Serafina's remarking with dignity that I was the friend of Mr. Theobald, he broke out into that fantastic French in which Italians so freely indulge, and declared with fervour that Mr. Theobald was a magnificent genius.

'I'm sure I don't know,' I answered with a shrug. 'If you're in a position to affirm it, you have the advantage of me. I've seen nothing from his hand but the bambino yonder, which certainly is fine.'

He declared that the bambino was a masterpiece, a pure Correggio. It was only a pity, he added with a knowing smile, that the sketch had not been made on some good bit of genuine old panel. The Signora Serafina hereupon protested that Mr. Theobald was the soul of honour, and that he would never lend himself to a deceit. 'I'm not a judge of genius,' she said, 'and I know nothing of pictures. I'm but a poor simple widow; but I know that the Signor Teobaldo has the heart of an angel and the virtue of a saint. He's my bene-factor,' she added sententiously. The after-glow of the somewhat sinister flush with which she had greeted me still lingered in her cheek, and perhaps did not favour her beauty; I could not but fancy it a wise custom of Theobald's to visit her only by candlelight. She was coarse, and her poor adorer was a poet.

'I have the greatest esteem for him,' I said; 'it is for this reason that I have been uneasy at not seeing him for ten days. Have you seen him? Is he perhaps ill?'

'Ill! Heaven forbid!' cried Serafina, with genuine vehemence.

Her companion uttered a rapid expletive, and reproached her with not having been to see him. She hesitated a moment; then she sim-pered the least bit and bridled. 'He comes to see me—without re-proach! But it would not be the same for me to go to him, though, indeed, you may almost call him a man of holy life.'

'He has the greatest admiration for you,' I said. 'He would have been honoured by your visit.'

She looked at me a moment sharply. 'More admiration than you. Admit that!' Of course I protested with all the eloquence at my command, and the Signora Serafina then confessed that she had taken no fancy to me on my former visit, and that, Theobald not having returned, she believed I had poisoned his mind against her. 'It would be no kindness to the poor gentleman, I can tell you that,' she said. 'He has come to see me every evening for years. It's a long friendship! No one knows him as well as I.'

'I don't pretend to know him, or to understand him,' I said. 'He's a mystery! Nevertheless he seems to me a little——' And I touched my forehead and waved my hand in the air.

Serafina glanced at her companion a moment, as if for inspiration.

He contented himself with shrugging his shoulders, as he filled his glass again. The Signora hereupon gave me a more softly insinuating smile than would have seemed likely to bloom on so candid a brow. 'It's for that that I love him!' she said. 'The world has so little kindness for such persons. It laughs at them, and despises them, and cheats them. He is too good for this wicked life! It's his fancy that he finds a little Paradise up here in my poor apartment. If he thinks so, how can I help it? He has a strange belief—really, I ought to be ashamed to tell you—that I resemble the Blessed Virgin: Heaven forgive me! I let him think what he pleases, so long as it makes him happy. He was very kind to me once, and I am not one that forgets a favour. So I receive him every evening civilly, and ask after his health, and let him look at me on this side and that! For that matter, I may say it without vanity, I was worth looking at once! And he's not always amusing, poor man! He sits sometimes for an hour without speaking a word, or else he talks away without stopping on art and nature, and beauty and duty, and fifty fine things that are all so much Latin to me. I beg you to understand that he has never said a word to me that I mightn't decently listen to. He may be a little cracked, but he's one of the saints.'

'Eh!' cried the man, 'the saints were all a little cracked!'

Serafina, I fancied, left part of her story untold; but she told enough of it to make poor Theobald's own statement seem intensely pathetic in its exalted simplicity. 'It's a strange fortune, certainly,' she went on, 'to have such a friend as this dear man,—a friend who's less than a lover and more than a friend.' I glanced at her companion, who preserved an impenetrable smile, twisted the end of his moustache, and disposed of a copious mouthful. Was *he* less than a lover? 'But what will you have?' Serafina pursued. 'In this hard world one mustn't ask too many questions; one must take what comes and keep what one gets. I've kept my good friend for twenty years, and I do hope that, at this time of day, Signore, you've not come to turn him against me!'

I assured her that I had no such design, and that I should vastly regret disturbing Mr. Theobald's habits or convictions. On the contrary, I was alarmed about him, and I should immediately go in search of him. She gave me his address and a florid account of her sufferings at his non-appearance. She had not been to him, for various reasons; chiefly because she was afraid of displeasing him, as he had always made such a mystery of his home. 'You might have sent this gentleman!' I ventured to suggest.

'Ah,' cried the gentleman, 'he admires the Signora Serafina, but he wouldn't admire me.' And then, confidentially, with his finger on his nose, 'He's a purist!'

I was about to withdraw, on the promise that I would inform the Signora Serafina of my friend's condition, when her companion, who had risen from table and girded his loins apparently for the onset, grasped me gently by the arm, and led me before the row of statuettes. 'I perceive by your conversation, signore, that you are a patron of the arts. Allow me to request your honourable attention for these modest products of my own ingenuity. They are brand-new, fresh from my *atelier*, and have never been exhibited in public. I have brought them here to receive the verdict of the Signora Serafina, who is a good critic, for all she may pretend to the contrary. I am the inventor of this peculiar style of statuette,—of subject, manner, material, everything. Touch them, I pray you; handle them; you needn't fear. Delicate as they look, it is impossible they should break! My various creations have met with great success. They are especially admired by Americans. I have sent them all over Europe, —to London, Paris, Vienna! You may have observed some little specimens in Paris, on the Boulevard, in a shop of which they constitute the specialty. There is always a crowd about the window. They form a very pleasing ornament for the mantel-shelf of a *jeune homme élégant,* for the boudoir of a *jolie femme.* You couldn't make a prettier present to a person with whom you wished to exchange a harmless joke. It is not classic art, signore, of course; but, between ourselves, isn't classic art sometimes rather a bore? Caricature, burlesque, *la charge,* as the French say, has hitherto been confined to paper, to the pen and pencil. Now, it has been my inspiration to introduce it into statuary. For this purpose I have invented a peculiar plastic compound which you will permit me not to divulge. That's my secret, signore! It's as light, you perceive, as cork, and yet as firm as alabaster! I frankly confess that I really pride myself as much on this little stroke of chemical ingenuity as upon the other element of novelty in my creations,—my types. What do you say to my types, signore? The idea is bold; does it strike you as happy? Cats and monkeys,—monkeys and cats,—all human life is there! Human life, of course, I mean, viewed with the eye of the satirist! To combine sculpture and satire, signore, has been my unprecedented ambition. I flatter myself that I have not egregiously failed.'

As this jaunty Juvenal of the chimney-piece delivered himself of his seductive allocution, he took up his little groups successively from the table, held them aloft, turned them about, rapped them with his knuckles, and gazed at them lovingly with his head on one side. They consisted each of a cat and a monkey, fantastically draped, in some preposterously sentimental conjunction. They exhibited a certain sameness of motive, and illustrated chiefly the different phases of what, in delicate terms, may be called gallantry and coquetry; but they were strikingly clever and expressive, and were at once very perfect cats and monkeys and very natural men and women. I confess, however, that they failed to amuse me. I was doubtless not in a mood to enjoy them, for they seemed to me peculiarly cynical and vulgar. Their imitative felicity was revolting. As I looked askance at the complacent little artist, brandishing them between finger and thumb, and caressing them with an amorous eye, he seemed to me himself little more than an exceptionally intelligent ape. I mustered an admiring grin, however, and he blew another blast. 'My figures are studied from life! I have a little menagerie of monkeys whose frolics I contemplate by the hour. As for the cats, one has only to look out of one's back window! Since I have begun to examine these expressive little brutes, I have made many profound observations. Speaking, signore, to a man of imagination, I may say that my little designs are not without a philosophy of their own. Truly, I don't know whether the cats and monkeys imitate us, or whether it's we who imitate them.' I congratulated him on his philosophy, and he resumed: 'You will do me the honour to admit that I have handled my subjects with delicacy. Eh, it was needed, signore! I have been free, but not licentious. Just a hint, you know! You may see as much or as little as you please. These little groups, however, are no measure of my invention. If you will favour me with a call at my studio, I think that you will admit that my combinations are really infinite. I likewise execute figures to command. You have perhaps some little motive,—the fruit of your own philosophy of life, signore,—which you would like to have interpreted. I can promise to work it up to your satisfaction; it shall be as malicious as you please. Allow me to present you with my card, and to remind you that my prices are moderate. Only sixty francs for a little group like that. My statuettes are as durable as bronze,—*aere perennius*, signore,—and, between ourselves, I think they are more amusing.'

As I pocketed his card, I glanced at the worthy Serafina, wondering whether she had an eye for contrasts. She had picked up one of the little couples and was tenderly dusting it with a feather broom.

What I had just seen and heard had so deepened my compassionate interest in my deluded friend, that I took a summary leave, and made my way directly to the house designated by the Signora Serafina. It was in an obscure corner of the opposite side of the town, and presented a sombre and squalid appearance. An old woman in the doorway, on my inquiring for Theobald, ushered me in with a

mumbled blessing and an expression of relief that the poor gentleman had a friend. His lodging seemed to consist of a single room
at the top of the house. On getting no answer to my knock, I opened
the door, supposing that he was absent; so that it gave me a certain
shock to find him sitting there helpless and dumb. He was seated
near the single window, facing an easel which supported a large
canvas. On my entering, he looked up at me blankly, without changing his position, which was that of absolute lassitude and dejection,
his arms loosely folded, his legs stretched before him, his head hanging on his breast. Advancing into the room, I perceived that his face
vividly corresponded with his attitude. He was pale, haggard, and
unshaven, and his dull and sunken eye gazed at me without a spark
of recognition. I had been afraid that he would greet me with fierce
reproaches, as the cruelly officious friend who had turned his peace
to bitterness, and I was relieved to find that my appearance awakened
no visible resentment. 'Don't you know me?' I asked, as I put out
my hand. 'Have you already forgotten me?'

He made no response, kept his position stupidly, and left me staring about the room. It spoke most plaintively for itself. Shabby,
sordid, naked, it contained, beyond the wretched bed, but the scant-
iest provision for personal comfort. It was bedroom at once and
studio,—a grim ghost of a studio. A few dusty casts and prints on the
walls, three or four old canvases turned face inward, and a rusty-
looking colour-box formed, with the easel at the window, the sum
of its appurtenances. The place savoured horribly of poverty. Its only
wealth was the picture on the easel, presumably the famous
Madonna. Averted as this was from the door, I was unable to see
its face; but at last, sickened by the vacant misery of the spot, I
passed behind Theobald, eagerly and tenderly, and yet I can hardly
say that I was surprised at what I found,—a canvas that was a mere
dead blank, cracked and discoloured by time. This was his immortal work! But though not surprised, I confess I was powerfully
moved, and I think that for five minutes I could not have trusted
myself to speak. At last, my silent nearness affected him; he stirred
and turned, and then rose and looked at me with a slowly kindling
eye. I murmured some kind, ineffective nothings about his being ill
and needing advice and care, but he seemed absorbed in the effort
to recall distinctly what had last passed between us. 'You were right,'
he said with a pitiful smile, 'I'm a dawdler! I'm a failure! I shall do
nothing more in this world. You opened my eyes, and, though the
truth is bitter, I bear you no grudge. Amen! I've been sitting here
for a week face to face with the truth, with the past, with my weakness and poverty and nullity. I shall never touch a brush! I believe

I've neither eaten nor slept. Look at that canvas!' he went on, as I relieved my emotion in the urgent request that he would come home with me and dine. 'That was to have contained my masterpiece! Isn't it a promising foundation? The elements of it are all *here*.' And he tapped his forehead with that mystic confidence which had marked the gesture before. 'If I could only transpose them into some brain that had the hand, the will! Since I've been sitting here taking stock of my intellects, I've come to believe that I have the material for a hundred masterpieces. But my hand is paralysed now, and they'll never be painted. I never began! I waited and waited to be worthier to begin, and wasted my life in preparation. While I fancied my creation was growing, it was dying. I've taken it all too hard! Michael Angelo didn't, when he went at the Lorenzo! He did his best at a venture, and his venture is immortal. *That's* mine!' And he pointed with a gesture I shall never forget at the empty canvas. 'I suppose we're a genus by ourselves in the providential scheme,— we talents that can't act, that can't do or dare! We take it out in talk, in plans and promises, in study, in visions! But our visions, let me tell you,' he cried, with a toss of his head, 'have a way of being brilliant, and a man hasn't lived in vain who has seen the things I have! Of course you'll not believe in them when that bit of worm-eaten cloth is all I have to show for them; but to convince you, to enchant and astound the world, I need only the hand of Raphael. I have his brain. A pity, you'll say, I haven't his modesty. Ah, let me babble now; it's all I have left! I'm the half of a genius! Where in the wide world is my other half? Lodged perhaps in the vulgar soul, the cunning, ready fingers of some dull copyist or some trivial artisan who turns out by the dozen his easy prodigies of touch! But it's not for me to sneer at him; he at least does something. He's not a dawdler! Well for me if I had been vulgar and clever and reckless, if I could have shut my eyes and dealt my stroke!'

What to say to the poor fellow, what to do for him, seemed hard to determine; I chiefly felt that I must break the spell of his present inaction, and remove him from the haunted atmosphere of the little room it seemed such cruel irony to call a studio. I cannot say I per-suaded him to come out with me; he simply suffered himself to be led, and when we began to walk in the open air I was able to measure his pitifully weakened condition. Nevertheless, he seemed in a cer-tain way to revive, and murmured at last that he would like to go to the Pitti Gallery. I shall never forget our melancholy stroll through those gorgeous halls, every picture on whose walls seemed, even to my own sympathetic vision, to glow with a sort of insolent renewal of strength and lustre. The eyes and lips of the great portraits seemed

to smile in ineffable scorn of the dejected pretender who had dreamed of competing with their glorious authors; the celestial candour,
even, of the Madonna in the Chair, as we paused in perfect silence
before her, was tinged with the sinister irony of the women of
Leonardo. Perfect silence indeed marked our whole progress,—the
silence of a deep farewell; for I felt in all my pulses, as Theobald,
leaning on my arm, dragged one heavy foot after the other, that he
was looking his last. When we came out, he was so exhausted that,
instead of taking him to my hotel to dine, I called a carriage and
drove him straight to his own poor lodging. He had sunk into an
extraordinary lethargy; he lay back in the carriage, with his eyes
closed, as pale as death, his faint breathing interrupted at intervals
by a sudden gasp, like a smothered sob or a vain attempt to speak.
With the help of the old woman who had admitted me before, and
who emerged from a dark back-court, I contrived to lead him up the
long steep staircase and lay him on his wretched bed. To her I gave
him in charge, while I prepared in all haste to seek a physician.
But she followed me out of the room with a pitiful clasping of her
hands.

'Poor, dear, blessed gentleman,' she murmured; 'is he dying?'

'Possibly. How long has he been thus?'

'Since a night he passed ten days ago. I came up in the morning
to make his poor bed, and found him sitting up in his clothes before
that great canvas he keeps there, and, poor, dear, strange man, says
his prayers to! He had not been to bed, nor since then, properly!
What has happened to him? Has he found out about the Serafina?'
she whispered with a glittering eye and a toothless grin.

'Prove at least that one old woman can be faithful,' I said, 'and
watch him well till I come back.' My return was delayed, through
the absence of the English physician on a round of visits, and my
vainly pursuing him from house to house before I overtook him. I
brought him to Theobald's bedside none too soon. A violent fever
had seized our patient, and the case was evidently grave. A couple
of hours later I knew that he had brain-fever. From this moment I
was with him constantly, but I am far from wishing to describe his
illness. Excessively painful to witness, it was happily brief. Life
burned out in delirium. A certain night that I passed at his pillow,
listening to his wild snatches of regret, of aspiration, of rapture and
awe at the phantasmal pictures with which his brain seemed to
swarm, recurs to my memory now like some stray page from a lost
masterpiece of tragedy. Before a week was over we had buried him
in the little Protestant cemetery on the way to Fiesole. The Signora
Serafina, whom I had caused to be informed of his illness, had come

in person, I was told, to inquire about its progress; but she was absent from his funeral, which was attended by but a scanty concourse of mourners. Half a dozen old Florentine sojourners, in spite of the prolonged estrangement which had preceded his death, had felt the kindly impulse to honour his grave. Among them was my friend Mrs. Coventry, whom I found, on my departure, waiting at her carriage door at the gate of the cemetery.

'Well,' she said, relieving at last with a significant smile the solemnity of our immediate greeting, 'and the great Madonna? Have you seen her, after all?'

'I've seen her,' I said; 'she's mine,—by bequest. But I shall never show her to you.'

'And why not, pray?'

'My dear Mrs. Coventry, you'd not understand her!'

'Upon my word, you're polite.'

'Excuse me; I'm sad and vexed and bitter.' And with reprehensible rudeness, I marched away. I was excessively impatient to leave Florence; my friend's dark spirit seemed diffused through all things. I had packed my trunk to start for Rome that night, and meanwhile, to beguile my unrest, I aimlessly paced the streets. Chance led me at last to the church of San Lorenzo. Remembering poor Theobald's phrase about Michael Angelo,—'he did his best at a venture,' —I went in and turned my steps to the chapel of the tombs. Viewing in sadness the sadness of its immortal treasures, I fancied, while I stood there, that the scene demanded no ampler commentary. As I passed through the church again to depart, a woman, turning away from one of the side-altars, met me face to face. The black shawl depending from her head draped picturesquely the handsome visage of the Signora Serafina. She stopped as she recognized me, and I saw that she wished to speak. Her eye was bright and her ample bosom heaved in a way that seemed to portend a certain sharpness of reproach. But the expression of my own face, apparently, drew the sting from her resentment, and she addressed me in a tone in which bitterness was tempered by a sort of dogged resignation. 'I know it was you, now, that separated us,' she said. 'It was a pity he ever brought you to see me! Of course, you couldn't think of me as he did. Well, the Lord gave him, the Lord has taken him. I've just paid for a nine days' mass for his soul. And I can tell you this, signore, I never deceived him. Who put it into his head that I was made to live on holy thoughts and fine phrases? It was his own fancy, and it pleased him to think so. Did he suffer much?' she added more softly, after a pause.

'His sufferings were great, but they were short.'

'And did he speak of me?' She had hesitated and dropped her eyes; she raised them with her question, and revealed in their sombre stillness a gleam of feminine confidence which, for the moment, revived and illumined her beauty. Poor Theobald! Whatever name he had given his passion, it was still her fine eyes that had charmed him.

'Be contented, madam,' I answered, gravely.

She dropped her eyes again and was silent. Then exhaling a full, rich sigh, as she gathered her shawl together: 'He was a magnificent genius!'

I bowed, and we separated.

Passing through a narrow side-street on my way back to my hotel, I perceived above a doorway a sign which it seemed to me I had read before. I suddenly remembered that it was identical with the superscription of a card that I had carried for an hour in my waistcoat-pocket. On the threshold stood the ingenious artist whose claims to public favour were thus distinctly signalized, smoking a pipe in the evening air, and giving the finishing polish with a bit of rag to one of his inimitable 'combinations'. I caught the expressive curl of a couple of tails. He recognized me, removed his little red cap with a most obsequious bow, and motioned me to enter his studio. I returned his bow and passed on, vexed with the apparition. For a week afterwards, whenever I was seized among the ruins of Roman greatness with some peculiarly poignant memory of Theobald's transcendent illusions and deplorable failure, I seemed to hear a fantastic, impertinent murmur, 'Cats and monkeys, monkeys and cats; all human life is there!'

The Sweetheart of M. Briseux

[First appeared in the *Galaxy*, vol. xv (June 1873), pp. 760–79. Not reprinted during James's lifetime.]

THE LITTLE PICTURE GALLERY AT M— IS A TYPICAL *musée de province*—cold, musty, unvisited, and enriched chiefly with miniature works by painters whose maturity was not to be powerful. The floors are tiled in brick, and the windows draped in faded moreen; the very light seems pale and neutral, as if the dismal lack-lustre atmosphere of the pictures were contagious. The subjects represented are of course of the familiar academic sort—the Wisdom of Solomon and the Fureurs d'Oreste; together with a few elegant landscapes exhibiting the last century view of nature, and half a dozen neat portraits of French gentlefolks of that period, in the act, as one may say, of taking the view in question. To me, I confess, the place had a melancholy charm, and I found none of the absurd old paintings too absurd to enjoy. There is always an agreeable finish in the French touch, even when the hand is not a master's. The catalogue, too, was prodigiously queer; a bit of very ancient literature, with comments, in the manner of the celebrated M. La Harpe. I wondered, as I turned its pages, into what measure of reprobation pictures and catalogue together had been compressed by that sole son of M—, who has achieved more than local renown in the arts. Conjecture was pertinent, for it was in these crepuscular halls that this deeply original artist must have heard the first early bird-notes of awakening genius : first, half credulously, as we may suppose, on festal Sundays, with his hand in his father's, gazing rosy and wide-eyed at the classical wrath of Achilles and the sallow flesh-tints of Dido; and later, with his hands in his pockets, an incipient critical frown and the mental vision of an Achilles somehow more in earnest and a Dido more deeply desirable. It was indeed doubly pertinent, for the little Musée had at last, after much watching and waiting and bargaining, become possessor of one of Briseux's pictures. I was promptly informed of the fact by the *concierge*, a person much reduced by years and chronic catarrh, but still robust enough to display his aesthetic culture to a foreigner presumably of distinction. He led me solemnly into the presence of the great work, and placed a chair for me in the proper light. The famous painter had left his native town early in life, before making his mark, and an inappreciative family—his father was a small apothecary with a proper admiration of the arts, but a horror of artists—had been at no pains to preserve his boyish sketches. The more fools they! The merest scrawl with his signature now brought hundreds of francs, and there were those of his blood still in the town with whom the francs were scarce enough. To obtain a serious picture had of course been no small affair, and little M—, though with the yearning heart of a mother, happened to have no scanty maternal savings. Yet the thing had been managed by subscription, and the picture paid for. To make the triumph complete, a fortnight after it had been hung on its nail, M. Briseux succumbs to a fever in Rome and his pictures rise to the most fantastic prices! This was the very work which had made the painter famous. The portrait of a Lady in a Yellow Shawl in the Salon of 1836 had *fait époque*. Every one had heard of the 'Yellow Shawl'; people talked of it as they did of the 'Chapeau de Paille' of Rubens or the 'Torn Glove' of Titian; or if they didn't, posterity would! Such was the discursive murmur of the concierge as I examined this precious specimen of Briseux's first manner; and there was a plaintive cadence in this last assurance, which seemed to denote a too vivid prevision of the harvest of tributary francs to be reaped by his successors in office. It would be graceless praise to say that a glimpse of the picture is worth your franc. It is a superb performance, and I spent half an hour before it in such serene enjoyment that I forgot the concierge was a bore.

It is a half-length portrait representing a young woman, not exactly beautiful, yet very far from plain, draped with a singularly simple elegance in a shawl of yellow silk embroidered with fantastic arabesque. She is dark and grave, her dress is dark, the background is of a sober tone, and this brilliant scarf glows splendidly by contrast. It seems indeed to irradiate luminous colour, and makes the picture brilliant in spite of its sombre accessories; and yet it leaves their full value to the tenderly glowing flesh portions. The portrait lacks a certain harmonious finish, that masterly interfusion of parts which the painter afterwards practised; the touch is hasty, and here and there a little heavy; but its splendid vivacity and energy, and the almost boyish good faith of some of its more venturesome strokes, make it a capital example of that momentous point in the history of genius when still tender promise blooms—in a night, as it were—into perfect force. It was little wonder that the picture had made a noise: judges of the more penetrating sort must have felt that it contained that invaluable something which an artist gives but once—the prime outgush of his effort—the flower of his originality. As I continued to look, however, I began to wonder whether it did not contain something better still—the reflection of a countenance very nearly as deep and ardent as the artist's talent. In spite of the expressive repose of the figure the brow and mouth wore a look of smothered agitation, the dark grey eye almost glittered, and the flash in the cheek burned ominously. Evidently this was the picture of something more than a yellow shawl. To the analytic eye it was the picture of a mind, or at least of a mood. 'Who was the lady?' I asked my companion.

He shrugged his shoulders, and for an instant looked uncertain. But as a Frenchman, he produced his hypothesis as follows: 'Mon Dieu! A sweetheart of M. Briseux!—*Ces artistes!*'

I left my place and passed into the adjoining rooms, where, as I have said, I found half an hour's diversion. On my return, my chair was occupied by a lady, apparently my only fellow-visitor. I noticed her no further than to see that, though comely, she was no longer young, that she was dressed in black, and that she was looking intently at the picture. Her intentness indeed at last attracted me, and while I lingered to gather a final impression, I covertly glanced at her. She was so far from being young that her hair was white, but with that charming and often premature brilliancy which belongs to fine brunettes. The concierge hovered near, narrating and expounding, and I fancied that her brief responses (for she asked no questions) betrayed an English accent. But I had doubtless no business to fancy anything, for my companion, as if with a sudden embarrassing sense of being watched, gathered her shawl about her, rose, and prepared to turn away. I should have immediately retreated, but that with this movement of hers our eyes met, and in the light of her rapid, just slightly deprecating glace, I read something which helped curiosity to get the better of politeness. She walked away, and I stood staring; and as she averted her head it seemed to me that my rather too manifest surprise had made her blush. I watched her slowly cross the room and pass into the next one, looking very vaguely at the pictures; and then addressed a keenly questioning glance at the 'Lady with the Yellow Shawl'. Her startlingly vivid eyes answered my question most distinctly. I was satisfied, and I left the Musée.

It would perhaps be more correct to say that I was wholly unsatisfied. I strolled at haphazard through the little town, and emerged, as a matter of course, on the local promenade. The promenade at M— is a most agreeable spot. It stretches along the top of the old town wall, over whose sturdy parapet, polished by the peaceful showers of many generations, you enjoy a view of the pale-hued but charming Provençal landscape. The middle of the rampart is adorned with a row of close-clipped lime-trees, with benches in the spaces between them; and, as you sit in the shade, the prospect is framed to your vision by the level parapet and the even limit of the far-projecting branches. What you see is therefore a long horizontal strip of landscape—a radiant stretch of white rocks and vaporous olives, scintillating in the southern light. Except a *bonne* or two, with a couple of children grubbing in the gravel, an idle apprentice in a blouse dozing on a bench, and a couple of red-legged soldiers leaning on the wall, I was the only lounger on the rampart, and this was a place to relish solitude. By nature a very sentimental traveller, there is nothing I like better than to light a cigar and lose myself in a meditative perception of local colour. I love to ruminate the picturesque, and the scene before me was redolent of it. On this occasion, however, the shady rampart and the shining distance were less interesting than a figure, disembodied but distinct, which soon obtruded itself on my attention. The mute assurance gathered before leaving the Musée had done as much to puzzle as to enlighten me. Was that modest and venerable person, then, the sweetheart of the illustrious Briseux? one of *ces artistes*, as rumour loudly proclaimed him, in the invidious as well as in the most honourable sense of the term. Plainly, she was the original of the portrait. In the days when her complexion would bear it, she had worn the yellow shawl. Time had changed, but not transformed her, as she must have fancied it had, to come and contemplate thus frankly this monument of her early charms. Why had she come? Was it accident, or was it vanity? How did it seem to her to find herself so strangely lifted out of her own possession and made a helpless spectator of her survival to posterity? The more I consulted my impression of her, the more certain I felt that she was no Frenchwoman, but a modest spinster of my own transatlantic race, on whom posterity had as little claim as this musty Musée, which indeed possessed much of that sepulchral chill which clings to such knowledge of us as posterity enjoys. I found it hard to reconcile the lady with herself, and it was with the restlessness of conjecture that I left my place and strolled to the further end of the rampart. Here conjecture paused, amazed at its opportunities; for M. Briseux's sweetheart was seated on a bench under the lime-trees. She was gazing almost as thoughtfully on the distant view as she had done on her portrait; but as I passed, she gave me a glance from which embarrassment seemed to have vanished. I slowly walked the length of the rampart again, and as I went an impulse, born somehow of the delicious mild air, the light-bathed landscape of rock and olive, and of the sense of a sort of fellowship in isolation in the midst of these deeply foreign influences, as well as of a curiosity which was after all but the frank recognition of an obvious fact, was transmuted into a decision sufficiently remarkable in a bashful man. I proceeded gravely to carry it out. I approached my companion and bowed. She acknowledged my bow with a look which, though not exactly mistrustful, seemed to demand an explanation. To give it, I seated myself beside her. Something in her face made explanation easy. I was sure that she was an old maid, and gently but frankly eccentric. Her age left her at liberty to be as frank as she chose, and though I was somewhat her junior, I had grey hairs enough in my moustache to warrant her in smiling at my almost ardent impatience. Her smile, when she perceived that my direct appeal was deeply respectful, broke into a genial laugh which completed our introduction. To her inner sense, as well, evidently, the grey indifference of the historic rampart, the olive-sown landscape, the sweet foreign climate, left the law very much in our own hands; and then moreover, as something in her eyes proclaimed, the well of memory in her soul had been so strongly stirred that it naturally overflowed. I fancy that she looked more like her portrait for that hour or two than she had done in twenty years. At any rate, it had come to seem, before many minutes, a delightful matter of course that I should sit there—a perfect stranger—listening to the story into which her broken responses to my first questions gradually shaped themselves. I should add that I had made a point of appearing a zealous student of the lamented Briseux. This was no more than the truth, and I proved categorically that I knew his works. We were thus pilgrims in the same faith, and licensed to discuss its mysteries. I repeat her story literally, and I surely don't transgress the proper limits of editorial zeal in supplying a single absent clause: she must in those days have been a wonderfully charming girl.

I have been spending the winter (she said) with my niece at Cannes, where I accidentally heard from an English gentleman interested in such matters, that Briseux's 'Yellow Shawl' had been purchased by this little Musée. He had stopped to see it on his way from Paris, and, though a famous *connoisseur*, poor man, do you know he never discovered what it took you but a moment to perceive? I didn't enlighten him, in spite of his kindness in explaining, 'Bradshaw' in hand, just how I might manage to diverge on my way to Paris and give a day to M—. I contented myself with telling him that I had known M. Briseux thirty years ago, and had chanced to have the first glimpse of his first masterpiece. Even this suggested nothing. But in fact, why should it have suggested anything? As I sat before the picture just now, I felt in all my pulses that I am *not* the person who stands masquerading there with that strangely cynical smile.

That poor girl is dead and buried; I should tell no falsehood in saying I'm not she. Yet as I looked at her, time seemed to roll backward and experience to repeat itself. Before me stood a pale young man in a ragged coat, with glowing dark eyes, brushing away at a great canvas, with gestures more like those of inspiration than any I have ever seen. I seemed to see myself—to *be* myself—muffled in that famous shawl, *posing* there for hours in a sort of fever that made me unconscious of fatigue. I've often wondered whether, during those memorable hours, I was more or less myself than usual, and whether the singular episode they brought forth was an act of folly or of transcendent reason. Perhaps you can tell me.

It was in Paris, in my twenty-first year. I had come abroad with Mrs. Staines, an old and valued friend of my mother's, who during the last days of her life, a year before, had consigned me appealingly to this lady's protection. But for Mrs. Staines, indeed, I should have been homeless. My brother had recently married, but not happily, and experiment had shown me that under his roof I was an indifferent peacemaker. Mrs. Staines was what is called a very superior person —a person with an aquiline nose, who wore gloves in the house, and gave you her ear to kiss. My mother, who considered her the wisest of women, had written her every week since their schooldays a crossed letter beginning 'My dearest Lucretia'; but it was my poor mother's nature to like being patronized and bullied. Mrs. Staines would send her by return of mail a budget of advice adapted to her 'station'—this being a considerate mode of allusion to the fact that she had married a very poor clergyman. Mrs. Staines received me, however, with such substantial kindness, that I should have had little grace to complain that the manner of it was frigid. When I knew her better I forgave her frigidity, for it was that of a disappointed woman. She was ambitious, and her ambitions had failed. She had married a very clever man, a rising young lawyer, of political tendencies, who promised to become famous. She would have enjoyed above all things being the wife of a legal luminary, and she would have insisted on his expanding to the first magnitude. She believed herself born, I think, to be the lawful Egeria of a cabinet minister. A cabinet minister poor Mr. Staines might have become if he had lived; but he broke down at thirty-five from overwork, and a year later his wife had to do double mourning. As time went on she transferred her hopes to her only boy; but here her disappointment lay the heavier on her heart that maternal pride had bidden it be for ever dumb. He would never tread in his father's steps, nor redeem his father's pledges. His genius—if genius it was—was bent in quite another way, and he was to be, not a useful, but an ornamental member of society. Extremely ornamental he seemed likely to become, and his mother found partial comfort as he grew older. He did his duty apparently in growing up so very handsome that, whatever else he might do, he would be praised less for that than for his good looks. They were those of a decorous young Apollo. When I first saw him, as he was leaving college, he might well have passed for an incipient great man. He had in perfection the *air* of distinction, and he carried it out in gesture and manner. Never was a handsomer, graver, better-bred young man. He was tall, slender, and fair, with the finest blonde hair curling close about his shapely head; a blue eye, as clear and cold as a winter's morning; a set of teeth so handsome that his infrequent smile might have seemed almost a matter of modesty; and a general expression of discretion and maturity which seemed to protest against the imputation of foppishness. After a while, probably, you would have found him too imperturbably neat and polite, and have liked him better if his manner had been sometimes at fault and his cravat occasionally awry. Me, I confess, he vastly impressed from the first, and I secretly worshipped him. I had never seen so fine a gentleman, and I doubted if the world contained such another. My experience of the world was small, and I had lived among what Harold Staines would have considered very shabby people—several of whom wore ill-brushed hats. I was, therefore, not sorry to find that I appreciated merit of the most refined sort; and in fact, ignorant though I was, my judgment was not at fault. Harold was perfectly honourable and amiable, and his only fault was that he looked wiser than he could reasonably be expected to be. In the evening especially, in a white cravat, leaning in a doorway, and overtopping the crowd by his whole handsome head, he seemed some inscrutable young diplomatist whose scepticism hadn't undermined his courtesy.

He had, through his mother, expectation of property sufficient to support him in ample ease; but though he had elegant tastes, idleness was not one of them, and he agreed with his mother that he ought to choose a profession. Then it was that she fully measured her disappointment. There had been nothing in her family but judges and bishops, and anything else was of questionable respectability. There was a great deal of talk on the matter between them; for superficially at least they were a most united pair, and if Harold had not asked her opinion from conviction he would have done so from politeness. In reality, I believe, there was but one person in the world whose opinion he greatly cared for—and that person was not Mrs. Staines; nor had it yet come to pass that he pretended for a while it was I. It was so far from being Mrs. Staines that one day, after a long talk, I found her leaving him in tears; and tears with this superior woman were an event of portentous rarity. Harold on the same day was not at home at dinner, and I thought the next day held his handsome head even higher than usual. I asked no questions, but a little later my curiosity was satisfied. Mrs. Staines informed me, with an air of dignity which evidently cost her some effort and seemed intended to deprecate criticism, that Harold had determined to be an—artist. 'It's not the career I should have preferred,' she said, 'but my son has talent—and respectability—which will make it honourable.' That Harold would do anything more for the profession of the brush than Raphael and Rembrandt had done, I was perhaps not prepared to affirm; but I answered that I was very glad, and that I wished him all success. Indeed, I was not surprised, for Mr. Staines had what in any one else would have been called a mania for pictures and bronzes, old snuff-boxes and candlesticks. He had not apparently used his pencil very freely; but he had recently procured—indeed, I think, he had himself designed—a 'sketching apparatus' of the most lavish ingenuity. He was now going to use it in earnest, and I remember reflecting with a good deal of satisfaction that the great white umbrella which formed its principal feature was large enough to protect his handsome complexion from the sun.

It was at this time I came to Mrs. Staines to stay indefinitely—with doubts and fears so few that I must have been either very ignorant or very confident. I had indeed an ample measure of the blessed simplicity of youth; but if I judged my situation imperfectly, I did so at any rate with a conscience. I was stoutly determined to receive no favours that I couldn't repay, and to be as quietly useful and gracefully agreeable as I could modestly devise occasion for. I was a homeless girl, but I was not a poor relation. My fortune was slender, but I was ready to go out into the world and seek a better, rather than fall into an attitude of irresponsive dependence. Mrs. Staines thought at first that I was dull and amiable, and that as a companion I would do no great credit to anything but her benevolence. Later, for a time, as I gave proofs of some sagacity and perhaps of some decision, I think she fancied me a schemer and—Heaven forgive her!—a hypocrite. But at last, evidently—although to the end, I believe, she continued to compliment my shrewdness at the expense of that feminine sweetness by which I should have preferred to commend myself—she decided that I was a person of the best intentions, and—here comes my story—that I would make a suitable wife for her son.

To this unexpectedly flattering conclusion, of course, she was slow in coming; it was the result of the winter we passed together after Harold had 'turned his attention', as his mother always publicly phrased it, 'to art'. He had declared that we must immediately go abroad that he might study the works of the masters. His mother, I believe, suggested that he might begin with the rudiments nearer home. But apparently he had mastered the rudiments, for she was overruled and we went to Rome. I don't know how many of the secrets of the masters Harold learned; but we passed a delightful winter. He began his studies with the solemn promptitude which he uesd in all things, and devoted a great deal of time to copying from the antique in the Vatican and the Capitol. He worked slowly, but with extraordinary precision and neatness, and finished his drawings with exquisite care. He was openly very little of a dogmatist, but on coming to know him you found that he had various principles of which he was extremely tenacious. Several of these related to the proportions of the human body, as ascertained by himself. They constituted, he affirmed, an infallible method for learning to draw. If other artists didn't know it, so much the worse for them. He applied this rare method persistently all winter, and carried away from Rome a huge portfolio full of neatly shaded statues and statuesque *contadini*. At first he had gone into a painter's studio with several other pupils, but he took no fancy to either his teacher or his companions, and came home one day in disgust, declaring that he had washed his hands of them. As he never talked about disagreeable things, he said nothing as to what had vexed him; but I guessed that he had received some mortal offence, and I was not surprised that he shouldn't care to fraternize with the common herd of art-students. They had long, untidy hair, and smoked bad tobacco; they lay no one knew where, and borrowed money and took liberties. Mr. Staines certainly was not a man to refuse a needy friend a napoleon, but he couldn't forgive a liberty. He took none with himself! We became very good friends, and it was especially for this that I liked him. Nothing is truer than that in the long run we like our opposites; they're a change and a rest from ourselves. I confess that my good intentions sometimes clashed with a fatal light-headedness, of which a fair share of trouble had not cured me. In moments of irritation I had a trick of giving the reins to my 'sarcasm'; so at least my partners in quadrilles had often called it. At my leisure I was sure to repent, and frank public amends followed fast on the heels of offence. Then I believe I was called generous—not only by my partners in quadrilles. But I had a secret admiration for people who were just, from the first and always, and whose demeanor seemed to shape itself with a sort of harmonious unity, like the outline of a beautiful statue. Harold Staines was a finished gentleman, as we used to say in those days, and I admired him the more that I still had ringing in my ears that eternal refrain of my schoolroom days—'My child, my child, when will you ever learn to be a lady?' He seemed to me an embodiment of the serene amenities of life, and I didn't know how very great a personage I thought him until I once overheard a young man in a crowd at St. Peter's call him *that confounded prig.* Then I came to the conclusion that it was a very coarse and vulgar world, and that Mr. Staines was too good for it.

This impression was not removed by—I hardly know what to call it—the gallant propriety of his conduct towards me. He had treated me at first with polite condescension, as a very young and rather humble person, whose presence in the house rested on his mother's somewhat eccentric benevolence, rather than on any very obvious merits of her own. But later, as my native merit, whatever it was, got the better of my shyness, he approached me, especially in company, with a sort of ceremonious consideration which seemed to give notice to the world that if his mother and he treated me as their equal— why, I *was* their equal. At last, one fine day in Rome, I learned that I had the honour to please him. It had seemed to me so little of a matter of course that I should captivate Mr. Staines, that for a moment I was actually disappointed, and felt disposed to tell him that I had expected more of his taste. But as I grew used to the idea, I found no fault with it, and I felt prodigiously honoured. I didn't take him for a man of genius, but his admiration pleased me more than if it had come in chorus from a dozen of the men of genius whom I had had pointed out to me at archaeological picnics. They somehow were covered with the world's rust and haunted with the world's errors, and certainly on any vital question could not be trusted to make their poor wives the same answers two days running. Besides, they were dreadfully ugly. Harold was consistency itself, and his superior manner and fine blonde beauty seemed a natural result of his spiritual serenity. The way he declared himself was very characteristic, and to some girls might have seemed prosaic. To my mind it had a peculiar dignity. I had asked him, a week before, as we stood on the platform before the Lateran, some question about the Claudian aqueduct, which he had been unable to answer at the moment, although on coming to Rome he had laid in a huge provision of books of reference which he consulted with unfailing diligence. 'I'll look it up,' he said gravely; but I thought no more about it, and a few days afterwards, when he asked me to ride with him on the Campagna, I never supposed I was to be treated to an archaeological lecture. It was worthy of a wiser listener. He led the way to a swelling mound, overlooking the long stretch of the aqueduct, and poured forth the result of his researches. This was surely not a trivial compliment; and it seemed to me a finer sort of homage than if he had offered me a fifty-franc bouquet or put his horse at a six-foot wall. He told me the number of the arches, and very possibly of the stones; his story bristled with learning. I listened respectfully and stared hard at the long ragged ruin, as if it had suddenly become intensely interesting. But it was Mr. Staines who was interesting: all honour to the man who kept his polite promises so handsomely! I said nothing when he paused, and after a few minutes was going to turn away my horse. Then he laid his hand on the bridle, and, in the same tone, as if he were still talking of the aqueduct, informed me of the state of his affections. I, in my unsuspectingness, had enslaved them, and it was proper that I should know he adored me. Proper! I have always remembered the word, though I was far from thinking then that it clashed with his eloquence. It often occurred to me after-wards as the key-note of his character. In a moment more, he form-ally offered himself.

Don't be surprised at these details: to be just I must be perfectly frank, and if I consented to tell you my story, it is because I fancied I should find profit in hearing it myself. As I speak my words come back to me. I left Rome engaged to Mr. Staines, subject to his mother's approval. He might dispense with it, I told him, but I could not, and as yet I had no reason to expect it. She would, of course, wish him to marry a woman of more consequence. Mine of late had risen in her eyes, but she could hardly regard me as yet as a possible daughter-in-law. With time I hoped to satisfy her and to re-ceive her blessing. Then I would ask for no further delay. We journeyed slowly up from Rome along the Mediterranean, stopping often for several days to allow Harold to sketch. He depicted moun-tains and villages with the same diligence as the statues in the Vatican, and presumably with the same success. As his winter's practice had given him great facility, he would dash off a magnificent landscape in a single morning. I always thought it strange that, being very sober in his speech and manner, he should be extremely fond of colour in art. Such at least was the fact, and these rapid water-colours were a wonderful medley. Crimson and azure, orange and emerald—nothing less would satisfy him. But, for that matter, nature in those regions has a dazzling brightness. So at least it had for a lively girl of twenty, just engaged. So it had for a certain time after-wards. I'll not deny, the lustrous sea and sky began vaguely to re-flect my own occasionally sombre mood. How to explain to you the process of my feeling at this time is more than I can say; how es-pecially to make you believe that I was neither perverse nor capri-cious. I give it up; I can only assure you that I observed my emotions,

even before I understood them, with painful surprise. I was not disillusioned, but an end had suddenly come to my elation. It was as
if my heart had had wings, which had been suddenly clipped. I
have never been especially fond of my own possessions, and I have
learned that if I wish to admire a thing in peace, I must remain at a
respectful distance. My happiness in Harold's affection reached its
climax too suddenly, and before I knew it I found myself wondering,
questioning, and doubting. It was no fault of his, certainly, and he
had promised me nothing that he was not ready to bestow. He was
all attention and decorous devotion. If there was a fault, it was mine,
for having judged like the very young and uninformed person I was.
Since my engagement I felt five years older, and the first use I made
of my maturity—cruel as it may seem—was to turn round and look
keenly at my lover and revise my judgment. His rigid urbanity was
still extremely impressive, but at times I could have fancied that I
was listening to a musical symphony, of which only certain brief, un-
resonant notes were audible. Was this all, and were there no others?
It occurred to me more than once, with a kind of dull dismay, in the
midst of my placid expectancy, that Harold's grave notes were the
beginning and the end of his character. If the human heart were a
less incurable sceptic, I might have been divinely happy. I sat by
my lover's side while he worked, gazing at the loveliest landscape
in the world, and admiring the imperturbable audacity with which he
attacked it. Sooner than I expected, these rather silent interviews, as
romantic certainly as scenery could make them, received Mrs.
Staines's sanction. She had guessed our secret, and disapproved of
nothing but its secrecy. She was satisfied with her son's choice, and
declared with great emphasis that she was not ambitious. She was
kindness itself (though, as you see, she indulged in no needless flattery), and I wondered that I could ever have thought her stern. From
this time forward she talked to me a great deal about her son; too
much, I might have thought, if I had cared less for the theme. I have
said I was not perverse. Do I judge myself too tenderly? Before long
I found something oppressive—something almost irritating—in the
frequency and complacency of Mrs Staines's maternal disquisitions.
One day, when she had been reminding me at greater length than
usual of what a prize I had drawn, I abruptly changed the subject in
the midst of a sentence, and left her staring at my petulance. She
was on the point, I think, of administering a reprimand, but she suppressed it and contented herself with approaching the topic more
cautiously in future. Here is another reminiscence. One morning (it
was near Spezia, I think) Harold had been sketching under a tree,
not far from the inn, and I sitting by and reading aloud from Shelley,

whom one might feel a kindness for there if nowhere else. We had had a little difference of opinion about one of the poems—the beautiful 'Stanzas written in Dejection near Naples', which you probably remember. Harold pronounced them childish. I thought the term ill-chosen, and remember saying, to reinforce my opinion, that though I was no judge of painting, I pretended to be of poetry. He told me (I have not forgotten his words) that 'I lacked cultivation in each department', and I believe I replied that I would rather lack cultivation than imagination. For a pair of lovers it was a very pretty quarrel as it stood. Shortly afterwards he discovered that he had left one of his brushes at the inn, and went off in search of it. He had trouble in finding it, and was absent for some time. His verdict on poor Shelley rang in my ears as I sat looking out on the blue iridescence of the sea, and murmuring the lines in which the poet has so wonderfully suggested it. Then I went and sat down on Harold's stool to see how he had rendered this enchanting effect. The picture was nearly finished, but unfortunately I had too little cultivation to enjoy it. The blue sea, however, seemed in all conscience blue enough. While I was comparing it with the far-fading azure of the original, I heard a voice behind me, and turning, saw two gentlemen from the inn, one of whom had been my neighbour the evening before at dinner. He was a foreigner, but he spoke English. On recognizing me he advanced gallantly, ushering his companion, and immediately fell into ecstasies over my picture. I informed him without delay that the picture was not mine; it was the work of Mr. Staines. Nothing daunted, he declared that it was pretty enough to be mine, and that I must have given suggestions; but his companion, a less superficial character apparently, and extremely nearsighted, after examining it minutely with his nose close to the paper, exclaimed with an annoying smile, 'Monsieur Staines? Surprising! I should have sworn it was the work of a *jeune fille*.'

The compliment was doubtful, and not calculated to restore my equanimity. As a *jeune fille* I suppose I ought to have been gratified, but as a betrothed I should have preferred Harold to paint like a man. I don't know how long after this it was that I allowed myself to wonder, by way of harmless conjecture, how a woman might feel who should find herself married to an ineffective mediocrity. Then I remembered—as if the case were my own—that I had never heard any one talk about his pictures, and that when I had seen them handed about before company by his mother, the buzz of admiration usual on such occasions seemed rather heavy-winged. But I quickly reminded myself that it was not because he painted better or worse that I cared for him, but because personally and morally he was the pink of perfection. This being settled, I fell to wondering whether one mightn't grow weary of perfection—whether (Heaven forgive me!) I was not already the least bit out of patience with Harold's. I could fancy him a trifle too absolute, too imperturbable, too prolific in cut-and-dried opinions. Had he settled everything, then, in his mind? Yes, he had certainly made the most of his time, and I could only admire his diligence. From the moment that I observed that he wasted no time in moods, or reveries, or intellectual pleasantry of any sort, I decided without appeal that he was not a man of genius; and yet, to listen to him at times, you would have vowed at least that he might be. He dealt out his opinions as if they were celestial manna, and nothing was more common than for him to say, 'You remember, a month ago, I told you so-and-so', meaning that he had laid down the law on some point and expected me to engrave it on my heart. It often happened that I had forgotten the lesson, and was obliged to ask him to repeat it; but it left me more unsatisfied than before. Harold would settle his shirt collar as if he considered that he had exhausted the subject, and I would take refuge in a silence which from day to day covered more treacherous conjectures. Nevertheless (strange as you may think it), I believe I should have decided that, Harold being a paragon, my doubts were immoral, if Mrs. Staines, after his cause might have been supposed to be gained, had not persisted in pleading it in season and out. I don't know whether she suspected my secret falterings, but she seemed to wish to secure me beyond relapse. I was so very modest for her son, that if I had been more worldly-wise, her enthusiasm might have alarmed me. Later I understood it; then I only understood that there was a general flavour of insinuation in her talk which made me vaguely uneasy. I did the poor lady injustice, and if I had been quicker-witted (and possibly harder-hearted) we might have become sworn allies. She judged her son less with a mother's tenderness than with a mother's zeal, and foresaw the world's verdict—which I won't anticipate! She perceived that he must depend upon a clever wife to float him into success; he would never prosper on his own merits. She did me the honour to believe me socially a sufficiently buoyant body for this arduous purpose, and must have felt it a thousand pities that she couldn't directly speak her mind. A thousand pities indeed! My answer would have been to the point, and would have saved us all a vast deal of pain. Meanwhile, trying half to convince and half to entangle me, she did everything to hasten our marriage.

If there had been anything less than the happiness of a lifetime at stake, I think I should have felt that I owed Harold a sort of reparation for thinking him too great a man, and should still have offered him an affection none the less genuine for being transposed into a minor key. But it was hard for a girl who had dreamed blissfully of a grandly sentimental union, to find herself suddenly face to face with a sternly rational one. When, therefore, Harold mentioned a certain day as the latest for which he thought it proper to wait, I found it impossible to assent, and asked for another month's delay. What I wished to wait for I could hardly have told. Possibly for the first glow of illusion to return; possibly for the last uneasy throb which told that illusion was ebbing away. Harold received this request very gravely, and inquired whether I doubted of his affection.

'No,' I said, 'I believe it's greater than I deserve.'

'Why then,' he asked, 'should you wait?'

'Suppose I were to doubt of my own?'

He looked as if I had said something in very bad taste, and I was almost frightened at his sense of security. But he at last consented to the delay. Perhaps on reflection he was alarmed, for the grave politeness with which he discharged his attentions took a still more formal turn, as if to remind me at every hour of the day that his was not a sentiment to be trifled with. To trifle, Heaven knows, was far enough from my thoughts; for I was fast losing my spirits, and I woke up one morning with the conviction that I was decidedly not happy.

We were to be married in Paris, where Harold had determined to spend six months in order that he might try his fortune again in the studio of a painter whom he especially esteemed—a certain Monsieur Martinet, an old man, and belonging, I believe, to a rather antiquated school of art. During our first days in Paris I went with Harold a great deal to the Louvre, where he was a very profitable companion. He had the history of the schools at his fingers' ends, and, as the phrase is, he knew what he liked. We had a fatal habit of not liking the same things; but I pretended to no critical insight, and desired nothing better than to agree with him. I listened devoutly to everything that could be said for Guido and Caravaggio. One day we were standing before the inscrutable 'Joconde' of Leonardo, a picture disagreeable to most women. I had been expressing my great aversion to the lady's countenance, which Harold on this occasion seemed to share. I was surprised therefore, when, after a pause, he said quietly, 'I believe I'll copy her.'

I hardly knew why I should have smiled, but I did, apparently to his annoyance. 'She must be very difficult,' I said. 'Try something easier.'

'I want something difficult,' he answered sternly.

'Truly?' I said. 'You mean what you say?'

'Why not?'

'Why then copy a portrait when you can copy an original?'

'What original?'

'Your betrothed! Paint my portrait. I promise to be difficult enough. Indeed, I'm surprised you should never have proposed it.' In fact the idea had just occurred to me; but I embraced it with a sort of relief. It seemed to me that it would somehow test my lover, and that if he succeeded, I might believe in him irremissibly. He stared a moment as if he had hardly understood me, and I completed my thought. 'Paint my portrait, and the day you finish it I'll fix our wedding day.'

The proposal was after all not very terrible, and before long he seemed to relish it. The next day he told me that he had composed his figure mentally, and that we might begin immediately. Circumstances favoured us, for he had for the time undisturbed all of M. Martinet's studio. This gentleman had gone into the country to paint a portrait, and Harold just then was his only pupil. Our first sitting took place without delay. At his request I brought with me a number of draperies, among which was the yellow shawl you have just been admiring. We wore such things then, just as we played on the harp and read 'Corinne'. I tried on my scarfs and veils, one after the other, but Harold was satisfied with none. The yellow shawl, in especial, he pronounced a meretricious ornament, and decided that I should be represented in a plain dark dress, with as few accessories as possible. He quoted with a bow the verse about beauty when unadorned, and began his work.

After the first day or two it progressed slowly, and I felt at moments as if I had saddled him with a cruel burden. He expressed no irritation, but he often looked puzzled and wearied, and sometimes would lay aside his brushes, fold his arms, and stand gazing at his work with a sort of vacant scowl which tried my patience. 'Frown at me,' I said more than once; 'don't frown at that blameless sheet of canvas. Don't spare me, though I confess it's not my fault if I'm hard to paint.' Thus admonished, he would turn towards me without smiling, often shading his eyes with his hand, and would walk slowly round the room, examining me at a distance. Then coming back to his easel, he would make half a dozen strokes and pause again, as if his impetus had already expired. For some time I was miserable; it seemed to me that I had been wonderfully wise to withhold my hand till the picture was finished. He begged I would not look at it, but I knew it was standing still. At last, one morning, after gazing at his work for some time in silence, he laid down his palette gravely, but with no further sign of discomposure than that he gently wiped his forehead with his pocket-handkerchief. 'You make me nervous,' he suddenly declared.

I fancied there was a tremor in his voice, and I began to pity him. I left my place and laid my hand on his arm. 'If it wearies you,' I said, 'give it up.'

He turned away and for some time made no answer. I knew what he was thinking about, and I suppose he knew that I knew it, and was hesitating to ask me seriously whether in giving up his picture he gave up something more. He decided apparently to give up nothing, but grasped his palette, and, with the short incisive gesture habitual to him, motioned me back to my seat. 'I'll bother no longer over the drawing,' he said; 'I'll begin to paint.' With his colours he was more prosperous, for the next day he told me that we were progressing fast.

We generally went together to the studio, but it happened one day that he was to be occupied during the early morning at the other end of Paris, and he arranged to meet me there. I was punctual, but he had not arrived, and I found myself face to face with my reluctant image. Opportunity served too well, and I looked at it in spite of his prohibition, meaning of course to confess my fault. It brought me less pleasure than faults are reputed to bring. The picture, as yet very slight and crude, was unpromising and unflattering. I chiefly distinguished a long white face with staring black eyes, and a terribly angular pair of arms. Was it in this unlovely form that I had impressed myself on Harold's vision? Absorbed by the question, it was some moments before I perceived that I was not alone. I heard a sound, looked round, and discovered a stranger, a young man, gazing over my shoulder at Harold's canvas. His gaze was intense and not expressive of pleasure, and some moment passed before he perceived that I had noticed him. He reminded me strongly of certain dishevelled copyists whom I had seen at work in the Louvre, and as I supposed he had some lawful errand in the studio, I contented myself with thinking that he hadn't the best manners in the world, and walked to the other end of the room. At last, as he continued to betray no definite intentions, I ventured to look at him again. He was young—twenty-five at most—and excessively shabby. I remember, among other details, that he had a black cravat wound two or three times round his neck, without any visible linen. He was short, thin, pale, and hungry-looking. As I turned towards him, he passed his hand through his hair, as if to do what he could to make himself presentable, and called my attention to his prodigious shock of thick black curls—a real *coiffure de rapin*. His face would have been meagre and vulgar, if from beneath their umbrageous locks there had not glanced an extraordinary pair of eyes—eyes really of fire. They were not tender nor appealing, but they glittered with a sort of feverish intelligence and penetration, and stamped their possessor not, as the French say, the first comer. He almost glared at me and stopped my words short.

'That's your portrait?' he asked, with a toss of his head.

I assented with dignity.

'It's bad, bad, bad!' he cried. 'Excuse my frankness, but it's really too bad. It's a waste of colours, of money, of time.'

His frankness certainly was extreme; but his words had an accent of ardent conviction which doesn't belong to commonplace impertinence. 'I don't know who you are, that I should value your opinion,' I said.

'Who I am? I'm an artist, mademoiselle. If I had money to buy visiting-cards, I would present you with one. But I haven't even money to buy colours—hardly to buy bread. I've talent—I've imagination—too much!—I've ideas—I've promise—I've a future; and yet the machine won't work—for want of fuel! I have to roam about with my hands in my pockets—to keep them warm—for want of the very tools of my trade. I've been a fool—an ignoble fool; I've thrown precious hours to the dogs and made enemies of precious friends. Six months ago I quarrelled with the père Martinet, who believed in me and would have been glad to keep me. *Il faut que jeunesse se passe*! Mine has passed at a rattling pace, ill-mounted though it was; we have parted company for ever. Now I only ask to do a man's work with a man's will. Meanwhile the père Martinet, justly provoked, has used his tongue so well that not a colourman in Paris will trust me. There's a situation! And yet what could I do with ten francs' worth of paint? I want a room and light and a model, and a dozen yards of satin tumbling about her feet. Bah! I shall have to want! There are things I want more. Behold the force of circumstances. I've come back with my pride in my pocket to make it up with the venerable author of the "Apotheosis of Molière", and ask him to lend me a louis.'

I arrested this vehement effusion by informing him that M. Martinet was out of town, and that for the present the studio was—private. But he seemed too much irritated to take my hint. 'That's not his work?' he went on, turning to the portrait. 'Martinet is bad, but is not as bad as that. *Quel genre*! You deserve, mademoiselle, to be better treated; you're an excellent model. Excuse me, once for all; I know I'm atrociously impudent. But I'm an artist, and I find it pitiful to see a fine great canvas besmeared in such a fashion as that! There ought to be a society for the protection of such things.'

I was at loss what to reply to this extraordinary explosion of contempt. Strange to say—it's the literal truth—I was neither annoyed nor disgusted; I simply felt myself growing extremely curious. This impudent little Bohemian was forcing me somehow to respect his opinion; he spoke with penetrating authority. Don't say that I was willing to be convinced; if you had been there, you would have let him speak. It would have been, of course, the part of propriety to request him in a chilling voice to leave the room, or to ring for the concierge, or to flee in horror. I did none of these things: I went back to the picture, and tried hard to see something in it which would make me passionately contradict him. But it seemed to exhale a mortal chill, and all I could say was: 'Bad—bad? How bad?'

'Ridiculously bad; impossibly bad! You're an angel of charity, mademoiselle, not to see it!'

'Is it weak—cold—ignorant?'

'Weak, cold, ignorant, stiff, empty, hopeless! And, on top of all, pretentious—oh, pretentious as the *façade* of the Madeleine!'

I endeavoured to force a sceptical smile. 'After all, monsieur, I'm not bound to believe you.'

'Evidently!' And he rubbed his forehead and looked gloomily round the room. 'But one thing I can tell you'—fixing me suddenly with his extraordinary eyes, which seemed to expand and glow with the vividness of prevision—'the day will come when people will fight for the honour of having believed me, and of having been the first. "I discovered him—I always said so. But for me you'd have to let the poor devil starve!" You'll hear the chorus! So now's your chance, mademoiselle! Here I stand, a man of genius if there ever was one, without a sou, without a friend, without a ray of reputation. Believe in me now, and you'll be the first, by many a day. You'd find it easier, you'll say, if I had a little more modesty. I assure you I don't go about blowing my trumpet in this fashion every day. This morning I'm in a kind of fever, and I've reached a crisis. I must do something—even make an ass of myself! I can't go on devouring my own heart. You see for these three months I've been *à sec*. I haven't dined every day. Perhaps a sinking at the stomach is propitious to inspiration: certainly, week by week, my brain has grown clearer, my imagination more restless, my desires more boundless, my visions more splendid! Within the last fortnight my last doubt has vanished, and I feel as strong as the sun in heaven! I roam about the streets and lounge in the public gardens for want of a better refuge, and everything I look at—the very sunshine in the gutter, the chimney-pots against the sky—seems a picture, a subject, an opportunity! I hang over the balustrade that runs before the pictures at the Louvre, and Titian and Correggio seem to turn pale, like people when you've guessed their secret. I don't know who the author of this masterpiece may be, but I fancy he would have more talent if he weren't so sure of his dinner. Do you know how I learned to look at things and use my eyes? By staring at the *charcutier's* windows when my pockets were empty. It's a great lesson to learn even the shape of a sausage and the colour of a ham. This gentleman, it's easy to see, hasn't noticed such matters. He goes by the sense of taste. *Voilà le monde!* I—I—I—'; and he slapped his forehead with a kind of dramatic fury—'here as you see me—ragged, helpless, hopeless, with my soul aching with ambition and my fingers itching for a brush—and *he*, standing up here after a good breakfast, in this perfect light, among pictures and tapestries and carvings, with you in your blooming beauty for a model, and painting that—sign-board.'

His violence was startling; I didn't know what might come next, and I took up my bonnet and mantle. He immediately protested with ardour. 'A moment's reflection, mademoiselle, will tell you that, with the appearance I present, I don't talk about your beauty *pour vous faire la cour*. I repeat with all respect, you're a model to make a painter's fortune. I doubt if you've many attitudes or much flexibility; but for once—the portrait of Mlle. X.—you're perfect.'

'I'm obliged to you for your—information,' I answered gravely. 'You see my artist is chosen. I expect him here at any moment, and I won't answer for his listening to you as patiently as I have done.'

'He's coming?' cried my visitor. '*Quelle chance!* I shall be charmed to meet him. I shall vastly enjoy seeing the human head from which that conception issued. I see him already: I construct the author from the work. He's tall and blonde, with eyes very much the colour of his own china-blue there. He wears straw-coloured whiskers, and doubtless he paints in straw-coloured gloves. In short, he's *un homme magnifique!*'

This was sarcasm run mad; but I listened to it and resented it as little as I enjoyed it. My companion seemed to possess a sort of demonic veracity of which the influence was irresistible. I questioned his sincerity so little that, if I offered him charity, it was with no intention of testing it. 'I dare say you've immense talent,' I said, 'but you've horrible manners. Nevertheless, I believe you will perceive that there is no reason why our conversation should continue; and I should pay you a poor compliment in thinking that you need to be bribed to withdraw. But since M. Martinet isn't here to lend you a louis, let me act for him.' And I laid the piece of gold on the table.

He looked at it hard for a moment and then at me, and I wondered whether he thought the gift too meagre. 'I won't go so far as to say that I'm proud,' he answered at last. 'But from a lady, *ma foi!* it's beggarly—it's humiliating. Excuse me then if I refuse; I mean to ask for something else. To do me justice, remember that I speak to you not as a man, but as an artist. Bestow your charity on the artist, and if it costs you an effort, remember that that is the charity which is of most account with heaven. Keep your louis; go and stand as you've been standing for this picture, in the same light and the same attitude, and then let me look at you for three little minutes.' As he spoke he drew from his pocket a ragged note-book and the stump of a pencil. 'The few scrawls I shall make here will be your alms.'

He spoke of effort, but it is a fact that I made little to comply. While I resumed my familiar attitude in front of Harold's canvas, he walked rapidly across the room and stooped over a chair upon which a mass of draperies had been carelessly tossed. In a moment I saw what had attracted him. He had caught a glimpse of the famous yellow scarf, glowing splendidly beneath a pile of darker stuffs. He pulled out the beautiful golden-hued tissue with furious alacrity, held it up before him and broke into an ecstasy of admiration. 'What a tone—what a glow—what a texture! In Heaven's name, put it on!' And without further ceremony he tossed it over my shoulders. I need hardly tell you that I obeyed but a natural instinct in gathering it into picturesque folds. He rushed away, and stood gazing and clapping his hands. 'The harmony is perfect—the effect sublime! You possess that thing and you bury it out of sight? Wear it, wear it, I entreat you—and your portrait—but ah!' and he glared angrily askance at the picture: 'you'll never wear it there!'

'We thought of using it, but it was given up.'

'Given up? *Quelle horreur!* He hadn't the pluck to attack it! Oh, if I could just take a brush at it and rub it in for him!' And, as if possessed by an uncontrollable impulse, he seized poor Harold's palette. But I made haste to stop his hand. He flung down the brushes, buried his face in his hands, and pressed back, I could fancy, the tears of baffled eagerness. 'You'll think me crazy!' he cried.

He was not crazy, to my sense; but he was a raging, aimless force, which I suddenly comprehended that I might use. I seemed to measure the full proportions of Harold's inefficiency, and to forsee the pitiful result of his undertaking. He wouldn't succumb, but he would doggedly finish his task and present me, in evidence of his claim, with a dreadful monument of his pretentious incapacity. Twenty strokes from this master-hand would make a difference; ten minutes' work would carry the picture forward. I thrust the palette into the young man's grasp again and looked at him solemnly.

'Paint away for your life,' I said; 'but promise me this: to succeed!'

He waved his hand in the air, despatched me with a glance to my place, and let himself loose on the canvas; there are no other words for his tremulous eagerness. A quarter of an hour passed in silence. As I watched his motions grow every moment broader and more sweeping, I could fancy myself listening to some ardent pianist, plunging deeper into a passionate symphony and devouring the key-board with outstretched arms. Flushed and dishevelled, consuming me almost with his ardent stare, daubing, murmuring, panting, he seemed indeed to be painting for life.

At last I heard a tread in the vestibule. I knew it was Harold's, and I hurried to look at the picture. How would he take it? I confess I was prepared for the worst. The picture spoke for itself. Harold's work had disappeared with magical rapidity, and even my unskilled eye perceived that a graceful and expressive figure had been powerfully sketched in. As Harold appeared, I turned to meet him. He seemed surprised at not finding me alone, and I laid my finger gravely on my lips and led him to the front of the canvas. The position of things was so singular that for some moments it baffled his comprehension. My companion finished what he was immediately concerned with; then with an obsequious bow laid down his brushes. 'It was a loan, monsieur,' he said. 'I return it with interest.'

Harold flushed to his eyes, and sat down in silence. I had expected him to be irritated; but this was more than irritation. At last: 'Explain this extraordinary performance,' he said in a low voice.

I felt pain, and yet somehow I felt no regret. The situation was tense, as the phrase is, and yet I almost relished it. 'This gentleman is a great artist,' I said boldly. 'Look for yourself. Your picture was lost; he has redeemed it.'

Harold looked at the intruder slowly from head to foot. 'Who is this person?' he demanded, as if he had not heard me.

The young man understood no English, but he apparently guessed at the question. 'My name is Pierre Briseux; let *that*' (pointing to his work) 'denote my profession. If you're affronted, monsieur, don't visit your displeasure on mademoiselle; I alone am responsible. You had got into a tight place; I wished to help you out of it; *sympathie de confrère*! I've done you no injury. I've made you a present of half a masterpiece. If I could only trust you not to spoil it!'

Harold's face betrayed his invincible disgust, and I saw that my offence was mortal. He had been wounded in his tenderest part, and his self-control was rapidly ebbing. His lips trembled, but he was too angry even to speak. Suddenly he seized a heavy brush which stood in a pot of dusky varnish, and I thought for a moment he was going to fling it at Briseux. He balanced it an instant, and then tossed it full in the face of the picture. I raised my hands to my face as if I felt the blow. Briseux, at least, felt it sorely. *'Malheureux!'* he cried. 'Are you blind as well? Don't you know a good thing when you see it? That's what I call a waste of material. *Allons*, you're very angry; let me explain. In meddling with your picture I certainly took a great liberty. My misery is my excuse. You have money, materials, models—everything but talent. No, no, you're no painter; it's impossible! There isn't an intelligent line on your canvas. I, on the other hand, am a born painter. I've talent and nothing more. I came here to see M. Martinet; learning he was absent, I stayed for very envy! I looked at your work, and found it a botch; at your empty stool and idle palette, and found them an immense temptation; at mademoiselle, and found her a perfect model. I persuaded, frightened, convinced her, and out of charity she gave me a five minutes' sitting. Once the brush in my hand, I felt the divine afflatus; I hoped for a miracle—that you'd never come back, that you'd be run over in the street, or have an attack of apoplexy. If you had only let me go on, I should have served you up a great work, monsieur—a work to which, in spite of your natural irritation, you wouldn't have dared to do a violence. You'd have been afraid of it. That's the sort of thing I meant to paint. If you could only believe me, you'd not regret it. Give me a start, and ten years hence I shall see you buying my pictures, and not thinking them dear. Oh, I thought I had my foot in the stirrup; I dreamed I was in the saddle and riding hard. But I've turned a somersault!'

I doubt that Harold, in his resentment, either understood M. Briseux's words or appreciated his sketch. He simply felt that he had been the victim of a monstrous aggression, in which I, in some pain-fully inexplicable way, had been half dupe and half accomplice. I was watching his anger and weighing its ominous significance. His cold fury, and the expression it threw into his face and gestures, told me more about him than weeks of placid love-making had done, and, following close upon my vivid sense of his incapacity, seemed sud-denly to cut the knot that bound us together, and over which my timid fingers had been fumbling. 'Put on your bonnet,' he said to me; 'get a carriage and go home.'

I can't describe his tone. It contained an assumption of my con-fusion and compliance, which made me feel that I ought to lose no time in undeceiving him. Nevertheless I felt cruelly perplexed, and almost afraid of his displeasure. Mechanically I took up my bonnet. As I held it in my hand, my eyes met those of our terrible companion, who was evidently trying to read the riddle of my relations with

Harold. Planted there with his trembling lips, his glittering, searching eyes, an indefinable something in his whole person that told of
joyous impulse arrested, but pausing only for a more triumphant
effort, he seemed a strangely eloquent embodiment of youthful
genius. I don't know whether he read in my glance a ray of sympathy,
but his lips formed a soundless 'Restez, madame', which quickened
the beating of my heart. The feeling that then invaded it I despair
of making you understand; yet it must help in your eyes to excuse me,
and it was so profound that often in memory it seems more real and
poignant than the things of the present. Poor little Briseux, ugly,
shabby, disreputable, seemed to me some appealing messenger from
the mysterious immensity of life; and Harold, beside him, comely,
elegant, imposing, justly indignant, seemed to me simply his narrow,
personal, ineffectual self. This was a wider generalization than the
feminine heart is used to. I flung my bonnet on the floor and burst
into tears.

'This is not an exhibition for a stranger,' said Harold grimly. 'Be
so good as to follow me.'

'You must excuse me; I can't follow you; I can't explain. I have
something more to say to M. Briseux. He's less of a stranger than you
think.'

'I'm to leave you here?' stammered Harold.

'It's the simplest way.'

'With that dirty little Frenchman?'

'What should I care for his being clean? It's his genius that interests me.'

Harold stared in dark amazement. 'Are you insane? Do you know
what you're doing?'

'An act, I believe, of real charity.'

'Charity begins at home. It's an act of desperate folly. Must I
command you to leave?'

'You've done that already. I can't obey you. If I were to do so, I
should pretend what isn't true; and, let me say it, it's to undeceive
you that I refuse.'

'I don't understand you,' cried Harold, 'nor to what spell this
meddlesome little beggar has subjected you! But I'm not a man to
be trifled with, you know, and this is my last request; my last, do
you understand? If you prefer the society of this abandoned person,
you're welcome, but you forfeit mine for ever. It's a choice! You give
up the man who has offered you an honourable affection, a name, a
fortune, who has trusted and cherished you, who stands ready to
make you a devoted husband. What you get the Lord knows!'

I had sunk into a chair. I listened in silence, and for some time answered nothing. His words were vividly true. He offered me much, and I gave up everything. He had played an honourable part, and I was playing a very strange one. I asked myself sternly whether I was ready to rise and take his arm and let him lead me blindfold through life. When I raised my eyes Briseux stood before me, and from the expression of his face I could have fancied he had guessed at the meaning of Harold's words. 'I'll make you immortal,' he murmured; 'I'll delight mankind—and I'll begin my own career!'

An ineffable prevision of the truth which after the lapse of years has brought about our meeting here seemed to raise me as if on wings, and made decision easy. We women are so habitually condemned by fate to act simply in what is called the domestic sphere, that there is something intoxicating in the opportunity to exert a far-reaching influence outside of it. To feel the charms of such an opportunity, one must perhaps be of a reprehensibly fanciful turn. Such at any rate was my mood for an hour. I seemed to be the end of an electric chain, of which the rest was throbbing away through time. I seemed to hold in my hand an immeasurable gift. 'We had better part on the spot,' I said to Harold. 'I've foreseen our parting for weeks, only it has come more abruptly. Forgive the abruptness. To myself the pretext seems better than to you; perhaps some day you'll appreciate it. A single question,' I added, 'Could you ever have finished my portrait?'

He looked at me askance for some moments, with a strange mistrust, as if I had suddenly developed some monstrous and sinister slyness; then catching his breath with a little groan—almost a shudder—he marched out of the room.

Briseux clasped his hands in ecstasy. 'You're magnificent!' he cried. 'If you could only look so for three hours!'

'To business,' I said sternly. 'If you don't paint a perfect picture, you're the most shameless of imposters.'

He had but a single sitting, but it was a long one; though how many hours it lasted, I doubt that either of us could have told. He painted till dusk, and then we had lamps. Before I left him I looked at the picture for the last and only time before seeing it today. It seemed to me as perfect as it seemed this morning, and I felt that my choice was justified and that Briseux's fortune was made. It gave me all the strength I needed for the immediate future. He was evidently of the same opinion and profoundly absorbed in it. When I bade him farewell, in very few words, he answered me almost absently. I had served his purpose and had already passed into that dusky limbo of unhonoured victims, the experience—intellectual and other —of genius. I left him the yellow shawl, that he might finish this part of his work at his leisure, and, as for the picture, I told him to keep it, for that I should have little pleasure in seeing it again. Then he stared a moment, but the next he was painting hard.

I had the next morning what under other circumstances I might call an explanation with Mr. Staines, an explanation in which I explained nothing to his satisfaction but that he had been hideously wronged, and that I was a demon of inconstancy. He wrapped himself in an icy silence, and, I think, expected some graceful effusion of humility. I many not have been humble, but I was considerate, and I perceived, for my reward, that the sore point with him was not that he had lost me, but that I had ventured to judge him. Mrs Staines's manner, on the other hand, puzzled me, so strange a mixture was it of half-disguised elation and undisguised sarcasm. At last I guessed her meaning. Harold, after all, had had an escape; instead of being the shrewd, practical girl she had thought me, I was a terribly romantic one! Perhaps she was right; I was romantic enough to make no further claim on her hospitality, and with as little delay as possible I returned home. A month later I received an enclosure of half a dozen cuttings from newspapers, scrawled boldly across with the signature of Pierre Briseux. The Paris *salon* had opened and the critics had spoken. They had not neglected the portrait of Mademoiselle X—. The picture was an immense success, and M. Briseux was famous. There were a few protesting voices, but it was evident that his career had begun. For Mademoiselle X— herself, I believe, there were none but compliments, several of which took the form of gallant conjecture as to her real identity. Mademoiselle X— was an assumed name, and according to more than one voice the lady was an imperious Russian princess with a distaste for vulgar publicity. You know the rest of M. Briseux's history. Since then he has painted real princesses by the dozen. He has delighted mankind rarely. As for his having made me immortal, I feel as if it were almost true. It must be an eternity since the thing happened—so very unreservedly I've described it!

The Last of the Valerii

[First appeared in the *Atlantic Monthly*, vol. xxxiii (January 1874), pp. 69–85. The tale was revised and reprinted in *A Passionate Pilgrim* (1875). The 1875 text was revised and reprinted in volume iii of *Stories Revived* (1885).]

I HAD HAD OCCASION TO DECLARE MORE THAN ONCE that if my god-daughter married a foreigner I should refuse to give her away. And yet when the young Conte Valerio was presented to me, in Rome, as her accepted and plighted lover, I found myself looking at the happy fellow, after a momentary stare of amazement, with a certain paternal benevolence; thinking, indeed, that from the picturesque point of view (she with her ycllow locks and he with his dusky ones) they were a strikingly well-assorted pair. She brought him up to me half proudly, half timidly, pushing him before her, and begging me with one of her dovelike glances to be very polite. I don't know that I am addicted to rudeness; but she was so deeply impressed with his grandeur that she thought it impossible to do him honour enough. The Conte Valerio's grandeur was perhaps nothing for a young American girl, who had the air and almost the habits of a princess, to sound her trumpet about; but she was desperately in love with him, and not only her heart, but her imagination, was touched. He was extremely handsome, and with a more significant sort of beauty than is common in the handsome Roman race. He had a sort of sunken depth of expression, and a grave, slow smile, suggesting no great quickness of wit, but an unimpassioned intensity of feeling which promised well for Martha's happiness. He had little of the light, inexpensive urbanity of his countrymen, and more of a sort of heavy sincerity in his gaze which seemed to suspend response until he was sure he understood you. He was perhaps a little stupid, and I fancied that to a political or aesthetic question the reply would be particularly slow. 'He is good and strong and brave,' the young girl however assured me; and I easily believed her. Strong the Conte Valerio certainly was; he had a head and throat like some of the busts in the Vatican. To my eye, which has looked at things now so long with the painter's purpose, it was a real perplexity to see such a throat rising out of the white cravat of the period. It sustained a head as massively round as that of the familiar bust of the Emperor Caracalla, and covered with the same dense sculptural crop of curls. The young man's hair grew superbly; it was such hair as the old Romans must have had when they walked bare-headed and bronzed about the world. It made a perfect arch over his low, clear forehead, and prolonged itself on cheek and chin in a close, crisp beard, strong with its own strength and unstiffened by the razor. Neither his nose nor his mouth was delicate; but they were powerful, shapely, and manly. His complexion was of a deep glowing brown which no emotion would alter, and his large lucid eyes seemed to stare at you like a pair of polished agates. He was of middle stature, and his chest was of so generous a girth that you half ex-pected to hear his linen crack with its even respirations. And yet, with his simple human smile, he looked neither like a young bullock nor a gladiator. His powerful voice was the least bit harsh, and his large, ceremonious reply to my compliment had the massive sonority with which civil speeches must have been uttered in the age of Augustus. I had always considered my god-daughter a very Ameri-can little person, in all delightful meanings of the word, and I doubted if this sturdy young Latin would understand the trans-atlantic element in her nature; but, evidently, he would make her a loyal and ardent lover. She seemed to me, in her blonde prettiness, so tender, so appealing, so bewitching, that it was impossible to be-lieve he had not more thoughts for all this than for the pretty fortune which it yet bothered me to believe that he must, like a good Italian, have taken the exact measure of. His own worldly goods consisted of the paternal estate, a villa within the walls of Rome, which his scanty funds had suffered to fall into sombre disrepair. 'It's the Villa she's in love with, quite as much as the Count,' said her mother. 'She dreams of converting the Count; that's all very well. But she dreams of refurnishing the Villa!'

The upholsterers were turned into it, I believe, before the wedding, and there was a great scrubbing and sweeping of saloons and raking and weeding of alleys and avenues. Martha made frequent visits of inspection while these ceremonies were taking place; but one day, on her return, she came into my little studio with an air of amusing horror. She had found them *scraping* the sarcophagus in the great ilex-walk; divesting it of its mossy coat, divesting it of the sacred green mould of the ages! This was their idea of making the Villa comfortable. She had made them transport it to the dampest place they could find; for next after that slow-coming, slow-going smile of her lover, it was the rusty complexion of his patrimonial marbles that she most prized. The young Count's conversion proceeded less rapidly, and indeed I believe that his betrothed brought little zeal to the affair. She loved him so devoutly that she believed no change of faith could better him, and she would have been willing for his sake to say her prayers to the sacred *Bambino* at Epiphany. But he had the good taste to demand no such sacrifice, and I was struck with the happy promise of a scene of which I was an accidental observer. It was at St. Peter's, one Friday afternoon, during the vesper service which takes place in the Chapel of the Choir. I met my goddaughter wandering happily on her lover's arm, her mother being established on her camp-stool near the chapel door. The crowd was collected thereabouts, and the body of the church was empty. Now and then the high voices of the singers escaped into the outer vastness and melted slowly away in the incense-thickened air. Something in the young girl's step and the clasp of her arm in her lover's told me that her contentment was perfect. As she threw back her head and gazed into the magnificent immensity of vault and dome, I felt that she was in that enviable mood in which all consciousness revolves on a single centre, and that her sense of the splendours around her was one with the ecstasy of her trust. They stopped before that sombre group of confessionals which proclaims so portentously the world's sinfulness, and Martha seemed to make some almost passionate protestation. A few minutes later I overtook them.

'Don't you agree with me, dear friend,' said the Count, who always addressed me with the most affectionate deference, 'that before I marry so pure and sweet a creature as this, I ought to go into one of those places and confess every sin I ever was guilty of,—every evil thought and impulse and desire of my grossly evil nature?'

Martha looked at him, half in deprecation, half in homage, with a look which seemed at once to insist that her lover could have no vices, and to plead that, if he had, there would be something magnificent in them. 'Listen to him!' she said, smiling. 'The list would be long, and if you waited to finish it, you would be late for the wedding! But if you confess your sins for me, it's only fair I should confess mine for you. Do you know what I have been saying to Camillo?' she added, turning to me with the half-filial confidence she had always shown me and with a rosy glow in her cheeks; 'that I want to do something more for him than girls commonly do for their lovers,—to take some step, to run some risk, to break some law, even! I'm willing to change my religion, if he bids me. There are moments when I'm terribly tired of simply staring at Catholicism; it will be a relief to come into a church to kneel. That's, after all, what they are meant for? Therefore, *Camillo mio*, if it casts a shade across your heart to think that I'm a heretic, I'll go and kneel down to that good old priest who has just entered the confessional yonder and say to him: "My father, I repent, I abjure, I believe. Baptize me in the only faith."'

'If it's as a compliment to the Count,' I said, 'it seems to me he ought to anticipate it by turning Protestant.'

She had spoken lightly and with a smile, and yet with an undertone of girlish ardour. The young man looked at her with a solemn, puzzled face and shook his head. 'Keep your religion,' he said. 'Every one his own. If you should attempt to embrace mine, I'm afraid you would close your arms about a shadow. I'm a poor Catholic! I don't understand all these chants and ceremonies and splendours. When I was a child I never could learn my catechism. My poor old confessor long ago gave me up; he told me I was a good boy but a *pagan*! You must not be a better Catholic than your husband. I don't understand your religion any better, but I beg you not to change it for mine. If it has helped to make you what you are it must be good.' And taking the young girl's hand, he was about to raise it affectionately to his lips; but suddenly remembering that they were in a place unaccordant with profane passions, he lowered it with a comical smile. 'Let us go!' he murmured, passing his hand over his forehead. 'This heavy atmosphere of St. Peter's always stupefies me.'

They were married in the month of May, and we separated for the summer, the Contessa's mamma going to illuminate the domestic circle in New York with her reflected dignity. When I returned to Rome in the autumn I found the young couple established at the Villa Valerio, which was being gradually reclaimed from its antique decay. I begged that the hand of improvement might be lightly laid on it, for as an unscrupulous old *genre* painter, with an eye to 'subjects', I preferred that ruin should accumulate. My god-daughter was quite of my way of thinking, and she had a capital sense of the picturesque. Advising with me often as to projected changes, she was sometimes more conservative than myself; and I more than once smiled at her archaelogical zeal, and declared that I believed she had married the Count because he was like a statue of the Decadence. I had a constant invitation to spend my days at the Villa, and my easel was always planted in one of the garden-walks. I grew to have a painter's passion for the place and to be intimate with every tangled shrub and twisted tree, every moss-coated vase and mouldy sarcophagus and sad, disfeatured bust of those grim old Romans who could so ill afford to become more meagre-visaged. The place was of small extent; but though there were many other villas more pretentious and splendid, none seemed to me more deeply picturesque, more romantically idle and untrimmed, more encumbered with precious antique rubbish, and haunted with half-historic echoes. It contained an old ilex-walk in which I used religiously to spend half an hour every day,—half an hour being, I confess, just as long as

I could stay without beginning to sneeze. The trees arched and inter-twisted here along their dusky vista in the quaintest symmetry; and as it was exposed uninterruptedly to the west, the low evening sun used to transfuse it with a sort of golden mist and play through it—over the leaves and knotty boughs and mossy marbles—with a thousand crimson fingers. It was filled with disinterred fragments of sculpture,—nameless statues and noseless heads and rough-hewn sarcophagi, which made it deliciously solemn. The statues used to stand there in the perpetual twilight like conscious things, brooding on their gathered memories. I used to linger about them, half ex-pecting they would speak and tell me their stony secrets—whisper heavily the whereabouts of their mouldering fellows, still un-recovered from the soil.

My god-daughter was idyllically happy and absolutely in love. I was obliged to confess that even rigid rules have their exceptions, and that now and then an Italian count is an honest fellow. Camillo was one to the core, and seemed quite content to be adored. Their life was a kind of childlike interchange of caresses, as candid and un-measured as those of a shepherd and shepherdess in a bucolic poem. To stroll in the ilex-walk and feel her husband's arm about her waist and his shoulder against her cheek; to roll cigarettes for him while he puffed them in the great marble-paved rotunda in the centre of the house; to fill his glass from an old rusty red amphora;—these graceful occupations satisfied the young Countess.

She rode with him sometimes in the tufty shadow of aqueducts and tombs, and sometimes suffered him to show his beautiful wife at Roman dinners and balls. She played dominoes with him after dinner, and carried out in a desultory way a daily scheme of reading him the newspapers. This observance was subject to fluctuations caused by the Count's invincible tendency to go to sleep,—a failing his wife never attempted to disguise or palliate. She would sit and brush the flies from him while he lay picturesquely snoozing, and, if I ventured near him, would place her finger on her lips and whisper that she thought her husband was as handsome asleep as awake. I confess I often felt tempted to reply to her that he was at least as entertaining, for the young man's happiness had not multi-plied the topics on which he readily conversed. He had plenty of good sense, and his opinions on practical matters were always worth having. He would often come and sit near me while I worked at my easel and offer a friendly criticism. His taste was a little crude, but his eye was excellent, and his measurement of the resemblance be-tween some point of my copy and the original as trustworthy as that of a mathematical instrument. But he seemed to me to have either a strange reserve or a strange simplicity; to be fundamentally un-furnished with 'ideas'. He had no beliefs, or hopes, or fears,—nothing but senses, appetites, and serenely luxurious tastes. As I watched him strolling about looking at his finger-nails, I often wondered whether he had anything that could properly be termed a soul, and whether good health and good-nature were not the sum of his attributes. 'It's lucky he's good-natured,' I used to say to myself; 'for if he were not, there is nothing in his conscience to keep him in order. If he had irritable nerves instead of quiet ones, he would strangle us as the young Hercules strangled the poor little snakes. He's the natural man! Happily, his nature is gentle and I can mix my colours at my ease.' I wondered what he thought about and what passed through his mind in the sunny leisure which seemed to shut him in from that modern work-a-day world of which, in spite of my passion for be-daubing old panels with ineffective portraiture of mouldy statues against screens of box, I still flattered myself I was a member. I went so far as to believe that he sometimes withdrew from the world al-together. He had moods in which his consciousness seemed so remote and his mind so irresponsive and dumb, that nothing but a powerful caress or a sudden violence was likely to arouse him. Even his lavish tenderness for his wife had a quality which I but half relished. Whether or no he had a soul himself, he seemed not to suspect that she had one. I took a godfatherly interest in what it had not always seemed to me crabbed and pedantic to talk of as her moral develop-ment. I fondly believed her to be a creature susceptible of the finer spiritual emotions. But what was becoming of her spiritual life in this interminable heathenish honeymoon? Some fine day she would find herself tired of the Count's *beaux yeux*, and make an appeal to his mind. She had, to my knowledge, plans of study, of charity, of worthily playing her part as a Contessa Valerio,—a position as to which the family records furnished the most memorable examples. But if the Count found the newspapers soporific, I doubted if he would turn Dante's pages very fast for his wife, or smile with much zest at the anecdotes of Vasari. How could he advise her, instruct her, sustain her? And if she became a mother, how could he share her responsibilities? He doubtless would assure his little son and heir a stout pair of arms and legs and a magnificent crop of curls, and sometimes remove his cigarette to kiss a dimpled spot; but I found it hard to picture him lending his voice to teach the lusty urchin his alphabet or his prayers, or the rudiments of infant virtue. One accomplishment indeed the Count possessed which could make him an agreeable playfellow: he carried in his pocket a collection of precious fragments of antique pavement,—

bits of porphyry and malachite and lapis and basalt,—disinterred on his own soil and brilliantly polished by use. With these you might see him occupied by the half-hour, playing the simple game of catch-and-toss, ranging them in a circle, tossing them in rotation, and catching them on the back of his hand. His skill was remarkable; he would send a stone five feet into the air, and pitch and catch and transpose the rest before he received it again. I watched with affectionate jealousy for the signs of a dawning sense, on Martha's part, that she was the least bit strangely mated. Once or twice, as the weeks went by, I fancied I read them, and that she looked at me with eyes which seemed to remember certain old talks of mine in which I had declared—with such verity as you please—that a French-man, an Italian, a Spaniard, might be a very good fellow, but that he never really respected the woman he pretended to love; but for the most part, I confess, these dusky broodings of mine spent themselves easily in the charmed atmosphere of our fine old Villa. We were out of the modern world and had no business with modern scruples. The place was so bright, so still, so sacred to the silent, imperturbable past, that drowsy contentment seemed a natural law; and sometimes when, as I sat at my work, I saw my companions passing arm-in-arm across the end of one of the long-drawn vistas and, turning back to my palette, found my colours dimmer for the radiant vision, I could easily believe that I was some loyal old chronicler of a perfectly poetical legend.

It was a help to ungrudging feelings that the Count, yielding to his wife's urgency, had undertaken a series of systematic excavations. To excavate is an expensive luxury, and neither Camillo nor his later forefathers had possessed the means for a disinterested pursuit of archaeology. But his young wife had persuaded herself that the much-trodden soil of the Villa was as full of buried treasures as a bride-cake of plums, and that it would be a pretty compliment to the ancient house which had accepted her as mistress to devote a portion of her dowry to bringing its mouldy honours to the light. I think she was not without a fancy that this liberal process would help to disinfect her Yankee dollars of the impertinent odour of trade. She took learned advice on the subject, and was soon ready to swear to you, proceeding from irrefutable premises, that a colossal gilt-bronze Minerva mentioned by Strabo was placidly awaiting resur-rection at a point twenty rods from the northwest angle of the house. She had a couple of grotesque old antiquaries to lunch, whom having plied with unwonted potations, she walked off their legs in the grounds; and though they agreed on nothing else in the world, they individually assured her that properly conducted researches would probably yield an unequalled harvest of discoveries. The Count had been not only indifferent, but even averse, to the scheme, and had more than once arrested his wife's complacent allusions to it by an unaccustomed acerbity of tone. 'Let them lie, the poor disinherited gods, the Minerva, the Apollo, the Ceres, you are so sure of finding,' he said, 'and don't break their rest. What do you want of them? We can't worship them. Would you put them on pedestals to stare and mock at them? If you can't believe in them, don't disturb them. Peace be with them!' I remember being a good deal impressed by a vigorous confession drawn from him by his wife's playfully declaring in answer to some remonstrances in this strain that he was veritably superstitious. 'Yes, by Bacchus, I am superstitious!' he cried. 'Too much so, perhaps! But I'm an old Italian, and you must take me as you find me. There have been things seen and done here which leave strange influences behind! They don't touch you doubtless, who come of another race. But they touch me, often, in the whisper of the leaves and the odour of the mouldy soil and the blank eyes of the old statues. I can't bear to look the statues in the face. I seem to see other strange eyes in the empty sockets, and I hardly know what they say to me. I call the poor old statues ghosts. In conscience, we've enough on the place already, lurking and peering in every shady nook. Don't dig up any more, or I won't answer for my wits!'

This account of Camillo's sensibilities was too fantastic not to seem to his wife almost a joke; and though I imagined there was more in it, he made a joke so seldom that I should have been sorry to cut short the poor girl's smile. With her smile she carried her point, and in a few days arrived a kind of explorer, with a dozen workmen armed with pickaxes and spades. For myself, I was secretly vexed at these energetic measures; for, though fond of disinterred statues, I disliked the disinterment and deplored the profane sounds which were henceforth to break the leisurely stillness of the gardens. I especially objected to the personage who conducted the operations, an ugly little dwarfish man who seemed altogether a subterranean genius, a mouldy gnome of the under world, and went prying about the grounds with a malicious smile which suggested more delight in the money the Signor Conte was going to bury than in the expected marbles and bronzes. When the first sod had been turned the Count's mood seemed to alter, and his curiosity got the better of his scruples. He sniffed delightedly the odour of the humid earth, and stood watching the workmen as they struck constantly deeper with a kindling wonder in his eyes. Whenever a pickaxe rang against a stone he would utter a sharp cry, and be deterred from jumping into the trench only by the little explorer's assurance that it was a false alarm. The near prospect of discoveries seemed to act upon his nerves, and I met him more than once strolling restlessly among his cedarn alleys, as if at last he had fallen a-thinking; he took me by the arm and made me walk with him, and discoursed ardently of the chance of a 'find'. I rather marvelled at his sudden zeal, and wondered whether he had an eye to the past or to the future—to the beauty of possible Minervas and Apollos or to their market value. Whenever the Count would come and denounce his little army of spadesmen, a set of loitering vagabonds, the little explorer would glance at me with a sarcastic twinkle which seemed to hint that excavations were a snare. We were kept some time in suspense, for several false beginnings were made. The earth was probed in the wrong places. The Count began to be discouraged and to prolong his abbreviated *siesta*. But the little explorer, who had his own ideas, shrewdly continued his labours; and as I sat at my easel I heard the spades ringing against the dislodged stones. Now and then I would pause, with an uncontrollable acceleration of my heartbeats. 'It *may* be,' I would say, 'that some marble masterpiece is stirring there beneath its lightening weight of earth! There are as good fish in the sea—I *may* be summoned to welcome another Antinous back to fame,—a Venus, a Faun, an Augustus!'

One morning it seemed to me that I had been hearing for half an hour a livelier movement of voices than usual, but as I was preoccupied with a puzzling bit of work I made no inquiries. Suddenly a shadow fell across my canvas, and I turned round. The little explorer stood beside me, with a glittering eye, cap in hand, his forehead bathed in perspiration. Resting in the hollow of his arm was an earth-stained fragment of marble. In answer to my questioning glance he held it up to me, and I saw it was a woman's shapely hand. 'Come!' he simply said, and led the way to the excavation. The workmen were so closely gathered round the open trench that I saw nothing till he made them divide. Then, full in the sun and flashing it back, almost, in spite of her mouldy incrustations, I beheld, propped up with stones against a heap of earth, a majestic marble image. She seemed to me almost colossal, though I afterwards perceived that she was of perfect human proportions. My pulses began to throb, for I felt she was something great, and that it was great to be among the first to know her. Her marvellous beauty gave her an almost human look, and her absent eyes seemed to wonder back at us. She was amply draped, so that I saw that she was not a Venus. 'She's a Juno,' said the explorer, decisively; and she seemed indeed an embodiment of celestial supremacy and repose. Her beautiful head, bound with a single band, could have bent only to give the nod of command; her eyes looked straight before her; her mouth was implacably grave; one hand, outstretched, appeared to have held a kind of imperial wand, the arm from which the other had been broken hung at her side with the most classical majesty. The workmanship was of the rarest finish, and though perhaps there was a sort of vaguely modern attempt at character in her expression, she was wrought, as a whole, in the large and simple manner of the Greek period. She was a masterpiece of skill and a marvel of preservation. 'Does the Count know?' I soon asked, for I had a guilty sense that our eyes were taking something from her.

'The Signor Conte is at his *siesta*,' said the explorer, with his sceptical grin. 'We don't like to disturb him.'

'Here he comes!' cried one of the workmen, and we made way for him. His *siesta* had evidently been suddenly broken, for his face was flushed and his hair disordered.

'Ah, my dream,—my dream was right then!' he cried, and stood staring at the image.

'What was your dream?' I asked, as his face seemed to betray more dismay than delight.

'That they'd found a Juno; and that she rose and came and laid her marble hand on mine—eh?' said the Count excitedly.

A kind of awe-struck, guttural *a-ah*! burst from the listening workmen.

'This is the hand!' said the little explorer, holding up his perfect fragment. 'I've had it this half-hour, so it can't have touched you.'

'But you're apparently right as to her being a Juno,' I said. 'Admire her at your leisure.' And I turned away; for if the Count was superstitious, I wished to leave him free to relieve himself. I repaired to the house to carry the news to my god-daughter, whom I found slumbering—dreamlessly, it appeared—over a great archaeological octavo. 'They've touched bottom,' I said. 'They've found a Juno of Praxiteles at the very least!' She dropped her octavo, and rang for a parasol. I described the statue, but not graphically, I presume, for Martha gave a little sarcastic grimace.

'A long, fluted *peplum*,' she said. 'How very odd! I don't believe she's beautiful.'

'She's beautiful enough, *figlioccia mia*,' I answered, 'to make you jealous.'

We found the Count standing before the resurgent goddess in fixed contemplation, with folded arms. He seemed to have recovered from the irritation of his dream, but I thought his face betrayed a still deeper emotion. He was pale, and gave no response as his wife caressingly clasped his arm. I'm not sure, however, that his wife's attitude was not a livelier tribute to the perfection of the image. She had been laughing at my rhapsody as we walked from the house, and I had bethought myself of a statement I had somewhere seen, that women lack the perception of the purest beauty. Martha, however, seemed slowly to measure our Juno's infinite stateliness. She gazed a long time silently, leaning against her husband, and then stepped half timidly down on the stones which formed a rough base for the figure. She laid her two rosy, ungloved hands upon the stony fingers of the goddess, and remained for some moments pressing them in her warm grasp, and fixing her living eyes upon the inexpressive brow. When she turned round her eyes were bright with an admiring tear,—a tear which her husband was too deeply absorbed to notice. He had apparently given orders that the workmen should be treated to a cask of wine, in honour of their discovery. It was now brought and opened on the spot, and the little explorer, having drawn the first glass, stepped forward, hat in hand, and obsequiously presented it to the Countess. She only moistened her lips with it and passed it to her husband. He raised it mechanically to his own; then suddenly he stopped, held it a moment aloft, and poured it out slowly and solemnly at the feet of the Juno.

'Why, it's a libation!' I cried. He made no answer and walked slowly away.

There was no more work done that day. The labourers lay on the grass, gazing with the native Roman relish of a fine piece of sculpture, but wasting no wine in pagan ceremonies. In the evening the Count paid the Juno another visit, and gave orders that on the morrow she should be transferred to the Casino. The Casino was a deserted garden-house, built in not ungraceful imitation of an Ionic temple, in which Camillo's ancestors must often have assembled to drink cool syrups from Venetian glasses, and listen to learned madrigals. It contained several dusty fragments of antique sculpture, and it was spacious enough to enclose that richer collection of which I began fondly to regard the Juno as but the nucleus. Here, with short delay, this fine creature was placed, serenely upright, a reversed funereal *cippus* forming a sufficiently solid pedestal. The little explorer, who seemed an expert in all the offices of restoration, rubbed her and scraped her with mysterious art, removed her earthy stains, and doubled the lustre of her beauty. Her mellow substance seemed to glow with a kind of renascent purity and bloom, and, but for her broken hand, you might have fancied she had just received the last stroke of the chisel. Her fame remained no secret. Within two or three days half a dozen inquisitive *cognoscenti* posted out to obtain sight of her. I happened to be present when the first of these gentlemen (a German in blue spectacles, with a portfolio under his arm) presented himself at the Villa. The Count, hearing his voice at the door, came forward and eyed him coldly from head to foot.

'Your new Juno, Signor Conte,' began the German, 'is, in my opinion, much more likely to be certain Proserpine——'

'I've neither a Juno nor a Proserpine to discuss with you,' said the Count curtly. 'You're misinformed.'

'You've dug up no statue?' cried the German. 'What a scandalous hoax!'

'None worthy of your learned attention. I'm sorry you should have the trouble of carrying your little note-book so far.' The Count had suddenly become witty!

'But you've something, surely. The rumour is running through Rome.'

'The rumour be damned!' cried the Count savagely. 'I've *nothing*, —do you understand? Be so good as to say so to your friends.'

The answer was explicit, and the poor archaeologist departed, tossing his flaxen mane. But I pitied him and ventured to remonstrate with the Count. 'She might as well be still in the earth, if no one is to see her,' I said.

'*I'm* to see her: that's enough!' he answered with the same unnatural harshness. Then, in a moment, as he caught me eyeing him askance in troubled surprise, 'I hated his great fortfolio. He was going to make some hideous drawing of her.'

'Ah, that touches me,' I said. 'I have been planning to make a little sketch.'

He was silent for some moments, after which he turned and grasped my arm, with less irritation, but with extraordinary gravity. 'Go in there towards twilight,' he said, 'and sit for an hour and look at her. I think you'll give up your sketch. If you don't, my good old friend,—you're welcome!'

I followed his advice, and, as a friend, I gave up my sketch. But an artist is an artist, and I secretly longed to attempt it. Orders strictly in accordance with the Count's reply to our German friend were given to the servants, who, with an easy Italian conscience and a gracious Italian persuasiveness, assured all subsequent inquirers that they had been regrettably misinformed. I have no doubt, indeed, that, in default of larger opportunity, they made condolence remunerative. Further excavation was, for the present, suspended, as implying an affront to the incomparable Juno. The workmen departed, but the little explorer still haunted the premises and sounded the soil for his own entertainment. One day he came to me with his usual ambiguous grimace. 'The beautiful hand of the Juno,' he murmured; 'what has become of it?'

'I've not seen it since you called me to look at her. I remember when I went away I saw it lying on the grass near the excavation.'

'Where I placed it myself! After that it disappeared. *Ecco!*'

'Do you suspect one of your workmen? Such a fragment as that would bring more *scudi* than most of them ever looked at.'

'Some, perhaps, are greater thieves than the others. But if I were to call up the worst of them and accuse him, the Count would interfere.'

'He must value that beautiful hand, nevertheless.'

The little expert in disinterment looked about him and winked. 'He values it so much that he himself purloined it. That's my belief, and I think that the less we say about it the better.'

'Purloined it, my dear sir? After all, it's his own property.'

'Not so much as that comes to. So beautiful a creature is more or less the property of every one; we've all a right to look at her. But the Count treats her as if she were a sacrosanct image of the Madonna. He keeps her under lock and key, and pays her solitary visits. What does he do, after all? When a beautiful woman is in stone, all you can do is to look at her. And what does he do with that precious hand? He keeps it in a silver box; he has made a relic of it!' And the little explorer began to titter grotesquely and walked away.

He left me musing uncomfortably, and wondering what the deuce he meant. The Count certainly chose to make a mystery of the Juno, but this seemed a natural incident of the first rapture of possession. I was willing to wait for a free access to her, and in the meantime I was glad to find that there was a limit to his constitutional apathy. But as the days elapsed I began to be conscious that his enjoyment was not communicative, but strangely cold and shy and sombre. That he should admire a marble goddess was no reason for his despising mankind, but he really seemed to be making invidious comparisons between us. From this untender proscription his charming wife was not excepted. At moments, when I tried to persuade myself that he was neither worse nor better company than usual, her face condemned my optimism. She said nothing, but she wore a constant look of pathetic perplexity. She sat at times with her eyes fixed on him with a kind of appealing remonstrance and tender curiosity, as if pitying surprise held resentment yet awhile in check. What passed between them in private, I had, of course, no warrant to inquire. Nothing, I imagined, and that was the misery. It was part of the misery, too, that he seemed impenetrable to these mute glances, and looked over her head with an air of superb abstraction. Occasion-

ally he noticed me looking at him in urgent deprecation, and then
for a moment his heavy eye would sparkle, half, as it seemed, in
defiant irony and half with a strangely stifled impulse to justify
himself. But from his wife he kept his face inexorably, cruelly
averted; and when she approached him with some persuasive caress,
he received it with an ill-concealed shudder. I inwardly protested and
raged. I grew to hate the Count and everything that belonged to
him. 'I was a thousand times right,' I cried; 'an Italian count may be
mighty fine, but he won't *wear*! Give us some wholesome young
fellow of our own blood, who'll play us none of these dusky Old-
World tricks. Painter as I am, I'll never recommend a picturesque
husband!' I lost my pleasure in the Villa, in the purple shadows
and glowing lights, the mossy marbles and the long-trailing profile
of the Alban Hills. My painting stood still; everything looked ugly.
I sat and fumbled with my palette, and seemed to be mixing mud
with my colours. My head was stuffed with dismal thoughts; an intolerable weight seemed to lie upon my heart. The Count became, to
my imagination, a dark efflorescence of the evil germs which history
had implanted in his line. No wonder he was foredoomed to be cruel.
Was not cruelty a tradition in his race, and crime an example? The
unholy passions of his forefathers stirred blindly in his untaught
nature and clamoured dumbly for an issue. What a heavy heritage
it seemed to me, as I reckoned it up in my melancholy musings, the
Count's interminable ancestry! Back to the profligate revival of arts
and vices,—back to the bloody medley of mediaeval wars,—back
through the long, fitfully-glaring dusk of the early ages to its ponderous origin in the solid Roman state,—back through all the darkness
of history,—it seemed to stretch, losing every feeblest claim on my
sympathies as it went. Such a record was in itself a curse; and my
poor girl had expected it to sit as lightly and gratefully on her
consciousness as her feather on her hat! I have little idea how long
this painful situation lasted. It seemed the longer from my god-
daughter's continued reserve, and my inability to offer her a word of
consolation. A sensitive woman, disappointed in marriage, exhausts
her own ingenuity before she takes counsel. The Count's preoccupations, whatever they were, made him increasingly restless; he came
and went at random, with nervous abruptness; he took long rides
alone, and, as I inferred, rarely went through the form of excusing
himself to his wife; and still, as time went on, he came no nearer
explaining his mystery. With the lapse of time, however, I confess
that my apprehensions began to be tempered with pity. If I had
expected to see him propitiate his urgent ancestry by a crime, now
that his native rectitude seemed resolute to deny them this satis-

faction, I felt a sort of comparative gratitude. A man couldn't be so gratuitously sombre without being unhappy. He had always treated me with that antique deference to a grizzled beard for which elderly men reserve the flames of their general tenderness for waning fashions, and I thought it possible he might suffer me to lay a healing hand upon his trouble. One evening, when I had taken leave of my god-daughter and given her my useless blessing in a silent kiss, I came out and found the Count sitting in the garden in the mild starlight, and staring at a mouldy Hermes, nestling in a clump of oleander. I sat down by him and informed him roundly that his conduct needed an explanation. He half turned his head, and his dark pupil gleamed an instant.

'I understand,' he said, 'you think me crazy!' And he tapped his forehead.

'No, not crazy, but unhappy. And if unhappiness runs its course too freely, of course our poor wits are sorely tried.'

He was silent awhile, and then, 'I'm not unhappy!' he cried abruptly. 'I'm prodigiously happy. You wouldn't believe the satisfaction I take in sitting here and staring at that old weather-worn Hermes. Formerly I used to be afraid of him: his frown used to remind me of a little bushy-browed old priest who taught me Latin and looked at me terribly over the book when I stumbled in my Virgil. But now it seems to me the friendliest, jolliest thing in the world, and suggests the most delightful images. He stood pouting his great lips in some old Roman's garden two thousand years ago. He saw the sandalled feet treading the alleys and the rose-crowned heads bending over the wine; he knew the old feasts and the old worship, the old Romans and the old gods. As I sit here he speaks to me, in his own dumb way, and describes it all! No, no, my friend, I'm the happiest of men!'

I had denied that I thought he was crazy, but I suddenly began to suspect it, for I found nothing reassuring in this singular rhapsody. The Hermes, for a wonder, had kept his nose; and when I reflected that my dear Countess was being neglected for this senseless pagan block, I secretly promised myself to come the next day with a hammer and deal him such a lusty blow as would make him too ridiculous for a sentimental tête-à-tête. Meanwhile, however, the Count's infatuation was no laughing matter, and I expressed my sincerest conviction when I said, after a pause, that I should recommend him to see either a priest or a physician.

He burst into uproarious laughter. 'A priest! What should I do with a priest, or he with me? I never loved them, and I feel less like beginning than ever. A priest, my dear friend,' he repeated, laying his hand on my arm, 'don't set a priest at me, if you value *his* sanity! My confession would frighten the poor man out of his wits. As for a doctor, I never was better in my life, and unless,' he added abruptly, rising, and eying me askance, 'you want to poison me, in Christian charity I advise you to leave me alone.'

Decidedly, the Count *was* unsound, and I had no heart, for some days, to go back to the Villa. How should I treat him, what stand should I take, what course did Martha's happiness and dignity demand? I wandered about Rome, revolving these questions, and one afternoon found myself in the Pantheon. A light spring shower had begun to fall, and I hurried for refuge into the great temple which its Christian altars have but half converted into a church. No Roman monument retains a deeper impress of ancient life, or verifies more forcibly the memory of these old beliefs which we are apt to regard as dim fables. The huge dusky dome seems to the spiritual ear to hold a vague reverberation of pagan worship, as a gathered shell holds the rumour of the sea. Three or four persons were scattered before the various altars; another stood near the centre, beneath the aperture in the dome. As I drew near I perceived he was the Count. He was planted with his hands behind him, looking up first at the heavy rain-clouds, as they crossed the great bull's-eye, and then down at the besprinkled circle on the pavement. In those days the pavement was rugged and cracked and magnificently old, and this ample space, in free communion with the weather, had become as mouldy and mossy and verdant as a strip of garden soil. A tender herbage had sprung up in the crevices of the slabs and the little microscopic shoots were twinkling in the rain. This great weather-current, through the unclosed apex of the temple, deadens most effectively the customary odours of incense and tallow, and transports one to a faith that was on friendly terms with nature. It seemed to have performed this office for the Count; his face wore an indefinable expression of ecstasy, and he was so rapt in contemplation that it was some time before he noticed me. The sun was struggling through the clouds without, and yet a thin rain continued to fall and came drifting down into our gloomy enclosure in a sort of illuminated drizzle. The Count watched it with the fascinated stare of a child watching a fountain, and then turned away, pressing his hand to his brow, and walked over to one of the ornamental altars. Here he again stood staring, but in a moment wheeled about and returned to his former place. Just then he recognized me, and perceived, I suppose, the puzzled gaze I must have fixed on him. He saluted me frankly with his hand, and at last came towards me. I fancied that he was in a kind of nervous tremor and was trying to appear calm.

'This is the best place in Rome,' he murmured. 'It's worth fifty St. Peters'. But do you know I never came here till the other day? I left it to the *forestieri*. They go about with their red books, and read about this and that, and think they know it. Ah! you must *feel* it, —feel the beauty and fitness of that great open skylight. Now, only the wind and the rain, the sun and the cold come down; but of old —of old'—and he touched my arm and gave me a strange smile— 'the pagan gods and goddesses used to come sailing through it and take their places at their altars. What a procession, when the eyes of faith could see it! Those are the things they have given us instead!' And he gave a pitiful shrug. 'I should like to pull down their pictures, overturn their candlesticks, and poison their holy-water!'

'My dear Count,' I said gently, 'you should tolerate people's honest beliefs. Would you renew the Inquisition, and in the interest of Jupiter and Mercury?'

'People wouldn't tolerate my belief, if they guessed it!' he cried. 'There's been a great talk about the pagan persecutions; but the Christians persecuted as well, and the old gods were worshipped in caves and woods as well as the new. And none the worse for that! It was in caves and woods and streams, in earth and air and water, they dwelt. And there—and here, too, in spite of all your Christian lustrations—a son of old Italy may find them still!'

He had said more than he meant, and his mask had fallen. I looked at him hard, and felt a sudden outgush of the compassion we always feel for a creature irresponsibly excited. I seemed to touch the source of his trouble, and my relief was great, for my discovery made me feel like bursting into laughter. But I contented myself with smiling benignantly. He looked back at me suspiciously, as if to judge how far he had betrayed himself; and in his glance I read, somehow, that he had a conscience we could take hold of. In my gratitude, I was ready to thank any gods he pleased. 'Take care, take care,' I said, 'you're saying things which if the sacristan there were to hear and report——!' And I passed my hand through his arm and led him away.

I was startled and shocked, but I was also amused and comforted. The Count had suddenly become for me a delightfully curious phenomenon, and I passed the rest of the day in meditating on the strange ineffacability of race-characteristics. A sturdy young Latin I had called Camillo; sturdier, indeed, than I had dreamed him. Discretion was now misplaced, and on the morrow I spoke to my god-daughter. She had lately been hoping, I think, that I would help her to unburden her heart, for she immediately gave way to tears, and confessed that she was miserable. 'At first,' she said, 'I thought it was fancy, and not his tenderness that was growing less, but my exactions that were growing greater. But suddenly it settled upon me like a mortal chill,—the conviction that he had ceased to care for me, that something had come between us. And the horrible thing has been the want of possible cause in my own conduct, or of other visible claim on his interest. I have racked my brain to discover what I had said or done or thought to displease him! And yet he goes about like a man too deeply injured to complain. He has never uttered a harsh word or given me a reproachful look. He has simply renounced me. I have dropped out of his life.'

She spoke with such an appealing tremor in her voice that I was on the point of telling her that I had guessed the riddle, and that this was half the battle. But I was afraid of her incredulity. My solution was so fantastic, so apparently far-fetched, so absurd, that I resolved to wait for convincing evidence. To obtain it, I continued to watch the Count, covertly and cautiously, but with a vigilance which disinterested curiosity now made doubly keen. I returned to my painting, and neglected no pretext for hovering about the gardens and the neighbourhood of the Casino. The Count, I think, suspected my designs, or at least my suspicions, and would have been glad to remember just what he had suffered himself to say to me in the Pantheon. But it deepened my interest in his extraordinary situation that, in so far as I could read his deeply brooding face, he seemed to have grudgingly pardoned me. He gave me a glance occasionally, as he passed me, in which a sort of dumb desire for help appeared to struggle with the instinct of mistrust. I was willing enough to help him, but the case was prodigiously delicate, and I wished to master the symptoms. Meanwhile I worked and waited and wondered. Ah! I wondered, you may be sure, with an interminable wonder; and, turn it over as I would, I couldn't get used to my idea. Sometimes it offered itself to me with a perverse fascination which deprived me of all wish to interfere. The Court took the form of a precious psychological study, and refined feeling seemed to dictate a tender respect for his delusion. I envied him the force of his imagination, and I used sometimes to close my eyes with a vague desire that when I opened them I might find Apollo under the opposite tree, lazily kissing his flute, or see Diana hurrying with long steps down the ilex-walk. But for the most part my host seemed to me simply an unhappy young man, with an unwholesome mental twist which should be smoothed away as speedily as possible. If the remedy was to match the disease, however, it would have to be an ingenious compound!

One evening, having bidden my god-daughter good-night, I had started on my usual walk to my lodgings in Rome. Five minutes after leaving the Villa gate I discovered that I had left my eye-glass —an object in constant use—behind me. I immediately remembered that, while painting, I had broken the string which fastened it round my neck, and had hooked it provisionally upon the twig of a flowering-almond tree within arm's reach. Shortly afterwards I had gathered up my things and retired, unmindful of the glass; and now, as I needed it to read the evening paper at the Caffè Greco, there was no alternative but to retrace my steps and detach it from its twig. I easily found it and lingered awhile to note the curious night-aspect of the spot I had been studying by daylight. The night was magnificent, and full-charged with the breath of the early Roman spring. The moon was rising fast and flinging her silver checkers into the heavy masses of shadow. Watching her at work, I strolled further and suddenly came in sight of the Casino. Just then the moon, which for a moment had been concealed, touched with a white ray a small marble figure which adorned the pediment of this rather factitious little structure. Its sudden illumination suggested that a rarer spectacle was at hand, and that the same influence must be vastly becoming to the imprisoned Juno. The door of the Casino was, as usual, locked, but the moonlight was flooding the high-placed windows so generously that my curiosity became obstinate—and inventive. I dragged a garden-seat round from the portico, placed it on end, and succeeded in climbing to the top of it and bringing myself abreast of one of the windows. The casement yielded to my pressure, turned on its hinges, and showed me the fancied scene,— Juno visited by Diana. The beautiful image stood bathed in the radiant flood and shining with a purity which made her most persuasively divine. If by day her mellow complexion suggested faded gold, her substance now might have passed for polished silver. The effect was almost terrible; beauty so eloquent could hardly be inanimate. This was my foremost observation. I leave you to fancy whether my next was less interesting. At some distance from the foot of the statue, just out of the light, I perceived a figure lying flat on the pavement, prostrate apparently with devotion I can hardly tell you how it completed the impressiveness of the scene. It marked the shining image as a goddess indeed, and seemed to throw a sort of conscious pride into her stony mask. I of course immediately recognized this recumbent worshipper as the Count, and while I stood gazing, as if to help me to read the full meaning of his attitude, the moonlight travelled forward and covered his breast and face. Then I saw that his eyes were closed, and that he was either asleep or swooning. Watching him attentively, I detected his even respirations, and judged there was no reason for alarm. The moonlight blanched his face, which seemed already pale with weariness. He had come into the presence of the Juno in obedience to that extraordinary need of which the symptoms had so woefully perplexed us, and, exhausted either by compliance or resistance, he had sunk down at her feet in a stupid sleep. The bright moonshine soon roused him, however; he muttered something and raised himself, vaguely staring. Then recognizing his situation, he rose and stood for some time gazing fixedly at the shining statue with an expression which I fancied was not that of wholly unprotesting devotion. He uttered a string of broken words of which I was unable to catch the meaning, and then, after another pause and a long, melancholy moan, he turned slowly to the door. As rapidly and noiselessly as possible I descended from my post of vigilance and passed behind the Casino, and in a moment I heard the sound of the closing lock and of his departing footsteps.

The next day, meeting the little explorer in the grounds, I shook my finger at him with what I meant he should consider portentous gravity. But he only grinned like the malicious earth-gnome to which I had always likened him, and twisted his moustache as if my menace were a capital joke. 'If you dig any more holes here,' I said, 'you shall be thrust into the deepest of them, and have the earth packed down on top of you. We have made enough dis-coveries, and we want no more statues. Your Juno has almost ruined us.'

He burst out laughing. 'I expected as much,' he cried, 'I had my notions!'

'What did you expect?'

'That the Signor Conte would begin and say his prayers to her.'

'Good heavens! Is the case so common? Why did you expect it?'

'On the contrary, the case is rare. But I've fumbled so long in the monstrous heritage of antiquity, that I have learned a multitude of secrets—learned that ancient relics may work modern miracles. There's a pagan element in all of us,—I don't speak for you, *illus-trissimi forestieri*,—and the old gods have still their worshippers. The old spirit still throbs here and there, and the Signor Conte has his share of it. He's a good fellow, but, between ourselves, he's an im-possible Christian!' And this singular personage resumed his im-pertinent hilarity.

'If your previsions were so distinct,' I said, 'you ought to have given me a hint of them. I should have sent your spadesmen walking!'

'Ah, but the Juno is so beautiful!'

'Her beauty be blasted! Can you tell me what has become of the Contessa's? To rival the Juno, she's turning to marble herself.'

He shrugged his shoulders. 'Ah, but the Juno is worth fifty thousand *scudi*!'

'I'd give a hundred thousand,' I said, 'to have her annihilated. Perhaps, after all, I shall want you to dig another hole.'

'At your service!' he answered, with a flourish; and we separated.

A couple of days later I dined, as I often did, with my host and hostess, and met the Count face to face for the first time since his prostration in the Casino. He bore the traces of it, and sat plunged in sombre distraction. I fancied that the path of the old faith was not strewn with flowers, and that the Juno was becoming daily a harder mistress to serve. Dinner was scarcely over before he rose from table and took up his hat. As he did so, passing near his wife, he faltered a moment, stopped and gave her—for the first time, I imagine—that vaguely imploring look which I had often caught. She moved her lips in inarticulate sympathy and put out her hands. He drew her towards him, kissed her with a kind of angry ardour, and strode away. The occasion was propitious, and further delay unnecessary.

'What I have to tell you is very strange,' I said to the Countess, 'very fantastic, very incredible. But perhaps you'll not find it so bad as you feared. Your enemy is the Juno. The Count—how shall I say it?—the Count takes her *au sérieux*.' She was silent; but after a moment she touched my arm with her hand, and I knew she meant that I had spoken her own belief. 'You admired his antique simplicity: you see how far it goes. He has reverted to the faith of his fathers. Dormant through the ages, that imperious statue has silently aroused it. He believes in the pedigrees you used to dog's-ear your School Mythology with trying to get by heart. In a word, dear child, Camillo is a pagan.'

'I suppose you'll be terribly shocked,' she answered, 'if I say that he's welcome to any faith, if he will only share it with me. I'll believe in Jupiter, if he'll bid me! My sorrow's not for that: let my husband be himself! My sorrow is for the gulf of silence and indifference that has burst open between us. His Juno's the reality: I'm the fiction!'

'I've lately become reconciled to this gulf of silence, and to your wearing for a while a fabulous character. After the fable the moral! The poor fellow has but half succumbed: the other half protests. The modern man is shut out in the darkness with his incomparable wife. How can he have failed to feel—vaguely and grossly, if it must have been, but in every throb of his heart—that you are a more perfect experiment of nature, a riper fruit of time, than those primitive persons for whom Juno was a terror and Venus an example? He pays you the compliment of believing you an inconvertible modern. He has crossed the Acheron, but he has left you behind, as a pledge to the present. We'll bring him back to redeem it. The old ancestral ghosts ought to be propitiated when a pretty creature like you has sacrificed the roses of her life. He has proved himself one of the Valerii; we shall see to it that he is the last, and yet that his decease shall leave the Conte Camillo in excellent health.'

I spoke with a confidence which I had partly felt, for it seemed to me that if the Count was to be touched it must be by the sense that his strange, spiritual excursion had not made his wife detest him. We talked long and to a hopeful end, for before I went away my goddaughter expressed the desire to go out and look at the Juno. 'I was afraid of her almost from the first,' she said, 'and have hardly seen her since she was set up in the Casino. Perhaps I can learn a lesson from her and guess the secret of her influence.'

For a moment I hesitated, with the fear that we might intrude upon the Count's devotions. Then, as something in the young girl's face suggested that she had thought of this and felt a sudden impulse to pluck victory from the heart of danger, I bravely offered her my arm. The night was cloudy, and on this occasion apparently the triumphant goddess was to depend upon her own lustre. But as we approached the Casino I saw that the door was ajar, and that there was lamp-light within. The lamp was suspended in front of the image, and it showed us that the place was empty. But the Count had lately been there. Before the statue stood a roughly extemporized altar, composed of a nameless fragment of antique marble, engraved with an illegible Greek inscription. We seemed really to stand in a pagan temple, and we gazed at the serene divinity with an impulse of spiritual reverence. It ought to have been deepened, I suppose, but it was rudely checked, by our observing a curious glitter on the face of the low altar. A second glance showed us it was blood!

My companion looked at me in pale horror, and turned away with a cry. A swarm of hideous conjectures pressed into my mind, and for a moment I was sickened. But at last I remembered that there is blood and blood, and the later Latins were not the anthropophagi.

'Be sure it's very innocent,' I said, 'a lamb, a kid, or a sucking calf!' But it was enough for her nerves and her conscience that it was a crimson trickle, and she returned to the house in great agitation. The rest of the night was not passed in a way to restore her to calmness. The Count had not come in, and she sat up for him from hour to hour. I remained with her and smoked my cigar as composedly as I might; but internally I wondered what in horror's name had become of him. Gradually, as the hours wore away, I shaped a vague interpretation of these dusky portents,—an interpretation none the less valid and devoutly desired for its being tolerably cheerful. The blood-drops on the altar, I mused, were the last instalment of his debt and the end of his delusion. They had been a happy necessity, for he was, after all, too gentle a creature not to hate himself for having shed them, not to abhor so cruelly insistent an idol. He had wandered away to recover himself in solitude, and he would come back to us with a repentant heart and an inquiring mind! I should certainly have believed all this more easily, however, if I could have heard his footstep in the hall. Towards dawn, as scepticism threatened to creep in with the grey light, I restlessly betook myself to the portico. Here in a few moments I saw him across the grass, heavy-footed, splashed with mud, and evidently excessively tired. He must have been walking all night; and his face denoted that his spirit had been as restless as his body. He passed near me, and before he entered the house he stopped, looked at me a moment, and then held out his hand. I grasped it warmly, and it seemed to me to throb with all that he could not speak.

'Will you see your wife?' I asked.

He passed his hand over his eyes and shook his head. 'Not now—not yet—some time!' he answered.

I was disappointed, but I convinced, I think, that he had cast out the devil. She felt, poor girl, a pardonable desire to celebrate the event. I returned to my lodging, spent the day in Rome, and came back to the Villa towards dusk. I was told that the Countess was in the grounds. I looked for her cautiously at first, for I thought it just possible I might interrupt the natural consequences of a reconciliation; but failing to meet her, I turned towards the Casino, and found myself face to face with the little explorer.

'Does your excellency happen to have twenty yards of stout rope about him?' he asked gravely.

'Do you want to hang yourself for the trouble you've stood sponsor to?' I answered.

'It's a hanging matter, I promise you. The Countess has given orders. You'll find her in the Casino. Sweet-voiced as she is, she knows how to make her orders understood.'

At the door of the Casino stood half a dozen of the labourers on the place, looking vaguely solemn, like outlying dependants at a superior funeral. The Countess was within, in a position which was an answer to the surveyor's riddle. She stood with her eyes fixed on the Juno, who had been removed from her pedestal and lay stretched in her magnificent length upon a rude litter.

'Do you understand?' she said. 'She's beautiful, she's noble, she's precious, but she must go back!' And, with a passionate gesture, she seemed to indicate an open grave.

I was hugely delighted, but I thought it discreet to stroke my chin and look sober, 'She's worth fifty thousand *scudi.*'

She shook her head sadly. 'If we were to sell her to the Pope and give the money to the poor, it wouldn't profit us. She must go back, —she must go back! We must smother her beauty in the dreadful earth. It makes me feel almost as if she were alive; but it came to me last night with overwhelming force, when my husband came in and refused to see me, that he'll not be himself as long as she is above ground. To cut the knot we must bury her! If I had only thought of it before!'

'Not before!' I said, shaking my head in turn. 'Heaven reward our sacrifice now!'

The little surveyor, when he reappeared, seemed hardly like an agent of the celestial influences, but he was deft and active, which was more to the point. Every now and then he uttered some half-articulate lament, by way of protest against the Countess's cruelty; but I saw him privately scanning the recumbent image with an eye which seemed to foresee a malicious glee in standing on a certain un-marked spot on the turf and grinning till people stared. He had brought back an abundance of rope, and having summoned his assistants, who vigorously lifted the litter, he led the way to the original excavation, which had been left unclosed with the project of further researches. By the time we reached the edge of the grave the evening had fallen and the beauty of our marble victim was shrouded in a dusky veil. No one spoke,—if not exactly for shame, at least for regret. Whatever our plea, our performance looked, at least, monstrously profane. The ropes were adjusted and the Juno was slowly lowered into her earthy bed. The Countess took a hand-ful of earth and dropped it solemnly on her breast. 'May it lie lightly, but for ever!' she said.

'Amen!' cried the little surveyor with a strange mocking inflection; and he gave us a bow, as he departed, which betrayed an agreeable consciousness of knowing where fifty thousand *scudi* were buried. His underlings had another cask of wine, the result of which, for them, was a suspension of all consciousness, and a subsequent irre-parable confusion of memory as to where they had plied their spades.

The Countess had not yet seen her husband, who had again ap-

parently betaken himself to communion with the great god Pan.
I was of course unwilling to leave her to encounter alone the results
of her momentous deed. She wandered into the drawing-room and
pretended to occupy herself with a bit of embroidery, but in reality
she was bravely composing herself for an 'explanation'. I took up a
book, but it held my attention as feebly. As the evening wore away
I heard a movement on the threshold and saw the Count lifting the
tapestried curtain which masked the door, and looking silently at his
wife. His eyes were brilliant, but not angry. He had missed the Juno
—and rejoiced! The Countess kept her eyes fixed on her work, and
drew her silken stitches like an image of wifely contentment. The
image seemed to fascinate him: he came in slowly, almost on tiptoe, walked to the chimney-piece, and stood there in a sort of rapt
contemplation. What had passed, what was passing, in his mind,
I leave to your own apprehension. My god-daughter's hand trembled
as it rose and fell, and the colour came into her cheek. At last she
raised her eyes and sustained the gaze in which all his returning
faith seemed concentrated. He hesitated a moment, as if her very
forgiveness kept the gulf open between them, and then he strode forward, fell on his two knees and buried his head in her lap. I departed
as the Count had come in, on tiptoe.

He never became, if you will, a thoroughly modern man; but one
day, years after, when a visitor to whom he was showing his cabinet
became inquisitive as to a marble hand, suspended in one of its inner
recesses, he looked grave and turned the lock on it. 'It is the hand of
a beautiful creature,' he said, 'whom I once greatly admired.'
   'Ah,—a Roman?' said the gentleman, with a smirk.
   'A Greek,' said the Count, with a frown.

Mme. De Mauves

IN TWO PARTS

[First appeared in the *Galaxy*, vol. xvii (February–March 1874), pp. 216–33, 354–74. The tale was revised and reprinted in *A Passionate Pilgrim* (1875). The 1875 text was revised and reprinted in volume i of *The Madonna of the Future* (1879). This text was later reproduced in volume xi of James's first 'Collective Edition' (1883). James finally revised the tale for the New York Edition where it appears in volume xiii (*The Reverberator*, Etc., 1908).]

PART I

I.

THE VIEW FROM THE TERRACE AT SAINT-GERMAIN-EN-Laye is immense and famous. Paris lies spread before you in dusky vastness, domed and fortified, glittering here and there through her light vapours, and girdled with her silver Seine. Behind you is a park of stately symmetry, and behind that a forest, where you may lounge through turfy avenues and light-checkered glades, and quite forget that you are within half an hour of the boulevards. One afternoon, however, in mid-spring, some five years ago, a young man seated on the terrace had chosen not to forget it. His eyes were fixed in idle wistfulness on the mighty human hive before him. He was fond of rural things, and he had come to Saint-Germain a week before to meet the spring half-way; but though he could boast of a six months' acquaintance with the great city, he never looked at it from his present standpoint without a feeling of painfully unsatisfied curiosity. There were moments when it seemed to him that not to be there just then was to miss some thrilling chapter of experience. And yet his winter's experience had been rather fruitless, and he had closed the book almost with a yawn. Though not in the least a cynic, he was what one may call a disappointed observer; and he never chose the right-hand road without beginning to suspect after an hour's wayfaring that the left would have been the interesting one. He now had a dozen minds to go to Paris for the evening, to dine at the Café Brébant, and to repair afterwards to the Gymnase and listen to the latest exposition of the duties of the injured husband. He would probably have risen to execute this project, if he had not observed a little girl who, wandering along the terrace, had suddenly stopped short and begun to gaze at him with round-eyed frankness. For a moment he was simply amused, for the child's face denoted helpless wonderment; the next he was agreeably surprised. 'Why this is my friend Maggie,' he said; 'I see you have not forgotten me.'

Maggie, after a short parley, was induced to seal her remembrance with a kiss. Invited then to explain her appearance at Saint-Germain, she embarked on a recital in which the general, according to the infantine method, was so fatally sacrificed to the particular, that Longmore looked about him for a superior source of information. He found it in Maggie's mamma, who was seated with another lady at the opposite end of the terrace; so, taking the child by the hand, he led her back to her companions.

Maggie's mamma was a young American lady, as you would immediately have perceived, with a pretty and friendly face and an expensive spring toilet. She greeted Longmore with surprised cordiality, mentioned his name to her friend, and bade him bring a chair and sit with them. The other lady, who, though equally young and perhaps even prettier, was dressed more soberly, remained silent, stroking the hair of the little girl, whom she had drawn against her knee. She had never heard of Longmore, but she now perceived that her companion had crossed the ocean with him, had met him afterwards in travelling, and (having left her husband in Wall street) was indebted to him for various small services.

Maggie's mamma turned from time to time and smiled at her friend with an air of invitation; the latter smiled back, and continued gracefully to say nothing.

For ten minutes Longmore felt a revival of interest in his interlocutress; then (as riddles are more amusing than commonplaces) it gave way to curiosity about her friend. His eyes wandered; her volubility was less suggestive than the latter's silence.

The stranger was perhaps not obviously a beauty nor obviously an American, but essentially both, on a closer scrutiny. She was slight and fair, and, though naturally pale, delicately flushed, apparently with recent excitement. What chiefly struck Longmore in her face was the union of a pair of beautifully gentle, almost heavy grey eyes, with a mouth peculiarly expressive and firm. Her forehead was a trifle more expansive than belongs to classic types, and her thick brown hair was dressed out of the fashion, which was just then very ugly. Her throat and bust were slender, but all the more in harmony with certain rapid, charming movements of the head, which she had a way of throwing back every now and then, with an air of attention and a sidelong glance from her dove-like eyes. She seemed at once alert and indifferent, contemplative and restless; and Longmore very soon discovered that if she was not a brilliant beauty, she was at least an extremely interesting one. This very impression made him magnanimous. He perceived that he had interrupted a confidential conversation, and he judged it discreet to withdraw, having first learned from Maggie's mamma—Mrs. Draper—that she was to take the six o'clock train back to Paris. He promised to meet her at the station.

He kept his appointment, and Mrs. Draper arrived betimes, accompanied by her friend. The latter, however, made her farewells at the door and drove away again, giving Longmore time only to raise his hat. 'Who is she?' he asked with visible ardour, as he brought Mrs. Draper her tickets.

'Come and see me tomorrow at the Hôtel de l'Empire,' she answered, 'and I will tell you all about her.' The force of this offer in making him punctual at the Hôtel de l'Empire Longmore doubtless never exactly measured; and it was perhaps well that he did not, for he found his friend, who was on the point of leaving Paris, so distracted by procrastinating milliners and perjured *lingères* that she had no wits left for disinterested narrative. 'You must find Saint-Germain dreadfully dull,' she said, as he was going. 'Why won't you come with me to London?'

'Introduce me to Mme. de Mauves,' he answered, 'and Saint-Germain will satisfy me.' All he had learned was the lady's name and residence.

'Ah! she, poor woman! will not make Saint-Germain cheerful for you. She's very unhappy.'

Longmore's further inquiries were arrested by the arrival of a young lady with a bandbox; but he went away with the promise of a note of introduction, to be immediately despatched to him at Saint-Germain.

He waited a week, but the note never came; and he declared that it was not for Mrs. Draper to complain of her milliner's treachery. He lounged on the terrace and walked in the forest, studied suburban street life, and made a languid attempt to investigate the records of the court of the exiled Stuarts; but he spent most of his time in wondering where Mme. de Mauves lived, and whether she ever walked on the terrace; sometimes, he finally discovered, for one afternoon towards dusk he perceived her leaning against the parapet, alone. In his momentary hesitation to approach her, it seemed to him that there was almost a shade of trepidation. But his curiosity was not diminished by the consciousness of this result of a quarter of an hour's acquaintance. She immediately recognized him on his drawing near, with the manner of a person unaccustomed to encounter a confusing variety of faces. Her dress, her expression, were the same as before; her charm was there, like that of sweet music on a second hearing. She soon made conversation easy by asking him for news of Mrs. Draper. Longmore told her that he was daily expecting news, and, after a pause, mentioned the promised note of introduction.

'It seems less necessary now,' he said—'for me, at least. But for you—I should have liked you to know the flattering things Mrs. Draper would probably have said about me.'

'If it arrives at last,' she answered, 'you must come and see me and bring it. If it doesn't, you must come without it.'

Then as she continued to linger, in spite of the thickening twilight, she explained that she was waiting for her husband, who was to arrive in the train from Paris, and who often passed along the terrace on his way home. Longmore well remembered that Mrs. Draper had pronounced her unhappy, and he found it convenient to suppose that this same husband made her so. Edified by his six months in Paris—'What else is possible,' he asked himself, 'for a sweet American girl who marries an unclean Frenchman?'

But this tender expectancy of her lord's return undermined his hypothesis, and it received a further check from the gentle eagerness with which she turned and greeted an approaching figure. Longmore beheld in the fading light a stoutish gentleman, on the fair side of forty, in a high light hat, whose countenance, indistinct against the sky, was adorned by a fantastically pointed moustache. M. de Mauves saluted his wife with punctilious gallantry, and, having bowed to Longmore, asked her several questions in French. Before taking his proffered arm to walk to their carriage, which was in waiting at the terrace gate, she introduced our hero as a friend of Mrs. Draper, and a fellow countryman, whom she hoped to see at home. M. de Mauves responded briefly, but civilly, in very fair English, and led his wife away.

Longmore watched him as he went, twisting his picturesque moustache, with a feeling of irritation which he certainly would have been at a loss to account for. The only conceivable cause was the light which M. de Mauves's good English cast upon his own bad French. For reasons involved apparently in the very structure of his being, Longmore found himself unable to speak the language tolerably. He admired and enjoyed it, but the very genius of awkwardness controlled his phraseology. But he reflected with satisfaction that Mme. de Mauves and he had a common idiom, and his vexation was effectually dispelled by his finding on his table that evening a letter from Mrs. Draper. It enclosed a short, formal missive to Mme. de

Mauves, but the epistle itself was copious and confidential. She had deferred writing till she reached London, where for a week, of course, she had found other amusements.

'I think it is these distracting English women,' she wrote, 'with their green barège gowns and their white stitched boots, who have reminded me in self-defence of my graceful friend at Saint-Germain and my promise to introduce you to her. I believe I told you that she was unhappy, and I wondered afterwards whether I had not been guilty of a breach of confidence. But you would have found it out for yourself, and besides, she told me no secrets. She declared she was the happiest creature in the world, and then, poor thing, she burst into tears, and I prayed to be delivered from such happiness. It's the miserable story of an American girl, born to be neither a slave nor a toy, marrying a profligate Frenchman, who believes that a woman *must* be one or the other. The silliest American woman is too good for the best foreigner, and the poorest of us have moral needs a Frenchman can't appreciate. She was romantic and wilful, and thought Americans were vulgar. Matrimonial felicity perhaps *is* vulgar; but I think nowadays she wishes she were a little less elegant. M. de Mauves cared, of course, for nothing but her money, which he's spending royally on his *menus plaisirs*. I hope you appreciate the compliment I pay you when I recommend you to go and "console an unhappy wife". I have never given a man such a proof of esteem, and if you were to disappoint me I should renounce the world. Prove to Mme. de Mauves that an American friend may mingle admiration and respect better than a French husband. She avoids society and lives quite alone, seeing no one but a horrible French sister-in-law. Do let me hear that you have drawn some of the sadness from that desperate smile of hers. Make her smile with a good conscience.'

These zealous admonitions left Longmore slightly disturbed. He found himself on the edge of a domestic tragedy, from which he instinctively recoiled. To call upon Mme. de Mauves, with his present knowledge, seemed a sort of fishing in troubled waters. He was a modest man, and yet he asked himself whether the effect of his attentions might not be to add to her burden. A flattering sense of unwonted opportunity, however, made him, with the lapse of time, more confident—possibly more reckless. It seemed a very inspiring idea to draw the sadness from his fair countrywoman's smile, and at least he hoped to persuade her that there was such a thing as an agreeable American. He immediately called upon her.

II.

She had been placed for her education, twelve years before, in a Parisian convent, by a widowed mamma, fonder of Homburg and Nice than of letting out tucks in the frocks of a vigorously growing daughter. Here, besides various elegant accomplishments—the art of wearing a train, of composing a bouquet, of presenting a cup of tea—she acquired a certain turn of the imagination which might have passed for a sign of precocious worldliness. She dreamed of marrying a title—not for the pleasure of hearing herself called Mme. la Vicomtesse (for which it seemed to her that she should never greatly care), but because she had a romantic belief that the best birth is the guarantee of an ideal delicacy of feeling. Romances are rarely shaped in such perfect good faith, and Euphemia's excuse was in the radical purity of her imagination. She was utterly incorruptible, and she cherished this pernicious conceit as if it had been a dogma revealed by a white-winged angel. Even after experience had given her a hundred rude hints, she found it easier to believe in fables, when they had a certain nobleness of meaning, than in well-attested but sordid facts. She believed that a gentleman with a long pedigree must be of necessity a very fine fellow, and that the consciousness of a picturesque family tradition imparts an exquisite tone to the character. *Noblesse oblige*, she thought, as regards yourself, and insures, as regards your wife. She had never spoken to a nobleman in her life, and these convictions were but a matter of transcendent theory. They were the fruit, in part, of the perusal of various ultramontane works of fiction—the only ones admitted to the convent library—in which the hero was always a legitimist vicomte who fought duels by the dozen, but went twice a month to confession; and in part of the perfumed gossip of her companions, many of them *filles de haut lieu*, who in the convent garden, after Sundays at home, depicted their brothers and cousins as Prince Charmings and young Paladins. Euphemia listened and said nothing; she shrouded her visions of matrimony under a coronet in religious mystery. She was not of that type of young lady who is easily induced to declare that her husband must be six feet high and a little near-sighted, part his hair in the middle, and have amber lights in his beard. To her companions she seemed to have a very pallid fancy; and even the fact that she was a sprig of the transatlantic democracy never sufficiently explained her apathy on social questions. She had a mental image of that son of the Crusaders who was to suffer her to adore him, but like many an artist who has produced a masterpiece of idealization, she shrank from exposing it to public criticism. It was the portrait of a gentleman rather ugly than handsome, and rather poor than rich. But his ugliness was to be nobly expressive, and his poverty delicately proud. Euphemia had a fortune of her own, which, at the proper time, after fixing on her in eloquent silence those fine eyes which were to soften the feudal severity of his visage, he was to accept with a world of stifled protestations. One condition alone she was to make—that his blood should be of the very finest strain. On this she would stake her happiness.

It so chanced that circumstances were to give convincing colour to this primitive logic.

Though little of a talker, Euphemia was an ardent listener, and there were moments when she fairly hung upon the lips of Mlle. Marie de Mauves. Her intimacy with this chosen schoolmate was, like most intimacies, based on their points of difference. Mlle. de Mauves was very positive, very shrewd, very ironical, very French— everything that Euphemia felt herself unpardonable in not being. During her Sundays *en ville* she had examined the world and judged it, and she imparted her impressions to our attentive heroine with an agreeable mixture of enthusiasm and scepticism. She was moreover a handsome and well-grown person, on whom Euphemia's ribbons and trinkets had a trick of looking better than on their slender pro- prietress. She had, finally, the supreme merit of being a rigorous example of the virtue of exalted birth, having as she did ancestors honourably mentioned by Joinville and Commines, and a stately grandmother with a hooked nose, who came up with her after the holidays from a veritable *castel* in Auvergne. It seemed to Euphemia that these attributes made her friend more at home in the world than if she had been the daughter of even the most prosperous grocer. A certain aristocratic impudence Mlle. de Mauves abundantly possessed, and her raids among her friend's finery were quite in the spirit of her baronial ancestors in the twelfth century—a spirit which Euphemia considered but a large way of understanding friendship— a freedom from small deference to the world's opinions which would sooner or later justify itself in acts of surprising magnanimity. Mlle. de Mauves perhaps enjoyed but slightly that easy attitude towards society which Euphemia envied her. She proved herself later in life such an accomplished schemer that her sense of having further heights to scale must have awakened early. Our heroine's ribbons and trinkets had much to do with the other's sisterly patronage, and her appealing pliancy of character even more; but the concluding motive of Marie's writing to her grandmamma to invite Euphemia for a three weeks' holiday to the *castel* in Auvergne, involved altogether superior considerations. Mlle. de Mauves was indeed at this time seventeen years of age, and presumably capable of general views; and Euphemia, who was hardly less, was a very well-grown subject for experiment, besides being pretty enough almost to pre-assure success. It is a proof of the sincerity of Euphemia's aspirations that the *castel* was not a shock to her faith. It was neither a cheerful nor a luxurious abode, but the young girl found it as delightful as a play. It had battered towers and an empty moat, a rusty drawbridge and a court paved with crooked, grass-grown slabs, over which the antique coachwheels of the old lady with the hooked nose seemed to awaken the echoes of the seventeenth century. Euphemia was not frightened out of her dream; she had the pleasure of seeing it assume the consistency of a flattering presentiment. She had a taste for old servants, old anecdotes, old furniture, faded household colours, and sweetly stale odours—musty treasures in which the Château de Mauves abounded. She made a dozen sketches in water-colours, after her conventional pattern; but sentimentally, as one may say, she was for ever sketching with a freer hand.

Old Mme. de Mauves had nothing severe but her nose, and she seemed to Euphemia, as indeed she was, a graciously venerable relic of an historic order of things. She took a great fancy to the young American, who was ready to sit all day at her feet and listen to anecdotes of the *bon temps* and quotations from the family chronicles. Mme. de Mauves was a very honest old woman, and uttered her thoughts with antique plainness. One day, after pushing back Euphemia's shining locks and blinking at her with some tenderness from under her spectacles, she declared, with an energetic shake of the head, that she didn't know what to make of her. And in answer to the young girl's startled blush—'I should like to advise you,' she said, 'but you seem to me so all of a piece that I am afraid that if I advise you, I shall spoil you. It's easy to see that you're not one of us. I don't know whether you're better, but you seem to me to listen to the murmur of your own young spirit, rather than to the voice from behind the confessional or to the whisper of opportunity. Young girls, in my day, when they were stupid, were very docile, but when they were clever, were very sly. You're clever enough, I imagine, and yet if I guessed all your secrets at this moment, is there one I should have to frown at? I can tell you a wickeder one than any you have discovered for yourself. If you expect to live in France, and you want to be happy, don't listen too hard to that little voice I just spoke of—the voice that is neither the curé's nor the world's. You'll fancy it saying things that it won't help your case to hear. They'll make you sad, and when you're sad you'll grow plain, and

when you're plain you'll grow bitter, and when you're bitter you'll
be very disagreeable. I was brought up to think that a woman's first
duty was to please, and the happiest women I've known have been
the ones who performed this duty faithfully. As you're not a
Catholic, I suppose you can't be a *dévote*; and if you don't take life
as a fifty years' mass, the only way to take it is as a game of skill.
Listen: not to lose, you must—I don't say cheat, but don't be too
sure your neighbour won't, and don't be shocked out of your self-
possession if he does. Don't lose, my dear; I beseech you, don't lose.
Be neither suspicious nor credulous; but if you find your neighbour
peeping, don't cry out, but very politely wait your own chance. I've
had my *revanche* more than once in my day, but I'm not sure that
the sweetest I could take against life as a whole would be to have
your blessed innocence profit by my experience.'

This was rather awful advice, but Euphemia understood it too
little to be either edified or frightened. She sat listening to it very
much as she would have listened to the speeches of an old lady in a
comedy, whose diction should picturesquely correspond to the pattern of her mantilla and the fashion of her headdress. Her indifference was doubly dangerous, for Mme. de Mauves spoke at the
prompting of coming events, and her words were the result of a
somewhat troubled conscience—a conscience which told her at once
that Euphemia was too tender a victim to be sacrificed to an ambition, and that the prosperity of her house was too precious a heritage
to be sacrificed to a scruple. The prosperity in question had suffered
repeated and grievous breaches, and the house De Mauves had been
pervaded by the cold comfort of an establishment in which people
were obliged to balance dinner-table allusions to feudal masters
against the absence of side dishes; a state of things the more regret-
table as the family was now mainly represented by a gentleman
whose appetite was large, and who justly maintained that its historic glories were not established by underfed heroes.

Three days after Euphemia's arrival, Richard de Mauves came
down from Paris to pay his respects to his grandmother, and treated
our heroine to her first encounter with a vicomte in the flesh. On
coming in he kissed his grandmother's hand, with a smile which
caused her to draw it away with dignity, and set Euphemia, who was
standing by, wondering what had happened between them. Her unanswered wonder was but the beginning of a life of bitter perplexity,
but the reader is free to know that the smile of M. de Mauves was a
reply to a certain postscript affixed by the old lady to a letter
promptly addressed to him by her granddaughter, after Euphemia
had been admitted to justify the latter's promises. Mlle. de Mauves

brought her letter to her grandmother for approval, but obtained no more than was expressed in a frigid nod. The old lady watched her with a sombre glance as she proceeded to seal the letter, and suddenly bade her open it again and bring her a pen.

'Your sister's flatteries are all nonsense,' she wrote; 'the young lady is far too good for you, *mauvais sujet*. If you have a conscience you'll not come and take possession of an angel of innocence.'

The young girl, who had read these lines, made up a little face as she redirected the letter; but she laid down her pen with a confident nod, which might have seemed to mean that, to the best of her belief, her brother had not a conscience.

'If you meant what you said,' the young man whispered to his grandmother on the first opportunity, 'it would have been simpler not to let her send the letter.'

It was perhaps because she was wounded by this cynical insinuation, that Mme. de Mauves remained in her own apartment during a greater part of Euphemia's stay, so that the latter's angelic innocence was left entirely to the vicomte's mercy. It suffered no worse mischance, however, than to be prompted to intenser communion with itself. M. de Mauves was the hero of the young girl's romance made real, and so completely accordant with this creature of her imagination, that she felt afraid of him, very much as she would have been of a supernatural apparition. He was thirty-five years old—young enough to suggest possibilities of ardent activity, and old enough to have formed opinions which a simple woman might deem it an intellectual privilege to listen to. He was perhaps a trifle handsomer than Euphemia's rather grim, Quixotic ideal, but a very few days reconciled her to his good looks, as they would have reconciled her to his ugliness. He was quiet, grave, and eminently distinguished. He spoke little, but his speeches, without being sententious, had a certain nobleness of tone which caused them to re-echo in the young girl's ears at the end of the day. He paid her very little direct attention, but his chance words—if he only asked her if she objected to his cigarette—were accompanied by a smile of extraordinary kindness.

It happened that shortly after his arrival, riding an unruly horse, which Euphemia with shy admiration had watched him mount in the castle yard, he was thrown with a violence which, without disparaging his skill, made him for a fortnight an interesting invalid, lounging in the library with a bandaged knee. To beguile his confinement, Euphemia was repeatedly induced to sing to him, which she did with a little natural tremor in her voice, which might have passed for an exquisite refinement of art. He never overwhelmed her with compliments, but he listened with unwandering attention, remembered all her melodies, and sat humming them to himself. While his imprisonment lasted, indeed, he passed hours in her company, and made her feel not unlike some unfriended artist who has suddenly gained the opportunity to devote a fortnight to the study of a great model. Euphemia studied with noiseless diligence what she supposed to be the 'character' of M. de Mauves, and the more she looked the more fine lights and shades she seemed to behold in this masterpiece of nature. M. de Mauves's character indeed, whether from a sense of being generously scrutinized, or for reasons which bid graceful defiance to analysis, had never been so amiable; it seemed really to reflect the purity of Euphemia's interpretation of it. There had been nothing especially to admire in the state of mind in which he left Paris—a hard determination to marry a young girl whose charms might or might not justify his sister's account of them, but who was mistress, at the worst, of a couple of hundred thousand francs a year. He had not counted out sentiment; if she pleased him, so much the better; but he had left a meagre margin for it, and he would hardly have admitted that so excellent a match could be improved by it. He was a placid sceptic, and it was a singular fate for a man who believed in nothing to be so tenderly believed in. What his original faith had been he could hardly have told you; for as he came back to his childhood's home to mend his fortunes by pretending to fall in love, he was a thoroughly perverted creature, and overlaid with more corruptions than a summer day's questioning of his conscience would have released him from. Ten years' pursuit of pleasure, which a bureau full of unpaid bills was all he had to show for, had pretty well stifled the natural lad, whose violent will and generous temper might have been shaped by other circumstances to a result which a romantic imagination might fairly accept as a late-blooming flower of hereditary honour. The Baron's violence had been subdued, and he had learned to be irreproachably polite; but he had lost the edge of his generosity, and his politeness, which in the long run society paid for, was hardly more than a form of luxurious egotism, like his fondness for cambric handkerchiefs, lavender gloves, and other fopperies by which shopkeepers remained out of pocket. In after years he was terribly polite to his wife. He had formed himself, as the phrase was, and the form prescribed to him by the society into which his birth and his tastes introduced him was marked by some peculiar features. That which mainly concerns us is its classification of the fairer half of humanity as objects not essentially different—say, from the light gloves one soils in an evening and throws away. To do M. de Mauves justice, he had in the course of time encountered such plentiful evidence of this pliant, glove-like quality in the feminine character, that idealism naturally seemed to him a losing game.

Euphemia, as he lay on his sofa, seemed by no means a refutation; she simply reminded him that very young women are generally innocent, and that this, on the whole, was the most charming stage of their development. Her innocence inspired him with profound respect, and it seemed to him that if he shortly became her husband it would be exposed to a danger the less. Old Mme. de Mauves, who flattered herself that in this whole matter she was being laudably rigid, might have learned a lesson from his gallant consideration. For a fortnight the Baron was almost a blushing boy again. He watched from behind the 'Figaro', and admired, and held his tongue. He was not in the least disposed towards a flirtation; he had no desire to trouble the waters he proposed to transfuse into the golden cup of matrimony. Sometimes a word, a look, a movement of Euphemia's, gave him the oddest sense of being, or of seeming at least, almost bashful; for she had a way of not dropping her eyes, according to the mysterious virginal mechanism, of not fluttering out of the room when she found him there alone, of treating him rather as a benignant than as a pernicious influence—a radiant frankness of demeanour, in fine, in spite of an evident natural reserve, which it seemed equally graceless not to make the subject of a compliment and indelicate not to take for granted. In this way there was wrought in the Baron's mind a vague, unwonted resonance of soft impressions, as we may call it, which indicated the transformation of 'sentiment' from a contingency into a fact. His imagination enjoyed it; he was very fond of music, and this reminded him of some of the best he had ever heard. In spite of the bore of being laid up with a lame knee, he was in a better humour than he had known for months; he lay smoking cigarettes and listening to the nightingales, with the comfortable smile of one of his country neighbours whose big ox should have taken the prize at a fair. Every now and then, with an impatient suspicion of the resemblance, he declared that he was pitifully *bête*; but he was under a charm which braved even the supreme penalty of seeming ridiculous. One morning he had half an hour's *tête-à-tête* with his grandmother's confessor, a soft-voiced old Abbé, whom for reasons of her own Mme. de Mauves had suddenly summoned, and had left waiting in the drawing-room while she rearranged her curls. His reverence, going up to the old lady, assured her that M. le Baron was in a most edifying state of mind, and a promising subject for the operation of grace. This was a pious interpretation of the Baron's momentary good-humour. He had always lazily wondered what priests were good for, and he now remembered, with a sense of especial obligation to the Abbé, that they were excellent for marrying people.

A day or two after this he left off his bandages, and tried to walk. He made his way into the garden and hobbled successfully along one of the alleys; but in the midst of his progress he was seized with a spasm of pain which forced him to stop and call for help. In an instant Euphemia came tripping along the path and offered him her arm with the frankest solicitude.

'Not to the house,' he said, taking it; 'further on, to the *bosquet*.' This choice was prompted by her having immediately confessed that she had seen him leave the house, had feared an accident, and had followed him on tiptoe.

'Why didn't you join me?' he had asked, giving her a look in which admiration was no longer disguised, and yet felt itself half at the mercy of her replying that a *jeune fille* should not be seen following a gentleman. But it drew a breath which filled its lungs for a long time afterwards, when she replied simply that if she had overtaken him he might have accepted her arm out of politeness, whereas she wished to have the pleasure of seeing him walk alone.

The *bosquet* was covered with an odorous tangle of blossoming vines, and a nightingale overhead was shaking out love notes with a profuseness which made the Baron consider his own conduct the perfection of propriety.

'In America,' he said, 'I have always heard that when a man wishes to marry a young girl, he offers himself simply, face to face, without any ceremony—without parents, and uncles, and cousins sitting round in a circle.'

'Why, I believe so,' said Euphemia staring, and too surprised to be alarmed.

'Very well, then,' said the Baron, 'suppose our *bosquet* here to be America. I offer you my hand, *à l'américaine*. It will make me intensely happy to have you accept it.'

Whether Euphemia's acceptance was in the American manner is more than I can say; I incline to think that for fluttering, grateful, trustful, softly-amazed young hearts, there is only one manner all over the world.

That evening, in the little turret chamber which it was her happiness to inhabit, she wrote a dutiful letter to her mamma, and had just sealed it when she was sent for by Mme. de Mauves. She found this ancient lady seated in her boudoir, in a lavender satin gown, with all her candles lighted, as if to celebrate her grandson's betrothal. 'Are you very happy?' Mme. de Mauves demanded, making Euphemia sit down before her.

'I'm almost afraid to say so,' said the young girl, 'lest I should wake myself up.'

'May you never wake up, *belle enfant*,' said the old lady solemnly. 'This is the first marriage ever made in our family in this way—by a Baron de Mauves proposing to a young girl in an arbour, like Jeannot and Jeannette. It has not been our way of doing things, and people may say it wants frankness. My grandson tells me he considers it the perfection of frankness. Very good. I'm a very old woman, and if your differences should ever be as frank as your agreement, I shouldn't like to see them. But I should be sorry to die and think you were going to be unhappy. You can't be, beyond a certain point; because, though in this world the Lord sometimes makes light of our expectations, he never altogether ignores our deserts. But you're very young and innocent, and easy to deceive. There never was a man in the world—among the saints themselves—as good as you believe the Baron. But he's a *galant homme* and a gentleman, and I've been talking to him tonight. To you I want to say this—that you're to forget the worldly rubbish I talked the other day about frivolous women being happy. It's not the kind of happiness that would suit you. Whatever befalls you, promise me this : to be yourself. The Baronne de Mauves will be none the worse for it. Yourself, understand, in spite of everything—bad precepts and bad examples, bad usage even. Be persistently and patiently yourself, and a De Mauves will do you justice.'

Euphemia remembered this speech in after years, and more than once, wearily closing her eyes, she seemed to see the old woman, sitting upright in her faded finery and smiling grimly, like one of the fates who sees the wheel of fortune turning up her favourite event. But at the moment it seemed to her simply to have the proper gravity of the occasion; this was the way, she supposed, in which lucky young girls were addressed on their engagement by wise old countesses.

At her convent, to which she immediately returned, she found a letter from her mother, which shocked her far more than the remarks of Mme. de Mauves. Who were these people, Mrs. Clive demanded, who had presumed to talk to her daughter of marriage without asking her leave? Questionable gentlefolk, plainly; the best French people never did such things. Euphemia would return straightway to her convent, shut herself up, and await her own arrival.

It took Mrs. Clive three weeks to travel from Nice to Paris, and during this time the young girl had no communication with her lover beyond accepting a bouquet of violets, marked with his initials and left by a female friend. 'I've not brought you up with such devoted care,' she declared to her daughter at their first interview, 'to marry a penniless Frenchman. I will take you straight home, and you will please to forget M. de Mauves.'

Mrs. Clive received that evening at her hotel a visit from the Baron which mitigated her wrath, but failed to modify her decision. He had very good manners, but she was sure he had horrible morals; and Mrs. Clive, who had been a very good-natured censor on her own account, felt a genuine spiritual need to sacrifice her daughter to propriety. She belonged to that large class of Americans who treat America as a kind of impossible allegiance, but are startled back into a sense of moral responsibility when they find Europeans taking them at their word. 'I know the type, my dear,' she said to her daughter with a sagacious nod. 'He'll not beat you; sometimes you'll wish he would.'

Euphemia remained solemnly silent; for the only answer she felt capable of making her mother was that her mind was too small a measure of things, and that the Baron's 'type' was one which it took some mystical illumination to appreciate. A person who confounded him with the common throng of her watering-place acquaintance was not a person to argue with. It seemed to Euphemia that she had no cause to plead; her cause was in the Lord's hands and her lover's.

M. de Mauves had been irritated and mortified by Mrs. Clive's opposition, and hardly knew how to handle an adversary who failed to perceive that a De Mauves of necessity gave more than he received. But he had obtained information on his return to Paris which exalted the uses of humility. Euphemia's fortune, wonderful to say, was greater than its fame, and in view of such a prize even a De Mauves could afford to take a snubbing.

The young man's tact, his deference, his urbane insistence, won a concession from Mrs. Clive. The engagement was to be suspended and her daughter was to return home, be brought out and receive the homage she was entitled to, and which would but too surely take a form dangerous to the Baron's suit. They were to exchange neither letters, nor mementoes, nor messages; but if at the end of two years Euphemia had refused offers enough to attest the permanence of her attachment, he should receive an invitation to address her again.

This decision was promulgated in the presence of the parties interested. The Baron bore himself gallantly, and looked at the young girl, expecting some tender protestation. But she only looked at him silently in return, neither weeping, nor smiling, nor putting out her hand. On this they separated; but as the Baron walked away, he declared to himself that, in spite of the confounded two years, he was a very happy fellow—to have a *fiancée* who to several millions of francs added such strangely beautiful eyes.

How many offers Euphemia refused but scantily concerns us—and how the Baron wore his two years away. He found that he needed pastimes, and, as pastimes were expensive, he added heavily to the list of debts to be cancelled by Euphemia's millions. Sometimes, in the thick of what he had once called pleasure with a keener conviction than now, he put to himself the case of their failing him after all; and then he remembered that last mute assurance of her eyes, and drew a long breath of such confidence as he felt in nothing else in the world save his own punctuality in an affair of honour.

At last, one morning, he took the express to Havre with a letter of Mrs. Clive's in his pocket, and ten days later made his bow to mother and daughter in New York. His stay was brief, and he was apparently unable to bring himself to view what Euphemia's uncle, Mr. Butterworth, who gave her away at the altar, called our great experiment in democratic self-government in a serious light. He smiled at everything, and seemed to regard the New World as a colossal *plaisanterie*. It is true that a perpetual smile was the most natural expression of countenance for a man about to marry Euphemia Clive.

III.

Longmore's first visit seemed to open to him so large an opportunity for tranquil enjoyment that he very soon paid a second, and, at the end of a fortnight, had spent a great many hours in the little drawing-room, which Mme. de Mauves rarely quitted except to drive or walk in the forest. She lived in an old-fashioned pavilion, between a high-walled court and an excessively artificial garden, beyond whose enclosure you saw a long line of tree-tops. Longmore liked the garden, and in the mild afternoons used to move his chair through the open window to the little terrace which overlooked it, while his hostess sat just within. After a while she came out and wandered through the narrow alleys and beside the thin-spouting fountain, and at last introduced him to a little gate in the garden wall, opening upon a lane which led into the forest. Hitherward, more than once, she wandered with him, bareheaded and meaning to go but twenty rods, but always strolling good-naturedly farther, and often taking a generous walk. They found a vast deal to talk about, and to the pleasure of finding the hours tread inaudibly away, Longmore was able to add the satisfaction of suspecting that he was a 'resource' for Mme. de Mauves. He had made her acquaintance with the sense, not altogether comfortable, that she was a woman with a painful secret, and that seeking her acquaintance would be like visiting at a house where there was an invalid who could bear no noise. But he very soon perceived that her sorrow, since sorrow it was, was not an aggressive one; that it was not fond of attitudes and ceremonies, and that her earnest wish was to forget it. He felt that even if Mrs. Draper had not told him she was unhappy, he would have guessed it; and yet he could hardly have pointed to his evidence. It was chiefly nega- tive—she never alluded to her husband. Beyond this it seemed to him simply that her whole being was pitched on a lower key than harmonious Nature meant; she was like a powerful singer who had lost her high notes. She never drooped nor sighed nor looked un- utterable things; she indulged in no dusky sarcasms against fate; she had, in short, none of the coquetry of unhappiness. But Long- more was sure that her gentle gaiety was the result of strenuous effort, and that she was trying to interest herself in his thoughts to escape from her own. If she had wished to irritate his curiosity and lead him to take her confidence by storm, nothing could have served her purpose better than this ingenuous reserve. He declared to him- self that there was a rare magnanimity in such ardent self-effacement, and that but one woman in ten thousand was capable of merging an intensely personal grief in thankless outward contemplation. Mme. de Mauves, he instinctively felt, was not sweeping the horizon for a compensation or a consoler; she had suffered a personal deception which had disgusted her with persons. She was not striving to balance her sorrow with some strongly-flavoured joy; for the present, she was trying to live with it, peaceably, reputably, and without scandal— turning the key on it occasionally, as you would on a companion liable to attacks of insanity. Longmore was a man of fine senses and of an active imagination, whose leading-strings had never been slipped. He began to see his hostess as a figure haunted by a shadow, which was somehow her intenser, more authentic self. This hovering mystery came to have for him an extraordinary charm. Her delicate beauty acquired to his eye the serious cast of certain blank-browed Greek statues, and sometimes, when his imagination more than his ear detected a vague tremor in the tone in which she attempted to make a friendly question seem to have behind it none of the hollow resonance of absent-mindedness, his marvelling eyes gave her an answer more eloquent, though much less to the point, than the one she demanded.

She gave him indeed much to wonder about, and, in his ignorance, he formed a dozen experimental theories upon the history of her marriage. She had married for love and staked her whole soul on it; of that he was convinced. She had not married a Frenchman to be near Paris and her base of supplies of millinery; he was sure she had seen conjugal happiness in a light of which her present life, with its conveniences for shopping and its moral aridity, was the absolute negation. But by what extraordinary process of the heart—through what mysterious intermission of that moral instinct which may keep pace with the heart, even when that organ is making unprecedented time—had she fixed her affections on an arrogantly frivolous Frenchman? Longmore needed no telling; he knew M. de Mauves was frivolous; it was stamped on his eyes, his nose, his mouth, his carriage. For French women Longmore had but a scanty kindness, or at least (what with him was very much the same thing) but a scanty gallantry; they all seemed to belong to the type of a certain fine lady to whom he had ventured to present a letter of introduction, and whom, directly after his first visit to her, he had set down in his notebook as 'metallic'. Why should Mme. de Mauves have chosen a French woman's lot—she whose character had a perfume which doesn't belong to even the brightest metals? He asked her one day frankly if it had cost her nothing to transplant herself—if she was not oppressed with a sense of irreconcilable difference from 'all these people'. She was silent awhile, and he fancied that she was hesitating as to whether she should resent so unceremonious an allusion to her husband. He almost wished she would; it would seem a proof that her deep reserve of sorrow had a limit.

'I almost grew up here,' she said at last, 'and it was here for me that those dreams of the future took shape that we all have when we cease to be very young. As matters stand, one may be very American and yet arrange it with one's conscience to live in Europe. My imagination perhaps—I had a little when I was younger—helped me to think I should find happiness here. And after all, for a woman, what does it signify? This is not America, perhaps, about me, but it's quite as little France. France is out there, beyond the garden, in the town, in the forest; but here, close about me, in my room and'— she paused a moment—'in my mind, it's a nameless country of my own. It's not her country,' she added, 'that makes a woman happy or unhappy.'

Mme. Clairin, Euphemia's sister-in-law, might have been supposed to have undertaken the graceful task of making Longmore ashamed of his uncivil jottings about her sex and nation. Mlle. de Mauves, bringing example to the confirmation of precept, had made a remunerative match and sacrificed her name to the millions of a prosperous and aspiring wholesale druggist—a gentleman liberal enough to consider his fortune a moderate price for being taken into circles unpervaded by pharmaceutic odours. His system, possibly, was sound, but his own application of it was unfortunate. M. Clairin's head was turned by his good luck. Having secured a fashionable wife, he adopted a fashionable vice and began to gamble at the Bourse. In an evil hour he lost heavily and staked heavily to recover himself. But he overtook his loss only by a greater one. Then he let everything go—his wits, his courage, his probity—everything that had made him what his ridiculous marriage had so promptly unmade. He walked up the rue Vivienne one day with his hands in his empty pockets, and stood for half an hour staring confusedly up and down the glittering boulevard. People brushed against him, and half a dozen carriages almost ran over him, until at last a policeman, who had been watching him for some time, took him by the arm and led him gently away. He looked at the man's cocked hat and sword with tears in his eyes; he hoped he was going to interpret to him the wrath of heaven—to execute the penalty of his dead weight of self-abhorrence. But the *sergent de ville* only stationed him in the embrasure of a door, out of harm's way, and walked away to supervise a financial contest between an old lady and a cabman. Poor M. Clairin had only been married a year, but he had had time to measure the lofty spirit of a De Mauves. After he had lost everything, he repaired to the house of a friend and asked for a night's lodging; and as his friend, who was simply his old head bookkeeper and lived in a small way, was put to some trouble to accommodate him—'You must excuse me,' Clairin said, 'but I can't go home. I'm afraid of my wife.' Towards morning he blew his brains out. His widow turned the remnants of his property to better account than could have been expected, and wore the very handsomest mourning. It was for this latter reason, perhaps, that she was obliged to retrench at other points and accept a temporary home under her brother's roof.

Fortune had played Mme. Clairin a terrible trick, but had found an adversary and not a victim. Though quite without beauty, she had always had what is called the grand air, and her air from this time forward was grander than ever. As she trailed about in her sable furbelows, tossing back her well-dressed head, and holding up her vigilant eyeglass, she seemed to be sweeping the whole field of society and asking herself where she should pluck her revenge. Suddenly she espied it, ready made to her hand, in poor Longmore's wealth and amiability. American dollars and American complaisance had made her brother's fortune; why shouldn't they make hers? She overestimated Longmore's wealth and misinterpreted his amiability; for she was sure that a man could not be so contented without being rich, nor so unassuming without being weak. He encountered her advances with a formal politeness which covered a great deal of unflattering discomposure. She made him feel acutely uncomfortable, and though he was at a loss to conceive how he could be an object of interest to a shrewd Parisienne, he had an indefinable sense of being enclosed in a magnetic circle, like the victim of an incantation. If Mme. Clairin could have fathomed his Puritanic soul, she would have laid by her wand and her book and admitted that he was an impossible subject. She gave him a kind of moral chill, and he never mentally alluded to her save as that dreadful woman—that terrible woman. He did justice to her grand air, but for his pleasure he preferred the small air of Mme. de Mauves; and he never made her his bow, after standing frigidly passive for five minutes to one of her gracious overtures to intimacy, without feeling a peculiar desire to ramble away into the forest, fling himself down on the warm grass, and, staring up at the blue sky, forget that there were any women in nature who didn't please like the swaying tree-tops. One day, on his arrival, she met him in the court and told him that her sister-in-law was shut up with a headache, and that his visit must be for her. He followed her into the drawing-room with the best grace at his command, and sat twirling his hat for half an hour. Suddenly he understood her; the caressing cadence of her voice was a distinct invitation to solicit the incomparable honour of her hand. He blushed to the roots of his hair and jumped up with uncontrollable alacrity; then, dropping a glance at Mme. Clairin, who sat watching him with hard eyes over the edge of her smile, as it were, perceived on her brow a flash of unforgiving wrath. It was not becoming, but his eyes lingered a moment, for it seemed to illuminate her character. What he saw there frightened him, and he felt himself murmuring, 'Poor Mme. de Mauves!' His departure was abrupt, and this time he really went into the forest and lay down on the grass.

After this he admired Mme. de Mauves more than ever; she seemed a brighter figure, dogged by a darker shadow. At the end of a month he received a letter from a friend with whom he had arranged a tour through the Low Countries, reminding him of his promise to meet him promptly at Brussels. It was only after his answer was posted that he fully measured the zeal with which he had declared that the journey must either be deferred or abandoned— that he could not possibly leave Saint-Germain. He took a walk in the forest, and asked himself if this was irrevocably true. If it was, surely his duty was to march straight home and pack his trunk.

Poor Webster, who, he knew, had counted ardently on this excursion, was an excellent fellow; six weeks ago he would have gone through fire and water to join Webster. It had never been in his books to throw overboard a friend whom he had loved for ten years for a married woman whom for six weeks he had—admired. It was certainly beyond question that he was lingering at Saint-Germain because this admirable married woman was there; but in the midst of all this admiration what had become of prudence? This was the conduct of a man prepared to fall utterly in love. If she was as unhappy as he believed, the love of such a man would help her very little more than his indifference; if she was less so, she needed no help and could dispense with his friendly offices. He was sure, moreover, that if she knew he was staying on her account, she would be extremely annoyed. But this very feeling had much to do with making it hard to go; her displeasure would only enhance the gentle stoicism which touched him to the heart. At moments, indeed, he assured himself that to linger was simply impertinent; it was indelicate to make a daily study of such a shrinking grief. But inclination answered that some day her self-support would fail, and he had a vision of this admirable creature calling vainly for help. He would be her friend, to any length; it was unworthy of both of them to think about 'consequences'. But he was a friend who carried about with him a muttering resentment that he had not known her five years earlier, and a brooding hostility to those who had anticipated him. It seemed one of fortune's most mocking strokes, that she should be surrounded by persons whose only merit was that they threw the charm of her character into radiant relief.

Longmore's growing irritation made it more and more difficult for him to see any other merit than this in the Baron de Mauves. And yet, disinterestedly, it would have been hard to give a name to the portentous vices which such an estimate implied, and there were times when our hero was almost persuaded against his finer judgment that he was really the most considerate of husbands, and that his wife liked melancholy for melancholy's sake. His manners were perfect, his urbanity was unbounded, and he seemed never to address her but, sentimentally speaking, hat in hand. His tone to Longmore (as the latter was perfectly aware) was that of a man of the world to a man not quite of the world; but what it lacked in deference it made up in easy friendliness. 'I can't thank you enough for having overcome my wife's shyness,' he more than once declared. 'If we left her to do as she pleased, she would bury herself alive. Come often, and bring someone else. She'll have nothing to do with my friends, but perhaps she'll accept yours.'

The Baron made these speeches with a remorseless placidity very amazing to our hero, who had an innocent belief that a man's head may point out to him the shortcomings of his heart and make him ashamed of them. He couldn't fancy him capable both of neglecting his wife and taking an almost humorous view of her suffering. Longmore had, at any rate, an exasperating sense that the Baron thought rather less of his wife than more, for that very same fine difference of nature which so deeply stirred his own sympathies. He was rarely present during Longmore's visits, and made a daily journey to Paris, where he had 'business', as he once mentioned—not in the least with a tone of apology. When he appeared, it was late in the evening, and with an imperturbable air of being on the best of terms with everyone and everything, which was peculiarly amazing if you happened to have a tacit quarrel with him. If he was a good fellow, he was surely a good fellow spoiled. Something he had, however, which Longmore vaguely envied—a kind of superb positiveness—a manner rounded and polished by the traditions of centuries—amenity exercised for his own sake and not his neighbours'—which seemed the result of something better than a good conscience—of a vigorous and unscrupulous temperament. The Baron was plainly not a moral man, and poor Longmore, who was, would have been glad to learn the secret of his luxurious serenity. What was it that enabled him, without being a monster with visibly cloven feet, exhaling brimstone, to misprize so cruelly a lovely wife, and to walk about the world with a smile under his moustache? It was the essential grossness of his imagination, which had nevertheless helped him to turn so many neat compliments. He could be very polite, and he could doubtless be supremely impertinent; but he was as unable to draw a moral inference of the finer strain, as a schoolboy who has been playing truant for a week to solve a problem in algebra. It was ten to one he didn't know his wife was unhappy; he and his brilliant sister had doubtless agreed to consider their companion a puritanical little person, of meagre aspirations and slender accomplishments, contented with looking at Paris from the terrace, and, as an especial treat, having a countryman very much like herself to supply her with homely transatlantic gossip. M. de Mauves was tired of his companion: he relished a higher flavour in female society. She was too modest, too simple, too delicate: she had too few arts, too little coquetry, too much charity. M. de Mauves, some day, lighting a cigar, had probably decided she was stupid. It was the same sort of taste, Longmore moralized, as the taste for Gérôme in painting, and for M. Gustave Flaubert in literature. The Baron was a pagan and his wife was a Christian, and between them, accordingly, was a gulf.

He was by race and instinct a *grand seigneur*. Longmore had often heard of this distinguished social type, and was properly grateful for an opportunity to examine it closely. It had certainly a picturesque boldness of outline, but it was fed from spiritual sources so remote from those of which he felt the living gush in his own soul, that he found himself gazing at it, in irreconcilable antipathy, across a dim historic mist. 'I'm a modern *bourgeois*,' he said, 'and not perhaps so good a judge of how far a pretty woman's tongue may go at supper without prejudice to her reputation. But I've not met one of the smartest of women without recognizing her and discovering that a certain sort of character offers better entertainment than Thérésa's songs, sung by a dissipated duchess. Wit for wit, I think mine carries me further.' It was easy indeed to perceive that, as became a *grand seigneur*, M. de Mauves had a stock of rigid notions. He would not especially have desired, perhaps, that his wife should compete in amateur operettas with the duchesses in question, chiefly of recent origin; but he held that a gentleman may take his amusement where he finds it, that he is quite at liberty not to find it at home; and that the wife of a De Mauves who should hang her head and have red eyes, and allow herself to make any other response to officious condolence than that her husband's amusements were his own affair, would have forfeited every claim to having her fingertips bowed over and kissed. And yet in spite of these sound principles, Longmore fancied that the Baron was more irritated than gratified by his wife's irreproachable reserve. Did it dimly occur to him that it was self-control and not self-effacement? She was a model to all the inferior matrons of his line, past and to come, and an occasional 'scene' from her at a convenient moment would have something reassuring—would attest her stupidity a trifle more forcibly than her excessive reasonableness.

Longmore would have given much to know the principle of her submissiveness, and he tried more than once, but with rather awkward timidity, to sound the mystery. She seemed to him to have been long resisting the force of cruel evidence, and, though she had succumbed to it at last, to have denied herself the right to complain, because if faith was gone her heroic generosity remained. He believed even that she was capable of reproaching herself with having expected too much, and of trying to persuade herself out of her bitterness by saying that her hopes had been illusions and that this was simply—life. 'I hate tragedy,' she once said to him; 'I have a really pusillanimous dread of moral suffering. I believe that—without base concessions—there is always some way of escaping from it. I had almost rather never smile all my life than have a single violent explosion of grief.' She lived evidently in nervous apprehension of being fatally convinced—of seeing to the end of her deception. Longmore, when he thought of this, felt an immense longing to offer her something of which she could be as sure as of the sun in heaven.

IV.

His friend Webster lost no time in accusing him of the basest infidelity, and asking him what he found at Saint-Germain to prefer to Van Eyck and Memling, Rubens, and Rembrandt. A day or two after the receipt of Webster's letter, he took a walk with Mme. de Mauves in the forest. They sat down on a fallen log, and she began to arrange into a bouquet the anemones and violets she had gathered. 'I have a letter,' he said at last, 'from a friend whom I some time ago promised to join at Brussels. The time has come—it has passed. It finds me terribly unwilling to leave Saint-Germain.'

She looked up with the candid interest which she always displayed in his affairs, but with no disposition, apparently, to make a personal application of his words. 'Saint-Germain is pleasant enough,' she said; 'but are you doing yourself justice? Won't you regret in future days that instead of travelling and seeing cities and monuments and museums and improving your mind, you sat here—for instance—on a log, pulling my flowers to pieces?'

'What I shall regret in future days,' he answered after some hesitation, 'is that I should have sat here and not spoken the truth on the matter. I am fond of museums and monuments and of improving my mind, and I'm particularly fond of my friend Webster. But I can't bring myself to leave Saint-Germain without asking you a question. You must forgive me if it's unfortunate, and be assured that curiosity was never more respectful. Are you really as unhappy as I imagine you to be?'

She had evidently not expected his question, and she greeted it with a startled blush. 'If I strike you as unhappy,' she said, 'I have been a poorer friend to you than I wished to be.'

'I, perhaps, have been a better friend of yours than you have supposed. I've admired your reserve, your courage, your studied gaiety. But I have felt the existence of something beneath them that was more *you*—more you as I wished to know you—than they were; something that I have believed to be an intense grief.'

She listened with great gravity, but without an air of offence, and he felt that while he had been timorously calculating the last consequences of friendship, she had placidly accepted them. 'You surprise me,' she said slowly, and her blush still lingered. 'But to refuse to answer you would confirm an impression which is evidently already too strong. An unhappiness that one can sit comfortably talking about, is an unhappiness with distinct limitations. If I were examined before a board of commissioners for investigating the felicity of mankind, I'm sure I should be pronounced a very fortunate woman.'

There was something delightfully gentle to him in her tone, and its softness seemed to deepen as she continued : 'But let me add, with all gratitude for your sympathy, that it's my own affair altogether. It needn't disturb you, Mr. Longmore, for I have often found myself in your company a very contented person.'

'You're a wonderful woman,' he said, 'and I admire you as I never have admired anyone. You're wiser than anything I, for one, can say to you; and what I ask of you is not to let me advise or console you, but simply thank you for letting me know you.' He had intended no such outburst as this, but his voice rang loud, and he felt a kind of unfamiliar joy as he uttered it.

She shook her head with some impatience. 'Let us be friends—as I supposed we were going to be—without protestations and fine words. To have you making bows to my wisdom—that would be real wretchedness. I can dispense with your admiration better than the Flemish painters can—better than Van Eyck and Rubens, in spite of all their worshippers. Go join your friend—see everything, enjoy everything, learn everything, and write me an excellent letter, brimming over with your impressions. I'm extremely fond of the Dutch painters,' she added with a slight faltering of the voice, which Longmore had noticed once before, and which he had interpreted as the sudden weariness of a spirit self-condemned to play a part.

'I don't believe you care about the Dutch painters at all,' he said with a laugh. 'But I shall certainly write you a letter.'

She rose and turned homeward, thoughtfully rearranging her flowers as she walked. Little was said; Longmore was asking himself, with a tremor in the unspoken words, whether all this meant simply that he was in love. He looked at the rooks wheeling against the golden-hued sky, between the tree-tops, but not at his companion, whose personal presence seemed lost in the felicity she had created. Mme. de Mauves was silent and grave, because she was painfully disappointed. A sentimental friendship she had not desired; her scheme had been to pass with Longmore as a placid creature with a good deal of leisure, which she was disposed to devote to profitable conversation of an impersonal sort. She liked him extremely, and felt that there was something in him to which, when she made up her girlish mind that a needy French baron was the ripest fruit of time, she had done very scanty justice. They went through the little gate in the garden wall and approached the house. On the terrace Mme. Clairin was entertaining a friend—a little elderly gentleman with a white moustache, and an order in his button-hole. Mme. de Mauves chose to pass round the house into the court; whereupon her sister-in-law, greeting Longmore with a commanding nod, lifted her eyeglass and stared at them as they went by. Longmore heard the little old gentleman uttering some old-fashioned epigram about *'la vieille galanterie française'*, and then, by a sudden impulse, he looked at Mme. de Mauves and wondered what she was doing in such a world. She stopped before the house, without asking him to come in. 'I hope,' she said, 'you'll consider my advice, and waste no more time at Saint-Germain.'

For an instant there rose to his lips some faded compliment about his time not being wasted, but it expired before the simple sincerity of her look. She stood there as gently serious as the angel of dis-interestedness, and Longmore felt as if he should insult her by treating her words as a bait for flattery. 'I shall start in a day or two,' he answered, 'but I won't promise you not to come back.'

'I hope not,' she said simply. 'I expect to be here a long time.'

'I shall come and say goodbye,' he rejoined; on which she nodded with a smile, and went in.

He turned away, and walked slowly homeward by the terrace. It seemed to him that to leave her thus, for a gain on which she herself insisted, was to know her better and admire her more. But he was in a vague ferment of feeling which her evasion of his question half an hour before had done more to deepen than to allay. Suddenly, on the terrace, he encountered M. de Mauves, who was leaning against the parapet finishing a cigar. The Baron, who, he fancied, had an air of peculiar affability, offered him his light-gloved hand. Longmore stopped; he felt a sudden angry desire to cry out to him that he had the loveliest wife in the world; that he ought to be ashamed of him-self not to know it; and that for all his shrewdness he had never looked into the depths of her eyes. The Baron, we know, considered that he had; but there was something in Euphemia's eyes now that was not there five years before. They talked for a while about various things, and M. de Mauves gave a humorous account of his visit to America. His tone was not soothing to Longmore's excited sensibilities. He seemed to consider the country a gigantic joke, and his urbanity only went so far as to admit that it was not a bad one. Longmore was not, by habit, an aggressive apologist for our institutions; but the Baron's narrative confirmed his worst impressions of French superficiality. He had understood nothing, he had felt nothing, he had learned nothing; and our hero, glancing askance at his aristocratic profile, declared that if the chief merit of a long pedigree was to leave one so vaingloriously stupid, he thanked his stars that the Longmores had emerged from obscurity in the present century, in the person of an enterprising lumber merchant. M. de Mauves dwelt of course on that prime oddity of ours—the liberty allowed to young girls; and related the history of his researches into the 'opportunities' it presented to French noblemen—researches in which, during a fortnight's stay, he seemed to have spent many agreeable hours. 'I am bound to admit,' he said, 'that in every case I was disarmed by the extreme candour of the young lady, and that they took care of themselves to better purpose than I have seen some mammas in France take care of them.' Longmore greeted this handsome concession with the grimmest of smiles, and damned his impertinent patronage.

Mentioning at last that he was about to leave Saint-Germain, he was surprised, without exactly being flattered, by the Baron's quickened attention. 'I'm very sorry,' the latter cried. 'I hoped we had you for the summer.' Longmore murmured something civil, and wondered why M. de Mauves should care whether he stayed or went. 'You were a diversion to Mme. de Mauves,' the Baron added. 'I assure you I mentally blessed your visits.'

'They were a great pleasure to me,' Longmore said gravely. 'Some day I expect to come back.'

'Pray do,' and the Baron laid his hand urgently on his arm. 'You see I have confidence in you!' Longmore was silent for a moment, and the Baron puffed his cigar for a while and watched the smoke. 'Mme. de Mauves,' he said at last, 'is a rather peculiar person.'

Longmore shifted his position, and wondered whether he was going to 'explain' Mme. de Mauves.

'Being as you are her fellow-countryman,' the Baron went on, 'I don't mind speaking frankly. She's just a little marked—the most charming woman in the world, as you see, but a little fanciful—a little *exaltée*. Now you see she has taken this extraordinary fancy for solitude. I can't get her to go anywhere—to see anyone. When my friends present themselves she's polite, but she's freezing. She doesn't do herself justice, and I expect every day to hear two or three of them say to me, "Your wife's *jolie à croquer*: what a pity she hasn't a little *esprit*." You must have found out that she has really a great deal. But to tell the whole truth, what she needs is to forget herself. She sits alone for hours poring over her English books and looking at life through that terrible grey veil which they always seem to me to fling over the world. I doubt if your English authors,' the Baron continued, with a serenity which Longmore afterwards characterized as sublime, 'are very sound reading for young married women. I don't pretend to know much about them; but I remember that not long after our marriage Mme. de Mauves undertook to read me one day a certain Wordsworth—a poet highly esteemed, it appears, *chez vous*. It seemed to me that she took me by the nape of the neck and forced my head for half an hour over a basin of *soupe aux choux*, and that one ought to ventilate the drawing-room before anyone called. But I suppose you know him—*ce génie là*. I think my wife never forgave me, and that it was a real shock to her to find she had married a man who had very much the same taste in literature as in cookery. But you're a man of general culture,' said the Baron, turning to Longmore and fixing his eyes on the seal on his watch-guard. 'You can talk about everything, and I'm sure you like Alfred de Musset as well as Wordsworth. Talk to her about everything, Alfred de Musset included. Bah! I forgot you're going. Come back then as soon as possible and talk about your travels. If Mme. de Mauves too would travel for a couple of months, it would do her good. It would enlarge her horizon'—and M. de Mauves made a series of short nervous jerks with his stick in the air—'it would wake up her imagination. She's too rigid, you know—it would show her that one may bend a trifle without breaking.' He paused a moment and gave two or three vigorous puffs. Then turning to his companion again, with a little nod and a confidential smile : 'I hope you admire my candour. I wouldn't say all this to one of us.'

Evening was coming on, and the lingering light seemed to float in the air in faintly golden motes. Longmore stood gazing at these luminous particles; he could almost have fancied them a swarm of humming insects, murmuring as a refrain, 'She has a great deal of *esprit*—she has a great deal of *esprit*.' 'Yes, she has a great deal,' he said mechanically, turning to the Baron. M. de Mauves glanced at him sharply, as if to ask what the deuce he was talking about. 'She has a great deal of intelligence,' said Longmore deliberately, 'a great deal of beauty, a great many virtues.'

M. de Mauves busied himself for a moment in lighting another cigar, and when he had finished, with a return of his confidential smile, 'I suspect you of thinking,' he said, 'that I don't do my wife justice. Take care—take care, young man; that's a dangerous assumption. In general, a man always does his wife justice. More than justice,' cried the Baron with a laugh—'that we keep for the wives of other men!'

Longmore afterwards remembered it in favour of the Baron's grace of address that he had not measured at this moment the dusky abyss over which it hovered. But a sort of deepening subterranean echo lingered on his spiritual ear. For the present his keenest sensation was a desire to get away and cry aloud that M. de Mauves was an arrogant fool. He bade him an abrupt good-night, which must serve also, he said, as goodbye.

'Decidedly then you go?' said M. de Mauves, almost peremptorily.

'Decidedly.'

'Of course you'll come and say goodbye to Mme. de Mauves.' His tone implied that the omission would be most uncivil; but there seemed to Longmore something so ludicrous in his taking a lesson in consideration from M. de Mauves, that he burst into a laugh. The Baron frowned, like a man for whom it was a new and most unpleasant sensation to be perplexed. 'You're a queer fellow,' he murmured, as Longmore turned away, not foreseeing that he would think him a very queer fellow indeed before he had done with him.

Longmore sat down to dinner at his hotel with his usual good intentions; but as he was lifting his first glass of wine to his lips, he suddenly fell to musing and set down his wine untasted. His reverie lasted long, and when he emerged from it, his fish was cold; but this mattered little, for his appetite was gone. That evening he packed his trunk with a kind of indignant energy. This was so effective that the operation was accomplished before bed-time, and as he was not in the least sleepy, he devoted the interval to writing two letters; one was a short note to Mme. de Mauves, which he entrusted to a servant, to be delivered the next morning. He had found it best, he said, to leave Saint-Germain immediately, but he expected to be back in Paris in the early autumn. The other letter was the result of his having remembered a day or two before that he had not yet complied with Mrs. Draper's injunction to give her an account of his impressions of her friend. The present occasion seemed propitious, and he wrote half a dozen pages. His tone, however, was grave, and Mrs. Draper, on receiving them, was slightly disappointed —she would have preferred a stronger flavour of rhapsody. But what chiefly concerns us is the concluding sentences.

'The only time she ever spoke to me of her marriage,' he wrote, 'she intimated that it had been a perfect lovematch. With all abatements, I suppose most marriages are; but in her case this would mean more, I think, than in that of most women; for her love was an absolute idealization. She believed her husband was a hero of rose-coloured romance, and he turns out to be not even a hero of very sad-coloured reality. For some time now she has been sounding her mistake, but I don't believe she has touched the bottom of it yet. She strikes me as a person who is begging off from full knowledge— who has struck a truce with painful truth, and is trying awhile the

experiment of living with closed eyes. In the dark she tries to see
again the gilding on her idol. Illusion of course is illusion, and one
must always pay for it; but there is something truly tragical in seeing
an earthly penalty levied on such divine folly as this. As for M.
de Mauves, he's a Frenchman to his fingers' ends; and I confess I should
dislike him for this if he were a much better man. He can't forgive
his wife for having married him too sentimentally and loved him
too well; for in some uncorrupted corner of his being he feels, I
suppose, that as she saw him, so he ought to have been. It's a perpetual vexation to him that a little American *bourgeoise* should have
fancied him a finer fellow than he is, or than he at all wants to be.
He hasn't a glimmering of real acquaintance with his wife; he can't
understand the stream of passion flowing so clear and still. To tell
the truth, I hardly can myself, but when I see the spectacle I can
admire it restlessly. M. de Mauves, at any rate, would like to have
the comfort of feeling that his wife was as corruptible as himself;
and you'll hardly believe me when I tell you that he goes about inti-
mating to gentlemen, whom he deems worthy of the knowledge, that
it would be a convenience to him to have them make love to her.'

PART II

V.

On reaching Paris, Longmore straightway purchased a Murray's
'Belgium', to help himself to believe that he would start on the
morrow for Brussels; but when the morrow came, it occurred to
him that, by way of preparation, he ought to acquaint himself
more intimately with the Flemish painters in the Louvre. This
took a whole morning, but it did little to hasten his departure.
He had abruptly left Saint-Germain, because it seemed to him
that respect for Mme. de Mauves demanded that he should leave
her husband no reason to suppose that he had understood him;
but now that he had satisfied this immediate need of delicacy,
he found himself thinking more and more ardently of Euphemia.
It was a poor expression of ardour to be lingering irresolutely on the
deserted boulevards, but he detested the idea of leaving Saint-
Germain five hundred miles behind him. He felt very foolish, nevertheless, and wandered about nervously, promising himself to take
the next train; but a dozen trains started, and Longmore was still
in Paris. This sentimental tumult was more than he had bargained
for, and, as he looked in the shop windows, he wondered whether

it was a 'passion'. He had never been fond of the word, and had grown up with a kind of horror of what it represented. He had hoped that when he fell in love, he should do it with an excellent conscience, with no greater agitation than a mild general glow of satisfaction. But here was a sentiment compounded of pity and anger, as well as admiration, and bristling with scruples and doubts. He had come abroad to enjoy the Flemish painters and all others; but what fair-tressed saint of Van Eyck or Memling was so appealing a figure as Mme. de Mauves? His restless steps carried him at last out of the long villa-bordered avenue which leads to the Bois de Boulogne.

Summer had fairly begun, and the drive beside the lake was empty, but there were various loungers on the benches and chairs, and the great café had an air of animation. Longmore's walk had given him an appetite, and he went into the establishment and demanded a dinner, remarking for the hundredth time, as he observed the smart little tables disposed in the open air, how much better this matter was ordered in France.

'Will monsieur dine in the garden or in the salon?' asked the waiter. Longmore chose the garden, and observing that a great vine of June roses was trained over the wall of the house, placed himself at a table near by, where the best of dinners was served him on the whitest of linen, in the most shining of porcelain. It so happened that his table was near a window, and that as he sat he could look into a corner of the salon. So it was that his attention rested on a lady seated just within the window, which was open, face to face, apparently, to a companion who was concealed by the curtain. She was a very pretty woman, and Longmore looked at her as often as was consistent with good manners. After a while he even began to wonder who she was, and to suspect that she was one of those ladies whom it is no breach of good manners to look at as often as you like. Longmore, too, if he had been so disposed, would have been the more free to give her all his attention, that her own was fixed upon the person opposite to her. She was what the French call a *belle brune*, and though our hero, who had rather a conservative taste in such matters, had no great relish for her bold outlines and even bolder colouring, he could not help admiring her expression of basking contentment.

She was evidently very happy, and her happiness gave her an air of innocence. The talk of her friend, whoever he was, abundantly suited her humour, for she sat listening to him with a broad, lazy smile, and interrupted him occasionally, while she crunched her bonbons, with a murmured response, presumably as broad, which seemed to deepen his eloquence. She drank a great deal of champagne and ate an immense number of strawberries, and was plainly altogether a person with an impartial relish for strawberries, champagne, and what she would have called *bêtises*.

They had half finished dinner when Longmore sat down, and he was still in his place when they rose. She had hung her bonnet on a nail above her chair, and her companion passed round the table to take it down for her. As he did so, she bent her head to look at a wine stain on her dress, and in the movement exposed the greater part of the back of a very handsome neck. The gentleman observed it, and observed also, apparently, that the room beyond them was empty; that he stood within eyeshot of Longmore, he failed to observe. He stooped suddenly and imprinted a gallant kiss on the fair expanse. Longmore then recognized M. de Mauves. The recipient of this vigorous tribute put on her bonnet, using his flushed smile as a mirror, and in a moment they passed through the garden, on their way to their carriage.

Then, for the first time, M. de Mauves perceived Longmore. He measured with a rapid glance the young man's relation to the open window, and checked himself in the impulse to stop and speak to him. He contented himself with bowing with great gravity as he opened the gate for his companion.

That evening Longmore made a railway journey, but not to Brussels. He had effectually ceased to care about Brussels; the only thing he now cared about was Mme. de Mauves. The atmosphere of his mind had had a sudden clearing up; pity and anger were still throbbing there, but they had space to rage at their pleasure, for doubts and scruples had abruptly departed. It was little, he felt, that he could interpose between her resignation and the unsparing harshness of her position; but that little, if it involved the sacrifice of everything that bound him to the tranquil past, it seemed to him that he could offer her with a rapture which at last made reflection a woefully halting substitute for faith. Nothing in his tranquil past had given such a zest to consciousness as the sense of tending with all his being to a single aim which bore him company on his journey to Saint-Germain. How to justify his return, how to explain his ardour, troubled him little. He was not sure, even, that he wished to be understood; he wished only to feel that it was by no fault of his that Mme. de Mauves was alone with the harshness of fate. He was conscious of no distinct desire to 'make love' to her; if he could have uttered the essence of his longing, he would have said that he wished her to remember that in a world coloured grey to her vision by disappointment, there was one vividly honest man. She might certainly have remembered it, however, without his coming back to remind her; and it is not to be denied that, as he packed his valise that evening, he wished immensely to hear the sound of her voice.

He waited the next day till his usual hour of calling—the late afternoon; but he learned at the door that Mme. de Mauves was not at home. The servant offered the information that she was walking in the forest. Longmore went through the garden and out of the little door into the lane, and, after half an hour's vain exploration, saw her coming towards him at the end of a green by-path. As he appeared, she stopped for a moment, as if to turn aside; then recognizing him, she slowly advanced, and he was soon shaking hands with her.

'Nothing has happened,' she said, looking at him fixedly. 'You're not ill?'

'Nothing, except that when I got to Paris I found how fond I had grown of Saint-Germain.'

She neither smiled nor looked flattered; it seemed indeed to Longmore that she was annoyed. But he was uncertain, for he immediately perceived that in his absence the whole character of her face had altered. It told him that something momentous had happened. It was no longer self-contained melancholy that he read in her eyes, but grief and agitation which had lately struggled with that passionate love of peace of which she had spoken to him, and forced it to know that deep experience is never peaceful. She was pale, and she had evidently been shedding tears. He felt his heart beating hard; he seemed now to know her secrets. She continued to look at him with a contracted brow, as if his return had given her a sense of responsibility too great to be disguised by a commonplace welcome. For some moments, as he turned and walked beside her, neither spoke; then abruptly—'Tell me truly, Mr. Longmore,' she said, 'why you have come back.'

He turned and looked at her with an air which startled her into a certainty of what she had feared. 'Because I've learned the real answer to the question I asked you the other day. You're not happy —you're too good to be happy on the terms offered you. Mme. de Mauves,' he went on with a gesture which protested against a gesture of her own, 'I can't be happy if you're not. I don't care for anything so long as I see such a depth of unconquerable sadness in your eyes. I found during three dreary days in Paris that the thing in the world I most care for is this daily privilege of seeing you. I know it's absolutely brutal to tell you I admire you; it's an insult to you to treat you as if you'd complained to me or appealed to me. But such a friendship as I waked up to there'—and he tossed his head towards the distant city—'is a potent force, I assure you; and when forces are compressed they explode. But if you had told me every trouble in your heart, it would have mattered little; I couldn't say more than I *must* say now—that if that in life from which you've hoped most has given you least, *my* devoted respect will refuse no service and betray no trust.'

She had begun to make marks in the earth with the point of her parasol; but she stopped and listened to him in perfect immobility. Rather, her immobility was not perfect; for when he stopped speaking a faint flush had stolen into her cheek. It told Longmore that she was moved, and his first perceiving it was the happiest instant of his life. She raised her eyes at last, and looked at him with what at first seemed a pleading dread of excessive emotion.

'Thank you—thank you!' she said, calmly enough; but the next moment her own emotion overcame her calmness, and she burst into tears. Her tears vanished as quickly as they came, but they did Longmore a world of good. He had always felt indefinably afraid of her; her being had somehow seemed fed by a deeper faith and a stronger will than his own; but her half-dozen smothered sobs showed him the bottom of her heart, and assured him that she was weak enough to be grateful.

'Excuse me,' she said; 'I'm too nervous to listen to you. I believe I could have faced an enemy today, but I can't endure a friend.'

'You're killing yourself with stoicism—that's my belief,' he cried. 'Listen to a friend for his own sake, if not for yours. I have never ventured to offer you an atom of compassion, and you can't accuse yourself of an abuse of charity.'

She looked about her with a kind of weary confusion which promised a reluctant attention. But suddenly perceiving by the wayside the fallen log on which they had rested a few evenings before, she went and sat down on it in impatient resignation, and looked at Longmore, as he stood silent, watching her, with a glance which seemed to urge that, if she was charitable now, he must be very wise.

'Something came to my knowledge yesterday,' he said as he sat down beside her, 'which gave me a supreme sense of your moral isolation. You are truth itself, and there is no truth about you. You believe in purity and duty and dignity, and you live in a world in which they are daily belied. I sometimes ask myself with a kind of rage how you ever came into such a world—and why the perversity of fate never let me know you before.'

'I like my "world" no better than you do, and it was not for its own sake I came into it. But what particular group of people is worth pinning one's faith upon? I confess it sometimes seems to me that men and women are very poor creatures. I suppose I'm romantic.

I have a most unfortunate taste for poetic fitness. Life is hard prose, which one must learn to read contentedly. I believe I once thought that all the prose was in America, which was very foolish. What I thought, what I believed, what I expected, when I was an ignorant girl, fatally addicted to falling in love with my own theories, is more than I can begin to tell you now. Sometimes, when I remember certain impulses, certain illusions of those days, they take away my breath, and I wonder my bedazzled visions didn't lead me into troubles greater than any I have now to lament. I had a conviction which you would probably smile at if I were to attempt to express it to you. It was a singular form for passionate faith to take, but it had all of the sweetness and the ardour of passionate faith. It led me to take a great step, and it lies behind me now in the distance like a shadow melting slowly in the light of experience. It has faded, but it has not vanished. Some feelings, I am sure, die only with ourselves; some illusions are as much the condition of our life as our heart-beats. They say that life itself is an illusion—that this world is a shadow of which the reality is yet to come. Life is all of a piece, then, and there is no shame in being miserably human. As for my "isolation", it doesn't greatly matter; it's the fault, in part, of my obstinacy. There have been times when I have been frantically distressed, and, to tell you the truth, wretchedly homesick, because my maid—a jewel of a maid—lied to me with every second breath. There have been moments when I have wished I was the daughter of a poor New England minister, living in a little white house under a couple of elms, and doing all the housework.'

She had begun to speak slowly, with an air of effort; but she went on quickly, as if talking were a relief. 'My marriage introduced me to people and things which seemed to me at first very strange and then very horrible, and then, to tell the truth, very contemptible. At first I expended a great deal of sorrow and dismay and pity on it all; but there soon came a time when I began to wonder whether it was worth one's tears. If I could tell you the eternal friendships I've seen broken, the inconsolable woes consoled, the jealousies and vanities leading off the dance, you would agree with me that tempers like yours and mine can understand neither such losses nor such compensations. A year ago, while I was in the country, a friend of mine was in despair at the infidelity of her husband; she wrote me a most tragical letter, and on my return to Paris I went immediately to see her. A week had elapsed, and, as I had seen stranger things, I thought she might have recovered her spirits. Not at all; she was still in despair—but at what? At the conduct, the abandoned, shameless conduct of Mme. de T. You'll imagine, of course, that Mme. de T, was the lady whom

my friend's husband preferred to his wife. Far from it; he had never
seen her. Who, then, was Mme. de T.? Mme. de T. was cruelly devoted to M. de V. And who was M. de V.? M. de V.—in two words,
my friend was cultivating two jealousies at once. I hardly know what
I said to her; something, at any rate, that she found unpardonable,
for she quite gave me up.

'Shortly afterwards my husband proposed we should cease to live
in Paris, and I gladly assented, for I believe I was falling into a
state of mind that made me a detestable companion. I should have
preferred to go quite into the country, into Auvergne, where my husband has a place. But to him Paris, in some degree, is necessary, and
Saint-Germain has been a sort of compromise.'

'A sort of compromise!' Longmore repeated. 'That's your whole
life.'

'It's the life of many people, of most people of quiet tastes, and
it's certainly better than acute distress. One is at loss theoretically to
defend a compromise; but if I found a poor creature clinging to
me from day to day, I should think it poor friendship to make him
lose his hold.' Mme. de Mauves had no sooner uttered these words
than she smiled faintly, as if to mitigate their personal application.

'Heaven forbid,' said Longmore, 'that one should do that unless one
has something better to offer. And yet I am haunted by a vision of a
life in which you should have found no compromises, for they are a
perversion of natures that tend only to goodness and rectitude. As I
see it, you should have found happiness serene, profound, complete;
a *femme de chambre*, not a jewel perhaps, but warranted to tell but
one fib a day; a society possibly rather provincial, but (in spite of your
poor opinion of mankind) a good deal of solid virtue; jealousies and
vanities very tame, and no particular iniquities and adulteries. A
husband,' he added after a moment, 'a husband of your own faith
and race and spiritual substance, who would have loved you well.'

She rose to her feet, shaking her head. 'You are very kind to go
to the expense of visions for me. Visions are vain things; we must
make the best of the reality.'

'And yet,' said Longmore, provoked by what seemed the very
wantonness of her patience, 'the reality, if I'm not mistaken, has very
recently taken a shape that keenly tests your philosophy.'

She seemed on the point of replying that his sympathy was too
zealous; but a couple of impatient tears in his eyes proved that it
was founded on a devotion to which it was impossible not to defer.
'Philosophy,' she said, 'I have none. Thank Heaven!' she cried, with
vehemence, 'I have none. I believe, Mr. Longmore,' she added in a
moment, 'that I have nothing on earth but a conscience—it's a good

time to tell you so—nothing but a dogged, clinging, inexpugnable conscience. Does that prove me to be indeed of your faith and race, and have you one for which you can say as much? I don't say it in vanity, for I believe that if my conscience will prevent me from doing anything very base, it will effectually prevent me from doing anything very fine.'

'I'm delighted to hear it,' cried Longmore. 'We are made for each other. It's very certain I shall never do anything fine. And yet I have fancied that in my case this inexpugnable organ you so eloquently describe might be blinded and gagged awhile, in a fine cause, if not turned out of doors. In yours,' he went on with the same appealing irony, 'is it absolutely invincible?'

But her fancy made no concession to his sarcasm. 'Don't laugh at your conscience,' she answered gravely; 'that's the only blasphemy I know.'

She had hardly spoken when she turned suddenly at an unexpected sound, and at the same moment Longmore heard a footstep in an adjacent by-path which crossed their own at a short distance from where they stood.

'It's M. de Mauves,' said Euphemia directly, and moved slowly forward. Longmore, wondering how she knew it, had overtaken her by the time her husband advanced into sight. A solitary walk in the forest was a pastime to which M. de Mauves was not addicted, but he seemed on this occasion to have resorted to it with some equanimity. He was smoking a fragrant cigar, and his thumb was thrust into the armhole of his waistcoat, with an air of contemplative serenity. He stopped short with surprise on seeing his wife and her companion, and Longmore considered his surprise impertinent. He glanced rapidly from one to the other, fixed Longmore's eye sharply for a single instant, and then lifted his hat with formal politeness.

'I was not aware,' he said, turning to Mme. de Mauves, 'that I might congratulate you on the return of monsieur.'

'You should have known it,' she answered gravely, 'if I had expected Mr. Longmore's return.'

She had become very pale, and Longmore felt that this was a first meeting after a stormy parting. 'My return was unexpected to myself,' he said. 'I came last evening.'

M. de Mauves smiled with extreme urbanity. 'It's needless for me to welcome you. Mme. de Mauves knows the duties of hospitality', and with another bow he continued his walk.

Mme. de Mauves and her companion returned slowly home, with few words, but, on Longmore's part at least, many thoughts. The Baron's appearance had given him an angry chill; it was a dusky cloud driving back the light which had begun to shine between himself and his companion.

He watched Euphemia narrowly as they went, and wondered what she had last had to suffer. Her husband's presence had checked her frankness, but nothing indicated that she had accepted the insulting meaning of his words. Matters were evidently at a crisis between them, and Longmore wondered vainly what it was on Euphemia's part that prevented an absolute rupture. What did she suspect?—how much did she know? To what was she resigned?—how much had she forgiven? How, above all, did she reconcile with knowledge, or with suspicion, that ineradicable tenderness of which she had just now all but assured him? 'She has loved him once,' Longmore said with a sinking of the heart, 'and with her to love once is to commit one's being for ever. Her husband thinks her too rigid! What would a poet call it?'

He relapsed with a kind of aching impotance into the sense of her being somehow beyond him, unattainable, immeasurable by his own fretful spirit. Suddenly he gave three passionate switches in the air with his cane, which made Mme. de Mauves look round. She could hardly have guessed that they meant that where ambition was so vain, it was an innocent compensation to plunge into worship.

Mme. de Mauves found in her drawing-room the little elderly Frenchman, M. de Chalumeau, whom Longmore had observed a few days before on the terrace. On this occasion too Mme. Clairin was entertaining him, but as her sister-in-law came in she surrendered her post and addressed herself to our hero. Longmore, at thirty, was still an ingenuous youth, and there was something in this lady's large coquetry which had the power of making him blush. He was surprised at finding he had not absolutely forfeited her favour by his deportment at their last interview, and a suspicion of her meaning to approach him on another line completed his uneasiness.

'So you've returned from Brussels,' she said, 'by way of the forest.'

'I've not been to Brussels. I returned yesterday from Paris by the only way—by the train.'

Mme. Clairin stared and laughed. 'I've never known a young man to be so fond of Saint-Germain. They generally declare it's horribly dull.'

'That's not very polite to you,' said Longmore, who was vexed at his blushes, and determined not to be abashed.

'Ah, what am I?' demanded Mme. Clairin, swinging open her fan. 'I'm the dullest thing here. They've not had your success with my sister-in-law.'

'It would have been very easy to have it. Mme. de Mauves is kindness itself.'

'To her own countrymen!'

Longmore remained silent; he hated the talk. Mme. Clairin looked
at him a moment, and then turned her head and surveyed Euphemia,
to whom M. de Chalumeau was serving up another epigram, which
she was receiving with a slight droop of the head and her eyes
absently wandering through the window. 'Don't pretend to tell me,'
she murmured suddenly, 'that you're not in love with that pretty
woman.'

'*Allons donc!*' cried Longmore, in the best French he had ever
uttered. He rose the next minute and took a hasty farewell.

VI.

He allowed several days to pass without going back; it seemed
delicate not to appear to regard his friend's frankness during their
last interview as a general invitation. This cost him a great effort, for
hopeless passions are not the most deferential; and he had, moreover, a constant fear that if, as he believed, the hour of supreme
'explanations' had come, the magic of her magnanimity might convert M. de Mauves. Vicious men, it was abundantly recorded, had
been so converted, as to be acceptable to God, and the something
divine in Euphemia's temper would sanctify any means she should
choose to employ. Her means, he kept repeating, were no business of his, and the essence of his admiration ought to be to
respect her freedom; but he felt as if he should turn away into a
world out of which most of the joy had departed, if her freedom,
after all, should spare him only a murmured 'Thank you'.

When he called again he found to his vexation that he was to run
the gauntlet of Mme. Clairin's officious hospitality. It was one of the
first mornings of perfect summer, and the drawing-room, through
the open windows, was flooded with a sweet confusion of odours and
bird-notes which filled him with the hope that Mme. de Mauves
would come out and spend half the day in the forest. But Mme.
Clairin, with her hair not yet dressed, emerged like a brassy discord
in a maze of melody.

At the same moment the servant returned with Euphemia's regrets;
she was indisposed and unable to see Mr. Longmore. The young
man knew that he looked disappointed, and that Mme. Clairin was
observing him, and this consciousness impelled her to give him a
glance of almost aggressive frigidity. This was apparently what she

desired. She wished to throw him off his balance, and if she was not mistaken, she had the means.

'Put down your hat, Mr. Longmore,' she said, 'and be polite for once. You were not at all polite the other day when I asked you that friendly question about the state of your heart.'

'I have no heart—to talk about,' said Longmore, uncompromisingly.

'As well say you've none at all. I advise you to cultivate a little eloquence; you may have use for it. That was not an idle question of mine; I don't ask idle questions. For a couple of months now that you've been coming and going among us, it seems to me that you have had very few to answer of any sort.'

'I have certainly been very well treated,' said Longmore.

Mme. Clairin was silent a moment, and then—'Have you never felt disposed to ask any?' she demanded.

Her look, her tone, were so charged with roundabout meanings that it seemed to Longmore as if even to understand her would savour of dishonest complicity. 'What is it you have to tell me?' he asked, frowning and blushing.

Mme. Clairin flushed. It is rather hard, when you come bearing yourself very much as the Sibyl when she came to the Roman king, to be treated as something worse than a vulgar gossip. 'I might tell you, Mr. Longmore,' she said, 'that you have as bad a *ton* as any young man I ever met. Where have you lived—what are your ideas? I wish to call your attention to a fact which it takes some delicacy to touch upon. You have noticed, I suppose, that my sister-in-law is not the happiest woman in the world.'

Longmore burned in silence.

Mme. Clairin looked slightly disappointed at his want of enthusiasm. Nevertheless—'You have formed, I suppose,' she continued, 'your conjectures on the causes of her—dissatisfaction.'

'Conjecture has been superfluous. I have seen the causes—or at least a specimen of them—with my own eyes.'

'I know perfectly what you mean. My brother, in a single word, is in love with other women—with another woman. I don't judge him; I don't judge my sister-in-law. I permit myself to say that in her position I would have managed otherwise. I would have kept my husband's affection, or I would have frankly done without it, before this. But my sister is an odd compound; I don't profess to understand her. Therefore it is, in a measure, that I appeal to you, her fellow countryman. Of course you'll be surprised at my way of looking at the matter, and I admit that it's a way in use only among people whose family traditions compel them to take a superior view of things.' Mme. Clairin paused, and Longmore wondered where her family traditions were going to lead her.

'Listen,' she went on. 'There has never been a De Mauves who has not given his wife the right to be jealous. We know our history for ages back, and the fact is established. It's a shame if you like, but it's something to have a shame with such a pedigree. The De Mauves are real Frenchmen, and their wives—I may say it—have been worthy of them. You may see all their portraits in our Château de Mauves; everyone of them an "injured" beauty, but not one of them hanging her head. Not one of them had the bad taste to be jealous, and yet not one in a dozen was guilty of an *escapade*—not one of them was talked about. There's good sense for you! How they managed—go and look at the dusky, faded canvases and pastels, and ask. They were *femmes d'esprit*. When they had a headache, they put on a little rouge and came to supper as usual; and when they had a heart-ache, they put a little rouge on their hearts. These are fine traditions, and it doesn't seem to me fair that a little American *bourgeoise* should come in and interrupt them, and should hang her photograph, with her obstinate little *air penché*, in the gallery of our shrewd fine ladies. A De Mauves must be a De Mauves.

'When she married my brother, I don't suppose she took him for a member of a *société de bonnes œuvres*. I don't say we're right; who is right? But we're as history has made us, and if anyone is to change, it had better be Mme. de Mauves herself.' Again Mme. Clairin paused and opened and closed her fan. 'Let her conform!' she said with amazing audacity.

Longmore's reply was ambiguous; he simply said 'Ah!'

Mme. Clairin's pious retrospect had apparently imparted an honest zeal to her indignation. 'For a long time,' she continued, 'my sister has been taking the attitude of an injured woman, affecting a disgust with the world and shutting herself up to read the "Imitation". I've never remarked on her conduct, but I've quite lost patience with it. When a woman with her prettiness lets her husband wander, she deserves her fate. I don't wish you to agree with me—on the contrary; but I call such a woman a goose. She must have bored him to death. What has passed between them for many months needn't concern us; what provocation my sister has had—monstrous, if you wish—what *ennui* my brother has suffered. It's enough that a week ago, just after you had ostensibly gone to Brussels, something happened to produce an explosion. She found a letter in his pocket —a photograph—a trinket—*que sais-je*? At any rate, the scene was terrible. I didn't listen at the keyhole, and I don't know what was said; but I have reason to believe that my brother was called to account as I fancy none of his ancestors have ever been—even by injured sweethearts.'

Longmore had leaned forward in silent attention with his elbows on his knees, and instinctively he dropped his face into his hands. 'Ah, poor woman!' he groaned.

'*Voilà!*' said Mme. Clarin. 'You pity her.'

'Pity her?' cried Longmore, looking up with ardent eyes and forgetting the spirit of Mme. Clairin's narrative in the miserable facts. 'Don't you?'

'A little. But I'm not acting sentimentally; I'm acting politically. I wish to arrange things—to see my brother free to do as he chooses—to see Euphemia contented. Do you understand me?'

'Very well, I think. You're the most immoral person I've lately had the privilege of conversing with.'

Mme. Clairin shrugged her shoulders. 'Possibly. When was there a great politician who was not immoral?'

'Nay,' said Longmore in the same tone. 'You're too superficial to be a great politician. You don't begin to know anything about Mme. de Mauves.'

Mme. Clairin inclined her head to one side, eyed Longmore sharply, mused a moment, and then smiled with an excellent imitation of intelligent compassion. 'It's not in my interest to contradict you.'

'It would be in your interest to learn, Mme. Clairin,' the young man went on with unceremonious candour, 'what honest men most admire in a woman—and to recognize it when you see it.'

Longmore certainly did injustice to her talents for diplomacy, for she covered her natural annoyance at this sally with a pretty piece of irony. 'So you *are* in love!' she quietly exclaimed.

Longmore was silent awhile. 'I wonder if you would understand me,' he said at last, 'if I were to tell you that I have for Mme. de Mauves the most devoted friendship?'

'You underrate my intelligence. But in that case you ought to exert your influence to put an end to these painful domestic scenes.'

'Do you suppose,' cried Longmore, 'that she talks to me about her domestic scenes?'

Mme. Clairin stared. 'Then your friendship isn't returned?' And as Longmore turned away, shaking his head, 'Now, at least,' she added, 'she will have something to tell you. I happen to know the upshot of my brother's last interview with his wife.' Longmore rose to his feet as a sort of protest against the indelicacy of the position into which he was being forced; but all that made him tender made him curious, and she caught in his averted eyes an expression which prompted her to strike her blow.

'My brother is monstrously in love with a certain person in Paris; of course he ought not to be; but he wouldn't be a De Mauves if he were not. It was this unsanctified passion that spoke. "Listen, madam," he cried at last; "let us live like people who understand life. It's unpleasant to be forced to say such things outright, but you have a way of bringing one down to the rudiments. I'm faithless, I'm heartless, I'm brutal, I'm everything horrible—it's understood. Take your revenge, console yourself; you're too pretty a woman to have anything to complain of. Here's a handsome young man sighing himself into a consumption for you. Listen to the poor fellow, and you'll find that virtue is none the less becoming for being good-natured. You'll see that it's not after all such a doleful world, and that there is even an advantage in having the most impudent of husbands."' Mme. Clairin paused; Longmore had turned very pale. 'You may believe it,' she said; 'the speech took place in my presence; things were done in order. And now, Mr. Longmore'—this with a smile which he was too troubled at the moment to appreciate, but which he remembered later with a kind of awe—'we count upon you.'

'He said this to her, face to face, as you say it to me now?' Longmore asked slowly after a silence.

'Word for word, and with the greatest politeness.'

'And Mme. de Mauves—what did she say?'

Mme. Clairin smiled again. 'To such a speech as that a woman says—nothing. She had been sitting with a piece of needlework, and I think she had not seen her husband since their quarrel the day before. He came in with the gravity of an ambassador, and I'm sure that when he made his *demande en mariage* his manner was not more respectful. He only wanted white gloves!' said Mme. Clairin. 'Euphemia sat silent a few moments drawing her stitches, and then without a word, without a glance, she walked out of the room. It was just what she should have done!'

'Yes,' Longmore repeated, 'it was just what she should have done.'

'And I, left alone with my brother, do you know what I said?'

Longmore shook his head. '*Mauvais sujet!*' he suggested.

'"You've done me the honour," I said, "to take this step in my presence. I don't pretend to qualify it. You know what you're about, and it's your own affair. But you may confide in my discretion." Do you think he has had reason to complain of it?' She received no answer; Longmore was slowly turning away and passing his gloves mechanically round the band of his hat. 'I hope,' she cried, 'you're not going to start for Brussels!'

Plainly, Longmore was deeply disturbed, and Mme. Clairin might
flatter herself on the success of her plea for old-fashioned manners.
And yet there was something that left her more puzzled than satisfied in the reflective tone with which he answered, 'No, I shall remain here for the present.' The processes of his mind seemed provokingly subterranean, and she would have fancied for a moment
that he was linked with her sister in some monstrous conspiracy of
asceticism.

'Come this evening,' she boldly resumed. 'The rest will take care of
itself. Meanwhile I shall take the liberty of telling my sister-in-law
that I have repeated—in short, that I have put you *au fait.*'

Longmore started and coloured, and she hardly knew whether he
was going to assent or to demur. 'Tell her what you please. Nothing
you can tell her will affect her conduct.'

'*Voyons!* Do you mean to tell me that a woman, young, pretty,
sentimental, neglected—insulted if you will——? I see you don't believe it. Believe simply in your own opportunity! But for heaven's
sake, if it's to lead anywhere, don't come back with that *visage de
croquemort.* You look as if you were going to bury your heart—not
to offer it to a pretty woman. You're much better when you smile.
Come, do yourself justice.'

'Yes,' he said, 'I must do myself justice.' And abruptly, with a
bow, he took his departure.

VII.

He felt when he found himself unobserved, in the open air, that
he must plunge into violent action, walk fast and far, and defer the
opportunity for thought. He strode away into the forest, swinging his
cane, throwing back his head, gazing away into the verdurous vistas,
and following the road without a purpose. He felt immensely excited,
but he could hardly have said whether his emotion was a pain or a
joy. It was joyous as all increase of freedom is joyous; something
seemed to have been knocked down across his path; his destiny
seemed to have rounded a cape and brought him into sight of an
open sea. But his freedom resolved itself somehow into the need of
despising all mankind, with a single exception; and the fact of Mme.
de Mauves inhabiting a planet contaminated by the presence of this
baser multitude kept his elation from seeming a pledge of ideal bliss.

But she was there, and circumstance now forced them to be intimate. She had ceased to have what men call a secret for him, and
this fact itself brought with it a sort of rapture. He had no prevision

that he should 'profit', in the vulgar sense, by the extraordinary
position into which they had been thrown; it might be but a cruel
trick of destiny to make hope a harsher mockery and renunciation
a keener suffering. But above all this rose the conviction that she
could do nothing that would not deepen his admiration.

It was this feeling that circumstance—unlovely as it was in itself—
was to force the beauty of her character into more perfect relief,
that made him stride along as if he were celebrating a kind of
spiritual festival. He rambled at random for a couple of hours, and
found at last that he had left the forest behind him and had wandered into an unfamiliar region. It was a perfectly rural scene, and the
still summer day gave it a charm which its meagre elements but half
accounted for.

Longmore thought he had never seen anything so characteristically French; all the French novels seemed to have described it, all
the French landscapists to have painted it. The fields and trees were
of a cool metallic green; the grass looked as if it might stain your
trousers, and the foliage your hands. The clear light had a sort of
mild greyness; the sunbeams were of silver rather than gold. A great
red-roofed, high-stacked farmhouse, with whitewashed walls and a
straggling yard, surveyed the high road, on one side, from behind a
transparent curtain of poplars. A narrow stream half choked with
emerald rushes and edged with grey aspens occupied the opposite
quarter. The meadows rolled and sloped away gently to the low
horizon, which was barely concealed by the continuous line of
clipped and marshalled trees. The prospect was not rich, but it had
a frank homeliness which touched the young man's fancy. It was full
of light atmosphere and diffused sunshine, and if it was prosaic, it
was soothing.

Longmore was disposed to walk further, and he advanced along
the road beneath the poplars. In twenty minutes he came to a village
which straggled away to the right, among orchards and *potagers*.
On the left, at a stone's throw from the road, stood a little pink-faced
inn, which reminded him that he had not breakfasted, having left
home with a prevision of hospitality from Mme. de Mauves. In the
inn he found a brick-tiled parlour and a hostess in *sabots* and a white
cap, whom, over the omelette she speedily served him—borrowing
license from the bottle of sound red wine which accompanied it—
he assured that she was a true artist. To reward his compliment, she
invited him to smoke his cigar in her little garden behind the house.

Here he found a *tonnelle* and a view of ripening crops, stretching
down to the stream. The tonnelle was rather close, and he preferred
to lounge on a bench against the pink wall, in the sun, which was not

too hot. Here, as he rested and gazed and mused, he fell into a train of thought which, in an indefinable fashion, was a soft influence from the scene about him. His heart, which had been beating fast for the past three hours, gradually checked its pulses and left him looking at life with a rather more level gaze. The homely tavern sounds coming out through the open windows, the sunny stillness of the fields and crops, which covered so much vigorous natural life, suggested very little that was transcendental, had very little to say about renunciation—nothing at all about spiritual zeal. They seemed to utter a message from plain ripe nature, to express the unperverted reality of things, to say that the common lot is not brilliantly amusing, and that the part of wisdom is to grasp frankly at experience, lest you miss it altogether. What reason there was for his falling a-wondering after this, whether a deeply wounded heart might be soothed and healed by such a scene, it would be difficult to explain; certain it is that, as he sat there, he had a waking dream of an unhappy woman strolling by the slow-flowing stream before him, and pulling down the blossoming boughs in the orchards. He mused and mused, and at last found himself feeling angry that he could not somehow think worse of Mme. de Mauves—or at any rate think otherwise. He could fairly claim that in a sentimental way he asked very little of life—he made modest demands on passion; why then should his only passion be born to ill-fortune? why should his first—his last—glimpse of positive happiness be so indissolubly linked with renunciation?

It is perhaps because, like many spirits of the same stock, he had in his composition a lurking principle of asceticism to whose authority he had ever paid an unquestioning respect, that he now felt all the vehemence of rebellion. To renounce—to renounce again—to renounce for ever—was this all that youth and longing and resolve were meant for? Was experience to be muffled and mutilated, like an indecent picture? Was a man to sit and deliberately condemn his future to be the blank memory of a regret, rather than the long reverberation of a joy? Sacrifice? The word was a trap for minds muddled by fear, an ignoble refuge of weakness. To insist now seemed not to dare, but simply to be, to live on possible terms.

His hostess came out to hang a cloth to dry on the hedge, and, though her guest was sitting quietly enough, she seemed to see in his kindled eyes a flattering testimony to the quality of her wine.

As she turned back into the house, she was met by a young man whom Longmore observed in spite of his preoccupation. He was evidently a member of that jovial fraternity of artists, whose very shabbiness has an affinity with the element of picturesqueness and unexpectedness in life, which provokes a great deal of unformulated envy among people foredoomed to be respectable.

Longmore was struck first with his looking like a very clever man, and then with his looking like a very happy one. The combination, as it was expressed in his face, might have arrested the attention of a less cynical philosopher. He had a slouched hat and a blonde beard, a light easel under one arm, and an unfinished sketch in oils under the other.

He stopped and stood talking for some moments to the landlady with a peculiarly good-humoured smile. They were discussing the possibilities of dinner; the hostess enumerated some very savoury ones, and he nodded briskly, assenting to everything. It couldn't be, Longmore thought, that he found such soft contentment in the prospect of lamb chops and spinach and a *tarte à la crème*. When the dinner had been ordered, he turned up his sketch, and the good woman fell a-wondering and looking off at the spot by the stream-side where he had made it.

Was it his work, Longmore wondered, that made him so happy? Was a strong talent the best thing in the world? The landlady went back to her kitchen, and the young painter stood as if he were waiting for something, beside the gate which opened upon the path across the fields. Longmore sat brooding and asking himself whether it was better to cultivate an art than to cultivate a passion. Before he had answered the question the painter had grown tired of waiting. He picked up a pebble, tossed it lightly into an upper window, and called, 'Claudine!'

Claudine appeared; Longmore heard her at the window, bidding the young man to have patience. 'But I'm losing my light,' he said; 'I must have my shadows in the same place as yesterday.'

'Go without me then,' Claudine answered; 'I will join you in ten minutes.' Her voice was fresh and young; it seemed to say to Longmore that she was as happy as her companion.

'Don't forget the Chénier,' cried the young man; and turning away, he passed out of the gate and followed the path across the fields until he disappeared among the trees by the side of the stream. Who was Claudine? Longmore vaguely wondered, and was she as pretty as her voice? Before long he had a chance to satisfy himself; she came out of the house with her hat and parasol, prepared to follow her companion. She had on a pink muslin dress and a little white hat, and she was as pretty as a Frenchwoman needs to be to be pleasing. She had a clear brown skin and a bright dark eye, and a step which seemed to keep time to some slow music, heard only by herself. Her hands were encumbered with various articles which she seemed to intend to carry with her. In one arm she held her parasol and a large roll of tapestry, and in the other a shawl and a heavy white umbrella, such as painters use for sketching. Meanwhile she was trying to thrust into her pocket a paper-covered volume which Longmore saw to be the 'Poems of André Chénier;' but in the effort she dropped the large umbrella, and uttered a half-smiling exclamation of disgust. Longmore stepped forward with a bow and picked up the umbrella, and as she, protesting her gratitude, put out her hand to take it, it seemed to him that she was unbecomingly overburdened.

'You have too much to carry,' he said; 'you must let me help you.'

'You're very good, monsieur,' she answered. 'My husband always forgets something. He can do nothing without his umbrella. He is *d'une étourderie*——.'

'You must allow me to carry the umbrella,' Longmore said. 'It's too heavy for a lady.'

She assented, after many compliments to his politeness; and he walked by her side into the meadow. She went lightly and rapidly, picking her steps and glancing forward to catch a glimpse of her husband. She was graceful, she was charming, she had an air of decision and yet of sweetness, and it seemed to Longmore that a young artist would work none the worse for having her seated at his side, reading Chénier's iambics. They were newly married, he supposed, and evidently their path of life had none of the mocking crookedness of some others. They asked little; but what need one ask more than such quiet summer days, with the creature one loves, by a shady stream, with art and books and a wide, unshadowed horizon? To spend such a morning, to stroll back to dinner in the red-tiled parlour of the inn, to ramble away again as the sun got low—all this was a vision of bliss which floated before him, only to torture him with a sense of the impossible. All Frenchwomen are not coquettes, he remarked, as he kept pace with his companion. She uttered a word now and then, for politeness' sake, but she never looked at him, and seemed not in the least to care that he was a well-favoured young man. She cared for nothing but the young artist in the shabby coat and the slouched hat, and for discovering where he had set up his easel.

This was soon done. He was encamped under the trees, close to the stream, and, in the diffused green shade of the little wood, seemed to be in no immediate need of his umbrella. He received a vivacious rebuke, however, for forgetting it, and was informed of what he owed to Longmore's complaisance. He was duly grateful; he thanked our hero warmly, and offered him a seat on the grass. But Longmore felt like a marplot, and lingered only long enough to glance at the young man's sketch, and to see it was a very clever rendering of the silvery stream and the vivid green rushes. The young wife had spread her shawl on the grass at the base of a tree, and meant to seat herself when Longmore had gone, and murmur Chénier's verses to the music of the gurgling stream. Longmore looked awhile from one to the other, barely stifled a sigh, bade them good morning, and took his departure.

He knew neither where to go nor what to do; he seemed afloat on the sea of ineffectual longing. He strolled slowly back to the inn, and in the doorway met the landlady coming back from the butcher's with the lamb chops for the dinner of her lodgers.

'Monsieur has made the acquaintance of the *dame* of our young painter,' she said with a broad smile—a smile too broad for malicious meanings. 'Monsieur has perhaps seen the young man's picture. It appears that he has a great deal of talent.'

'His picture was very pretty,' said Longmore, 'but his *dame* was prettier still.'

'She's a very nice little woman; but I pity her all the more.'

'I don't see why she's to be pitied,' said Longmore; 'they seem a very happy couple.'

The landlady gave a knowing nod. 'Don't trust to it, monsieur! Those artists—*ça n'a pas de principes*! From one day to another he can plant her there! I know them, *allez*. I've had them here very often; one year with one, another year with another.'

Longmore was puzzled for a moment. Then, 'You mean she's not his wife?' he asked.

She shrugged her shoulders. 'What shall I tell you? They are not *des hommes sérieux*, those gentlemen! They don't engage themselves for an eternity. It's none of my business, and I've no wish to speak ill of madame. She's a very nice little woman, and she loves her *jeune homme* to distraction.'

'Who is she?' asked Longmore. 'What do you know about her?'

'Nothing for certain; but it's my belief that she's better than he. I've even gone so far as to believe that she's a lady—a true lady— and that she has given up a great many things for him. I do the best I can for them, but I don't believe she's been obliged all her life to content herself with a dinner of two courses.' And she turned over her lamb chops tenderly, as if to say that though a good cook could imagine better things, yet if you could have but one course, lamb chops had much in their favour. 'I shall cook them with bread crumbs. *Voilà les femmes, monsieur!*'

Longmore turned away with the feeling that women were indeed a measureless mystery, and that it was hard to say whether there was greater beauty in their strength or in their weakness. He walked back to Saint-Germain, more slowly than he had come, with less philosophic resignation to *any* event, and more of the urgent egotism of the passion which philosophers call the supremely selfish one. Every now and then the episode of the happy young painter, and the charming woman who had given up a great many things for him, rose vividly in his mind, and seemed to mock his moral unrest like some obtrusive vision of unattainable bliss.

The landlady's gossip cast no shadow on its brightness; her voice seemed that of the vulgar chorus of the uninitiated, which stands always ready with its gross prose rendering of the inspired passages in human action. Was it possible a man could take *that* from a woman—take all that lent lightness to that other woman's footstep and intensity to her glance—and not give her the absolute certainty of a devotion as unalterable as God's sunlight? Was it possible that such a rapturous union had the seeds of trouble—that the charm of such a perfect accord could be broken by anything but death? Longmore felt an immense desire to cry out a thousand times 'No!' for it seemed to him at last that he was somehow spiritually the same as the young painter, and that the latter's companion had the soul of Mme. de Mauves.

The heat of the sun, as he walked along, became oppressive, and when he re-entered the forest he turned aside into the deepest shade he could find, and stretched himself on the mossy ground at the foot of a great beech. He lay for awhile staring up into the verdurous dusk overhead, and trying to conceive Mme. de Mauves hastening towards some quiet stream-side where he waited, as he had seen that trusting creature do an hour before. It would be hard to say how well he succeeded; but the effort soothed him rather than excited him, and as he had had a good deal both of moral and physical fatigue, he sank at last into a quiet sleep.

While he slept he had a strange, vivid dream. He seemed to be in a wood, very much like the one on which his eyes had lately closed; but the wood was divided by the murmuring stream he had left an hour before. He was walking up and down, he thought, restlessly and in intense expectation of some momentous event. Suddenly, at a distance, through the trees, he saw the gleam of a woman's dress, and hurried forward to meet her. As he advanced he recognized her, but he saw at the same time that she was on the opposite bank of the river. She seemed at first not to notice him, but when they were opposite each other she stopped and looked at him very gravely and pityingly. She made him no motion that he should cross the stream, but he wished greatly to stand by her side. He knew the water was deep, and it seemed to him that he knew that he should have to plunge, and that he feared that when he rose to the surface she would have disappeared. Nevertheless he was going to plunge, when a boat turned into the current from above and came swiftly towards them, guided by an oarsman, who was sitting so that they could not see his face. He brought the boat to the bank where Longmore stood; the latter stepped in, and with a few strokes they touched the opposite shore. Longmore got out, and, though he was sure he had crossed the stream, Mme. de Mauves was not there. He turned with a kind of agony and saw that now she was on the other bank—the one he had left. She gave him a grave, silent glance, and walked away up the stream. The boat and the boatman resumed their course, but after going a short distance they stopped, and the boatman turned back and looked at the still divided couple. Then Longmore recognized him—just as he had recognized him a few days before at the café in the Bois de Boulogne.

VIII.

He must have slept some time after he ceased dreaming, for he had no immediate memory of his dream. It came back to him later, after he had roused himself and had walked nearly home. No great ingenuity was needed to make it seem a rather striking allegory, and it haunted and oppressed him for the rest of the day. He took refuge, however, in his quickened conviction that the only sound policy in life is to grasp unsparingly at happiness; and it seemed no more than one of the vigorous measures dictated by such a policy, to return that evening to Mme. de Mauves. And yet when he had decided to do so, and had carefully dressed himself, he felt an irresistible nervous tremor which made it easier to linger at his open window, wondering, with a strange mixture of dread and desire, whether Mme. Clarin had told her sister-in-law what she had told him. . . . His presence now might be simply a gratuitous cause of suffering; and yet his absence might seem to imply that it was in the power of circumstances to make them ashamed to meet each other's eyes. He sat a long time with his head in his hands, lost in a painful confusion of hopes and questionings. He felt at moments as if he could throttle Mme. Clairin, and yet he could not help asking himself whether it was not possible that she might have done him a service. It was late when he left the hotel, and as he entered the gate of the other house his heart was beating so that he was sure his voice would show it.

The servant ushered him into the drawing-room, which was empty, with the lamp burning low. But the long windows were open, and their light curtains swaying in a soft, warm wind, and Longmore stepped out upon the terrace. There he found Mme. de Mauves alone, slowly pacing up and down. She was dressed in white, very simply, and her hair was arranged, not as she usually wore it, but in a single loose coil, like that of a person unprepared for company.

She stopped when she saw Longmore, seemed slightly startled, uttered an exclamation, and stood waiting for him to speak. He looked at her, tried to say something, but found no words. He knew it was awkward, it was offensive, to stand silent, gazing; but he could not say what was suitable, and he dared not say what he wished.

Her face was indistinct in the dim light, but he could see that her eyes were fixed on him, and he wondered what they expressed. Did they warn him, did they plead or did they confess to a sense of provocation? For an instant his head swam; he felt as if it would make all things clear to stride forward and fold her in his arms. But a moment later he was still standing looking at her; he had not moved; he knew that she had spoken, but he had not understood her.

'You were here this morning,' she continued, and now, slowly, the meaning of her words came to him. 'I had a bad headache and had to shut myself up.' She spoke in her usual voice.

Longmore mastered his agitation and answered her without betraying himself: 'I hope you are better now.'

'Yes, thank you, I'm better—much better.'

He was silent a moment, and she moved away to a chair and seated herself. After a pause he followed her and stood before her, leaning against the balustrade of the terrace. 'I hoped you might have been able to come out for the morning into the forest. I went alone; it was a lovely day, and I took a long walk.'

'It was a lovely day,' she said absently, and sat with her eyes lowered, slowly opening and closing her fan. Longmore, as he watched her, felt more and more sure that her sister-in-law had seen her since her interview with him; that her attitude towards him was changed. It was this same something that chilled the ardour with which he had come, or at least converted the dozen passionate speeches which kept rising to his lips into a kind of reverential silence. No, certainly, he couldn't clasp her to his arms now, any more than some early worshipper could have clasped the marble statue in his temple. But Longmore's statue spoke at last, with a full human voice, and even with a shade of human hesitation.

She looked up, and it seemed to him that her eyes shone through the dusk.

'I'm very glad you came this evening,' she said. 'I have a particular reason for being glad. I half expected you, and yet I thought it possible you might not come.'

'As I have been feeling all day,' Longmore answered, 'it was impossible I shouldn't come. I have spent the day in thinking of you.'

She made no immediate reply, but continued to open and close her fan thoughtfully. At last—'I have something to say to you,' she said abruptly. 'I want you to know to a certainty that I have a very high opinion of you.' Longmore started and shifted his position. To what was she coming? But he said nothing, and she went on.

'I take a great interest in you; there's no reason why I shouldn't say it—I have a great friendship for you.'

He began to laugh; he hardly knew why, unless that this seemed the very mockery of coldness. But she continued without heeding him.

'You know, I suppose, that a great disappointment always implies a great confidence—a great hope?'

'I have hoped,' he said, 'hoped strongly, but doubtless never rationally enough to have a right to bemoan my disappointment.'

'You do yourself injustice. I have such confidence in your reason, that I should be greatly disappointed if I were to find it wanting.'

'I really almost believe that you are amusing yourself at my expense,' cried Longmore. 'My reason? Reason is a mere word. The only reality in the world is *feeling*!'

She rose to her feet and looked at him gravely. His eyes by this time were accustomed to the imperfect light, and he could see that her look was reproachful, and yet that it was beseechingly kind. She shook her head impatiently, and laid her fan upon his arm with a strong pressure.

'If that were so, it would be a weary world. I know your feeling, however, nearly enough. You needn't try to express it. It's enough that it gives me the right to ask a favour of you—to make an urgent, a solemn request.'

'Make it; I listen.'

'*Don't disappoint me.* If you *don't* understand me now, you will tomorrow, or very soon. When I said just now that I had a very high opinion of you, I meant it very seriously. It was not a vain compliment. I believe that there is no appeal one may make to your generosity which can remain long unanswered. If this were to happen—if I were to find you selfish where I thought you generous, narrow where I thought you large'—and she spoke slowly, with her voice lingering with emphasis on each of these words—'vulgar where I thought you rare—I should think worse of human nature. I should suffer—I should suffer keenly. I should say to myself in the dull days of the future, "There was one man who might have done so and so; and he, too, failed." But this shall not be. You have made too good an impression on me not to make the very best. If you wish to please me for ever, there's a way.'

She was standing close to him, with her dress touching him, her eyes fixed on his. As she went on her manner grew strangely intense, and she had the singular appearance of a woman preaching reason with a kind of passion. Longmore was confused, dazzled, almost bewildered. The intention of her words was all remonstrance, refusal, dismissal; but her presence there, so close, so urgent, so personal, seemed a distracting mockery of it. She had never been so lovely. In her white dress, with her pale face and deeply lighted eyes, she seemed the very spirit of the summer night. When she had ceased speaking, she drew a long breath; Longmore felt it on his cheek, and it stirred in his whole being a sudden, rapturous conjecture. Were her words, in their soft severity, a mere delusive spell, meant to throw into relief her almost ghostly beauty, and was this the only truth, the only reality, the only law?

He closed his eyes and felt that she was watching him, not without pain and perplexity herself. He looked at her again, met her own eyes, and saw a tear in each of them. Then this last suggestion of his desire seemed to die away with a stifled murmur, and her beauty, more and more radiant in the darkness, rose before him as a symbol of something vague which was yet more beautiful than itself.

'I may understand you tomorrow,' he said, 'but I don't understand you now.'

'And yet I took counsel with myself today and asked myself how I had best speak to you. On one side, I might have refused to see you at all.' Longmore made a violent movement, and she added: 'In that case I should have written to you. I might see you, I thought, and simply say to you that there were excellent reasons why we should part, and that I begged this visit should be your last. This I inclined to do; what made me decide otherwise was—simply friendship! I said to myself that I should be glad to remember in future days—not that I had dismissed you, but that you had gone away out of the fullness of your own wisdom.'

'The fullness—the fullness,' cried Longmore.

'I'm prepared, if necessary,' Mme. de Mauves continued after a pause, 'to fall back upon my strict right. But, as I said before, I shall be greatly disappointed, if I am obliged to.'

'When I hear you say that,' Longmore answered, 'I feel so angry, so horribly irritated, that I wonder it is not easy to leave you without more words.'

'If you should go away in anger, this idea of mine about our parting would be but half realized. No, I don't want to think of you as angry; I don't want even to think of you as making a serious sacrifice. I want to think of you as——'

'You want to think of me as a creature who never has existed—who never can exist! A creature who knew you without loving you—who left you without regretting you!'

She turned impatiently away and walked to the other end of the terrace. When she came back, he saw that her impatience had become a cold sternness. She stood before him again, looking at him from head to foot, in deep reproachfulness, almost in scorn. Beneath her glance he felt a kind of shame. He coloured; she observed it, and withheld something she was about to say. She turned away again, walked to the other end of the terrace, and stood there looking away into the garden. It seemed to him that she had guessed he understood her, and slowly—slowly—half as the fruit of his vague self-reproach—he did understand her. She was giving him a chance to do gallantly what it seemed unworthy of both of them he should do meanly.

She liked him, she must have liked him greatly, to wish so to spare him, to go to the trouble of conceiving an ideal of conduct for him. With this sense of her friendship—her strong friendship she had just called it—Longmore's soul rose with a new flight, and suddenly felt itself breathing a clearer air. The words ceased to seem a mere bribe to his ardour; they were charged with warmth themselves; they were a present happiness. He moved rapidly towards her with a feeling that this was something he might immediately enjoy.

They were separated by two-thirds of the length of the terrace, and he had to pass the drawing-room window. As he did so he started with an exclamation. Mme. Clairin stood posted there, watching him. Conscious, apparently, that she might be suspected of eaves-dropping, she stepped forward with a smile and looked from Longmore to his hostess.

'Such a *tête-à-tête* as that,' she said, 'one owes no apology for interrupting. One ought to come in for good manners.'

Mme. de Mauves turned round, but she answered nothing. She looked straight at Longmore, and her eyes had extraordinary eloquence. He was not exactly sure, indeed, what she meant them to say; but they seemed to say plainly something of this kind: 'Call it what you will, what you have to urge upon me is the thing which this

woman can best conceive. What I ask of you is something she can't.'
They seemed, somehow, to beg him to suffer her to be herself, and to
intimate that that self was as little as possible like Mme. Clairin. He
felt an immense answering desire not to do anything which would
seem natural to this lady. He had laid his hat and cane on the parapet of the terrace. He took them up, offered his hand to Mme. de
Mauves with a simple good night, bowed silently to Mme. Clairin,
and departed.

IX.

He went home, and without lighting his candle flung himself on
his bed. But he got no sleep till morning; he lay hour after hour
tossing, thinking, wondering; his mind had never been so active. It
seemed to him that Euphemia had laid on him in those last moments a kind of inspiring charge, and that she had expressed herself
almost as largely as if she had listened assentingly to an assurance of
his love. It was neither easy nor delightful perfectly to understand
her; but little by little her perfect meaning sank into his mind and
soothed it with a sense of opportunity, which somehow stifled his
sense of loss. For, to begin with, she meant that she could love him in
no degree or contingency, in no imaginable future. This was absolute;
he felt that he could alter it no more than he could veil with a wish
the starry sky he lay gazing at through his open window. He wondered what it was, in the background of her life, that she grasped so
closely: a sense of duty, unquenchable to the end? a love that no
offence could trample out? 'Good heavens!' he thought, 'is the
world so rich in the purest pearls of passion that such tenderness
as that can be wasted for ever—poured away without a sigh into
bottomless darkness?' Had she, in spite of the loathsome present,
some precious memory which masked a shrinking hope? Was she
prepared to submit to everything and yet to believe? Was it strength,
was in weakness, was it a vulgar fear, was it conviction, conscience,
constancy?
Longmore sank back with a sigh and an oppressive feeling that
it was vain to guess at such a woman's motives. He only felt that
those of Mme. de Mauves were buried deep in her soul, and that they
must be of some fine temper, not of a base one. He had a dim, overwhelming sense of a sort of invulnerable constancy being the supreme
law of her character—a constancy which still found a foothold
among crumbling ruins. 'She has loved once,' he said to himself as
he rose and wandered to his window; 'that's for ever. Yes, yes—if she

loved again she would be *common.*' He stood for a long time looking out into the starlit silence of the town and the forest, and thinking of what life would have been if *his* constancy had met her un-
pledged. But life was this, now, and he must live. It was living keenly
to stand there with a petition from such a woman to resolve. He
was not to disappoint her, he was to justify a conception which it
had beguiled her weariness to shape. Longmore's imagination
swelled; he threw back his head and seemed to be looking for Mme.
de Mauves's conception among the blinking mocking stars. But it
came to him rather on the mild night wind, as it wandered in over
the housetops, which covered the rest of so many heavy human
hearts. What she asked he felt that she was asking not for her own
sake (she feared nothing, she needed nothing), but for that of his
own happiness and his own character. He must assent to destiny.
Why else was he young and strong, intelligent and resolute? He must
not give it to her to reproach him with thinking that she had a moment's attention for his love—to plead, to argue, to break off in bitterness; he must see everything from above, her indifference and his
own ardour; he must prove his strength, he must do the handsome
thing; he must decide that the handsome thing was to submit to the
inevitable, to be supremely delicate, to spare her all pain, to stifle
his passion, to ask no compensation, to depart without delay and try
to believe that wisdom is its own reward. All this, neither more nor
less, it was a matter of friendship with Mme. de Mauves to expect of
him. And what should he gain by it? He should have pleased her!
. . . He flung himself on his bed again, fell asleep at last, and slept till
morning.

Before noon the next day he had made up his mind that he would
leave Saint-Germain at once. It seemed easier to leave without seeing
her, and yet if he might ask a grain of 'compensation', it would be
five minutes face to face with her. He passed a restless day. Wherever
he went he seemed to see her standing before him in the dusky halo
of evening, and looking at him with an air of still negation more
intoxicating than the most passionate self-surrender. He must certainly go, and yet it was hideously hard. He compromised and went
to Paris to spend the rest of the day. He strolled along the boulevards and looked at the shops, sat awhile in the Tuileries gardens
and looked at the shabby unfortunates for whom this only was
nature and summer; but simply felt, as a result of it all, that it was a
very dusty, dreary, lonely world into which Mme. de Mauves was
turning him away.

In a sombre mood he made his way back to the boulevards and sat
down at a table on the great plain of hot asphalt, before a café. Night

came on, the lamps were lighted, the tables near him found occupants, and Paris began to wear that peculiar evening look of hers which seems to say, in the flare of windows and theatre doors, and the muffled rumble of swift-rolling carriages, that this is no world for you unless you have your pockets lined and your scruples drugged. Longmore, however, had neither scruples nor desires; he looked at the swarming city for the first time with an easy sense of repaying its indifference. Before long a carriage drove up to the pavement directly in front of him, and remained standing for several minutes without its occupant getting out. It was one of those neat, plain coupés, drawn by a single powerful horse, in which one is apt to imagine a pale, handsome woman, buried among silk cushions, and yawning as she sees the gas lamps glittering in the gutters. At last the door opened and out stepped M. de Mauves. He stopped and leaned on the window for some time, talking in an excited manner to a person within. At last he gave a nod and the carriage rolled away. He stood swinging his cane and looking up and down the boulevard, with the air of a man fumbling, as one may say, with the loose change of time. He turned towards the café and was apparently, for want of anything better worth his attention, about to seat himself at one of the tables, when he perceived Longmore. He wavered an instant, and then, without a change in his nonchalant gait, strolled towards him with a bow and a vague smile.

It was the first time they had met since their encounter in the forest after Longmore's false start for Brussels. Mme. Clairin's revelations, as we may call them, had not made the Baron especially present to his mind; he had another office for his emotions than disgust. But as M. de Mauves came towards him he felt deep in his heart that he hated him. He noticed, however, for the first time, a shadow upon the Baron's cool placidity, and his delight at finding that somewhere at last the shoe pinched *him*, mingled with his impulse to be as provokingly impenetrable as possible, enabled him to return the other's greeting with all his own self-possession.

M. de Mauves sat down, and the two men looked at each other across the table, exchanging formal greetings, which did little to make their mutual scrutiny seem gracious. Longmore had no reason to suppose that the Baron knew of his sister's revelations. He was sure that M. de Mauves cared very little about his opinions, and yet he had a sense that there was that in his eyes which would have made the Baron change colour if keener suspicion had helped him to read it. M. de Mauves did not change colour, but he looked at Longmore with a half-defiant intentness, which betrayed at once an irritating memory of the episode in the Bois de Boulogne, and such vigilant curiosity as was natural to a gentleman who had entrusted his 'honour' to another gentleman's magnanimity—or to his artlessness. It would appear that Longmore seemed to the Baron to possess these virtues in rather scantier measure than a few days before; for the cloud deepened on his face, and he turned away and frowned as he lighted a cigar.

The person in the coupé, Longmore thought, whether or no the same person as the heroine of the episode of the Bois de Boulogne, was not a source of unalloyed delight. Longmore had dark blue eyes, of admirable lucidity—truth-telling eyes which had in his childhood always made his harshest taskmasters smile at his nursery fibs. An observer watching the two men, and knowing something of their relations, would certainly have said that what he saw in those eyes must not a little have puzzled and tormented M. de Mauves. They judged him, they mocked him, they eluded him, they threatened him, they triumphed over him, they treated him as no pair of eyes had ever treated him. The Baron's scheme had been to make no one happy but himself, and here was Longmore already, if looks were to be trusted, primed for an enterprise more inspiring than the finest of his own achievements. Was this candid young provincial but a *faux bonhomme* after all? He had puzzled the Baron before, and this was once too often.

M. de Mauves hated to seem preoccupied, and he took up the evening paper to help himself to look indifferent. As he glanced over it he uttered some cold commonplace on the political situation, which gave Longmore an easy opportunity of replying by an ironical sally, which made him seem for the moment provokingly at his ease. And yet our hero was far from being master of the situation. The Baron's ill humour did him good, as far as it pointed to a want of harmony with the lady in the coupé, but it disturbed him sorely as he began to suspect that it possibly meant jealousy of himself. It passed through his mind that jealousy is a passion with a double face, and that in some of its moods it bears a plausible likeness to affection. It recurred to him painfully that the Baron might grow ashamed of his proposed 'arrangement' with his wife, and he felt that it would be far more tolerable in the future to think of his continued turpitude than of his repentance. The two men sat for half an hour exchanging meagre small talk, the Baron feeling a nervous need of playing the spy, and Longmore indulging a merciless relish of his discomfort. The frigid interview was broken however by the arrival of a friend of M. de Mauves—a tall, pale, consumptive-looking dandy, who filled the air with the odour of heliotrope. He looked up and down the boulevard wearily, examined the Baron's toilet from head to foot, then surveyed his own in the same fashion, and at last announced languidly that the Duchess was in town! M. de Mauves must come with him to call; she had abused him dreadfully a couple of evenings before—a sure sign she wanted to see him.

'I depend upon you,' said M. de Mauves's friend with an infantine drawl, 'to put her *en train.*'

M. de Mauves resisted, and protested that he was *d'une humeur massacrante*; but at last he allowed himself to be drawn to his feet, and stood looking irresolutely—awkwardly for M. de Mauves—at Longmore. 'You'll excuse me,' he said dryly; 'you, too, probably, have occupation for the evening?'

'None but to catch my train,' Longmore answered, looking at his watch.

'Ah, you go back to Saint-Germain?'

'In half an hour.'

M. de Mauves seemed on the point of disengaging himself from his companion's arm, which was locked in his own; but on the latter uttering some persuasive murmur, he lifted his hat formally and turned away.

Longmore packed his trunk the next day with dogged heroism and wandered off to the terrace, to try and beguile the restlessness with which he waited for evening; for he wished to see Mme. de Mauves for the last time at the hour of long shadows and pale, pink, reflected lights, as he had almost always seen her. Destiny, however, took no account of this mild plea for poetic justice; it was his fortune to meet her on the terrace sitting under a tree, alone. It was an hour when the place was almost empty; the day was warm, but as he took his place beside her a light breeze stirred the leafy edges on the broad circle of shadow in which she sat. She looked at him with candid anxiety, and he immediately told her that he should leave Saint-Germain that evening—that he must bid her good-bye. Her eye expanded and brightened for a moment as he spoke; but she said nothing and turned her glance away towards distant Paris, as it lay twinkling and flashing through its hot exhalations. 'I have a request to make of you,' he added: 'that you think of me as a man who has felt much and claimed little.'

She drew a long breath, which almost suggested pain. 'I can't think of you as unhappy. It's impossible. You've a life to lead, you've duties, talents, and interests. I shall hear of your career. And then,' she continued after a pause and with the deepest seriousness, 'one can't be unhappy through having a better opinion of a friend, instead of a worse.'

For a moment he failed to understand her. 'Do you mean that

there can be varying degrees in my opinion of you?'

She rose and pushed away her chair. 'I mean,' she said quickly, 'that it's better to have done nothing in bitterness—nothing in passion.' And she began to walk.

Longmore followed her, without answering. But he took off his hat and with his pocket-handkerchief wiped his forehead. 'Where shall you go? what shall you do?' he asked at last, abruptly.

'Do? I shall do as I've always done—except perhaps that I shall go for a while to Auvergne.'

'I shall go to America. I have done with Europe for the present.'

She glanced at him as he walked beside her after he had spoken these words, and then bent her eyes for a long time on the ground. At last, seeing that she was going far, she stopped and put out her hand. 'Good-bye,' she said; 'may you have all the happiness you deserve!'

He took her hand and looked at her, but something was passing in him that made it impossible to return her hand's light pressure. Something of infinite value was floating past him, and he had taken an oath not to raise a finger to stop it. It was borne by the strong current of the world's great life and not of his own small one. Mme. de Mauves disengaged her hand, gathered her shawl, and smiled at him almost as you would do at a child you should wish to encourage. Several moments later he was still standing watching her receding figure. When it had disappeared, he shook himself, walked rapidly back to his hotel, and without waiting for the evening train paid his bill and departed.

Later in the day M. de Mauves came into his wife's drawing-room, where she sat waiting to be summoned to dinner. He was dressed with a scrupulous freshness which seemed to indicate an intention of dining out. He walked up and down for some moments in silence, then rang the bell for a servant, and went out into the hall to meet him. He ordered the carriage to take him to the station, paused a moment with his hand on the knob of the door, dismissed the servant angrily as the latter lingered observing him, re-entered the drawing-room, resumed his restless walk, and at last stopped abruptly before his wife, who had taken up a book. 'May I ask the favour,' he said with evident effort, in spite of a forced smile of easy courtesty, 'of having a question answered?'

'It's a favour I never refused,' Mme. de Mauves replied.

'Very true. Do you expect this evening a visit from Mr. Longmore?'

'Mr. Longmore,' said his wife, 'has left Saint-Germain.' M. de

Mauves started and his smile expired. 'Mr. Longmore,' his wife continued, 'has gone to America.'

M. de Mauves stared a moment, flushed deeply, and turned away. Then recovering himself—'Had anything happened?' he asked. 'Had he a sudden call?'

But his question received no answer. At the same moment the servant threw open the door and announced dinner; Mme. Clairin rustled in, rubbing her white hands, Mme. de Mauves passed silently into the dining-room, and he stood frowning and wondering. Before long he went out upon the terrace and continued his uneasy walk. At the end of a quarter of an hour the servant came to inform him that the carriage was at the door. 'Send it away,' he said curtly. 'I shall not use it.' When the ladies had half finished dinner he went in and joined them, with a formal apology to his wife for his tardiness.

The dishes were brought back, but he hardly tasted them; on the other hand, he drank a great deal of wine. There was little talk; what there was was supplied by Mme. Clairin. Twice she saw her brother's eyes fixed on her own, over his wine-glass, with a piercing, questioning glance. She replied by an elevation of the eyebrows, which did the office of a shrug of the shoulders. M. de Mauves was left alone to finish his wine; he sat over it for more than an hour, and let the darkness gather about him. At last the servant came in with a letter and lighted a candle. The letter was a telegram, which M. de Mauves, when he had read it, burnt at the candle. After five minutes' meditation, he wrote a message on the back of a visiting-card and gave it to the servant to carry to the office. The man knew quite as much as his master suspected about the lady to whom the message was addressed; but its contents puzzled him; they consisted of the single word '*Impossible*'. As the evening passed without her brother reappearing in the drawing-room, Mme. Clairin came to him where he sat, by his solitary candle. He took no notice of her presence for some time; but he was the one person to whom she allowed this license. At last, speaking in a peremptory tone, 'The American has gone home at an hour's notice,' he said. 'What does it mean?'

Mme. Clairin now gave free play to the shrug she had been obliged to suppress at the table. 'It means that I have a sister-in-law whom I haven't the honour to understand.'

He said nothing more, and silently allowed her to depart, as if it had been her duty to provide him with an explanation and he was disgusted with her levity. When she had gone, he went into the garden and walked up and down, smoking. He saw his wife sitting alone on the terrace, but remained below strolling along the narrow paths. He remained a long time. It became late and Mme. de Mauves disappeared. Towards midnight he dropped upon a bench tired, with a kind of angry sigh. It was sinking into his mind that he, too, did not understand Mme. Clairin's sister-in-law.

Longmore was obliged to wait a week in London for a ship. It was very hot, and he went out for a day to Richmond. In the garden of the hotel at which he dined he met his friend Mrs. Draper, who was staying there. She made eager inquiry about Mme. de Mauves, but Longmore at first, as they sat looking out at the famous view of the Thames, parried her questions and confined himself to small talk. At last she said she was afraid he had something to conceal; whereupon, after a pause, he asked her if she remembered recommending him, in the letter she sent to him at Saint-Germain, to draw the sadness from her friend's smile. 'The last I saw of her was her smile,' said he —'when I bade her good-bye.'

'I remember urging you to "console" her,' Mrs. Draper answered, 'and I wondered afterwards whether—a model of discretion as you are—I hadn't given you rather foolish advice.'

'She has her consolation in herself,' he said; 'she needs none that any one else can offer her. That's for troubles for which—be it more, be it less—our own folly has to answer. Mme. de Mauves hasn't a grain of folly left.'

'Ah, don't say that!' murmured Mrs. Draper. 'Just a little folly is very graceful.'

Longmore rose to go, with a quick nervous movement. 'Don't talk of grace,' he said, 'till you have measured *her* reason.'

For two years after his return to America he heard nothing of Mme. de Mauves. That he thought of her intently, constantly, I need hardly say: most people wondered why such a clever young man should not 'devote' himself to something; but to himself he seemed absorbingly occupied. He never wrote to her; he believed that she preferred it. At last he heard that Mrs. Draper had come home, and he immediately called on her.

'Of course,' she said after the first greetings, 'you are dying for news of Mme. de Mauves. Prepare yourself for something strange. I heard from her two or three times during the year after your return. She left Saint-Germain and went to live in the country, on some old property of her husband's. She wrote me very kind little notes, but I felt somehow that—in spite of what you said about "consolation"—they were the notes of a very sad woman. The only advice I could have given her was to leave her wretch of a husband and come back to her own land and her own people. But this I didn't feel free to do, and yet it made me so miserable not to be able to help her that I preferred to let our correspondence die a natural death. I had no news of her for a year. Last summer, however, I met at Vichy a clever young Frenchman whom I accidentally learned to be a friend of Euphemia's lovely sister-in-law, Mme. Clairin. I lost no time in asking him what he knew about Mme. de Mauves—a countrywoman of mine and an old friend. "I congratulate you on possessing her friendship," I answered. "That's the charming little woman who killed her husband." You may imagine that I promptly asked for an explanation, and he proceeded to relate to me what he called the whole story. M. de Mauves had *fait quelques folies*, which his wife had taken absurdly to heart. He had repented and asked her forgiveness, which she had inexorably refused. She was very pretty, and severity, apparently, suited her style; for whether or no her husband had been in love with her before, he fell madly in love with her now. He was the proudest man in France, but he had begged her on his knees to be readmitted to favour. All in vain! She was stone, she was ice, she was outraged virtue. People noticed a great change in him: he gave up society, ceased to care for anything, looked shockingly. One fine day they learned that he had blown out his brains. My friend had the story of course from Mme. Clairin.'

Longmore was strongly moved, and his first impulse after he had recovered his composure was to return immediately to Europe. But several years have passed, and he still lingers at home. The truth is, that in the midst of all the ardent tenderness of his memory of Mme. de Mauves, he has become conscious of a singular feeling, for which awe would be hardly too strong a name.

Adina

IN TWO PARTS

[First appeared in the *Scribner's Monthly*, vol. viii (May–June 1874), pp. 33–43, 181–91. Not reprinted during James's lifetime.]

PART I

WE HAD BEEN TALKING OF SAM SCROPE ROUND THE FIRE—mindful, such of us, of the rule *de mortuis*. Our host, however, had said nothing; rather to my surprise, as I knew he had been particularly intimate with our friend. But when our group had dispersed, and I remained alone with him, he brightened the fire, offered me another cigar, puffed his own awhile with a retrospective air, and told me the following tale:

Eighteen years ago Scrope and I were together in Rome. It was the beginning of my acquaintance with him, and I had grown fond of him, as a mild, meditative youth often does of an active, irreverent, caustic one. He had in those days the germs of the eccentricities,—not to call them by a hard name,—which made him afterwards the most intolerable of the friends we did not absolutely break with; he was already, as they say, a crooked stick. He was cynical, perverse, conceited, obstinate, brilliantly clever. But he was young, and youth, happily, makes many of our vices innocent. Scrope had his merits, or our friendship would not have ripened. He was not an amiable man, but he was an honest one—in spite of the odd caprice I have to relate; and half my kindness for him was based in a feeling that at bottom, in spite of his vanity, he enjoyed his own irritability as little as other people. It was his fancy to pretend that he enjoyed nothing, and that what sentimental travellers call picturesqueness was a weariness to his spirit; but the world was new to him and the charm of fine things often took him by surprise and stole a march on his premature cynicism. He was an observer in spite of himself, and in his happy moods, thanks to his capital memory and ample information, an excellent critic and most profitable companion. He was a punctilious classical scholar. My boyish journal, kept in those days, is stuffed with learned allusions; they are all Scrope's. I brought to the service of my Roman experience much

more loose sentiment than rigid science. It was indeed a jocular bargain between us that in our wanderings, picturesque and archaeological, I should undertake the sentimental business—the raptures, the
reflections, the sketching, the quoting from Byron. He considered me
absurdly Byronic, and when, in the manner of tourists at that period,
I breathed poetic sighs over the subjection of Italy to the foreign
foe, he used to swear that Italy had got no more than she deserved,
that she was a land of vagabonds and declaimers, and that he had
yet to see an Italian whom he would call a man. I quoted to him
from Alfieri that the 'human plant' grew stronger in Italy than anywhere else, and he retorted that nothing grew strong there but lying
and cheating, laziness, beggary and vermin. Of course we each said
more than we believed. If we met a shepherd on the Campagna,
leaning on his crook and gazing at us darkly from under the shadow
of his matted locks, I would proclaim that he was the handsomest
fellow in the world, and demand of Scrope to stop and let me sketch
him. Scrope would confound him for a filthy scare-crow and me for
a drivelling album-poet. When I stopped in the street to stare up
at some mouldering *palazzo* with a patched petticoat hanging to
dry from the drawing-room window, and assured him that its
haunted disrepair was dearer to my soul than the neat barred front of
my Aunt Esther's model mansion in Mount Vernon street, he would
seize me by the arm and march me off, pinching me till I shook
myself free, and whelming me, my soul and my *palazzo*, in a ludicrous torrent of abuse. The truth was that the picturesque of Italy,
both in man and in nature, fretted him, depressed him, strangely.
He was consciously a harsh note in the midst of so many mellow
harmonies everything seemed to say to him—'Don't you wish you
were as easy, as loveable, as carelessly beautiful as we?' In the bottom of his heart he did wish it. To appreciate the bitterness of this
dumb disrelish of the Italian atmosphere, you must remember how
very ugly the poor fellow was. He was uglier at twenty than at forty,
for as he grew older it became the fashion to say that his crooked
features were 'distinguished'. But twenty years ago, in the infancy
of modern aesthetics, he could not have passed for even a bizarre
form of ornament. In a single word, poor Scrope looked *common*:
that was where the shoe pinched. Now you know that in Italy almost
everything has, to the outer sense, what artists call style.

In spite of our clashing theories, our frienship *did* ripen, and we
spent together many hours, deeply seasoned with the sense of youth
and freedom. The best of these, perhaps, were those we passed on
horseback, on the Campagna; you remember such hours; you remember those days of early winter, when the sun is as strong as that

of a New England June, and the bare, purple-drawn slopes and
hollows lie bathed in the yellow light of Italy. On such a day, Scrope
and I mounted our horses in the grassy terrace before St. John
Lateran, and rode away across the broad meadows over which the
Claudian Aqueduct drags its slow length—stumbling and lapsing
here and there, as it goes, beneath the burden of the centuries. We
rode a long distance—well towards Albano, and at last stopped near
a low fragment of ruin, which seemed to be all that was left of an
ancient tower. Was it indeed ancient, or was it a relic of one of the
numerous mediaeval fortresses, with which the grassy desert of the
Campagna is studded? This was one of the questions which Scrope,
as a competent classicist, liked to ponder; though when I called his
attention to the picturesque effect of the fringe of wild plants which
crowned the ruin, and detached their clear filaments in the deep blue
air, he shrugged his shoulders, and said they only helped the brick-
work to crumble. We tethered our horses to a wild fig tree hard by,
and strolled around the tower. Suddenly, on the sunny side of it,
we came upon a figure asleep on the grass. A young man lay there, all
unconscious, with his head upon a pile of weed-smothered stones.
A rusty gun was on the ground beside him, and an empty game-bag,
lying near it, told of his being an unlucky sportsman. His heavy
sleep seemed to point to a long morning's fruitless tramp. And yet
he must have been either very unskilled, or very little in earnest, for
the Campagna is alive with small game every month in the year—
or was, at least, twenty years ago. It was no more than I owed to my
reputation for Byronism to discover a careless, youthful grace in the
young fellow's attitude. One of his legs was flung over the other; one
of his arms was thrust back under his head, and the other resting
loosely on the grass; his head drooped backward, and exposed a
strong, young throat; his hat was pulled over his eyes, so that we
could see nothing but his mouth and chin. 'An American rustic
asleep is an ugly fellow,' said I, 'but this young Roman clodhopper,
as he lies snoring there, is really statuesque'; 'clodhopper' was for
argument—for our rustic Endymion, judging by his garments, was
something better than a mere peasant. He turned uneasily, as we
stood above him, and muttered something. 'It's not fair to wake
him,' I said, and passed my arm into Scrope's, to lead him away; but
he resisted, and I saw that something had struck him.

In his change of position, our picturesque friend had opened the
hand which was resting on the grass. The palm, turned upward, contained a dull-coloured oval object, of the size of a small snuff-box.
'What has he got there?' I said to Scope; but Scrope only answered
by bending over and looking at it. 'Really, we are taking great

liberties with the poor fellow,' I said. 'Let him finish his nap in peace.'
And I was on the point of walking away. But my voice had aroused
him; he lifted his hand, and, with the movement, the object I have
compared to a snuff-box caught the light, and emitted a dull flash.

'It's a gem,' said Scrope, 'recently disinterred and encrusted with
dirt.'

The young man awoke in earnest, pushed back his hat, stared at
us, and slowly sat up. He rubbed his eyes, to see if he were not still
dreaming, then glanced at the gem, if gem it was, thrust his hand
mechanically into his pocket, and gave us a broad smile. 'Gentle,
serene Italian nature!' I exclaimed. 'A young New England farmer,
whom we should have disturbed in this fashion, would wake up with
an oath and a kick.'

'I mean to test his gentleness,' said Scrope. 'I'm determined to see
what he has got there.' Scrope was very fond of small *bric-à-brac*, and
had ransacked every curiosity shop in Rome. It was an oddity among
his many oddities, but it agreed well enough with the rest of them.
What he looked for and relished in old prints and old china was
not, generally, beauty of form nor romantic association; it was elaborate and patient workmanship, fine engraving, skilful method.

'Good day,' I said to our young man; 'we didn't mean to interrupt
you.'

He shook himself, got up, and stood before us, looking out from
under his thick curls, and still frankly smiling. There was something
very simple,—a trifle silly,—in his smile, and I wondered whether
he was not under-witted. He was young, but he was not a mere lad.
His eyes were dark and heavy, but they gleamed with a friendly
light, and his parted lips showed the glitter of his strong, white
teeth. His complexion was of a fine, deep brown, just removed from
coarseness by that vague suffused pallor common among Italians.
He had the frame of a young Hercules; he was altogether as handsome a vagabond as you could wish for the foreground of a pastoral
landscape.

'You've not earned your rest,' said Scrope, pointing to his empty
game-bag; 'you've got no birds.'

He looked at the bag and at Scrope, and then scratched his head
and laughed. 'I don't want to kill them,' he said. 'I bring out my gun
because it's stupid to walk about pulling a straw! And then my
uncle is always grumbling at me for not doing something. When he
sees me leave the house with my gun, he thinks I may, at least, get
my dinner. He didn't know the lock's broke; even if I had powder
and shot, the old blunderbuss wouldn't go off. When I'm hungry I
go to sleep.' And he glanced, with his handsome grin, at his recent

couch. 'The birds might come and perch on my nose, and not wake me up. My uncle never thinks of asking me what I have brought home for supper. He is a holy man, and lives on black bread and beans.'

'Who is your uncle?' I inquired.

'The Padre Girolamo at Lariccia.'

He looked at our hats and whips, asked us a dozen questions about our ride, our horses, and what we paid for them, our nationality, and our way of life in Rome, and at last walked away to caress our browsing animals and scratch their noses. 'He has got something precious there,' Scrope said, as we strolled after him. 'He has evidently found it in the ground. The Campagna is full of treasures yet.' As we overtook our new acquaintance he thrust his indistinguishable prize behind him, and gave a foolish laugh, which tried my companion's patience. 'The fellow's an idiot!' he cried. 'Does he think I want to snatch the thing?'

'What is it you've got there?' I asked kindly.

'Which hand will you have?' he said, still laughing.

'The right.'

'The left,' said Scrope, as he hesitated.

He fumbled behind him a moment more, and then produced his treasure with a flourish. Scrope took it, wiped it off carefully with his handkerchief, and bent his near-sighted eyes over it. I left him to examine it. It was more interested in watching the Padre Girolamo's nephew. The latter stood looking at my friend gravely, while Scrope rubbed and scratched the little black stone, breathed upon it and held it up to the light. He frowned and scratched his head; he was evidently trying to concentrate his wits on the fine account he expected Scrope to give of it. When I glanced towards Scrope, I found he had flushed excitedly, and I immediately bent my nose over it too. It was of about the size of a small hen's-egg, of a dull brown colour, stained and encrusted by long burial, and deeply corrugated on one surface. Scrope paid no heed to my questions, but continued to scrape and polish. At last—'How did you come by this thing?' he asked dryly.

'I found it in the earth, a couple of miles from here, this morning.' And the young fellow put out his hand nervously, to take it back. Scrope resisted a moment, but thought better, and surrendered it. As an old mouser, he began instinctively to play at indifference. Our companion looked hard at the little stone, turned it over and over, then thrust it behind him again, with his simple-souled laugh.

'Here's a precious chance,' murmured Scrope.

'But in Heaven's name, what is it,' I demanded, impatiently.

'Don't ask me. I don't care to phrase the conjecture audibly—it's immense—if it's what I think it is; and here stands this giggling lout with a prior claim to it. What shall I do with him? I should like to knock him in the head and with the butt end of his blunder-buss.'

'I suppose he'll sell you the thing, if you offer him enough.'

'Enough? What does he know about enough? He doesn't know a topaz from a turnip.'

'Is it a topaz, then?'

'Hold your tongue, and don't mention names. He must sell it as a turnip. Make him tell you just where he found it.'

He told us very frankly, still smiling from ear to ear. He had observed in a solitary ilex-tree, of great age, the traces of a recent lightning-stroke. (A week of unseasonably sultry weather had, in fact some days before, culminated in a terrific thunder-storm.) The tree had been shivered and killed, and the earth turned up at its foot. The bolt, burying itself, had dug a deep, straight hole, in which one might have planted a stake. 'I don't know why,' said our friend, 'but as I stood looking at it, I thrust the muzzle of my old gun into the aperture. It descended for some distance and stopped with a strange noise, as if it were striking a metallic surface. I rammed it up and down, and heard the same noise. Then I said to myself—"Something is hidden there—*quattrini*, perhaps; let us see." I made a spade of one of the shivered ilex-boughs, dug, and scraped and scratched; and, in twenty minutes, fished up a little, rotten, iron box. It was so rotten that the lid and sides were as thin as letter-paper. When I gave them a knock, they crumbled. It was filled with other bits of iron of the same sort, which seemed to have formed the com-partments of a case, and, with the damp earth, which had oozed in through the holes and crevices. In the middle lay this stone, embedded in earth and mould. There was nothing else. I broke the box to pieces and kept the stone. *Ecco!*'

Scrope, with a shrug, repossessed himself of the mouldy treasure, and our friend, as he gave it up, declared it was a thousand years old. Julius Caesar had worn it in his crown!

'Julius Caesar wore no crown, my dear friend,' said Scrope ur-banely. 'It may be a thousand years old, and it may be ten. It may be an—agate, and it may be a flint! I don't know. But if you will sell it on the chance?——' And he tossed it three times high into the air, and caught it as it fell.

'I have my idea it's precious,' said the young man. 'Precious things are found here every day—why shouldn't I stumble on something as well as another? Why should the lightning strike just that spot, and no other? It was sent there by my patron, the blessed Saint Angelo!'

He was not such a simpleton, after all; or rather he was a puzzling mixture of simplicity and sense. 'If you really want the thing,' I said to Scrope, 'make him an offer, and have done with it.'

' "Have done with it", is easily said. How little do you suppose he will take?'

'I haven't the smallest idea of its value.'

'Its value has nothing to do with the matter. Estimate it at its value and we may as well put it back into its hole—of its probable value, he knows nothing; he need never know,' and Scrope, musing an instant, counted, and flung them down on the grass, ten silver *scudi*—the same number of dollars. Angelo,—he virtually told us his name,—watched them fall, one by one, but made no movement to pick them up. But his eyes brightened; his simplicity and his shrewdness were debating the question. The little heap of silver was most agreeable; to make a poor bargain, on the other hand, was not. He looked at Scrope with a dumb appeal to his fairness which quite touched me. It touched Scrope, too, a trifle; for, after a moment's hesitation, he flung down another *scudi*. Angelo gave a puzzled sigh, and Scrope turned short about and began to mount. In another moment we were both in the saddle. Angelo stood looking at his money. 'Are you satisfied?' said my companion, curtly.

The young fellow gave a strange smile. 'Have *you* a good conscience?' he demanded.

'Hang your impudence!' cried Scrope, very red. 'What's my conscience to you?' And he thrust in his spurs and galloped away. I waved my hand to our friend and followed more slowly. Before long I turned in the saddle and looked back. Angelo was standing as we had left him, staring after us, with his money evidently yet untouched. But, of course, he would pick it up!

I rode along with my friend in silence; I was wondering over his off-hand justice. I was youthful enough to shrink from being thought a Puritan or a casuist, but it seemed to me that I scented sophistry in Scrope's double valuation of Angelo's treasure. If it was a prize for him, it was a prize for Angelo, and ten *scudi*,—and one over,—was meager payment for a prize. It cost me some discomfort to find rigid Sam Scrope, of all men, capable of a piece of bargaining which needed to be ingeniously explained. Such as it was, he offered his explanation at last—half angrily, as if he knew his logic was rather grotesque. 'Say it out; say it, for Heaven's sake!' he cried. 'I know what you're thinking—I've played that pretty-faced simpleton a trick, eh?—and I'm no better than a swindler, evidently! Let me tell you, once for all, that I'm not ashamed of having got my prize

cheap. It was ten *scudi* or nothing! If I had offered a farthing more
I should have opened those sleepy eyes of his. It was a case to pocket
one's scruples and *act*. That silly boy was not to be trusted with the
keeping of such a prize for another half hour; the deuce knows what
might have become of it. I rescued it in the interest of art, of
science, of taste. The proper price of the thing I couldn't have
dreamed of offering; where was I to raise ten thousand dollars to buy
a bauble? Say I had offered a hundred—forthwith our picturesque
friend, thick-witted though he is, would have pricked up his ears and
held fast! He would have asked time to reflect and take advice, and
he would have hurried back to his village and to his uncle, the
shrewd old priest, Padre Girolamo. The wise-heads of the place would
have held a conclave, and decided—I don't know what; that they
must go up to Rome and see Signor Castillani, or the director of the
Papal excavations. Some knowing person would have got wind of
the affair, and whispered to the Padre Girolamo that his handsome
nephew had been guided by a miracle to a fortune, and might marry
a *contessina*. And when all was done, where should I be for my
pains? As it is, I discriminate; I look at the matter all round, and I
decide. I get my prize; the ingenious Angelo gets a month's carouse,
—he'll enjoy it,—and goes to sleep again. Pleasant dreams to him!
What does he want of money? Money would have corrupted him!
I've saved the *contessina*, too; I'm sure he would have beaten her. So,
if we're all satisfied, is it for you to look black? My mind's at ease;
I'm neither richer nor poorer. I'm not poorer, because against my
eleven *scudi* may stand the sense of having given a harmless treat
to an innocent lad; I'm not richer, because,—I hope you understand,
—I mean never to turn my stone into money. There it is that delicacy
comes in. It's a stone and nothing more; and all the income I shall
derive from it will be enjoying the way people open their eyes and
hold their breath when I make it sparkle under the lamp, and tell
them just what stone it is.'

'What stone is it, then, in the name of all that's demoralizing?'
I asked, with ardour.

Scrope broke into a gleeful chuckle, and patted me on the arm.
'*Pazienza*! Wait till we get under the lamp, some evening, and then
I'll make it sparkle and tell you. I must be sure first,' he added, with
sudden gravity.

But it was the feverish elation of his tone, and not its gravity, that
struck me. I began to hate the stone; it seemed to have corrupted
him. His ingenious account of his motives left something vaguely
unexplained—almost inexplicable. There are dusky corners in the
simplest natures; strange, moral involutions in the healthiest.

Scrope was not simple, and, in virtue of his defiant self-consciousness, he might have been called morbid; so that I came to consider his injustice in this particular case as the fruit of a vicious seed which I find it hard to name. Everything in Italy seemed mutely to reproach him with his meagre faculty of pleasing; the indefinable gracefulness of nature and man murmured for ever in his ears that he was an angular cynic. This was the real motive of his intolerance of my sympathetic rhapsodies, and it prompted him now to regale himself, once for all, with the sense of an advantage wrested, if not by fair means, then by foul, from some sentient form of irritating Italian felicity. This is a rather metaphysical account of the matter; at the time I guessed the secret, without phrasing it.

Scrope carried his stone to no appraiser, and asked no archaeological advice about it. He quietly informed himself, as if from general curiosity, as to the best methods of cleansing, polishing, and restoring antique gems, laid in a provision of delicate tools and acids, turned the key in his door, and took the measure of his prize. I asked him no questions, but I saw that he was intensely preoccupied, and was becoming daily better convinced that it was a rare one. He went about whistling and humming odd scraps of song, like a lover freshly accepted. Whenever I heard him I had a sudden vision of our friend Angelo staring blankly after us, as we rode away like a pair of ravishers in a German ballad. Scrope and I lodged in the same house, and one evening, at the end of a week, after I had gone to bed, he made his way into my room, and shook me out of my slumbers as if the house were on fire. I guessed his errand before he had told it, shuffled on my dressing-gown, and hurried to his own apartment. 'I couldn't wait till morning,' he said, 'I've just given it the last touch; there it lies in its imperial beauty!'

There it lay, indeed, under the lamp, flashing back the light from its glowing heart—a splendid golden topaz on a cushion of white velvet. He thrust a magnifying glass into my hand, and pushed me into a chair by the table. I saw the surface of the stone was worked in elaborate intaglio, but I was not prepared for the portentous character of image and legend. In the centre was a full-length naked figure, which I supposed at first to be a pagan deity. Then I saw the orb of sovereignty in one outstretched hand, the chiselled imperial sceptre in the other, and the laurel-crown on the low-browed head. All round the face of the stone, near the edges, ran a chain of carven figures—warriors, and horses, and chariots, and young men and women interlaced in elaborate confusion. Over the head of the image, within this concave frieze, stood the inscription:

DIVUS TIBERIUS CÆSAR TOTIUS ORBIS IMPERATOR.

The workmanship was extraordinarily delicate; beneath the powerful glass I held in my hand, the figures revealed the perfection and
finish of the most renowned of antique marbles. The colour of the
stone was superb, and, now that its purity had been restored, its
size seemed prodigious. It was in every way a gem among gems, a
priceless treasure.

'Don't you think it was worth while getting up to shake hands with
the Emperor Tiberius?' cried Scrope, after observing my surprise.
'Shabby Nineteenth Century Yankees, as we are, we are having our
audience. Down on your knees, barbarian, we're in a tremendous
presence! Haven't I worked all these days and nights, with my little
rags and files, to some purpose? I've annulled the centuries—I've
resuscitated a *totius orbis imperator*. Do you conceive, do you apprehend, does your heart thump against your ribs? Not as it should,
evidently. This is where Caesar wore it, dull modern—here, on his
breast, near the shoulder, framed in chiselled gold, circled about
with pearls as big as plums, clasping together the two sides of his
gold-stiffened mantle. It was the agraffe of the imperial purple.
Tremble, sir!' and he took up the splendid jewel, and held it against
my breast. 'No doubts—no objections—no reflections—or we're mortal enemies. How do I know it—where's my warrant? It simply must
be! It's too precious to have been anything else. It's the finest
intaglio in the world. It has told me its secret; it has lain whispering
classic Latin to me by the hour all this week past.'

'And has it told you how it came to be buried in its iron box?'

'It has told me everything—more than I can tell you now. Content
yourself for the present with admiring it.'

Admire it I did for a long time. Certainly, if Scrope's hypothesis
was not sound, it ought to have been, and if the Emperor Tiberius
had never worn the topaz in his mantle, he was by so much the
less imperial. But the design, the legend, the shape of the stone,
were all very cogent evidence that the gem had played a great part.
'Yes, surely,' I said, 'it's the finest of known intaglios.'

Scrope was silent a while. 'Say of unknown,' he answered at last.
'No one shall ever know it. You I hereby hold pledged to secrecy. I
shall show it to no one else—except to my mistress, if I ever have
one. I paid for the chance of its turning out something great. I
couldn't pay for the renown of possessing it. That only a princely
fortune could have purchased. To be known as the owner of the
finest intaglio in the world would make a great man of me, and
that would hardly be fair to our friend Angelo. I shall sink the

glory, and cherish my treasure for its simple artistic worth.'

'And how would you express that simple artistic worth in Roman *scudi.*'

'It's impossible. Fix upon any sum you please.'

I looked again at the golden topaz, gleaming in its velvet nest; and I felt that there could be no successful effort to conceal such a magnificent negation of obscurity. 'I recommend you,' I said at last, 'to think twice before showing it to your mistress.'

I had no idea, when I spoke, that my words were timely; for I had vaguely taken for granted that my friend was foredoomed to dispense with this graceful appendage, very much as Peter Schlemihl, in the tale, was condemned to have no shadow. Nevertheless, before a month had passed, he was in a fair way to become engaged to a charming girl. 'Juxtaposition is much,' says Clough; especially juxtaposition, he implies, in foreign countries; and in Scrope's case it had been particularly close. His cousin, Mrs. Waddington, arrived in Rome, and with her a young girl who, though really no relative, offered him all the opportunities of cousinship, added to the remoter charm of a young lady to whom he had to be introduced. Adina Waddington was her companion's stepdaughter, the elder lady having, some eight years before, married a widower with a little girl. Mr. Waddington had recently died, and the two ladies were just emerging from their deep mourning. These dusky emblems of a common grief helped them to seem united, as indeed they really were, although Mrs. Waddington was but ten years older than her stepdaughter. She was an excellent woman, without a fault that I know of, but that of thinking all the world as good as herself and keeping dinner waiting sometimes while she sketched the sunset. She was stout and fresh-coloured, she laughed and talked rather loud, and generally, in galleries and temples, caused a good many stiff British necks to turn round.

She had a mania for excursions, and at Frascati and Tivoli she inflicted her goodhumoured ponderosity on diminutive donkeys with a relish which seemed to prove that a passion for scenery, like all our passions, is capable of making the best of us pitiless. I had often heard Scrope say that he detested boisterous women, but he forgave his cousin her fine spirits, and stepped into his place as her natural escort and adviser. In the vulgar sense he was not selfish; he had a very definite theory as to the sacrifices a gentleman should make to formal courtesy; but I was nevertheless surprised at the easy terms on which the two ladies secured his services. The key to the mystery was the one which fits so many locks; he was in love with Miss Waddington. There was a sweet stillness about her which balanced the widow's exuberance. Her pretty name of Adina seemed to me to have somehow a mystic fitness to her personality. She was short and slight and blonde, and her black dress gave a sort of infantine bloom to her fairness. She wore her auburn hair twisted into a thousand fantastic braids, like a coiffure in a Renaissance drawing, and she looked out at you from grave blue eyes, in which, behind a cold shyness, there seemed to lurk a tremulous promise to be franker when she knew you better. She never consented to know me well enough to be very frank; she talked very little, and we hardly exchanged a dozen words a day; but I confess that I found a perturbing charm in those eyes. As it was all in silence, though, there was no harm.

Scrope, however, ventured to tell his love—or, at least, to hint at it eloquently enough. I was not so deeply smitten as to be jealous, and I drew a breath of relief when I guessed his secret. It made me think better of him again. The stand he had taken about poor Angelo's gem, in spite of my efforts to account for it philosophically, had given an uncomfortable twist to our friendship. I asked myself if he really had no heart; I even wondered whether there was not a screw loose in his intellect. But here was a hearty, healthy, natural passion, such as only an honest man could feel—such as no man could feel without being the better for it. I began to hope that the sunshine of his fine sentiment would melt away his aversion to giving Angelo his dues. He was charmed, soul and sense, and for a couple of months he really forgot himself, and ceased to send forth his unsweetened wit to do battle for his ugly face. His happiness rarely made him 'gush', as they say; but I could see that he was vastly contented with his prospects. More than once, when we were together, he broke into a kind of nervous, fantastic laugh, over his own thoughts; and on his refusal to part with them for the penny which one offers under those circumstances, I said to myself that this was humorous surprise at his good luck. How had *he* come to please that exquisite creature? Of course, I learned even less from the young girl about her own view of the case; but Mrs. Waddington and I, not being in love with each other, had nothing to do but to gossip about our companions whenever (which was very often) they consigned us to a *tête-à-tête*.

'She tells me nothing,' the good-humoured widow said; 'and if I'm to know the answer to a riddle, I must have it in black and white. My cousin is not what is called "attractive", but I think Adina, nevertheless, is interested in him. How do you and I know how passion may transfigure and exalt him? And who shall say beforehand what a fanciful young girl shall do with that terrible little piece of machinery she calls her heart? Adina is a strange child; she is fanciful without being capricious. For all I know, she may admire my cousin for his very ugliness and queerness. She has decided, very likely, that she wants an "intellectual" husband, and if Mr. Scrope is not handsome, nor frivolous, nor over-polite, there's a greater chance of his being wise.' Why Adina should have listened to my friend, however, was her own business. Listen to him she did, and with a sweet attentiveness which may well have flattered and charmed him.

We rarely spoke of the imperial topaz; it seemed not a subject for light allusions. It might properly make a man feel solemn to possess it; the mere memory of its lustre lay like a weight on my own conscience. I had felt, as we lost sight of our friend Angelo that, in one way or another, we should hear of him again; but the weeks passed by without his re-appearing, and my conjectures as to the sequel, on his side, of his remarkable bargain remained quite unanswered. Christmas arrived, and with it the usual ceremonies. Scrope and I took the requisite vigorous measures,—it was a matter, you know, of fists and elbows and knees,—and obtained places for the two ladies at the Midnight Mass at the Sistine Chapel. Mrs. Waddington was my especial charge, and on coming out we found we had lost sight of our companions in the crowd. We waited awhile in the Colonnade, but they were not among the passers, and we supposed that they had gone home independently, and expected us to do likewise. But on reaching Mrs. Waddington's lodging we found they had not come in. As their prolonged absence demanded an explanation, it occurred to me that they had wandered into Saint Peter's, with many others of the attendants at the Mass, and were watching the tapers twinkle in its dusky immensity. It was not perfectly regular that a young lady should be wandering about at three o'clock in the morning with a very 'unattractive' young man; but 'after all,' said Mrs. Waddington, 'she's almost his cousin.' By the time they returned she was much more. I went home, went to bed, and slept as late as the Christmas bells would allow me. On rising, I knocked at Scrope's door to wish him the compliments of the season, but on his coming to open it for me, perceived that such common-place greetings were quite below the mark. He was but half undressed, and had flung himself, on his return, on the outside of his bed. He had gone with Adina, as I supposed, into Saint Peter's, and they had found the twinkling tapers as picturesque as need be. He walked about the room for some time restlessly, and I saw that he had something to say. At last he brought it out. 'I say, I'm accepted. I'm engaged. I'm what's called a happy man.'

Of course I wished him joy on the news; and could assure him, with ardent conviction, that he had chosen well. Miss Waddington was the loveliest, the purest, the most interesting of young girls. I could see that he was grateful for my sympathy, but he disliked 'expansion', and he contented himself, as he shook hands with me, with simply saying—'Oh yes; she's the right thing.' He took two or three more turns about the room, and then suddenly stopped before his toilet-table, and pulled out a tray in his dressing-case. There lay the great intaglio; larger even than I should have dared to boast. 'That would be a pretty thing to offer one's *fiancée*,' he said, after gazing at it for some time. 'How could she wear it—how could one have it set?'

'There could be but one way,' I said; 'as a massive medallion, depending from a necklace. It certainly would light up the world more, on the bosom of a beautiful woman, than thrust away here, among your brushes and razors. But, to my sense, only a beauty of a certain type could properly wear it—a splendid, dusky beauty, with the brow of a Roman Empress, and the shoulders of an antique statue. A fair, slender girl, with blue eyes, and sweet smile, would seem, somehow, to be overweighted by it, and if I were to see it hung, for instance, round Miss Waddington's white neck, I should feel as if it were pulling her down to the ground, and giving her a mysterious pain.'

He was a trifle annoyed, I think, by this rather fine-spun objection; but he smiled as he closed the tray. 'Adina may not have the shoulders of the Venus of Milo,' he said, 'but I hope it will take more than a bauble like this to make her stoop.'

I don't always go to church on Christmas Day; but I have a life-long habit of taking a solitary walk, in all weathers, and harbouring Christian thoughts if they come. This was a Southern Christmas, without snow on the ground, or sleigh-bells in the air, or the smoke of crowded firesides rising into a cold, blue sky. The day was mild, and almost warm, the sky grey and sunless. If I was disposed towards Christmas thoughts, I confess, I sought them among Pagan memories. I strolled about the forums, and then walked along to the Coliseum. It was empty, save for a single figure, sitting on the steps at the foot of the cross in the centre—a young man, apparently, leaning forward, motionless, with his elbows on his knees, and his head buried in his hands. As he neither stirred nor observed me when I passed near him, I said to myself that, brooding there so intensely in the shadow of the sign of redemption, he might pass for an image of youthful remorse. Then, as he never moved, I wondered whether it was not a deeper passion even than repentance. Suddenly he looked up, and I recognized our friend Angelo—not immediately, but in response to a gradual movement of recognition in his own face. But seven weeks had passed since our meeting, and yet he looked three years older. It seemed to me that he had lost flesh, and gained expression. His simple-souled smile was gone; there was no trace of it in the shy mistrust of his greeting. He looked graver, manlier, and very much less rustic. He was equipped in new garments of a pretentious pattern, though they were carelessly worn, and bespattered with mud. I remember he had a flaming orange necktie, which harmonized admirably with his picturesque colouring. Evidently he was greatly altered; as much altered as if he had made a voyage round the world. I offered him my hand, and asked if he remembered me.

'*Per Dio!*' he cried. 'With good reason.' Even his voice seemed changed; it was fuller and harsher. He bore us a grudge. I wondered how his eyes had been opened. He fixed them on me with a dumb reproachfuless, which was half appealing and half ominous. He had been brooding and brooding on his meagre bargain till the sense of wrong had become a kind of smothered fear. I observed all this with poignant compassion, for it seemed to me that he had parted with something more precious even than his imperial intaglio. He had lost his boyish ignorance—that pastoral peace of mind which had suffered him to doze there so gracefully with his head among the flowers. But even in his resentment he was simple still. 'Where is the other one—your friend?' he asked.

'He's at home—he's still in Rome.'

'And the stone—what has he done with it?'

'Nothing. He has it still.'

He shook his head dolefully. 'Will he give it back to me for twenty-five *scudi*?'

'I'm afraid not. He values it.'

'I believe so. Will he let me see it?'

'That you must ask him. He shows it to no one.'

'He's afraid of being robbed, eh? That proves its value! He hasn't shown it to a jeweller—to a, what do they call them?—a lapidary?'

'To no one. You must believe me.'

'But he has cleaned it, and polished it, and discovered what it is?'

'It's very old. It's hard to say.'

'Very old! Of course it's old. There are more years in it than it brought me *scudi*. What does it look like? Is it red, blue, green, yellow?'

'Well, my friend,' I said, after a moment's hesitation, 'it's yellow.'

He gave me a searching stare; then quickly—'It's what's called a topaz,' he cried.

'Yes, it's what's called a topaz.'

'And it's sculptured—that I could see! It's an intaglio. Oh, I know the names, and I've paid enough for my learning. What's the figure? A king's head—or a Pope's, perhaps, eh? Or the portrait of some beautiful woman that you read about?'

'It is the figure of an Emperor.'

'What is his name?'

'Tiberius.'

'*Corpo di Cristo!*' his face flushed, and his eyes filled with angry tears.

'Come,' I said, 'I see you're sorry to have parted with the stone. Someone has been talking to you, and making you discontented.'

'Every one, *per Dio!* Like the finished fool I was, I couldn't keep my folly to myself. I went home with my eleven *scudi,* thinking I should never see the end of them. The first thing I did was to buy a gilt hairpin from a peddler, and give it to the Ninetta—a young girl of my village, with whom I had a friendship. She stuck it into her braids, and looked at herself in the glass, and then asked how I had suddenly got so rich! "Oh, I'm richer than you suppose," said I, and showed her my money, and told her the story of the stone. She is a very clever girl, and it would take a knowing fellow to have the last word with her. She laughed in my face, and told me I was an idiot, that the stone was surely worth five hundred *scudi*; that my *forestiere* was a pitiless rascal; that I ought to have brought it away, and shown it to my elders and betters; in fine, that I might take her word for it, I had held a fortune in my hand, and thrown it to the dogs. And, to wind up this sweet speech, she took out her hairpin, and tossed it into my face. She never wished to see me again; she had as lief marry a blind beggar at a cross-road. What was I to say? She had a sister who was waiting-maid to a fine lady in Rome,—a *marchesa,*—who had a priceless necklace made of fine old stones picked up on the Campagna. I went away hanging my head, and cursing my folly: I flung my money down in the dirt, and spat upon it! At last, to ease my spirit, I went to drink a *foglietta* at the wine-shop. There I found three or four young fellows I knew; I treated them all round; I hated my money, and wanted to get rid of it. Of course they too wanted to know how I came by my full pockets. I told them the truth. I hoped they would give me a better account of things than that vixen of a Ninetta. But they knocked their glasses on the table, and jeered at me in chorus. Any donkey, out a-grazing, if he had turned up such a treasure with his nose, would have taken it in his teeth and brought it home to his master. This was cold comfort; I drowned my rage in wine. I emptied one flask after another; for the first time in my life I got drunk. But I can't speak of that night! The next day I took what was left of my money to my uncle, and told him to give it to the poor, to buy new candlesticks for his church, or to say masses for the redemption of my blaspheming soul. He looked at it very hard, and hoped I had come by it honestly. I was in for it; I told *him* too! He listened to me in silence, looking at me over his spectacles. When I had done, he turned over the money in his hands, and then sat for three minutes with his eyes closed. Suddenly he thrust it back into my own hands. "Keep it—keep it, my son," he said, "your wits will never help you to a supper, make the most of what you've got?" Since then, do you see, I've been in a fever. I can think of nothing else but the fortune I've lost.'

'Oh, a fortune!' I said, deprecatingly. 'You exaggerate.'

'It would have been a fortune to me. A voice keeps ringing in my ear night and day, and telling me I could have got a thousand *scudi* for it.'

'I'm afraid I blushed; I turned away a moment; when I looked at the young man again, his face had kindled. 'Tiberius, eh? A Roman emperor sculptured on a big topaz—that's fortune enough for me! Your friend's a rascal—do you know that? I don't say it for you; I like your face, and I believe that, if you can, you'll help me. But your friend is an ugly little monster. I don't know why the devil I trusted him; I saw he wished me no good. Yet, if ever there was a harmless fellow, I was. *Ecco!* it's my fate. That's very well to say; I say it and say it, but it helps me no more than an empty glass helps your thirst. I'm not harmless now. If I meet your friend, and he refuses me justice, I won't answer for these two hands. You see—they're strong; I could easily strangle him! Oh, at first I shall speak him fair, but if he turns me off, and answers me with English oaths, I shall think only of my *revenge!*' And with a passionate gesture he pulled off his hat, and flung it on the ground, and stood wiping the perspiration from his forehead.

I answered him briefly but kindly enough. I told him to leave his case in my hands, go back to Lariccia and try and find some occupation which would divert him from his grievance. I confess that even as I gave this respectable advice, I but half believed in it. It was none of poor Angelo's mission to arrive at virtue through tribulation. His indolent nature, active only in immediate feeling, would have found my prescription of wholesome labour more intolerable even than his wrong. He stared gloomily and made no answer, but he saw that I had his interests at heart, and he promised me, at least, to leave Rome, and believe that I would fairly plead his cause. If I had good news for him I was to address him at Lariccia. It was thus I learned his full name,—a name, certainly, that ought to have been to its wearer a sort of talisman against trouble,—Angelo Beati.

PART II

Sam Scrope looked extremely annoyed when I began to tell him of my encounter with our friend, and I saw there was still a cantankerous something in the depths of his heart intensely hostile to fairness. It was characteristic of his peculiar temper that his happiness, as an accepted lover, had not disposed him to graceful concessions. He treated his bliss as his own private property, and was as little in the humour to diffuse its influence as he would have been to send out in charity a choice dish from an unfinished dinner. Nevertheless, I think he might have stiffly admitted that there was a grain of reason in Angelo's claim, if I had not been too indiscreetly accurate in my report of our interview. I had been impressed, indeed, with something picturesquely tragic in the poor boy's condition, and, to do perfect justice to the picture, I told him he had flung down his hat on the earth as a gauntlet of defiance and talked about his *revenge*. Scrope hereupon looked fiercely disgusted and pronounced him a theatrical jackanapes; but he authorized me to drop him a line saying that he would speak with him a couple of days later. I was surprised at Scrope's consenting to see him, but I perceived that he was making a conscientious effort to shirk none of the disagreeables of the matter. 'I won't have him stamping and shouting in the house here,' he said. 'I'll also meet him at the Coliseum.' He named his hour and I despatched to Lariccia three lines of incorrect but courteous Italian.

It was better,—far better,—that they should not have met. What passed between them Scrope requested me on his return to excuse him from repeating; suffice it that Angelo was an impudent puppy, and that he hoped never to hear of him again. Had Angelo, at last, I asked, received any compensation? 'Not a farthing!' cried Scrope, and walked out of the room. Evidently the two young men had been a source of immitigable offence to each other. Angelo had promised to speak to him fair, and I inclined to believe had done so; but the very change in his appearance, by seeming to challenge my companion's sympathy in too peremptory a fashion, had had the irritating effect of a menace. Scrope had been contemptuous, and his awkward, ungracious Italian had doubtless made him seem more so. One can't handle Italians with contempt; those who know them have learned what may be done with a moderate amount of superficial concession. Angelo had replied in wrath, and, as I afterwards learned, had demanded, as a right, the restitution of the topaz in exchange for the sum received for it. Scrope had rejoined that if he took that tone he should get nothing at all, and the injured youth had retorted with reckless and insulting threats. What had prevented them from coming to blows, I know not, no sign of flinching, certainly, on my companion's part. Face to face, he had not seemed to Angelo so easy to strangle, and that saving grain of discretion which mingles with all Italian passion had whispered to the young man to postpone his revenge. Without taking a melodramatic view of things, it seemed to me that Scrope had an evil chance in waiting for him. I had, perhaps, no definite vision of a cloaked assassin lurking under a dark archway, but I thought it perfectly possible that Angelo might make himself intolerably disagreeable. His simply telling his story up and down Rome to whomsoever would listen to him, might be a grave annoyance; though indeed Scrope had the advantage that most people might refuse to believe in the existence of a gem of which its owner was so little inclined to boast. The whole situation, at all events, made me extremely nervous. I cursed my companion one day for a hungrier Jew than Shylock, and pitied him the next as the victim of a moral hallucination. If we gave him time, he *would* come to his senses; he would repay poor Angelo with interest. Meanwhile, however, I could do nothing, for I felt that it was worse than useless to suggest to Scrope that he was in danger. He would have scorned the idea of a ranting Italian making him swerve an inch from his chosen path.

I am unable to say whether Angelo's 'imprudence' had seemed to relieve him, generally, from his vow to conceal the intaglio; a few words, at all events, from Miss Waddington, a couple of evenings later, reminded me of the original reservation he had made to the vow. Mrs. Waddington was at the piano, deciphering a new piece of music, and Scrope, who was fond of a puzzle as a puzzle, was pretending, half jocosely, to superintend and correct her. 'I've seen it,' Adina said to me, with grave, expanded eyes; 'I've seen the wonderful topaz. He says you are in the secret. He won't tell me how he came by it. Honestly, I hope.'

I tried to laugh. 'You mustn't investigate too closely the honesty of hunters for antiquities. It's hardly dishonest in their code to treat loose cameos and snuff-boxes as pickpockets treat purses.'

She looked at me in shy surprise, as if I had made a really cruel joke. 'He says that I must wear it one of these days as a medallion,' she went on. 'But I shall not. The stone is beautiful, but I should feel most uncomfortable in carrying the Emperor Tiberius so near my heart. Wasn't he one of the bad Emperors—one of the worst? It is almost a pollution to have a thing that *he* had looked at and touched coming to one in such direct descent. His image almost spoils for me the beauty of the stone and I'm very glad Mr. Scrope keeps it out of sight.' This seemed a very becoming state of mind in a blonde angel of New England origin.

The days passed by and Angelo's 'revenge' still hung fire. Scrope never met his fate at a short turning of one of the dusky Roman streets; he came in punctually every evening at eleven o'clock. I wondered whether our brooding friend had already spent the sinister force of a nature formed to be lazily contented. I hoped so, but I was wrong. We had gone to walk one afternoon,—the ladies, Scrope and I,—in the charming Villa Borghese, and, to escape from the rattle of the fashionable world and its distraction, we had wandered away to an unfrequented corner where the old mouldering wall and the slim black cypresses and the untrodden grass made, beneath the splendid Roman sky, the most harmonious of pictures. Of course there was a mossy stone hemicycle not far off, and cracked benches with griffins' feet, where one might sit and gossip and watch the lizards scamper in the sun. We had done so for some half an hour when Adina espied the first violet of the year glimmering at the root of a cypress. She made haste to rise and gather it, and then wandered further, in the hope of giving it a few companions. Scrope sat and watched her as she moved slowly away, trailing her long shadow on the grass and drooping her head from side to side in her charming quest. It was not, I know, that he felt no impulse to join her; but that he was in love, for the moment, with looking at her from where he sat. Her search carried her some distance and at last she passed out of sight behind a bend in the villa wall. Mrs. Waddington proposed in a few moments that we should overtake her, and we moved forward. We had not advanced many paces before she re-appeared, glancing over her shoulder as she came towards us with an air of suppressed perturbation. In an instant I saw she was being followed; a man was close behind her—a man in whom my second glance recognized Angelo Beati. Adina was pale; something had evidently passed between them. By the time she had met us, we were also face to face with Angelo. He was pale, as well, and, between these two pallors, Scrope had flushed crimson. I was afraid of an explosion and stepped towards Angelo to avert it. But to my surprise, he was evidently following another line. He turned the

cloudy brightness of his eyes upon each of us and poised his hand in
the air as if to say, in answer to my unspoken charge—'Leave me
alone, I know what I am about.' I exchanged a glance with Scrope,
urging him to pass on with the ladies and let me deal with the
intruder. Miss Waddington stopped; she was gazing at Angelo with
soft intentness. Her lover, to lead her away, grasped her arm almost
rudely, and as she went with him I saw her faintly flushing. Mrs.
Waddington, unsuspicious of evil, saw nothing but a very handsome young man. 'What a beautiful creature for a sketch!' I heard
her exclaim, as she followed her step-daughter.

'I'm not going to make a noise,' said Angelo, with a sombre smile;
'don't be frightened! I know what good manners are. These three
weeks now that I've been hanging about Rome, I've learned to play
the gentleman. Who is that young lady?'

'My dear young man, it's none of your business. I hope you had not
the hardihood to speak to her.'

He was silent a moment, looking after her as she retreated on her
companion's arm. 'Yes, I spoke to her—and she understood me.
Keep quiet; I said nothing she mightn't hear. But such as it was,
she understood it. She's your friend's *amica*; I know that. I've been
watching you for half an hour from behind those trees. She is wonderfully beautiful. Farewell; I wish you no harm, but tell your
friend I've not forgotten *him*. I'm only awaiting my chance; I think
it will come. I don't want to kill him; I want to give him some hurt
that he'll survive and *feel*—for ever!' He was turning away, but he
paused and watched my companions till they disappeared. At last—
'He has more than his share of good luck,' he said, with a sort of
forced coldness. 'A topaz—and a pearl! both at once! Eh, farewell!'
And he walked rapidly away, waving his hand. I let him go. I was
unsatisfied, but his unexpected sobriety left me nothing to say.

When a startling event comes to pass, we are apt to waste a good
deal of time in trying to recollect the correct signs and portents
which preceded it, and when they seem fewer than they should be,
we don't scruple to imagine them—we invent them after the fact.
Therefore it is that I don't pretend to be sure that I was particularly
struck, from this time forward, with something strange in our quiet
Adina. She had always seemed to me vaguely, innocently strange;
it was part of her charm that in the daily noiseless movement of her
life a mystic undertone seemed to murmur—'You don't half know
me!' Perhaps we three prosaic mortals were not quite worthy to
know her: yet I believe that if a practised man of the world had
whispered to me, one day, over his wine, after Miss Waddington
had rustled away from the table, that *there* was a young lady who,

sooner or later, would treat her friends to a first class surprise, I should have laid my finger on his sleeve and told him with a smile that he phrased my own thought. Was she more silent than usual, was she preoccupied, was she melancholy, was she restless? Picturesquely, she ought to have been all these things; but in fact, she was still to the unillumined eye simply a very pretty blonde maiden, who smiled more than she spoke, and accepted her lover's devotion with a charming demureness which savoured much more of humility than of condescension. It seemed to me useless to repeat to Scrope the young Italian's declaration that he had spoken to her, and poor Sam never intimated to me either that he had questioned her in suspicion of the fact, or that she had offered him any account of it. I was sure, however, that something must have passed between the young girl and her lover in the way of question and answer, and I privately wondered what the deuce Angelo had meant by saying she had understood him. What had she understood? Surely not the story of Scrope's acquisition of the gem; for granting—what was unlikely —that Angelo had had time to impart it, it was unnatural that Adina should not have frankly demanded an explanation. At last I broke the ice and asked Scrope if he supposed Miss Waddington had reason to connect the great intaglio with the picturesque young man she had met in the Villa Borghese.

My question caused him visible discomfort. 'Picturesque?' he growled. 'Did she tell you she thought him picturesque?'

'By no means. But he is! You must at least allow him that.'

'He hadn't brushed his hair for a week—if that's what you mean. But it's a charm which I doubt that Adina appreciates. But she has certainly taken,' he added in a moment, 'an unaccountable dislike to the topaz. She says the Emperor Tiberius spoils it for her. It's carrying historical antipathies rather far: I supposed nothing could spoil a fine gem for a pretty woman. It appears,' he finally said, 'that that rascal spoke to her.'

'What did he say?'

'He asked her if she was engaged to me.'

'And what did she answer?'

'Nothing.'

'I suppose she was frightened.'

'She might have been; but she says she was not. He begged her not to be; he told her he was a poor harmless fellow looking for justice. She left him, without speaking. I told her he was crazy—it's not a lie.'

'Possibly!' I rejoined. Then, as a last attempt—'You know it wouldn't be quite a lie,' I added, 'to say that *you* are not absolutely sane. You're very erratic about the topaz; obstinacy, pushed under certain circumstances beyond a certain point, bears a dangerous likeness to craziness.'

I suppose that if one could reason with a mule it would make him rather more mulish to know one called him stubborn. Scrope gave me a chilling grin. 'I deny your circumstances. If I'm mad, I claim the madman's privilege of believing myself peculiarly sane. If you wish to preach to me, you must catch me in a lucid interval.'

The breath of early spring in Rome, though magical, as you know, in its visible influence on the dark old city, is often rather trying to the foreign constitution. After a fortnight of uninterrupted sirocco, Mrs. Waddington's fine spirits confessed to depression. She was afraid, of course, that she was going to have 'the fever', and made haste to consult a physician. He reassured her, told her she simply needed change of air, and recommended a month at Albano. To Albano, accordingly, the two ladies repaired, under Scrope's escort. Mrs. Waddington kindly urged my going with them; but I was detained in Rome by the arrival of some relations of my own, for whom I was obliged to play *cicerone*. I could only promise to make an occasional visit to Albano. My uncle and his three daughters were magnificent sight-seers, and gave me plenty to do; nevertheless, at the end of a week I was able to redeem my promise. I found my friends lodging at the inn, and the two ladies doing their best to merge the sense of dirty stone floors and crumpled yellow table-cloth in ecstatic contemplation, from their windows, of the great misty sea-like level of the Campagna. The view apart, they were passing delightful days. You remember the loveliness of the place and its picturesque neighbourhood of strange old mountain towns. The country was blooming with early flowers and foliage, and my friends lived in the open air. Mrs. Waddington sketched in water colours. Adina gathered wild nosegays, and Scrope hovered contentedly between them—not without an occasional frank stricture on the elder lady's use of her pigments and Adina's combinations of narcissus and cyclamen. All seemed to me very happy and, without ill-nature, I felt almost tempted to wonder whether the most desirable gift of the gods is not a thick-and-thin conviction of one's own impeccability. Yet even a lover with a bad conscience might be cheated into a disbelief in retribution by the unbargained sweetness of such a presence in his life as Adina Waddington's.

I spent the night at Albano, but as I had pledged myself to go the next morning to a *funzione* with my fair cousins in Rome,— 'fair' is for rhetoric; but they were excellent girls,—I was obliged to rise and start at dawn. Scrope had offered to go with me part of the way, and walk back to the inn before breakfast; but I declined to accept so onerous a favour, and departed alone in the early twilight. A rickety diligence made the transit across the Campagna, and I had a five minutes' walk to the post-office, while it stood waiting for its freight. I made my way through the little garden of the inn, as this saved me some steps. At the sound of my tread on the gravel, a figure rose slowly from a bench at the foot of a crippled grim statue, and I found myself staring at Angelo Beati. I greeted him with an exclamation, which was virtually a challenge of his right to be there. He stood and looked at me fixedly, with a strangely defiant, unembarrassed smile, and at last, in answer to my repeated inquiry as to what the deuce he was about, he said he supposed he had a right to take a stroll in a neighbour's garden.

'A neighbour?' said I. 'How——?'

'Eh, *per Dio*! don't I live at Lariccia?' And he laughed in almost as simple a fashion as when we had awaked him from his dreamless sleep in the meadows.

I had had so many other demands on my attention during my friend's absence that it never occurred to me that Scrope had lodged himself in the very jaws of the enemy. But I began to believe that, after all, the enemy was very harmless. If Angelo confined his machinations to sitting about in damp gardens at malarial hours, Scrope would not be the first to suffer. I had fancied at first that his sense of injury had made a man of him; but there seemed still to hang about him a sort of a romantic ineffectiveness. His painful impulsion towards maturity had lasted but a day and he had become again an irresponsible lounger in Arcady. But he must have had an Arcadian constitution to brave the Roman dews at that rate. 'And you came here for a purpose,' I said. 'It ought to be a very good one to warrant your spending your nights out of doors in this silly fashion. If you are not careful you'll get the fever and die, and that will be the end of everything.'

He seemed grateful for my interest in his health. 'No, no, *Signorino mio*, I'll not get the fever. I've a fever here'—and he struck a blow on his breast—'that's a safeguard against the other. I've had a purpose in coming here, but you'll never guess it. Leave me alone; I shan't harm you! But now that day is beginning, I must go; I must not be seen.'

I grasped him by the arm, looked at him hard and tried to penetrate his meaning. He met my eyes frankly and gave a little contented laugh. Whatever his secret was, he was not ashamed of it; I saw with some satisfaction that it was teaching him patience. Something in his face, in the impression it gave me of his nature, reassured

me, at the same time, that it contradicted my hypothesis of a moment before. There was no evil in it and no malignity, but a deep,
insistent, natural desire which seemed to be slumbering for the
time in a mysterious prevision of success. He thought, apparently,
that his face was telling too much. He gave another little laugh,
and began to whistle softly. 'You are meant for something better,'
I said, 'than to skulk about here like a burglar. How would you like
to go to America and do some honest work?' I had an absurd momentary vision of helping him on his way, and giving him a letter
of introduction to my brother-in-law, who was in the hardware
business.

He took off his hat and passed his hand through his hair. 'You
think, then, I am meant for something good?'

'If you will! If you'll give up your idle idea of "revenge" and trust
to time to right your wrong.'

'Give it up?—Impossible!' he said, grimly. 'Ask me rather to chop
off my arm. This is the same thing. It's part of my life. I *have* trusted
to time—I've waited four long months, and yet here I stand as poor
and helpless as at the beginning. No, no, I'm not to be treated like
a dog. If he had been just, I would have done anything for him. I'm
not a bad fellow; I never had an unkind thought. Very likely I was
too simple, too stupid, too contented with being poor and shabby.
The Lord does with us as he pleases; he thought I needed a little
shaking up. I've got it, surely! But did your friend take counsel of
the Lord? No, no! He took counsel of his own selfishness, and he
thought himself clever enough to steal the sweet and never taste the
bitter. But the bitter will come; and it will be my sweet.'

'That's fine talk! Tell me in three words what it means.'

'*Aspetti*!—If you are going to Rome by the coach, as I suppose,
you should be moving. You may lose your place. I have an idea we
shall meet again.' He walked away, and in a moment I heard the
great iron gate of the garden creaking on its iron hinges.

I was puzzled, and for a moment, I had a dozen minds to stop
over with my friends. But on the one hand, I saw no definite way
in which I could preserve them from annoyance; and on the other,
I was confidently expected in Rome. Besides, might not the dusky
cloud be the sooner dissipated by letting Angelo's project,—substance or shadow, whatever it was,—play itself out? To Rome accordingly I returned; but for several days I was haunted with a suspicion that something ugly, something sad, something strange, at
any rate, was taking place at Albano. At last it became so oppressive
that I hired a light carriage and drove back again. I reached the inn
towards the close of the afternoon, and but half expected to find

my friends at home. They had in fact gone out to walk, and the
landlord had not noticed in what direction. I had nothing to do but
to stroll about the dirty little town till their return. Do you remember the Capuchin convent at the edge of the Alban lake? I
walked up to it and, seeing the door of the church still open, made
my way in. The dusk had gathered in the corners, but the altar, for
some pious reason, was glowing with an unusual number of candles.
They twinkled picturesquely in the gloom; here and there a kneeling figure defined itself vaguely; it was a pretty piece of chiaroscuro,
and I sat down to enjoy it. Presently I noticed the look of intense
devotion of a young woman sitting near me. Her hands were clasped
on her kness, her head thrown back and her eyes fixed in strange
expansion on the shining altar. We make out pictures, you know,
in the glow of the hearth at home; this young girl seemed to be reading an ecstatic vision in the light of the tapers. Her expression was
so peculiar that for some moments it disguised her face and left me
to perceive with a sudden shock that I was watching Adina Waddington. I looked round for her companions, but she was evidently
alone. It seemed to me then that I had no right to watch her covertly,
and yet I was indisposed either to disturb her or to retire and leave
her. The evening was approaching; how came it that she was un-
accompanied? I concluded that she was waiting for the others;
Scrope, perhaps, had gone in to see the sunset from the terrace of
the convent garden—a privilege denied to ladies; and Mrs. Waddington was lingering outside the church to take memoranda for a sketch.
I turned away, walked round the church and approached the young
girl on the other side. This time my nearness aroused her. She removed her eyes from the altar, looked at me, let them rest on my
face, and yet gave no sign of recognition. But at last she slowly rose
and I saw that she knew me. Was she turning Catholic and preparing to give up her heretical friends? I greeted her, but she continued to look at me with intense gravity, as if her thoughts were
urging her beyond frivolous civilities. She seemed not in the least
flurried—as I had feared she would be—at having been observed; she
was preoccupied, excited, in a deeper fashion. In suspecting that
something strange was happening at Albano, apparently I was not
far wrong—'What are you doing, my dear young lady,' I asked
brusquely, 'in this lonely church?'
    'I'm asking for light,' she said.
    'I hope you've found it!' I answered smiling.
    'I think so!' and she moved towards the door. 'I'm alone,' she
added, 'will you take me home?' She accepted my arm and we passed
out; but in front of the church she paused. 'Tell me,' she said sud-

denly, 'are you a very intimate friend of Mr. Scrope's?'

'You must ask him,' I answered, 'if he considers me so. I at least aspire to the honour.' The intensity of her manner embarrassed me, and I tried to take refuge in jocosity.

'Tell me then this: will he bear a disappointment—a keen disappointment?'

She seemed to appeal to me to say yes! But I felt that she had a project in hand, and I had no warrant to give her a license. I looked at her a moment; her solemn eyes seemed to grow and grow till they made her whole face a mute entreaty. 'No,' I said resolutely, 'decidedly not!'

She gave a heavy sigh and we walked on. She seemed buried in her thoughts; she gave no heed to my attempts at conversation, and I had to wait till we reached the inn for an explanation of her solitary visit to Capuccini. Her companions had come in, and from them, after their welcome, I learned that the three had gone out together, but that Adina had presently complained of fatigue, and obtained leave to go home. 'If I break down on the way,' she had said, 'I will go into a church to rest.' They had been surprised at not finding her at the inn, and were grateful for my having met her. Evidently, they, too, had discovered that the young girl was in a singular mood. Mrs. Waddington had a forced smile, and Scrope had no smile at all. Adina quietly sat down to her needlework, and we confessed, even tacitly, to no suspicion of her being 'nervous'. Common nervousness it certainly was not; she bent her head calmly over her embroidery, and drew her stitches with a hand innocent of the slightest tremor. At last we had dinner; it passed somewhat oppressively, and I was thankful for Scrope's proposal, afterwards, to go and smoke a cigar in the garden. Poor Scrope was unhappy; I could see that, but I hardly ventured to hope that he would tell me off-hand what was the matter with Adina. It naturally occurred to me that she had shown a disposition to retract her engagement. I gave him a dozen chances to say so, but he evidently could not trust himself to utter his fears. To give an impetus to our conversation, I reminded him of his nearness to Lariccia, and asked whether he had had a glimpse of Angelo Beati.

'Several,' he said. 'He has passed me in the village, or on the roads, some half a dozen times. He gives me an impudent stare and goes his way. He takes it out in looking daggers from his dark eyes; you see how much there is to be feared from him!'

'He doesn't quite take it out,' I presently said, 'in looking daggers. He hangs about the inn at night; he roams about the garden while you're in bed, as if he thought that he might give you bad dreams by staring at your windows.' And I described our recent interview at dawn.

Scrope stared in great surprise, then slowly flushed in rising anger. 'Curse the meddling idiot!' he cried. 'If he doesn't know where to stop, I'll show him.'

'Buy him off!' I said sturdily.

'I'll buy him a horsewhip and give it to him over his broad back!'

I put my hands in my pockets, I believe, and strolled away, whistling. Come what might, I washed my hands of mediation! But it was not irritation, for I felt a strange, half-reasoned increase of pity for my friend's want of pliancy. He stood puffing his cigar gloomily, and by way of showing him that I didn't altogether give up, I asked him at last whether it had yet been settled when he should marry. He had told me shortly before that this was still an open question, and that Miss Waddington preferred to leave it so.

He made no immediate answer, but looked at me hard, 'Why do you ask—just now?'

'Why, my dear fellow, friendly curiosity——' I began.

He tossed the end of his cigar nervously upon the ground. 'No, no; it's not friendly curiosity!' he cried. 'You've noticed something—you suspect something!'

Since he insisted, I confessed that I did. 'That beautiful girl,' I said, 'seems to me agitated and preoccupied; I wondered whether you had been having a quarrel.'

He seemed relieved at being pressed to speak.

'That beautiful girl is a puzzle. I don't know what's the matter with her; it's all very painful; she's a very strange creature. I never dreamed there was an obstacle to our happiness—to our union. She has never protested and promised; it's not her way, nor her nature; she is always humble, passive, gentle; but always extremely grateful for every sign of tenderness. Till within three or four days ago, she seemed to me more so than ever; her habitual gentleness took the form of a sort of shrinking, almost suffering, deprecation of my attentions, my *petits soins*, my lover's nonsense. It was as if they oppressed and mortified her—and she would have liked me to bear more lightly. I did not see directly that it was not the excess of my devotion, but my devotion itself—the very fact of my love and her engagement that pained her. When I did it was a blow in the face. I don't know what under heaven I've done! Women are fathomless creatures. And yet Adina is not capricious, in the common sense. Mrs. Waddington told me that it was a "girl's mood", that we must not seem to heed it—it would pass over. I've been waiting, but the situation doesn't mend; you've guessed at trouble without a hint. So these are *peines d'amour?*' he went on, after brooding a moment. 'I didn't know how fiercely I was in love!'

I don't remember with what well-meaning foolishness I was going to attempt to console him; Mrs. Waddington suddenly appeared and drew him aside. After a moment's murmured talk with her, he went rapidly into the house. She remained with me and, as she seemed greatly perplexed, and we had, moreover, often discussed our companion's situation and prospects, I immediately told her that Scrope had just been relating his present troubles. 'They are very unexpected,' she cried. 'It's thunder in a clear sky. Just now Adina laid down her work and told me solemnly that she would like to see Mr. Scrope alone; would I kindly call him? Would she kindly tell me, I inquired, what in common sense was the matter with her, and what she proposed to say to him. She looked at me a moment as if I were a child of five years old interrupting family prayers; then came up gently and kissed me, and said I would know everything in good time. Does she mean to stand there in that same ghostly fashion and tell him that, on the whole, she has decided not to marry him? What has the poor man done?'

'She has ceased to love him,' I suggested.

'Why ceased, all of a sudden?'

'Perhaps it's not so sudden as you suppose. Such things have happened, in young women's hearts, as a gradual revision of a first impression.'

'Yes, but not without a particular motive—another fancy. Adina is fanciful, that I know; with all respect be it said, it was fanciful to accept poor Sam to begin with. But her choice deliberately made, what has put her out of humour with it?—in a word the only possible explanation would be that our young lady has transferred her affections. But it's impossible!'

'Absolutely so?' I asked.

'Absolutely. Judge for yourself. To whom, pray? She hasn't seen another man in a month. Who could have so mysteriously charmed her? The little hunchback who brings us mandarin oranges every morning? Perhaps she has lost her heart to Prince Doria! I believe he has been staying at his villa yonder.'

I found no smile for this mild sarcasm. I was wondering—wondering. 'Has she literally seen no one else?' I asked when my wonderings left me breath.

'I can't answer for whom she may have *seen*; she's not blind. But she has spoken to no one else, nor been spoken to; that's very certain. Love at sight—at sight only—used to be common in the novels I devoured when I was fifteen; but I doubt whether it exists anywhere else.'

I had a question on my tongue's end, but I hesitated some time to risk it. I debated some time in silence and at last I uttered it, with a prefatory apology. 'On which side of the house is Adina's room?'

'Pray, what are you coming to?' said my companion. 'On this side.'

'It looks into the garden?'

'There it is in the second story.'

'Be so good—which one?'

'The third window—the one with the shutters tied back with a handkerchief.'

The shutters and the handkerchief suddenly acquired a mysterious fascination for me. I looked at them for some time, and when I glanced back at my companion our eyes met. I don't know what she thought—what she thought I thought. I thought it *might* be out of a novel—such a thing as love at sight; such a thing as an unspoken dialogue, between a handsome young Italian with a 'wrong', in a starlit garden, and a fanciful western maid at a window. From her own sudden impression Mrs. Waddington seemed slowly to recoil. She gathered her shawl about her, shivered, and turned towards the house. 'The thing to do,' I said, offering my arm, 'is to leave Albano tomorrow.'

On the inner staircase we paused; Mrs. Waddington was loth to interrupt Adina's interview with Scrope. While she was hesitating whither to turn, the door of her sitting-room opened, and the young girl passed out. Scrope stood behind her, very pale, his face distorted with an emotion he was determined to repress. She herself was pale, but her eyes were lighted up like two wind-blown torches. Meeting the elder lady, she stopped, stood for a moment, looking down and hesitating, and then took Mrs. Waddington's two hands and silently kissed her. She turned to me, put out her hand, and said 'Good night!' I shook it, I imagine, with sensible ardour, for somehow, I was deeply impressed. There was a nameless force in the girl, before which one had to stand back. She lingered but an instant and rapidly disappeared towards her room, in the dusky corridor. Mrs. Waddington laid her hand kindly upon Scrope's arm and led him back into the parlour. He evidently was not going to be plaintive; his pride was rankling and burning, and it seasoned his self-control.

'Our engagement is at an end,' he simply said.

Mrs. Waddington folded her hands. 'And for what reason?'

'None.'

It was cruel, certainly; but what could we say? Mrs. Waddington sank upon the sofa and gazed at the poor fellow in mute, motherly compassion. Her large, caressing pity irritated him; he took up a book and sat down with his back to her. I took up another, but I couldn't read; I sat noticing that he never turned his own page. Mrs. Waddington at last transferred her gaze uneasily, appealingly, to me; she moved about restlessly in her place; she was trying to shape my vague intimations in the garden into something palpable to common credulity. I could give her now no explanation that would not have been a gratuitous offence to Scrope. But I felt more and more nervous; my own vague previsions oppressed me. I flung down my book at last, and left the room. In the corridor Mrs. Waddington overtook me, and requested me to tell her what I meant by my extraordinary allusions to—'in plain English,' she said, 'to an intrigue.'

'It would be needless, and it would be painful,' I answered, 'to tell you now and here. But promise to return to Rome tomorrow. There we can take breath and talk.'

'Oh, we shall bundle off, I promise!' she cried. And we separated. I mounted the stairs to go to my room; as I did so I heard her dress rustling in the corridor, undecidedly. Then came the sound of a knock; she had stopped at Adina's door. Involuntarily I paused and listened. There was a silence, and then another knock; another silence and a third knock; after this, despairing, apparently, of obtaining admission, she moved away, and I went to my room. It was useless going to bed; I knew I should not sleep. I stood a long time at my open window, wondering whether I had anything to say to Scrope. At the end of half an hour I wandered down into the garden again, and strolled through all the alleys. They were empty, and there was a light in Adina's window. No; it seemed to me that there was nothing I could bring myself to say to Scrope, but that he should leave Albano the next day, and Rome and Italy as soon after as possible, wait a year, and then try his fortune with Miss Waddington again. Towards morning, I *did* sleep.

Breakfast was served in Mrs. Waddington's parlour, and Scrope appeared punctually, as neatly shaved and brushed as if he were still under tribute to a pair of blue eyes. He really, of course, felt less serene than he looked. It can never be comfortable to meet at breakfast the young lady who has rejected you overnight. Mrs. Waddington kept us waiting some time, but at last she entered with surprising energy. Her comely face was flushed from brow to chin, and in her hand she clasped a crumpled note. She flung herself upon the sofa and burst into tears; I had only time to turn the grinning *cameriera* out of the room. 'She's gone, gone, gone!' she cried, among her sobs. 'Oh the crazy, wicked, ungrateful girl!'

Scrope, of course, knew no more than a tea-pot what she meant; but I understood her more promptly—and yet I believe I gave a long whistle. Scrope stood staring at her as she thrust out the crumpled note: that she meant that Adina—that Adina had left us in the night—was too large a horror for his unprepared sense. His dumb amazement was an almost touching sign of the absence of a thought which could have injured the girl. He saw by my face that I knew something, and he let me draw the note from Mrs. Waddington's hand and read it aloud:

Good-bye to everything! Think me crazy if you will. I could never explain. Only forget me and believe that I am happy, happy, happy!
Adina Beati.

I laid my hand on his shoulder; even yet he seemed powerless to apprehend. 'Angelo Beati,' I said gravely, 'has at last taken his revenge!'

'Angelo Beati!' he cried. 'An Italian beggar! It's a lie!'

I shook my head and patted his shoulder. 'He has insisted on payment. He's a clever fellow!'

He saw that I knew, and slowly, distractedly he answered with a burning blush!

It was a most extraordinary occurrence; we had ample time to say so, and to say so again, and yet never really to understand it. Neither of my companions ever saw the young girl again; Scrope never mentioned her but once. He went about for a week in absolute silence; when at last he spoke I saw that the fold was taken, that he was going to be a professional cynic for the rest of his days. Mrs. Waddington was a good-natured woman, as I have said, and, better still, she was a just woman. But I assure you, she never forgave her step-daughter. In after years, as I grew older, I took an increasing satisfaction in having assisted, as they say, at this episode. As mere *action*, it seemed to me really superb, and in judging of human nature I often weighed it mentally against the perpetual spectacle of strong impulses frittered in weakness and perverted by prudence. There has been no prudence here, certainly, but there has been ardent, full-blown, positive passion. We see the one every day, the other once in five years. More than once I ventured to ventilate this heresy before the kindly widow, but she always stopped me short, 'The thing was odious,' she said; 'I thank heaven the girl's father did not live to see it.'

We didn't finish that dismal day at Albano, but returned in the evening to Rome. Before our departure I had an interview with the Padre Girolamo of Lariccia, who failed to strike me as the holy man whom his nephew had described. He was a swarthy, snuffy little old

priest, with a dishonest eye—quite capable, I believed, of teaching
his handsome nephew to play his cards. But I had no reproaches to
waste upon him; I simply wished to know whither Angelo had taken
the young girl. I obtained the information with difficulty and only
after a solemn promise that if Adina should reiterate, *viva voce*, to
a person delegated by her friends, the statement that she was happy,
they would take no steps to recover possession of her. She was in
Rome, and in that holy city they should leave her. 'Remember,' said
the Padre, very softly, 'that she is of age, and her own mistress, and
can do what she likes with her money;—she has a good deal of it,
eh?' She had less than he thought, but evidently the Padre knew
his ground. It was he, he admitted, who had united the young couple
in marriage, the day before; the ceremony had taken place in the
little old circular church on the hill, at Albano, at five o'clock in the
morning. 'You see, Signor,' he said, slowly rubbing his yellow hands,
'she had taken a great fancy!' I gave him no chance, by any remark
of my own, to remind me that Angelo had a grudge to satisfy, but he
professed the assurance that his nephew was the sweetest fellow in
the world. I heard and departed in silence; my curiosity, at least, had
not yet done with Angelo.

Mrs. Waddington, also, had more of this sentiment than she confessed to; her kindness wondered, under protest of her indignation,
how on earth the young girl was living, and whether the smells on
her staircase were very bad indeed. It was, therefore, at her tacit request that I repaired to the lodging of the young pair, in the neighbourhood of the Piazza Barberini. The quarters were modest, but
they looked into the quaint old gardens of the Capuchin Friars; and
in the way of smells, I observed nothing worse than the heavy breath
of a great bunch of pinks in a green jug on the window sill. Angelo
stood there, pulling one of the pinks to pieces, and looking quite the
proper hero of his romance. He eyed me shyly and a trifle coldly at
first, as if he were prepared to stand firm against a possible blowing
up; but when he saw that I chose to make no allusions whatever
to the past, he suffered his dark brow to betray his serene contentment. I was no more disposed than I had been a week before, to call
him a bad fellow; but he was a mystery,—his character was as great
an enigma as the method of his courtship. That he was in love I
don't pretend to say; but I think he had already forgotten how his
happiness had come to him, and that he was basking in a sort of
primitive natural, sensuous delight in being adored. It was like the
warm sunshine, or like plenty of good wine. I don't believe his fortune in the least surprised him; at the bottom of every genuine
Roman heart,—even if it beats beneath a beggar's rags,—you'll find

an ineradicable belief that we are all barbarians, and made to pay them tribute. He was welcome to all his grotesque superstitions, but what sort of a future did they promise for Adina? I asked leave to speak with her; he shrugged his shoulders, said she was free to choose, and went into an adjoining room with my proposal. Her choice apparently was difficult; I waited sometime, wondering how she would look on the other side of the ugly chasm she had so audaciously leaped. She came in at last, and I immediately saw that she was vexed by my visit. She wished to utterly forget her past. She was pale and very grave; she seemed to wear a frigid mask of reserve. If she had seemed to me a singular creature before, it didn't help me to understand her to see her there, beside her extraordinary husband. My eyes went from one to the other and, I suppose, betrayed my reflections; she suddenly begged me to inform her of my errand.

'I have been asked,' I said, 'to inquire whether you are contented. Mrs. Waddington is unwilling to leave Rome while there is a chance of your——' I hesitated for a word, and she interrupted me.

'Of my repentance, is what you mean to say?' She fixed her eyes on the ground for a moment, then suddenly raised them. 'Mrs. Waddington may leave Rome,' she said softly. I turned in silence, but waited a moment for some slight message of farewell. 'I only ask to be forgotten!' she added, seeing me stand.

Love is said to be *par excellence* the egotistical passion; if so, Adina was far gone. 'I can't promise to forget you,' I said; 'you and my friend here deserve to be remembered!'

She turned away; Angelo seemed relieved at the cessation of our English. He opened the door for me, and stood for a moment with a significant, conscious smile.

'She's happy, eh?' he asked.

'So she says!'

He laid his hand on my arm, 'So am I!—She's better than the topaz!'

'You're a queer fellow!' I cried; and, pushing past him, I hurried away.

Mrs. Waddington gave her step-daughter another chance to repent, for she lingered in Rome a fortnight more. She was disappointed at my being able to bring her no information as to how Adina had eluded observation—how she had played her game and kept her secret. My own belief was that there had been a very small amount of courtship, and that until she stole out of the house the morning before her flight, to meet the Padre Girolamo and his nephew at the church, she had barely heard the sound of her lover's voice. There had been signs, and glances, and other unspoken vows, two or three notes, perhaps. Exactly who Angelo was, and what had originally secured for us the honour of his attentions, Mrs. Waddington never learned; it was enough for her that he was a friendless, picturesque Italian. Where everything was a painful puzzle, a shade or two, more or less, of obscurity hardly mattered. Scrope, of course, never attempted to account for his own blindness, though to his silent thoughts it must have seemed bitterly strange. He spoke of Adina, as I said, but once.

He knew by instinct, by divination,—for I had not told him,—that I had been to see her, and late on the evening following my visit, he proposed to me to take a stroll through the streets. It was a soft, damp night, with vague, scattered cloud masses, through which the moon was slowly drifting. A warm south wind had found its way into the dusky heart of the city. 'Let us go to St. Peter's,' he said, 'and see the fountains play in the fitful moonshine.' When we reached the bridge of St. Angelo, he paused and leaned some time on the parapet, looking over into the Tiber. At last, suddenly raising himself— 'You've seen her?' he asked.

'Yes.'

'What did she say?'

'She said she was happy.'

He was silent, and we walked on. Half-way over the bridge he stopped again and gazed at the river. Then he drew a small velvet case from his pocket, opened it, and let something shine in the moonlight. It was the beautiful, the imperial, the baleful topaz. He looked at me and I knew what his look meant. It made my heart beat, but I did not say—no! It had been a curse, the golden gem, with its cruel emblems; let it return to the mouldering under-world of the Roman past! I shook his hand firmly, he stretched out the other and, with a great flourish, tossed the glittering jewel into the dusky river. There it lies! Some day, I suppose, they will dredge the Tiber for treasures, and, possibly, disinter our topaz, and recognize it. But who will guess at this passionate human interlude to its burial of centuries?

Professor Fargo

[First appeared in the *Galaxy*, vol. xviii (August 1874), pp. 233-53. Not reprinted during James's lifetime.]

I.

THE LITTLE TOWN OF P— IS OFF THE RAILWAY, AND reached by a coach drive of twenty-five miles, which the primitive condition of the road makes a trial to the flesh, and the dullness of the landscape a weariness to the spirit. It was therefore not balm to my bruises, physical or intellectual, to find, on my arrival, that the gentleman for whose sake I had undertaken the journey had just posted off in a light buggy for a three days' holiday. After venting my disappointment in a variety of profitless expletives, I decided that the only course worthy of the elastic philosophy of a commercial traveller was to take a room at the local tavern and await his return. P— was obviously not an exhilarating place of residence, but I had out-weathered darker hours, and I reflected that having, as the phrase is, a bone to pick with my correspondent, a little accumulated irritation would arm me for the combat. Moreover, I had been rattling about for three months by rail; I was mortally tired, and the prospect of spending a few days beyond earshot of the steam whistle was not unwelcome. A certain audible, rural hush seemed to hang over the little town, and there was nothing apparently to prevent my giving it the whole of my attention. I lounged awhile in the tavern porch, but my presence seemed only to deepen the spell of silence on that customary group of jaundiced ruminants who were tilting their chairs hard by. I measured thrice, in its length, the dusty plank sidewalk of the main street, counted the hollyhocks in the front yards, and read the names on the little glass door-plates; and finally, in despair, I visited the cemetery. Although we were at the end of September, the day was hot, and this youthful institution boasted but a scanty growth of funereal umbrage. No weeping willow, no dusky cypress offered a friendly shelter to the meditative visitor. The yellow grass and the white tombstones glared in the hot light, and though I felt very little merrier than a graveyard ghost, I stayed hardly longer than one who should have mistaken his hour. But I am fond of reading country epitaphs, and I promised myself to come back when the sun was lower. On my way back to the inn I found myself, on a lately opened cross street, face to face with the town hall, and pausing approached its threshold with hopes of entertainment scarcely less ardent than those which, during a journey abroad, had guided my steps towards some old civic palace of France or Italy. There was, of course, no liveried minion to check my advance, and I made my way unchallenged into the large, bare room which occupied the body of the edifice. It was the accustomed theatre of town meetings, caucuses, and other solemn services, but it seemed just now to have been claimed for profaner uses. An itinerant lecturer, of a boisterous type, was unpacking his budget and preparing his *mise en scène*. This seemed to consist simply of a small table and three chairs in a row, and of a dingy specimen of our national standard, to whose awkward festoons, suspended against the blank wall at the rear of the platform, the orator in person was endeavouring to impart a more artistic grace. Another personage on the floor was engaged in scrawling the date of the performance, in red chalk, upon a number of printed handbills. He silently thrust one of these documents at me as I passed, and I saw with some elation that I had a resource for my evening. The latter half of the page consisted of extracts from village newspapers, setting forth the merits of the entertainments. The headings alone, as I remember them, ran somewhat in this fashion:

A MESSAGE FROM THE SPIRIT WORLD.
THE HIGHER MATHEMATICS MADE EASY TO LADIES AND CHILDREN.
A NEW REVELATION! A NEW SCIENCE!
GREAT MORAL AND SCIENTIFIC COMBINATION.
PROFESSOR FARGO, THE INFALLIBLE WAKING MEDIUM AND
MAGICIAN, CLAIRVOYANT, PROPHET, AND SEER!
COLONEL GIFFORD, THE FAMOUS LIGHTNING CALCULATOR AND
MATHEMATICAL REFORMER!

This was the substance of the programme, but there were a great many incidental *fioriture* which I have forgotten. By the time I had mastered them, however, for the occasion, the individual who was repairing the tattered flag, turned round, perceived me, and showed me a countenace which could belong only to an 'infallible waking medium'. It was not, indeed, that Professor Fargo had the abstracted and emaciated aspect which tradition attributes to pro-phets and visionaries. On the contrary, the fleshly element in his composition seemed, superficially, to enjoy a luxurious preponder-ance over the spiritual. He was tall and corpulent, and wore an air of aggressive robustness. A mass of reddish hair was tossed back from his forehead in a leonine fashion, and a lustrous auburn beard dif-fused itself complacently over an expansive but by no means immaculate shirt front. He was dressed in a black evening suit, of a tarnished elegance, and it was in keeping with the festal pattern of his garments, that on the right forefinger of a large, fat hand, he should wear an immense turquoise ring. His intimate connection with the conjuring class was stamped upon his whole person; but to a superficial glance he might have seemed a representative of its grosser accomplishments. You could have fancied him, in spangled fleshings, looking down the lion's mouth, or cracking the ring-master's whip at the circus, while Mlle. Josephine jumped through the hoops. It was his eyes, when you fairly met them, that proved him an artist on a higher line. They were eyes which had peeped into stranger places than even lions' mouths. Their pretension, I know, was to pierce the veil of futurity; but if this was founded, I could only say that the vision of Ezekiel and Jeremiah was but an-other name for consummate Yankee shrewdness. They were, in a single word, the most impudent pair of eyes I ever beheld, and it was the especial sign of their impudence that they seemed somehow to undertake to persuade you of their disinterested benevolence. Being of a fine reddish brown colour, it was probable that several young women that evening would pronounce them magnificent. Perceiving, apparently, that I had not the rustic physiognomy of a citizen of P—, Professor Fargo deemed my patronage worth securing. He advanced to the cope of the platform with his hands in his pockets, and gave me a familiar nod.

'Mind you come tonight, young man!' he said, jocosely imperious.

'Very likely I shall,' I answered. 'Anything in the world to help me through an evening at P—.'

'Oh, you won't want your money back,' the Professor rejoined. 'Mine is a first-class entertainment; none of your shuffling break-downs. We are perfect, my friends and I, in our respective parts. If you are fond of a good, stiff, intellectual problem, we'll give you some-thing to think about.' The Professor spoke very slowly and benign-antly, and his full, sonorous voice rolled away through the empty hall. He evidently liked to hear it himself; he balanced himself on his toes and surveyed the scene of his impending exploits. 'I don't blow my own trumpet,' he went on; 'I'm a modest man; you'll see for your-self what I can do. But I should like to direct your attention to my friend the Colonel. *He's* a rare old gentleman to find in a travelling show! The most remarkable old gentleman, perhaps, that ever ad-dressed a promiscuous audience. You needn't be afraid of the higher mathematics; it's all made as pretty as a game of billiards. It's his own daughter does the sums. We don't put her down in the bills, for motives of delicacy; but I'll tell you for your private satisfaction that she is an exquisite young creature of seventeen.'

It was not every day that I found myself in familiar conversation with a prophet, and the opportunity of obtaining a glimpse of the inner mechanism of the profession was too precious to be neglected. I questioned the Professor about his travels, his expenses, his profits, and the mingled emotions of the itinerant showman's lot; and then, taking the bull by the horns, I asked him whether, between ourselves, an accomplished medium had not to be also a tolerable conjurer? He leaned his head on one side and stood stroking his beard, and looking at me between lids shrewdly half closed. Then he gave a little dry chuckle, which expressed, at my choice, compassion either for my disbelief in his miracles or my faith in his urbanity.

'I confess frankly,' I said, 'that I'm a sceptic. I don't believe in messages from the spirit world. I don't believe that even the depressing prospect of immortality is capable of converting people who talked plain sense here on earth into the authors of the inflated platitudes which people of your profession pretend to transmit from them. I don't believe people who have expressed themselves for a lifetime in excellent English can ever be content with conversation by raps on the dinner table. I don't believe that you know anything more about the future world than you do about the penal code of China. My impression is that you don't believe so yourself. I can hardly expect you, of course, to take the wind out of your own sails. What I should vastly like you to do is, to tell me *viva voce*, in so many words, that your intentions are pure and your miracles genuine.'

The Professor remained silent, still caressing his prophetic beard. At last, in a benevolent drawl, 'Have you got any dear friend in the spirit land?' he asked.

'I don't know what you call the spirit land,' I answered. 'Several of my friends have died.'

'Would you like to see 'em?' the Professor promptly demanded.

'No, I confess I shouldn't!'

The Professor shook his head.

'You've not a rich nature,' he rejoined blandly.

'It depends on what you call rich. I possess on some points a wealth of curiosity. It would gratify me peculiarly to have you say outright, standing there on your own platform, that you're an honest man.'

It seemed to give him pleasure to trifle with my longing for this sensation. 'I'll give you leave,' he said, for all answer, 'to tie my hands into the tightest knot you can invent—and then I'll make your great-grandfather come in and stop the clock. You know I couldn't stop a clock, perched up on a mantel shelf five feet high, with my heels.'

'I don't know,' said I. 'I fancy you're very clever.'

'Cleverness has nothing to do with it. I've great magnetism.'

'You'd magnetize my great-grandfather down from Heaven?'

'Yes, sir, if I could establish communication. You'll see tonight what I can do. I'll satisfy you. If I don't, I shall be happy to give you a private sitting. I'm also a healing medium. You don't happen to have a toothache? I'd set you down there and pull it right out, as I'd pull off your boot.'

In compliment to this possibility, I could only make him my bow. His, at least, was a 'rich nature'. I bade him farewell, with the assurance that, sceptic as I was, I would applaud him impartially in the evening. I had reached the top of the hall, on my way out, when I heard him give a low, mellifluous whistle. I turned round, and he beckoned to me to return. I walked back, and he leaned forward from the platform, uplifting his stout forefinger. 'I simply desire to remark,' he said, 'that I'm an honest man!'

On my reurn to the hotel I found that my impatience for the Professor's further elucidation of his honesty made the interval look long. Fortune, however, assisted me to traverse it at an elastic pace. Rummaging idly on a bookshelf in the tavern parlour, I found, amid a pile of farmers' almanacs and Methodist tracts, a tattered volume of 'Don Quixote'. I repaired to my room, tilted back my chair, and communed deliciously with the ingenious hidalgo. Here was 'magnetism' superior even to that of Professor Fargo. It proved so effective that I lost all note of time, and, at last on looking at my watch, perceived that dinner must have been over for an hour. Of 'service' at this unsophisticated hostelry there was but a rigidly democratic measure, and if I chose to cultivate a too elegant absence of eagerness for beefsteak pie and huckleberry pudding, the young lady in long, tight ringlets and short sleeves, who administered these delicacies in the dining-room, was altogether too haughty a spirit to urge them on my attention. So I sat alone and ate them cold. After dinner I returned for an hour to La Mancha, and then strolled forth, according to my morning's vow, to see the headstones in the cemetery cast longer shadows. I was disappointed in the epitaphs; they were posterior to the age of theological *naïveté*. The cemetery covered the two opposed sides of a hill, and on walking up to the ridge and looking over it, I discovered that I was not the only visitor. Two persons had chosen the spot for a quiet talk. One of them was a young girl, dressed in black, and seated on a headstone, with her face turned towards me. In spite of her attitude, however, she seemed not to perceive me, wrapt as she was in attention to her companion—a tall, stout fellow, standing before her, with his back to me. They were at too great a distance for me to hear their talk, and indeed in a few minutes I began to fancy they were not speaking. Nevertheless, the young girl's eyes remained fixed on the man's face; he was holding her spellbound by an influence best known to himself. She was very pretty. Her hat was off, and she was holding it in her lap; her lips were parted, and her eyes fixed intently on her companion's face. Suddenly she gave a bright, quick smile, made a rapid gesture in the air, and laid her forefinger on her lips. The movement, and the manner of it, told her story. She was deaf and dumb, and the man had been talking to her with his fingers. I would willingly have looked at her longer, but I turned away in delicacy, and walked in another direction. As I was leaving the cemetery, however, I saw her advancing with her companion to take the path which led to the gate. The man's face was now turned to me, and I straightway recognized it, in spite of the high peaked white hat which surmounted it. It was natural enough, I suppose, to find Professor Fargo in a graveyard; as the simplest expedient for ascertaining what goes on beyond the tomb might seem to be to get as close as possible to the hither cope of it. Besides, if he was to treat the townsfolk to messages from their buried relatives, it was not amiss to 'get up' a few names and dates by the perusal of the local epitaphs. As he passed me, however, and flourished his hand in the air by way of salutation, there was a fine absence in his glance of any admission that he had been caught cheating. This, too, was natural enough; what surprised me was that such a vulgar fellow should be mated with so charming a companion. She gave me, as she passed, the trustfully unshrinking glance of those poor mortals who are obliged to listen, as one may say, with their eyes. Her dress was scanty and simple, but there was delicacy in her mobile features. Who was she, and how had *he* got hold of her? After all, it was none of my business; but as they passed on, walking rather briskly, and I strolled after them, watching the Professor's ponderous tread and the gliding footfall of the young girl, I began to wonder whether he might not be right—might not, in truth, have that about him which would induce the most venerable of my ancestors to revert from eternity and stop the clock.

II.

His handbills had done their office, and the Town Hall, when I entered it that evening, was filled with a solemnly expectant auditory. P— was evidently for the evening a cluster of empty houses. While my companions scanned the stage for the shadow of coming events, I found ample pastime in perusing the social physiognomy of the town. A shadow presently appeared in the person of a stout young countryman, armed with an accordian, from which he extracted an ingenious variety of lamentable sounds. Soon after this mysterious prelude, the Professor marshalled out his forces. They consisted, first and foremost, of himself, his leonine *chevelure*, his black dress suit, and his turquoise ring, and then of an old gentleman who walked in gravely and stiffly, without the Professor's portentous salaam to the audience, bearing on his arm a young girl in black. The Professor managed somehow, by pushing about the chairs, turning up the lamps, and giving a twist to the patriotic drapery in the background, to make his audience feel his presence very intimately. His assistants rested themselves tranquilly against the wall. It took me but a short time to discover that the young girl was none other than the companion of the Professor's tour of inspection in the cemetery, and then I remembered that he had spoken in the morning of the gentleman who performed the mathematical miracles being assisted by his daughter. The young girl's infirmity, and her pretty face, promised to impart a picturesque interest to this portion of the exhibition; but meanwhile I inferred from certain ill-suppressed murmurs, and a good deal of vigorous pantomime among the female spectators, that she was found wanting in the more immediate picturesqueness demanded of a young lady attached to a show. Her plain black dress found no favour; the admission fee had justified the expectation of a good deal of trimming and several bracelets. She, however, poor girl, sat indifferent in her place, leaning her head back rather wearily against the wall, and looking as if, were she disposed, she might count without trouble all the queer bonnets among her judges. Her father sat upright beside her, with a cane between his knees and his two hands crossed on the knob. He was a man of sixty-five—tall, lean, pale, and serious. The lamp hanging above his head deepened the shadows on his face, and transformed it into a sort of pictorial mask. He was very bald, and his forehead, which was high and handsome, wore in the lamplight the gleam of old ivory. The sockets of his eyes were in deep shadow, and out of them his pupils gazed straight before him, with the glow of smouldering fire. His high-arched nose cast a long shadow over his mouth and chin, and two intensified wrinkles, beside his moustache, made him look strangely tragic. With his tragic look, moreover, he seemed strangely familiar. His daughter and the Professor I regarded as old friends; but where had I met this striking specimen of antique melancholy? Though his gaze seemed fixed, I imagined it was covertly wandering over the audience. At last it appeared to me that it met mine, and that its sombre glow emitted a spark of recognition

of my extra-provincial and inferentially more discriminating character. The next moment I identified him—he was Don Quixote in
the flesh; Don Quixote, with his sallow Spanish colouring, his high-
browed, gentlemanly visage, his wrinkles, his moustache, and his
sadness.

Professor Fargo's lecture was very bad. I had expected he would
talk a good deal of nonsense, but I had imagined it would be cleverer
nonsense. Very possibly there was a deeper cleverness in it than I
perceived, and that, in his extreme shrewdness, he was giving his
audience exactly what they preferred. It is an ascertained fact, I
believe, that rural assemblies have a relish for the respectably ponderous, and an honest pride in the fact that they cannot be bored.
The Professor, I suppose, felt the pulse of his listeners, and detected
treasures of latent sympathy in their solemn, irresponsive silence. I
should have said the performance was falling dead, but the Professor
probably would have claimed that this was the rapture of attention
and awe. He certainly kept very meagrely the promise of his
grandiloquent programme, and gave us a pound of precept to a
grain of example. His miracles were exclusively miracles of rhetoric.
He discoursed upon the earth life and the summer land, and related
surprising anecdotes of his intimacy with the inhabitants of the
latter region; but to my disappointment, the evening passed away
without his really bringing us face to face with a ghost. A number
of 'prominent citizens' were induced to step upon the platform
and be magnetized, but the sturdy agricultural temperament
of P— showed no great pliancy under the Professor's manual blandishments. The attempt was generally a failure—the only brilliant
feature being the fine impudence with which the operator lodged
the responsibility of the *fiasco* upon what he called his victim's
low development. With three or four young girls the thing was a
trifle better. One of them closed her eyes and shivered; another
had a fearful access of nervous giggling; another burst into tears,
and was restored to her companions with an admonitory wink.
As everyone knew everyone else and everyone else's family history,
some sensation was probably produced by half a dozen happy guesses
as to the Christian names and last maladies of certain defunct
town worthies. Another deputation of the prominent citizens ascended the platform and wrote the names of departed friends on
small bits of paper, which they threw into a hat. The Professor then
folded his arms and clutched his beard, as if he were invoking inspiration. At last he approached the young girl, who sat in the background, took her hand, and led her forward. She picked the papers
out of the hat, and held them up one by one, for the Professor to look

at. 'There is no possible collusion,' he said with a flourish, as he presented her to the audience. 'The young lady is a deaf-mute!' On a gesture of her companion she passed the paper to one of the contemplative grey heads who represented the scientific curiosity of P—, and he verified the Professor's guess. The Professor risked an 'Abijah' or a 'Melinda', and it turned out generally to be an Ezekiel or a Hepzibah. Three several times, however, the performer's genius triumphed; whereupon, the audience not being up to the mark, he gave himself a vigorous round of applause. He concluded with the admission that the spirits were shy before such a crowd, but that he would do much better for the ladies and gentlemen individually, if they would call on him at the hotel.

It was all terribly vulgar rubbish, and I was glad when it was over. While it lasted, the old gentleman behind continued to sit motionless, seeming neither to see, to hear, nor to understand. I wondered what he thought of it, and just what it cost his self-respect to give it the sanction of his presence. It seemed, indeed, as if mentally he were not present; as if by an intense effort he had succeeded in making consciousness a blank, and was awaiting his own turn in a kind of trance. Once only he moved—when the Professor came and took his daughter by the hand. He gave an imperceptible start, controlled himself, then, dropping his hand a little, closed his eyes and kept them closed until she returned to his side. There was an intermission, during which the Professor walked about the platform, shaking his mane and wiping his forehead, and surveying the audience with an air of lofty benevolence, as if, having sown the seed, he was expecting to see it germinate on the spot. At last he rapped on the table and introduced the old gentleman—Colonel Gifford, the Great Mathematical Magician and Lightning Calculator; after which he retreated in turn to the background—if a gentleman with tossing mane and flowing beard, that turquoise ring, and generally expansive and importunate presence, could be said to be, under any circumstances, in the background. The old gentleman came forward and made his bow, and the young girl placed herself beside him, simply, unaffectedly, with her hands hanging and crossed in front of her—with all the childish grace and serenity of Mignon in 'Wilhelm Meister', as we see her grouped with the old harper. Colonel Gifford's performance gave me an exquisite pleasure, which I am bound to confess was quite independent of its intrinsic merits. These, I am afraid, were at once too numerous and too scanty to have made it a popular success. It was a very ingenious piece of scientific contrivance, but it was meagrely adapted to tickle the ears of the groundlings. If one had read it—the substance of it—in a handsomely printed pamphlet, under the lamp, of a wet evening when no one was likely to call, one would have been charmed at once with the quaint vivacity of the author's mode of statement, and with the unexpected agility of one's own intellect. But in spite of an obvious effort to commend himself to understandings more familiar with the rule of thumb than with the differential calculus, Colonel Gifford remained benignantly but formidably unintelligible. He had devised—so far as I understood it—an extension of the multiplication table to enormous factors, by which he expected to effect a revolution in the whole science of accounts. There was the theory, which rather lost itself, thanks to his discursive fervour in the mists of the higher mathematics, and there was the practice, which, thanks to his daughter's co-operation, was much more gracefully concrete. The interesting thing to me was the speaker's personality, not his system. Although evidently a very positive old man, he had a singularly simple, unpretentious tone. His intensity of faith in the supreme importance of his doctrine gave his manner a sort of reverential hush. The echoes of Professor Fargo's windy verbiage increased the charms of his mild sincerity. He spoke in a feeble, tremulous voice, which every now and then quavered upward with excitement, and then subsided into a weary, plaintive cadence. He was an old gentleman of a single idea, but his one idea was a religion. It was impossible not to feel a kindness for him, and imagine that he excited among his auditors something of the vague good will—half pity and half reverence—that uncorrupted souls entertain for those neat, keen-eyed, elderly people who are rumoured to have strange ways and say strange things—to be 'cracked', in short, like a fine bit of porcelain which will hold together only so long as you don't push it about. But it was upon the young girl, when once she had given them a taste of her capacity, that they bestowed their frankest admiration. Now that she stood forward in the bright light, I could observe the character of her prettiness. It was no brilliant beauty, but a sort of meagre, attenuated, angular grace, the delicacy and fragility of the characteristic American type. Her chest was flat, her neck extremely thin, her visage narrow, and her forehead high and prominent. But her fair hair encircled her head in such fleecy tresses, her cheeks had such a pale pink flush, her eyes such an appealing innocence, her attitude such a quaint unconscious felicity, that one watched her with a kind of upstart belief that to such a stainless little spirit the working of miracles might be really possible. A couple of blackboards were hung against the wall, on one of which the old man rapidly chalked a problem—choosing one, of course, on the level of the brighter minds in theaudience. The young girl glanced at it, and before we could count ten dashed off a great bold answer on the other tablet. The brighter minds were then invited to verify, and the young lady was invariably found to have hit the mark. She was in fact a little arithmetical fairy, and her father made her perform a series of gymnastics among numbers as brilliant in their way as the vocal flourishes and roulades of an accomplished singer. Communicating with her altogether by the blackboard, he drew from her a host of examples of the beauty of his system of trancendent multiplication. A person present was requested to furnish two enormous numbers, one to multiply the other. The old man wrote them out. After standing an instant meditative and just touching her forehead with her forefinger, she chalked down the prodigious result. Her father then performed rapidly, on the blackboard, the operation according to his own system (which she had employed mentally), and finally satisfied every one by repeating it in the roundabout fashion actually in use. This was all Colonel Gifford's witchcraft. It sounds very ponderous, but it was really very charming, and I had an agreeable sense of titillation in the finer parts of my intellectual mechanism. I felt more like a thinking creature. I had never supposed I was coming to P— to take a lesson in culture.

It seemed on the morrow as if, at any rate, I was to take a lesson in patience. It was a Sunday, and I awoke to hear the rain pattering against my window panes. A rainy Sunday at P— was a prospect to depress the most elastic mind. But as I stepped into my slippers, I bethought myself of my unfinished volume of 'Don Quixote', and promised myself to borrow from Sancho Panza a philosophic proverb or so applicable to my situation. 'Don Quixote' consoled me, as it turned out, in an unexpected fashion. On descending to the dining-room of the inn, while I mentally balanced the contending claims of muddy coffee and sour green tea, I found that my last evening's friends were also enjoying the hospitality of the establishment. It was the only inn in the place, and it would already have occurred to a more investigating mind that we were fellow-lodgers. The Professor, happily, was absent; and it seemed only reasonable that a ghost-seer should lie in bed late of a morning. The melancholy old mathematician was seated at the breakfast table cutting his dry toast into geometrical figures. He gave me a formal bow as I entered, and proceeded to dip his sodden polygons into his tea. The young girl was at the window leaning her forehead against the pane, and looking out into the sea of yellow mud in the village street. I had not been in the room a couple of minutes when, seeming in spite of her deafness to feel that I was near, she turned straight round and looked at me. She wore no trace of fatigue from her public labours, but was the same clear-eyed, noiseless little sprite as before. I observed that, by daylight, her black dress was very shabby, and her father's frock coat, buttoned with military precision up to his chin, had long since exchanged its original lustre for the melancholy brilliancy imparted by desperate brushing. I was afraid that Professor Fargo was either a niggardly *impresario*, or that the great 'moral and scientific combination' was not always as remunerative as it seemed to have been at P—. While I was making these reflections the Professor entered, with an exhilaration of manner which I conceived to be a tribute to unwonted success.

'Well, sir,' he cried, as his eyes fell upon me, 'what do you say to it now? I hope we did things handsomely, eh? I hope you call that a solid entertainment. This young man, you must know, is one of the scoffers,' he went on, turning to the Colonel. 'He came yesterday and bearded the lion in his den. He snaps his fingers at spirits, suspects me of foul play, and would like me to admit, in my private character, that you and I are a couple of sharpers. I hope we satisfied you!'

The Colonel went on dipping his toast into his tea, looking grave and saying nothing. 'Poor man!' I said to myself; 'he despises his colleague—and so do I. I beg your pardon,' I cried with warmth; 'I would like nothing of the kind. I was extremely interested in this gentleman's exhibition', and I made the Colonel a bow. 'It seemed to me remarkable for its perfect good faith and truthfulness.'

'Many thanks for the compliment,' said the Professor. 'As much as to say the Colonel's an apostle, and I'm a rascal. Have it as you please; if so, I'm a hardened one!' he declared with a great slap on his pocket; 'and anyhow, you know, it's all one concern,' and the Professor betook himself to the window where Miss Gifford was standing. She had not looked round at him on his entrance, as she had done at me. The Colonel, in response to my compliment, looked across at me with mild benignity, and I assured him afresh of my admiration. He listened silently, stirring his tea; his face betrayed an odd mixture of confidence and deprecation; as if he thought it just possible that I might be laughing at him, but that if I was not, it was extremely delightful. I continued to insist on its being distinctively *his* half of the performance that had pleased me; so that, gradually convinced of my respectful sympathy, he seemed tacitly to intimate that, if we were only alone and he knew me a little better, it would do him a world of good to talk it all over. I determined to give him a chance at the earliest moment. The Professor, meanwhile, waiting for his breakfast, remained at the window experimenting in the deaf and dumb alphabet with the young girl. It took him, as an amateur, a long time to form his sentences, but he went on bravely, brandishing his large, plump knuckles before her face. She seemed very patient of his slowness, and stood watching his gestures with the same intense earnestness I had caught a glimpse of in the cemetery. Most of my female friends enjoy an unimpeded use of their tongues, and I was unable from experience to appreciate his situation; but I could easily fancy what a delightful sense of intimacy there must be in this noiseless exchange of long looks with a pretty creature towards whom all *tendresse* of attitude might be conveniently attributed to compassion. Before long the Colonel pushed away his cup, turned about, folded his arms, and fixed his eyes with a frown on the Professor. It seemed to me that I read in his glance a complete revelation of moral torture. The stress of fortune had made them associates, but the Colonel jealously guarded the limits of their private intimacy. The Professor, with all his audacity, suffered himself to be reminded of them. He suddenly pulled out his watch and clamoured for his coffee, and was soon seated at a repast which indicated that the prophetic temperament requires a generous diet. The young girl roamed about the room, looking idly at this and that, as if she were used to doing nothing. When she met my eye, she smiled brightly, after a moment's gravity, as if she were also used to saying to people, mentally, 'Yes, I know I'm a strange little creature, but you must not be afraid of me.' The Professor had hardly got that array of innumerable little dishes, of the form and dimensions of soap-trays, with which one is served in the rural hostelries of New England, well under contribution, before a young lady was introduced who had come to request him to raise a ghost—a resolute young lady, with several ringlets and a huge ancestral umbrella, whose matutinal appetite for the supernatural had not been quenched by the raw autumnal storm. She produced very frankly a 'tin-type' of a florid young man, actually deceased, and demanded to be confronted with his ghost. The day was beginning well for the Professor. He gallantly requested her to be seated, and promised her every satisfaction. While he was hastily despatching his breakfast, the Colonel's daughter made acquaintance with her bereaved sister. She drew the young man's portrait gently out of her hand, examined it, and then shook her head with a little grimace of displeasure. The young woman laughed good-naturedly, and screamed into her ear that she didn't believe she was a bit deaf and dumb. At the announcement the Colonel, who, after eyeing her while she stated her credulous errand with solemn compassion, had turned away to the window, as if to spare himself the spectacle of his colleague's unblushing pretensions, turned back again and eyed her coldly from head to foot. 'I recommend you, madam,' he said sternly, 'to reserve your suspicions for an occasion in which they may be more pertinent.'

Later in the morning I found him still in the dining-room with his daughter. Professor Fargo, he said, was in the parlour, raising ghosts by the dozen; and after a little pause he gave an angry laugh, as if his suppressed irritation were causing him more than usual discomfort. He was walking up and down, with slow, restless steps, and smoking a frugal pipe. I took the liberty of offering him a good cigar, and while he puffed it gratefully, the need to justify himself for his odd partnership slowly gathered force. 'It would be a satisfaction for me to tell you, sir,' he said at last, looking at me with eyes that fairly glittered with the pleasure of hearing himself speak the words, 'that my connection with Professor Fargo implies no—no'— and he paused for a moment—'no intellectual approval of his extraordinary pretensions. This, of course, is between ourselves. You're a stranger to me, and it's doubtless the height of indiscretion in me to take you into my confidence. My subsistence depends on my not quarrelling with my companion. If you were to repeat to him that I went about undermining the faith, the extremely retributive faith, as you see' (and he nodded towards the parlour door), 'of his audiences, he would of course dissolve our partnership and I should be adrift again, trying to get my heavy boat in tow. I should perhaps feel like an honest man again, but meanwhile, probably, I should starve. Misfortune,' he added bitterly, 'makes strange bedfellows; and I have been unfortunate!'

There was so much melancholy meaning in this declaration that I asked him frankly who and what he was. He puffed his cigar vigorously for some moments without replying, and at last turned his fine old furrowed visage upon me through a cloud of smoke. 'I'm a fanatic. I feed on illusions and cherish ambitions which will never butter my bread. Don't be afraid; I won't buttonhole *you*; but I have a head full of schemes which I believe the world would be the happier for giving a little quiet attention to. I'm an inventor; and like all inventors whose devices are of value, I believe that my particular contrivance would be the salvation of a misguided world. I have looked a good deal into many things, but my latest hobby is the system of computation of which I tried to give a sketch last night. I'm afraid you didn't understand a word of it, but I assure you it's a very beautiful thing. If it could only get a fair hearing and be thoroughly propagated and adopted, it would save our toiling human race a prodigious deal of ungrateful labour. In America alone, I have calculated, it would save the business community about 23,000 hours in the course of ten years. If time is money, they are worth saving.

But there I go! You oughtn't to ask me to talk about myself. Myself is my ideas!'

A little judicious questioning, however, drew from him a number of facts of a more immediate personal kind. His colonelship, he intimated, was held by the inglorious tenure of militia service, and was only put forward to help him to make a figure on Professor Fargo's platform. It was part of the general humbuggery of the attempt to *bribe* people to listen to wholesome truths—truths the neglect of which was its own chastisement. 'I have always had a passion for scientific research, and I have squandered my substance in experiments which the world called fruitless. They were curious, they were beautiful, they were divine! But they wouldn't turn any-one's mill or grind anyone's corn, and I was treated like a mediaeval alchemist, astray in the modern world. Chemistry, physics, mathe-matics, philology, medicine—I've dug deep in them all. Each, in turn, has been a passion to which I've given my days and my nights. But apparently I haven't the art of finding favour for my ideas—of sweet-ening the draught so that people will drink it. So here I am, after all my vigils and ventures, an obscure old man, ruined in fortune, broken down in health and sadly diminished in hope, trying hard to keep afloat by rowing in the same boat as a gentleman who turns tables and raises ghosts. I'm a proud man, sir, and a devotee of the exact sciences. You may imagine what I suffer. I little fancied ten years ago that I was ever going to make capital, on a mountebank's booth, of the pathetic infirmity of my daughter.'

The young girl, while her father talked, sat gazing at him in wist-ful surprise. I inferred from it that this expansive mood was rare; she wondered what long story he was telling. As he mentioned her, I gave her a sudden glance. Perceiving it, she blushed slightly and turned away. The movement seemed at variance with what I had supposed to be her characteristic indifference to observation. 'I have a good reason,' he said, 'for treating her with more than the tender-ness which such an infirmity usually commands. At the time of my marriage, and for some time after, I was performing a series of curious chemical researches. My wife was a wonderfully pretty little creature. She used to come tripping and rustling about my labora-tory, asking questions of the most comical ignorance, peeping and rummaging everywhere, raising the lids of jars, and making faces at the bad smells. One day while she was in the room I stepped out on the balcony to examine something which I had placed to dry in the sun. Suddenly I heard a terrific explosion; it smashed the window-glass into atoms. Rushing in, I found my wife in a swoon on the floor. A compound which I had placed to heat on a furnace had been left

too long; I had underestimated its activity. My wife was not visibly
injured, but when she came to her senses again, she found she had
lost her hearing. It never returned. Shortly afterwards my daughter
was born—born the poor deaf creature you see. I lost my wife and
I gave up chemistry. As I advanced in life, I became convinced that
my ruling passion was mathematics. I've gone into them very deeply;
I consider them the noblest acquisition of the human mind, and I
don't hesitate to say that I have profound and original views on the
subject. If you have a head for such things, I could open great vistas
to you. But I'm afraid you haven't! Ay, it's a desperately weak-witted
generation. The world has a horror of concentrated thought; it
wants the pill to be sugared; it wants everything to be made easy; it
prefers the brazen foolery that you and I sat through last night to
the divine harmonies of the infinite science of numbers. That's why
I'm a beggar, droning out my dreary petition and pushing forth my
little girl to catch the coppers. That's why I've had to strike a partnership with a vulgar charlatan. I was a long time coming to it, but I'm
well in for it now. I won't tell you how, from rebuff to rebuff, from
failure to failure, through hope deferred and justice denied, I have
finally come to this. It would overtax both your sympathy and your
credulity. You wouldn't believe the stories I could relate of the impenetrable stupidity of mankind, of the leaden empire of Routine. I
squandered my property, I confess it, but not in the vulgar way. It
was a carnival of high research, a long debauch of experiment. When
I had melted down my last cent in the consuming crucible, I thought
the world might be willing to pay me something for my results. The
world had better uses for its money than the purchase of sovereign
truth! I became a solicitor; I went from door to door, offering people a
choice of twenty superb formulated schemes, the paltriest of which
contained the germs of a peaceful revolution. The poor unpatented
visions are at this hour all in a bundle up stairs in my trunk. In the
midst of my troubles I had the ineffable pleasure of finding that my
little girl was a genius. I don't know why it should have been a pleasure; her poor father's genius stood there before me as a warning. But
it was a delight to find that her little imprisoned, soundless mind was
not a blank. She had inherited my passion for numbers. My folly had
taken a precious faculty from her; it was but just I should give her
another. She was in good hands for becoming perfect. Her gift is a
rare one among women, but she is not of the common feminine stuff.
She's very simple—strangely simple in some ways. She has never been
talked to by women about petticoats, nor by men about love. She
doesn't reason; her skill at figures is a kind of intuition. One day it
came into my head that I might lecture for a livelihood. I had listened

to windy orators, in crowded halls, who had less to say than I. So I lectured, sometimes to twenty people, sometimes to five, once to no one at all. One morning, some six months ago, I was waited upon by my friend there. He told me frankly that he had a show which didn't draw as powerfully as it deserved, and proposed that, as I also seemed unable to catch the public ear, we should combine our forces and carry popularity by storm. His entertainment, alone, was rather thin; mine also seemed to lack the desirable consistency; but a mixture of the two might produce an effective compound. I had but five dollars in my pocket. I disliked the man, and I believe in spiritualism about as much as I believe that the sun goes round the earth. But we must live, and I made a bargain. It was a very poor bargain, but it keeps us alive. I took a few hints from the Professor, and brightened up my lucky formulas a little. Still, we had terribly thin houses. I couldn't play the mountebank; it's a faculty I lack. At last the Professor bethought himself that I possessed the golden goose. From the mountebank's point of view a pretty little deaf and dumb daughter, who could work miracles on the blackboard, was a treasure to a practical mind. The idea of dragging my poor child and her pathetic idiosyncrasies before the world was extremely repulsive to me; but the Professor laid the case before the little maid herself, and at the end of a fortnight she informed him that she was ready to make her curtsy on the platform as a "lightning calculator". I consented to let her try, and you see that she succeeded. She draws, not powerfully, but sufficiently, and we manage to keep afloat.'

Half an hour later the Professor returned from his morning's labours—flushed, dishevelled, rubbing his hands, evidently in high good humour. The Colonel immediately became silent and grave, asked no questions, and, when dinner was served shortly afterwards, refused everything and sat with a melancholy frown and his eyes fixed on his plate. His comrade was plainly a terrible thorn in his side. I was curious, on the other hand, to know how the Colonel affected the Professor, and I soon discovered that the latter was by no means his exuberant impudent self within the radius of his colleague's pregnant silence. If there was little love lost between them, the ranting charlatan was at least held in check by an indefinable respect for his companion's probity. He was a fool, doubtless, with his careful statements and his incapacity to take a humorous view of human credulity; but, somehow, he was a venerable fool, and the Professor, as a social personage, without the inspiration of a lecture-room more or less irritatingly interspaced, and with that pale, grave old mathmetician sitting by like a marble monument to Veracity, lacked the courage to ventilate his peculiar pretensions. On this occasion, however, he swallowed the Colonel's tacit protest with a wry face. I don't know what he had brought to pass in the darkened parlour; whatever it was, it had agreeably stimulated his confidence in his resources. We had been joined, moreover, at dinner by half a dozen travellers of less oppressively sceptical mould than the Colonel, and under these circumstances it was peculiarly trying to have to veil one's brighter genius. There was undischarged thunder in the air.

The rain ceased in the afternoon, and the sun leaped out and set the thousand puddles of the village street a-flashing. I found the Colonel sitting under the tavern porch with a village urchin between his knees, to whom he seemed to be imparting the rudiments of mathematical science. The little boy had a bulging forehead, a prodigious number of freckles, and the general aspect of a juvenile Newton. Being present at the Colonel's lecture, he had been fired with a laudable curiosity to know more, and learning that Professor Fargo imparted information *à domicile*, had ventured to believe that his colleague did likewise. The child's father, a great, gaunt, brown-faced farmer, with a yellow tuft on his chin, stood by, blushing at the audacity of his son and heir, but grinning delightedly at his brightness. The poor Colonel, whose meed of recognition had as yet been so meagre, was vastly tickled by this expression of infantine sympathy, and discoursed to the little prodigy with the most condescending benevolence. Certainly, as the boy grows up, the most vivid of his childhood memories will be that of the old man with glowing eyes and a softened voice coming from under his white moustache— the voice which held him stock-still for a whole half hour, and assured him afterwards that he was a little Trojan. When the lesson was over, I proposed a walk to the Colonel, and we wandered away out of the village. The afternoon, as it waned, became glorious; the heavy clouds, broken and dispersed, sailed through the glowing sky like high-prowed galleys, draped in purple and silver. I, on my side, shall never forget the Colonel's excited talk, nor how at last, as we sat on a rocky ridge looking off to the sunset, he fairly unburdened his conscience.

'Yes, sir!' he said; 'it's a base concession to the ignoble need of keeping body and soul together. Sometimes I feel as if I couldn't stand it another hour—as if it were better to break with the impudent rascal and sink or swim as fate decrees, than get a hearing for the truth at such a cost. It's all very well holding my tongue and insisting that I, at least, make no claims for the man's vile frauds; my connection with him is itself a sanction, and my presence at his damnable mummeries an outrage to the purity of truth. You see I have the misfortune to believe in something, to *know* something, and to think it makes a difference whether people feed, intellectually, on poisoned garbage or on the ripe, sweet fruit of true science! I shut my eyes every night, and lock my jaws, and clench my teeth, but I can't help hearing the man's windy rubbish. It's a tissue of scandalous lies, from beginning to end. I know them all by heart by this time, and I verily believe I could stand up and rattle them off myself. They ring in my ears all day, and I have horrible dreams at night of crouching under a table with a long cloth, and tapping on the top of it. The Professor stands outside swearing to the audience that it's the ghost of Archimedes. Then I begin to suffocate, and overturn the table, and appear before a thousand people as the accomplice of the impostor. There are times when the value of my own unheeded message to mankind seems so vast, so immeasurable, that I am ready to believe that any means are lawful which may enable me to utter it; that if one's ship is set to sail for the golden islands, even a flaunting buccaneer may tow it into the open sea. In such moods, when I sit there against the wall, in the shade, closing my eyes and trying not to hear—I really *don't* hear! My mind is a myriad miles away—floating, soaring on the wings of invention. But all of a sudden the odiousness of my position comes over me, and I can't believe my senses that it's verily I who sit there—I to whom a grain of scientific truth is more precious than a mountain of gold!'

He was silent a long time, and I myself hardly knew what consolation to offer him. The most friendly part was simply to let him expend his bitterness to the last drop. 'But that's not the worst,' he resumed after a while. 'The worst is that I hate the greasy rascal to come near my daughter, and that, living and travelling together as we do, he's never far off. At first he used to engage a small child beforehand to hold up his little folded papers for him; but a few weeks ago it came into his head that it would give the affair an even greater air of innocence, if he could make use of my poor girl. It does, I believe, and it tells, and I've been brought so low that I sit by night after night and endure it. She, on her side, dreams of no harm, and takes the Professor for an oracle and his lecture for a masterpiece. I have never undeceived her, for I have no desire to teach her that there are such things ar falsity and impurity. Except that our perpetual railway journeys give her bad headaches, she supposes that we lead a life of pure felicity. But some fine day our enterprising friend will be wanting to put her into a pink dress and a garland of artificial flowers, and then, with God's help, we shall part company!'

My silence, in reply to this last burst of confidence, implied the most deferential assent; but I was privately wondering whether 'the little maid' was so perfectly ignorant of evil as the old man supposed.

I remembered the episode at the cemetery the day before, and doubted greatly whether her father had countenanced it. With his sentiments touching the Professor, this was most unlikely. The young girl, then, had a secret, and it gave me real discomfort to think this coarse fellow should keep the key of it. I feared that the poor Colonel was yoked to his colleague more cruelly than he knew. On our return to the inn this impression was vividly confirmed. Dusk had fallen when we entered the public room, and in the grey light which pervaded it two figures at one of the windows escaped immediate recognition. But in a moment one of them advanced, and in the sonorous accents of Professor Fargo hoped that we had enjoyed our expedition. The Colonel started and stared, and left me to answer. He sat down heavily on the sofa; in a moment his daughter came over and sat beside him, placing her hand gently on his knee. But he let it lie, and remained motionless, resting his hot head on his cane. The Professor withdrew promptly, but with a swagger which suggested to my sense that he could now afford to treat his vanity to a dose of revenge for the old man's contempt.

Late in the evening I came down stairs again, and as I passed along the hall I heard Professor Fargo perorating vigorously in the bar-room. Evidently he had an audience, and the scene was probably curious. Drawing near, I found this gifted man erect on the floor, addressing an assemblage of the convivial spirits of P—. In an extended hand he brandished a glass of smoking whisky and water; with the other he caressed his rounded periods. He had evidently been drinking freely, and I perceived that even the prophetic vision was liable to obfuscation. It had been a brilliant day for him; fortune smiled, and he felt strong. A dozen rustic loafers, of various degrees of inveteracy, were listening to him with a speechless solemnity, which may have been partly faith, but was certainly partly rum. In a corner, out of the way, sat the Colonel, with an unfinished glass before him. The Professor waved his hand as I appeared, with magnificent hospitality, and resumed his discourse.

'Let me say, gentlemen,' he cried, 'that it's not my peculiar influence with the departed that I chiefly value; for, after all, you know, a ghost is but a ghost. It can't do much any way. You can't touch it, half the time you can't see it. If it happens to be the spirit of a pretty girl, you know, this makes you kind of mad. The great thing now is to be able to exercise a mysterious influence over living organisms. You can do it with your eye, you can do it with your voice, you can do it with certain motions of your hand—as thus, you perceive; you can do it with nothing at all by just setting your mind on it. That is, of course, some people can do it; not very many—certain rich, powerful, sympathetic natures that you now and then come across. It's called magnetism. Various works have been written on the subject, and various explanations offered, but they don't amount to much. All you can say is that it's just magnetism, and that you've either got it or you haven't got it. Now the Lord has seen fit to bestow it on me. It's a great responsibility, but I try to make a noble use of it. I can do all sorts of things. I can find out things. I can make people confess. I can make 'em sick and I can make 'em well. I can make 'em in love—what do you say to that? I can take 'em out of love again, and make 'em swear they wouldn't marry the loved object, not if they were paid for it. How it is I do it I confess I can't tell you. I just say to myself, "Come now, Professor, we'll fix this one or that one." It's a free gift. It's magnetism, in short. Some folks call it animal magnetism, but I call it spiritual magnetism.'

There was a profound silence; the air seemed charged with that whimsical retention of speech which is such a common form of American sociability. I looked askance at the Colonel; it seemed to me that he was paler than usual, and that his eyes were really fierce. Professor Fargo turned about to the bar to replenish his glass, and the old man slowly rose and came out into the middle of the room. He looked round at the company; he evidently meant to say something. He stood silent for some moments, and I saw that he was in a tremor of excitement. 'You've listened to what this gentleman has been saying?' he began. 'I won't say, have you understood it? It's not to be understood. Some of you, perhaps, saw me last night sitting on the platform while Professor Fargo said his say. You know that we are partners—that for convenience's sake we work together. I wish to say that you are not therefore to believe that I assent to the doctrines he has just promulgated. "Doctrines" is a flattering name for them. I speak in the name of science. Science recognizes no such thing as "spiritual magnetism"; no such thing as mysterious fascinations; no such thing as spirit-rappings and ghost-raisings. I owe it to my conscience to say so. I can't remain there and see you all sit mum when this gentleman concludes such a monstrous piece of talk. I have it on my conscience to assure you that no intelligent man, woman, or child need fear to be made to do anything against his own will by the supernatural operation of the will of Professor Fargo.'

If there had been silence on the conclusion of Professor Fargo's harangue, what shall I say of the audible absence of commentary which followed the Colonel's remarks? There was an intense curiosity —I felt it myself—to see what a clever fellow like the Professor would do. The Colonel stood there wiping his forehead, as if, having thrown down the gauntlet, he were prepared to defend it. The Professor looked at him with his head on one side, and a smile which was an excellent imitation of genial tolerance. 'My dear sir,' he cried, 'I'm glad you've eased your mind. I knew you wanted to; I hope you feel better. With your leave, we won't go into the philosophy of the dispute. It was George Washington, I believe, who said that people should wash their dirty linen at home. You don't endorse my views—you're welcome. If you weren't a very polite old gentleman, I know you'd like to say that, in a single word, they're the views of a quack. Now, in a single word, I deny it. You deny the existence of the magnetic power; I reply that I personally possess it, and that if you'll give me a little more time, I'll force you to say that there's something in it. I'll force you to say I can do something. These gentlemen here can't witness the consummation, but at least they can hear my promise. I promise you evidence. You go by facts: I'll give you facts. I'd like just to have you remark before our friends here, that you'll take account of them!'

The Colonel stood still, wiping his forehead. He had even less prevision than I of the character of the Professor's projected facts, but of course he could make but one answer. He bowed gravely to the Professor and to the company. 'I shall never refuse,' he said, 'to examine serious evidence.' 'Whatever,' he added, after a moment, 'it might cost my prejudices.'

III.

The Colonel's incorruptible conservatism had done me good mentally, and his personal situation had deeply interested me. As I bade him farewell the next day—the 'Combination' had been heralded in a neighbouring town—I wished him heartily that what was so painfully crooked in the latter might be straightened out in time. He shook his head sadly, and answered that his time was up.

He was often in my thoughts for the next six weeks, but I got no tidings of him. Meanwhile I too was leading an ambulant life, and travelling from town to town in a cause which demanded a good deal of ready-made eloquence. I didn't exactly pretend that the regeneration of society depended on its acceptance of my wares, but I devoted a good deal of fellow feeling to the Colonel's experiences as an uncredited solicitor. At the beginning of the winter I found myself in New York. One evening, as I wandered along a certain avenue, undedicated to gentility, I perceived, in the flare of a gas-lamp, on a placard beside a doorway, the name and attributes of Professor Fargo. I immediately stopped and read the manifesto. It was even more grandiloquent than the yellow hand-bill at P—; for to over-top concurrence in the metropolis one must mount upon very high stilts indeed. The 'Combination' still subsisted, and Colonel Gifford brought up the rear. I observed with interest that his daughter now figured in an independent and extremely ornamental paragraph. Above the door was a blue lamp, and beneath the lamp the in-scription 'Excelsior Hall'. No one was going in, but as I stood there a young man in a white overcoat, with his hat on his nose, came out and planted himself viciously, with a tell-tale yawn, in the doorway. The poor Colonel had lost an auditor; I was determined he should have a substitute. Paying my fee and making my way into the room, I found that the situation was indeed one in which units rated high. There were not more than twenty people present, and the appearance of this meagre group was not in striking harmony with the state-ment on the placard without, that Professor Fargo's entertainment was thronged with the intellect and fashion of the metropolis. The Professor was on the platform, unfolding his budget of miracles; be-hind him, as at P—, sat the Colonel and his daughter. The Professor was evidently depressed by the preponderance of empty benches, and carried off his revelations with an indifferent grace. Disappoint-ment made him brutal. He was heavy, vulgar, slipshod; he stumbled in his periods, and bungled more than once in his guesses when the folded papers with the names were put into the hat. His brow wore a vicious, sullen look, which seemed to deepen the expression of melancholy patience in his companions. I trembled for my friends. The Colonel had told me that his bargain with his impresario was a poor one, and I was sure that if, when the 'Combination' was in a run of luck, as it had been at P—, his dividend was scanty, he was paying a heavy share of penalty for the present eclipse of fortune. I sat down near the door, where the hall was shrouded in a thrifty dimness, so that I had no fear of being recognized. The Professor evidently was reckless—a fact which rather puzzled me in so shrewd a man. When he had brought his own performance to an un-applauded close, instead of making his customary speech on behalf of his coadjutor, he dropped into a chair and gaped at the face of his audience. But the Colonel, after a pause, threw himself into the breach—or rather lowered himself into it with stately gravity—and addressed his humble listeners (half of whom were asleep) as if they had been the flower of the Intellect and Fashion. But if his manner was the old one, his discourse was new. He had too many ideas to repeat himself, and, although those which he now attempted to ex-pound were still above the level of my frivolous apprehension, this unbargained abundance of inspiration half convinced me that his claim to original genius was just. If there had been something grotesquely sad in his appeal to the irresponsive intellect of P——, it was almost intolerably dismal to sit there and see him grappling with the dusky void of Excelsior Hall. The sleepers waked up, or turned over, at least, when Miss Gifford came forward. She wore, as yet, neither a pink dress nor an artificial garland, but it seemed to me that I detected here and there an embryonic hint of these ornaments—a ruffle round her neck, a coloured sash over her black dress, a curl or two more in her hair. But her manner was as childish, as simple and serene as ever; the empty benches had no weary meaning for her.

I confess that in spite of my personal interest in my friend, the entertainment seemed woefully long; more than once I was on the point of departing, and awaiting the conclusion in the street. But I had not the heart to inflict upon the poor Colonel the sight of a retreating spectator. When at last my twenty companions had shuffled away, I made my way to the platform and renewed acquaintance with the trio. The Professor nodded with uncompromising familiarity, the Colonel seemed cordially glad to see me, and his daughter, as I made her my bow, gazed at me with even more than usual of her clear-eyed frankness. She seemed to wonder what my reappearance meant for them. It meant, to begin with, that I went the next day to see the Colonel at his lodging. It was a terribly modest little lodging, but he did me the honours with a grace which showed that he had an old habit of hospitality. He admitted frankly that the 'Combination' had lately been doing a very poor business, but he made the admission with a gloomy stoicism which showed me that he had been looking the event full in the face, and had assented to it helplessly. They had gone their round in the country, with varying success. They had the misfortune to have a circus keeping just in advance of them, and beside the gorgeous pictorial placards of this establishment, their own superior promises, even when swimming in a deluge of exclamation points, seemed pitifully vague. 'What are my daughter and I,' said the Colonel, 'after the educated elephant and the female trapezist? What even is the Professor, after the great American clown?' Their profits, however, had been kept fairly above the minimum, and victory would still have hovered about their banners if they had been content to invoke her in the smaller towns. The Professor, however, in spite of remonstrance, had suddenly steered for New York, and what New York was doing for them I had seen the night before. The last half dozen performances had not paid for the room and the gas. The Colonel told me that he was bound by contract for five more lectures. but that when these were delivered he would dissolve the partnership. The Professor, in insisting on coming to the city, had shown a signal want of shrewdness; and when his shrewdness failed him, what had you left? What to attempt himself, the Colonel couldn't imagine. 'At the worst,' he said, 'my daughter can go into an asylum, and I can go into the poor-house.' On my asking him whether his colleague had yet established, according to his vow, the verities of 'spiritual magnetism', he stared in surprise and seemed quite to have forgotten the Professor's engagement to convert him. 'Oh, I've let him off,' he said, shaking his head. 'He was tipsy when he made the promise, and I expect to hear no more about it.'

I was very busy, and the pensive old man was gloomy company; but his characters and his fortunes had such a melancholy interest that I found time to pay him several visits. He evidently was thankful to be diverted from his sombre self-consciousness and his paternal anxiety, and, when once he was aroused from the dogged resignation in which he seemed plunged, enjoyed vastly the chance to expatiate on his multitudinous and irrealizable theories, Most of the time his meaning was a cloud bank to me, but I listened, assented, applauded; I felt the charm of pure intellectual passion. I incline to believe that he had excogitated some extremely valuable ideas. We took long walks through the crowded streets. The Colonel was indefatigable, in spite of his leanness and pallor. He strode along with great steps, talking so loud, half the time, in his high, quavering voice, that even the eager pedestrians in the lower latitudes of Broadway slackened pace to glance back at him. He declared that the crowded streets gave him a strange exhilaration, and the mighty human hum of the great city quickened his heart-beats almost to pain. More than once he stopped short, on the edge of a kerbstone or in the middle of a crossing, and laying his hand on my arm, with a deeper glow beneath his white eyebrows, broke into a kind of rhapsody of transcendental thought. 'It's for all these millions I would work, if they would let me!' he cried. 'It's to the life of great cities my schemes are addressed. It's to make millions wiser and better that I stand pleading my cause so long after I have earned my rest.' One day he seemed taciturn and preoccupied. He talked much less than usual, noticed nothing, and walked with his eyes on the pavement. I imagined that, in a phrase with which he had made me familiar, he had caught the tail of an idea and was holding it fast, in spite of its slippery contortions. As we neared his lodging at the end of our walk, he stopped abruptly in the middle of the street, and I had to give him a violent pull to rescue him from a rattling butcher's cart. When we reached the pavement he stopped again, grasped me by the hand, and fixed his eyes on me with a very extraordinary exaltation. We were at the top of the shabby cross-street in which he had found a shelter. A row of squalid tenements faced us, and half a dozen little Irish ragamuffins were sprawling beneath our feet, between their doorways and the gutter. 'Eureka! Eureka!' he cried. 'I've found it—I've found it!' And on my asking him what he had found, 'Something science has groped for, for ages—the solution of the incalculable! Perhaps, too, my fortune; certainly my immortality! Quick, quick! Before it vanishes I must get at my pen.' And he hurried me along to his dingy little dwelling. On the doorstep he paused. 'I can't tell you now,' he cried. 'I must fling it down in black and white. But for heaven's sake, come tonight to the lecture, and in the first flush of apprehension I think I can knock off a statement!' To the lecture I promised to come. At the same moment I raised my eyes and beheld in the window of the Colonel's apartment the ominous visage of Professor Fargo. I had been kindled by the Colonel's ardour, but somehow I was suddenly chilled by the presence of the Professor. I feared that, be the brilliancy of my friend's sudden illumination what it might, the shock of meeting his unloved *confrère* under his own roof would loosen his grasp of his idea. I found a pretext for keeping him standing a moment, and observed that the Professor disappeared. The next moment the door opened and he stepped forth. He had put on his hat, I suppose, hastily; it was cocked towards one side with a jauntiness which seemed the climax of his habitual swagger. He was evidently in better spirits than when I listened to him at Excelsior Hall; but neither the Professor's smiles nor his frowns were those of an honest man. He bestowed on my companion and me one of the most expansive of the former, gave his hat a cock in the opposite direction, and was about to pass on. But suddenly bethinking himself, he paused and drew from his pocket a small yellow ticket, which he presented to me. It was admission to Excelsior Hall.

'If you can use this tonight,' he said, 'I think you'll see something out of the common.' This intimation, accompanied with a wink of extreme suggestiveness, seemed to indicate that the Professor also, by a singular coincidence, had had a flash of artistic inspiration. But giving me no further clue, he rapidly went his way. As I shook hands in farewell with the Colonel, I saw that the light of the old man's new inspiration had gone out in angry wonderment over the Professor's errand with his daughter.

I can hardly define the vague apprehensiveness which led me to make that evening a peculiarly prompt appearance at Excelsior Hall. There was no one there when I arrived, and for half an hour the solitude remained unbroken. At last a shabby little man came in and sat down on the last bench, in the shade. We remained a while staring

at the white wall behind the three empty chairs of the performers
and listening to the gas-burners, which were hissing with an expressiveness which, under the circumstances, was most distressing. At
last my companion left his place and strolled down the aisle. He
stopped before the platform, turned about, surveyed the capacity of
the room, and muttered something between a groan and an imprecation. Then he came back towards me and stopped. He had a
dirty shirt-front, a scrubby beard, a small, wrathful black eye, and a
nose unmistakably Judaic.

'If you don't want to sit and be lectured at all alone,' he said, 'I
guess you'd better go.'

I expressed a hope that some one would turn up yet, and said that
I preferred to remain, in any event, as I had a particular interest in
the performance.

'A particular interest?' he cried; 'that's about what I've got. I've
got the rent of my room to collect. This thing has been going on
here for three weeks now, and I haven't seen the first dollar of *my*
profits. It's been going down hill steady, and I think the Professor,
and the Colonel, and the deaf and dumb young woman had better
shut up shop. They ain't appreciated; they'd better try some other
line. There's mighty little to this thing, anyway; it ain't what I
call an attractive exhibition. I've got an offer for the premises for a
month from the Canadian Giantess, and I mean to ask the present
company to pay me down and vacate.'

It looked, certainly, as if the 'Combination' would have some difficulty in meeting its engagements. The Professor's head emerged
inquiringly from a door behind the stage and disappeared, after a
brief communion with the vacuity of the scene. In a few minutes,
however, the customary trio came forth and seated itself gravely on
the platform. The Professor thrust his thumbs into his waistcoat
and drummed on the floor with his toes, as if it cost his shrewdness a
painful effort to play any longer at expectation. The Colonel sat stiff
and solemn, with his eyes on the ground. The young girl gazed forth
upon the ungrateful void with her characteristically irresponsible
tranquillity. For myself, after listening some ten minutes more for
an advancing tread, I leaned my elbows on the back of the bench
before me and buried my head; I couldn't bear any longer to look
at the Colonel. At last I heard a scramble behind me, and looking
round, say my little Jew erecting himself on his feet on a bench.

'Gentlemen!' he cried out, 'I don't address the young woman; I'm
told she can't hear. I suppose the man with the biggest audience
has a right to speak. The amount of money in this hall tonight is
just thirty cents—unless, indeed, my friend here is on the free list.

Now it stands to reason that you can't pay your night's expenses out of thirty cents. I think we might as well turn down some of this gas; we can still see to settle our little account. To have it paid will gratify me considerably more than anything you can do there. I don't judge your entertainment; I've no doubt it's a very smart thing. But it's very evident it don't suit this city. It's too intellectual. I've got something else in view—I don't mind telling you it's the Canadian Giantess. It is going to open tomorrow with a matinée, and I want to put some props under that platform. So you'd better pay this young man his money back, and go home to supper. But before you leave, I'll trouble you for the sum of ninety-three dollars and eighty-seven cents.'

The Professor stroked his beard; the Colonel didn't move. The little Jew descended from his perch and approached the platform with his bill in his hand. In a moment I followed him.

'We're a failure,' said the Professor, at last. 'Very well! I'm not discouraged; I'm a practical man. I've got an idea in my head by which, six months hence, I expect to fill the Academy of Music.' Then, after a pause, turning to his companion, 'Colonel, do you happen to have ninety-three dollars and eighty-seven cents?'

The Colonel slowly raised his eyes and looked at him; I shall never forget the look.

'Seriously speaking,' the Professor went on, daunted but for an instant, 'you're liable for half the debt. But I'll assume your share on a certain condition. I have in my head the plan of another entertainment. Our friend here is right; we have been too intellectual. Very good!' and he nodded at the empty benches. 'I've learned the lesson. Henceforth I'm going to be sensational. My great sensation' —and he paused a moment to engage again the eye of the Colonel, who presently looked vaguely up at him—'is this young lady!' and he thrust out a hand towards Miss Gifford. 'Allow me to exhibit your daughter for a month, in my own way and according to my own notions, and I assume your debt.'

The young girl dropped her eyes on the ground, but kept her place. She had evidently been schooled. The Colonel slowly got up, glaring and trembling with indignation. I wished to cut the knot, and I interrupted his answer. 'Your inducement is null,' I said to the Professor. 'I assume the Colonel's debt. It shall be paid this moment.'

Professor Fargo gave an honestly gleeful grin; this was better even than the Colonel's assent. 'You refuse your consent then,' he demanded of the old man, 'to your daughter's appearance under my exclusive management.'

'Utterly!' cried the Colonel.

'You are aware, I suppose, that she's of age?'

The Colonel stared at me with a groan, 'What under heaven is the fellow coming to?'

'To this!' responded the Professor; and he fixed his eye for a moment on the young girl. She immediately looked up at him, rose, advanced, and stood before him. Her face betrayed no painful consciousness of what she was doing, and I have often wondered how far, in her strangely simple mood and nature, her consciousness on this occasion was a guilty one. I never ascertained. This was the most unerring stroke I had seen the Professor perform. The poor child fixed her charming eyes on his gross, flushed face, and awaited his commands. She was fascinated; she had no will of her own. 'You'll be so good as to choose,' the Professor went on, addressing her in spite of her deafness, 'between your father and me. He says we're to part. I say you're to follow me. What do you say?'

For all answer, after caressing him a moment with her gentle gaze, she dropped before him on her knees. The Colonel sprang towards her with a sort of howl of rage and grief, but she jumped up, retreated, and tripped down the steps of the platform into the room. She rapidly made her way to the door. There she paused and looked back at us. Her father stood staring after her in helpless bewilderment. The Professor disappeared into the little ante-room behind the stage, and came back in a moment jamming his hat over his eyes and carrying the young girl's shawl. He reached the edge of the platform, and then, stopping, shook the forefinger with the turquoise ring at the Colonel.

'What do you say now?' he cried. 'Is spiritual magnetism a humbug?'

The little Jew rushed after him, shrieking and brandishing the unpaid bill; but the Professor cleared at half a dozen strides the interval which divided him from the door, caught the young girl round the waist, and made a triumphant escape. Half an hour later the Colonel and I left the little Jew staring distractedly at his unretributed gas-burners.

I walked home with the old man, and, having led him into his shabby refuge, suffered him to make his way alone, with groans, and tears, and imprecations, into his daughter's empty room. At last he came tottering out again; it seemed as if he were going mad. I brought him away by force, and he passed the night in my own quarters. He had spoken shortly before of the prospect of an asylum for his daughter, but it became evident that the asylum would have to be for him.

I sometimes go to see him. He spends his days covering little square sheets of paper with algebraic signs, but I am assured by his superintendent, who understands the matter, that they represent no coherent mathematical operation. I never treated myself to the 'sensation' of attending Professor Fargo's new entertainment.

Eugene Pickering
IN TWO PARTS

[First appeared in the *Atlantic Monthly*, vol. xxxiv (October–November 1874), pp. 397–410, 513–26. The tale was revised and reprinted in *A Passionate Pilgrim* (1875). The 1875 text was revised and reprinted in volume ii of *The Madonna of the Future* (1879). This text was later reproduced in volume xiv of James's first 'Collective Edition' (1883).]

PART I

IT WAS AT HOMBURG, SEVERAL YEARS AGO, BEFORE THE play had been suppressed. The evening was very warm, and all the world was gathered on the terrace of the Kursaal and the esplanade below it, to listen to the excellent orchestra; or half the world, rather, for the crowd was equally dense in the gaming rooms, around the tables. Everywhere the crowd was great. The night was perfect, the season was at its height, the open windows of the Kursaal sent long shafts of unnatural light into the dusky woods, and now and then, in the intervals of the music, one might almost hear the clink of the napoleons and the metallic call of the *croupiers* rise above the watching silence of the saloons. I had been strolling with a friend, and we at last prepared to sit down. Chairs, however, were scarce. I had captured one, but it seemed no easy matter to find a mate for it. I was on the point of giving up in despair and proposing an adjournment to the damask divans of the Kursaal, when I observed a young man lounging back on one of the objects of my quest, with his feet supported on the rounds of another. This was more than his share of luxury, and I promptly approached him. He evidently belonged to the race which has the credit of knowing best, at home and abroad, how to make itself comfortable; but something in his appearance suggested that his present attitude was the result of inadvertence rather than of egotism. He was staring at the conductor of the orchestra and listening intently to the music. His hands were locked round his long legs, and his mouth was half open, with rather a foolish air. 'There are so few chairs,' I said, 'that I must beg you to surrender this second one.' He started, stared, blushed, pushed the chair away with awkward alacrity, and murmured something about not having noticed that he had it.

'What an odd-looking youth!' said my companion, who had

watched me, as I seated myself beside her.

'Yes, he's odd-looking; but what is odder still is that I've seen him before, that his face is familiar to me, and yet that I can't place him.' The orchestra was playing the Prayer from Der Freischütz, but Weber's lovely music only deepened the blank of memory. Who the deuce was he? where, when, how, had I known him? It seemed extraordinary that a face should be at once so familiar and so strange. We had our backs turned to him, so that I could not look at him again. When the music ceased, we left our places and I went to consign my friend to her mamma on the terrace. In passing, I saw that my young man had departed; I concluded that he only strikingly resembled some one I knew. But who in the world was it he resembled? The ladies went off to their lodgings, which were near by, and I turned into the gaming rooms and hovered about the circle at roulette. Gradually, I filtered through to the inner edge, near the table, and, looking round, saw my puzzling friend stationed opposite to me. He was watching the game, with his hands in his pockets; but singularly enough, now that I observed him at my leisure, the look of familiarity quite faded from his face. What had made us call his appearance odd was his great length and leanness of limb, his long, white neck, his blue, prominent eyes, and his in-genuous, unconscious absorption in the scene before him. He was not handsome, certainly, but he looked peculiarly amiable, and if his overt wonderment savoured a trifle of rurality, it was an agreeable contrast to the hard, inexpressive masks about him. He was the ver-dent offshoot, I said to myself, of some ancient, rigid stem; he had been brought up in the quietest of homes, and was having his first glimpse of life. I was curious to see whether he would put anything on the table; he evidently felt the temptation, but he seemed para-lysed by chronic embarrassment. He stood gazing at the rattling cross-fire of losses and gains, shaking his loose gold in his pocket, and every now and then passing his hand nervously over his eyes.

Most of the spectators were too attentive to the play to have many thoughts for each other; but before long I noticed a lady who evi-dently had an eye for her neighbours as well as for the table. She was seated about half-way between my friend and me, and I presently observed that she was trying to catch his eye. Though at Homburg, as people said, 'one could never be sure', I yet doubted whether this lady was one of those whose especial vocation it was to catch a gentleman's eye. She was youthful rather than elderly, and pretty rather than plain; indeed, a few minutes later, when I saw her smile, I thought her wonderfully pretty. She had a charm-ing grey eye and a good deal of blonde hair, disposed in picturesque disorder; and though her features were meagre and her complexion faded, she gave one a sense of sentimental, artificial gracefulness. She was dressed in white muslin very much puffed and frilled, but a trifle the worse for wear, relieved here and there by a pale blue ribbon. I used to flatter myself on guessing at people's nationality by their faces, and, as a rule, I guessed aright. This faded, crumpled, vaporous beauty, I conceived, was a German—such a German, somehow, as I had seen imaged in literature. Was she not a friend of poets, a correspondent of philosophers, a muse, a priestess of aesthetics— something in the way of a Bettina, a Rahel? My conjectures, however, were speedily merged in wonderment as to what my diffident friend was making of her. She caught his eye at last, and raising an ungloved hand, covered altogether with blue-gemmed rings,—turquoises, sapphires, and lapis,—she beckoned him to come to her. The gesture was executed with a sort of practised coolness and accompanied with an appealing smile. He stared a moment, rather blankly, unable to suppose that the invitation was addressed to him; then, as it was immediately repeated, with a good deal of intensity, he blushed to the roots of his hair, wavered awkwardly, and at last made his way to the lady's chair. By the time he reached it he was crimson and wiping his forehead with his pocket-handkerchief. She tilted back, looked up at him with the same smile, laid two fingers on his sleeve, and said something, interrogatively, to which he replied by a shake of the head. She was asking him, evidently, if he had ever played, and he was saying no. Old players have a fancy that when luck has turned her back on them, they can put her into good humour again by having their stakes placed by an absolute novice. Our young man's physiognomy had seemed to his new acquaintance to express the perfection of inexperience, and, like a practical woman, she had determined to make him serve her turn. Unlike most of her neighbours, she had no little pile of gold before her, but she drew from her pocket a double napoleon, put it into his hand, and bade him place it on a number of his own choosing. He was evidently filled with a sort of delightful trouble; he enjoyed the adventure, but he shrank from the hazard. I would have staked the coin on its being his companion's last; for although she still smiled, intently, as she watched his hesitation, there was anything but indifference in her pale, pretty face. Suddenly, in desperation, he reached over and laid the piece on the table. My attention was diverted at this moment by my having to make way for a lady with a great many flounces, before me, to give up her chair to a rustling friend to whom she had promised it; when I again looked across at the lady in white muslin, she was drawing in a very goodly pile of gold with her little blue-gemmed claw. Good luck and bad, at the Homburg tables, were equally undemonstrative, and this fair adventuress rewarded her young friend for the sacrifice of his innocence with a single, rapid, upward smile. He had innocence enough left, however, to look round the table with a gleeful, conscious laugh, in the midst of which his eyes encountered my own. Then, suddenly, the familiar look which had vanished from his face flickered up unmistakably; it was the boyish laugh of a boyhood's friend. Stupid fellow that I was, I had been looking at Eugene Pickering!

Though I lingered on for some time longer, he failed to recognize me. Recognition, I think, had kindled a smile in my own face; but less fortunate than he, I suppose my smile had ceased to be boyish. Now that luck had faced about again, his companion played for herself—played and won hand over hand. At last she seemed disposed to rest on her gains, and proceeded to bury them in the folds of her muslin. Pickering had staked nothing for himself, but as he saw her prepare to withdraw, he offered her a double napoleon and begged her to place it. She shook her head with great decision, and seemed to bid him put it up again; but he, still blushing a good deal, urged her with awkward ardour, and she at last took it from him, looked at him a moment fixedly, and laid it on a number; a moment later the croupier was raking it in. She gave the young man a little nod which seemed to say, 'I told you so'; he glanced round the table again and laughed; she left her chair and he made a way for her through the crowd. Before going home I took a turn on the terrace and looked down on the esplanade. The lamps were out, but the warm starlight vaguely illumined a dozen figures scattered in couples. One of these figures, I thought, was a lady in a white dress.

I had no intention of letting Pickering go without reminding him of our old acquaintance. He had been a very droll boy, and I was curious to see what had become of his drollery. I looked for him the next morning at two or three of the hotels, and at last discovered his whereabouts. But he was out, the waiter said; he had gone to walk an hour before. I went my way, confident that I should meet him in the evening. It was the rule with the Homburg world to spend its evenings at the Kursaal, and Pickering, apparently, had already discovered a good reason for not being an exception. One of the charms of Homburg is the fact that of a hot day you may walk about for a whole afternoon in unbroken shade. The umbrageous gardens of the Kursaal mingle with the charming Hardtwald, which, in turn, melts away into the wooded slopes of the Taunus Mountains. To the Hardtwald I bent my steps, and strolled for an hour through mossy glades and the still, perpendicular gloom of the fir-woods. Suddenly, on the grassy margin of a by-path, I came upon a young man stretched at his length in the sun-checkered shade and kicking his heels towards a patch of blue sky. My step was so noiseless on the turf, that before he saw me, I had time to recognize Pickering again. He looked as if he had been lounging there for some time; his hair was tossed about as if he had been sleeping; on the grass near him, beside his hat and stick, lay a sealed letter. When he perceived me he jerked himself forward, and I stood looking at him without elucidating,—purposely, to give him a chance to recognize me. He put on his glasses, being awkwardly near-sighted, and stared up at me with an air of general trustfulness, but without a sign of knowing me. So at last I introduced myself. Then he jumped up and grasped my hands and stared and blushed and laughed and began a dozen random questions, ending with a demand as to how in the world I had known him.

'Why, you're not changed so utterly,' I said, 'and after all, it's but fifteen years since you used to do my Latin exercises for me.'

'Not changed, eh?' he answered, still smiling and yet speaking with a sort of ingenuous dismay.

Then I remembered that poor Pickering had been in those Latin days a victim of juvenile irony. He used to bring a bottle of medicine to school and take a dose in a glass of water before lunch; and every day at two o'clock, half an hour before the rest of us were liberated, an old nurse with bushy eyebrows came and fetched him away in a carriage. His extremely fair complexion, his nurse, and his bottle of medicine, which suggested a vague analogy with the phial of poison in the tragedy, caused him to be called Juliet. Certainly, Romeo's sweetheart hardly suffered more; she was not, at least, a standing joke in Verona. Remembering these things, I hastened to say to Pickering that I hoped he was still the same good fellow who used to do my Latin for me. 'We were capital friends, you know,' I went on, 'then and afterwards.'

'Yes, we were very good friends,' he said, 'and that makes it the stranger I shouldn't have known you. For you know as a boy I never had many friends, nor as a man either. You see,' he added, passing his hand over his eyes, 'I'm half dazed and bewildered at finding myself for the first time—alone.' And he jerked back his shoulders nervously and threw up his head, as if to settle himself in an unwonted position. I wondered whether the old nurse with the bushy eyebrows had remained attached to his person up to a recent period, and discovered presently that, virtually at least, she had. We had the whole summer day before us, and we sat down on the grass together and overhauled our old memories. It was as if we had stumbled upon an ancient cupboard in some dusky corner, and rummaged out a heap of childish playthings—tin soldiers and torn storybooks, jack-knives and Chinese puzzles. This is what we remembered, between us.

He had made but a short stay at school—not because he was tormented, for he thought it so fine to be at school at all that he held his tongue at home about the sufferings incurred through the medicine bottle; but because his father thought he was learning bad manners. This he imparted to me in confidence at the time, and I remember how it increased my oppressive awe of Mr. Pickering, who had appeared to me, in glimpses, as a sort of high priest of the proprieties. Mr. Pickering was a widower—a fact which seemed to produce in him a sort of preternatural concentration of parental dignity. He was a majestic man, with a hooked nose, a keen, dark eye, very large whiskers, and notions of his own as to how a boy—or his boy, at any rate—should be brought up. First and foremost, he was to be a 'gentleman', which seemed to mean, chiefly, that he was always to wear a muffler and gloves, and be sent to bed, after a supper of bread and milk, at eight o'clock. School-life, on experiment, seemed hostile to these observances, and Eugene was taken home again, to be moulded into urbanity beneath the parental eye. A tutor was provided for him, and a single select companion was prescribed. The choice, mysteriously, fell upon me, born as I was under quite another star; my parents were appealed to, and I was allowed for a few months to have my lessons with Eugene. The tutor, I think, must have been rather a snob, for Eugene was treated like a prince, while I got all the questions and the raps with the ruler. And yet I remember never being jealous of my happier comrade, and striking up, for the time, a huge boyish friendship. He had a watch and a pony and a great store of picture-books, but my envy of these luxuries was tempered by a vague compassion, which left me free to be generous. I could go out to play alone, I could button my jacket myself, and sit up till I was sleepy. Poor Pickering could never take a step without a prior petition, or spend half an hour in the garden without a formal report of it when he came in. My parents, who had no desire to see me inoculated with importunate virtues, sent me back to school at the end of six months. After that I never saw Eugene. His father went to live in the country, to protect the lad's morals, and Eugene faded, in reminiscence, into a pale image of the depressing effects of education. I think I vaguely supposed that he would melt into thin air, and indeed began gradually to doubt of his existence and to regard him as one of the foolish things one ceased to believe in as one grew older. It seemed natural that I should have no more news of him. Our present meeting was my first assurance that he had really survived all that muffling and coddling.

I observed him now with a good deal of interest, for he was a rare phenomenon—the fruit of a system persistently and uninterruptedly applied. He struck me, in a fashion, like certain young monks I had seen in Italy; he had the same candid, unsophisticated, cloister face. His education had been really almost monastic. It had found him, evidently, a very compliant, yielding subject; his gentle, affectionate spirit was not one of those that need to be broken. It had bequeathed him, now that he stood on the threshold of the great world, an extraordinary freshness of impression and alertness of desire, and I confess that, as I looked at him and met his transparent blue eye, I trembled for the unwarned innocence of such a soul. I became aware, gradually, that the world had already wrought a certain work upon him and roused him to a restless, troubled self-consciousness. Everything about him pointed to an experience from which he had been debarred; his whole organism trembled with a dawning sense of unsuspected possibilities of feeling. This appealing tremor was indeed outwardly visible. He kept shifting himself about on the grass, thrusting his hands through his hair, wiping a light perspiration from his forehead, breaking out to say something and rushing off to something else. Our sudden meeting had greatly excited him, and I saw that I was likely to profit by a certain overflow of sentimental fermentation. I could do so with a good conscience, for all this trepidation filled me with a great friendliness.

'It's nearly fifteen years, as you say,' he began, 'since you used to call me "butter-fingers" for always missing the ball. That's a long time to give an account of, and yet they have been, for me, such eventless, monotonous years, that I could almost tell their history in ten words. You, I suppose, have had all kinds of adventures and travelled over half the world. I remember you had a turn for deeds of daring; I used to think you a little Captain Cook in roundabouts, for climbing the garden-fence to get the ball, when I had let it fly over. I climbed no fences then or since. You remember my father, I suppose, and the great care he took of me? I lost him some five months ago. From those boyish days up to his death we were always together. I don't think that in fifteen years we spent half a dozen hours apart. We lived in the country, winter and summer, seeing but three or four people. I had a succession of tutors, and a library to browse about in; I assure you I'm a tremendous scholar. It was a dull life for a growing boy, and a duller life for a young man grown, but I never knew it. I was perfectly happy.' He spoke of his father at some length and with a respect which I privately declined to emulate. Mr. Pickering had been, to my sense, a cold egotist, unable to conceive of any larger vocation for his son than to become a mechanical reflection of himself. 'I know I've been strangely brought up,' said my friend, 'and that the result is something grotesque; but my education, piece by piece, in detail, became one of my father's personal habits, as it were. He took a fancy to it at first through his intense affection for my mother and the sort of worship he paid her memory. She died at my birth, and as I grew up, it seems that I bore an extraordinary likeness to her. Besides, my father had a great many theories; he prided himself on his conservative opinions; he thought the usual American *laissez aller* in education was a very vulgar practice, and that children were not to grow up like dusty thorns by the wayside. So you see,' Pickering went on, smiling and blushing, and yet with something of the irony of vain regret, 'I'm a regular garden plant. I've been watched and watered and pruned, and, if there is any virtue in tending, I ought to take the prize at a flower-show. Some three years ago my father's health broke down and he was kept very much within doors. So, although I was a man grown, I lived altogether at home. If I was out of his sight for a quarter of an hour he sent for me. He had severe attacks of neuralgia, and he used to sit at his window, basking in the sun. He kept an opera-glass at hand, and when I was out in the garden he used to watch me with it. A few days before his death, I was twenty-seven years old, and the most innocent youth, I suppose, on the continent. After he died I missed him greatly,' Pickering continued, evidently with no intention of making an epigram. 'I stayed at home, in a sort of dull stupor. It seemed as if life offered itself to me for the first time, and yet as if I didn't know how to take hold of it.'

He uttered all this with a frank eagerness which increased as he talked, and there was a singular contrast between the meagre experience he described and a certain radiant intelligence which I seemed to perceive in his glance and tone. Evidently, he was a clever fellow, and his natural faculties were excellent. I imagined he had read a great deal, and achieved, in some degree, in restless intellectual conjecture, the freedom he was condemned to ignore in practice. Opportunity was now offering a meaning to the empty forms with which his imagination was stored, but it appeared to him dimly, through the veil of his personal diffidence.

'I've not sailed round the world, as you suppose,' I said, 'but I confess I envy you the novelties you are going to behold. Coming to Homburg, you have plunged *in medias res.*'

He glanced at me, to see if my remark contained an allusion, and hesitated a moment. 'Yes, I know it. I came to Bremen in the steamer with a very friendly German, who undertook to initiate me into the glories and mysteries of the fatherland. At this season, he said, I must begin with Homburg. I landed but a fortnight ago, and here I am.' Again he hesitated, as if he were going to add something about the scene at the Kursaal; but suddenly, nervously he took up the letter which was lying beside him, looked hard at the seal, with a troubled frown, and then flung it back on the grass with a sigh.

'How long do you expect to be in Europe?' I asked.

'Six months, I supposed when I came. But not so long—now!' And he let his eyes wander to the letter again.

'And where shall you go—what shall you do?'

'Everywhere, everything, I should have said yesterday. But now it is different.'

I glanced at the letter interrogatively, and he gravely picked it up and put it into his pocket. We talked for a while longer, but I saw that he had suddenly become preoccupied; that he was apparently weighing an impulse to break some last barrier of reserve. At last he suddenly laid his hand on my arm, looked at me a moment appealingly, and cried, 'Upon my word, I should like to tell you everything.'

'Tell me everything, by all means,' I answered, smiling. 'I desire nothing better than to lie here in the shade and hear everything!'

'Ah, but the question is, will you understand it? No matter; you think me a queer fellow already. It's not easy, either, to tell you what I feel—not easy for so queer a fellow as I to tell you in how many he's queer!' He got up and walked away a moment, passing his hand over his eyes, then came back rapidly and flung himself on the grass again. 'I said just now I always supposed I was happy; it's true; but now that my eyes are open, I see I was only stultified. I was like a poodle dog, led about by a blue ribbon, and scoured and combed and fed on slops. It wasn't life; life is learning to know one's self, and in that sense I've lived more in the past six weeks than in all the years that preceded them. I'm filled with this feverish sense of liberation; it keeps rising to my head like the fumes of strong wine. I find I'm an active, sentient, intelligent creature, with desires, with passions, with possible convictions—even with what I never dreamed of, a possible will of my own! I find there is a world to know, a life to lead, men and women to form a thousand relations with. It all lies there like a great surging sea, where we must plunge and dive and feel the breeze and breast the waves. I stand shivering here on the brink, staring, longing, wondering, charmed by the smell of the brine and yet afraid of the water. The world beckons and smiles and calls, but a nameless influence from the past, that I can neither wholly obey nor wholly contemn, seems to hold me back. I'm full of impulses, but, somehow, I'm not full of strength. Life seems inspiring at certain moments, but it seems terrible and unsafe; and I ask myself why I should wantonly measure myself with merciless forces, when I have learned so well how to stand aside and let them pass. Why shouldn't I turn my back upon it all and go home to—what awaits me?—to that sightless, soundless country life, and long days spent among old books? But if a man *is* weak, he doesn't want to assent beforehand to his weakness; he wants to taste whatever sweetness there may be in paying for the knowledge. So it is there comes and comes again this irresistible impulse to take my plunge, to let myself swing, to go where liberty leads me.' He paused a moment, fixing me with his excited eyes, and perhaps perceived in my own an irrepressible smile at his intensity. ' "Swing ahead, in Heaven's name," you want to say, "and much good may it do you." I don't know whether you are laughing at my trepidation or at what possibly strikes you as my depravity. I doubt,' he went on gravely, 'whether I have an inclination towards wrong-doing; if I have, I'm sure I shan't prosper in it. I honestly believe I may safely take out a licence to amuse myself. But it isn't that I think of, any more than I dream of playing with suffering. Pleasure and pain are empty words to me; what I long for is knowledge—some other knowledge than comes to us in formal, colourless, impersonal precept. You would understand all this better if you could breathe for an hour the musty in-door atmosphere in which I have always lived. To break a window and let in light and air,—I feel as if at last I must *act!*'

'Act, by all means, now and always, when you have a chance,' I answered. 'But don't take things too hard, now or ever. Your long seclusion makes you think the world better worth knowing than you're likely to find it. A man with as good a head and heart as yours has a very ample world within himself, and I'm no believer in art for art, nor in what's called "life" for life's sake. Nevertheless, take your plunge, and come and tell me whether you've found the pearl of wisdom.' He frowned a little, as if he thought my sympathy a trifle meagre. I shook him by the hand and laughed. 'The pearl of wisdom,' I cried, 'is love; honest love is the most convenient concentration of experience! I advise you to fall in love.' He gave me no smile in response, but drew from his pocket the letter of which I've spoken, held it up, and shook it solemnly. 'What is it?' I asked.

'It's my sentence!'

'Not of death, I hope!'

'Of marriage.'

'With whom?'

'With a person I don't love.'

This was serious. I stopped smiling and begged him to explain.

'It's the singular part of my story,' he said at last. 'It will remind you of an old-fashioned romance. Such as I sit here, talking in this wild way, and tossing off invitations to destiny, my destiny is settled and sealed. I'm engaged—I'm given in marriage. It's a bequest of the past—the past I never said nay to! The marriage was arranged by my father, years ago, when I was a boy. The young girl's father was his particular friend; he was also a widower, and was bringing up his daughter, on his side, in the same rigid seclusion in which I was spending my days. To this day, I'm unacquainted with the origin of the bond of union between our respective progenitors. Mr. Vernor was largely engaged in business, and I imagine that once upon a time he found himself in a financial strait and was helped through it by my father's coming forward with a heavy loan, on which, in his situation, he could offer no security but his word. Of this my father was quite capable. He was a man of dogmas, and he was sure to have a precept adapted to the conduct of a gentleman towards a friend in pecuniary embarrassment. What's more, he was sure to adhere to it. Mr. Vernor, I believe, got on his feet, paid his debt, and vowed my father an eternal gratitude. His little daughter was the apple of his eye, and he pledged himself to bring her up to be the wife of his benefactor's son. So our fate was fixed, parentally, and we have been educated for each other. I've not seen my betrothed since she was a very plain-faced little girl in a sticky pinafore, hugging a one-armed doll—of the male sex, I believe—as big as herself. Mr. Vernor is in what's called the Eastern trade, and has been living these many years at Smyrna. Isabel has grown up there in a white-walled garden, in an orange grove, between her father and her governess. She is a good deal my junior; six months ago she was seventeen; when she is eighteen we're to marry!'

He related all this calmly enough, without the accent of complaint, dryly rather and doggedly, as if he were weary of thinking of it, 'It's a romance indeed,' I said, 'for these dull days, and I heartily congratulate you. It's not every young man who finds, on reaching the marrying age, a wife kept in cotton for him. A thousand to one Miss Vernor is charming; I wonder you don't post off to Smyrna.'

'You're joking,' he answered, with a wounded air, 'and I am terribly serious. Let me tell you the rest. I never suspected this tender conspiracy till something less than a year ago. My father, wishing to provide against his death, informed me of it, solemnly. I was neither elated nor depressed; I received it, as I remember, with a sort of emotion which varied only in degree from that with which I could have hailed the announcement that he had ordered me a dozen new shirts. I supposed that it was under some such punctual, superterrestrial dispensation as this that all young men were married. Novels and poems indeed said otherwise; but novels and poems were one thing and life was another. A short time afterwards he introduced me to a photograph of my predestined, who has a pretty, but an extremely inanimate face. After this his health failed rapidly. One night I was sitting, as I habitually sat for hours, in his dimly lighted room, near his bed, to which he had been confined for a week. He had not spoken for some time, and I supposed he was asleep, but happening to look at him I saw his eyes wide open and fixed on me strangely. He was smiling benignantly, intensely, and in a moment he beckoned to me. Then, on my going to him—"I feel that I shan't last long," he said, "but I am willing to die when I think how comfortably I have arranged your future." He was talking of death, and anything but grief at that moment was doubtless impious and monstrous; but there came into my heart for the first time a throbbing sense of being over-governed. I said nothing, and he thought my silence was all sorrow. "I shan't live to see you married," he went on, "but since the foundation is laid, that little signifies; it would be a selfish pleasure, and I have never had a thought but for your own personal advantage. To foresee your future, in its main outline, to know to a certainty that you'll be safely domiciled here, with a wife approved by our judgment, cultivating the moral fruit of which I have sown the seed—this will content me. But, my son, I wish to clear this bright vision from the shadow of a doubt. I believe in your docility; I believe I may trust the salutary force of your respect for my memory. But I must remember that when I am removed, you will stand here alone, face to face with a myriad nameless temptations to perversity. The fumes of unrighteous pride may rise into your brain and tempt you, in the interest of a vain delusion which it will call your independence, to shatter the edifice I have so laboriously constructed. So I must ask you for a promise—the solemn promise you owe my condition." And he grasped my hand : "You will follow the path I have marked; you will be faithful to the young girl whom an influence as devoted as that which has governed your own young life has moulded into everything amiable; you will marry Isabel Vernor." There was something portentous in this rigid summons. I was frightened. I drew away my hand and asked to be trusted without any such terrible vow. My reluctance startled my father into a suspicion that the vain delusion of independence had already been whispering to me. He sat up in his bed and looked at me with eyes which seemed to foresee a lifetime of odious ingratitude. I felt the reproach; I feel it now. I promised! And even now I don't regret my promise nor complain of my father's tenacity. I feel, somehow, as if the seeds of ultimate rest had been sown in those unsuspecting years—as if after many days I might gather the mellow fruit. But after many days! I'll keep my promise, I'll obey; but I want to *live* first!'

'My dear fellow, you're living now. All this passionate consciousness of your situation is a very ardent life. I wish I could say as much for my own.'

'I want to forget my situation. I want to spend three months without thinking of the past or the future, grasping whatever the present offers me. Yesterday, I thought I was in a fair way to sail with the tide. But this morning comes this memento!' And he held up his letter again.

'What is it?'

'A letter from Smyrna.'

'I see you have not yet broken the seal.'

'No, nor do I mean to, for the present. It contains bad news.'

'What do you call bad news?'

'News that I'm expected in Smyrna in three weeks. News that Mr. Vernor disapproves of my roving about the world. News that his daughter is standing expectant at the altar.'

'Isn't this pure conjecture?'

'Conjecture, possibly, but safe conjecture. As soon as I looked at the letter, something smote me at the heart. Look at the device on the seal, and I'm sure you'll find it's *Tarry not!*' And he flung the letter on the grass.

'Upon my word, you had better open it,' I said.

'If I were to open it and read my summons, do you know what I should do? I should march home and ask the *Oberkellner* how one gets to Smyrna, pack my trunk, take my ticket, and not stop till I arrived. I know I should; it would be the fascination of habit. The only way, therefore, to wander to my rope's end is to leave the letter unread.'

'In your place,' I said, 'curiosity would make me open it.'

He shook his head. 'I have no curiosity! For these many weeks the idea of my marriage has ceased to be a novelty, and I have contemplated it mentally, in every possible light. I fear nothing from that side, but I do fear something from conscience. I want my hands tied. Will you do me a favour? Pick up the letter, put it into your pocket, and keep it till I ask you for it. When I do, you may know that I am at my rope's end.'

I took the letter, smiling. 'And how long is your rope to be? The Homburg season doesn't last for ever.'

'Does it last a month? Let that be my season! A month hence you'll give it back to me.'

'Tomorrow, if you say so. Meanwhile, let it rest in peace!' And I consigned it to the most sacred interstice of my pocket-book. To say that I was disposed to humour the poor fellow would seem to be saying that I thought his demand fantastic. It was his situation, by no fault of his own, that was fantastic, and he was only trying to be natural. He watched me put away the letter, and when it had disappeared gave a soft sigh of relief. The sigh was natural and yet it set me thinking. His general recoil from an immediate responsibility imposed by others might be wholesome enough; but if there was an old grievance on one side, was there not possibly a new-born delusion on the other? It would be unkind to withhold a reflection that might serve as a warning; so I told him, abruptly, that I had been an undiscovered spectator, the night before, of his exploits at roulette.

He blushed deeply, but he met my eyes with the same radiant frankness.

'Ah, you saw then,' he cried, 'that wonderful lady?'

'Wonderful she was indeed. I saw her afterwards, too, sitting on the terrace in the starlight. I imagine she was not alone.'

'No indeed, I was with her—for nearly an hour. Then I walked home with her.'

'Verily! And did you go in?'

'No, she said it was too late to ask me; though in a general way, she declared she did not stand upon ceremony.'

'She did herself injustice. When it came to losing your money for you, she made you insist.'

'Ah, you noticed that too?' cried Pickering, still quite unconfused. 'I felt as if the whole table was staring at me; but her manner was so gracious and reassuring that I concluded she was doing nothing unusual. She confessed, however, afterwards, that she is very eccentric. The world began to call her so, she said, before she ever dreamed of it, and at last, finding that she had the reputation, in spite of herself, she resolved to enjoy its privileges. Now, she does what she chooses.'

'In other words, she is a lady with no reputation to lose?'

Pickering seemed puzzled, and smiled a little. 'Isn't that what you say of bad women?'

'Of some—of those who are found out.'

'Well,' he said, still smiling, 'I haven't yet found out Madame Blumenthal.'

'If that's her name, I suppose she's German.'

'Yes; but she speaks English so well that you might almost doubt it. She is very clever. Her husband's dead.'

I laughed, involuntarily, at the conjunction of these facts, and Pickering's clear glance seemed to question my mirth. 'You have been so bluntly frank with me,' I said, 'that I too must be frank. Tell me, if you can, whether this clever Madame Blumenthal, whose husband is dead, has given an edge to your desire for a suspension of communication with Smyrna.'

He seemed to ponder my question, unshrinkingly. 'I think not,' he said, at last. 'I've had the desire for three months; I've known Madame Blumenthal for less than twenty-four hours.'

'Very true. But when you found this letter of yours on your plate at breakfast, did you seem for a moment to see Madame Blumenthal sitting opposite?'

'Opposite?' he repeated, frowning gently.

'Opposite, my dear fellow, or anywhere in the neighbourhood. In a word, does she interest you?'

'Very much!' he cried, with his frown clearing away.

'Amen!' I answered, jumping up with a laugh. 'And now, if we are to see the world in a month, there is no time to lose. Let us begin with the Hardtwald.'

Pickering rose and we strolled away into the forest, talking of lighter things. At last we reached the edge of the wood, sat down on a fallen log, and looked out across an interval of meadow at the long wooded waves of the Taunus. What my friend was thinking of, I can't say; I was revolving his quaint history and letting my wonderment wander away to Smyrna. Suddenly I remembered that he possessed a portrait of the young girl who was waiting for him there in a white-walled garden. I asked him if he had it with him. He said nothing, but gravely took out his pocket-book and drew forth a small photograph. It represented, as the poet says, a simple maiden in her flower—a slight young girl, with a certain childish roundness of contour. There was no ease in her posture; she was standing, stiffly and shyly, for her likeness; she wore a short-waisted white dress; her arms hung at her sides and her hands were clasped in front; her head was bent downward a little, and her dark eyes fixed. But her awkwardness was as pretty as that of some angular seraph in a mediaeval carving, and in her sober gaze there seemed to lurk the questioning gleam of childhood. 'What is this for?' her charming eyes appeared to ask; 'why have I been decked, for this ceremony, in a white frock and amber beads?'

'Gracious powers!' I said to myself; 'what an enchanting thing is innocence!'

'That portrait was taken a year and a half ago,' said Pickering, as if with an effort to be perfectly just. 'By this time, I suppose, she looks a little wiser.'

'Not much, I hope,' I said, as I gave it back. 'She's lovely!'

'Yes, poor girl, she's lovely—no doubt!' And he put the thing away without looking at it.

We were silent for some moments. At last, abruptly: 'My dear fellow,' I said, 'I should take some satisfaction in seeing you immediately leave Homburg.'

'Immediately?'

'Today—as soon as you can get ready.'

He looked at me, surprised, and little by little he blushed. 'There's something I've not told you,' he said; 'something that your saying that Madame Blumenthal has no reputation to lose has made me half afraid to tell you.'

'I think I can guess it. Madame Blumenthal has asked you to come and check her numbers for her at roulette again.'

'Not at all!' cried Pickering, with a smile of triumph. 'She says that she plays no more, for the present. She has asked me to come and take tea with her this evening.'

'Ah, then,' I said, very gravely, 'of course you can't leave Homburg.'

He answered nothing, but looked askance at me, as if he were expecting me to laugh. 'Urge it strongly,' he said in a moment. 'Say it's my duty—command me.'

I didn't quite understand him, but, feathering the shaft with a harmless expletive, I told him that unless he followed my advice, I would never speak to him again.

He got up, stood before me, and struck the ground with his stick. 'Good!' he cried. 'I wanted an occasion to break a rule—to leap an obstacle. Here it is! I stay!'

I made him a mock bow for his energy. 'That's very fine,' I said; 'but now, to put you in a proper mood for Madame Blumenthal's tea, we'll go and listen to the band play Schubert under the lindens.' And we walked back through the woods.

I went to see Pickering the next day, at his inn, and on knocking, as directed, at his door, was surprised to hear the sound of a loud voice within. My knock remained unnoticed, so I presently introduced myself. I found no company, but I discovered my friend walking up and down the room and apparently declaiming to himself from a little volume bound in white vellum. He greeted me heartily, threw his book on the table, and said that he was taking a German lesson.

'And who is your teacher?' I asked, glancing at the book.

He rather avoided meeting my eye as he answered, after an instant's delay, 'Madame Blumenthal.'

'Indeed! Has she written a grammar?' I inquired.

'It's not a grammar; it's a tragedy.' And he handed me the book.

I opened it, and beheld, in delicate type, in a very large margin, a *Trauerspiel* in five acts, entitled 'Cleopatra'. There were a great many marginal corrections and annotations, apparently from the author's hand; the speeches were very long, and there was an inordinate number of soliloquies by the heroine. One of them, I remember, towards the end of the play, began in this fashion:

'What, after all, is life but sensation, and sensation but deception? —reality that pales before the light of one's dreams, as Octavia's dull beauty fades beside mine? But let me believe in some intenser bliss and seek it in the arms of death!'

'It seems decidedly passionate,' I said. 'Has the tragedy ever been acted?'

'Never in public; but Madame Blumenthal tells me that she had it played at her own house in Berlin, and that she herself undertook the part of the heroine.'

Pickering's unworldly life had not been of a sort to sharpen his perception of the ridiculous, but it seemed to me an unmistakable sign of his being under the charm that this information was very soberly offered. He was preoccupied, and irresponsive to my experimental observations on vulgar topics—the hot weather, the inn, the advent of Adelina Patti. At last he uttered his thoughts, and announced that Madame Blumenthal had turned out an extraordinarily interesting woman. He seemed to have quite forgotten our long talk in the Hardtwald, and betrayed no sense of this being a confession that he had taken his plunge and was floating with the current. He only remembered that I had spoken slightingly of the lady and hinted that it behoved me to amend my opinion. I had received the day before so strong an impression of a sort of spiritual fastidiousness in my friend's nature that, on hearing now the striking of a new hour, as it were, in his consciousness, and observing how the echoes of the past were immediately quenched in its music, I said to myself that it had certainly taken a delicate hand to regulate that fine machinery. No doubt Madame Blumenthal was a clever woman. It is a good German custom, at Homburg, to spend the hour preceding dinner in listening to the orchestra in the Kurgarten, Mozart and Beethoven; for organisms in which the interfusion of soul and sense is peculiarly mysterious, are a vigorous stimulus to the appetite. Pickering and I conformed, as we had done the day before, to the fashion, and when we were seated under the trees, he began to expatiate on his friend's merits.

'I don't know whether she is eccentric or not,' he said; 'to me every one seems eccentric, and it's not for me, yet awhile, to measure people by my narrow precedents. I never saw a gaming table in my life before, and supposed that a gamester was, of necessity, some dusky villain with an evil eye. In Germany, says Madame Blumenthal, people play at roulette as they play at billiards, and her own venerable mother originally taught her the rules of the game. It is a recognized source of subsistence for decent people with small means. But I confess Madame Blumenthal might do worse things than play roulette, and yet make them harmonious and beautiful. I have never been in the habit of thinking positive beauty the most excellent thing in a woman. I have always said to myself that if my heart was ever to be captured it would be by a sort of general grace—a sweetness of motion and tone—on which one could count for soothing impressions, as one counts on a musical instrument that is perfectly in tune. Madame Blumenthal has it—this grace that soothes and satisfies; and it seems the more perfect that it keeps order and harmony in a character really passionately ardent and active. With her multifarious impulses and accomplishments nothing would be easier than that she should seem restless and over-eager and importunate. You will know her, and I leave you to judge whether she does. She has every gift, and culture has done everything for each. What goes on in her mind, I of course can't say; what reaches the observer—the admirer—is simply a penetrating perfume of intelligence, mingled with a penetrating perfume of sympathy.'

'Madame Blumenthal,' I said, smiling, 'might be the loveliest woman in the world, and you the object of her choicest favours, and yet what I should most envy you would be, not your peerless friend, but your beautiful imagination.'

'That's a polite way of calling me a fool,' said Pickering. 'You're a sceptic, a cynic, a satirist! I hope I shall be a long time coming to that.'

'You'll make the journey fast if you travel by express trains. But pray tell me, have you ventured to intimate to Madame Blumenthal your high opinion of her?'

'I don't know what I may have said. She listens even better than she talks, and I think it possible I may have made her listen to a great deal of nonsense. For after the first words I exchanged with her I was conscious of an extraordinary evaporation of all my old diffidence. I have, in truth, I suppose,' he added, in a moment, 'owing to my peculiar circumstances, a great accumulated fund of un-

uttered things of all sorts to get rid of. Last evening, sitting there
before that lovely woman, they came swarming to my lips. Very
likely I poured them all out. I have a sense of having enshrouded
myself in a sort of mist of talk, and of seeing her lovely eyes shining
through it opposite to me, like stars above a miasmatic frog-pond.'
And here, if I remember rightly, Pickering broke off into an ardent
parenthesis, and declared that Madame Blumenthal's eyes had something in them that he had never seen in any others. 'It was a jumble
of crudities and inanities,' he went on, 'which must have seemed to
her terribly farcical; but I feel the wiser and the stronger, somehow,
for having poured them out before her; and I imagine I might have
gone far without finding another woman in whom such an exhibition
would have provoked so little of mere cold amusement.'

'Madame Blumenthal, on the contrary,' I surmised, 'entered into
your situation with warmth.'

'Exactly so—the greatest! She's wise, she knows, she has felt, she
has suffered, and now she understands!'

'She told you, I imagine, that she understood you to a *t*, and she
offered to be your guide, philosopher, and friend.'

'She spoke to me,' Pickering answered, after a pause, 'as I had
never been spoken to before, and she offered me, in effect, formally,
all the offices of a woman's friendship.'

'Which you as formally accepted?'

'To you the scene sounds absurd, I suppose, but allow me to say,
I don't care!' Pickering cried, with an air of genial aggression which
was the most inoffensive thing in the world. 'I was very much moved;
I was, in fact, very much excited. I tried to say something, but I
couldn't; I had had plenty to say before, but now I stammered and
bungled, and at last I took refuge in an abrupt retreat.'

'Meanwhile she had dropped her tragedy into your pocket!'

'Not at all. I had seen it on the table before she came in. Afterwards she kindly offered to read German aloud with me, for the
accent, two or three times a week. "What shall we begin with?" she
asked. "With this!" I said, and held up the book. And she let me
take it to look it over.'

I was neither a cynic nor a satirist, but even if I had been, I might
have had my claws clipped by Pickering's assurance, before we
parted, that Madame Blumenthal wished to know me and expected
him to introduce me. Among the foolish things which, according
to his own account, he had uttered, were some generous words in my
praise, to which she had civilly replied. I confess I was curious to
see her, but I begged that the introduction should not be immediate.
I wished, on the one hand, to let Pickering work out his destiny with-

out temptation, on my part, to play Providence; and on the other
hand I had at Homburg a group of friends with whom for another
week I had promised to spend my leisure hours. For some days I
saw little of Pickering, though we met at the Kursaal and strolled
occasionally in the park. I watched, in spite of my desire to let him
alone, for the signs and portents of the world's action upon him—
of that portion of the world, in especial, which Madame Blumenthal
had gathered up into her comprehensive soul. He seemed very
happy, and gave me in a dozen ways an impression of increased self-
confidence and maturity. His mind was admirably active, and always,
after a quarter of an hour's talk with him, I asked myself what
experience could really do, that seclusion had not, to make it bright
and fine. Every now and then I was struck with his deep enjoyment
of some new spectacle,—often trifling enough,—something foreign,
local, picturesque, some detail of manner, some accident of scenery;
and of the infinite freedom with which he felt he could go and
come and rove and linger and observe it all. It was an expansion, an
awakening, a coming to manhood in a graver fashion; as one might
arrive somewhere, after delays, in some quiet after-hour which should
transmute disappointment into gratitude for the preternatural vividness of first impressions. Each time I met him he spoke a little less
of Madame Blumenthal, but let me know generally that he saw
her often, and continued to admire her—tremendously! I was forced
to admit to myself, in spite of preconceptions, that if she was really
the ruling star of this serene efflorescence, she must be a very fine
woman. Pickering had the air of an ingenuous young philosopher
sitting at the feet of an austere muse, and not of a sentimental
spendthrift dangling about some supreme incarnation of levity.

PART II

Madame Blumenthal seemed, for the time, to have abjured the
Kursaal, and I never caught a glimpse of her. Her young friend, apparently, was an interesting study; she wished to pursue it un-
diverted.

She reappeared, however, at last, one evening at the opera, where
from my chair I perceived her in a box, looking extremely pretty.
Adelina Patti was singing, and after the rising of the curtain I was
occupied with the stage; but on looking round when it fell for the
entr'acte, I saw that the authoress of 'Cleopatra' had been joined by
her young admirer. He was sitting a little behind her, leaning forward, looking over her shoulder and listening, while she, slowly

moving her fan to and fro and letting her eye wander over the house, was apparently talking of this person and that. No doubt she was saying sharp things; but Pickering was not laughing; his eyes were following her covert indications; his mouth was half open, as it always was when he was interested; he looked intensely serious. I was glad that, having her back to him, she was unable to see how he looked. It seemed the proper moment to present myself and make her my bow; but just as I was about to leave my place, a gentleman, whom in a moment I perceived to be an old acquaintance, came to occupy the next chair. Recognition and mutual greetings followed, and I was forced to postpone my visit to Madame Blumenthal. I was not sorry, for it very soon occurred to me that Niedermeyer would be just the man to give me a fair prose version of Pickering's lyrical tributes to his friend. He was an Austrian by birth, and had formerly lived about Europe a great deal, in a series of small diplomatic posts. England especially he had often visited, and he spoke the language almost without accent. I had once spent three rainy days with him in the house of an English friend, in the country. He was a sharp observer and a good deal of a gossip; he knew a little something about everyone, and about some people everything. His knowledge on social matters generally had the flavour of all German science; it was copious, minute, exhaustive. 'Do tell me,' I said, as we stood looking round the house, 'who and what is the lady in white, with the young man sitting behind her.'

'Who?' he answered, dropping his glass. 'Madame Blumenthal! What? It would take long to say. Be introduced; it's easily done; you'll find her charming. Then, after a week, you'll tell me what she is.'

'Perhaps I shouldn't. My friend there has known her a week, and I don't think he is yet able to give an accurate account of her.'

He raised his glass again, and after looking awhile, 'I'm afraid your friend is a little—what do you call it?—a little "soft". Poor fellow! he's not the first. I've never known this lady that she had not some eligible youth hovering about in some such attitude as that, undergoing the softening process. She looks wonderfully well, from here. It's extraordinary how those women last!'

'You don't mean, I take it, when you talk about "those women", that Madame Blumenthal is not embalmed, for duration, in a certain dilution of respectability?'

'Yes and no. The sort of atmosphere that surrounds her is entirely of her own making. There is no reason, in her antecedents, that people should lower their voice when they speak of her. But some women are never at their ease till they have given some odd twist

or other to their position before the world. The attitude of upright
virtue is unbecoming, like sitting too straight in a *fauteuil*. Don't
ask me for opinions, however; content yourself with a few facts, and
an anecdote. Madame Blumenthal is Prussian, and very well born. I
remember her mother, an old Westphalian Gräfin, with principles
marshalled out like Frederick the Great's grenadiers. She was poor,
however, and her principles were an insufficient dowry for Anastasia,
who was married very young to a shabby Jew, twice her own age. He
was supposed to have money, but I'm afraid he had less than was
nominated in the bond, or else that his pretty young wife spent it
very fast. She has been a widow these six or eight years, and living,
I imagine, in rather a hand to mouth fashion. I suppose she is some
thirty-four or five years old. In winter one hears of her in Berlin,
giving little suppers to the artistic rabble there; in summer one often
sees her across the green table at Ems and Wiesbaden. She's very
clever, and her cleverness has spoiled her. A year after her marriage
she published a novel, with her views on matrimony, in the George
Sand manner, but really out-Heroding Herod. No doubt she was very
unhappy; Blumenthal was an old beast. Since then she has published
a lot of stuff—novels and poems and pamphlets on every conceivable
theme, from the conversion of Lola Montez, to the Hegelian philosophy. Her talk is much better than her writing. Her radical theories
on matrimony made people think lightly of her at a time when her
rebellion against it was probably theoretic. She had a taste for spin-
ning fine phrases, she drove her shuttle, and when she came to the
end of her yarn, she found that society had turned its back. She
tossed her head, declared that at last she could breathe the air of
freedom, and formally announced her adhesion to an "intellectual"
life. This meant unlimited *camaraderie* with scribblers and daubers,
Hegelian philosophers, and Hungarian pianists waiting for engagements. But she has been admired also by a great many really clever
men; there was a time, in fact, when she turned a head as well set
on its shoulders as this one!' And Niedermeyer tapped his forehead.
'She has a great charm, and, literally, I know no harm of her. Yet for
all that, I'm not going to speak to her; I'm not going near her box.
I'm going to leave her to say, if she does me the honour to observe
the omission, that I too have gone over to the Philistines. 'Tis not
that; it is that there is something sinister about the woman. I'm too
old to have it frighten me, but I'm good-natured enough to have it
pain me. Her quarrel with society has brought her no happiness, and
her outward charm is only the mask of a dangerous discontent. Her
imagination is lodged where her heart should be! So long as you
amuse it, well and good; she's radiant. But the moment you let it

flag, she's capable of dropping you without a pang. If you land on your feet, you're so much the wiser, simply; but there have been two or three, I believe, who have almost broken their necks in the fall.'

'You're reversing your promise,' I said, 'and giving me an opinion, but not an anecdote.'

'This is my anecdote. A year ago a friend of mine made her acquaintance in Berlin, and though he was no longer a young man and had never been what's called a susceptible one, he took a great fancy to Madame Blumenthal. He's a major in the Prussian artillery—grizzled, grave, a trifle severe, a man every way firm in the faith of his father's. It's a proof of Anastasia's charm that such a man should have got into the way of calling on her every day for a month. But the major was in love, or next door to it! Every day that he called he found her scribbling away at a little ormolu table on a lot of half-sheets of note paper. She used to bid him sit down and hold his tongue for a quarter of an hour, till she had finished her chapter; she was writing a novel, and it was promised to a publisher. Clorinda, she confided to him, was the name of the injured heroine. The major, I imagine, had never read a work of fiction in his life, but he knew by hearsay that Madame Blumenthal's literature, when put forth in pink covers, was subversive of several respectable institutions. Besides, he didn't believe in women knowing how to write at all, and it irritated him to see this prolific being scribbling away under his nose for the press; irritated him the more that, as I say, he was in love with her and that he ventured to believe she had a kindness for his years and his honours. And yet she was not such a woman as he could easily ask to marry him. The result of all this was that he fell into the way of railing at her intellectual pursuits and saying he should like to run his sword through her pile of papers. A woman was clever enough when she could guess her husband's wishes, and learned enough when she could spell out her prayer-book. At last, one day, Madame Blumenthal flung down her pen and announced in triumph that she had finished her novel. Clorinda had danced her dance. The major, by way of congratulating her, declared that her novel was coquetry and vanity and that she propagated various paradoxes on purpose to make a noise in the world and look picturesque and impassioned. He added, however, that he loved her in spite of her follies, and that if she would formally abjure them he would as formally offer her his hand. They say that in certain cases women like being frightened and snubbed. I don't know, I'm sure; I don't know how much pleasure, on this occasion, was mingled with Anastasia's wrath. But her wrath was very quiet, and the major assured me it made her look terribly handsome. "I have told you before," she says, "that I write from an inner need. I write to unburden my heart, to satisfy my conscience. You call my poor efforts coquetry, vanity, the desire to produce a sensation. I can prove to you that it is the quiet labour itself I care for, and not the world's more or less flattering attention to it!" And seizing the manuscript of Clorinda she thrusts it into the fire. The major stands staring, and the first thing he knows she is sweeping him a great courtesy and bidding him farewell for ever. Left alone and recovering his wits, he fishes out Clorinda from the embers and then proceeds to thump vigorously at the lady's door. But it never opened, and from that day to the day three months ago when he told me the tale, he had not beheld her again.'

'By Jove, it's a striking story,' I said. 'But the question is, what does it prove?'

'Several things. First (what I was careful not to tell my friend), that Madame Blumenthal cared for him a trifle more than he supposed; second, that he cares for her more than ever; third, that the performance was a master stroke and that her allowing him to force an interview upon her again is only a question of time.'

'And last?' I asked.

'This is another anecdote. The other day, Unter den Linden, I saw on a bookseller's counter a little pink-covered romance: "Sophronia", by Madame Blumenthal. Glancing through it, I observed an extraordinary abuse of asterisks; every two or three pages the narrative was adorned with a portentous blank, crossed with a row of stars.'

'Well, but poor Clorinda?' I objected, as Niedermeyer paused.

'Sophronia, my dear fellow, is simply Clorinda renamed by the baptism of fire. The fair author comes back, of course, and finds Clorinda tumbled upon the floor, a good deal scorched, but on the whole more frightened than hurt. She picks her up, brushes her off, and sends her to the printer. Wherever the flames had burnt a hole, she swings a constellation! But if the major is prepared to drop a penitent tear over the ashes of Clorinda, I shan't whisper to him that the urn is empty.'

Even Adelina Patti's singing, for the next half-hour, but half availed to divert me from my quickened curiosity to behold Madame Blumenthal face to face. As soon as the curtain had fallen again, I repaired to her box and was ushered in by Pickering with zealous hospitality. His glowing smile seemed to say to me, 'Ay, look for yourself, and adore!' Nothing could have been more gracious than the lady's greeting, and I found, somewhat to my surprise, that her prettiness lost nothing on a nearer view. Her eyes indeed were the finest I have ever seen—the softest, the deepest, the most intensely responsive. In spite of something faded and jaded in her physiognomy, her movements, her smile, and the tone of her voice, especially when she laughed, had an almost girlish frankness and spontaneity. She looked at you very hard with her radiant grey eyes, and she indulged in talking in a super-abundance of restless, zealous gestures, as if to make you take her meaning in a certain very particular and rather superfine sense. I wondered whether after a while this might not fatigue one's attention; then, meeting her charming eyes, I said, No! not for ages, at least. She was very clever, and, as Pickering had said, she spoke English admirably. I told her, as I took my seat beside her, of the fine things I had heard about her from my friend, and she listened, letting me run on some time, and exaggerate a little, with her fine eyes fixed full upon me. 'Really?' she suddenly said, turning short upon Pickering, who stood behind us, and looking at him in the same way, 'is that the way you talk about me?'

He blushed to his eyes, and I repented. She suddenly began to laugh; it was then I observed how sweet her voice was in laughter. We talked after this of various matters, and in a little while I complimented her on her excellent English and asked if she had learned it in England.

'Heaven forbid!' she cried. 'I've never been there and wish never to go. I should never get on with the'—I wondered what she was going to say; the fogs, the smoke, or whist with sixpenny stakes?—'I should never get on,' she said, 'with the Aristocracy! I'm a fierce democrat, I'm not ashamed of it. I hold opinions which would make my ancestors turn in their graves. I was born in the lap of feudalism. I'm a daughter of the crusaders. But I'm a revolutionist! I have a passion for freedom—boundless, infinite, ineffable freedom. It's to your great country I should like to go. I should like to see the wonderful spectacle of a great people free to do everything it chooses, and yet never doing anything wrong!'

I replied, modestly, that, after all, both our freedom and our virtue had their limits, and she turned quickly about and shook her fan with a dramatic gesture at Pickering. 'No matter, no matter!' she cried, 'I should like to see the country which produced that wonderful young man. I think of it as a sort of Arcadia—a land of the golden age. He's so delightfully innocent! In this stupid old Germany, if a young man is innocent, he's a fool; he has no brains; he's not a bit interesting. But Mr. Pickering says the most naïf things, and after I have laughed five minutes at their simplicity, it suddenly occurs to me that they are very wise, and I think them over for a week. True!'

she went on, nodding at him. 'I call them inspired solecisms, and I treasure them up. Remember that when I next laugh at you!'

Glancing at Pickering, I was prompted to believe that he was in a state of beatific exaltation which weighed Madame Blumenthal's smiles and frowns in an equal balance. They were equally hers, they were links alike in the golden chain. He looked at me with eyes that seemed to say, 'Did you ever hear such wit? Did you ever see such grace?' I imagine he was but vaguely conscious of the meaning of her words; her gestures, her voice and glance, made an irrestistible harmony. There is something painful in the spectacle of absolute enthralment, even to an excellent cause. I gave no response to Pickering's challenge, but embarked upon some formal tribute to the merits of Adelina Patti's singing. Madame Blumenthal, as became a 'revolutionist', was obliged to confess that she could see no charm in it; it was meagre, it was trivial, it lacked soul. 'You must know that in music, too,' she said, 'I think for myself!' And she began with a great many flourishes of her fan to expound what it was she thought. Remarkable things, doubtless; but I cannot answer for it, for in the midst of the exposition, the curtain rose again. 'You can't be a great artist without a great passion!' Madame Blumenthal was affirming. Before I had time to assent, Madame Patti's voice rose wheeling like a skylark, and rained down its silver notes. 'Ah, give me that art,' I whispered, 'and I'll leave you your passion!' and I departed for my own place in the orchestra. I wondered afterwards whether the speech had seemed rude, and inferred that it had not, on receiving a friendly nod from the lady, in the lobby, as the theatre was emptying itself. She was on Pickering's arm, and he was taking her to her carriage. Distances are short at Homburg, but the night was rainy, and Madame Blumenthal exhibited a very pretty satin-shod foot as a reason why, though but a penniless creature, she should not walk home. Pickering left us together a moment while he went to hail the vehicle, and my companion seized the opportunity, as she said, to beg me to be so very kind as to come and see her. It was for a particular reason! It was reason enough for me, of course I answered, that I could grasp at the shadow of a permission. She looked at me a moment with that extraordinary gaze of hers, which seemed so absolutely audacious in its candour, and answered that I paid more compliments than our young friend there, but that she was sure I was not half so sincere. 'But it's about him I want to talk,' she said. 'I want to ask you many things; I want you to tell me all about him. He interests me, but you see my sympathies are so in-tense, my imagination is so lively, that I don't trust my own impressions. They've misled me more than once!' And she gave a little tragic shudder.

I promised to come and compare notes with her, and we bade her farewell at her carriage door. Pickering and I remained a while, walking up and down the long glazed gallery of the Kursaal. I had not taken many steps before I became aware that I was beside a man in the very extremity of love. 'Isn't she wonderful?' he asked, with an implicit confidence in my sympathy which it cost me some ingenuity to elude. If he was really in love, well and good! For although, now that I had seen her, I stood ready to confess to large possibilities of fascination on Madame Blumenthal's part, and even to certain possibilities of sincerity of which I reserved the precise admeasurement, yet it seemed to me less ominous to have him give the reins to his imagination than it would have been to see him stand off and cultivate an 'admiration' which should pique itself on being discriminating. It was on his fundamental simplicity that I counted for a happy termination of his experiment, and the former of these alternatives seemed to me to prove most in its favour. I resolved to hold my tongue and let him run his course. He had a great deal to say about his happiness, about the days passing like hours, the hours like minutes, and about Madame Blumenthal being a 'revelation'. 'She was nothing tonight,' he said, 'nothing to what she sometimes is in the way of brilliancy—in the way of repartee. If you could only hear her when she tells her adventures!'

'Adventures?' I inquired. 'Has she had adventures?'

'Of the most wonderful sort!' cried Pickering, with rapture. 'She hasn't vegetated, like me! She has lived in the tumult of life. When I listen to her reminiscences, it's like hearing the mingled shadowy suggestions of conflict and trouble in one of Beethoven's symphonies, as they lose themselves in a triumphant harmony of faith and strength!'

I could only bow, but I desired to know before we separated what he had done with that troublesome conscience of his. 'I suppose you know, my dear fellow,' I said, 'that you're simply in love. That's what they call your state of mind.'

He replied with a brightening eye, as if he were delighted to hear it. 'So Madame Blumenthal told me,' he cried, 'only this morning!' And seeing, I suppose, that I was slightly puzzled, 'I went to drive with her,' he continued; 'we drove to Königstein, to see the old castle. We scrambled up into the heart of the ruin and sat for an hour in one of the crumbling old courts. Something in the solemn stillness of the place unloosed my tongue, and while she sat on an ivied stone, on the edge of the plunging wall, I stood there and made a speech. She

listened to me, looking at me, breaking off little bits of stone and
letting them drop down into the valley. At last she got up and
nodded at me two or three times silently, with a smile, as if she were
applauding me for a solo on the violin. "You're in love," she said.
"It's a perfect case!" And for some time she said nothing more.
But before we left the place she told me that she owed me an
answer to my speech. She thanked me heartily, but she was afraid
that if she took me at my word she would be taking advantage of my
inexperience. I had known few women, I was too easily pleased, I
thought her better than she really was. She had great faults; I must
know her longer and find them out; I must compare her with other
women—women younger, simpler, more innocent, more ignorant;
and then if I still did her the honour to think well of her, she would
listen to me again. I told her that I was not afraid of preferring any
woman in the world to her, and then she repeated, "Happy man,
happy man! you're in love, you're in love!"'

I called upon Madame Blumenthal a couple of days later, in some
agitation of thought. It has been proved that there are, here and
there, in the world, such people as sincere attitudinizers; certain characters cultivate fictitious emotions in perfect good faith. Even if this
clever lady enjoyed poor Pickering's bedazzlement, it was conceivable that, taking vanity and charity together, she should care more
for his welfare than for her own entertainment, and her offer to abide
by the result of hazardous comparison with other women was a finer
stroke than her fame—and indeed than probability—had seemed to
foreshadow. She received me in a shabby little sitting-room, littered
with uncut books and newspapers, many of which I saw at a glance
were French. One side of it was occupied by an open piano, surmounted by a jar full of white roses. They perfumed the air; they
seemed to me to exhale the pure aroma of Pickering's devotion.
Buried in an arm-chair, the object of this devotion was reading the
'Revue des Deux Mondes'. The purpose of my visit was not to admire Madame Blumenthal on my own account, but to ascertain how
far I might safely leave her to work her will upon my friend. She
had impugned my sincerity the evening of the opera, and I was careful on this occasion to abstain from compliments and not to place
her on her guard against my penetration. It is needless to narrate our
interview in detail; indeed, to tell the perfect truth, I was punished for
my ambition to read her too clearly by a temporary eclipse of my own
perspicacity. She sat there so questioning, so perceptive, so genial, so
generous, and so pretty withal, that I was quite ready at the end of
half an hour to shake hands with Pickering on her being a wonderful woman. I have never liked to linger, in memory on that half-hour.

The result of it was to prove that there were many more things in the composition of a woman who, as Niedermeyer said, had lodged her imagination in the place of her heart, than were dreamt of in my philosophy. Yet, as I sat there stroking my hat and balancing the account between nature and art in my affable hostess, I felt like a very competent philosopher. She had said she wished me to tell her everything about our friend, and she questioned me, categorically, as to his family, his fortune, his antecedents, and his character. All this was natural in a woman who had received a passionate declaration of love, and it was expressed with an air of charmed solicitude, a radiant confidence that there was really no mistake about his being a supremely fine fellow, and that if I chose to be explicit, I might deepen her conviction to disinterested ecstasy, which might have almost inspired me to invent a good opinion, if I had not had one at hand. I told her that she really knew Pickering better than I did, and that until we met at Homburg, I had not seen him since he was a boy.

'But he talks to you freely,' she answered; 'I know you're his confidant. He has told me certainly a great many things, but I always feel as if he were keeping something back—as if he were holding something behind him, and showing me only one hand at once. He seems often to be hovering on the edge of a secret. I have had several friendships in my life—thank Heaven! but I have had none more dear to me than this one. Yet in the midst of it I have the painful sense of my friend being half afraid of me—of his thinking me terrible, strange, perhaps a trifle out of my wits. Poor me! If he only knew what a plain good soul I am, and how I only want to know him and befriend him!'

These words were full of a plaintive magnanimity which made mistrust seem cruel. How much better I might play providence over Pickering's experiments with life, if I could engage the fine instincts of this charming woman on the providential side! Pickering's secret was, of course, his engagement to Miss Vernor; it was natural enough that he should have been unable to bring himself to talk of it to Madame Blumenthal. The simple sweetness of this young girl's face had not faded from my memory; I couldn't rid myself of the fancy that in going further Pickering might fare much worse. Madame Blumenthal's professions seemed a virtual promise to agree with me, and after a momentary hesitation I said that my friend had, in fact, a substantial secret, and that it appeared to me enlightened friendship to put her into possession of it. In as few words as possible I told her that Pickering stood pledged by filial piety to marry a young lady at Smyrna. She listened intently to my story; when I had finished it there was a faint flush of excitement in each of her cheeks. She broke out into a dozen exclamations of admiration and compassion. 'What a wonderful tale—what a romantic situation! No wonder poor Mr. Pickering seemed restless and unsatisfied—no wonder he wished to put off the day of submission. And the poor little girl at Smyrna— waiting there for the young Western prince like the heroine of an Eastern tale! She would give the world to see her photograph; did I think Mr. Pickering would show it to her? But never fear; she would ask nothing indiscreet! Yes, it was a marvellous story, and if she had invented it herself, people would have said it was absurdly improbable.' She left her seat and took several turns about the room, smiling to herself and uttering little German cries of wonderment. Suddenly she stopped before the piano and broke into a little laugh; the next moment she buried her face in the great bouquet of roses. It was time I should go, but I was indisposed to leave her without obtaining some definite assurance that, as far as pity was concerned, she pitied the young girl at Smyrna more than the young man at Homburg. 'Of course you appreciate,' I said, rising, 'my hopes in telling you all this.'

She had taken one of the roses from the vase and was arranging it in the front of her dress. Suddenly, looking up, 'Leave it to me, leave it to me!' she cried. 'I'm interested!' And with her little blue-gemmed hand she tapped her forehead. 'I'm interested—don't interfere!'

And with this I had to content myself. But more than once, for the day following, I repented of my zeal, and wondered whether a providence with a white rose in her bosom might not turn out a trifle too human. In the evening, at the Kursaal, I looked for Pickering, but he was not visible, and I reflected that my revelation had not as yet, at any rate, seemed to Madame Blumenthal a reason for prescribing a cooling-term to his passion. Very late, as I was turning away, I saw him arrive—with no small satisfaction, for I had determined to let him know immediately in what way I had attempted to serve him. But he straightway passed his arm through my own and led me off towards the gardens. I saw that he was too excited to allow me prior speech.

'I've burnt my ships!' he cried, when we were out of earshot of the crowd. 'I've told her everything. I've insisted that it's simple torture for me to wait, with this idle view of loving her less. It's well enough for her to ask it, but I feel strong enough now to override her reluctance. I've cast off the mill-stone from round my neck. I care for nothing, I know nothing but that I love her with every pulse of my being—and that everything else has been a hideous dream, from which she may wake me into blissful morning with a single word!'

I held him off at arms-length and looked at him gravely. 'You have told her, you mean, of your engagement to Miss Vernor?'

'The whole story! I've given it up—I've thrown it to the winds. I've broken utterly with the past. It may rise in its grave and give me its curse, but it can't frighten me now. I've a right to be happy, I've a right to be free, I've a right not to bury myself alive. It wasn't *I* who promised! I wasn't born then. I myself, my soul, my mind, my option—all this is but a month old! Ah,' he went on, 'if you knew the difference it makes—this having chosen and broken and spoken! I'm twice the man I was yesterday! Yesterday I was afraid of her; there was a kind of mocking mystery of knowledge and cleverness about her which oppressed me in the midst of my love. But now I'm afraid of nothing but of being too happy.'

I stood silent, to let him spend his eloquence. But he paused a moment, and took off his hat and fanned himself. 'Let me perfectly understand,' I said at last. 'You've asked Madame Blumenthal to be your wife?'

'The wife of my intelligent choice.'

'And does she consent?'

'She asks three days to decide.'

'Call it four! She has known your secret since this morning. I'm bound to let you know I told her.'

'So much the better!' cried Pickering, without apparent resentment or surprise. 'It's not a brilliant offer for such a woman, and in spite of what I have at stake I feel that it would be brutal to press her.'

'What does she say,' I asked in a moment, 'to your breaking your promise?'

Pickering was too much in love for false shame. 'She tells me,' he answered bravely, 'that she loves me too much to find courage to condemn me. She agrees with me that I have a right to be happy. I ask no exemption from the common law. What I claim is simply freedom to try to be!'

Of course I was puzzled; it was not in that fashion that I had expected Madame Blumenthal to make use of my information. But the matter now was quite out of my hands, and all I could do was to bid my companion not work himself into a fever over either fortune.

The next day I had a visit from Niedermeyer, on whom, after our talk at the opera, I had left a card. We gossiped a while, and at last he said suddenly: 'By the way, I have a sequel to the history of Clorinda. The major is in Homburg!'

'Indeed!' said I. 'Since when?'

'These three days.'

'And what is he doing?'

'He seems,' said Niedermeyer with a laugh, 'to be chiefly occupied in sending flowers to Madame Blumenthal. That is, I went with him the morning of his arrival to choose a nosegay, and nothing would suit him but a small haystack of white roses. I hope it was received.'

'I can assure you it was,' I cried. 'I saw the lady fairly nestling her head in it. But I advise the major not to build upon that. He has a rival.'

'Do you mean the soft young man of the other night?'

'Pickering is soft, if you will, but his softness seems to have served him. He has offered her everything, and she has not yet refused it.' I had handed my visitor a cigar and he was puffing it in silence. At last he abruptly asked if I had been introduced to Madame Blumenthal, and, on my affirmative, inquired what I thought of her. 'I'll not tell you,' I said, 'or you'll call *me* soft.'

He knocked away his ashes, eying me askance. 'I've noticed your friend about,' he said, 'and even if you had not told me, I should have known he was in love. After he has left his adored, his face wears for the rest of the day the expression with which he has risen from her feet, and more than once I've felt like touching his elbow, as you would that of a man who has inadvertently come into a drawing-room in his overshoes. You say he has offered our friend everything; but, my dear fellow, he hasn't everything to offer her. He's as amiable, evidently, as the morning, but madame has no taste for daylight.'

'I assure you,' said I, 'Pickering is a very interesting fellow.'

'Ah, there it is! Hasn't he some story or other? isn't he an orphan, or natural child, or consumptive, or contingent heir to great estates? She'll read his little story to the end, and close the book very tenderly and smooth down the cover, and then, when he least expects it, she'll toss it into the dusty limbo of all her old romances. She'll let him dangle, but she'll let him drop!'

'Upon my word,' I cried with heat, 'if she does, she'll be a very unprincipled little creature!'

Niedermeyer shrugged his shoulders. 'I never said she was a saint!'

Shrewd as I felt Niedermeyer to be, I was not prepared to take his simple word for this consummation, and in the evening I received a communication which fortified my doubts. It was a note from Pickering, and it ran as follows:

'My dear Friend,—I have every hope of being happy, but I am to go to Wiesbaden to learn my fate. Madame Blumenthal goes thither this afternoon to spend a few days, and she allows me to accompany her. Give me your good wishes; you shall hear of the event.   E.P.'

One of the diversions of Homburg for new-comers is to dine in rotation at the different *tables d'hôtes*. It so happened that, a couple of days later, Niedermeyer took pot-luck at my hotel and secured a seat beside my own. As we took our places I found a letter on my plate, and, as it was postmarked Wiesbaden, I lost no time in opening it. It contained but three lines:

'I'm happy—I'm accepted—an hour ago. I can hardly believe it's your poor old   E.P.'

I placed the note before Niedermeyer: not exactly in triumph, but with the alacrity of all privileged confutation. He looked at it much longer than was needful to read it, stroking down his beard gravely, and I felt it was not so easy to confute an ex-disciple of Metternich. At last, folding the note and handing it back, 'Has your friend mentioned,' he asked, 'Madame Blumenthal's errand at Wiesbaden?'

'You look very wise. I give it up!' said I.

'She's gone there to make the major follow her. He went by the next train.'

'And has the major, on his side, dropped you a line?'

'He's not a letter-writer.'

'Well,' said I, pocketing my letter, 'with this document in my hand I'm bound to reserve my judgment. We'll have a bottle of Johannisberg, and drink to the triumph of virtue.'

For a whole week more I heard nothing from Pickering—somewhat to my surprise, and, as the days went by, not a little to my discomposure. I had expected that his bliss would continue to overflow in an occasional brief bulletin, and his silence was possibly an indication that it had been clouded. At last I wrote to his hotel at Wiesbaden, but received no answer; whereupon, as my next resource, I repaired to his former lodging at Homburg, where I thought it possible he had left property which he would sooner or later send for. There I learned that he had indeed just telegraphed from Cologne for his baggage. To Cologne I immediately dispatched a line of inquiry as to his prosperity and the cause of his silence. The next day I received three words in answer—a simple, uncommented request that I would come to him. I lost no time, and reached him in the course of a few hours. It was dark when I arrived, and the city was sheeted in a cold, autumnal rain. Pickering had stumbled, with an indifference which was itself a symptom of distress, on a certain musty old Mainzerhof, and I found him sitting over a smouldering fire in a vast, dingy chamber, which looked as if it had grown grey with watching the *ennui* of ten generations of travellers. Looking at him, as he rose on my entrance, I saw that he was in extreme tribulation. He was pale and haggard; his face was five years older. Now, at least, in all conscience, he had tasted of the cup of life. I was anxious to know what had turned it so suddenly to bitterness; but I spared him all importunate curiosity, and let him take his time. I assented, tacitly, to the symptoms of his trouble, and we made for a while a feeble effort to discuss the picturesqueness of Cologne. At last he rose and stood a long time looking into the fire, while I slowly paced the length of the dusky room.

'Well!' he said as I came back; 'I wanted knowledge, and I certainly know something I didn't a month ago.' And herewith, calmly and succinctly enough, as if dismay had worn itself out, he related the history of the foregoing days. He touched lightly on details; he evidently never was to be as eloquent again as he had been during the prosperity of his suit. He had been accepted one evening, as explicitly as his imagination could desire, and had gone forth in his rapture and roamed about till nearly morning in the gardens of the Conversation-House, taking the stars and the perfumes of the summer night into his confidence. 'It's worth it all, almost,' he said, 'to have been wound up for an hour to that celestial pitch. No man, I'm sure, can ever know it but once.' The next morning he had repaired to Madame Blumenthal's lodging and had been met, to his amazement, by a naked refusal to see him. He had strode about for a couple of hours—in another mood—and then had returned to the charge. The servant handed him a three-cornered note; it contained these words : 'Leave me alone today; I'll give you ten minutes tomorrow evening.' Of the next thirty-six hours he could give no coherent account, but at the appointed time Madame Blumenthal had received him. Almost before she spoke there had come to him a sense of the depth of his folly in supposing he knew her. 'One has heard all one's days,' he said, 'of people removing the mask; it's one of the stock phrases of romance. Well, there she stood with her mask in her hand. Her face,' he went on, gravely, after a pause, 'her face was horrible!' 'I give you ten minutes,' she had said, pointing to the clock. 'Make your scene, tear your hair, brandish your dagger!' And she had sat down and folded her arms. 'It's not a joke,' she cried, 'it's dead earnest; let's get through with it. You're dismissed! Have you nothing to say?' He had stammered some frantic demand for an explanation; and she had risen and come near him, looking at him from head to feet, very pale, and evidently more excited than

she wished to have him see. 'I've done with you!' she said with a
smile; 'you ought to have done with me! It has all been delightful,
but there are excellent reasons why it should come to an end.' 'You've
been playing a part, then,' he had gasped out; 'you never cared for
me?' 'Yes; till I knew you; till I saw how far you'd go. But now the
story's finished; we've reached the *dénoûement*. We'll close the book
and be good friends.' 'To see how far I would go?' he had repeated.
'You led me on, meaning all the while to do *this*?' 'I led you on, if
you will. I received your visits in season and out! Sometimes they
were very entertaining; sometimes they bored me fearfully. But you
were such a very curious case of—what shall I call it?—of enthusiasm,
that I determined to take good and bad together. I wanted to make
you commit yourself unmistakably. I should have preferred not to
bring you to this place: but that too was necessary. Of course I
can't marry you; I can do better. Thank your fate for it. You've
thought wonders of me for a month, but your good-humour wouldn't
last. I'm too old and too wise; you're too young and too foolish. It
seems to me that I've been very good to you; I've entertained you
to the top of your bent, and, except perhaps that I'm a little *brusque*
just now, you've nothing to complain of. I would have let you down
more gently if I could have taken another month to it; but circumstances have forced my hand. Abuse me, revile me, if you like. I'll
make every allowance!' Pickering listened to all this intently enough
to perceive that, as if by some sudden natural cataclysm, the ground
had broken away at his feet, and that he must recoil. He turned
away in dumb amazement. 'I don't know how I seemed to be taking
it,' he said, 'but she seemed really to desire—I don't know why—
something in the way of reproach and vituperation. But I couldn't,
in that way, have uttered a syllable. I was sickened; I wanted to get
away into the air—to shake her off and come to my senses.' "Have you
nothing, nothing, nothing to say?" she cried, as I stood with my hand
on the door. "Haven't I treated you to talk enough?" I believe I
answered. "You'll write to me then, when you get home?" "I think
not," said I. "Six months hence, I fancy, you'll come and see me!"
"Never!" said I. "That's a confession of stupidity," she answered.
"It means that, even on reflection, you'll never understand the philosophy of my conduct." The word "philosophy" seemed so strange
that I verily believe I smiled. "I've given you," she went on, "all
that you gave me. Your passion was an affair of the head." "I only
wish you had told me sooner," I exclaimed, "that you considered it
so!" And I went my way. The next day I came down the Rhine. I
sat all day on the boat, not knowing where I was going, where to get
off. I was in a kind of ague of terror; it seemed to me I had seen

something infernal. At last I saw the cathedral towers here looming over the city. They seemed to say something to me, and when the boat stopped, I came ashore. I've been here a week: I haven't slept at night—and yet it has been a week of rest!'

It seemed to me that he was in a fair way to recover, and that his own philosophy, if left to take its time, was adequate to the occasion. After his story was told I referred to his grievance but once—that evening, later, as we were about to separate for the night. 'Suffer me to say,' I said, 'that there was some truth in *her* account of your relations. You were using her, intellectually, and all the while, without your knowing it, she was using you. It was diamond cut diamond. Her needs were the more superficial and she came to an end first.' He frowned and turned uneasily away, but he offered no denial. I waited a few moments, to see if he would remember, before we parted, that he had a claim to make upon me. But he seemed to have forgotten it.

The next day we strolled about the picturesque old city, and of course, before long, went into the cathedral. Pickering said little; he seemed intent upon his own thoughts. He sat down beside a pillar near a chapel, in front of a gorgeous window, and, leaving him to his meditations, I wandered through the church. When I came back I saw he had something to say. But before he had spoken, I laid my hand on his shoulder and looked at him with a significant smile. He slowly bent his head and dropped his eyes, with a mixture of assent and humility. I drew forth his letter from where it had lain untouched for a month, placed it silently on his knee, and left him to deal with it alone.

Half an hour later I returned to the same place, but he had gone, and one of the sacristans, hovering about and seeing me looking for Pickering, said he thought he had left the church. I found him in his gloomy chamber at the inn, pacing slowly up and down. I should doubtless have been at a loss to say just what effect I expected his letter to produce; but his actual aspect surprised me. He was flushed, excited, a trifle irritated.

'Evidently,' I said, 'you've read your letter.'

'I owe you a report of it,' he answered. 'When I gave it to you a month ago, I did my friends injustice.'

'You called it a "summons", I remember.'

'I was a great fool! It's a release!'

'From your engagement?'

'From everything! The letter, of course, is from Mr. Vernor. He desires to let me know at the earliest moment, that his daughter, informed for the first time a week before of what was expected of her, positively refuses to be bound by the contract or to assent to my being bound. She had been given a week to reflect and had spent it in inconsolable tears. She had resisted every form of persuasion; from compulsion, writes Mr. Vernor, he naturally shrinks. The young lady considers the arrangement "horrible". After accepting her duties cut and dried all her life, she presumes at last to have a taste of her own. I confess I'm surprised; I had been given to believe that she was idiotically passive and would remain so to the end of the chapter. Not a bit! She has insisted on my being formally dismissed, and her father intimates that in case of non-compliance she threatens him with an attack of brain fever. Mr. Vernor condoles with me handsomely, and lets me know that the young lady's attitude has been a great shock to his own nerves. He adds that he will not aggravate such regret as I may do him the honour to entertain, by any allusion to his daughter's charms and to the magnitude of my loss, and he concludes with the hope that, for the comfort of all concerned, I may already have amused my fancy with other "views". He reminds me in a postscript that, in spite of this painful occurrence, the son of his most valued friend will always be a welcome visitor at his house. I am free, he observes; I have my life before me; he recommends an extensive course of travel. Should my wanderings lead me to the East, he hopes that no false embarrassment will deter me from presenting myself at Smyrna. He will ensure me at least a friendly reception. It's a very polite letter.'

Polite as the letter was, Pickering seemed to find no great exhilaration in having this famous burden so handsomely lifted from his conscience. He fell a-brooding over his liberation in a manner which you might have deemed proper to a renewed sense of bondage. 'Bad news' he had called his letter originally, and yet, now that its contents proved to be in flat contradiction to his foreboding, there was no impulsive voice to reverse the formula and declare the news was good. The wings of impulse in the poor fellow had of late been terribly clipped. It was an obvious reflection, of course, that if he had not been so doggedly sure of the matter a month before, and had gone through the form of breaking Mr. Vernor's seal, he might have escaped the purgatory of Madame Blumenthal's blandishments. But I left him to moralize in private; I had no desire, as the phrase is, to rub it in. My thoughts, moreover, were following another train; I was saying to myself that if to those gentle graces of which her young visage had offered to my fancy the blooming promise, Miss Vernor added in this striking measure the capacity for magnanimous action, the amendment to my friend's career had been less happy than the rough draft. Presently, turning about, I saw him looking at the young lady's photograph. 'Of course, now,' he said, "I have no right to keep it!' And before I could ask for another glimpse of it, he had thrust it into the fire.

'I am sorry to be saying it just now,' I observed after a while, 'but I shouldn't wonder if Miss Vernor were a lovely creature.'

'Go and find out,' he answered gloomily. 'The coast is clear. My part,' he presently added, 'is to forget her. It oughtn't to be hard. But don't you think,' he went on suddenly, 'that for a poor fellow who asked nothing of fortune but leave to sit down in a quiet corner, it has been rather a cruel pushing about?'

Cruel indeed, I declared, and he certainly had the right to demand a clean page on the book of fate, and a fresh start. Mr. Vernor's advice was sound; he should seek diversion in the grand tour of Europe. If he would allow it to the zeal of my sympathy, I would go with him on his way. Pickering assented without enthusiasm; he had the discomfited look of a man who, having gone to some cost to make a good appearance in a drawing-room, should find the door suddenly slammed in his face. We started on our journey, however, and little by little his enthusiasm returned. He was too capable of enjoying fine things to remain permanently irresponsive, and after a fortnight spent among pictures and monuments and antiquities, I felt that I was seeing him for the first time in his best and healthiest mood. He had had a fever and then he had had a chill; the pendulum had swung right and left in a manner rather trying to the machine; but now, at last, it was working back to an even, natural beat. He recovered in a measure the ample speech with which he had fanned his flame at Homburg, and talked about things with something of the same passionate freshness. One day when I was laid up at the inn at Bruges with a lame foot, he came home and treated me to a rhapsody about a certain meek-faced virgin of Hans Memling, which seemed to me sounder sense than his compliments to Madame Blumenthal. He had his dull days and his sombre moods—hours of irresistible retrospect; but I let them come and go without remonstrance, because I fancied they always left him a trifle more alert and resolute. One evening, however, he sat hanging his head in so doleful a fashion that I took the bull by the horns and told him he had by this time surely paid his debt to penitence, and owed it to himself to banish that woman for ever from his thoughts.

He looked up, staring; and then with a deep blush: 'That woman?' he said. 'I was not thinking of Madame Blumenthal!'

After this I gave another construction to his melancholy. Taking him with his hopes and fears, at the end of six weeks of active observation and keen sensation, Pickering was as fine a fellow as need be.

We made our way down to Italy and spent a fortnight at Venice. There something happened which I had been confidently expecting; I had said to myself that it was merely a question of time. We had passed the day at Torcello, and came floating back in the glow of the sunset, with measured oar-strokes. 'I'm well on the way,' Pickering said, 'I think I'll go!'

We had not spoken for an hour, and I naturally asked him, Where? His answer was delayed by our getting in to the Piazzetta. I stepped ashore first and then turned to help him. As he took my hand he met my eyes, consciously, and it came: 'To Smyrna!'

A couple of days later he started. I had risked the conjecture that Miss Vernor was a lovely creature, and six months afterwards he wrote me that I was right.

TEXTUAL VARIANTS

Introduction
A Passionate Pilgrim   (1871/1875/1884/1885/1908)
At Isella   (1871/?)
Master Eustace   (1871/1885)
The Madonna of the Future   (1873/1875/1879/1908)
The Last of the Valerii   (1874/1875/1885)
Mme. De Mauves   (1874/1875/1879/1908)
Eugene Pickering   (1874/1875/1879)

INTRODUCTION

In preparing this record of all substantive variants in the seven revised tales of the period some decisions of an editorial nature had to be taken: this introduction explains those decisions.

The variants listed below are keyed to the periodical versions of the tales—the original creations of which all later changes are, so to speak, offshoots—as reprinted in the present edition. I have taken all book editions of a tale published during James's lifetime and subjected them to textual comparison with the periodical text. The substantive variants that the collation revealed have been compiled in this record.

The overall authority of the revisions examined cannot be questioned: the five collections—*A Passionate Pilgrim, The Madonna of the Future, Stories Revived, The Siege of London* and the New York Edition—where the revised versions of the tales first appeared, were all prepared by James himself. The authority of individual instances of alteration, however, is impossible to establish as only one—and a half-finished at that—of the seven manuscript revisions has survived.[1] In the absence of such evidence for comparison, the problem becomes a critical one. Needless to say, all substantive variants listed have been critically examined from the viewpoint of style and structure, and were found to conform to the context of meanings established in the originals. Remarkably few misprints have been noticed in the revised editions.

The decision to ignore all accidentals—variants of punctuation, contractions (I have/I've), expanded forms (I've/ I have), paragraph division, spelling variants, etc.,—is, of course, arbitrary. It is influenced by two factors. First, it is extremely difficult, if not altogether impossible, to record the variants of punctuation in a complex and large body of multiple texts such as the 112 tales of Henry James. Secondly, as readers of James know, in the matter of punctuation he was not very consistent. The difference between the early system of punctuation and that of the New York Edition is so great that the latter cannot be treated as anything but a new, highly idiosyncratic style. It was decided, therefore, to treat this aspect of the revisions separately in an essay to appear in the final volume of the edition. For the present it should suffice to say that the revised texts are lightly punctuated, and that most contractions have been expanded in them. Although I have generally ignored the accidentals, the

[1] See headnote to 'At Isella' above.

punctuation variants in all substantively revised passages have been recorded.

Each of the seven lists opens with a brief headnote which singles out the texts that have been collated. The note does not mention that sample collations of all available reprints of the revised editions have been taken privately. For works with more than one revised form, capital letters of the alphabet have been used as identifying symbols for the various stages of revision. (I should hasten to add that on this matter I am having to depart from the method followed in the first volume of this edition, where initial letters of the titles are used as identifying symbols. Because of the increased multiplicity of the texts involved in the present volume, and the rather lengthy form of most of the titles, alphabetical symbols seemed the simpler of the two alternatives.) These symbols are explained in the first note and later appear against each entry. In most cases, the first note is followed by another set of notes which record the revised division of chapters, revised names of the characters, and similar other peculiarities of the revision.

For each entry the page and line references are to the text in the present edition. The usual square bracket divides the original from the revised form. Wherever possible, I have tried to divide the revisions into very small units of text, the original form of which is indicated preceding the square bracket. In the case of longer passages, however, three dots (...) have been used to cover the matter, of all lengths, left out. The ellipses cover not only substantive matter but also punctuation, including full stops and quotation marks.

James often makes changes towards the end of his sentences and these usually add new matter. In recording such additions, the full stop at the end of the original sentence has *not* been indicated—unless the revised form closes with a different punctuation mark. The same treatment has been given to all punctuation marks coming *at the end* of a passage which has been revised without any change in the original punctuation mark.

A frequent, and significant, feature of the revisions is the readjustment of editorial directions in the dialogues—the changes made in the placing of such fictional props as 'he said', 'she said', etc. Since many of these alterations affect only the directions, and not the speeches, a method had to be evolved to avoid long passages of unrevised matter. The following should explain the procedure adopted to deal with the problem. If, for example,

'No, I do not agree with you.'

is changed to

'No,' he said, 'I do not agree with you.'

the list would record the variant thus:

No, I do not] No,' he said, 'I do not

In other words, in the case of revisions involving dialogue, *only the relevant part* of the quotation marks has been indicated. And the same principle is employed in recording revisions where James has added something before or after a speech, or has omitted the stage direction. Also, in order to save space, the usual practice of transcribing dialogue in separate units has not been kept.

Finally, a few words about the 'definitive' version of 'A Passionate Pilgrim' which has not been included in the collation. The tale exists in five versions, at least two of which are so different from the original, and, significantly, all three from each other, that no *orderly* collation of all five seemed possible without giving the enterprise a volume to itself. I have, therefore, in order to save space and avoid confusion, collated only four texts—the first four—and have reproduced the version in the New York Edition here in an Appendix.

A PASSIONATE PILGRIM

Notes:

1. The variants recorded below are based on a collation of the original serial text of the tale (*Atlantic Monthly*, 1871) and *three* of its four revised versions in *A Passionate Pilgrim* (1875)—hereinafter mentioned as A; *The Siege of London* (1884)—hereinafter mentioned as B; and *Stories Revived* (1885)—hereinafter mentioned as C. For reasons briefly explained in the textual Introduction, the final, New York Edition text of this tale—its fourth revision—is not included in the collation but is reproduced in its entirety in this volume.

2. Where there are small differences between two otherwise identical, *revised* readings, these are indicated in square brackets.

3. The following, in texts B and C, are the revised forms of two proper names; John Simmons] Abijah Simmons BC; Herefordshire] Slant-shire B; Slopeshire C

IN TWO PARTS] om. ABC

PART I] I. ABC

42:10	very] om. BC
10	decorum] 'attendance', BC
12	mown ... in my] cut a BC
12	British] English BC
14	England] the motherland BC
16–17	gaze ... unamazed] discover romantic meanings in it BC
19	delectable] characteristic BC
19–20	which I ... depths] I never have got to the bottom of BC
20	the] its A
20	virgin] om. BC
21	primary] early BC
43:3	fatal ... say] intimate, as the French say, than his enjoyment, for instance BC
6	and] in BC
6	small] narrow BC
8	each] om. ABC
9	narrow] meagre BC
9	esteemed] denominated ABC
10	the little ... constituted] these rigid receptacles BC
12	the several ... hungriness] no less than four [pairs C] of active British elbows BC
30	rhubarb tart] charlotte-russe AB; *salade de saison* C
36–7	I took ... fellow-lodger] after I had looked at him a moment, I supposed to be a fellow-lodger, and probably

the only one   BC

44:3   brow] well-drawn brows   BC

5   hung ... black] reposed a soft, horizontal   BC

5   black] dark   A

8   elegant] attenuated   ABC

10   forward] om.   ABC

11   purpose] intentions   BC

12   with ... half-mourning] and he might have been in mourning   BC

13   unmarried ... Englishman] a bachelor, he was out of health, he was not indigenous to the soil   BC

14–15   momentarily ... tones] momentarily in tones barely audible   BC

17–18   of a certain ... which] slightly of certain sceptical, cosmopolitan Russians whom   BC

18–19   weighing this hypothesis] considering this facile problem   BC

22   possible] impecunious   A; potential   BC

23   bent on vacancy; the] wandering over the dingy ornaments of the room. The   BC

24   concave frontage] concavity   BC

25   penny-ha'penny] ha'penny   BC

29   high] vague   BC

30   an American] a transatlantic   BC

34–45:1   that, through no ... drum. They were] that the crumbs of their conversation were scattered pretty freely abroad; I could hear almost all they said, without straining to catch it, over the top of the partition that divided us. Occasionally their voices dropped, as if they remembered that their topic was private, but the mystery pieced itself together, as if on purpose to entertain me. Their utterance was pitched in that key which may, in English air, be called foreign, in spite of resemblances of orthography. The voices were   BC

44:36–7   its flavours with those] its savour with that   A

44:40   at it] it   A

45:12   It's ... for ever] It won't be so long as—some things have been   BC

13   same old] same cheerful old   ABC

14   die] give up the ghost   BC

18   them] these animals   BC

22   man] creature   ABC

27–8   Am I not] Ain't I   BC

29–30   Mr. Simmons ... But the next,] Mr. Simmon's brightness appeared to flicker a moment in this gust of despair; but the next it was burning steady again.   BC

32	feelings ... nothing] sentiment. Sentiment won't do any-thing BC
36	you are] you're quite BC
36	You got] You never got BC
41	John] Abijah BC
42	devil] demon of perversity BC
43	scamp] rogue ABC
46:1	stout] sturdy ABC
2	very] dreadful BC
6	morbid man] morbid, mooning man BC
8–9	like a blasted fool] more like a wandering maniac than a member of our best society BC
12	I was a ... written] Well, I was a kind of sentimental myself when I wrote BC
12–13	infernal meddlesome benevolence] always wishing so to please folks BC
23–4	to call ... pretty one] that one of these London fellows will look at. It looked at first as if you had a rather seductive case BC
25	preposterous benevolence] liking to please folk BC
26–8	to experience ... Come] to be distinguished with some-thing; it proved to be with his beverage. 'This beer is awfully nasty, as you say here,' he remarked to the waiter. 'I guess I'll have some brandy.—Come BC
28	sherry] brandy A
29	settle ... Benevolence] jump right on top of you! My natural urbanity BC
32–3	poor ... Yankee] horrid low American BC
39	stamping] tearing round BC
42	untender benediction] ambiguous compliment BC
47:3–4	smile ... emanation!] way they smile, these big-wigs in the Inns of Court—that's what they call 'em—when they want to let you know there's no help for you. I guess it would take it out of you to be simpered at that way. BC
4	would ... emanation!] wouldn't stand being sniffed at in that fashion. A
5–6	distinguished ... forearmed] usurping cousin, and he evi-dently knew there was something in the wind BC
7	forth] out BC
15	mysterious] unencouraging—or unencouraged— BC
16	noting] being able to see BC
19	Lawyer Simmons] Abijah Simmons BC
24–5	I fancied ... sherry] and I imagined there was a certain tenderness in his gaze; but I am not sure whether this was pity or whether it was beer and brandy BC
25	sherry] brandy A
26–7	some ... pitch,] a native who might be struck with his

cleverness, he lifted his voice a little and gave it an
ironical ring   BC
26   some unnoticeable] an impossible   A
33   sherry] brandy   ABC
41   your money] the cash   BC
48:2   enormous] tremendous   BC
5   the ocean] that beastly ocean   BC
9   die] leave for another place   BC
12–19   Mr. Simmons ... If you'll] Mr. Simmons was silent a
moment. 'Well, you *are* sick!' he exclaimed presently. 'All
I can say is that if you are going to talk about prussic acid
and that sort of thing, we cease to occupy common ground.
You can't get a dose of prussic acid for nothing, you
know. Look here, Searle: if you'll   BC
16   much for] much even for   A
16   as yet ... piety] easy morality   A
21–2   willed ... that I stay] made up my mind to anything before,'
he said, 'but I think it's made up now. I shall stay   BC
23   leave] departure   BC
23   poor old] wretched little   BC
26–7   So I ... Europe] I meant I was sick for a home. Don't I
belong here? Haven't I longed to get here all my life?
Haven't I counted the months and the years till I should
be able to go to Europe, as they say   BC
27   it, am ... again?] here, must I just back out? No, no, I'll
move on.   BC
28   enough for] enough money for   BC
30   last me out] see me through   BC
32   English yew] old gnarled, black yew   BC
33   thus] so   BC
36   pleasure ... decreed, I] pleasure, if I would just go and
look. I declined to look, but took number 12 at a venture,
and   BC
41   dreamed of it so much] thought of it so often   BC
49:1–2   an unhandsome ... malice] a grin that made his upper lip
look more than ever glazed with [denuded by   C] the
razor, and jerked the ugly ornament of his chin into the
air   BC
3   a Miss Searle] a certain Miss Searle   BC
5   suppose ... marry!] you talk of moving on. You might
move on the damsel.   BC
6   silence. Simmons] silence, and Simmons   BC
8   crimson and his] crimson; his   BC
11   insisted on my coming to] represented to me that I ought,
in justice to him, to come and   BC
13   Adelina Patti] Madame Bosio   ABC
14   vaguely fancying] for it had occurred to me that   BC

16–17   sunk in ... delayed] fast asleep and dreaming perhaps of Abijah Simmons   BC

17   sleep long delayed] tardy sleep   A

18–19   face, pale ... delicacy] closed eyes, in the dim lamplight, looked even more helpless and resigned, and I seemed to see the fine grain of his nature in his unconscious mask   BC

20   sleep. Standing] sleep, and standing   BC

20   benignant] benevolent   BC

21–4   amid the ... waiterhood] in one of the little prandial pews I have described, the melancholy waiter, with his whiskered chin, too, reposing on the blankness of his shirt-front   BC

22   refectory boxes] dining stalls   A

26–7   upward vista] dusky shaft   BC

27   from which] where   BC

28–9   an antique] a rattling   BC

29–30   watched ... distant] leaned on their elbows for many a year, I made out the far-off,   BC

34   the innocent object] the object   BC

37   running] moving   BC

38–41   snatching ... association] catching all kinds of romantic impressions by the way. To the ingenious American eye the grimy complexion of the British metropolis often flushes with the tints of association   BC

41–50:1   my impatient ... fixed upon] I became conscious of a wish to see something green, and thinking over the excursions recommended to the innocent [ingenuous C] stranger, determined [decided C] to take the train to   BC

50:5   multitudinous rooms] apartments   BC

7   grand] om.   ABC

8   flavour] effect   BC

9   great] om.   BC

11   and] om.   BC

12   decorous] rigid   BC

13   vast] big,   BC

15   attested] symbolized   BC

15   balustrade, the] balustrade, and the   BC

17   side] om.   BC

17   recesses, the] recesses, rise the   BC

20–1   the misty ... portraits] misty park. The brown walls are dimly illumined by innumerable portraits   BC

20   grandly] gravely   A

25–33   long-drawn ... devout contemplation] processional interior is unspeakably stale and sad. The tints of all things have both faded and darkened, and you taste the chill of the place as you walk from room to room. It was still early in

the day and in the season, and I flattered myself that I
was the only visitor. This idea, however, was dispelled
suddenly by my coming upon a person standing motionless BC

32	apparently] om. A
34	person] victim of an evaporated spell BC
35	at] of BC
36–7	I detected ... seeing] he looked as if he would be very glad to answer me, were I to speak to him. But he did not wait for this. The next moment, seeing BC
36	a sort] an air A
38	ascertaining it] satisfying him BC
41	a light piece of work] slight BC
42	a little ... think] was evidently a little abashed BC
51 : 1–2	weak and] infirm but that he was BC
4–5	culture ... grace] cultivation, but with a certain natural love of pleasant things BC
6	true] genuine BC
7–8	marks ... gross] is a sign of our transatlantic taste. His perceptions were delicate, his opinions were probably rather primitive BC
9	I too was an American] I was a fellow-citizen BC
11	rest of the palace] other apartments BC
12	vast] large BC
14	apartments] tenements BC
16	these] the BC
18–19	dim horticultural closets] somewhat stuffy bowers C
19	many a turn] several turns BC
20–3	spacious level ... substructures] quiet terrace, looking down on the floral figures of the rest of the garden and on the stoutly woven tapestry of creeping plants which muffles the foundations BC
21	stout-fibred] stoutly woven A
21–3	compacted ... substructures] vine and blossom which muffles the foundations A
24–6	upon that ... palace] in front of it and felt the protection and security of the place BC
26–7	of hammered ... gardens] into one of the little private gardens A; into one of the green enclosures B; into one of the mossy cages C
30–1	had an ... merits] would probably have had an opinion on the virtue BC
31	merits] virtue A
32	so exquisite in life] in life so exquisite BC
33	to the ... consciousness] om. BC
33	burden] savour A; quality BC
34–6	perception ... at home] appreciation [relish A] of local

colour makes comrades of strangers   ABC

36–8   vague ... to give] enjoyment; he scowled gently, as if it gave   BC

37   wooed] scanned   A

41   found ... inn] entered an inn which I pretended, very sincerely, to find excellent   BC

52 : 3–4   You're ... one!'] I am afraid you are rather out of health,' I said. 'Yes, sir, I'm incurable.'   BC

6   broad] om.   BC

6   Bushey Park. After] Bushey Park, and after   BC

7–14   the huge ... of the past] the hazy vista of the great avenue of horse-chestnuts   A; the celebrated avenue of horse-chestnuts   BC

15–18   mind, with ... your being] mind seems to swallow the whole sum of its impressions at a gulp. You take in the whole place, whatever it is. You feel England; you feel Italy; and the sensation, for the moment, is accompanied with a sort of excitement   BC

16   asserts] achieves   A

17   sensation] reflection   A

17–18   stirs ... your being] has an extraordinary poignancy   A

20   arrival] disembarkation   BC

20   come] arrive   BC

21   excellent] tolerable   BC

22   came now ... tread] arrived now with irresistible force   BC

23   my visions] one's early reveries   BC

24   deep-hued ... ordered] ripeness of its   BC

25   palace] residence   BC

25   copings] facings   BC

26   tell of ... past] make the past definite and massive   BC

27–8   tavern of gentility] taverns with figurative names   BC

28–31   parsonage ... ghosts] mossy roofs, looked like the property of a feudal lord   BC

29–31   hamlet; the ... ghosts] hamlet.   A

32   read ... prose] perused the British classics   BC

33–53 : 4 English poets ... world to herself.'] the poets; and I seemed to feel the buried generations in the dense and elastic sod. These reflections came in some form or other from my lips, as I gather, remembering it, from a remark of my companion's.   BC

53 : 5–6   me,' ... 'in] me, in   BC

9–15   home—a few ... earlier in life] home used to call me a cockney. But it wasn't true,' he went on; 'if it had been. I should have made my way over here long ago   BC

17–18   my learning ... time] it was merely a question of time that I should learn his story   BC

19   impart] unfold   ABC

23	get them all back] recover everything BC
35	inexorable solitude] deadly silence BC
36	patted ... on the] laid my hand on my friend's BC
39	lovely] little BC
41	American] alien BC
41	the sweetest incident] one of the prettiest incidents BC
43	looked] glanced BC
54 : 1–2	her whip ... alarm] the hunting-crop with which she was armed; whereupon she reined up and looked shyly at us and at the instrument BC
3	whip] crop BC
4	devotion] civility BC
5–6	a whispered 'Thanks!'] softly murmured gratitude, BC
6	elastic] quiet BC
8–9	his face ... of your having] he too was blushing, 'I don't think you have BC
12	and watched] and, as the sun began to sink, watched BC
12–13	turning to ... sun] powder itself with gold BC
18	a light ... darkness] strangely clear, in spite of the thickness of the air BC
20	of the British tramp] about the British tramp in the British novel BC
21–2	to bear ... tourist-gaze] my historic consciousness to bear upon the present specimen ABC
24	cap, with greasy] bonnet, with greasy A; bonnet, with false-looking BC
29	green stuff] vegetables BC
30–1	a singular ... He] an extraordinary mixture of the brutal and the insinuating. He too, like everything else, BC
32–3	Never was ... fixedness] He was the completest vagabond I had ever encountered. There was a richness BC
34	awe] respect C
35	an artist in vagrancy] a great artist or actor BC
41–2	responsive ... 'if] at him and at each other, and to our imagination his appeal had almost the force of a command. 'I wonder if BC
42	enough.'] enough?' I murmured. BC
55 : 3	a tramp] a tramp like him BC
4	Upon ... spoke.] om. BC
4	you, my] you, 'anyway', my BC
5	you] you—please BC
6	A sudden ... so that] The colour rose again to his pale face, and BC
9	New York ... lived] New York. I have lived in New York A; New York and I have lived there all my life BC
10	nothing] nothing, at all BC

11	protested] remarked, smiling BC
17–19	Of what ... behind] What I might have been—once—there is nothing left to show. I was rotten before I was ripe BC
18	fatal tide] steady current A
20–2	will and ... sentiment] having a little character and purpose. But I hadn't even a little. I had nothing but nice tastes, as they call them, and fine sympathies and sentiments BC
22–3	New York ... sentiments] New York today and you'll find the tattered remnants of these things BC
28–33	God and ... married] the immortality of the soul. The soul is immortal, certainly—if you have got one; but most people haven't BC
36	money and my wit] early wealth BC
40	incredible] incredible—upon my word BC
40–56:3	Hampton Court ... I shall be dry] these old places then. I hadn't seen any form. I should tell you I used to be an awful [a precious C] fool At present I am not even a fool—I am nothing at all, as I have told you BC
55:43	elegant] incomparable A
56:3	be dry] be high and dry A
6	those theorizers] those dreary theorizers A; those fatuous theorizers BC
7–8	damning ... end of it] right one, because that looks bad for them BC
9	a gentler world] a world arranged on different lines BC
12	soul for the picturesque] passion for old forms B; passion for ancient rites C
13	found it nowhere. I found] found them nowhere—found C
21	vulgar idleness] crude dissipation BC
23	abroad] over here BC
24	unwell] out of health BC
25	as] om. ABC
27–8	cherished ... the past] which has danced before the eyes of my family, at odd moments, every [any C] time these BC
28–9	It's ... define] I confess it's very shadowy and desperately hard to follow BC
30	mastered it] got the hang of it BC
31	you'll] you BC
32–3	got my ... nine as] tried to commit the 'points' of our case to memory, as I used to get nine times nine by heart as BC
36	since] ago BC
37–9	sort of ... strong point] man who once got me out of a

dreadful mess—not that I had done any harm—a sharp
American lawyer, an extremely common fellow, but with
a great deal of *flair*, as they say in New York   BC

41 pretended right] these vague pretentions of ours   BC

43 mighty] monstrous   BC

57 : 1–2 vastly ... my life] greatly surprised if I were unable to
do something. This was the greatest push I had ever got
in my life; I took a deliberate step, for the first time   BC

7 precipitate] idiotic   BC

11 I doubted ... claim] I didn't really believe I had any
case   BC

15 loved] got on with beautifully   BC

21 you,' ... 'to] you to   BC

21 request. But] request,' I said. 'But   BC

28 mind and spirits] low spirits   BC

35 claim.'] vague pretensions, as you call them, and pretenders, to me, have always been an attractive class. But
their first duty is to be gallant.' 'Their first duty is to be
definite, to understand what they want,' he answered with
a languid smile.   BC

36 expound ... it alone.] trace our pedigree now. I'll try
some day, but it's a sad muddle. There's no doubt, however, that we are a very old race. But   BC

37 myself] om.   BC

38 short off] in two   BC

38 of my expectancy] from which everything hangs   BC

39–40 in this ... bestowal of] this hard world is no place for   BC

40–1 doubt, I fancy, that,] doubt that   BC

58 : 3 utmost right is] ideas are   BC

4 eighty-five thousand] a hundred and thirty thousand   BC

4 eight-five] a hundred and thirty   BC

12 Herefordshire] Slantshire   B; Slopeshire   C

13 pondered awhile. 'I'm] reflected a little. 'Yes, as I tell you,
I am   BC

14–15 this Lockley Park, Herefordshire] Lockley Park in Slant-
shire [Slopeshire   C]   BC

18 heart,' ... 'to] heart to   BC

19 alone. But] alone,' he said. 'But   BC

21–7 felt to ... Their influence] were equally conscious of that
intellectual pressure which London exerts upon those
pilgrims from the west who feel it to be the mother-city
of their race, the distributing heart of their traditional
life. Certain characteristics of London, certain aspects,
phases, expressions, are more suggestive to an American
soul [American   C] than anything else in Europe. The
influence of these things   BC

24–6 There are ... Europe holds] Certain London characteristics

—monuments, relics, hints of history, local moods and memories—are more deeply suggestive to an American soul than anything else in Europe   A

29   passionate] morbid   BC

30   and social] the social   BC

30   its] om.   BC

30–8   now to tremble ... pretty figure] to flicker up and illuminate his face and his talk. We looked up the topography of Slantshire [Slopeshire   C] in a county-guide, which spoke highly, as the phrase is, of Lockley Park   BC

32   new] strange   A

32   birth] renascence   A

34–5   select publication] big red book   A

36–7   range ... Herefordshire] range,—though in which county I forget   A

38   pretty] handsome   A

39   abode at] abode, our journey ended, at   BC

41–2   tenderly ... Englishness of] handed up as straight as possible to outsiders athirst with fast travelling. We stopped, here for simple admiration of   BC

42   the very Englishness of] sheer admiration of   A

43   and its decent] its homely   A; its hospitable   BC

59:2–3   prepared to ... journey] prepared to execute the especial purpose of our pilgrimage   B; proceeded to the particular business that had drawn us on   C

3–5   In this ... force] This admirable region is [The region I allude to is   BC] a compendium of the general physiognomy of England   ABC

5   subtle] latent   C

6–8   magical ... love replied] way we scarcely knew whether we were looking at it for the first or last time, made it appeal to us at every step   BC

6   its multitudinous] multitudinous   A

7–8   simple ... replied] natural affection answered   A

11–12   was streaked ... thousand-fold] was streaked with a ranker freshness   A; had been washed over with a lighter brush   BC

13–14   hills ... summits,] hills, from the summits of which   BC

15   vast range] scope   BC

16–18   flats of ... Hereford] hedgy flats and the copse-checkered slopes   BC

18–21   From their ... composite colour.] om.   ABC

22   large] om.   BC

22–4   cathedral towers ... the ineffable] towers of cathedrals rose sharply out of a reddish blur of houses, taking the mild   BC

24–31   'Out of England ... animated clouds] We took an immense deal of notice of this same solar reserve, and found in it only a refinement of art. The sky never was empty and never idle; the clouds were continually at play for our benefit   BC

28–9   the English earth ... effects] the complex English earth A

32   compacted] condensed   BC

33–7   in innumerable ... or escapes in] blotting the azure [blue   BC] with sullen rain-spots, stretching, breeze-fretted, into dappled fields of grey, bursting into a storm [an explosion   BC] of light or melting into   ABC

38–9   summits ... slopes of] ridge of the downs, and descended through slanting, oblique   BC

40–1   rural village ... meadows] russet village beckoned us from the interstices of the hedges   BC

43   and privacy,] om.   BC

60:2   height of hedges] barriers of hawthorn   BC

3   now jostled] now rather rudely jostled   BC

5   stands in] stands there in   BC

5–9   at the receipt ... home! Its] doggedly submitting to be pointed out and sketched. It is a wonderful image of the domiciliary conditions of the past. It is cruelly complete; its [of the past—cruelly complete; with   C]   BC

8–9   complete ... Its] complete; its   A

9   great] om.   ABC

10   its many gables, seem] its gables, seem   AB; gables, that seem   C

12   proportions ... wondering] proportions [pieces   C] to notify the scowling   BC

13–14   still prefer ... modern day] retain their opacity as a part of the primitive idea of defence   BC

15   patched and] patched, so   C

18–20   and above all ... history,—] om.   ABC

21   synthesis] symbol   BC

32–3   stile ... him] stile, and he had the merit of being not only a ploughboy but a Gainsborough   BC

32   Mulready] Gainsborough   A

34   lay ... woof] wandered like a streak drawn by a finger over the surface of the stuff   BC

39–40   headstones ... overcome] headstones and protrusions that had settled and sunk. The whole scene spoke so of a long tradition of worship, that my sensitive companion was quite overcome   BC

41   cried] murmured   BC

41   first church] first real church   BC

43   saw ... kind] saw a church of statelier proportions   A; visited a place of worship more commodious   BC

61 : 1–2   a region . . . incidents] such a mist of local colour   ABC

6   viewed . . . reflected] looked down at the reflection of the solid minster   BC

6   calm] solid   A

8   phaetons] curricles   ABC

9   swansdown boas and lace] their sandals, and   BC

10   about the gentle] about the mellow   B; in the gravelled C

12–13   far aloft . . . field] clinging far aloft to the quiet sides   BC

14   bold architectural] perpendicular   BC

15   graciously] irresistibly   BC

15   witnesses of nature] dials   BC

18–19   marries . . . church] dovetails with cloister and choir   BC

21   haunted such] gone and come through   BC

24   Park] om.   BC

27–8   its vast . . . dells] its enclosure the declining spurs of the hills continued to undulate and subside   BC

27   vast] broad   A

32   and wild] om.   BC

33   the stern] that angular   BC

33–4   property . . . welcome] property put on such an air of innocence   A; landlordism muffle itself in so many concessions   BC

36   refinement . . . climes] purity unknown in climates where fine weather is cheap   BC

39–41   foot . . . rare] foot—distilled from an alchemist's crucibles [crucible   C]   BC

40–1   recorded . . . rare.] recorded!   A

41   external region] liberal margin   BC

41   very] om.   ABC

62 : 2   Hence] Here   C

2   dark . . . among] rich grey front of the Tudor-time, above   BC

4–5   a proscribed . . . hovering] an exiled prince who has come back on tiptoe, hovering   BC

6   think,' . . . 'of] think of   BC

7   years! I] years!' he answered. 'I   BC

7   what might] but what might   C

8   you] a man   BC

9–10   you happy,' . . . to believe] him perfectly happy, independent of other things, I should [rather   C] hesitate to believe,' I said. 'But it's hard to suppose   BC

9   believe] suppose   A

15–16   my bit of . . . turf] the rest of my life away on this turf of the middle-ages   BC

16–17   yon moated grange] that old hall, or grange or court— what in the name of enchantment do you call it?—   BC

17	turning] he turned C
19	torment] distraction BC
20	near ... servant] within call a decent lad BC
21	gardens ... house] gardens, and who might have been an underling in the stables BC
22	admittance] admittance to the house BC
24	of the mansion] om. BC
26	shall] must BC
26	a third] another ABC
27–31	specimen ... fulness] production of some four hundred years ago: a multitudinous cluster of gables and porches, projections and recesses, brown old surfaces nestling under their ivy, and mottled roofs that testified not to seasons but to centuries BC
28–31	huge brick ... fulness] multitudinous cluster of gables and porches, oriels and turrets, screens of ivy and pinnacles of state A
32	adjacent domain] place BC
33	person ... habillé] person BC
34	statement] assertion BC
35	that] said BC
36–7	following directly upon] following so directly upon A; following so directly on BC
37–8	seemed ... pertinent] was rather resented by my companion BC
40	deferential] diplomatic BC
42–3	Standing ... impulse] as I stood with the pencil in my hand a temptation entered into it BC
43	weighing] considering BC
63 : 1	yielded to it. I] let the pencil obey, and BC
1	name] name the words BC
3	attended] waited upon BC
4	dowdy clean cap] clean, dowdy cap BC
8–9	constituent ... manor] constituent properties of a great house B; proper features of a great mansion C
12–13	and a ... places] a couple of Gainsboroughs, hung there with high complacency BC
13–15	The great ... furniture.] om. ABC
15	about silent] about, scarcely speaking BC
17	and asked no question] on what we saw, and asked but a question or two BC
17	him at a certain moment] him, at last ABC
20	an antique buffet] a great crédence BC
21–2	huge ... colours] plates of every shape, with their glaze of happy colour BC
23	came to] seemed to rise before BC
25–8	had bargained ... palace] been waited on at his inn by

persuasive toymen   BC

29–30   showed ... irony:] showed me a blush which I felt, I think, more than he.   BC

31   while] when   C

32   the] a   C

34   majolica-ware] majolica   ABC

36–7   old young ... *chinoiseries*] ancient young buck [contemporary dandy   C] who had a taste for foreign gimcracks BC

39   *demi-jour*] twilight   ABC

40   say,' ... 'in] say in   BC

41   this] this sort of thing   BC

42   one of ... majolicas] some of their infernal crockery   BC

64:7   the chimney-piece of which] whose chimney-piece   BC

13   buck,' ... 'who] buck who   BC

13–14   majolica-ware ... Italy.'] majolica out of Italy.' A; majolica out of Italy,' I suggested.   BC

15   staring] without any wonder   BC

19   gazing] staring   BC

21   deuce] devil   C

24   have] om.   BC

29   lovely] beautiful   BC

29–30   Kinsman] Dear kinsman   BC

32–4   forlorn ... its youth] about in misery till it got another incarnation—in this poor trunk!' And he tapped his hollow chest. 'Here it has rattled about these forty years, beating its wings against its rickety cage, begging to be taken home again   BC

33–4   racking its wretched casing] shaking its rickety cage   A

35–8   Let me ... My] Now, at last, the poor spirit can escape!' The housekeeper, very timorously, endeavoured to practise a smile. The scene was really embarrassing, and my   BC

41   with a timid air] without confidence   BC

43   Searle ... marvelling] Searle stared at her as if one of the pictures had stepped out of its frame   BC

65:1   mistaken,' ... 'one] mistaken, one   BC

2   Searle.'] Searle,' the lady said.   BC

5   receive it] —not to see him   BC

6   interrupt] intrude upon   C

8   interruption] intrusion   C

9   are] come   BC

9   America] that America   B

12   took] suddenly took   BC

14   are] must be   BC

15   an extremely modest] a thoroughly diffident   BC

16–17   proceed ... overture] make advances without help   BC

17–18   foot. I fancied I] foot, and I fancied I   B: foot, and I

	could easily C
19	heiress] mistress BC
19	manorial acres and] hereditary BC
20	thirty-three] thirty-five C
21–2	with ... her shape] and full of a kind of slim robustness BC
22–3	blue eye ... comely] grey eye, a considerable quantity of very light brown hair and a smiling, well-formed mouth BC
27–8	glance and accent] expression and tone C
28	simple, too] very shy and BC
29	been fancying] prefigured to himself BC
30	plain] not obtrusively fair BC
31	by the grace of] with ABC
32	avow] claim ABC
33	in the least] om. BC
34	doing so] knowing anything about me BC
35–6	anew and smiled] and smiled anew BC
38	though] however ABC
39	of a Clement Searle] that a Clement Searle was BC
40	I hardly] But, you know, I hardly BC
43	shy] hesitating BC
66:2	as] so C
3	the show] what there is, I think BC
5	of the great] of a great BC
6	silent and shy] dumb and abashed C
7	a great] an C
8	small-talk] conversation BC
9–10	mansion. Meanwhile I] mansion, and as I did so I C
10–14	small beauty ... massive luxury] no brilliancy of expression or manner; there was something infelicitous and unexpected [meagre and provincial C] in her dress; yet she pleased me well. There was about her a sturdy [She had a sort of antique C] sweetness, a homely fragrance of old traditions. To be so simple, among those complicated treasures BC
16	many ... home] such places as that BC
17	Belle ... Dormant] Sleeping Beauty in the Wood BC
19	no light scrutiny] a curiosity that was not artfully veiled BC
19–29	The best possible ... but once?'] 'I should like so to go abroad!' she exclaimed suddenly, as if she meant us to take the speech for an expression of interest in ourselves. 'Have you never been?' I inquired. BC
22–3	gracieuseté] amenity A
31	this] that C
32	Here ... born] I was born in this house BC

33	I fancy I'm] one gets BC
34–5	It's extremely] Of course it's very BC
42	who would ... estates] who of course would have had everything BC
43	I'm ... now] that makes me heir, [the heir C] as they have done something—I don't quite know what—to the entail BC
67:3	a rambling ... vapidity] rambling eagerness BC
5	curate] vicar BC
5	inducted] presented to the living BC
6	sound orthodox] quite safe BC
11	ripely verdant] mellow C
13–14	a potential ... Miss Burney] the heroine of a last-century novel BC
16	away,' ... 'without] away without BC
16	us?'] us?' she inquired. BC
31	At least] I am afraid BC
33	way,' ... 'tell] way, tell BC
34	America!'] America,' he said to me. BC
38–9	eye. I read ... interested] eye. I thought I read in her glance [eye; it began to be plain enough C] that she was interested in her curious cousin BC
40–2	London ... tact] London, and which, in a very crude form had reference to his making a match with this lady. If only Miss Searle could be induced to think of that, and if one had the tact to manipulate her a little BC
43	sentiment] the flower of romantic affection BC
68:1	but] only BC
1	lurked] seemed to shape itself BC
5–7	'And yet ... know how] 'And yet he doesn't look in the least an Englishman,' said Miss Searle. 'Oh, it isn't his looks, poor fellow.' 'Of course looks are not everything BC
8	looks and] om. BC
11–14	without children ... travel on?'] all alone in the world.' 'Has he much property?' 'None to speak of.' 'But he has means to travel about.' BC
14	on] om. A
16	in poor] in very poor BC
17	fancied] supposed BC
18	He's better, though,] But he is better BC
20	Poor fellow] Dear me—poor man BC
20	fancied] thought BC
20	her] Miss Searle's BC
21	off] away BC
22	a modest man] very modest C
27	out. I] out, while I BC

27   on the terrace] om. BC
28   our friend] our appreciative friend C
29   a splendid peacock] the familiar fowl of gardens—a
        splendid specimen— BC
31   him] the gorgeous fowl A; the gorgeous biped BC
32   parapet] ledge C
34–5   very . . . gardenry] genius of stately places BC
35–6   tickled so cunningly] flattered ABC
36–7   and esplanades] om. BC
39   autumnal leaves] over autumnal leaves B; over grass or
        gravel C
69:3   else by] else—not by BC
10   book full] collection C
15   horrors] that won't do BC
15   done] managed BC
17   and then . . . laugh] laughing at his idea C
19   luxury] picturesqueness ABC
22   something!] something extraordinary. C
23   here! when I think] here— C
24   through those glades] under the beeches BC
27   immortal picturesqueness] intense experience A; rich
        experience of life— BC
28   vehemence] agitation C
30–1   that . . . over-excited] he was really losing his head BC
31   evoked] called up there BC
35   blessed oriel] dear little window BC
36   casement] oriel BC
37   cunningly] om. ABC
39   my room] my little room C
40   maiden's] woman's ABC
40–3   the forgotten . . . cousins!] all the dear faces—all of them
        so mild and yet so proud—that have looked out of that
        lattice, and of all the old-time women's lives whose prin-
        cipal view of the world has been this quiet park! Every
        one of them was a cousin of mine. BC

PART II] II. ABC

70:1   great] large BC
6   you the soul] you to be the spirit BC
8–9   worship] delight in BC
11–12   *Belle . . . Dormant*] Sleeping Beauty BC
15   said] announced C
16   Dear Me!] Oh, what shall I do? C
23   to have my companion] that my companion should BC
26   world,' . . . 'did] world did BC

26	here?'] here?' asked Searle. BC
27–8	'He learned ... Simmons and] I answered that he had probably learned from his solicitor of the visit of his[1] friend Simmons. 'Simmons and BC
29	England. Simmons] England,' I said. 'Simmons BC
35–7	his nobler ... fractional] he has been very much struck with what the legal people have had to say for you, and that he wishes to have the originality of making over to you your partial BC
36	these] the A
38	*Je m'y perds*] I give it up ABC
71 : 1–2	bespoken ... well] told them to see about a room for you BC
8–9	most ... little] low, narrow ABC
9	horizontal] om. BC
14	placidly reverted] dropped on his breast BC
15	early excitement. I] rhapsodies, and I ABC
17	light parting] light, expressive parting C
18	brightness and peace] mental soundness ABC
27	her,' ... 'than] her than BC
27	her. Get] her,' I said. 'Get BC
31	You're ... man] Oh, you are all right BC
32–3	had spent ... told me] told me that he had spent the hours of my absence BC
34	must already be] must be very BC
41	a smaller ... one] others, smaller and more convenient, C
72 : 1	ducal] royal BC
1	the great] a great BC
2	alabaster] marble [white marble BC], yellowed by time ABC
3	stood] was BC
4	knew her not] scarcely knew her ABC
5	profoundly] remarkably BC
14	bow] curious little sharp stare BC
16	short ... less] very limited stature, which was less BC
16	stature, less] stature, which was less A
17	flaming] preternatural ABC
17–19	The former ... abundant,] They intermingled over his ears and ABC
20–2	His beard ... in water.] om. ABC
25–6	finely ... wrinkles] wrinkles finely [sharply C] etched and scratched, BC

---

[1] Texts B and C have 'your' for 'his', which does not make sense in the revised context of the passage and belongs to the original text, where the passage is treated as a dialogue. Apparently, James himself introduced the error when he carried out the second revision, and failed to spot it when he returned to the tale for the third.

26	cunning] refined C
27	The complexion ... fifty] It was the complexion of a man of sixty ABC
28–9	In harmony ... eyes] His eyes BC
30	with a sort of] had a kind of auburn glow, a BC
30	but] and were BC
32	tone] aspect ABC
32	almost,] om. BC
32–3	in which ... encased] which made a sort of frame for it BC
33–5	smile which ... to command,'] queer, quick, defiant, perfunctory, preoccupied smile, BC
34	single] official A
37	fancied] perceived BC
37–8	our excursion ... Of how] we had yet encountered. How BC
38	revealed to us] introduced to us A
40	small suspicion] not suspected, BC
41–3	distinctly ... mistrust] became aware, without his giving me the least sign, that he was placing himself on the defensive BC
42–3	stiffen ... mistrust] place himself, morally speaking, on the defensive A
43–73 : 1	Mr. Searle ... *simpatico*] Mr. Searle sympathetic BC
73 : 1	*simpatico*] sympathetic A
1	fancied] guessed BC
2	Miss Searle apprehended] his sister apprehended B; his sister entered into C
6–7	pale and her eyes] pale, her eyes were BC
7	signs and tokens] betrayals ABC
9	rare] om. B
9	the rare picturesqueness of] something complimentary and commemorative in C
12	cunning] om. BC
13	dressed in the] dressed in some B; habited in some C
13–15	a beautiful ... *bouillonnement*;] sea-green crape and silk, BC
17	stately] dull BC
17	the grand ... fashion] an air of admirable elegance A; a festive air BC
19	heavy] rounded ABC
19–20	necklace of heavy] single circle of large BC
20	with her into] in with her to BC
22	sportively] jocosely BC
24	most exacting] very difficult BC
25	heavily charged] embarrassing BC
26	a strong] the BC

28   shadowy ... self-esteem] languid will. The poor fellow tried to take himself more seriously than he had done even in his best days   BC

28   will, poor fellow,] will. The poor fellow sat   A

30–1   pretence ... words] propriety, and shown her the [shown the   C] bottom of his fantastic heart   ABC

32   double-distilled] consumate   BC

33   flattering] om.   ABC

34   peace] security   ABC

34   then] accordingly   BC

34–6   turn painfully ... elder world] screw himself round, as it were, to take a new point of view. He set himself the task of appearing very American, in order that his appreciation of everything Mr. Searle represented,   BC

34   painfully] faithfully   A

35   assert] prove   A

36   at heart] om.   A

37–8   to find him] him to be   BC

38   poised ... amenity] finely adjusted urbanity   A; exaggerated urbanity   BC

39–40   likely ... at all] so harmless   BC

42   exotic] transatlantic   BC

42   Mr. Searle] Our host   ABC

43   decency] delicacy   C

74:2   proportion] admixture   BC

5   I felt] I, for my part, felt   ABC

6–7   be strained ... shoulders] suffer from [be disfigured by   C] the extrusion of even such inconsiderable particles as ourselves   BC

8   way,' ... 'of] way,' said our host, 'of   A; way of   BC

9   America; but] America,' Mr. Searle said, 'but   BC

17   have] make   C

18   he has ... now.] you have kept him alive by one of those beastly processes—I think you have 'em over there: what do you call it, 'putting up' things?   BC

19   nice] wise   ABC

21   against] to   BC

22   wrought a great evil!] did a wrong   BC

28   Unfold ... tale] Do tell us all about it   BC

30–1   own ... force] resources   BC

32   five] long   BC

35   grotesque] peculiar   BC

39   older] elder   C

40   utmost fondness] greatest affection   BC

75:3   fancy] suspect   C

5   discharged] opened   BC

7–8   possessed ... trick] had a character which appears to have

	gone out of fashion in my family now-a-days; she was what the French call a *maîtresse-femme* BC
9	a number of] every so many BC
10	given ... will] sharpened her temper and her will BC
11	were ... amiss] had another object, and this object she began to hate BC
12	importunities] urgency A; purpose BC
14	secret and] secret, of course he loved A; secret. If he loved in secret, of course he loved BC
14–15	about sombre ... preoccupied] about the place, sombre, sullen, brooding BC
15	fatal indiscretion] rashness BC
18	did he] did so, he BC
21	fair rejected] rejected one BC
21	Clement] Clement Searle BC
23	great] big BC
25–6	there came ... quickening of] something happened which quickened BC
28	and made] and, making BC
29	guest. She poured] guest, poured BC
29–30	of Hereford] out of some little hole in Gloucestershire BC
33	reckoned too fondly] been a second time too trustful ABC
39	There] Mr. Searle related this anecdote in the tone of a very cultivated man, and when he ceased there BC
40	a great pity] much emotion BC
76:1	hugely tickled] immensely gratified BC
1	this poor ghost] the *revenant* C
5	then smiling superbly:] then, with a subtle sneer, BC
10	chilled] checked BC
10–11	frigid contact] influence BC
11	glow ... fire] ferment and crepitate BC
12	mind his *p*'s and *q*'s] steer his cockle-shell ABC
13–14	the passionate ... heart] his passionate satisfaction in the scene about him A; his passionate appreciation of the scene around him BC
16	resented ... egotism] been annoyed by the way he reverted constantly to himself BC
18	an immense] a kind of irresistible [irresponsible C] BC
19	the manner ... speech] every thing that passed his lips BC
20	very soul of it] essence of his discourse BC
21–4	rich facts ... the trees] poetry of his companion's situation and of the [and the BC] contrasted prosiness of their attitude ABC
25	demanded] suddenly inquired BC
28	nail it down] make it fast BC
34	a grey] a little grey C

34	said Miss Searle] Miss Searle remarked BC
36	little glass] hand-glass C
38	ten] many ABC
39	said] interposed BC
40	hence] from last Thursday, BC
40	forty-three.'] forty-three,' she answered. AB; forty-four,' she answered. C
43	of an] om. BC
77:3	these ... years] this wasted period BC
9–10	You're ... circumstances'] You are reduced—you are—a—straitened BC
11–13	vastly ... circumstances at all!'] much amused at hearing his bleak situation depicted in semi-tones. 'Reduced to nothing!' he cried with a long, light laugh; 'straitened to the clothes on my back!' B; much amused at hearing his bleak situation depicted in semi-tones. 'Reduced to nothing; straitened to the clothes on my back!' C
18	with a twinkle in his eye] in an inscrutable, humorous manner, C
21	keen] penetrating BC
23	circumstances] wardrobe BC
24	said] cried BC
24–5	are ... Park] wardrobe is immense. He could dress up a regiment BC
25–6	a rather ... drinkable] rather more champagne—I admit that the champagne was good BC
29	harshness] bravado B; rashness C
30	from table] from the table ABC
32–3	The night ... destiny] The romantic, the fatal, the critical, night BC
32	experience] fatality A
34	region] portion BC
37–8	panellings] wainscots BC
40	vastness] variety BC
78:1	became] became almost BC
2	Miss Searle] his sister BC
4	metaphysically, at least] metaphysically ABC
5	great] tall BC
7–8	bits ... treasures] carvings and cornices BC
8–9	house. He ... wit the] house to perfection. He touched upon a hundred traditions and memories, and sketched very vividly several BC
10	anecdotes] *historiettes* C
10–11	an almost ... neatness] remarkable art BC
14	time,' ... 'you] time you BC
15	friends.'] friends,' I remarked. BC
16–17	homely candid gaze] kind little eyes BC

20	He's ... man.] He is really very odd! BC
21	singular] odd BC
24–5	rich, mellow] sweet-sounding BC
26	was] used to be BC
27	playing] practising BC
28	fancy] sensibilities BC
29–30	charged ... forces,] precarious BC
30	wholly ... rejoice] to be glad BC
31	now,' ... 'seems] now seems BC
31	shape. It will] shape,' I said. 'It will BC
32	part, Miss Searle, if] part if BC
33	soundness and serenity] all that he ought to be BC
35–6	You see ... doubtless,] I daresay you see in him now BC
39	respect] esteem BC
40	puzzled ... gaze] pathetic little frown BC
41	poor me] poor stupid me BC
79 : 1–2	with a ... meaning] if I had been reproaching her with her insignificance BC
3	begun now] begun to live now BC
4–5	outside ... foreigner.)] else than your old-fashioned habits. Excuse me if I seem rather meddlesome; you know we Americans are very rough. BC
7	fancy] believe BC
11	arrival,' ... 'is] arrival is BC
11	disturbance.'] disturbance,' she said at last. BC
12	recognizing] coming to meet BC
14	after a fashion!] in a certain sense. BC
15	proper] right and just C
20	And hereupon I] I could not help C
21–3	felt a dull ... demanded.] relieved [relieving C] myself— at least by the tone of my voice—of the antipathy with which, decidedly, this gentleman had inspired me. 'Not perhaps that we should get on so well together!' BC
24	tearful] long shuddering BC
26	I looked at him.] om. C
27	rococo] chiselled BC
29–33	Shall I ... watched. I] It was evident that I too was being overlooked [supervised C], and I determined I BC
31	villain] sneak A
34	watched] suspected C
36–7	the glance ... pain] a glance which begged me to spare her BC
37	me] me—please don't C
38	verge of ... ground] edge of a place where the ground had suddenly fallen away, BC
40	beckon her forward] assist her to jump BC
42	O, dreadful] oh, what a dreadful BC

80 : 5   most] very   BC
7   I gave ... look.] om.   BC
15   Mistress] Mrs.   BC
16   who did ... pleased] *qui se passait ses fantaisies*   BC
18–19   Fair ... What] Pretty Mrs. Margaret, you must have been a woman of courage! Upon my word, she looks like Miss Searle! Pray go on. What   BC
18   I honour you] my compliments   A
23   Mistress] Mrs.   BC
24   to Cynthia] to a certain Cynthia   BC
26   been confined] had a baby   BC
27   and neglected] and dreadfully neglected   BC
28   effusion] production   BC
31–3   'This was ... un-English!'] Then he remarked—'This was the only lady of the family who ever looked at [was taken in by   C] an adventurer.'   BC
35   of the lady's heavy] of the heroine's   BC
36   zeal] expression   C
37–8   This utterance ... zeal.] om.   BC
38   Mistress] Mrs.   BC
38–9   he cried, and] my friend returned; and he   BC
41   You've found] You found   B; You have found   C
41   cousin,' ... vengeance.'] cousin with a vengeance,' I said, laughing.   BC
42   said my host] my host repeated   BC
81 : 3–4 so!' and ... I] so! He tells me, he is an invalid,' he added in a moment, 'I   BC
5   fancied] supposed   C
6   hours.' ... 'he's] hours he is   BC
7   place and your] beautiful house, and your   B; beautiful house, your extreme   C
8   little shapeless] vague   BC
9   many an ... announce] Englishmen of a certain class sometimes recognize   BC
14   was] were   BC
14–15   been prompted ... he was] opened himself to any one, as if the process were monstrous disagreeable, and he were   BC
22   style] sort   BC
27   deuce] devil   BC
28   has he established this] why the devil has he put forward this   BC
29   utterance] inquiry   BC
32   amazed] surprised   BC
34–5   struck ... blow] been wanting in form   BC
36   seldom ... shock as] been more disgusted than I can say, BC
37   monstrous] extraordinary   BC

39–40	passion] admiration C
40	respect it] respect my place, BC
41	imagination] loyalty C
42	life, myself] life, my heaven B; conscience, my life C
42–3	concede ... of it to] make a great hole in it for A; divide it up at this time of day with BC
43	means, without] means, without appearance, without C
82 : 1	stranger] pretender BC
1	an adventurer] a mountebank C
7	really absurd] om. BC
9	base] unworthy BC
10	and of conscience] and conscience BC
14	keen] sharp C
15	radiant] flamboyant A; strange red BC
15–16	with the ... sensation] om. ABC
17	whispered] shouted BC
17	it] it—let him bring it into court C
19	noble porch] porch AB; portico C
23	then] om. BC
24–5	on the threshold] at the entrance C
26	faltered] faltering BC
28	plated salver] silver tray BC
29	salver] tray BC
31	fine sense ... explosion] quick, nervous prevision of a catastrophe BC
32	match] match to the train BC
32	extending salver] extending the salver C
40	(The housekeeper.)] This lady [personage C], I afterwards learned, was our friend the housekeeper. BC
83 : 1–2	completely ... courtesy] with his equilibrium completely restored by the crisis BC
1	a scene] the sense A
4–6	exasperated ... a servant] so exasperated that I was afraid he would snatch Mrs. Horridge's missive BC
8	cried] exclaimed BC
10	disgusted] very angry BC
12	thing] document BC
14	Heaven's ... 'what] the name of decency,' cried Searle, 'what A; the name of decency, what BC
15	mean?'] mean?' Searle broke out. BC
16	break out upon] open fire on BC
18	high-pitched and angry] high-pitched, contentious C
19	dressing-gown] wrapper C
20	heavy] thick C
23	butler of infinite] butler of remarkable A; person of remarkable BC
24	celerity] agility BC

35	them and left] them, leaving BC
35–7	An inexorable ... unhandsomeness,] But there was something even in her patience which seemed to him to mock him, so that he flushed crimson with rage and spite BC
37	You're a child] You always were an idiot BC
39–40	twisted ... frown] blighted and distorted C
42	asked, plaintively] inquired plaintively B; inquired very plaintively C
84 : 1	rounded integrity] stability ABC
4	home] house BC
5	break my diamond!] share my land [property BC] with you? ABC
5	infernal] preposterous BC
12	on] on in the same infuriated tone BC
12–13	practised] plotted BC
14	practise against] intrigue with BC
15	softly roared] groaned BC
18–19	thus to think of us] to think of us so ABC
20	you!] *you* as you would like, BC
22	pursued] went on BC
25	furious] insane BC
28	vastly improved] improved a good deal BC
30–1	flaming *chevelure*] brilliant head BC
33	species] sort BC
36	imbecile] hypocrite BC
38	—to—] om. BC
42	carriage wheels] wheels of the carriage BC
43	the footman] a footman BC
85 : 3	a grand] the grandest BC
3–4	which ... laughter] om. BC
4	added;] added artlessly, BC
9	said her brother] her brother broke in C
13	was a ... warning. I] was only a word of warning. It was to tell you to go. I BC
18	said] cried ABC
21–2	and crossed] and we crossed BC
24	cried our host] cried her brother AB; her brother went on C
27	foolish] ridiculous A
27	O foolish man] Oh, you ridiculous man B; You very ridiculous man C
28	shall] will BC
28	screamed] shouted C
30	And this gentle verb] And this soft vocable A; And this grim participle B; This grim participle C
32	whence] from which BC
33	free] unencumbered ABC

33	of] with ABC
41	a restless walk] restlessly up and down BC
86:3	sweet Margaret Searle] poor Margaret BC
6	solitude, in a romance] world quite detached BC
7–8	fairer ... loquacity] prettier, more attractive. I found my-self talking all kinds of nonsense BC
8	gone far] gone very far BC
11	huge conviction] sense—it was odd how it came over me then [there C]—of the reality of my connection with the place BC
11–12	"It exists ... said.] om. BC²
12	forgone it] given it up BC
13	it from your heart!] me for my sacrifice. BC
14	cried, "it ... trouble.] cried, 'it will make every thing right. B; asked, 'will it make everything right? C
14	solve] repair A
15	marriage," ... "the trouble] marriage, the whole difficulty BC
16	ocean.'] ocean,' I answered. BC
17	deep,] om. BC
17–18	shatter ... she said] wake us up and show us our folly. 'I love you, but I shall never see you again,' she cried BC
23	fancied] believed BC
24	of a stubborn wakefulness] that I should not close my eyes BC
24–5	set my fire a-blazing] stirred my fire BC
35	Make it ... truest!] om. BC
37–8	A woman ... a ghost!] A ghost, sir! Do you understand? ABC
39	great] kind of BC
41	can't] can BC
41	even] om. BC
42	with a great blow] quickly BC
42	then] om. BC
87:2	in it ... before him] in it; then I got on my knees C
5	waited ... throat] waited there, very curious for what he would say BC
7–8	with ... lives] om. BC
10–11	—waves ... Maker!'] —into waves [surges C]—and know all the secrets of things, and all the reasons, and all the mysteries!' BC
12	candle—far] candle.—No, far ABC
13	Young, dreadfully] Young and wonderfully BC
15	dead dark] wet-looking BC

² The speech which follows this passage properly answers the question posed in it; but, for some curious reason, the question itself is dropped in B and C, making the readings there mildly absurd.

18	and spoke] and she spoke BC
19	right me] put an end to my shame BC
21	Heaven and earth] Bless us and save us BC
22	make] made BC
22–3	discredit it] turn it into ridicule BC
23	irresistible] om. BC
24	immense sensation] own agitation A; excitement BC
27	wits] common sense BC
28	bad] evil A; om. BC
29	tacitly established] easily agreed BC
31–2	especially to obviate] above all to preserve him from BC
32	hugely] om. ABC
32–3	about with multitudinous] up in the BC
33	left] om. BC
35	kind of] om. BC
39	vast] om. BC
40	gaze … firelight] look, without blinking, into the fire BC
41	that blighted maid] the little woman with the muff BC
43	drooping black] distorted BC
43	transcendent] extraordinary BC
88:1	high] om. BC
1–2	in the … his brow] as the red light flickered over him BC
3	nursed by … Duchess] laid up after one of his exploits BC
5	the birds] the awakened birds BC
5–6	twitter … unperturbed,] twitter, and Searle, unperturbed, sat BC
5	of another day] om. A
6	look; I] look and I BC
9	gazed … time] looked at me for a long time BC
10	strange, innocent] kind of innocent BC
12	nothing] nothing of any consequence C
13	deemed myself] supposed myself to be BC
14	personage!] great exception BC
14	I'm … men!] om. BC
15	Sleep] If sleep BC
15	eyes: I] eyes, I BC
16	perfect] om. BC
17	was] were BC
18–23	an essential … investing sentinels] old habits of gentle behaviour [confirmed habits of mildness C] that I did not fear he would prove unmanageable BC
22–3	finding … sentinels] finding an issue A
24	grotesque] curious BC
24	an end] a close BC
24	appeared] was BC
25	rise from] get out of C

26–7	from an apparent inability] being apparently unable BC
28	doubt of my living] don't think I shall live BC
29	brave] good BC
29	the best] any BC
30	my near ... death] that they are getting ready for me on the other side of the grave BC
31–3	On my ... narcotic] When I said something about [touched the question of C] breakfast he replied that he had his breakfast in his pocket; and he drew from his travelling-bag a phial of morphine ABC
32–3	some habitual narcotic] morphine A
34	and apparently] much BC
35–6	a ghost-encumbered comrade] not only a man with a grievance, but a man with a ghost BC
40	imagined] supposed BC
42	Of Oxford ... detail] Of this remarkable spot I shall not attempt to speak with any order, or indeed with any reason BC
89 : 1–2	thoughts ... words] emotions it kindles in the mind of the western pilgrim, are too rich and various to be expressed in the halting rhythm of prose BC
1	thoughts it generates] emotions it stirs A
2–9	It seems to ... of its effect.] om. BC
5	Truly, no] No A
7	braver] finer A
10–16	streets innumerable ... lesser states] small, oblique streets in which the long grey, battered, public face of the colleges seems to be watching for noises that may break upon the stillness of study, you feel it to be the most dignified, the most educated of cities. Over all of it, through all of it, the great corporate fact of the University, slowly throbs like some steady bass in a concerted piece, like the mediaeval, mystical presence of the Empire in the old states of Germany BC
10	streets innumerable] various streets A
11–12	a mediaeval vacancy,] om. A
16	Gothic] perpendicular BC
18	fancy] imagination BC
19	perceive] discover BC
20–21	grateful ... eyes] that bookish eyes like to rest upon BC
22	noble and] om. BC
23	the admonitory ... great name] her own good manners BC
25	strolled vaguely] strolled eagerly A; wandered BC
27	embossed ... shaftings] delicately fluted and embossed BC
30	little] low BC

30–2	that dim ... faster and] the dim little court that nestles beneath the tower, where BC
33	ivy ... than] ivy than BC
33	Oxford ... thence] Oxford, and passed BC
34	great] quiet BC
34	gaunt stone images along] little sculptured monsters along A; small sculptured monsters on BC
35–6	arcade ... founders] arcade ABC
38–9	the influence ... imagination] he would take Oxford too hard, as he took everything BC
40	hard] difficult BC
41–2	perception and illusion] what he saw and what he imagined BC
42	confound] mingle BC
90 : 1–2	speak ... Old-World] talk altogether in the character of his old-time BC
1–2	Old World] old-time A
3	all Oxford] the whole place BC
4–5	paced ... the hour] walked up and down this cloister with the undergraduates of the last century BC
6	them] early attachments BC
8–9	there are ... old haunt] some of the foundation-stones are loosened; some of the breaches will have to be repaired! Mine was the old unregenerate University, the home BC
9	precedent] invidious distinctions C
12–13	his ... to ebb] he had lost the little that remained of his strength BC
13	labour] effort C
13–14	any large exploration] regular sight-seeing ABC
17	almost] om. BC
18	Lockley Park] the home of the Searles BC
18–19	a broad ... satisfaction] an unruffled resignation BC
20	the depths ... lake] an old-fashioned mirror BC
21	—worthy ... name!—] om. ABC
23	to 'Iffey ... the hill,'] om. ABC
25	the heart need demand] could be desired BC
26	mighty lads of England] *belle jeunesse* of England B; young, the happy generation C
27	immense] muscular BC
27	magnificent in their youth] magnificent, fresh C
28–9	solitude ... honours] a singleness that nursed ambitions BC
29	pregnant] portentious A
30–1	When ... motion] When, in conjunction with all this magnificent sport [beautiful physical life BC] ABC
31–2	verdant ... sanctities] lawns and bowers, the silvery sanctities B; perfumed privacy C

32	esteem] consider B
32–3	esteem ... salted] hold that to be young in this incomparable country is to be doubly—infinitely—blessed C
34–5	on three successive days] om. C
35	various gardens] scholastic domains A; scholastic shades BC
36–9	The perfect ... disbelief.] om. ABC
39	These ... domains] They ABC
39	seemed to us the] struck us as the C
39	possible] om. ABC
40	fruits] fruit C
43	centenary vines] immemorial plants B; unrecorded plants C
43–91 : 1	perfumes ... memories] nightingales and memories—a sort of hum of tradition; C
91 : 1	memories] traditions B
2	if tenderly ... pressure] if to spare it the injury C
5	vast] green BC
9	worshipping] dreaming A; in fascinated *flânerie*, BC
9–10	college ... broods] college façade [face of the college BC] here perhaps broods ABC
11–13	fell into ... Every student] dropped into fitful talk and spun his fancies into golden figures. Every collegian BC
12–13	felicity ... reproduce] felicity, compounded of the oddest mixture of wisdom and folly A
15–19	My friend's ... blindness.] om. ABC
20	all,' ... 'a] all a BC
20	lie? Mightn't] lie?' he demanded. 'Mightn't BC
24	framed] invented BC
33	Oxford] such a place BC
38	deeper] cleverer BC
39–40	feel a certain ... voice] take it as a sort of affront to my dignity ABC
42	our parts] our meagre little parts BC
43	bow to] accept BC
92 : 2	a *mise en scène*] decorations C
4	concoct] invent BC
5	mysteries] traditions BC
7–8	the obligations here contracted] such obligations ABC
9–12	bear ... Americans.] may go through life with her blessing: but if you let it stand unhonoured, you are a worse barbarian than we! ABC
15	corridors and cloisters] cloisters and halls BC
16	close] end BC
17	ending] close BC
18	a sterner] the general BC

18–19   gathered ... history] dropped into less bottomless traps BC

26   mullion and open casement] cornice and the lattice   BC

27   a Pylades of mine] my *fidus Achates*   A; my bosom friend BC

28   mullion] cornice   BC

29   Pylades] *fidus Achates*   A; bosom friend   BC

30   pledged] committed   BC

34–5   surprising ... magniloquence] really artistic in my poor friend's divagations   BC

35   poor] om.   BC

35   *flâneur*] loafer   A; dandy   BC

37   shy] om.   BC

40   more ... tenuous] thinner and more transparent   **ABC**

40   unallayed] om.   ABC

93 : 6–8   vagaries ... society] extravagance, partly from seeing him get worse under the pressure—applied without scruple by the juvenile class—of champagne and an admiring circle C

7   them] his state   B

9   fancied] supposed   BC

11   firmness] dignity   BC

11   most melting *bonhomie*] desire to fraternise   C

11–12   respect. Two] respect. If they didn't think him a lunatic they certainly thought him a celebrity of the Occident. Two   BC

16   He dined] Making the acquaintance of several tutors and fellows, he dined   ABC

17–18   brevity and relish] unction   ABC

18   at the ... entertainments] after a symposium indiscreetly prolonged   C

20   and looking] looking   ABC

20   and exhausted] om.   ABC

21–2   stubbornly] rigidly   BC

28   look and feel] eat and drink   BC

31   an article: it] a convenience: it   A; a convenience, and it BC

33   one ... spot] one on the spot at liberty   BC

34–5   had come ... cold] now had a perpetual chill   BC

39   the hotel doors] the doors of the hotels   BC

40   hopeless doubt] poor prospect   C

94 : 1   with untender curtness] a little ungraciously   C

5–6   He ... 'seedy'.] To describe him in the slang of our native land, he was a 'dead-beat'.   BC

9   experience] tribulations   C

10   turned to purple] assumed a tinge   C

10   sandy] reddish   C

17–18	a rounded ... equal] such a bow as one man of the world might make to another BC
19–20	perfect ... speech] refinement of his tone A; superiority of his accent BC
23	said to] asked of BC
25	Wadham ... college] one of the colleges, 'That used to be my place BC
29	Wadham] My college BC
30	Wadham] my college BC
35	degenerate ... Wadham] perverted product of a liberal education BC
40	smiled ... companion] gave our companion a glance of intelligence BC
43	lattice] casement BC
95 : 1–2	bosky resorts in] planted places of BC
3	façade] front BC
5	he broke out] the latter broke out C
9	English,' ... 'are] English are C
9	——impayables] really fabulous ABC
10	protest against] despise A; abhor BC
20–21	Wadham College as] om. BC
22	Wadham College as] om. BC
26	clapping his hands] with great seriousness C
27	drop further] drop any further BC
28–9	there's ... lot] I too am at the very bottom of the hole BC
30	Save ... of] Well, sir, there's a difference between BC
36	'point,' ... 'of] point of BC
37	figures.'] figures,' he said. BC
40	great gravity] all consideration C
96 : 15	Wadham gardens] the most delicious corner of the ancient world BC
16	America] Yankeeland BC
17	Wadham ... well] Delicious corners are very well, and so is the ancient world BC
20	there] in Yankeeland BC
21	a sort of ... energy] feeble force BC
27	England] old England BC
31	amiss] out of the way BC
35	gentleman,' ... 'fancied] gentleman fancied BC
38	America.'] America,' I said. BC
97 : 5	account] importance whatever B; importance whatever, Mr. Rawson C
6	address] sally BC
10–11	to his light dishonour] if he didn't gain by it BC
18–19	by ... emotion] with his agitation B
18–19	tinged ... emotion] dyed by his agitation C

24	of chances] of last chances BC
28	I've no ideas] Oh, I have no opinions BC
29	for England] for old England ABC
40	*séance*] little session BC
41	little hand-rail] handle BC
98:1	were ... front of] passed C
2	a potent ... puddings] an aroma of old-fashioned cookery, and other restorative things C
5	a colossal dinner] the best dinner they can give you BC
6	immortal health] eternal rest BC
7–8	momentarily irresponsive fingers] fingers momentarily irresponsive C
11	succulent flavour] savoury character BC
11	spot] establishment C
13	Chambertin] the yellow seal BC
20	a cruelly extorted] the very dregs of his BC
28	person, a sweet person] woman, a sweet woman BC
32–3	Need a man eat his] Why should one eat one's C
33	before his hanging] the day he [one C] is hanged BC
36	Release] Help me out with ABC
38	*dying*] *sinking* BC
42	weakness ... complete] exhaustion had become so total [great BC] ABC
99:2–3	the memories ... jumble] in a ghastly [sinister BC] jumble the memories of the past weeks and those of bygone years ABC
7	mighty] enormous BC
9	Nay] No BC
12	elegance] foppery C
13	shirt-buttons and scarf-pins] odds and ends of goldsmith's work BC
24	descend] send ABC
25	was] were BC
27	grave] suppressed ABC
29	high fraternal greeting] human message BC
30	Great God] Lord have mercy BC
33	trinkets; let] battered relics; you can sell them; let BC
34	memories] mementoes C
37	our friend] the poor man C
38	here] here, I will stay with you and wait on you BC
43	Lord,' ... 'who] Lord, who BC
100:1	exhausted] quite used up BC
3	broad] rough ABC
8	lit] lighted BC
11	widely] wide BC
15	moment] instant C

25	some grim ... justice] poetic justice having been grimly shuffled away ABC
31	bedside ... withdrew] bedside, while the doctor withdrew BC
43	me,' ... colours!'] me wear colours!' he said. BC
101:2	attested] assured us of B
4	mightiest] blackest and widest BC
5	older] hoarier ABC

Notes:

1. The variants recorded below are based on a collation of the original serial text of the tale (*Galaxy*, 1871) and its revised version, only half-finished and in manuscript, now in the James collection in the Houghton Library at Harvard University (see headnote to the tale, p. 102).

2. The opening six pages revised by James show three section divisions: these occur at 106:10; 109:31; 111:35.

102:6–7	of my ... the rage] of my complexion would not resist the rage
13	penury] paucity
24–103:1	was Catholic Switzerland] part of Switzerland was Catholic; that made it seem more foreign
16	hereabouts] in this region
20	to fancy] to try to think
28	Milan] Milano
33–7	how ... and deed!] how, now that I saw my way out of it, I became reconciled to Switzerland.
41	from the rushing] out of the liquid
41	a palpable] an evident
104:1	note 'sensations'] receive impressions
8	was society] society was
23	in the land] on the level
27	was ... way] had not absolutely started
27	land] level
31	toil] process
32	mighty] om.
32	grand] om.
33	loneliness] solitude
34–5	desecration ... inviolable] desecration of the altitudes. As if they made much difference in the altitudes
41	takes ... colour] grows more and more perpendicular
43	perfect] om.
105:1	lifts and] om.
2	scenic] om.
2	fancy] album and the stage
6	generate] evoke
8–10	You ... itself.] om.
14	shuddering] indignant
18	broad] rich
18	possible] om.
20	profoundly] really
26–7	Something short of] A little way below
30	tarried] halted

34	being at] being only at
39	hard] om.
106 : 11–12	Its ... grandeur.] om.
13	reaches] efforts
14–15	some ... genius] an attempt to engineer for the sake of engineering
17	perfect] om.
17–18	beneath ... sun] by the crudest sunshine
19	billowy] crumpled
24–5	lustre ... blackness] glare of the sky grows black
31	superbly] merrily
35	brother] other
38	gently] om.
41–2	dramatically ... in tone] theatrically speaking, a succession of asides
42	a friend] an acquaintance
43	those] the friends
107 : 1	and appealing] and of appealing
4–5	transposed ... *thus!*] obedient to orders inscrutably superior.
6	treated ... travelled] made such haste to treat me as a
8	the ... travel] new dangers, new mysteries
12	relish ... things] delight in his freedom
16	snickering] chuckling
25	By] At
25	apace] in company
32	to] at
34	bless] favour
34–5	blessed ... words] of the happiest
41–2	a field ... lazuli] acres of sapphire
42–3	the beauty ... immensity] a luxury of greenness; the view is as soft as it is huge
108 : 2	proper ... grimness] the steepness of things
3–4	seemed ... serenity] fairly twinkled with the fine weather
5	along] round
6	towards] which was crowned with
7	crowned with topaz] om.
13	cities to] cities such establishments
14	chilly] chill
15	snowland] level of the snow
18	solemn and pleasant] perceptible
21	especial] om.
22	the premonition ... passed] the name of all the future hours I should pass
24	cold] rigid
24	face] countenance
24	defiant] om.

28	impart] om.
29	an ... Catholicism] make Catholicism partly an address to the nose
109:31	divine] enchanting
33	melt] lapse
35	tend downward] tend steadily downward
35	unbroken] om.
36	fancy a] suppose that a
37	crept ... upward] clambered towards the heights
39	deemed] thought
43	bright Italian] om.
110:2	slope] side
2	road] om.
6	nears ... less] is not postponed
12	blue. The] blue while the
14–15	din ... tunnel] din.
15	the Gorge of Gondo] this gorge of gorges
16	The ... climate] Emanations of mildness
17–18	Lo! suddenly ... sensation:] Sensations more definite are not wanting: as for instance the sight, by the still wayside, of
20	above this inscribed] superscribed
23	thumped] rapped on
24	the mountain echoes] the echoes [in] the hills
25	of peasants] om.
26	her own ... of her] her only bottle and her
30	utterly] perfectly
31	simply ... brow] with her tender eyes
33–4	its long-drawn] complicated
34–5	keeps ... Lombardy] compresses itself, as if to make more of a surprise of the loveliness to which it yields at last
111:2–4	cerulean ... picture] tight blue legs, in the future, were to ornament so many crooked streets
8	the dark eyed] a languid
10	beyond stood] beyond this stood
11	seemed to me] struck me
20	where of] of which
22–3	vastly ... broom] much refreshed by an application of soap-suds
26–7	cap, with little] cap; little

[The revision ends abruptly with a mark, in James's hand, indicating a new section division a few lines below the last variant listed above.]

MASTER EUSTACE

Notes:

1. The variants recorded below are based on a collation of the original serial text of the tale (*Galaxy*, 1871) and its revised version in *Stories Revived* (1885).

2. In the revised text the tale is divided into vi sections. Section i begins at 127:1; section ii at 131:14; section iii at 135:9; section iv at 139:36; section v at 143:36; and section vi at 147:43.

127:2	a delicate] an
5	a quiet] a very quiet
14	sciences] science
20	service] bondage very
21	that] if
21	fairly measured] fully appreciated
22	that] om.
23	estimated] measured
27	pretty ... But] attractive woman; but
29–31	light of ... languor),] fluttering, with frequent gestures and not many words,
34–5	seemed compounded of] been made up of
36	making her] putting her together
36–128:1	that wholesome ... weighted] the harder, heavier parts, the selfishness, the ambition, the power to insist and to calculate
128:5	her soul] her very soul
6	trouble] distresses
6	was] were
9	of hers] om.
10	her ... sorrow] it
12	had] had been
14	intimated] mentioned
16	obvious] manifest
17	fancied] suspected
30	but little like] not at all in the manner of
35	lodged] situated
36–7	wore an ... authority] presented himself as a little man who would take a line of his own
37	to] who would ever
37–8	evil, but to snatch] evil; he would snatch
42	eyes] eye
43–129:1	in spite of ... to be] with every possible relaxation of the nursery-code my place never became in the least a sinecure
129:9	dinners] dinner

17	caressing] fondling
21	moonshiny] perverse
23–4	exacts and denies] requires and refuses
24	wicked and hideous] wicked
32	as] what
36	bright and inaccessible] bright, inaccessible
40–2	or the ... illusion] or found himself the final morbid little offshoot of a long line of despots, he couldn't have had a greater idea of his prerogative
42–130:1	I pierced ... punctures.] om.
130:2	graceful] extra
2	legal] regular
3–4	permit this ... asked;] allow things, if his leave had been asked,
4	of conflicting] of a conflicting
5–7	Poor puny ... of privileges!] om.
9–10	I found ... fancied it] If he liked me and confided in me, I had worked hard for it—I had to 'live up' to it. He thought it
12–13	to have ... see-saw] to make me joggle with him on the see-saw (sitting close to the middle),
15	by ... favour] at his liking me
17	demanded ... licence] required a great margin
20	seemed to ... picturesque] had a kind of personal distinction
24–5	fairly practised] practised properly
25	as neatly ... wished] with wonderful expression
32	an air which they] a melody they
34	fancy] imagine
35	big, superbly-expectant eyes] big eyes
36	poor little] om.
37	mercy ... impotence] for breath
39	and] om.
39	my prisoners, my] dragons, dungeons and
41	pitifully prosaic] dreadfully below the mark
41	always] om.
42	gape] yawn
131:2	dreadfully] remarkably
5	secretly thanked it, for] was secretly thankful, because
6	which] that
8	stirring] exciting
10	cool and] om.
13	you had] you *had* lost
19	dozen] other
22	a teacher] an instructor
24	enjoy] minister to
24	concurrence] competition

26	categorically] punctually
28	told their love] 'told' it
30	and alike distasteful] all very untidy paws
34	fashion] manner
36–7	Nay ... hideous] But she never would have forgiven herself a flirtation
37–8	a brave little passion of] her
38	a general] her general
41–2	in fact ... from it] it inspired her, in fact, with a kind of terror
132:2–3	her floating ... anchorage] she was always very explicit
8	love] such feelings
14	Defiant ... the world] Impatient as she was of being 'made up to', she exposed herself very little to such dangers, and almost never went into the world
22	frankest] best
24	seemed] was
24	to hang] suspended
24–5	I fancied it growing] it appeared to grow
27	so that] as if
27–8	drop or melt away] drop away or melt away
30	this inviolate ... my] I had fits of immense
31	tenderness] affection
31–2	it never unduly irritated it] I never pried, never pressed her
34–5	proclaimed] insisted
36	vastly content] exceedingly glad
37	lonesome days] monotonous years
133:2	fantastic] extraordinary
4	and] om.
10	discretion] effect
14	took on the graces of] carried himself like
23–4	deepened her mourning but] made her mourning more marked, and
25	declared] used to say
31	invocation] appeal
38	a point] a single point
134:1	largely] most of the time
2	most of the time] there were whole days that
9–10	fancy ... evoked] imagination and the scenes it presented to him
10	beatific] ecstatic
11	before him] on which he would enter some day
12	consummate] prosperous
13	prosperity] popularity
14	ideal shapes] tinted pictures
18	sweet] sweeter
20	deftly] promptly

29	worse. It] worse, and it
30	sturdy seraph tussled] superior spirit (a sort of human conscience) tussled
33	intelligence] cleverness
33	to their depths] om.
38–9	a croaking ... gossip] the croaking of the frogs in the pond
42	spools] reels
135:3	charm: he ... frank] charm: he was magnificently candid
4	rank] interlaced
5	like young] like fine young
6	sunset] sunrise
6	uttered] expressed
6	and uttered] expressed
7	vengeance. It] revenges. They
8	it] them
10	vista] train
12	needs] opinions
15	shrewd] keen
21	imperiously ... to do] frequently called upon to do
27	forecast] anticipate our
28	of misery] of our misery
31	kind of tremor of] sort of mild
36	vulgar] common
39	fancied] supposed
42	comfortable] gratified
136:1	supercelestial] pre-established
2	I fancied] It seemed to me
3	cope] edge
8	these shuffled] those shuffled-off
10	immediate displeasure] handy dissatisfaction
12–13	He ... father] The boy knew that he
14–15	pleasure! the boy ... fancying] pleasure, Eustace thought, as if he had believed
16	pleasure] pleasures
19	pleasures] most marked tastes
20–21	shaping ... father's] arranging his life to resemble his father's
23	arranged] paraded
24	had turned seventeen] was seventeen years old
30	got] om.
40	people are, here] Americans are
137:3–4	You'll see] Vous allez voir
5	distracted] embarrassed
8	attitude ... contemplation] tremulous reserve
16	fancy it a kind] believe it to be a kind

19–20	of counsel ... absence] of good counsel, in regard to these plans of Eustace's
21	wore] put on
21–2	devout postulant] very faithful believer
23	adviser] monitor
24	favoured ... schemes] should fall in with his own projects
31	that] om.
33–4	frantic ... fears] perpetual scruples and fears
36–7	deemed ... of travel] too limp and battered to be a bear-leader in distant lands
38–9	claimed ... manner] was represented to know the world as well as he knew books
40–1	serene ... loss] friendly and good humoured that we cried for him in advance
43	yet] as soon as I am out of sight
138:10	his pleasure-taking] the recreations of his age
19	aroused] excited
23	herewith] om.
24	but I fancied] and I could see that
26	intense as ... painful] violent as to be painful to behold
32	blonde] fair
37	lodging] residence
38	here] he
38–9	My poor ... greeting] I suppose I was flattered by the notice he took of so humble a personage
41–2	begged to ... himself] hoped very much I would be indulgent to him
42	thanked] repaid
42	household zeal] domestic service
139:2–3	mutual ... effusions] old memories and references
5	so deep and ... exchanged] in which words might pass
13	would] might easily
17–18	extremely ... circumstances.] very powerful, like a large man somewhat 'reduced'.
26–9	has with ... masculine mind] is more touching when the eye is alive and sees what the ear loses
30	blessed] resigned
31	share] enter into
34	*bonhomie* ... opinion] brightness, guessed your opinion with a glance,
35	more wittily] better
36	odd to] odd now to
37	loss; at] loss, and at
38	patience; it was] patience, but after all, it was
39	a logic all its own] private reasons
39	But she] She
42	undefined secret] element of mystery

140 : 2	best of the mystery] principal part of the secret
3	Mr. Cope, I imagined,] I made up my mind that Mr. Cope
5	untender] revolting
16	them] the pair
19	they] my companions
20	zeal] eagerness
25–6	the echo of] om.
26	happiness] improved condition
28	spoken too frankly] been too precipitate
29	wholesome ... travel] larger life of the grand tour
32	her ... scope] the boy, embraced everything that concerned her
36	hot] sultry
37	old] om.
39	old man] tutor
42	fancied] thought
141 : 5	vast relish] great liking
8	agog] in a flutter
11	bondage] servitude
12	easily] wisely
15	smile] air
18	to] to be married to
20	with ... manner] almost defiantly
28	with] in
32	labour ... order] affair to put things to rights
33	strangers] agents
38	blaspheme!] object,
142 : 4	deepening of her] om.
9	deeply] exceedingly
14	wholesome profit] advantages
15	pity that] pity indeed that
15–16	wholesome profit] things that were good for him
16	ventured] venture
16	high esteem for] worship of
18	counsel and support] some higher authority
18–19	grant ... in it] be respectful when there was something really to respect
22	He'll ... knees.] om.
24–5	jealousy] perversity
25	place] just put
25	instinct] delicacy
27	harly as] hardly so
30	grave ... bow] few proper, grateful words
30	was preoccupied] was much preoccupied
39–40	excited ... He turned] excited, and he turned
41	authority] influence
41	Plead] Argue

143:4	most] highly
5	vastly immensely
15	made] finished
17	roaring] bristling
18	letter. A] letter, and a
19	they] my companions
22	wedding] nuptials
22	continue unbroken] last all summer
29	grave] solemn
35	vastly] greatly
35	seaside] cooling
40	amazingly] extraordinarily
144:17	tremor] trepidation
20–1	with a ... as a trace] as if he wanted to pick out some offensive trace
22	hideous] horrible
25	welcome,' ... 'if I ask] welcome if I ask
26	suddenly.'] suddenly,' I ventured to say.
42	with fierce] with a kind of fierce
145:21–2	Bound ... You needn't] Wrapped in cotton and then exposed—you needn't
23	but bald folly] that is not idiotic
25	agony] rancour
34	madam] you goose
42	deemed it my] regarded it as my
146:2	of her sojourn] where she was staying
2–3	started ... receipt of] should start as soon as she received
4	were days] were the days
5–6	terrible ... rage] almost insane in his resentment
8	his chamber door] the door of his room
18–19	bore ... temper] told me how he had raved up and down
26	brave] courageous
32–3	yet ... dread] eagerness
36	and passed] and he passed
36	side] lateral
147:5	you've betrayed ... *insulted* me] betrayed me—dishonoured me
20	broken] ruined
24	Heaven] heavens
27	heal] cure
28	healed!] cured.
33	eyed] glared at
34	enforced] pressed upon him
34–5	by ... authority] in the kindest, wisest, firmest way
37	bravely] straight
39	shaken] om.
40	resounding] passionate

41	urged] repeated
148:1	but] only
3	ringing] quivering
7	serve] be of any use
14	heart] nature
15	I'm disillusioned] I have seen something too dreadful
17	the . . . soul.] his character—isn't it his character?
20	garrulous] talkative
23	cope] edge
28	chamber] room
40	impassioned] quickened
42	exhaled] flashed
149:4	from . . . soul] with a supreme disappointment
8	summon . . . husband] make her husband come to her
9–10	in momentary silence] silent for the moment
13	untender gaze] vicious expression
14–15	adjuring . . . suddenly] forcing them somehow apart, when suddenly
17	dismiss fond patience] say that he had been patient enough
19	vastly amazed] immensely surprised
23	escutcheon] scutcheon
23	to strong] to take strong
32	breathed her last] drew her last breath
36	crimson] burning red

THE MADONNA OF THE FUTURE

Notes:

1. The variants recorded below are based on a collation of the original serial text of the tale (*Atlantic Monthly*, 1873) and its three revised versions in *A Passionate Pilgrim* (1875)—hereinafter mentioned as A; *The Madonna of the Future* (1879)—hereinafter mentioned as B; and *The Reverberator*, Etc. (1908)—hereinafter mentioned as C.

2. In text C, the tale is divided into three sections. Section i begins at 202 : 1; section ii at 211 : 22; and section iii at 213 : 18.

202 : 4	the best] perfection BC
4	been showing] shown C
6	one] single BC
6–7	apparently relapsed] appeared to relapse C
7	fatal mediocrity] obscurity and mediocrity BC
8	phenomenon] inconsequence C
8	observed,] noted C
8	sat] sit C
12	and] and who C
13	he didn't] didn't C
17	little picture] precious object in circulation C
21–2	finding ... circle] then finding us under the spell C
22	had sunk] sank BC
24	at me,] om. C
24	tender] om. BC
26	two fine] two very fine C
29	the city] such a place C
203 : 5	like] as B; even as C
6	At its base, in its] At its base, in the AB; At the base, in the great C
9	shining] who shone C
9–10	some young ... David] some embodied Defiance. In a moment I recognized him as Michael Angelo's David A; a sentinel who has taken the alarm. In a moment I recognized him as Michael Angelo's *David* B; a sentinel roused by some alarm and in whom I at once recognized Michael Angelo's famous David C
11	his sinister] his heroic sinister C
12	stationed] poised C
14–15	graceful; gentle, almost] graceful, markedly gentle almost C
16	name is Perseus] name—as, unlike the great David, he still stands there—is Perseus C
22	good] proper C
22	a sort] some fashion C

24   gleamed] shimmered   C
24   mediaeval berretta] beretto of the *cinquecento*   C
25   asked me] proceeded to appeal to me   C
26   seemed picturesque] was romantic   C
27   there in this] in that   C
29   were not] wasn't   C
29–30   flourishing] who flourishes   C
30   resentful of] resents   C
31   fantasy] analogy   BC
31   plausible] complete   BC
31–2   the fine ... embarrassed] the brilliant tirade with which
          he greeted my embarrassed   AB; his breaking into dis-
          course as I threw myself diffidently back upon   C
204:3–4   know I fancy—I fancy] take my refreshing idea   C
5   I fancy] my idea that   C
10   contemplation] attention   BC
10–11   we might witness] well, witness   C
16–17   fancied you, too, were] seemed to take you too for   C
19   charm; your] charm, and your   C
20   reflections have only] remarks have only   B; remarks,' I
          declared, 'have only   C
21–2   he rejoined, with a bow] he rejoined, with an expressive
          smile   B; he returned with flattering frankness   C
24–5   to pay ... Beautiful] to render homage to these blest
          objects   C
26–7   an American ... prodigiously to] the most characteristic
          of compatriots. He would *have* to be one of 'us', of the
          famished race—for we were at least a pair—to take the
          situation so to   C
30   New-Yorkers,' ... 'have been] New-Yorkers have been   B;
          New-Yorkers have often been   C
31   art!'] art!' he answered urbanely.   BC
32   this midnight reverie] his irrepressible passion   C
33   enterprise, and was] enterprise?—was   C
40   indisposed] loth   C
40   that] om.   C
41   stroll] proceed   C
205:1   slowly about] far and wide   C
2   sort of] positively   C
3   and wondered] wondering   C
3   was] might be   C
4–5   his American origin] an origin identical with my own   C
5   Art!' he cried 'We are] Art! We're   C
10   force] power   B; force   C
13   circumstance] conditions   C
16   answered] made answer   C
17   pretty] easy   C

18	nutritive soil] nursing air, of a kindly soil C
19–20	and all ... part is] of the things that help. The only thing that helps is C
25–6	he cried, with a tender smile]—my friend rose to it beautifully C
28	complainers,—querulous cynics] complainers—impotent cynics B; complainers, of the falsely fastidious, C
31	undertaken a] undertaken, believe me, a C
35	fantasy] illustration BC
36–7	of my nervous nights,] of my—shall I say inspired?— nights: C
40	moonlight, and] moonlight; it C
42	that] om. C
43	Michael] Buonarotti BC
206 : 1–3	deeply versed ... lovely city into] really to know his Florence through and through and had no need to tell me he loved her. I saw he was an old devotee and had taken her even from the first to C
4	declared. 'It's] put it—'it's C
5	intellectually] intellectually and aesthetically speaking C
11–12	I asked, with amenity] I asked sympathetically B; I found myself too interested to keep from asking C
13–14	sense!' ... 'I have] sense! I've C
18	mite] grain C
19	and eyed] eying C
22	the line] that divine line BC
32	upon] on C
32–3	aesthetic haunts of Florence] pictorial haunts of Florence B; art-haunts of the so rich little city C
35	perfect works] world famous things BC
36	two] om. ABC
36	railing which] rail that C
37	he] om. C
38	superb triptych] superb neighbouring triptych C
207 : 1	a deep ... perhaps,] he coloured for the consciousness of what I brought back: he recalled perhaps C
3	frankness which] friendliness which B; frankness that C
3	not a] no C
4	ardent *chevelure*] great nimbus of red hair C
6	far] much C
6	he] om. C
7	gesture] attitude C
7	the quite] quite the C
9	obvious than glorious] conceivable doubtless than commendable C
11	which] that C

12	which ... affect] that members of his craft sometimes affect C
14	pallid leanness of visage] pale facial spareness C
17	eloquence] flow C
19	youth!' And] youth!'—with which C
21	cream of the gallery] flower of the array C
21	But before] Before C
21–2	he pressed ... gave it] however, I felt him squeeze me and give it C
24–5	my friend ... an extremely] he might have been didn't seem to me even then to concern me—it so served that he was an C
25–6	opinions, theories, and sympathies] opinions and theories, sympathies and aversions C
26–9	He was ... felicities of chance] He inclined more than I approved to the sentimental proposition, was too fond, I thought, of superfine shades and of discovering subtle intentions and extracting quintessences C
29	the shallow felicities of chance] shallow places B
31	too deep for intellectual security] that were not for my breasting C
32	happy judgement] frequent felicities C
33	this worshipful company] all such worshipful companies C
34	so devoted ... opportunity] his systematic and exhaustive attack C
38	mood] om. C
39–40	clevernesses] cleverness BC
208:1	pastoral, sceptical Italian] broken-bridged pastoral classical C
2–3	the intellect,] the taste or the faith C
5	taste] attitude C
6	Michael] Michael Angelo B; Michael C
8–9	accident, as one may call it, which] accident or privilege which C
10	those] the C
10	chambers of the Pitti Palace] extent of the Pitti C
13	a sort of inviolate] an inviolate C
14	passed along the gallery] paced the clear tunnel C
16	ducal ... Ducal] grand-ducal, the palatial saloons. Grand-ducal C
17–18	it must be ... that, with] they must be pronounced imperfect show-rooms, since, thanks to C
20–1	and you ... atmosphere] so that you see them in a deep diffused lustre C
21	saloons] chambers C

23	mellow canvas and dusky gilding] toned canvas and gleaming gold C
28	Madonna in the Chair] Madonna of the Chair C
29	seemed to ... the one] was to strike me at once as the work C
31	effect] success BC
32	result, which ... works] result that sometimes faintly invalidates noble efforts C
34–5	rounded softness,] a softness as rounded and C
36–7	melts away ... knows not] imposes on the spectator a spell of submission which he scarce knows C
40	on earth] among men C
209:4	among men,] here below C
14	I answered] I fear I profanely asked C
23	perfume] fragrance BC
27–8	I said ... 'is a] —and I really but wanted to draw him further out—'an idealist is a C
32	upon me] on me at first C
32–3	angrily, but ... gravely] angrily, but perceiving the genial savour of my sarcasm, he smiled gravely B; angrily—then saw that I was but sowing the false to reap the true C
40	caresses and flatters] intensifies C
41–2	his portrait] his inimitable portrait C
43	Ariel above] Ariel hovered above B; Ariel in the play hovers above C
210:3	see] have C
3	woo] cultivate BC
8	in after] through all the C
10–11	hanging ... living] keeping pace with the restless centuries and the changing world; of living C
12	and hand that are part of] and a hand that belong to C
13–14	generations ... purity] generations; of making beauty more and more a force and purity more and more C
15	said smiling] smiled C
20–1	is a profane touch] to be then as calculating and commercial as any other C
22	hand in hand] arm in arm BC
25–7	My companion ... confidence:] My friend momentarily stared—he shivered and shook his ears under this bucketful of cold water. But he bravely kept up his high tone. C
27	demand!' he cried; 'that] demand—that C
28	but] only C
29	this] their C
36	world, that] world such an C
39	pure,] free C
211:5	cried] laughed C

9   salute] make my bow to   A; pay my respects to   BC
10–11   He blushed ... resignation] His face, at this, had a flush
             of consciousness, and he seemed to sigh half in protest,
             half in resignation   C
11   in so many words] by name   BC
13   even] om.   C
15–16   at,—laughed ... crimson] at, positively laughed at, sir!'—
             and his poor guilty blush deepened   C
20   talents] limitations   C
22   sternly sincere] admirably candid   C
23   impertinent] to savour just then of indiscretion   C
24   ask them] put as many as I would   C
25   by appointment, to see the sights] under agreement that he
             should help me to intimacy with the little treasure-city   C
26–7   the city ... galleries] it so well and had studied it with
             so pious a patience   C
27   versed in] versed both in   C
28–9   lesser memories ... altogether ideal] its minor memories.
             he had become in short so fond and familiar a Florentine,
             that he was an ideal   C
30–1   my Murray ... commentary] dryer documents at home
             and learn what I wanted from his lips and his example   C
31–2   like a lover ... he had] as a devoted old lover might still
             speak of an old incomparable mistress who remained proof
             against time; he liked to describe how he had   C
33–4   talk of all ... 'but,] make all cities of the feminine gender,
             but   C
35   Chicago] Chicago, as London, as Liverpool   C
35   true woman] perfect lady   BC
36   a lad in his teens] some sensitive aspiring youth   C
37–8   It's ... she creates] She fills you with a sort of aspiring
             gallantry   B; She fills you with a presumptuous gallantry
             C
39   life, apparently, and] life and   BC
41   frivolous self] uninstructed years   C
42   hours ... been, to] hours to   BC
43   many ... those] them in historic streets and consecrated
             nooks, in churches and convents and galleries, spent them
             above all in study of those   C
212:2   wonder whether] find in   C
2–3   art ... fragrance] art a fragrance   C
4   sepulchral] mortuary   C
5   and] where we   C
5–6   sitting there like] sit like   C
6   brooding] brood   C
11   seem like] resemble   C
12   dark chapels] obscure shrines   C

14	carving] sculpture C
15	prodigious] remarkable BC
15–16	was a ... reverie] was a pretext for some wildly idealistic rhapsody or reverie AB; became a pretext for one of his high-flown excursions C
17	end] lead him BC
17	in] to BC
19–20	a monomaniac ... his character] a natural rhapsodist, or even a harmless madman; and I found the play of his temper, his humour and his candid and unworldly character as quaint C
22	own little] boundless C
23	the world] the accidents of life C
24–8	often thought ... fever] sometimes questioned the reality of an artistic virtue, an aesthetic purity, on which some profane experience hadn't rubbed off a little more. It was hard to have to accept him as of our own hard-headed stock; but after all there could be no better sign of his American star than the completeness of his reaction in favour of vague profits C
25	vastly] greatly B
28	same fantastic] high aesthetic AB
28	devotion was a sign] worship was a mark C
29–30	to European ... with comfort] within sight of the temple take their opportunities more for granted C
32–4	was vastly ... 'magnificent'.] was very much more generous than just, and his mildest terms of approbation were 'stupendous', 'transcendent', and 'incomparable'. B; rather ignored proportion and degree; his recognitions had a generous publicity, his discriminations were all discoveries. C
33–4	'glorious' ... 'magnificent'.] 'stupendous', 'transcendent', and 'incomparable'. A
34	admiration] appreciation C
34	him no] him in fine no C
35–6	frank as ... altogether] with all this overflow of opinion and gestures he remained in himself C
36–8	professions ... background] professions were practically, somehow, all masks and screens, and his personal allusions, as to his ambiguous background, mere wavings of the dim lantern C
39	proud, and] proud, in other words, and C
40	poor; yet he] poor, and yet C
213:3	moved] prompted ABC
3	seemed ... which] seemed always hungry, and this B; appeared for the most part hungry, and this C
4	a 'redeeming vice.'] human grossness. BC

5   asking ... questions] never seeming to cross a certain line with him   C

7   as it were] if I might   C

8   grave smile. 'We're] bravery that never languished; 'I think we can't be said not to be   C

10   They're *suggestive!*] They bring me in a harvest of incentives.   C

12   it, and] it—he   C

14   knew the ... gather with] knew—in connection with something to be done—of the rapture of observing and remembering, of applying one's notes. I take in at   C

15   colour or relief!] colour, for style.   C

18   was ... Florence] Had been introduced meanwhile   C

19–20   the foreign residents] strangers of supposed distinction   C

20   she] om.   C

22–3   an aesthetic flavour] a high aesthetic pitch   C

24   Pitti Palace *au petit pied*] miniature Pitti Palace   C

26   parlour] drawing-room   BC

27   Backed] Surrounded   BC

28   showing] covered with   BC

29   panels, our hostess] backgrounds, our hostess   B; backgrounds, she   C

29   sort of] social   C

30–1   huge miniature copy] huge, if reduced, copy   C

32–3   knew ... Mr. Theobald] knew among our compatriots in the place a certain eccentric but charming Mr. Theobald   C

34   him!' she exclaimed; 'know] him, know   C

34   Theobald! All] Theobald?'—her answer was as public as if I had owed it to the bell-crier. 'All   C

39   cried] asked   C

39   his madonna] his wondrous Madonna   C

42   Florence and took us] Florence and took the town   AB; Florence—that is on our little colony here—and took the town   C

43   and poor, dear America was] and the poor dear United States were   B; and our poor dear barbarous country was   C

214:2   alas, but not] alas—it's his difficulty—appears to have to do duty for   C

3   upon] on   C

4   on] from   C

4   all] om.   C

5   Joconde] Gioconda   C

7   mysterious and inscrutable] "esoteric" and indescribable   C

7–9   Mysterious ... master never] Well, it has all remained esoteric, and nobody can describe what nobody has ever seen. The months, the years have passed and the miracle has hung fire; our master has never   C

10   He passed] He has passed   C

11–12   he talked ... but he] he has talked more about his subject —about every subject—than any human being before has ever talked about anything, but has   C

16   admit] recognize   C

21   it has ... gusto] that the man has particularly enjoyed doing it   C

28   inexpensive] light   C

29   Hereupon the poor man] On that the poor dear man   C

30   an *âme méconnue*] a martyr to his opinions   C

35–6   he wouldn't ... I fancy] he doesn't see his way to paint her in the style of Titian's Flora. I'm afraid   C

42   It is a ... now that] It's ever so long now since   C

215:2   masterly] grand   C

4   fine idea] striking idea   AB; *trouvaille*   C

5   the] om.   C

7   heaven] goodness   C

8–9   blush,' my hostess frankly continued] blush'—my friend freely proceeded—   C

11   credulity, only] credulity. Only   BC

11–12   to give you a] this   C

15   whether] om.   C

16–17   I fancy ... in that tale] I shouldn't myself be surprised if, when one runs him to earth, one finds scarce more than in that terrible little tale   C

20   pungent recital] bold sketch   C

21   and was ... with certain] it set the seal on   C

22–3   a clever ... generous one] not only a clever woman, but presumably a generous one   B; satirical, but was neither unveracious nor vindictive   C

27   immediately] at once   C

28–30   and gave me ... and heartless,] with a sadder, though perhaps sharper, look than had ever yet come into his face. 'Has she got *you* into training? She's a most vain woman. She's empty and scheming   C

32   think that] suppose   C

35   Buddhism] the stock-market   C

35–6   words,' he ... pause] things,' he more vehemently went on   C

37   mendacious] humbugging   C

37   of hers,] om.   C

39   days, to show to] days, and let her hand it round among   ABC

39–40   in plain ... impostor!] you're a low fraud and that they must have nothing to do with you.   C

39   English you're] English that you are   B

41   accuracy] understanding of our poor friend   C

216:1   gate] gates   BC

2   which seems a most fitting avenue] which seem a very fitting avenue   B; the most fitting of avenues   C

3   lingering repose] lingering repose¹   AB; rest and thought¹ C [the footnote in ABC refers to a date: 1869]

7   its] theirs   C

9   into] in   C

9   the little ... dropped] this choicest handful of the spoils of time has been stored away for keeping   C

12   rarely played work] work rarely played   C

13   I had half] I half   BC

13   observed] noted   C

15-16   said, smiling] put to him   C

25   find a charm in] hold out against   C

26   response] answer   C

30   I was] myself   C

31-2   I could ... informed me,] if the question was of his giving me such an exhibition I would accept it on the terms he should impose, he made known to me—   C

34   a soul!] a beautiful soul.   C

35   cried] said   C

35-6   fortunate. And ... conjunction] fortunate, I shall rejoice to witness the conjunction   A; fortunate, and that is a most attractive description   B; fortunate. I'm not less so, but you do keep cards up your sleeve   C

37   he answered] he went on   B; he returned   C

37   a lesson] a revelation, a lesson   C

41   sort of] om.   C

42   contemplated ... my friend] studied and admired her. Therefore what I'm doing for you—well, my friend, is friendship   C

217:2   you perhaps will] you'll perhaps   C

2   upon it] on what I show you   C

3   interpretation] appreciation   C

5-6   the very ... edifice] its highest flight   C

6   beauty ... exalted] beauty seemed as loftily exalted   B; worshipped human type seemed hung as far   C

7-8   the Belle aux ... tower-top] his artistic ideal was lifted above the usual practice of men   B; his artistic ideal was lifted over the usual practice of men   C

9   and, flinging open] where, opening   C

9   door, ushered] door, he ushered   C

10   seemed] affected me as   C

13   Theobald] my guide   C

14	calmly ... but] with a serene smile; then C
15	a kind of] om. C
15–16	Theobald ... kissed it,] He stepped nearer, taking her hand and kissing it C
18	I thought she blushed] had, I thought, a perfectly human change of colour C
19	*Ecco la Serafina*] Behold the Serafina AB; This is the sublime Serafina C
19–20	said Theobald ... 'This] —Theobald frankly waved me forward. 'And this C
23	of great] of a great BC
25	towards] to C
26	as to] about C
28	embroidery] needlework C
29	some portion of an] one of the pieces of some C
29	yellow] ivory C
31	which I hesitated] I couldn't know C
40	denote] express but C
218:3–4	perceived, after recovering] recognized as soon as I had recovered C
5	beauty] appearance C
5	a sort] the sort C
6	essential charm] greater merit C
11	her head was] her head were B; this head were C
12	and the] and they were the B; and all the C
15	nature and the] nature, with the C
17	sort of] om. C
20	greatly, and yet with a large] greatly, yet with a considerable C
21–2	belonged ... and had] was the very mark of her complexion and form, and C
22	it] them C
23	a rather vulgar] rather a vulgar C
29	fetched] addressed himself to C
30	from] on C
30–1	placed, lighted, on] lighted and transferred to C
31–2	brighter ... elderly woman] improved clearness I made our hostess out a very mature person C
33	grey; she was simply] grey, but she was thick and C
33–4	'soul' ... promised] beautiful soul my friend had promised me C
34	scarcely] scarce C
34–5	was no deeper ... matronly] dwelt in no deeper principle than some accident of quietude, some matronly C
36	would] should BC
36	declare that that] pronounce her C
37	was nothing more than] nothing more inward than C

37	constantly] always C
38–40	It occurred ... needlewoman] It might have been even a slightly more sinister symptom, for in spite of her apparently admirable dullness this object of our all-candid homage practically C
42	*au sérieux*] seriously BC
219:4	respectful] reverent AB; discreet C
5	youth] swain BC
9	needlework] stitching C
11	friend] admirer C
18	Finely, finely] Oh in their own fine quiet way C
21–2	then tapping ... had used a] then, repeating the vivid reference to the contents of our poor friend's head she had used a C
24	answered, with a smile] was amused in spite of myself C
25	it,] what I say C
26	*bambino*] *santo bambino* C
28	festooned] fastened B; attached C
32	was executed] had been thrown off C
32	power, and yet seemed] directness, but was none the less C
33	sort of] om. C
34	in the midst ... boldness] mingled with its boldness AB; which yet didn't weaken its expression C
36	whom] om. C
36–7	Signor Teobaldo gave] Signor Teobaldo, a generous person if ever there was one, gave C
37	beside] besides BC
38	time and admired it vastly] time and admired it immensely B; time—certainly it had charm C
39	Theobald,] our friend C
40–1	would hold] would bravely hold C
41	extreme pleasure] joy C
42	hands, and his] hands—his C
42–3	It moved ... with the] I had apparently quickened his C
220:1	made his adieux to] took leave of C
4	perceived] felt C
8	divine] sublime C
9	fervour] anxiety C
10	'It's ... beauty!'] 'It is certainly good solid beauty!' I answered. A; 'It is certainly an excellent style of good looks!' I answered. B; 'She's certainly a fine figure of a woman,' I answered without ceremony. C
15	I think] I'm sure C
16	coming in] coming back C
18	hand. I] hand and I C
20	money] money and received what I gave her with the

holy sweetness with which the Santissima Vergine receives
the offerings of the faithful   C

20   that] om.   C

23   and] but   C

25–6   I felt ... vision] It was as if I had had like one of the
monkish artists of old a miraculous vision   C

26   convent] monkish   B

26   them] the poor creatures   ABC

29   consecrate the pathos] sanctify the sadness and sweetness
BC

30   that] om.   C

31   held] lifted   C

31   minutes, and] minutes—so as not to lose him *all*—and   C

37   religion!] instinctive imperturbable piety.   C

38   knows I've] yet knows that I've   BC

39   of it] what I think of it   C

39–41   observed ... And was] taken in the extraordinary clearness and modesty of her looks. Was   C

43–221:1   little; my] little, I've made her my own, my   C

221:3   much] om.   C

5–6   really had ... slowly] really—since that first time—made
her *pose*,' he said with a shade of awkwardness   C

7–8   had her ... my easel] put her to the inconvenience—so to
call it—to which I'd have put a common model   C

10–11   a piece of ... to regret] a headlong exclamation. I was
destined to regret it   ABC

14   Madonna!] maiden mother.   C

18–19   you don't ... twenty] you don't take her for a woman of
twenty   B; you don't take her for anything *but* mature   C

20   looking] looked   C

23   you truly] you really and truly   C

23   blind?'] blind?' he demanded.   C

27   seemed to me almost a] struck me almost as a   C

28   answered] returned   C

28–9   you're deceived] you're rather unfortunately deceived   C

30   but, I protest, that was] but you see that must have been
C

31   *beaux restes*] *de beaux restes*   AB; fine things left   C

32   I broke] But I broke   C

34–5   'De beaux restes? ... English. I] ' "Fine things left?" ' he
stared. 'Do you speak as if other people had helped themselves—?' 'Why my dear man,' I smiled, 'the years have
helped themselves! But she has what the French call—
don't they? *de beaux restes*?' Oh how he gaped and how
something seemed to roll over him! I   C

35   up] om.   C

35   of *beaux restes*] of *de beaux restes*   ABC

36	murmured] re-echoed C
37	at] by C
39	proclaim] pronounce BC
40	and I hereby] and hereby C
42	stared, but he seemed scarcely] kept staring, but seemed scarce C
222 : 6	seemed to roll] surged C
11	I said, smiling,] I smiled C
15	cried] vowed C
15	No, in] No, no, in C
16	here!' and he tapped] *here!'* And he tapped AB; *here!'* And he smote C
22	moment, and then] moment—then C
26	river] Arno C
26	that] om. C
29	should ... Theobald] had really startled poor Theobald B; had really startled him C
35	or strolling] or even strolling C
37	barouche and phaeton] the open-carriages C
39	that I had] I might have C
40–1	impetus ... paralysed it] push to his talent, or at least to his faith, I had done it a real harm C
41	that I had] I might have C
223 : 1	to the last had] had to the last C
1	mystery] secret C
1	altogether] om. C
2	where to look for him] how to follow him up C
3	beauty of the Mercato Vecchio] object of his homage who neighboured with the Mercato Vecchio C
5	and] perhaps C
6–7	behold ... pass for] set eyes once more on the ripe enchantress who had made twenty years, as he had said, pass like C
7	for] as AB
9–10	and ... whether] and, while I hesitated C
11	kettle] cooking-pot C
13	entered] reached C
15	and before it] before which C
16	dealing justice] doing execution BC
17	friendly proximity] intimate nearness C
18	entered] arrived C
29	immediately ... Signora] forthwith felt sure that the sublime C
30	even] still C
34	recalled her prudence] stimulated her prudence AB; made her prudent C
34	I was welcome, she said] I must put myself at my ease C

36	which was almost amiable] that had turned to the gracious C
39	he] om.
40	*forestiere*] *forestiero* C
40	wiry] active C
41	*retroussé*] tossed up ABC
41–2	and ... moustache] conscious of many things at once, and the cocked-up moustache of a trooper C
42–3	a little ... smoking-cap] one of the loose velvet caps affected by sculptors in damp studios C
224 : 1	brilliant slippers] bright 'worked' slippers C
3	in which Italians] of which certain Italians B; of which Italians C
3	so freely ... with fervour] are so insistently lavish and declared with fervour AB; are sometimes so insistently lavish, declaring without reserve C
8	declared] had it C
8	masterpiece, a pure Correggio] masterpiece—in the maniera Correggiesca C
9	smile] laugh BC
10	genuine] honeycombed ABC
11	Signora] stately AB; sublime C
12	that he ... deceit] didn't lend himself to that style of manufacture C
14	but] om. C
14	I know ... Signor Teobaldo] I'm sure *nostro signore* C
15–16	my benefactor] my great benefactor C
16	added sententiously] made no secret of it C
18	fancy] judge C
20	was] om. C
21	said] stated C
21	this] that C
22	that] om. C
22	been uneasy] been so uneasy C
26	she] om. C
34	the Signora Serafina] my mysterious hostess AB; my ambiguous hostess C
35	Theobald] our friend C
39	as well as I] as I do C
40–1	him,' ... Nevertheless] him. I can only esteem and—I think I may say—love him. Nevertheless C
43	a moment, as if for] as for C
225 : 1	as] while C
2	Signora] *padrona* AB; padrona C
2–4	gave me a ... bow. 'It's] treated me to a look of more meaning than quite consorted with her noble blankness. 'Ah but it's C

4	him!' she said. 'The] him! The C
6	fancy] blest imagination C
9	Blessed Virgin: Heaven] Madonna Santissima, heaven C
11	that] who C
15	poor man] poveretto C
17	on] about C
17	and] about C
19	decently] honourably C
20	the saints] the blessed saints BC
21	Eh!] Eh, eh, C
21	the saints] the blessed saints BC
22	fancied] surmised C
22–4	but she told ... simplicity] what she said sufficed to make poor Theobald's own statement still more affecting than I had already found its strained simplicity C
26	lover and more] lover, yet more C
26	friend] brother C
26–8	companion, who ... mouthful] comrade who continued to smirk in a mystifying manner while he twisted the ends of his moustache between his copious mouthfuls C
31	good friend] *amorso* C
34	that] om. C
34	design] intention C
36	and I should immediately] and would at once C
41	I ventured] I however ventured C
42	the Signora Serafina] Madonna Serafina C
226:1	me.] me whom he doesn't take for Saint Joseph! C
1	with] om. C
2	He's a purist] His taste's terribly severe C
3	on the promise] after having promised BC
3–4	the Signora Serafina] our hostess C
11–12	the Signora Serafina] this dear lady ABC
14	them; you] them freely—you BC
17	Americans] the American *conoscenti* C
18	observed] noticed C
19	the Boulevard, in a] the *grand boulevard* '—he aimed at the French sound of the words—'in a C
21–2	*jeune homme élégant*] gay young bachelor ABC
22	*jolie femme*] pretty woman ABC
23	wished] should wish C
26	as the French says,] om. C
38	that] om. C
39–40	delivered ... allocution,] thus persuasively proceeded C
40	seductive] persuasive AB
42	lovingly with his] lovingly, his C
43	each of] each, with a vengeance, of C
43	fantastically] occasionally C

227:3	delicate ... coquetry] fine terms, might have been called the amorous advance and the amorous alarm C
5	perfect cats and monkeys] dreadful little beasts C
10–11	an amorous ... himself] the fondest eye, he struck me as himself C
14	contemplate] follow C
22–3	signore! ... Just] *signore mio.* I've been just a bit free, but not too free—eh, *dica?* Just a scrap of C
23	licentious!] too free—eh? AB
26	think that you will] think you'll C
28	own] om. ABC
30	be as malicious] have as many high lights and sharp accents C
35	glanced at the worthy Serafina] glanced at Madonna Serafina AB; turned an eye on Madonna Serafina C
36	an eye] a sense C
39–40	and made] making BC
40–1	the Signora Serafina] this remarkable woman ABC
42	An old woman] A withered crone, C
43	ushered me in] welcomed me C
228:1–2	that the ... a friend] at the poor gentleman having a friend AB; at the poor gentleman's having at last a caller C
2	seemed] appeared C
4	that he was] him C
5	sitting there] but seated C
5	He was seated] His chair was C
10–11	room, I ... corresponded with] room I saw how vividly his face answered to C
13	I had been afraid] My fear had been C
14	friend] patron ABC
14	peace] contentment BC
15	that my appearance awakened] my appearance excite C
16	I asked, as I put] —I put C
18	response, kept] response, but kept C
19	spoke most plaintively] spoke, the poor place, all plaintively C
25	place] whole scene C
25	poverty] indigence C
28	the vacant misery of the spot] my impression of vacant misery C
29–30	tenderly ... say that] tenderly. I can hardly say that AB; tenderly. I can scarcely say C
32	But though] Though ABC
35	rose and looked] rose, looking C
35–6	slowly kindling eye] slow return of intelligence C
42	with the truth, with the past] with it, the terrible truth,

	face to face with the past C
229:2	in the] in an B; by an C
5–6	had marked the gesture before] had so often marked the gesture for me before C
7	had] has BC
11	begin, and wasted] begin—I wasted C
12	was dying] was only dying C
12	it all] the whole business C
17	do or dare] do nor dare ABC
18	plans and promises, in study] study, in plans and promises C
20–1	I have] I have seen B; *I've* seen C
23–4	I have his brain] His brain I already have BC
24	say, I haven't] say, that I haven't BC
24–5	me babble] me boast and babble BC
31	dealt my stroke] taken my leap BC
33	that] om. C
34	remove ... atmosphere] draw him out of the haunted air C
35	seemed] was BC
36	out] forth C
37–8	open air ... condition] warm light of day I was able to appreciate his great weakness C
37	measure] appreciate B
38–9	a certain ... that he] a manner to revive; he even murmured to me at last that he C
39	would] should BC
41–2	seemed, even ... a sort of] glowed, to my stricken sight, with an C
43	seemed] appeared B; reflected C
230:1	to smile in ineffable] for me a pitying C
2	glorious authors; the] triumphant authors; the AB; triumphant authors. The C
3	in the] of the BC
4	was tinged with the sinister irony] broke into the strange smile C
9	carriage] cab C
10–11	an extraordinary] the deepest C
11	carriage,] vehicle C
13	sudden] om. C
17	seek a physician] call in a doctor C
20	murmured;] wailed— C
21	thus] so bad C
22	a night] a certain night BC
24	great canvas] great dirty canvas C
24	there, and, poor,] there. Poor, AB; there. Poor C

24–5	man, says his prayers to] man he says his prayers to it ABC
25	bed ... properly!] bed—not even since then, as you may say. C
26	the Serafina] *quella cattiva donna* C
27	whispered] panted C
30	physician on] physician, who was away on BC
30–1	visits ... pursuing him] visits and whom I vainly pursued BC
33	and the] whose C
34	later I knew that] later on I knew C
35	wishing to describe] wishing fully to report C
37	A certain night] One night B; One night in particular C
40	recurs] comes back BC
42–3	The Signora Serafina/ Madonna Serafina C
43	illness] state C
231:2	by but] but by C
4	which] that C
6–7	at her carriage door at] in her carriage at BC
9	great Madonna] greatest of all Madonnas C
14	My dear Mrs. Coventry,] Because C
15	'Upon] She rather glared at me. 'Upon
16	Excuse] Pardon C
17	excessively] om. C
18	dark spirit ... things] blighted spirit met my eyes in all aspects C
24	fancied,] could say to myself C
25	the scene demanded] they needed BC
25	commentary] commentary than those simple words C
26	depart] leave it BC
28	picturesquely] becomingly C
28–9	visage of the Signora Serafina] visage of Madonna Serafina AB; face of Madonna Serafina C
30	that] om. C
30	eye was bright] brow was lighted C
32	the] some C
32	own face, apparently,] own then C
34	a sort of dogged resignation] an acceptance of the anti-climax that had been after all so long and so wondrously postponed C
35	that] who C
41	fancy] imagination C
42	softly, after] softly and after C
232:4	illumined] enhanced C
8	dropped her eyes] lowered her lids C
11	bowed, and] bowed assent and C
13	perceived] noted C

13   which] that   C
14   that it was] it for   C
22   bow] salute   BC
23–4   of Roman greatness] of triumphant Rome   ABC
25–6   hear a ... murmur,] catch the other so impertinent and so cynical echo: C

THE LAST OF THE VALERII

Notes:

1. The variants recorded below are based on a collation of the original serial text of the tale (*Atlantic Monthly*, 1874) and its two revised versions in *A Passionate Pilgrim* (1875)—hereinafter mentioned as A—and *Stories Revived* (1885)—hereinafter mentioned as B.

2. The following, in text B, is the revised form of a proper name; only the first occurrence of this form in that text is recorded: Camillo] Marco B

259:7	picturesque] pictorial B
11	am ... rudeness] am particularly addicted to rudeness A; usually miss that effect B
13	perhaps] doubtless AB
17–18	a more ... is common] a beauty which was less a matter of mere fortunate surface than usually happens B
19–21	He had ... of feeling] There was a latent tenderness in his admirable mask, and his grave, slow smile, if it suggested no great nimbleness of wit, spoke of a manly constancy B
23	more ... sincerity] there was a kind of stupid sincerity B
23	gaze which] gaze; it B
24	perhaps] certainly B
25	stupid] dense B
26	reply] response AB
30–1	perplexity] annoyance B
260:6	and manly] masculine B
16	delightful] honourable B
19	blonde] tinted B
21	the pretty] the equally pretty B
35	divesting] disencrusting AB
261:1	at Epiphany] at the feast of the Epiphany B
3	promise] significance B
6	happily] serenely B
7	chapel door] entrance of the place B
17	confessionals] polyglot confessionals B
18	world's sinfulness] sinfulness of the world B
25–6	a look] an eye B
32	Camillo] Marco B
35	lovers ... step] intended—to take some great step B
36	I'm willing] I am quite willing B
38	That's, after all,] That, after all, is B
262:2	turning Protestant] giving up, for you, something equally important B
7–8	I'm a poor Catholic] I am not a good Catholic, a good Christian B

11	a better Catholic] more devout B
21	circle . . . with] circle, beyond the sea, with B
23	being gradually] now partly B
25	*genre*] om. B
25	painter, with] painter of ruins and relics, with B
26	ruin should accumulate] crumbling things should be allowed to crumble at their ease B
27–8	thinking . . . picturesque] thinking; she had a high appreciation of antiquity B
29	conservative than myself;] conservative even than I, B
30	and declared] declaring B
39	deeply picturesque] exquisitely romantic B
40–2	romantically . . . ilex-walk] haunted by the ghosts of the past. There were memories in the fragrance of the untended flowers, in the hum of the insects. It contained, among other idle, untrimmed departments, an old ilex-walk B
263 : 2	here along their] over the B
2	quaintest] most perfect B
9	there] om. B
10	gathered memories] long observations B
10	about] near B
12	heavily] hoarsely B
16	an honest fellow] as genuine as possible B
17	one to the . . . adored] a perfect original (not a copy), and seemed quite content to be appreciated B
18	kind of] om. AB
18–19	unmeasured] natural B
25	tufty] grassy AB
28	daily] om. B
29	newspapers] daily papers B
32	picturesquely snoozing] statuesquely snoring B
35	to her] om. B
36	least as] least quite as B
38	practical matters were always] any practical matter was usually B
40	criticism] criticism on what I was doing B
41	resemblance] correspondence B
42	point . . . original] feature of my sketch and the object I was trying to reproduce B
264 : 1	strange] still stranger B
2	'ideas'.] anything remotely resembling an idea. B
2	or hopes, or] nor hopes nor AB
3	and] om. B
4	looking] while he looked B
6	sum of hit attributes] sum of his advantages A; sum total of his advantages B

10	young] infant AB
11	gentle and I] gentle; I AB
13	leisure which] idleness that B
13	that] the B
19	dumb] inarticulate B
19–20	a powerful caress or a sudden] some fresh endearment or some sudden B
20	was likely] could have power B
20	lavish] om. B
21	I but half relished] made me uneasy B
23–5	what it .... development] the development of her immortal part B
25–6	the finer spiritual emotions] a moral life B
26	spiritual] moral B
31	memorable] inspiring AB
32	if he] whether he B
35	became] should become B
36	assure] transmit B
265:4	and] om. B
9	strangely] oddly B
14–15	love; but ... mine] love. For the most part, however, these dusky broodings of mine A; love. For the most part, however, my alarms, suspicions, prejudices, B
16	fine old Villa] romantic home A; romantic, our classical home B
23–4	believe ... poetical] have believed that I was some old monkish chronicler or copyist, engaged in illuminating a mediaeval B
40	grotesque] asthmatic B
43	properly conducted researches] researches properly conducted B
266:2	averse,] unfriendly B
10	vigorous] om. B
11–12	veritably] absolutely A; really and truly B
16	they touch me, often] me they touch often B
26	cut ... smile] convert the poor girl's smile into a suspicion B
27	explorer] archaeological detective A; archaeological expert, or commissioner, B
28	workmen armed] workmen, who bristled B
30	the disinterment] to see the soil disturbed, B
31	break the leisurely] jar upon the sleepy AB
32–3	operations, an ugly little] operations—a little ugly, B
34	a mouldy] an earthy AB
38	alter,] change very much B
43	the little explorer's assurance] some assurance on the part of the little expert B

267:3-4   had fallen a-thinking; he] had fallen a thinking. He   A;
            too had learned how to reflect. He   B

4-5   and discoursed ardently of] having much to say about   B

5   marvelled] wondered   B

6   zeal, and wondered] eagerness, and asked myself   B

7   beauty] intrinsic interest   B

8-11   would come ... were a snare] came down to the place and
            —as he very often did—began to berate his little army of
            spadesmen for dawdling, the diminutive person who super-
            intended the operations would glance at me with a sar-
            castic twinkle which seemed to hint that excavations were
            sometimes a snare   B

9   spadesmen, a set] spadesmen for a set   A

11   some time] a good while   B

12   made. The earth was] made—the earth   B

13-14   began to be ... the little explorer] was discouraged—the
            resumption of his naps testified to it. But the master-digger
            B

14   explorer] expert   A

16   ringing against] making their gay sound as they touched
            B

20   sea—I *may* be summoned] sea as ever were caught! what
            if I should be summoned   B

26   explorer] excavator   B

33   mouldy] dusky   AB

36   of perfect human proportions] only of the proportions of a
            woman exceptionally tall   B

37   felt she] felt that she   B

37-8   great ... great] great and it was a high privilege   B

38   marvellous] finished   B

41   explorer] excavator   A; expert   B

268:4   classical] queenly   B

5   rarest finish] greatest delicacy   B

6   a sort of ... expression] more in her than usual of a
            certain personal expression   B

11   explorer] *padrone*   B

13   we made] we promptly made   B

20   a Juno;] a wonderful Juno,   B

21   mine—eh?] mine. Is that it!   B

22-4   A kind of ... explorer] An awestruck 'Santissima Vergine!'
            burst from one of the listening workmen. 'Yes, Signor
            Conte, this is the hand!' said the superintendent   B

25   it this] it safe here this   B

28   I wished to ... himself] I didn't wish to embarrass him by
            my observation   B

31-2   a Juno of Praxiteles] something Phidian or Praxitelian   B

37–8	enough ... jealous.'] enough to make you jealous, *figlioccia mia*,' I replied. B
41	irritation] impression B
43	caressingly] affectionately B
269:3	a statement] an assertion B
7	on] upon B
10–11	inexpressive] sightless B
12	an admiring ... absorbed] the tear which deep admiration sometimes calls forth and which, in this case, her husband was too much absorbed B
15	explorer] expert B
30–1	learned madrigals] madrigals and other *concetti* B
35–6	little explorer] small superintendent B
36	an expert] a thorough adept B
38	and doubled] gave her back B
38	mellow substance] firm, fine surface B
41	fame] presence B
270:25	I have] I too have AB
33	it] one AB
37	regrettably] lamentably B
39	excavation was] operations were B
41	explorer] adept B
271:3–4	remember when] remember that when B
4	I saw it lying] it was lying AB
5	Ecco] *Pare impossibile* B
9	worst of them] greatest rascal of the lot B
12	The ... disinterment] My friend the resurrectionist B
20	you] he A; one B
22–3	And ... titter] And this cynical personage began to chuckle AB
23	and] as he B
27	a free access to] permission to approach B
32	mankind, but] mankind; yet AB
33	untender] ridiculous B
36	her ... optimism] the expression of her face contradicted this superficial view B
37	constant] om. B
37	pathetic] really touching B
38–9	appealing ... curiosity] imploring curiosity AB
39	pitying ... check] for the present she were too much surprised to be angry B
41	imagined] suspected B
42	seemed] was B
272:1–2	noticed me ... his heavy] seemed to notice that I too didn't know what to make of his condition, and then for a moment his dull B
2–3	seemed ... impulse to] appeared, with a kind of sinister

	irony, and half with an impulse strangely stifled, as soon as he felt it, to B
4	inexorably, cruelly] inexorably AB
5	persuasive caress] melancholy attempt at fondness B
6–7	I inwardly ... I grew] The situation struck me as tremendously queer, and I grew B
11–12	Painter ... husband] Artist as I have aspired to be, I will never again recommend a husband with traditions B
12–13	purple ... lights] violet shadows and amber lights B
17	seemed to ... The Count] settled itself on my heart. The poor Count B
21	stirred blindly] revived, incurably, B
28	history,—it seemed to stretch] history it stretched itself B
28	feeblest] om. B
30	poor] dear B
33	continued reserve,] persistent reticence B
35	counsel] counsel of others B
40	time] the months B
41	apprehensions] anxiety B
41	pity] compassion B
42	urgent] inexorable B
42	a crime] the commission of a misdeed B
43	native ... deny] honest nature appeared to have refused B
273 : 1	comparative] grudging AB
2	gratuitously ... unhappy] infernally blue without being, however little he might confess it, in want of sympathy B
4	flames] flower A; cream B
5	might suffer me to] would suffer me at last to B
7	my useless ... kiss] in a silent kiss, my rather ineffectual blessing B
9	nestling] planted B
10	roundly] in definite terms B
11	needed] required B
16	our ... tried] it's a great strain upon the mind B
18	prodigiously] tremendously B
21	little] om. B
28	Romans] believers B
274 : 9	revolving] turning over B
11	great temple] big rotunda B
13–15	or verifies ... dim fables] or verifies more forcibly those prodigious beliefs which we are apt to regard as dim fables A; or has more of the form of the antique faiths whose temples were nobler than their gods B
16	gathered shell] shell picked up on the beach B
19	he] this AB
28	unclosed apex of the temple] uncapped vault AB
28	most] om. B

30	friendly terms] terms of reciprocity B
38	ornamental altars] rather perfunctory altars B
41	puzzled] curious B
42	saluted me frankly] waved me a greeting B
42–275:2	I fancied . . . appear calm] He was in a state of nervous exaltation—doing his best to appear natural B
275:5	books] books and their opera-glasses B
10	come sailing] descend B
41	Camillo; sturdier] poor Marco; and he was sturdier B
42	misplaced] out of place B
276:2–3	was fancy] was all fancy AB
3	tenderness] affection B
6	horrible] puzzling AB
7–8	other . . . interest] any sign that there is another woman in the case AB
13	an appealing tremor] a pathetic little quiver B
19	doubly] intensely AB
25–6	seemed to] seemed—half contemptuously—to B
26	grudgingly pardoned me] forgiven me B
27	sort] kind B
28	instinct of mistrust] conviction that such a one as I would never even understand him B
29	prodigiously] exceedingly B
41	an unwholesome] a morbid B
42	should] ought to B
277:2	ingenious compound] extraordinary dose B
3	had] om. B
4	Rome] the Corso B
9	tree within arm's reach] which happened to be near me B
17	work] play AB
21	Its sudden illumination] The way it leaped into prominence B
24	was flooding] flooded B
29	the fancied scene] what I had been looking for AB
30	Juno visited by Diana] a transfiguration B
31	radiant flood and] cold radiance, B
31–3	which made . . . polished silver] that made her convincingly divine. If by day her rich paleness suggested faded gold, she now had a complexion like silver slightly dimmed B
34	eloquent] expressive B
41–3	I of course . . . gazing] Of course, in this recumbent worshipper I immediately recognized the Count, and while I lingered there B
278:3	detected] perceived B
6–7	extraordinary need] fabulous passion AB
7	so woefully . . . us, and] given us so much to wonder at, and B

9	The bright moonshine] The lunar influence B
12	shining statue] glowing image A; brilliant image B
13	fancied] suspected B
20	meeting the … grounds] meeting in the garden the functionary who had conducted the excavation B
20	explorer] antiquarian A
21–2	what I … gravity] an intention of portentous gravity B
23	likened] compared AB
29	much,' … 'I had] much—I had B
31	did you expect] was your notion B
43	distinct,' … 'you] distinct, you B
279:1	them. I] them,' I said. 'I B
7	thousand,' … 'to] thousand to B
9	and we separated] while I turned my back upon him B
12–13	sat plunged … I fancied] was uncommonly taciturn and absent. It appeared to me B
13	old] antique AB
18	I had] I myself had B
20	a kind of angry ardour] an almost brutal violence B
23	very fantastic] very improbable B
24	feared. Your] feared. There *is* a woman in the case! Your AB
29	through the ages] for so many centuries B
29	statue] image B
30	aroused] evoked B
32	Camillo is a pagan.] Marco is an anthropomorphist. Do you know what that means? B
37	burst open] opened itself B
39	wearing … character] fading for a while into a fiction A; losing for a while your importance B
41	incomparable] irreproachable B
280:2–3	an example] a model B
3–4	inconvertible] unconvertible B
7	roses] fragrance A; best elements B
9	decease] passing away B
11	a] om. AB
11	confidence … felt] confidence, and partly felt it B
18	her … influence] her—perhaps I can guess how she charms him AB
19	with the] from the B
20	young] poor AB
21	she had] she too had B
27	But the] But evidently the B
29	nameless] shapeless B
31	and we] and as we B
31–2	with … reverence] I think we each of us felt for a moment the breath of superstition B

32	deepened] quickened B
33	checked] arrested B
39	the later ... anthropophagi] the Latins were posterior to the cannibals A; that in the best time the ancient Romans offered no human victims B
42	great] sad A; immense B
281:2	her and smoked] her—smoking B
4	shaped] arrived at B
5	dusky portents] strange practices B
6	devoutly ... tolerably] less welcome for being comparatively B
9	gentle] generous B
14	as] om. AB
15	light, I] light, and I AB
22	could not speak] could not utter A; was unable to utter B
31	interrupt] intrude upon B
33	little explorer] mocking little commissioner B
42	outlying] outstanding AB
282:6	indicate] represent B
8	sober] scrupulous B
14	as long] so long B
19	surveyor] expert B
28	unclosed with] unclosed, owing to B
37	mocking] sneering B
283:9–10	Juno—and rejoiced] Juno—and drawn a long breath AB
11	stitches ... contentment] threads like an image of domestic tranquility B
13–14	in ... contemplation] awhile, giving her, askance, an immense deal of attention B
27	said] asked B

MME. DE MAUVES

Notes:

1. The variants recorded below are based on a collation of the original serial text of the tale (*Galaxy*, 1874) and its three revised versions in *A Passionate Pilgrim* (1875)—hereinafter mentioned as A; *The Madonna of the Future* (1879)—hereinafter mentioned as B; and *The Reverberator*, Etc., (1908)—hereinafter mentioned as C.

2. In texts A, B, and C, the abbreviations, Mme. and Mlle., have been expanded and the original Mrs. Clive is changed to Mrs. Cleve. These variants are ignored in the record.

IN TWO PARTS] om. ABC

PART I] om. ABC

284:9	chosen not to forget it] chosen not to forget this AB; preferred to keep this in mind C
14–15	standpoint ... curiosity] vantage without a sense of curiosity still unappeased C
21	interesting one] better C
23	and to repair] and repair C
25	observed] noticed C
285:3	for] om. C
3	denoted] denoting such C
15–16	an expensive spring toilet] a great elegance of fresh finery C
16–17	surprised cordiality, mentioned] amazement and joy, mentioning C
17	bade] bidding C
18	who, though equally] in whom, though she was equally C
19	was dressed more soberly] muslins and laces and feathers were less of a feature C
21	perceived] took in C
24	various small] sundry C
25–6	her friend] this lady C
28	minutes Longmore] minutes, meanwhile, Longmore C
28–9	interlocutress] old acquaintance C
29	as riddles] as mild riddles C
29	than commonplace] than mere commonplaces C
31	was less suggestive than the latter's] shook a sort of sweetness out of the friend's C
33	but essentially ... scrutiny] but she was essentially both, on a closer scrutiny B; but essentially both for the really seeing eye C

34	pale, delicately] pale, she was delicately B; pale, was delicately C
34–5	apparently with recent excitement] just now, as by the effect of late agitation C
36	heavy] languid ABC
37	peculiarly expressive and firm] that was all expression and intention C
39	was] om. C
39–40	which was ... ugly] just then even more ugly than usual C
286 : 3	an extremely interesting] a most attaching C
4	perceived that] was certain C
5	he] om. C
13	Mrs. Draper] the traveller C
17	that he did not] he was vague C
19–20	she had ... narrative] coherence had quite deserted her C
21	she said ... going] she nevertheless had the presence of mind to say as he was going C
24	will satisfy] will quite satisfy C
26–7	woman! will ... for you] woman, won't make your affair a carnival C
27	unhappy.'] unhappy,' said Mrs. Draper. C
32	He waited] He then waited C
32–3	declared that it was not] felt how little it was C
33	her milliner's treachery] engagements unperformed C
38	finally discovered,] was at last able to recognize; C
39	perceived ... alone] made her out from a distance, arrested there alone and leaning against the low wall C
40–1	her, it ... there was] her there was C
42	diminished ... this result] chilled by such a measure of the effect C
43	immediately recognized him] at once recovered their connection C
287 : 1–2	with the manner ... faces] with the manner of a person unaccustomed to encounter an embarrassing variety of faces B; and showed it with the frankness of a person unprovided with a great choice of contacts C
3	was there] came out C
3	sweet] fine C
8	flattering] good C
8–9	Mrs. Draper] our friend C
9	said] been able to say C
12	linger, in spite of] linger through C
16	pronounced her unhappy] spoken of uneasy things in her life C
16	convenient to suppose] natural to guess C

17   made her so] was the source of them   C
18   asked himself] put it   C
19   unclean Frenchman] unholy foreigner   C
20   tender expectancy of] quiet dependence on   C
20–1   undermined his hypothesis] rather shook his shrewdness
            C
21   gentle eagerness] free confidence   C
22   and greeted] to greet   C
23   beheld] distinguished   C
24   light] grey   C
24–5   indistinct ... moustache] obscure as yet against the quar-
            ter from which it came, mainly presented to view the large
            outward twist of its moustache   C
28   proffered] offered   C
28–9   the terrace gate] the gate of the terrace   BC
29–30   and a] and also a   C
30   to see at home] they might have the pleasure of seeing, as
            she said, *chez eux*   C
31   very] om.   C
33–6   twisting his ... bad French] renewing the curl of his main
            facial feature—watched him with an irritation devoid of
            any mentionable ground. His own pretext for gnashing his
            teeth would have been in his apprehension that this gentle-
            man's worst English might prove a matter to shame his
            own best French   C
38–40   himself ... satisfaction] a colloquial use of that idiom as
            insecure as the back of a restive horse, and was obliged to
            take his exercise, as he was aware, with more tension than
            grace. He reflected meanwhile with comfort   C
41   idiom] tongue   C
41–2   vexation ... by his] anxiety yielded to his relief at   C
288:4–6   these distracting ... my graceful] the sight of so many
            women here who don't look at all like her that has re-
            minded me by the law of contraries of my charming   BC
7   her. I] her,' she wrote. 'I   BC
7–8   told ... unhappy] spoke to you of her rather blighted
            state   C
9–10   have found ... she was] certainly have arrived at guesses
            of your own, and, besides, she has never told me her
            secrets. The only one she ever pretended to was that
            she's   C
11   and then ... burst] after assuring me of which, poor
            thing, she went off   C
12   and I] so that I   C
13–17   to be neither ... appreciate] neither to submit basely nor
            to rebel crookedly marrying a shining sinful Frenchman
            who believes a woman must do one or the other of those

things. The lightest of *us* have a ballast that they can't
imagine, and the poorest a moral imagination that they
don't require   C

16–17   moral needs ... appreciate] moral needs that the cleverest
          Frenchman is quite unable to appreciate   B
17–18   wilful, and thought] perverse—she thought   BC
18–19   Americans were ... elegant] the world she had been
          brought up in too vulgar or at least too prosaic. To have a
          decent home-life isn't perhaps the greatest of adventures;
          but I think she wishes nowadays she hadn't gone in quite
          so desperately for thrills   C
22–3   "console ... proof of] cheer up a lady domestically dejected.
          Believe me, I've given no other man a proof of this   C
24   and] so   C
24   disappoint me ... the world] take me in an inferior sense
          I would never speak to you again   C
25–6   Mme. de Mauves ... husband] this fine sore creature that
          our manners may have all the grace without wanting to
          make such selfish terms for it   C
28–9   drawn some ... conscience] made her patience a little less
          absent-minded. Make her *want* to forget; make her like
          you   C
30   These zealous ... disturbed] This ingenious appeal left
          the young man uneasy   C
31–2   on the edge ... recoiled] in the presence of more compli-
          cations than had been in his reckoning   C
32   upon] on   C
33   seemed a sort of] struck him as akin to   C
33–4   a modest man] of modest composition   C
34–5   the effect ... to add] an appearance of attentions from any
          gallant gentleman mightn't give another twist   C
35   burden] tribulation   A; discomfort   B; tangle   C
36   however, made] however—of such a possible value con-
          stituted for him as he had never before been invited to
          rise to—made   C
37–8   It seemed ... smile] It was too inspiring not to act upon the
          idea of kindling a truer light in his fair country-woman's
          slow smile   C
39–40   there was ... American] even a raw representative of the
          social order she had not done justice to was not necessarily
          a mere fortuitous collocation of atoms   C
40   upon] on   C
289:1   twelve] fourteen   ABC
2   mamma, fonder] mamma who was fonder   BC
8   a title] a man of hierarchical 'rank'   C
9   that] om.   C
10–11   best birth is the] enjoyment of inherited and transmitted

consideration, consideration attached to the fact of birth, would be the direct   C

11   feeling. Romances] feeling. She supposed it would be found that the state of being noble does actually enforce the famous obligation. Romances   C

12   shaped] constructed   B; worked out   C

12   perfect] transcendent   C

13   in the ... imagination] the primitive purity of her imagination   B; the prime purity of her moral vision   C

13   utterly] profoundly   A; essentially   BC

14   cherished] took   C

14   conceit as] conceit to her bosom very much as   C

19–21   that the consciousness ... Noblesse oblige] enjoyment of a chance to carry further a family chronicle begun ever so far back must be, as a consciousness, a source of the most beautiful impulses. It wasn't therefore only that noblesse oblige   C

22   and insures, as regards] but that it ensures as nothing else does in respect to   C

22   never spoken] never, at the start, spoken   C

23–4   transcendent] extravagant   C

28   perfumed] strong social scent of the   C

32   religious mystery] the silence that mostly surrounds all ecstatic faith   C

36   she seemed ... pallid fancy] her flights of fancy seemed short, rather, and poor and untutored   C

290 : 4 Euphemia] She   C

6   which] that   C

8–9   his blood ... strain] he should have 'race' in a state as documented as it was possible to have it   C

9–10   happiness. It ... were] happiness; and it was so to happen that several accidents conspired   C

11   primitive logic] artless philosophy   C

12   Though little ... listener] Inclined to long pauses and slow approaches herself, Euphemia was a great sitter at the feet of breathless volubility   C

14–15   was, like ... of difference] was founded on the perception —all her own—that their differences were just the right ones   C

17   in] for   C

27   Euphemia] our own young woman   C

32–3   which Euphemia considered but a] regarded by Euphemia but as a   C

34–5   small deference ... later justify] conformities without style, and one that would sooner or later express   C

35–7   Mlle. de Mauves ... society which] Mademoiselle de Mauves herself perhaps was but partially conscious of that sweet security which   B; There doubtless prevailed in the breast of Mademoiselle de Mauves herself a dimmer vision of the large securities that   C

37 proved herself] was to become   C

38 such an accomplished] so accomplished a   C

39–41 must have ... more; but the] might well have waked up early. The especially fine appearance made by our heroine's ribbons and trinkets as her friend wore them ministered to pleasure on both sides, and the spell was not of a nature to be menaced by the young American's general gentleness. The   C

43–291 : 1 Auvergne ... superior] Auvergne involved, however, the subtlest   C

291 : 1 was indeed] indeed,   C

2 presumably] om.   C

2–5 general views; and, ... success] views as wide as her wants, was as proper a figure as could possibly have been found for the foreground of a scene artfully designed; and Euphemia, whose years were of like number, asked herself if a right harmony with such a place mightn't come by humble prayer   C

5 Euphemia's] the latter's   C

7–8 the young ... a play.] it was as full of wonders as a box of old heirlooms or objects 'willed'.   C

10 old] om.   C

12–13 it assume ... presentiment] all the easier passages translated into truth, as the learner of a language begins with the common words   C

20–2 Euphemia, as indeed ... American,] Euphemia—what indeed she had every claim to pass for—the very image and pattern of an 'historical character'. Belonging to a great order of things, she patronised the young stranger   C

24 woman, and] woman; she   C

25 antique] ancient   C

26 at her] om.   C

27 under her spectacles] behind an immense *face-à-main* that acted as for the relegation of the girl herself to the glass case of a museum   C

28 her] such a little person   C

29 young girl's startled blush] little person's evident wonder C

30 that] om.   C

32–5 listen to the ... stupid, were] have been wound up by some key that isn't kept by your governess or your confessor or even your mother, but that you wear by a fine black ribbon round your own neck. Little persons in my day— when they were stupid they were   C

36	clever, were] clever they were C
39–41	expect too live ... the world's] wish to live at ease in the *doux pays de France* don't trouble too much about the key of your conscience or even about your conscience itself —I mean your own particular one C
40	want] wish B
42	that] om. C
292:2	very disagreeable] *peu aimable* C
3	was] is BC
3	please] be infinitely so C
4	the ones] in fact those C
7	Listen : not to lose, you] Listen to this. Not to lose at the game of life, you BC
7	don't be] not be BC
8	don't be] not be BC
10	but] and BC
11	but] only C
12	*revanche*] revenge C
12	I'm not sure that] I really think that B; I really think C
13	take ... whole] take, *en somme*, against the past I've known, C
15	awful] bewildering BC
18	picturesquely] strikingly C
18–19	pattern] form C
19	mantilla] high-backed armchair C
19	headdress] coif C
21	prompting] instance C
22–3	somewhat ... Euphemia was] worry of scruples—scruples in the light of which Euphemia was on the one hand C
24	that] om. C
24	her house was] her own house on the other C
25	a scruple] an hesitation C
26	house De Mauves] house of De Mauves AB; menaced institution C
26–7	had been pervaded by the] been over much pervaded by that C
27	of an establishment] om. C
28	were] are C
28	masters] ancestors ABC
29–30	more regrettable] sorrier C
32	were not] had not been B; hadn't been C
33	Richard de Mauves came] Richard de Mauves, coming C
34	and] om. C
35	vicomte] gentilhomme ABC
36	coming in] appearing C
38	wondering what had] to ask herself what could have C
39	life of bitter perplexity] long chain of puzzlements C

41	certain] om. C
42	promptly] om. C
42	after Euphemia] as soon as the girl C
293:3	a sombre glance as] this coldness while C
3	and] then C
6	*mauvais sujet*] *mauvais sujet* beyond redemption C
6	a conscience] a particle of conscience BC
7	take possession] disturb the repose BC
8	young girl] other relative of the subject of this warning C
9	redirected the letter] freshly indited the address C
10–11	seemed to ... conscience] denoted that by her judgement her brother was appealed to on the ground of a principle that didn't exist in him C
12	'If] And 'if C
12	man whispered] man on his side observed C
13	the first] his first private C
14	let her send] have sent C
15–16	It was ... apartment] Put out of humour perhaps by this gross impugnment of her sincerity, the head of the family kept her room on pretexts C
18	entirely to the vicomte's] entirely to the Baron's AB; all to her grandson's C
22	him, very much] him almost C
23	supernatural apparition] figure in a framed picture who should have stepped down from the wall C
23	thirty-five years old] now thirty-five B; now thirty-three C
25	which] that C
28	as they] as effectually they BC
29	to his ugliness] to a characterized want of them C
29	and] om. BC
30	speeches] remarks C
31	certain] om. C
31	which] that C
33	if] when C
37	Euphemia with] Euphemia had with C
37	had] om. C
41	Euphemia] the accomplished young stranger C
41	sing to him] sing for him C
42	little] small C
42	in her voice, which] that C
43	an exquisite refinement of art] the finish of vocal art C
294:1	unwandering] unfailing C
2	sat] would sit C
4	and made] making C
10	being generously scrutinized] being so generously and intensely taken for granted C

11	so amiable] so much on show, even to the very casual critic lodged, as might be said, in an out-of-the-way corner of it C
12	interpretation of it] pious opinion C
14	hard determination] settled resolve C
14	girl] person C
18–19	and he would] and would C
20	placid] robust and serene C
24	perverted] perverse C
26	released him from] put to flight BC
29–31	other circumstances ... violence had] a different pressure to some such showing as would have justified a romantic faith. So should he have exhaled the natural fragrance of a late-blooming flower of hereditary honour. His violence indeed had C
33	edge] fineness BC
35	cambric handkerchiefs] ciphered pocket-handkerchiefs C
39	tastes introduced] tastes had introduced C
42–3	the light gloves ... and throws] those very lavender gloves that are soiled in an evening and thrown C
295:1–2	such plentiful ... character] in the feminine character such plentiful evidence of its pliant softness and fine adjustability C
4	seemed] struck him as C
4	a refutation] contradictory C
6	this, on] this on C
6	was] is B; om. C
6–7	charming ... development] potent source of their attraction C
7–8	inspired him ... respect] moved him to perfect consideration C
10	being] very BC
11–12	might have ... almost] might almost have taken a lesson from the delicacy he practised. For two or three weeks her grandson was well-nigh C
13	and admired, and] he admired and desired and C
14	was] found himself C
14	disposed towards] moved to C
14–15	desire] wish C
16	movement] gesture C
21	benignant] glorious C
22	in spite of an evident] despite an infinite C
23	equally] at once C
23–4	make the subject of a compliment] be complimentary about C
25	there was] had been C
25	Baron's] young man's C

26–7	indicated the ... into a fact] resembled the happy stir of the change from dreaming pleasantly to waking happily C
26–7	tranformation] transmutation AB
28	enjoyed it] was touched C
28–9	this reminded ... best] he now seemed to give easy ear to some of the sweetest C
32	comfortable] satisfied C
35	that he was] himself C
35	which] that C
41	M. le Baron] M. le Comte C
42	a promising] the likeliest C
43	pious] theological BC
43	the Baron's ... good-humour] the Count's unusual equanimity C
296:6	he was seized with] was pulled up by C
22	vines] creepers BC
23–4	profuseness ... perfection] profusion that made the Count feel his own conduct the last word C
25	'In America,' ... that when] 'I've always heard that in America, when C
26–7	face, without any] face and without C
27	uncles, and] uncles and aunts and C
31	then,' ... 'suppose] then—suppose C
31	*bosquet*] arbour C
32	America] your great sensible country C
33	have] see B; feel C
38	little] massive C
38	which] om. C
41–297:1	gown, with ... betrothal] gown and with her candles all lighted as for the keeping of some fête C
297:1	Mme. de Mauves] the old woman C
3	so,' ... 'lest] so, lest C
5	said the old lady solemnly] Madame de Mauves grandly returned C
7	Baron] Comte C
9–10	considers ... Very good] regards it—for the conditions—as the perfection of good taste. Very well C
11	frank] marked BC
11	agreement] agreements C
12	like] care C
13	be, beyond] be, my dear, beyond C
16	deceive] dazzle C
17–18	the Baron] my grandson C
20–1	frivolous women being happy] the happiness of frivolous women C
21	suit you] suit you, *ma toute-belle* C

22	to be yourself] to be, to remain, your own sincere little self only, charming in your own serious little way C
22	Baronne] Comtesse C
23	Yourself] Your brave little self C
24	bad usage even] bad fortune and even bad usage C
25	yourself, and a De Mauves] just what the good God has made you, and even one of us—and one of those who is most what we *are*— C
31	seemed ... have] had for her simply C
33–4	countesses] women of quality ABC
36	shocked] disconcerted C
298:5	a penniless] a presumptuous and penniless C
5	will] shall C
6	to] om. C
7–8	the Baron which mitigated] this personage which softened C
10	Mrs. Clive] the lady C
11	genuine spiritual] deep and real C
13	treat ... allegiance] make light of America in familiar discourse A; make light of their native land in familiar discourse BC
14	moral responsibility] having blasphemed C
16	sagacious] competent C
19	her mother] om. C
19	her mind] her mother's mind C
20	that the ... one which] her lover's type an historic, a social masterpiece that C
23–4	seemed to ... had no] struck the girl she had simply no C
24	her lover's] in those of M. de Mauves C
25	M. de Mauves] This agent of Providence C
27	a De Mauves of necessity gave] a member of his family gave of necessity C
30–1	a De Mauves] a member of his family C
33	suspended] put off BC
35–6	would but ... Baron's suit] might well take a form representing peril to the suit of this first headlong aspirant C
41	Baron] Count C
41–2	and looked ... expecting] looking at his young friend as if he expected C
299:1	the Baron] M. de Mauves C
3	a very happy fellow] one of the luckiest of men C
6	the Baron] the young man C
6	that he needed] he required C
8	millions] fortune C
11	eyes,] pale face C
19	in democratic] of democratic C

23–4	an opportunity ... enjoyment] a range of quiet pleasure C
25	a great many] uncounted C
31	little] smooth C
32	After ... wandered] Presently she would come out and wander C
34	introduced] introduce C
34	little] private C
34	garden] high C
34–5	opening upon] the opening to C
35	into] to ABC
35–6	Hitherward ... wandered] Hitherwards she more than once strolled C
37	strolling] going C
37–8	taking a generous walk] stretching it to the freedom of a *promenade* C
38	found a vast deal] discovered many things AB; found many things C
39	finding ... away,] feeling the hours slip along like some silver stream C
300:3	altogether comfortable] wholly inspiring C
4	secret, and] twist in her life and C
6	perceived] recognized C
6–7	sorrow ... aggressive one] grievance, if grievance it was, was not aggressive C
8	her earnest wish was to forget it] her most earnest wish was to remember it as little as possible C
10	he could ... It was] that he couldn't have pointed to his proof. The evidence was C
12	on] in C
13	meant] had designed C
15	she indulged ... fate] she dealt no sarcastic digs at her fate C
16	coquetry ... But] conscious graces of the woman wronged. Only C
17–18	the result ... was trying] but the milder or sharper flush of a settled ache, and that she but tried C
18–19	to escape] in order to escape C
21–4	ingenuous reserve ... contemplation] studied discretion. He measured the rare magnanimity of self-effacement so deliberate, he felt how few women were capable of exchanging a luxurious woe for a thankless effort C
25	instinctively] himself C
27	which] that C
27–8	striving ... strongly-flavoured joy] planning to get the worth of her trouble back in some other way C
28	strongly-flavoured] strongly-seasoned B

29	trying] proposing C
32	an active ... leading-strings] a speculative spirit, leading-strings that C
33	see] regard ABC
34	intenser, more] intenser and more C
34–5	hovering ... have] lurking duality in her put on C
43	gave him indeed] supplied him indeed with C
43	and] so that he fitted C
301 : 1	he formed] om. C
1–2	experimental ... marriage] experimental theories on the subject of her marriage B; high-flown theories to her apparent history C
3	married a Frenchman] changed her allegiance C
5	conjugal happiness] her perpetrated mistake C
9	that] this BC
10	arrogantly] insolently C
11	knew] knew that C
12	frivolous; it was] both cynical and shallow; these things were C
12–15	his carriage ... gallantry] his voice, his gesture, his step. Of Frenchwomen themselves, when all was said, our young man, full of nursed discriminations, went in no small fear C
19–20	character ... to even] character had a perfume which is absent from even B; nature had an atmospheric envelope absent even from C
23–5	She was silent ... her husband] She replied nothing at first, till he feared she might think it her duty to resent a question that made light of all her husband's importances C
26	deep reserve of sorrow] policy of silence C
28	dreams] visions C
29	cease to be very young] begin to think or to dream beyond mere playtime C
33	America, perhaps, about me] America, no—this element C
34–5	garden, in the town, in] garden, France is in the town and C
36	nameless country] nameless, and doubtless not at all remarkable, little country C
39	might have, might meanwhile have C
302 : 2	consider] regard C
2	taken] towed ABC
4	was unfortunate] to be deplored C
5–6	a fashionable] an aristocratic ABC
6	a fashionable] an aristocratic ABC
7	and staked] and then staked C

8–9	overtook ... Then he let] was to learn that the law of compensation works with no such pleasing simplicity, and he rolled to the dark bottom of his folly. There he felt C
10	ridiculous] fatuous C
11	one day] om. C
12	for] om. C
13	glittering] brave C
17	he was going to interpret to him] for some practical application of C
18	heaven ... penalty of his] heaven, something that would express violently his C
19	But the ... only] The *sergent de ville*, however, only C
20	away] off C
23	lofty spirit of a De Mauves] great spirit of true children of the *anciens preux* C
23–4	After he had lost everything] When night had fallen ABC
27	excuse] pardon C
27	Clairin] the poor man C
37	forward] forth C
39	vigilant eyeglass] vigilant long-handled eyeglass C
303 : 1	Longmore's] the C
1	his] the C
2	that] om. C
2	not] neither C
3	unassuming] 'backward' C
3	He encountered] Longmore met C
4	which covered a great] that covered a good C
5	acutely] deeply C
7	shrewd] sharp C
8	like] of having become C
10	admitted ... was an] dismissed him for an C
11	kind of] om. C
12	mentally alluded to her] named her to himself C
12	terrible] awful C
20	arrival] arrival at the house C
20	and told him] with the news C
24	the] her C
24	cadence ... distinct] cadences were so almost explicit an C
25	incomparable] charming C
28	the edge] the thin edge C
29	becoming] pleasing in itself C
30	illuminate] show off C
31	there] in the picture C
31–2	murmuring,] murmur C
34	this] which C

34	Mme. de Mauves] his young countrywoman C
34–5	she seemed ... darker shadow] she seemed a brighter figure, with a darker shadow appended to it B; her intrinsic clearnes shone out to him even through the darker shade cast over it C
38	meet him promptly] keep their tryst C
41	that] since C
42–3	was irrevocably ... his trunk] were indeed portentously true. Such a truth somehow made it surely his duty to march straight home and put together his effects C
42	was] were B
42	was] were B
304 : 1	an excellent fellow] the best of men C
3	fire and water] anything C
4	loved for ten] loved ten C
5	for six ... admired] he had six weeks—well, admired C
6	was lingering] hung on C
8	all this] so much C
8	prudence] his fine old power to conclude C
9	prepared ... love] drifting rapidly into passion B; not judging but drifting, and he had pretended never to drift C
9	was] were BC
10	love] passion B; active sympathy C
11	was] were BC
12	friendly offices] professions C
14	But this very feeling had] This very feeling indeed had C
15–16	only ... stoicism which] be the flush on the snow of the high cold stoicism that C
16	moments, indeed,] moments withal C
17	to linger was] staying to watch her—and what else did it come to?—was C
17–18	indelicate ... But] gross to keep tugging at the cover of a book so intentionally closed. Then C
20	admirable] exquisite C
20–1	would be] would just be C
21	length; it] length and it C
21	both of them] either C
22	But he] He C
22–3	friend ... he had not] friend, however, who nursed a brooding regret for his not having C
24	and a brooding ... who had] as well as a particular objection to those who had smartly C
26–7	the charm of her character] every side of her, as she turned in her pain, C
28	Longmore's] Our young man's C
29	the Baron de Mauves] Richard de Mauves C

31	portentous ... implied] pitiless perversity lighted by such a conclusion C
32	our hero] Longmore C
34	his wife ... His] it was not a man's fault if his wife's love of life had pitched itself once for all in the minor key. The Count's C
35	urbanity was unbounded] discretion irreproachable
36	her] his companion C
38–9	deference] true frankness C
39	friendliness] form C
41	would bury herself alive] would—in her youth and her beauty—bury herself all absurdly alive C
42	someone else] your good friends and compatriots—some of them are so amusing C
42–3	my friends ... accept yours] mine, but perhaps you'll be able to offer her better *son affaire* C
43	accept] look at B
305:1	The Baron] M. de Mauves C
1	remorseless placidity] bright assurance C
4–5	capable ... her suffering] formed both to neglect his wife and to take the derisive view of her minding it C
6–7	the Baron ... more, for] the Baron thought rather the less of his wife on account of B; this nobleman thought rather the less of their interesting friend on account of C
9	Longmore's visits] the sessions of the American visitor C
9	and made] and he made BC
10–11	'business,' ... mentioned—not] *de gros soucis d'affaires* as he once mentioned—with an all-embracing flourish and not C
11	with a] in the C
14	amazing] annoying ABC
15	a good fellow ... spoiled] an honest man, he was an honest man somehow spoiled for confidence C
16	which Longmore] that his critic C
16–17	envied ... positiveness—] envied, something in his address, splendidly positive, C
17–18	traditions of centuries—] habit of conversation and the friction of full experience, C
18	amenity] an amenity A; an urbanity BC
18	sake ... neighbours'—] sake, not for his neighbour's, C
19–21	result of ... moral man] fruit of one of those strong temperaments that rule the inward scene better than the best conscience. The Count had plainly no sense for morals C
21–2	was, would ... serenity] had the finest, would have been glad to borrow his recipe for appearing then so to range the whole scale of the senses C
23	without] short of C
23–4	feet, exhaling] feet and exhaling C

24	lovely wife,] nature like his wife's C
25	a smile under his moustache] a candid smile under his moustache B; such a handsome invincible grin C
27	turn ... compliments] such a store of neat speeches C
27	very] highly C
28	he could] could C
28	supremely] damnably C
28–30	he was as ... in algebra] the life of the spirit was a world as closed to him as the world of great music to a man without an ear C
31	know his wife was unhappy] in the least understand how his wife felt C
31	brilliant] smooth C
32	consider their companion] regard their relative as C
33–4	slender accomplishments, contented] few talents, content C
34	an especial] a special C
35–6	supply her ... gossip] regale her with innocent echoes of their native wit C
37	relished ... society] liked women who could, frankly, amuse him better C
38	modest, too simple, too delicate] dim, too delicate, too modest C
39–40	M. de Mauves ... was stupid] Lighting a cigar some day while he summed up his situation, her husband had probably decided she was incurably stupid C
40–1	same sort of taste, Longmore] same taste, in essence, our young man C
41	Gérôme] M. Gérôme and M. Baudry C
42	M. Gustave Fleubert] M. Charles Baudelaire B; M. Gustave Flaubert and M. Charles Baudelaire C
43	was] om. C
43	them, accordingly, was a] them an impassable C
306:2	this distinguished social] that historic C
3–4	certainly ... boldness] its elegance C
4	it was fed from] depended on C
7	across] through C
9	without ... reputation] before the mirrors properly crack to hear C
10	smartest] sweetest AB; rarest C
10–12	her and ... entertainment than] her, without making my reflection that, charm for charm, such a *manière d'être* is more 'fetching' even than the worst of C
14–15	rigid notions] social principles BC
17	chiefly of] for the most part of comparatively C
19	the wife of a De Mauves] even an adoptive daughter of his house C

23–4	these sound principles] this definite faith BC
24–5	fancied ... reserve] figured him much inconvenienced by the Countess's avoidance of betrayals C
26	it] the principle of this reserve C
28	convenient moment] manageable hour C
28–9	have something] have had something C
29	attest] have attested C
29–30	a trifle more ... reasonableness] a trifle more forcibly than her inscrutable tranquillity AB; rather better than this mere polish of her patience C
31–2	know ... submissiveness] be able to guess how this latter secret worked C
32–4	but with ... long resisting] though timidly and awkwardly enough, to make out the game she was playing. She struck him as having long resisted C
34–5	though ... to have] as though succumbing to it at last, having C
35–6	the right ... generosity] on simple grounds of generosity the right to complain. Her faith might have perished, but the sense of her own old deep perversity C
37	even that she was] her thus quite C
39	illusions and that this] vanities and follies and that what was before her C
40–1	I have a ... suffering. I believe] I'm a dreadful coward about having to suffer or to bleed. I've always tried to believe C
42–307 : 1	there is ... of grief] such extremities may always somehow be dodged or indefinitely postponed. I should be willing to buy myself off, from having ever to be *overwhelmed*, by giving up—well, any amusement you like C
306 : 42	I had] I would B
307 : 3	an immense longing] the force of his desire C
5	Webster lost] Webster meanwhile lost C
6	and asking] and in asking C
6	at Saint-Germain] at suburban Saint-Germain C
8	Webster's] this friend's C
11	letter] word here C
12	at] in C
14	candid] immediate C
14	which] om. C
14	displayed] showed C
15	disposition, apparently,] hint of a disposition C
16–17	enough,' ... 'but] enough, but C
17	Won't you] Shall you not B; Shan't you C
19	you sat] you simply sat C
20	log, pulling] log and pulled C
22–3	here and ... on the matter] here—sat here so much—and

never have shown what's the matter with me   C

26 unfortunate] discreet   BC

29–30 question ... blush] appeal, and, making her change colour, it took her unprepared   C

30 she said] she none the less simply said   C

33 supposed. I've] supposed,' he returned. 'I've   C

36 something ... intense grief] something that I have believed to be a constant sorrow   AB; some trouble in you that I've permitted myself to hate and resent   C

37 with great gravity] all gravely   C

39 placidly] serenely   B; quietly enough   C

308 : 1 blush] flush   C

2 an impression] an impression on your part   B; some impression in you   C

2 which is evidently already] even now much   C

3 An unhappiness that] Any "trouble"—if you mean any unhappiness—that   C

5 investigating] testing   C

7–8 delightfully ... to deepen] that deeply touched him in her tone, and this quality pierced further   C

10 Mr. Longmore, for I have] my dear sir,' she wound up with a certain quaintness of gaiety, 'for I've   C

11 a very contented person] contented enough and diverted enough   C

12 You're] Well, you're   C

12 he said] the young man declared   C

12–13 I never have] I've never   C

17 a kind of] an   C

20 making bows] paying compliments   BC

26 a slight ... which] the faintest quaver in the world, an impressible break of voice that   C

27 once] once or twice   C

27 which he] om.   C

28 weariness of] weariness, the controlled convulsion, of   C

29 about the Dutch painters at all] a button about the Dutch painters   B; a button for the Dutch painters   C

30 with a laugh] with an unhesitating laugh   AB

33 a tremor] an agitation of his own   C

37–8 grave ... sentimental] grave—she felt she had almost grossly failed and she was proportionately disappointed. An emotional   C

39 Longmore] her visitor   C

41–2 extremely ... in him] extremely, she felt in him the living force of something   C

43 French Baron] nobleman   C

309 : 1 very scanty] too scant   C

6 a commanding] an authoritative   C

9	and then,] —then C
11	without] not C
12	hope,' she ... waste] hope you will act upon my advice,' she said, 'and waste B; hope you'll act on my advice and waste C
17	Longmore felt as if] it seemed to him C
21–2	he rejoined ... smile, and] he returned—which she appeared to accept with a smile as she C
23	turned away, and] stood a moment, then C
25	in] aware of C
27–8	Suddenly, on the terrace] In the midst of it suddenly, on the great terrace of the Château C
28–9	who was ... parapet] planted there against the parapet and C
29	Baron] Count C
29	fancied] thought he made out C
30	light-gloved] fair, plump A; white plump BC
31	sudden angry] sharp, a sore C
32	loveliest] most precious C
33	shrewdness] grand assurance C
33–4	looked into] looked down into C
34	The Baron, we know] Richard de Mauves, we have seen C
34	that] om. C
35	was something ... was not] was doubtless now something in this young woman's eyes that had not been C
36–7	They ... account of] The two men conversed formally enough, and M. de Mauves threw off a light bright remark or two about C
39	consider] have found C
39–40	urbanity ... bad one] blandness went but so far as to allow that jokes on that scale are indeed inexhaustible C
41	our institutions] his native institutions B; the seat of his origin C
41–2	Baron's narrative] Count's easy diagnosis C
42	impressions] estimate C
43	he had] om. C
43	he had] om. C
310:1	our hero] his critic C
3	vaingloriously] fatuously BC
3	his stars that] goodness C
4	century, in] century and in C
5	lumber merchant] timber-merchant BC
6–8	ours—the liberty ... noblemen—researches] the American order—the liberty allowed the fairer half of the unmarried young, and confessed to some personal study of the 'occasions' it offered to the speculative visitor; a line of research C

9   seemed to have spent many] had clearly spent his most   C
15   Mentioning at] Mentioning, however, at   C
16   the Baron's] his interlocutor's   C
17   I'm very] I am so very   BC
17   sorry,' the latter cried. 'I hoped] sorry; I hoped   C
18   the summer] the whole summer   BC
20   You were a diversion] You were a distraction   B; You've
         been a real resource   C
20   Baron] Count   C
21   you I mentally] you I've mentally   C
24   Baron ... his arm] Count made a great and friendly point
         of it   C
25   I have confidence] the confidence I have   C
25–6   was silent ... the Baron] said nothing and M. de Mauves
         C
26   for a while] reflectively   ABC
27   peculiar] singular   ABC
28   Longmore] And then while our young man   C
28   was] were   B
30   the Baron went on] this lady's husband pursued   C
31   just] om.   C
31   marked] morbid   AB; overstrained   C
32–3   fanciful—a little *exaltée*] fanciful—a little *entêtée*   B;
         volontaire and morbid   C
35   she's polite ... freezing] she is perfectly polite, but she is
         simply freezing   B; she's perfectly polite, but it cures
         them of coming again   C
41   grey veil which] brown fog which   AB; brown fog   C
41   always] om.   C
41–2   me to] me—don't they?—to   C
42–3   Baron continued,] Count went on   C
311:4   day a] day some passages from a   C
5   It ... she took] It was as if she had taken   C
6   forced] held   BC
6–7   *soupe aux choux*, and that one] *soupe aux choux*; I felt as
         if we   C
8   *ce génie là*. I think my] *ce génie-là*. Every nation has its
         own ideals of every kind, but when I remember some of
         our charming writers! I think at all events my   C
11   culture,' said the Baron] culture—a man of the world,' said
         the Baron   B; culture, a man of the world,' said M. de
         Mauves   C
12   and fixing his eyes on] but looking hard at   C
12   on his] of his   BC
14   Wordsworth] Monsieur Wordsworth   BC
14   everything] everything you can   C
15   forgot you're] forgot that you are   B

16	talk about] report on C
16–17	Mme. de Mauves] my wife C
17	travel . . . months] make a little voyage BC
17–18	her good] her great good C
20	rigid] much of one piece C
21	that one] how much one C
21	a trifle] om. C
23	a little nod . . . smile] eyebrows expressively raised C
24	I wouldn't say all this] I beg you to believe I wouldn't say such things C
25	coming on,] at hand C
25–6	float in the air in] charge the air with C
28	murmuring as] the chorus of C
30	Baron] Count C
32	deliberately] quietly C
36	thinking,' . . . 'that] thinking that BC
37	justice. Take] justice,' he said. 'Take B; justice,' he made answer. 'Take C
39	cried . . . a laugh] the Count laughed C
41	it] om. C
41–2	the Baron's grace of address] the Baron's fine manner B; his friend's fine manner C
43	sort of] om. C
312:1	echo lingered] echo, loudest at the last, lingered C
3	an arrogant fool] no better than a pompous dunce C
3	must] was to BC
5	said . . . peremptorily] It was spoken almost with the note of irritation C
7	Of course] But of course C
7	said goodbye to Mme. de Mauves.] take leave—? C
8	tone] manner C
8	most] very B; om. C
9	Longmore] Longmore himself C
10	burst into] put the appeal by with C
11	Baron] Count C
11	like a . . . it was] as if it were C
11	most] om. C
12	to be perplexed . . . fellow,'] for him to be left at a loss. 'Ah you people have your *façons*!' C
13	would] should BC
14	think him . . . fellow indeed] learn still more about his *façons* C
16	as he was] in the act of C
17	his wine] the liquor C
17	His reverie] This mood C
19	this] that C
20	a kind of] an C

23	one was] one of them C

23   one was] one of them   C

24   to be delivered] for delivery   C

26   be back in] return to   C

26   in the early autumn] early in the autumn   C

29   impressions] impression   C

31   receiving them] reading him over   C

32   a stronger flavour of rhapsody] he should have 'raved' a little more   C

33   sentences] passage   C

36–7   most marriages ... more, I think,] this is what most marriages take themselves to be; but it would mean in her case, I think, more   C

38   was] to be   C

41   touched the bottom of it yet] yet touched the bottom   C

43   struck a truce with painful] patched up a peace with some painful   C

313:5   a Frenchman] a shallow Frenchman   C

7   sentimentally] extravagantly   C

8–9   for in some ... as she saw] since he feels, I suppose, in some uncorrupted corner of his being that as she originally saw   C

9–10   It's a perpetual vexation to him] It disagrees with him somewhere   C

14   can] can understand it   B; understand it   C

14–15   spectacle ... restlessly] spectacle I can admire it furiously   AB; sight I find I greatly admire it   C

15–16   M. de Mauves ... corruptible] The Count at any rate would have enjoyed the comfort of believing his wife as bad a case   C

16   was] is   B

17   tell you that] assure you   C

18   deems worthy of the knowledge] thinks it concern   C

19   to have them make love to her] that they should make love to her   B; they should make love to Madame de Mauves   C

PART II] om.   ABC

23   that, by ... ought to] that he ought by way of preparation to   C

27   demanded that] required   C

27   leave] allow   AB; bequeath   C

28   suppose ... understood him] suppose he had, as it were, taken a low hint   C

29   satisfied ... delicacy] satisfied the behest of delicacy,   B; deferred to that scruple   C

30	Euphemia] his friend C
32	deserted boulevards] forsaken boulevard C
35	train; but a] train. ABC
35	started, and Longmore] started, however, and he C
36	sentimental tumult] inward ache C
37	looked in] looked at C
37–314 : 1	whether it was] if it represented C
314 : 2	a kind of ... represented] much mistrust of what it stood for C
3	fell in love,] should fall in love, B; should fall 'really' in love C
4–5	no greater ... But here was] plenty of confidence and joy, doubtless, but no strange soreness, no pangs nor regrets. Here was C
4–5	general glow of satisfaction] suffusion of cheerfulness B
5	compounded] concocted BC
6	as admiration] as of admiration BC
6	doubts] doubts and fears C
8	appealing] interesting BC
9	Mme. de Mauves] the lonely lady of Saint-Germain C
16	observed] admired C
17–18	better this matter was ordered] better they ordered this matter AB; better (than anywhere else) they ordered this matter C
19–20	asked the waiter] the waiter blandly asked C
20	vine] cluster BC
23	linen, in] linen and in C
27	to] with BC
30	and to] and finally to C
32	Longmore,] Our young man C
34	opposite to] facing C
35	our hero] Longmore C
36	had no great relish for] was but half-charmed by C
37	bolder colouring] braver complexion C
41	lazy] idle C
42	interrupted him occasionally] interrupting him fitfully C
315 : 1	seemed to deepen his eloquence] appeared to have the effect of launching him again C
4	she would] she doubtless would C
14	Longmore] In the author of this tribute Longmore C
14–15	M. de Mauves ... this vigorous tribute] Richard de Mauves. The lady to whom it had been rendered C
18	perceived Longmore] became aware of his wife's young friend C
19	the young man's] this spectator's C
21	with great gravity] all imperturbably C
24	about] for C

24–5	the only ... The atmosphere] all he cared for in the world now was Madame de Mauves. The air C
29–30	unsparing harshness] indignity BC
31–2	it seemed to him that] om. BC
32–3	reflection a woefully halting] reflection appear a woefully halting B; stiff resistance a terribly inferior C
34–5	the sense ... on his journey] this happy sense of choosing to go straight back BC
37	was not sure, even, that] wasn't even sure C
38	feel that it was by no] show how little by any C
39	that Mme. de Mauves was alone] Madame de Mauves was alone so C
39	harshness] ugliness AB
42–3	disappointment] the sense of her mistake C
316:2–3	packed his valise that evening,] waited for the morrow BC
3	he wished immensely to hear] he longed immensely for C
5	Mme. de Mauves] the mistress of the house C
6–7	walking in] walking a little way in C
7	little] small C
10	for] om. C
11	he was ... with her] had presently taken the hand he held out C
12	looking at him fixedly] with her beautiful eyes on him C
17	was annoyed] took his reappearance with no pleasure C
18	perceived] noted C
19	altered. It told him that] changed. It showed him C
21	that] the C
22	of which ... to him] ruling her before all things else C
23	it] her C
24	she] om. C
24	beating] beat C
25	know her secrets] touch her secret C
26	contracted] clouded C
26–7	given ... responsibility] surrounded her with complications C
27	commonplace] colourless C
31	He ... at her] He inclined himself to her, almost pulling up again, C
31	which] that C
36	happy if you're not] happy, you know, when you are as little so as I make you out C
37	see such a ... your eyes] see such an unfathomable sadness in your eyes B; only feel helpless and sore about you C
38	three] those C
38–9	the world] life C

40	absolutely] very BC
43	you; and when] you. When C
317:1	compressed] stupidly stifled C
1	explode. But if you] explode. However,' he went on, 'if you C
4	*my* devoted respect] this devoted respect of mine BC
7–9	immobility. Rather ... cheek. It told] immobility—immobility save for the appearance by the time he had stopped speaking of a flush in her guarded clearness. Such as it was it told C
9	that] om. C
10	instant] moment C
11–12	looked at him ... excessive emotion] they uttered a plea for non-insistence that unspeakably touched him C
14	overcame her calmness,] baffled this pretence, a convulsion shook her for ten seconds C
19	assured him that] convinced him C
22	faced] encountered B; dealt with C
22	endure] bear up under C
23	my belief,] what is the matter with you! BC
25	ventured] presumed C
27–8	with a kind ... promised] as under the constraint of this appeal, but it promised him C
28	But suddenly perceiving] Noting, however, C
30–2	in impatient ... seemed to urge] with a resigned grace while the young man, silent before her and watching her, took from her the mute assurance C
32	must be] must at least be C
34–5	a supreme ... isolation] an intense impression of your loneliness BC
37–8	I sometimes ... of rage] I ask myself with vain rage C
40	'I like] She waited a little; she looked down, straight before her. 'I like C
42	that] om. C
43	I'm romantic] I'm too romantic and always was C
318:1	a most] an BC
2	which] and BC
2	read contentedly] read prose contentedly BC
2–3	thought that all the prose was] supposed all the prose to be C
8	wonder ... didn't lead] wonder that my false point of view hasn't led BC
13–14	now in the distance like a shadow] now, far off, a vague deceptive form C
14	slowly] om. C
19	"isolation,"] loneliness BC
27	an air of] reserve and C

28 quickly, as if talking were] quickly and as if talk were at last C

30 very contemptible] of very little importance C

32 whether it was] whether it were B; if it were C

34–5 leading off the dance] scrambling for precedence B; scrambling to outdo each other C

36 losses] troubles BC

38 tragical] dolorous BC

43 Mme. de T] —well of a lady I'll call Madame de T C

319:3 M. de V.—in two words] M. de V. was—well, in two words again C

8–9 was falling into a state of mind] had taken a turn of spirits C

11 place] house BC

12 a sort of] a conscious C

13 A sort of] A conscious C

13 Longmore repeated] Longmore expressively repeated C

15 people, of most] people,' she made prompt answer—'of most C

17 a compromise] compromises C

17–19 clinging to ... Mme. de Mauves] who had managed to invent one, I should think it questionable friendship to expose its weak side.' Madame de Mauves B; who had managed to arrive at one I should think myself not urgently called to expose its weak side.' But she C

18 me] one A

20 smiled ... mitigate their] laughed all amicably, as if to mitigate their too C

21 forbid,' said Longmore, 'that one] forbid that one B; forbid one C

22 to offer. And yet] to offer,' said Longmore. And yet B; to offer,' Longmore returned. 'And yet C

22 a vision] the dream C

33 of visions] of such dazzling visions C

34 reality] reality we happen to be in for C

36 reality ... has very] reality *you* "happen to be in for" has, if I'm not in error, very C

39–40 that it was] it C

40 to which ... to defer] of which it was impossible to make light B; of which she mightn't make light C

41 Philosophy,] Ah philosophy? C

41 said] echoed C

320:1 dogged ... inexpugnable] dogged, obstinate, clinging BC

3 one for] one yourself for C

3 say it] speak C

4 will] may C

5 me from] me also from C

7	cried Longmore. 'We are] her friend returned with high emphasis—'that proves we're C
8	I shall] I too shall ABC
8	never do anything fine] never cut a great romantic figure C
9–10	this inexpugnable ... describe] this unaccommodating organ B; the unaccommodating organ we speak of C
10	fine] really good C
12	invincible] inexpugnable B; beyond being "squared" C
13	her fancy] she BC
13	sarcasm] tone C
17	Longmore] he C
20	said Euphemia directly, and] she said at once; with which she C
21	it] without seeing C
22	advanced into sight] came into view C
25	his thumb was thrust] had thrust his thumb C
26	an air ... serenity] the air of a man thinking at his ease C
28	Longmore ... impertinent] to Longmore his surprise seemed impertinent B; his surprise had for Longmore even the pitch of impertinence C
29	Longmore's eye sharply for] the young man's own look sharply C
33	should have] should at once have C
33	she answered gravely] she immediately answered C
34	Mr. Longmore's return] such a pleasure C
35	become] turned C
35	that this was] this to be C
36	a stormy parting] some commotion C
37	he said] he said to her husband C
37	last evening] back last night C
38	smiled ... urbanity] seemed to express such satisfaction as could consort with a limited interest C
39	welcome you] make you welcome C
41–321:2	Mme. de Mauves ... companion] She pursued her homeward course with her friend, neither of them pretending much not to consent to appear silent. The Count's few moments with them had both chilled Longmore and angered him, casting a shadow across a prospect which had somehow, just before, begun to open and almost to brighten C
321:1	driving back] reabsorbing AB
3	Euphemia] his companion C
5–7	frankness, but ... Longmore wondered] disposition to talk, though nothing betrayed she had recognized his making a point at her expense. Yet if matters were none

	the less plainly at a crisis between them he could but wonder C
5	frankness] disposition to talk B
5	accepted] acknowledged B
7	Euphemia's] her C
8	an absolute] some practical protest or some C
11	ineradicable ... which] intense consideration C
12	him] him she entertained C
13–14	one's being] one's self B; herself C
14	Her husband] Her clever husband C;
14	rigid!] stiff! B; prim. C
14	a poet] a stupid poet C
16	a kind of] om. C
18	spirit] logic BC
20–1	that they ... into worship] their signifying that where ambition was so vain the next best thing to it was the very ardour of hopelessness C
22	Mme. de Mauves] She C
28	coquetry ... him blush] assured attack that fairly intimidated him C
28–9	surprised] doubtless not as reassured as he ought to have been C
30	deportment at] want of resource during C
30	meaning] being prepared BC
31	uneasiness] distress C
32	Brussels,' ... 'by] Brussels by BC
32	forest.'] forest?' she said. B; forest?' she archly asked. C
35	stared and laughed] was infinitely struck C
35	young man] person at all expérimentée C
38–9	who was vexed at his blushes,] vexed at his lack of superior form C
40	am I?' ... her fan] have I to do with it?' Madame Clairin brightly wailed C
41	had your] had, other gentlemen, your C
322:3	'To her] She swung open her great fan. 'To her C
4	talk. Mme. Clairin] tone of this conversation. Madame Clairin B; tone of this conversation. The speaker C
5	moment,] little C
5	turned ... Euphemia] took in their hostess C
7	she was ... slight droop] the charming creature received with a droop C
7	her] om. C
8	absently wandering] that strayed C
9	she murmured suddenly] Madame Clairin suddenly exhaled C
11	best French] most inspired French C
13–14	it seemed ... to appear] it seemed delicate to appear not

	B; it was of a sublime suitability to appear not C
14	his friend's] Madame de Mauves' B
15	This cost] The sacrifice cost C
16	not the most deferential] exactly not the most patient C
17	believed, the] believed, deep within the circle round which he could only hover, the C
21	Euphemia's temper] this lady's composition C
24	respect her freedom] allow her to do as she liked BC
25–6	her freedom ... 'Thank you.'] she should like, after all, to see nothing more in his interest in her than might be re-paid by a murmured 'Thank you.' B; she should like, after all, to see nothing more in his interest in her than might be repaid by mere current social coin. C
27	he called again] at last he went back C
30	a sweet] such a C
31	which filled him with] as might warrant C
32	come out ... the day in] renew with him for an hour or two the exploration of C
32–3	But Mme. Clairin, with her hair] Her sister-in-law, how-ever, whose hair was C
35	Euphemia's] his mistresses's C
36	she was] she begged to be excused, she was C
36	and unable] and was unable B
37–9	that he looked ... him a glance] just how disappointed he looked and just what Madame Clairin thought of it, and this consciousness determined in him an attitude C
323:2	she had the means] knew exactly how C
6–7	said Longmore, uncompromisingly] he returned with as little grace C
11	that] om. C
13	said Longmore] he still dryly allowed C
14	Mme. Clairin ... and then—] His companion waited ever so little to bring out: C
15	she demanded.] om. C
16	roundabout] insidious C
17	that it ... if even] as to make him feel that even C
19	asked, frowning and blushing] cried with a flushed frown C
20	Mme. Clairin flushed] Her own colour rose at the question C
23	Mr. Longmore] monsieur C
23	said] returned C
25	I wish to] A stupid one of my own—possibly!—has been to C
25	which] that C
28	Longmore burned in silence] Longmore assented with a gesture AB; 'Oh!'—Longmore made short work of it C

29–30   Mme. Clairin ... Nevertheless—] She seemed to measure
           his intelligence a little uncertainly.   C

30–1   she continued] she nevertheless continued   C

31   conjectures ... dissatisfaction.] conception of the grounds
           of her discontent?   C

32   Conjecture ... causes] It hasn't required much forming.
           The grounds   C

33   with my own eyes] have simply stared me in the face   C

34   'I know ... My brother] Madame Clairin considered a
           moment with her eyes on him. 'Yes—*ces choses-là se
           voient.* My brother.   C

34   is] has the deplorable habit of falling   C

35   other women—with another woman] another woman
           AB;   other women   C

36   I permit] I only permit   C

37   I would have] I would either have   BC

38–9   it, before this] it   BC

43–324 : 1   family traditions ... view of things] history—that of a
           race—has cultivated in them the sense for high political
           solutions   C

324 : 1   Mme. Clairin] She   C

1–2   her family traditions were] the history of her race was   C

3   'Listen,' ... 'There has] But she clearly saw her course.
           'There has   C

3   De Mauves who] *galant homme* among us, I fear, who,   C

4   wife the] wife, even when she was very charming, the   C

5   a shame] not a very edifying one   C

6   a shame with such a pedigree] scandals with pedigrees—if
           you can't have them with attenuations   C

6–7   The De Mauves are real Frenchmen] Our men have been
           real Frenchmen   B; Our men have been Frenchmen of
           France   C

8   worthy of them] of no meaner blood   C

8–9   in our Château de Mauves;] at our house in Auvergne;   B;
           at our poor charming old house—   C

10   them had] them ever had   C

11–12   was guilty ... for you!] ever consented to an indiscretion—
           allowed herself, I mean, to be talked about. *Voilà comme
           elles ont su s'arranger.*   C

13   managed] did it   C

14   *femmes d'esprit*] dear brave women of wit   C

16   put a ... their hearts] touched up that quarter with just
           such another brush   C

17   fine traditions, and] great traditions, and   B; great trad-
           itions and charming precedents, I hold, and   C

18–19   interrupt them ... with her] pretend to alter them, and
           should hang her photograph, with her   B; pretend to

alter them—all to hang her modern photograph and her
C

20   fine ladies] great-grandmothers   C

20   A De Mauves must be a De Mauves] a De Mauves must
be of the old race   B; She should fall into line, she should
keep up the tone   C

24   Mme. de Mauves herself] my sister-in-law herself   B; our
charming, but not accommodating, friend   C

25   paused and] paused, again she   C

25   her fan] her great modern fan, which clattered like the
screen of a shop-window   C

25   conform] keep up the tone   C

26   said with amazing audacity] prodigiously repeated   C

27   Longmore's reply ... 'Ah!'] Longmore felt himself gape,
but he gasped an 'Ah!' to cover it.   C

28   pious retrospect] historical retrospect   B; dip into the
family annals   C

30   sister] *belle-sœur*   C

31–2   the 'Imitation.'] free-thinking books.   BC

32   remarked] permitted myself any observation   B; permitted myself, you may believe, the least observation   C

32–3   I've ... with it] I can't accept it as the last word either of
taste or of tact   C

34   wander,] stray away   BC

34   deserves her] deserves no small part of her   C

35   a goose] a pure noodle   C

41–2   the scene was terrible] there was a grand scene   C

43   my brother] my poor brother   C

43–325:1   called to account] hauled over the coals   C

325:2   injured sweethearts] injured mistresses   B; angry ladies
who weren't their wives   C

4   instinctively] now instinctively   B; now, impulsively,   C

5   he groaned.] om.   C

8   Mme. Clairin's narrative] the story to which he had been
treated   C

10–11   politically. I wish to] politically. We have always been a
political family. I wish to   B; scientifically. We've always
been capable of ideas. I want to   C

12   Euphemia] his wife   C

13   think. You're] think,' the young man said, 'You're   C

15   shrugged her shoulders] took it calmly   C

15   there] ever   C

16   politician who was] peacemaker   C

17   Nay] Ah no   BC

17   said ... tone] Longmore protested   C

18   politician] peacemaker   C

20   Mme. Clairin] She   C

20–1	eyed Longmore sharply,] while her fine eyes kept her visitor in view; she C
21–2	with an ... compassion] as with a certain compassionate patience C
24	Mme. Clairin] madam C
24–5	the young man ... candour] he resolutely returned C
27–9	Longmore ... piece of irony] She was wonderful—she waited a moment C
29	quietly exclaimed] then effectively brought out C
30	Longmore was silent awhile] For a moment he thought of getting up, but he decided to stay C
32	devoted friendship] devoted and most respectful friendship C
35	suppose,' ... 'that she talks] suppose that she talks B; imagine she talks C
36	scenes?'] scenes?' cried Longmore. B; scenes?' Longmore cried. C
37	Mme. Clairin] His companion C
38	Longmore ... his head] he but ambiguously threw up his hands C
41	sort of] om. C
41–2	into which he was being forced] in which he found himself B; into which he had been drawn C
326:1	which] that C
3	monstrously in love] absurdly entangled C
4	a De Mauves] my brother BC
5	unsanctified] irregular BC
5	spoke] dictated his words BC
5–6	Listen, madam] Listen to me, madam BC
10	pretty] charming C
12	the poor fellow,] your poor compatriot C
17	said] amazingly pursued C
18	Mr. Longmore] monsieur C
18	smile] wondrous strained grimace C
20	upon] on C
21	He] Her husband C
21–2	Longmore asked slowly] he asked C
23	greatest] most perfect C
27	her husband] Richard C
30	Mme. Clairin] Longmore's friend C
31	Euphemia] My *belle-sœur* C
32	she] om. C
34	Longmore] the young man C
41	Longmore ... passing his] her visitor had slowly averted himself; he passed his C
327:1	Longmore was deeply] he was much C
2	flatter] congratulate BC

4	reflective] colourless C
5–6	seemed provokingly subterranean] were unsociably private C
6	would] could be BC
7	her sister] their difficult friend C
9	boldly] nevertheless bravely C
12–13	Longmore started ... to demur] He had a start but he controlled himself, speaking quietly enough C
16	insulted] wronged C
17	opportunity! But] opportunity!' she went on. 'But C
20	smile] smile—you're very nice then BC
22	'Yes,' he said ... And] He remained a moment face to face with her, but his expression didn't change. 'I shall do myself justice,' he, however, after an instant made answer; and C
24	unobserved, in the open air] unobserved and outside C
27	gazing away] casting his eyes C
27	the] om. C
29–30	he could ... or a joy] could have given no straight name to his agitation C
30	joyous] a joy C
31	knocked down across] cleared out of BC
31	path; his] path and his C
32	seemed] appeared AB; om. C
33	But his ... somehow] But it was a pain in the degree in which his freedom somehow resolved itself C
34	of] that C
35	inhabiting] inhabited C
35	this] the C
36	his] om. C
37	But she was there] There she was, at any rate C
37	circumstance] circumstances BC
328:5	deepen his admiration] quicken his attachment C
6–7	feeling that ... was to] conviction that gross accident—all odious in itself—would C
6	unlovely] odious B
7–8	relief, that] relief for him that C
8	kind of] om. C
9	festival] feast C
9	random] hazard C
9–10	and found] finding C
12	charm which] charm for which ABC
13	for] om. ABC
14	Longmore] He C
17	your] his C
18	your] his C
18	sort of] om. C

19	sunbeams ... than gold] sheen of silver, not of gold, was in the work-a-day sun C
26	it] om. C
27	which] that C
28	sunshine] clearness C
29	was soothing] was somehow sociable C
38	which] that C
39	that] om. C
41	ripening] tinted C
329:5	a rather] rather a C
5	homely] friendly C
7	fields and crops] yellowing grain C
8	suggested ... had very] conveyed no strained nor high-pitched message, had C
9–10	seemed ... from] communicated the sense of C
10	to express] expressed C
11	to say] declared C
13–14	falling a-wondering] beginning to wonder C
16	is] was C
16	had a waking dream] dreamt, awake, C
17	strolling] who strolled C
17–18	and pulling] and who pulled C
18	blossoming] fruit-laden BC
19	feeling] quite C
21	a sentimental] the romantic C
22	he] om. C
27–8	asceticism ... authority he] sacrifice, sacrifice for sacrifice's sake, to the authority of which he C
28	an unquestioning respect] due deference C
30	resolve] ardour C
34	reverberation of a joy] possession of a treasure C
37	a cloth to dry] a moist cloth C
38	seemed to see] might have imagined C
41	whom] of whom C
41	observed] took note C
41	preoccupation] high distraction C
43–330:2	with the element ... to be respectable] with the un-established and unexpected in life—the element often gazed at with a certain wistfulness out of the curtained windows even of the highest respectability C
330:1	life, which provokes a great deal of] life—that element which provokes so much B
4	very happy] contented C
5	of a] of even a AB
6	cynical philosopher] exasperated reasoner C
6	blonde] yellow C
9–10	landlady ... smile] landlady, while something pleasant

played in his face   C

13 soft contentment] ideal ease   C

14 *tarte à la crème*] *croûte aux fruits*   BC

16–17 a-wondering ... had made of it] to admiring and comparing, to picking up, off by the stream-side, the objects represented   C

16 off] away   B

22 whether it was] if it weren't probably   C

23 an art] one of the arts   B; the arts   C

23 a passion] one of the passions   B; the passions   C

24–5 He picked] He had picked   C

26 called,] called familiarly   C

28 to have] cultivate   C

31–2 seemed to say ... as happy] represented almost aggressively to Longmore that she was as pleased   C

33–4 man; and turning away, he] man, who, turning away,   C

36 was Claudine] might Claudine be   C

40 a Frenchwoman needs to be] suffices almost any Frenchwoman   C

42–3 which seemed ... by herself] that made walking as light a matter as being blown—and this even though she happened to be at the moment not a little over-weighted   C

43–331 : 1 which she seemed ... with her] involved in her pursuit of her friend   C

331 : 2 tapestry] needlework   ABC

5 but] and   C

6 she dropped] dropping   C

6 uttered a half-smiling] marking this with a half-smiling   C

7 with a bow] om.   BC

9–10 it seemed ... overburdened] he recognized her as too obliging to the young man who had preceded her   C

15–16 said. 'It's too heavy] risked; 'there's too much of it   C

21 sweetness] accommodation   C

21 Longmore] our friend   C

25 one] to   C

26–7 days, with the ... unshadowed] days by a shady stream, with a comrade all amiability, to say nothing of art and books and a wide unmenaced   C

30 bliss] delight   C

31 are] were   C

32 remarked] noted   C

35 well-favoured young man] well-favoured and well dressed young man   C

39–40 seemed to be in no] couldn't have felt   C

40 vivacious] free   C

332 : 1 like] himself   C

2   it was a very clever] in it an easy   C
5   Longmore had gone, and] he had left them, meant to   C
6   stream] river   ABC
6   one to] one of these lucky persons to   C
11   and in the doorway met] where, in the doorway, he met   C
11   coming back] returning   C
14   broad smile] free smile   C
14   too broad] too free   C
16   he has ... talent] he's *d'une jolie force*   C
17   picture was very pretty] picture's very charming   C
17–18   was prettier still] is more charming still   C
20   said Longmore;] Longmore pleaded.   C
26   was puzzled for a moment] was at first puzzled   C
28   shrugged her shoulders] took it responsibly   C
29–30   themselves for an] for   C
31   She's ... woman] She's *gentille*—but *gentille*   C
33   Who is she] Who then is so distinguished a young woman   C
35   a true lady] a *vraie dame*   C
37–8   she's been ... content herself] she has had all her life to **put up**   C
41   cook] do   C
333 : 1–2 whether there ... weakness] in which of their forms of perversity there was most merit   C
5   which philosophers call] pronounced by philosophers   C
6   Every now and then] Now and then   C
10   gossip cast] gossip had cast   BC
13   in] of   BC
15   intensity to her glance—] grace to her surrender
16   God's sunlight] the process of the sun   ABC
17   such a rapturous union] so clear a harmony   C
18   such a perfect accord] so perfect union   C
20–1   spiritually ... had the soul] only a graver equivalent of the young lover and that rustling Claudine was a lighter sketch   C
22   Mme. de Mauves] Euphemia de Mauves   A; Euphemia B; Madame de Mauves   C
27   to conceive ... hastening] mentally to see his friend at Saint-Germain hurry   C
29   do] hurry   C
30   him] om.   C
33   he slept ... vivid] he slept moreover he had a strange and vivid   C
38   the gleam] a gleam   C
39   and hurried forward] on which he hastened   C
40   opposite] other   C
41–2   were opposite each other] had come to opposite places   C

43	motion] sign C
43	should] must C
334:1	greatly] unutterably C
2	that] om. C
2	that] how C
3	plunge] breast it C
3	that] how C
17	café] restaurant BC
19	his dream] this vision C
20–1	ingenuity] arrangement C
21	rather] om. C
30	told] repeated to C
31	cause of suffering] annoyance BC
35	questionings] ambiguities C
36	he] om. C
37	whether it was not] whether it were not B; if it weren't C
37	that] om. C
37	might have] had C
335:1	was beating] beat C
1	so that] so fast that BC
3–4	empty, with] empty and with C
5–6	and Longmore stepped] so that Longmore immediately stepped BC
7	up and down] its length C
9	coil, like that of a person] coil and as if she were C
10	Longmore, seemed slightly startled] her friend, showed some surprise C
11–12	He looked at her, tried] He tried, with his eyes on her C
13	silent, gazing] gazing at her BC
14	he dared not] mightn't C
15–16	could see ... eyes were] felt her eyes C
16	he] om. C
18	felt as if] was sure C
20	standing looking at] dumb there before C
21	that] om. C
21	her] om. C
24	in] with C
28	was silent a moment,] waited again C
29–30	stood ... against] leaned closer to her, against C
35	sure that] assured C
37–8	chilled the ardour] hampered the desire C
38–40	the dozen ... reverential silence] all his imagined freedom of speech about it to a final hush of wonder C
41	early] antique BC
336:1	that] om. C
3	evening,' she said. 'I have a] evening—and I've a C

6	I have been feeling all day] the case has been present to me C
7	the day] every minute of the day C
9	something to] something important to C
10	said abruptly] resumed with decision C
11	started and shifted] gave an uneasy shift to C
14	have] feel C
15	laugh;] laugh, all awkwardly— C
15	that] because C
16	mockery of coldness] irony of detachment C
16–17	continued without heeding him.] went on in her way: C
20	I have hoped] I've certainly hoped C
22	'You do] There was something troubled in her face that seemed all the while to burn clearer. 'You do C
22	reason,] fairness of mind C
24	that] om. C
25–6	cried Longmore ... in the world] the young man cried. 'My fairness of mind? Of all the question-begging terms!' he laughed. 'The only thing for one's mind to be fair to C
26	*feeling*] the thing one *feels* BC
27	gravely] hard C
29	her look was ... it was] if she was urgent she was yet C
30	laid] came near enough to lay C
30	upon] on C
32–3	your feeling, however, nearly enough] what you feel, however, nearly enough B; enough, however, of your probable attitude C
34	it gives] your sincerity gives C
34	urgent] intense C
38	very high] high C
39	you, I] you, you see I C
39	seriously. It] seriously,' she explained. 'It C
40	that] om. C
41	which] that C
43	with] om. C
337:1	with emphasis] with all emphasis C
3	suffer—I should suffer keenly] take it, I assure you, very hard indeed C
9–11	manner grew ... a kind of passion] tone became, to his sense, extraordinary, and she offered the odd spectacle of a beautiful woman preaching reason with the most communicative and irresistible passion C
11–12	confused, dazzled, almost] dazzled, but mystified and C
13	presence there] presence and effect there C
14	seemed] om. C
14	mockery] contradiction ABC
16	eyes] brow C

17	Longmore] he C
18–19	rapturous ... Were her] perverse imagination. Were not her C
19	soft severity] high impossible rigour C
19–20	delusive spell, meant] challenge to his sincerity, a mere precaution of her pride, meant C
20	was this] wasn't this C
21	reality, the only law] law, the only thing to take account of C
22	that she was watching] her watch C
24	a tear in each of them] them fill with strange tears C
24–5	suggestion ... to die] sophistry of his great desire for her knew itself touched as a bubble is pricked; it died C
36–7	simply friendship!] well, simply that I like you so. C
38	had dismissed] had, in the horrible phrase, got rid of C
39	wisdom] wisdom and the excellence of your own taste C
40	The fullness—the fullness,] Ah wisdom and taste! C
40	cried Longmore] the poor young man wailed C
42	upon] on C
43	to] to do that BC
338: 1	hear you say that] listen to your horrible and unnatural lucidity C
2	horribly irritated] merely sore and sick C
2	it is not easy to] I don't BC
5	half realized. No, I] half-realized,' she returned with no drop in her ardour. 'No, I C
6	angry] feeling a great pain C
6	serious] great C
7	as] om. C
8	You want ... never has] As a creature who never has AB; As a stupid brute who has never C
9	exist! A] exist!' he broke in. 'A C
9	knew] could know C
10	left] could leave C
10	regretting] for ever missing C
12–13	become a cold sternness] grown sharp and almost hard C
14–16	foot, in deep ... was about] foot and without consideration now; so that as the effect of it he felt his assurance finally quite sink. This then she took from him, withholding in consequence something she had meant C
16	turned away again] moved off afresh C
17–18	looking away into] with her face to C
18	It seemed ... guessed] She assumed that C
19–20	his vague ... her] this mute pressure, he let everything go but the rage of a purpose somehow still to please her C
23	liked ... wish] must have 'liked' him indeed, as she said, to wish C

25–6 friendship ... Longmore's soul] tenderness still in her dreadful consistency, his spirit C

27 breathing a] breathe C

27 The words] Her profession C

28 ardour; they were] eagerness; it was C

28 warmth themselves] ardour themselves AB; eagerness itself C

28–9 they were a present happiness] it was a present reward and would somehow last C

29–30 with a feeling ... he might] as with the sense of a gage that he might sublimely yet C

33–4 posted there, watching him] framed in the opening as if, though just arriving on the scene, she too were already aware of its interest C

34–5 eavesdropping,] having watched them C

35–6 Longmore to his hostess] one to the other C

37 that,' she said, 'one] that one C

39 turned round, but she] turned to her, but C

40–1 had extraordinary eloquence] shone with a lustre that struck him as divine C

42 they seemed ... this kind:] it translated itself to something that would do. C

43 you have to] you have wanted to C

43 which] om. C

339:1 can't,] can't begin to! C

2 be herself] be triumphantly herself C

3 intimate that ... Mme. Clairin] intimate—yet this too all decently—how little that self was of Madame Clairin's particular swelling measure C

4–5 anything which would seem natural] anything then that might seem probable or *prévu* C

5 cane] stick BC

7–8 and departed] and found his way, with tingling ears, out of the place C

12 that Euphemia] his friend C

12 laid on] given B

13 a kind of ... that she had] an inspiring commission, and that she had AB; a heavy charge and had C

14 largely] handsomely C

14 assentingly] complacently C

15 perfectly] thoroughly ABC

19–20 absolute; he ... it no more] absolute—he knew he could no more alter it C

20–1 veil ... starry sky] transpose the constellations A; pull down the constellations B; pull down one of the constellations C

21–2 wondered what] wondered to what C

22–3	that she ... sense of duty,] that she had so attached her-self to. A sense of duty B; she had so dedicated herself. A conception of duty C
24	offence] outrage BC
24	trample out] stifle BC
24	Good heavens] Great heaven C
24	thought,] groaned; C
27	loathsome] detestable ABC
28	which masked a shrinking hope] which contained the germ of a shrinking hope AB; that still kept the door of pos-sibility open C
34	Mme. de Mauves] this one C
35	some fine temper, not of a base one] the noblest, and con-tain nothing base B; the noblest, must contain nothing base C
35–7	a dim, overwhelming ... her character] his hard impres-sion that endless constancy was all her law C
37	which] that C
39	that's] and that's C
340:2	the forest] forest BC
3–4	hers unpledged] hers before this had happened B; her own in earlier days C
4	living keenly] living, really, C
5	a petition ... resolve] such a request from such a woman still ringing in one's ears B; such a faith even in one's self still flung over one by such hands C
6	which] om. C
7	shape] form C
7–8	Longmore's imagination swelled] Longmore's imagination expanded B; His imagination embraced it C
8–9	Mme. de Mauve's] his friend's C
10	as it wandered] wandering BC
12	felt ... asking] seemed to feel her ask C
16	that she had] she had had C
17	love—to plead] love, give it to her to plead C
19	he] om. C
20	he] om. C
22	delay and try] waiting and to try C
24	matter of ... Mme. de Mauves] matter of beautiful friend-ship with him for her C
25	he gain] he himself gain C
26	He flung] Well, he flung C
28	the] om. C
28	that he would] to C
29	easier to leave] easiest to go C
30	ask a] ask for a C
30	it] this C

32	seemed to see her standing] saw her stand C
33	and looking] saw her look C
36–7	boulevards and looked at] boulevard and paused sightlessly before C
39	felt] felt afresh C
39–40	that it . . . world into] the dusty dreary lonely world to C
40–1	was turning him away] had consigned him C
42	boulevards] centre of motion C
43	on the great . . . a café] before a café door, on the great plain of hot asphalt C
341 : 1	came on] arrived C
2–3	that peculiar . . . say] that evening grimace of hers that seems to tell C
3	windows and] plate glass and of C
3	and] om. C
4	that] how C
5	scruples drugged] delicacies perverted C
7	swarming city] great preoccupied place C
10	without . . . out] without its occupant descending B; without sign from its occupant C
11–12	one is apt to imagine] the *flâneur* figures C
14	M. de Mauves] Richard de Mauves C
18	may say, with] might say C
21	perceived] noticed C
22–3	change in . . . vague smile] shade of difference in his careless gait, advanced to the accompaniment of a thin recognition C
26	we may call] he might have regarded C
26	Baron] Count C
27–8	had another . . . But as] had had another call to meet than the call of disgust. But now, as C
28–9	deep in . . . hated him] deep in his heart that he abhorred him AB; abhorrence well up C
29	noticed] made out C
30	shadow upon . . . placidity] cloud on this nobleman's superior clearness C
30	his] a C
31	that] the shoe C
31–3	the shoe pinched . . . own self possession] pinching *him*, mingled with the resolve to be blank and unaccommodating, enabled him to meet the occasion with due promptness C
32	provokingly] exasperatingly AB
35	greetings, which] remarks that C
36	make their . . . gracious] lend grace to their encounter C
37	that the Baron] the Count C
37	revelations] intimations B; various interventions C

38	that] om. C
39	that ... his eyes] of something grim in his own New York face C
40	the Baron] him C
40–1	him to read it] it to be read there C
42	Longmore ... betrayed] his wife's so oddly, so more than naturally (wouldn't it be?) detached friend with an intentness that betrayed C
342:3	would] might C
3–4	Longmore seemed ... measure] these virtues shone out of our young man less engagingly or reassuringly C
4–5	for the ... and he] the shadow at any rate fell darker across the brow of his critic, who C
5–6	as he lighted] while lighting C
7	Longmore thought] he accordingly judged C
10	lucidity—truth-telling] clarity, settled truth-telling C
11	nursery fibs] primitive fibs B; notion of a subterfuge C
13	saw] had at last both to recognize and to miss C
15–16	judged him ... threatened him] took possession of him, they laid him out, they measured him in that state of flatness C
17	had ever treated him] had perhaps ever treated any member of his family before C
17	Baron's] Count's C
17–18	make no ... himself, and] provide for a positive state of ease on the part of no one save himself, but C
18–20	looks were ... own achievements] appearances perhaps not appreciable to the vulgar meant anything, primed as for some prospect of pleasure more than Parisian C
20	provincial] barbarian ABC
21–2	puzzled ... too often.] never really quite satisfied his occasional host, but was he now, for a climax, to leave him almost gaping? C
23	M. de Mauves ... and he] M. de Mauves, as if hating to seem preoccupied, C
24	look] seem C
25	uttered] threw off C
25–7	cold commonplace ... at his ease] perfunctory allusion to the crisis—the political—which enabled Longmore to reply with perfect veracity that, with other things to think about, he had had no attention to spare for it C
26	an easy] a fair B
27	provokingly] aggressively AB
28–9	was far from ... him good, as] was in truth far from secure against rueful reflection. The Count's ruffled state was a comfort so C
29–31	a want of ... jealousy of himself] the possibility that the

lady in the coupé might be proving too many for him; but it ministered to no vindictive sweetness for Longmore so far as it should perhaps represent rising jealousy   C

33-4   in some of ... the Baron] on one of its sides it may sometimes almost look generous. It glimmered upon him odiously M. de Mauves   C

35   proposed 'arrangement'] political compact   ABC

35-6   that it ... tolerable in the] how far more tolerable it would be in   C

36-7   his continued ... repentance] him as always impertinent than to think of him as occasionally contrite   C

37-40   sat for ... however by] pretended meanwhile for half an hour to outsit each other conveniently; and the end—at that rate—might have been distant had not the tension in some degree yielded to   C

38   meagre] stinted   AB

39   merciless] ferocious   AB

40   The frigid interview was broken] These rigid courtesies were interrupted   A; These thin amenities were interrupted   B

43-343 : 1   Baron's ... same fashion] Count's garments in some detail, then appeared to refer restlessly to his own   C

343 : 2   languidly] resignedly   C

5-6   said M. de Mauves ... infantine drawl] said with an infantine drawl this specimen of an order Longmore felt he had never had occasion so intimately to appreciate   C

7   and] he   C

9   irresolutely] awkwardly   ABC

10   said dryly] appeared to find some difficulty in saying   C

12   Longmore answered, looking] And our friend looked   C

17   latter] latter's   C

18   formally] stiffly   ABC

20-1   packed his ... and wandered] the next day wandered   BC

22   for evening] for the evening   C

22   for] om.   C

23-4   pale, pink, reflected lights] pale reflected amber lights   C

25   mild] humble   ABC

25   his fortune] appointed him   C

26-7   on the terrace ... place was] seated by the great walk under a tree and alone. The hour made the place   C

28   on the] of the   B; of their   C

29   shadow in which she sat] shadow   C

29-30   with ... immediately] almost with no pretence of not having believed herself already rid of him, and he at once   C

31-2   evening—that ... for a moment] evening, but must first bid her farewell. Her face lighted a moment, he fancied, C

31	good-bye] farewell AB
33	nothing ... towards distant] nothing, only turning it off to far C
33	as it] which C
34	its] om. C
35	added : 'that] added. 'That C
38	It's] That is B; That's C
39	and] inspirations, C
40	continued ... seriousness] pursued after a pause, though as if it had before this quite been settled between them C
344 : 5	answering] answering at first C
7	he asked at last, abruptly] he simply asked at last C
9	Auvergne] my husband's old home C
10	America] *my* old one C
10	present.'] present,' the young man added. C
13	At last ... was going] But suddenly, as if aware of her going too C
14	Good-bye,' she said; 'may] Good-bye. May C
16	and looked at] with his eyes on C
16	passing] at work C
17	return ... pressure] deal in the easy way with her touch C
19	oath not] oath, with which any such case interfered, not C
21	her hand] herself C
21	her shawl,] in her long scarf C
23–4	standing ... figure] there watching her leave him and leave him C
24	it had disappeared,] she was out of sight C
24	rapidly] at once C
28–30	was dressed ... dining out] had dressed as he usually didn't dress for dining at home C
37	of easy courtesy] as of allusion to a large past exercise of the very best taste C
39	Mme. de Mauves] she C
345 : 1	started and] waited, but C
3–4	stared a moment ... 'Had anything] took it—a rare thing for him—with confessed, if momentary, intellectual indigence. But he raised, as it were, the wind. 'Has anything C
9	and he ... wondering] but he remained outside—outside of more things, clearly, than his mere *salle-à-manger* C
10	out upon] forth to C
11	inform him] let him know C
12	the] his C
12	curtly] without hesitation C
13	went in] returned C
14	tardiness] inconsequence C

15–16	on the other ... of wine] he drank on the other hand more wine than usual C
16–17	talk; what ... Twice she] talk, scarcely a convivial sound save the occasional expressive appreciative 'M-m-m!' of Madame Claïrin over the succulence of some dish. Twice this lady C
18–19	with a ... glance] put to her a question she knew she should have to irritate him later on by not being able to answer C
19	replied by] replied, for the present at least, by C
19–20	eyebrows ... shoulders] eyebrows that resembled even to her own humour the vain raising of an umbrella in anticipation of a storm C
27	message] telegram ABC
29	brother] brother's C
32–3	he was the ... 'The American has] this affected her as unexpected indulgence. At last, however, he spoke with a particular harshness. '*Ce jeunne mufle* has C
34	notice,' he said. 'What] notice. What the devil C
35–6	gave free ... at the table] felt thankful for her umbrella C
38–9	her to depart, as if it had] her, after a little, to depart. It had C
40	levity] blankness; but she was—if there was no more to come—getting off easily C
41	down, smoking] down with his cigar C
41	sitting] seated C
42–3	below ... paths] below, wandering, turning, pausing, lingering C
43	became] grew C
346:2	kind of angry sigh] long vague exhalation of unrest C
2	mind] spirit C
5	for a] one C
9	small talk] other topics C
12	she sent to him] she had addressed him C
13	said he] he said C
15	answered] returned C
16	a] om. C
17	given ... advice] cut you out work for which you wouldn't thank me C
18	he said] the young man said C
22	murmured Mrs. Draper]—Mrs. Draper knowingly protested C
22–3	folly is very] folly's often very C
24	go, with a quick nervous movement] go—she somehow annoyed him C
30–1	that she preferred it] she wouldn't have 'liked' it C

36	return] seeing her C
39	very sad] wretched C
40	wretch] scamp C
347 : 3–4	Euphemia's lovely sister-in-law] Euphemia's charming sister-in-law B; that charming sister of the Count's C
6	possessing her friendship] the friendship of such a person C
7	charming] terrible C
8	that] om. C
8–9	proceeded to relate to me what] told me—from his point of view—what C
12	severity, apparently, suited] severity must have suited C
19	learned that] discovered C
25–6	feeling, for which ... strong a name] feeling—a feeling for which awe would be hardly too strong a name AB; feeling—a feeling of wonder, of uncertainty, of awe C

EUGENE PICKERING

Notes:

1. The variants recorded below are based on a collation of the original serial text of the tale (*Atlantic Monthly*, 1874) and its two revised versions in *A Passionate Pilgrim* (1875)—hereinafter mentioned as A—and *The Madonna of the Future* (1879)—hereinafter mentioned as B.

2. The serial text appeared in two instalments: that division is retained in the revised texts.

PART I] I. AB
IN TWO PARTS] om. AB

413:2	play] gaming AB
15	damask divans] silken ottomans B
414:27	and was] and he was B
30–1	rattling cross-fire] chinking complexity B
39	was] were B
43	blonde] yellow B
415:8	imaged] imagined B
27	an absolute novice] a novice B
416:2	fair] happy B
19	urged] pressed B
30	droll] singular B
31	drollery] singularity B
32	last discovered] last I discovered B
417:8	elucidating,—] introducing myself— B
25	phial of poison] sleeping-potion B
35	I'm ... bewildered] I'm dazed and bewildered A; I am rather dazed, rather bewildered B
418:22	upon] on B
28	a huge boyish friendship] one of those friendships of childhood B
33	a prior petition] asking leave B
419:4	like] as B
43	cold] frigid B
420:1–2	to become ... himself] to strive to reproduce so irreproachable a model B
19	for me] some one after me B
33	achieved] recovered AB
421:29	poodle dog, led] poodle-dog that is led B
43	contemn] resist AB
422:9–11	there comes ... to let] that it comes back—this irresistible impulse to take my plunge—to let B
13	intensity] perplexity B

15	trepidation] scruples B
28	seclusion] confinement B
423:4	invitations] provocations B
6	I never ... nay to] I had no hand in B
9	rigid] severe B
17	a precept ... to] a rule of life—as clear as if it had been written out in his beautiful copper-plate hand—adapted to B
33	indeed,' I said, 'for] indeed, for B
33	days, and I] days,' I said, 'and I B
35	cotton] a box of rose-leaves B
39	tender] superior B
424:1	dozen] set of B
1–3	that it ... were married.] that was the way that all marriages were made; I had heard of their being made in heaven, and what was my father but a divinity? B
3	said otherwise] talked about falling in love B
20–1	had a ... advantage] thought of myself but in you B
23	our] my AB
28	myriad] hundred B
30	vain delusion] vulgar theory B
37–8	There was ... summons] This was pretty "steep" as we used to say at school B
40	vain delusion] vulgar theory B
425:2	rest] repose B
35	these many weeks] a long time now B
426:6	demand] request B
17–18	radiant frankness] clear good-humour B
19	you saw then,' he cried, 'that] then you saw that B
24	Verily] Ah B
25–6	in ... declared] she remarked that in a general way B
31	concluded] supposed B
38	puzzled, and smiled] puzzled; he smiled B
427:1–2	might almost doubt it] wouldn't know it B
7	an edge] a point B
15	he repeated ... gently.] om. B
18	with his ... away] joyously B
26	revolving ... history] meditating on his queer biography B
38	sober] timid B
40	decked] dressed up B
428:4	lovely] very sweet B
5	lovely] very sweet B
17	check her ... again] play her game for her again B
19	plays] means to play B
25	command me] that I *must* B
30–1	an obstacle] a barrier B

429:4	I inquired.] om. B
6	in a] with a B
7	a *Trauerspiel*] an *Historisches Trauerspiel* B
24	preoccupied, and irresponsive] preoccupied, he was irresponsive B
26–7	last he ... turned out] last, uttering his thoughts, he announced that Madame Blumenthal had proved to be B
32	and hinted] and he now hinted B
37	regulate] wind up B
38	machinery] machine B
430:6	gamester] gambler B
11–12	play roulette] play at roulette B
14	was] were B
20–1	multifarious ... accomplishments] eager nature and her innumerable accomplishments, B
22	over-eager ... importunate] aggressive B
23	does.] does seem so! B
26–7	penetrating ... perfume of sympathy] sort of fragrant emanation of intelligence and sympathy B
431:2	lovely] charming B
5	stars above ... frog-pond] fog-lamps at sea B
9	which] they B
10	terribly farcical] great rubbish B
10	feel] felt B
11	having ... her; and] having fired off all my guns—they could hurt nobody now if they hit—and B
16–17	She's ... suffered] She has felt and suffered B
18	to a *t*] as if she had made you B
21	me ... formally,] me formally B
25	cried,] spoke B
25	aggression] defiance B
29	took ... retreat] bolted out of the room B
37	had my ... clipped] been disarmed B
42–3	immediate ... to let] immediate, for I wished to let B
43–432:3	without temptation ... hours] alone B
432:4	Pickering] him B
7–8	especial ... soul] especial, of which Madame Blumenthal had constituted herself the agent B
12	seclusion had not] innocence had not done B
13	Every now and then] om. B
14–16	some new ... and of the] the whole spectacle of foreign life—its novelty, its picturesqueness, its light and shade—and with the B
18–21	to manhood ... impressions] to moral manhood B
22	but let] but he let B
23	her—tremendously!] her. B
24	was] were B

25	serene efflorescence] happy season B
25	fine] superior B
31–2	study; she ... undiverted] study, and the studious mind prefers seclusion B
433:13	lyrical] lyric B
21	flavour] quality B
30	an accurate] a coherent B
33	she ... some] she had not had some B
39	dilution] infusion B
40	sort of] om. B
42	lower] drop B
43	odd] damnable B
434:3–4	and an] and with an B
8	shabby] vicious B
11	and living] and has lived B
13	thirty ... old] six or eight-and-thirty years of age B
17–18	matrimony ... Herod] matrimony, in the George Sand manner—beating the drum to Madame Sand's trumpet B
20	stuff] literature B
22–3	radical ... matrimony made] *conjugophobia*—I can't call it by any other name—made B
24	it was ... theoretic] it was probably only theoretic A; marriage was probably only theoretic B
27	the air] the sacred air B
28	her adhesion to] that she had embraced B
30–1	pianists waiting for engagements] pianists B
39	to have it frighten] for it to frighten B
435:12–13	way of ... a month] habit of going to see her every day of his life B
23	prolific being] inky goddess AB
23–4	scribbling ... press;] correcting proof-sheets under his nose— B
31–2	spell ... prayerbook] read him the newspapers B
34	danced her dance] expired in the arms of—some one else than her husband B
35–7	coquetry ... impassioned] immoral rubbish, and that her love of vicious paradoxes was only a peculiarly depraved form of coquetry B
37	impassioned] passionate A
39–40	in certain ... snubbed] women like to be snubbed by military men B
43	terribly handsome] uncommonly pretty B
436:5	manuscript] history B
29	comes] came B
29	finds] found B
437:6	in talking] while she talked B
6	zealous] rather affected little B

	8	rather] om. B
	10	No! ... least] Not for a long time B
	13	run] go B
	30	boundless ... freedom.] my idea of happiness is to die on a great barricade! B
	35	virtue] good conduct B
	41	most naïf] freshest B
	42	simplicity,] freshness B
438:8		I imagine] It seemed to me that B
	9	irresistible] absorbing B
	12–13	embarked ... the merits] made some remark upon the charm B
	17	expound] explain B
	19	exposition,] explanation B
	28	at] in AB
	30	creature] widow B
	35	that I ... permission] that she had given me leave B
	37	answered] rejoined B
439:9		was] were B
	12–13	I reserved ... admeasurement] my appreciation was vague B
	13–16	to have ... discriminating] that he should be simply smitten than that his admiration should pique itself on being discriminating B
	18	to prove ... favour] the simpler B
	28–9	mingled ... trouble in] opening tumult of AB
	30	they lose themselves] it loses itself AB
	30–1	faith and strength] beauty and faith AB
	32	bow] lift my eyebrows B
	35	they call] they happen to call B
	37	me,' he cried, 'only] me only B
440:19		attitudinizers] impostors B
	19–20	characters cultivate] characters who cultivate B
	25–6	fame ... foreshadow] reputation had led me to expect B
	39	ambition ... too clearly] rash attempt to surprise her, B
	42	shake ... being] subscribe to the most comprehensive of Pickering's rhapsodies. She was certainly B
441:7–8		me, categorically, as] me as B
	12	supremely fine fellow] most distinguished young man B
	14	inspired] provoked B
	14–15	at hand] ready made B
	35	fancy] suspicion B
	38	a momentary] some B
	39–40	it appeared ... of it] perhaps I might do him a good turn by putting her in possession of it B
442:17–18		'Of course ... all this.'] 'Of course you know what I wished in telling you this.' I said, rising. 'She is evidently a charm-

ing creature, and the best thing he can do is to marry her. I wished to interest you in that view of it.'   B

22–3	I'm interested ... interfere] I am deeply interested B
24–5	for the day following] the next day B
35	prior speech] to speak first B
443:26	say,' ... 'to your] say to your B
27	promise?'] promise?' I asked in a moment. B
28–9	me,' ... 'that] me that B
41	in] at B
444:24	He's as amiable, evidently,] He evidently is as amiable B
24	madame] the lady B
26	you,' ... 'Pickering] you Pickering B
26	fellow.'] fellow,' I said. B
31	of all ... romances] of her other romances B
38	consummation] event B
445:2	event] result B
10	old] friend B
12	privileged] felicitous B
14	an ex-disciple] a pupil of the school AB
15–16	mentioned,' ... 'Madame] mentioned Madame B
16	Wiesbaden?'] Wiesbaden?' he asked. B
28	an occasional] om. B
28	bulletin] bulletins B
34	baggage] luggage B
446:19	assented ... trouble] accepted tacitly his tacit confession of distress B
17	be as eloquent] gush as freely AB
17	been] done AB
40	let's get ... with it] let us have it over B
447:1	wished to have him see] wished him to see B
11	enthusiasm] sincerity B
15	better. Thank] better. So can you, for that matter; thank B
22	revile] curse B
31–2	as I stood ... the door] as if she were disappointed, while I stood with my hand on the door B
38	you," she went on, "all] you all B
39	gave me.] gave me," she went on. B
39	Your passion] "Your passion B
40	sooner," ... "that] sooner that B
41	so!"] so!" I exclaimed. B
448:7	was told I] was once told I B
9	say,' ... 'that] say that B
10	relations. You] relations,' I said. 'You B
12	came ... first] got tired of the game first B
13	he offered no denial] without contradicting me B
25–6	I drew forth ... a month] I drew forth from where it had

	lain untouched for a month the letter he had given me to keep B
32–3	his letter] the letter from Smyrna B
36	I owe . . . of it] It is proper I should tell you what is in it B
43	was] had been B
449 : 6	presumes] pretends B
8	idiotically passive] stupidly submissive B
9	bit!] bit of it. B
13	own] om. B
23	He will . . . me] He can promise me B
27	conscience] spirit B
27	fell a-brooding] began to brood B
34	doggedly sure] stiffly certain B
36	blandishments] sub-acid blandishments B
450 : 5	lovely] charming B
7	part,' . . . 'is] part is B
7	forget her. It] forget her,' he presently added. 'It B
13–14	seek diversion . . . sympathy] amuse himself with a long journey. If it would be any comfort to him B
16	discomfited] embarrassed B
26	the ample speech] the generous eloquence AB
37	and owed] and that he owed B
451 : 12	lovely] charming B

APPENDIX I
A Passionate Pilgrim: The Text in the New York Edition.

[A few small errors in the text have been corrected.]

I

INTENDING to sail for America in the early part of June, I determined to
spend the interval of six weeks in England, to which country my mind's
eye only had as yet been introduced. I had formed in Italy and France a
resolute preference for old inns, considering that what they sometimes cost
the ungratified body they repay the delighted mind. On my arrival in
London, therefore, I lodged at a certain antique hostelry, much to the
east of Temple Bar, deep in the quarter that I had inevitably figured as
the Johnsonian. Here, on the first evening of my stay, I descended to the
little coffee-room and bespoke my dinner of the genius of 'attendance' in
the person of the solitary waiter. No sooner had I crossed the threshold of
this retreat than I felt I had cut a golden-ripe crop of English 'impressions'. The coffee-room of the Red Lion, like so many other places and
things I was destined to see in the motherland, seemed to have been waiting for long years, with just that sturdy sufferance of time written on its
visage, for me to come and extract the romantic essence of it.

The latent preparedness of the American mind even for the most
characteristic features of English life was a matter I meanwhile failed to
get to the bottom of. The roots of it are indeed so deeply buried in the
soil of our early culture that, without some great upheaval of feeling, we
are at a loss to say exactly when and where and how it begins. It makes
an American's enjoyment of England an emotion more searching than
anything Continental. I had seen the coffee-room of the Red Lion years
ago, at home—at Saragossa, Illinois—in books, in visions, in dreams, in
Dickens, in Smollett, in Boswell. It was small and subdivided into six
narrow compartments by a series of perpendicular screens of mahogany,
something higher than a man's stature, furnished on either side with a
meagre uncushioned ledge, denominated in ancient Britain a seat. In
each of these rigid receptacles was a narrow table—a table expected under
stress to accommodate no less than four pairs of active British elbows.
High pressure indeed had passed away from the Red Lion for ever. It now
knew only that of memories and ghosts and atmosphere. Round the room
there marched, breast-high, a magnificent panelling of mahogany, so
dark with time and so polished with unremitted friction that by gazing a
while into its lucid blackness I made out the dim reflexion of a party of
wigged gentlemen in knee-breeches just arrived from York by the coach.
On the dark yellow walls, coated by the fumes of English coal, of English
mutton, of Scotch whisky, were a dozen melancholy prints, sallow-toned
with age—the Derby favourite of the year 1807, the Bank of England, her
Majesty the Queen. On the floor was a Turkey carpet—as old as the
mahogany almost, as the Bank of England, as the Queen—into which the

waiter had in his lonely revolutions trodden so many massive soot-flakes
and drops of overflowing beer that the glowing looms of Smyrna would
certainly not have recognized it. To say that I ordered my dinner of this
archaic type would be altogether to misrepresent the process owing to
which, having dreamed of lamb and spinach and a *salad de saison*, I sat
down in penitence to a mutton-chop and a rice pudding. Bracing my feet
against the cross-beam of my little oaken table, I opposed to the
mahogany partition behind me the vigorous dorsal resistance that must
have expressed the old-English idea of repose. The sturdy screen refused
even to creak, but my poor Yankee joints made up the deficiency.

While I was waiting there for my chop there came into the room a
person whom, after I had looked at him a moment, I supposed to be a
fellow lodger and probably the only one. He seemed, like myself, to have
submitted to proposals for dinner; the table on the other side of my partition had been prepared to receive him. He walked up to the fire, exposed
his back to it, and, after consulting his watch, looked directly out of the
window and indirectly at me. He was a man of something less than
middle age and more than middle stature, though indeed you would
have called him neither young nor tall. He was chiefly remarkable for his
emphasized leanness. His hair, very thin on the summit of his head, was
dark, short, and fine. His eye was of a pale turbid grey, unsuited, perhaps,
to his dark hair and well-drawn brows, but not altogether out of harmony with his colourless bilious complexion. His nose was aquiline and
delicate; beneath it his moustache languished much rather than bristled.
His mouth and chin were negative, or at the most provisional; not vulgar,
doubtless, but ineffectually refined. A cold fatal gentlemanly weakness
was expressed indeed in his attenuated person. His eye was restless and
deprecating; his whole physiognomy, his manner of shifting his weight
from foot to foot, the spiritless droop of his head, told of exhausted intentions, of a will relaxed. His dress was neat and 'toned down'—he
might have been in mourning. I made up my mind on three points: he
was a bachelor, he was out of health, he was not indigenous to the soil.
The waiter approached him, and they conversed in accents barely audible.
I heard the words 'claret', 'sherry' with a tentative inflexion, and finally
'beer' with its last letter changed to 'ah'. Perhaps he was a Russian in
reduced circumstances; he reminded me slightly of certain sceptical cos-
mopolite Russians whom I had met on the Continent.

While in my extravagant way I followed this train—for you see I was
interested—there appeared a short brisk man with reddish-brown hair,
with a vulgar nose, a sharp blue eye, and a red beard confined to his lower
jaw and chin. My putative Russian, still in possession of the rug, let his
mild gaze stray over the dingy ornaments of the room. The other drew
near, and his umbrella dealt a playful poke at the concave melancholy
waistcoat. 'A penny ha'penny for your thoughts!'

My friend, as I call him, uttered an exclamation, stared, then laid his
two hands on the other's shoulders. The latter looked round at me keenly,
compassing me in a momentary glance. I read in its own vague light that

this was a transatlantic eyebeam; and with such confidence that I hardly needed to see its owner, as he prepared, with his companion, to seat himself at the table adjoining my own, take from his overcoat-pocket three New York newspapers and lay them beside his plate. As my neighbours proceeded to dine I felt the crumbs of their conversation scattered pretty freely abroad. I could hear almost all they said, without straining to catch it, over the top of the partition that divided us. Occasionally their voices dropped to recovery of discretion, but the mystery pieced itself together as if on purpose to entertain me. Their speech was pitched in the key that may in English air be called alien in spite of a few coincidences. The voices were American, however, with a difference; and I had no hesitation in assigning the softer and clearer sound to the pale thin gentleman, whom I decidedly preferred to his comrade. The latter began to question him about his voyage.

'Horrible, horrible! I was deadly sick from the hour we left New York.'

'Well, you do look considerably reduced,' said the second-comer.

'Reduced! I've been on the verge of the grave. I haven't slept six hours for three weeks.' This was said with great gravity. 'Well, I've made the voyage for the last time.'

'The plague you have! You mean to locate here permanently?'

'Oh it won't be so very permanent!'

There was a pause; after which: 'You're the same merry old boy, Searle. Going to give up the ghost tomorrow, eh?'

'I almost wish I were.'

'You're not so sweet on England then? I've heard people say at home that you dress and talk and act like an Englishman. But I know these people here and I know you. You're not one of this crowd, Clement Searle, not you. You'll go under here, sir; you'll go under as sure as my name's Simmons.'

Following this I heard a sudden clatter as of the drop of a knife and fork. 'Well, you're a delicate sort of creature, if it *is* your ugly name! I've been wandering about all day in this accursed city, ready to cry with homesickness and heartsickness and every possible sort of sickness, and thinking, in the absence of anything better, of meeting you here this evening and of your uttering some sound of cheer and comfort and giving me some glimmer of hope. Go under? Ain't I under now! I can't do more than get under the ground!'

Mr. Simmons's superior brightness appeared to flicker a moment in this gust of despair, but the next it was burning steady again. '*Don't* cry, Searle,' I heard him say. 'Remember the waiter. I've grown Englishman enough for that. For heaven's sake don't let's have any nerves. Nerves won't do anything for you here. It's best to come to the point. Tell me in three words what you expect of me.'

I heard another movement, as if poor Searle had collapsed in his chair. 'Upon my word, sir, you're quite inconceivable. You never got my letter?'

'Yes, I got your letter. I was never sorrier to get anything in my life.'

At this declaration Mr. Searle rattled out an oath, which it was well perhaps that I but partially heard. 'Abijah Simmons,' he then cried, 'what demon of perversity possesses you? Are you going to betray me here in a foreign land, to turn out a false friend, a heartless rogue?'

'Go on, sir,' said sturdy Simmons. 'Pour it all out. I'll wait till you've done. Your beer's lovely,' he observed independently to the waiter. 'I'll have some more.'

'For God's sake explain yourself!' his companion appealed.

There was a pause, at the end of which I heard Mr. Simmons set down his empty tankard with emphasis. 'You poor morbid mooning man,' he resumed, 'I don't want to say anything to make you feel sore. I regularly pity you. But you must allow that you've acted more like a confirmed crank than a member of our best society—in which every one's so sensible.'

Mr. Searle seemed to have made an effort to compose himself. 'Be so good as to tell me then what was the meaning of your letter.'

'Well, you had got on *my* nerves, if you want to know, when I wrote it. It came of my always wishing so to please folks. I had much better have let you alone. To tell you the plain truth I never was so horrified in my life as when I found that on the strength of my few kind words you had come out here to seek your fortune.'

'What then did you expect me to do?'

'I expected you to wait patiently till I had made further inquiries and had written you again.'

'And you've made further inquiries now?'

'Inquiries! I've committed assaults.'

'And you find I've no claim?'

'No claim that one of *these* big bugs will look at. It struck me at first that you had rather a neat little case. I confess the look of it took hold of me——'

'Thanks to your liking so to please folks!'

Mr. Simmons appeared for a moment at odds with something; it proved to be with his liquor. 'I rather think your beer's too good to be true,' he said to the waiter. 'I guess I'll take water. Come, old man,' he resumed, 'don't challenge me to the arts of debate, or you'll have me right down on you, and then you *will* feel me. My native sweetness, as I say, was part of it. The idea that if I put the thing through it would be a very pretty feather in my cap and a very pretty penny in my purse was part of it. And the satisfaction of seeing a horrid low American walk right into an old English estate was a good deal of it. Upon my word, Searle, when I think of it I wish with all my heart that, extravagant vain man as you are, I *could*, for the charm of it, put you through! I should hardly care what you did with the blamed place when you got it. I could leave you alone to turn it into Yankee notions—into ducks and drakes as they call 'em here. I should like to see you tearing round over it and kicking up its sacred dust in their very faces!'

'You don't know me one little bit,' said Mr. Searle, rather shirking, I thought, the burden of this tribute and for all response to the ambiguity of the compliment.

'I should be very glad to think I didn't, sir. I've been to no small amount of personal inconvenience for you. I've pushed my way right up to the headspring. I've got the best opinion that's to be had. The best opinion that's to be had just gives you one leer over its spectacles. I guess that look will fix you if you ever get it straight. I've been able to tap, indirectly,' Mr. Simmons went on, 'the solicitor of your usurping cousin, and he evidently knows something to be in the wind. It seems your elder brother twenty years ago put out a feeler. So you're not to have the glory of even making them sit up.'

'I never made any one sit up,' I heard Mr. Searle plead. 'I shouldn't begin at this time of day. I should approach the subject like a gentleman.'

'Well, if you want very much to do something like a gentleman you've got a capital chance. Take your disappointment like a gentleman.'

I had finished my dinner and had become keenly interested in poor Mr. Searle's unencouraging—or unencouraged—claim; so interested that I at last hated to hear his trouble reflected in his voice without being able —all respectfully!—to follow it in his face. I left my place, went over to the fire, took up the evening paper, and established a post of observation behind it.

His cold counsellor was in the act of choosing a soft chop from the dish —an act accompanied by a great deal of prying and poking with that gentleman's own fork. My disillusioned compatriot had pushed away his plate; he sat with his elbows on the table, gloomily nursing his head with his hands. His companion watched him and then seemed to wonder—to do Mr. Simmons justice—how he could least ungracefully give him up. 'I say, Searle,'—and for my benefit, I think, taking me for a native ingenuous enough to be dazzled by his wit, he lifted his voice a little and gave it an ironical ring—'in this country it's the inestimable privilege of a loyal citizen, under whatsoever stress of pleasure or of pain, to make a point of eating his dinner.'

Mr. Searle gave his plate another push. 'Anything may happen now. I don't care a straw.'

'You ought to care. Have another chop and you *will* care. Have some better tipple. Take my advice!' Mr. Simmons went on.

My friend—I adopt that name for him—gazed from between his two hands coldly before him. 'I've had enough of your advice.'

'A little more,' said Simmons mildly; 'I shan't trouble you again. What do you mean to do?'

'Nothing.'

'Oh come!'

'Nothing, nothing, nothing!'

'Nothing but starve. How about meeting expenses?'

'Why do you ask?' said my friend. 'You don't care.'

'My dear fellow, if you want to make me offer you twenty pounds you set most clumsily about it. You said just now I don't know you,' Mr.

Simmons went on. 'Possibly. Come back with me then,' he said kindly enough, 'and let's improve our acquaintance.'

'I won't go back. I shall never go back.'

'Never?'

'Never.'

Mr. Simmons thought it shrewdly over. 'Well, you *are* sick!' he exclaimed presently. 'All I can say is that if you're working out a plan for cold poison, or for any other act of desperation, you had better give it right up. You can't get a dose of the commonest kind of cold poison for nothing, you know. Look here, Searle'—and the worthy man made what struck me as a very decent appeal. 'If you'll consent to return home with me by the steamer of the twenty-third I'll pay your passage down. More than that, I'll pay for your beer.'

My poor gentleman met it. 'I believe I never made up my mind to anything before, but I think it's made up now. I shall stay here till I take my departure for a newer world than any patched-up newness of ours. It's an odd feeling—I rather like it! What should I do at home?'

'You said just now you were homesick.'

'I meant I was sick for a home. Don't I belong here? Haven't I longed to get here all my life? Haven't I counted the months and the years till I should be able to "go" as we say? And now that I've "gone", that is that I've come, must I just back out? No, no, I'll move on. I'm much obliged to you for your offer. I've enough money for the present. I've about my person some forty pounds' worth of British gold, and the same amount, say, of the toughness of the heaven-sent idiot. They'll see me through together! After they're gone I shall lay my head in some English churchyard, beside some ivied tower, beneath an old gnarled black yew.'

I had so far distinctly followed the dialogue; but at this point the landlord entered and, begging my pardon, would suggest that number 12, a most superior apartment, having now been vacated, it would give him pleasure if I would look in. I declined to look in, but agreed for number 12 at a venture and gave myself again, with dissimulation, to my friends. They had got up; Simmons had put on his overcoat; he stood polishing his rusty black hat with his napkin. 'Do you mean to go down to the place?' he asked.

'Possibly. I've thought of it so often that I should like to see it.'

'Shall you call on Mr. Searle?'

'Heaven forbid!'

'Something has just occurred to me,' Simmons pursued with a grin that made his upper lip look more than ever denuded by the razor and jerked the ugly ornament of his chin into the air. 'There's a certain Miss Searle, the old man's sister.'

'Well?' my gentleman quavered.

'Well, sir!—you talk of moving on. You might move on the damsel.'

Mr. Searle frowned in silence and his companion gave him a tap on the stomach. 'Line those ribs a bit first!' He blushed crimson; his eyes filled with tears. 'You *are* a coarse brute,' he said. The scene quite harrowed

me, but I was prevented from seeing it through by the reappearance of
the landlord on behalf of number 12. He represented to me that I ought
in justice to him to come and see how tidy they *had* made it. Half an hour
afterwards I was rattling along in a hansom towards Covent Garden,
where I heard Madame Bosio in *The Barber of Seville*. On my return
from the opera I went into the coffee-room; it had occurred to me I might
catch there another glimpse of Mr. Searle. I was not disappointed. I found
him seated before the fire with his head sunk on his breast: he slept,
dreaming perhaps of Abijah Simmons. I watched him for some moments.
His closed eyes, in the dim lamplight, looked even more helpless and resigned, and I seemed to see the fine grain of his nature in his unconscious
mask. They say fortune comes while we sleep, and, standing there, I felt
really tender enough—though otherwise most unqualified—to be poor
Mr. Searle's fortune. As I walked away I noted in one of the little prandial
pews I have described the melancholy waiter, whose whiskered chin also
reposed on the bulge of his shirt-front. I lingered a moment beside the
old inn-yard in which, upon a time, the coaches and post-chaises found
space to turn and disgorge. Above the dusky shaft of the enclosing galleries, where lounging lodgers and crumpled chambermaids and all the
picturesque domesticity of a rattling tavern must have leaned on their
elbows for many a year, I made out the far-off lurid twinkle of the
London constellations. At the foot of the stairs, enshrined in the glittering
niche of her well-appointed bar, the landlady sat napping like some
solemn idol amid votive brass and plate.

The next morning, not finding the subject of my benevolent curiosity
in the coffee-room, I learned from the waiter that he had ordered breakfast in bed. Into this asylum I was not yet prepared to pursue him. I
spent the morning in the streets, partly under pressure of business, but
catching all kinds of romantic impressions by the way. To the searching
American eye there is no tint of association with which the great grimy
face of London doesn't flush. As the afternoon approached, however, I
began to yearn for some site more gracefully classic than what surrounded
me, and, thinking over the excursions recommended to the ingenuous
stranger, decided to take the train to Hampton Court. The day was the
more propitious that it yielded just that dim subaqueous light which
sleeps so fondly upon the English landscape.

At the end of an hour I found myself wandering through the apartments of the great palace. They follow each other in infinite succession,
with no great variety of interest or aspect, but with persistent pomp and a
fine specific effect. They are exactly of their various times. You pass from
painted and panelled bedchambers and closets, anterooms, drawing-
rooms, council-rooms, through king's suite, queen's suite, prince's suite,
until you feel yourself move through the appointed hours and stages of
some rigid monarchical day. On one side are the old monumental upholsteries, the big cold tarnished beds and canopies, with the circumference
of disapparelled royalty symbolized by a gilded balustrade, and the great
carved and yawning chimney-places where dukes-in-waiting may have

warmed their weary heels; on the other, in deep recesses, rise the immense windows, the framed and draped embrasures where the sovereign whispered and favourites smiled, looking out on terraced gardens and misty park. The brown walls are dimly illumined by innumerable portraits of courtiers and captains, more especially with various members of the Batavian *entourage* of William of Orange, the restorer of the palace; with good store too of the lily-bosomed models of Lely and Kneller. The whole tone of this processional interior is singularly stale and sad. The tints of all things have both faded and darkened—you taste the chill of the place as you walk from room to room. It was still early in the day and in the season, and I flattered myself that I was the only visitor. This complacency, however, dropped at sight of a person standing motionless before a simpering countess of Sir Peter Lely's creation. On hearing my footstep this victim of an evaporated spell turned his head and I recognized my fellow lodger of the Red Lion. I was apparently recognized as well; he looked as if he could scarce wait for me to be kind to him, and in fact didn't wait. Seeing I had a catalogue he asked me the name of the portrait. On my satisfying him he appealed, rather timidly, as to my opinion of the lady.

'Well,' said I, not quite timidly enough perhaps, 'I confess she strikes me as no great matter.'

He remained silent and was evidently a little abashed. As we strolled away he stole a sidelong glance of farewell at his leering shepherdess. To speak with him face to face was to feel keenly that he was no less interesting than infirm. We talked of our inn, of London, of the palace; he uttered his mind freely, but seemed to struggle with a weight of depression. It was an honest mind enough, with no great cultivation but with a certain natural love of excellent things. I foresaw that I should find him quite to the manner born—to ours; full of glimpses and responses, of deserts and desolations. His perceptions would be fine and his opinions pathetic; I should moreover take refuge from his sense of proportion in his sense of humour, and then refuge from *that*, ah me!—in what? On my telling him that I was a fellow citizen he stopped short, deeply touched, and, silently passing his arm into my own, suffered me to lead him through the other apartments and down into the gardens. A large gravelled platform stretches itself before the basement of the palace, taking the afternoon sun. Parts of the great structure are reserved for private use and habitation, occupied by state-pensioners, reduced gentlewomen in receipt of the Queen's bounty, and other deserving persons. Many of the apartments have their dependent gardens, and here and there, between the verdure-coated walls, you catch a glimpse of these somewhat stuffy bowers. My companion and I measured more than once this long expanse, looking down on the floral figures of the rest of the affair and on the stoutly-woven tapestry of creeping plants that muffle the foundations of the huge red pile. I thought of the various images of old-world gentility which, early and late, must have strolled in front of it and felt the protection and security of the place. We peeped through an antique grating into one of the mossy cages and saw an old lady with a black mantilla on her head, a decanter of water in one hand and a crutch in the other, come forth, followed by three little dogs and a cat, to sprinkle a plant. She would probably have had an opinion on the virtue of Queen Caroline. Feeling these things together made us quickly, made us extraordinarily, intimate. My companion seemed to ache with his impression; he scowled, all gently, as if it gave him pain. I proposed at last that we should dine somewhere on the spot and take a late train to town. We made our way out of the gardens into the adjoining village, where we entered an inn which I pronounced, very sincerely, exactly what we wanted. Mr. Searle had approached our board as shyly as if it had been a cold bath; but, gradually warming to his work, he declared at the end of half an hour that for the first time in a month he enjoyed his victuals.

'I'm afraid you're rather out of health,' I risked.

'Yes, sir—I'm an incurable.'

The little village of Hampton Court stands clustered about the entrance of Bushey Park, and after we had dined we lounged along into the celebrated avenue of horse-chestnuts. There is a rare emotion, familiar to every intelligent traveller, in which the mind seems to swallow the sum total of its impressions at a gulp. You take in the whole place, whatever it be. You feel England, you feel Italy, and the sensation involves for the moment a kind of thrill. I had known it from time to time in Italy and had opened my soul to it as to the spirit of the Lord. Since my landing in England I had been waiting for it to arrive. A bottle of tolerable Burgundy, at dinner, had perhaps unlocked to it the gates of sense; it arrived now with irresistible force. Just the scene around me was the England of one's early reveries. Over against us, amid the ripeness of its gardens, the dark red residence, with its formal facings and its vacant windows, seemed to make the past definite and massive; the little village, nestling between park and palace, around a patch of turfy common, with its taverns of figurative names, its ivy-towered church, its mossy roofs, looked like the property of a feudal lord. It was in this dark composite light that I had read the British classics; it was this mild moist air that had blown from the pages of the poets; while I seemed to feel the buried generations in the dense and elastic sod. And that I must have testified in some form or other to what I have called my thrill I gather, remembering it, from a remark of my companion's.

'You've the advantage over me in coming to all this with an educated eye. You already know what old things can be. I've never known it but by report. I've always fancied I should like it. In a small way at home, of course, I did try to stand by my idea of it. I must be a conservative by nature. People at home used to call me a cockney and a fribble. But it wasn't true,' he went on; 'if it had been I should have made my way over here long ago: before—before——'. He paused, and his head dropped sadly on his breast.

The bottle of Burgundy had loosened his tongue; I had but to choose my time for learning his story. Something told me that I had gained his confidence and that, so far as attention and attitude might go, I was 'in' for responsibilities. But somehow I didn't dread them. 'Before you lost your health,' I suggested.

'Before I lost my health,' he answered. 'And my property—the little I had. And my ambition. And any power to take myself seriously.'

'Come!' I cried. 'You shall recover everything. This tonic English climate will wind you up in a month. And *then* see how you'll take yourself—and how I shall take you!'

'Oh,' he gratefully smiled, 'I may turn to dust in your hands! I should like,' he presently pursued, 'to be an old genteel pensioner, lodged over there in the palace and spending my days in maundering about these vistas. I should go every morning, at the hour when it gets the sun, into that long gallery where all those pretty women of Lely's are hung—I know you despise them!—and stroll up and down and say something kind to them. Poor precious forsaken creatures! So flattered and courted in their day, so neglected now! Offering up their shoulders and ringlets and smiles to that musty deadly silence!'

I laid my hand on my friend's shoulder. 'Oh sir, you're all right!'

Just at this moment there came cantering down the shallow glade of the avenue a young girl on a fine black horse—one of those little budding gentlewomen, perfectly mounted and equipped, who form to alien eyes one of the prettiest incidents of English scenery. She had distanced her servant and, as she came abreast of us, turned slightly in her saddle and glanced back at him. In the movement she dropped the hunting-crop with which she was armed; whereupon she reined up and looked shyly at us and at the implement. 'This is something better than a Lely,' I said. Searle hastened forward, picked up the crop and, with a particular courtesy that became him, handed it back to the rider. Fluttered and blushing she reached forward, took it with a quick sweet sound, and the next moment was bounding over the quiet turf. Searle stood watching her; the servant, as he passed us, touched his hat. When my friend turned towards me again I saw that he too was blushing. 'Oh sir, you're all right,' I repeated.

At a short distance from where we had stopped was an old stone bench. We went and sat down on it and, as the sun began to sink, watched the light mist powder itself with gold. 'We ought to be thinking of the train back to London, I suppose,' I at last said.

'Oh hang the train!' sighed my companion.

'Willingly. There could be no better spot than this to feel the English evening stand still.' So we lingered, and the twilight hung about us, strangely clear in spite of the thickness of the air. As we sat there came into view an apparition unmistakeable from afar as an immemorial vagrant —the disowned, in his own rich way, of all the English ages. As he approached us he slackened pace and finally halted, touching his cap. He was a man of middle age, clad in a greasy bonnet with false-looking earlocks depending from its sides. Round his neck was a grimy red scarf, tucked into his waistcoat; his coat and trousers had a remote affinity with those of a reduced hostler. In one hand he had a stick; on his arm he bore a tattered basket, with a handful of withered vegetables at the bottom. His face was pale haggard and degraded beyond description—as base as a counterfeit coin, yet as modelled somehow as a tragic mask. He too, like everything else, had a history. From what height had he fallen, from what depth had he risen? He was the perfect symbol of generated constituted baseness; and I felt before him in presence of a great artist or actor.

'For God's sake, gentlemen,' he said in the raucous tone of weather-beaten poverty, the tone of chronic sore-throat exacerbated by perpetual gin, 'for God's sake, gentlemen, have pity on a poor fern-collector!'—turning up his stale daisies. 'Food hasn't passed my lips, gentlemen, for the last three days.'

We gaped at him and at each other, and to our imagination his appeal had almost the force of a command. 'I wonder if half-a-crown would help?' I privately wailed. And our fasting botanist went limping away through the park with the grace of controlled stupefaction still further enriching his outline.

'I feel as if I had seen my *Doppelgänger*,' said Searle. 'He reminds me of myself. What am I but a mere figure in the landscape, a wandering minstrel or picker of daisies?'

'What are you "anyway", my friend?' I thereupon took occasion to ask. 'Who are you? kindly tell me.'

The colour rose again to his pale face and I feared I had offended him. He poked a moment at the sod with the point of his umbrella before answering. 'Who am I?' he said at last. 'My name is Clement Searle. I was born in New York, and that's the beginning and the end of me.'

'Ah not the end!' I made bold to plead.

'Then it's because I *have* no end—any more than an ill-written book. I just stop anywhere; which means I'm a failure,' the poor man all lucidly and unreservedly pursued : 'a failure, as hopeless and helpless, sir, as any that ever swallowed up the slender investments of the widow and the orphan. I don't pay five cents on the dollar. What I might have been—once!—there's nothing left to show. I was rotten before I was ripe. To begin with, certainly, I wasn't a fountain of wisdom. All the more reason for a definite channel—for having a little character and purpose. But I hadn't even a little. I had nothing but nice tastes, as they call them, and fine sympathies and sentiments. Take a turn through New York today and you'll find the tattered remnants of these things dangling on every bush and fluttering in every breeze; the men to whom I lent money, the women to whom I made love, the friends I trusted, the follies I invented, the poisonous fumes of pleasure amid which nothing was worth a thought but the manhood they stifled! It was my fault that I believed in pleasure here below. I believe in it still, but as I believe in the immortality of the soul. The soul is immortal, certainly—if you've got one; but most people haven't. Pleasure would be right if it were pleasure straight through; but it never is. My taste was to be the best in the world; well, perhaps it was. I

had a little money; it went the way of my little wit. Here in my pocket I
have the scant dregs of it. I should tell you I was the biggest kind of ass.
Just now that description would flatter me; it would assume there's something left of me. But the ghost of a donkey—what's that? I think,' he
went on with a charming turn and as if striking off his real explanation, 'I
should have been all right in a world arranged on different lines. Before
heaven, sir—whoever you are—I'm in practice so absurdly tender-hearted
that I can afford to say it: I entered upon life a perfect gentleman. I had
the love of old forms and pleasant rites, and I found them nowhere—
found a world all hard lines and harsh lights, without shade, without
composition, as they say of pictures, without the lovely mystery of colour.
To furnish colour I melted down the very substance of my soul. I went
about with my brush, touching up and toning down; a very pretty
chiaroscuro you'll find in my track! Sitting here in this old park, in this
old country, I feel that I hover on the misty verge of what might have
been! I should have been born here and not there; here my makeshift
distinctions would have found things they'd have been true of. How it was
I never got free is more than I can say. It might have cut the knot, but
the knot was too tight. I was always out of health or in debt or somehow
desperately dangling. Besides, I had a horror of the great black sickening
sea. A year ago I was reminded of the existence of an old claim to an
English estate, which has danced before the eyes of my family, at odd
moments, any time these eighty years. I confess it's a bit of a muddle
and a tangle, and am by no means sure that to this hour I've got the hang
of it. You look as if you had a clear head: some other time, if you consent,
we'll have a go at it, such as it is, together. Poverty was staring me in the
face; I sat down and tried to commit the "points" of our case to memory,
as I used too get nine-times-nine by heart as a boy. I dreamed of it for
six months, half-expecting to wake up some fine morning and hear
through a latticed casement the cawing of an English rookery. A couple
of months ago there came out to England on business of his own a man
who once got me out of a dreadful mess (not that I had hurt anyone but
myself), a legal practitioner in our courts, a very rough diamond, but with
a great deal of *flair*, as they say in New York. It was with him yesterday
you saw me dining. He undertook, as he called it, to "nose round" and see
if anything could be made of our questionable but possible show. The
matter had never seriously been taken up. A month later I got a letter
from Simmons assuring me that it seemed a very good show indeed and
that he should be greatly surprised if I were unable to do something.
This was the greatest push I had ever got in my life; I took a deliberate
step, for the first time; I sailed for England. I've been here three days:
they've seemed three months. After keeping me waiting for thirty-six
hours my legal adviser makes his appearance last night and states to me,
with his mouth full of mutton, that I haven't a leg to stand on, that my
claim is moonshine, and that I must do penance and take a ticket for six
more days of purgatory with his presence thrown in. My friend, my friend
—shall I say I was disappointed? I'm already resigned. I didn't really

believe I had any case. I felt in my deeper consciousness that it was the crowning illusion of a life of illusions. Well, it was a pretty one. Poor legal adviser!—I forgive him with all my heart. But for him I shouldn't be sitting in this place, in this air, under these impressions. This is a world I could have got on with beautifully. There's an immense charm in its having been kept for the last. After it nothing else would have been tolerable. I shall now have a month of it, I hope, which won't be long enough for it to "go back" on me. There's one thing!'—and here, pausing, he laid his hand on mine; I rose and stood before him—'I wish it were possible you should be with me to the end.'

'I promise you to leave you only when you kick me downstairs.' But I suggested my terms. 'It must be on condition of your omitting from your conversation this intolerable flavour of mortality. I know nothing of "ends". I'm all for beginnings.'

He kept on me his sad weak eyes. Then with a faint smile: 'Don't cut down a man you find hanging. He has had a reason for it. I'm bankrupt.'

'Oh health's money!' I said. 'Get well, and the rest will take care of itself. I'm interested in your questionable claim—it's the question that's the charm; and pretenders, to anything big enough, have always been, for me, an attractive class. Only their first duty's to be gallant.'

'Their first duty's to understand their own points and to know their own mind,' he returned with hopeless lucidity. 'Don't ask me to climb our family tree now,' he added; 'I fear I haven't the head for it. I'll try some day—if it will bear my weight; or yours added to mine. There's no doubt, however, that we, as they say, go back. But I know nothing of business. If I were to take the matter in hand I should break in two the poor little silken thread from which everything hangs. In a better world than this I think I should be listened to. But the wind doesn't set to ideal justice. There's no doubt that a hundred years ago we suffered a palpable wrong. Yet we made no appeal at the time, and the dust of a century now lies heaped upon our silence. Let it rest!'

'What then,' I asked, 'is the estimated value of your interest?'

'We were instructed from the first to accept compromise. Compared with the whole property our ideas have been small. We were once advised in the sense of a hundred and thirty thousand dollars. Why a hundred and thirty I'm sure I don't know. Don't beguile me into figures.'

'Allow me one more question,' I said. 'Who's actually in possession?'

'A certain Mr. Richard Searle. I know nothing about him.'

'He's in some way related to you?'

'Our great-grandfathers were half-brothers. What does that make us?'

'Twentieth cousins, say. And where does your twentieth cousin live?'

'At a place called Lackley—in Middleshire.'

I thought it over. 'Well, suppose we look up Lackley in Middleshire!'

He got straight up. 'Go and see it?'

'Go and see it.'

'Well,' he said, 'with you I'll go anywhere.'

On our return to town we determined to spend three days there together and then proceed to our errand. We were as conscious one as the other of that deeper mystic appeal made by London to those superstitious pilgrims who feel it the mother-city of their race, the distributing heart of their traditional life. Certain characteristics of the dusky Babylon, certain aspects, phases, features, 'say' more to the American spiritual ear than anything else in Europe. The influence of these things on Searle it charmed me to note. His observation I soon saw to be, as I pronounced it to him, searching and caressing. His almost morbid appetite for any over-scoring of time, well-nigh extinct from long inanition, threw the flush of its revival into his face and his talk.

II

WE looked out the topography of Middleshire in a county-guide, which spoke highly, as the phrase is, of Lackley Park, and took up our abode, our journey ended, at a wayside inn where, in the days of leisure, the coach must have stopped for luncheon and burnished pewters of rustic ale been handed up as straight as possible to outsiders athirst with the sense of speed. We stopped here for mere gaping joy of its steep-thatched roof, its latticed windows, its hospitable porch, and allowed a couple of days to elapse in vague undirected strolls and sweet sentimental observ-ance of the land before approaching the particular business that had drawn us on. The region I allude to is a compendium of the general physiognomy of England. The noble friendliness of the scenery, its latent old-friendliness, the way we scarcely knew whether we were looking at it for the first time or the last time, made it arrest us at every step. The countryside, in the full warm rains of the last of April, had burst into sudden perfect spring. The dark walls of the hedgerows had turned into blooming screens, the sodden verdure of lawn and meadow been washed over with a lighter brush. We went forth without loss of time for a walk on the great grassy hills, smooth arrested central billows of some primitive upheaval, from the summits of which you find half England unrolled at your feet. A dozen broad counties, within the scope of your vision, com-mingle their green exhalations. Closely beneath us lay the dark rich hedgy flats and the copse-chequered slopes, white with the blossom of apples. At widely opposite points of the expanse two great towers of cathedrals rose sharply out of a reddish blur of habitation, taking the mild English light.

We gave an irrepressible attention to this same solar reserve, and found in it only a refinement of art. The sky never was empty and never idle; the clouds were continually at play for our benefit. Over against us, from our station on the hills, we saw them piled and dissolved, condensed and shifted, blotting the blue with sullen rain-spots, stretching, breeze-fretted, into dappled fields of grey, bursting into an explosion of light or melting into a drizzle of silver. We made our way along the rounded ridge of the downs and reached, by a descent, through slanting angular fields, green to cottage-doors, a russet village that beckoned us from the heart of the maze in which the hedges wrapped it up. Close beside it, I admit, the roaring train bounces out of a hole in the hills; yet there broods upon this charming hamlet an old-time quietude that makes a violation of confidence of naming it so far away. We struck through a narrow lane, a green lane, dim with its barriers of hawthorn; it led us to a superb old farmhouse, now rather rudely jostled by the multiplied roads and by-ways that have reduced its ancient appanage. It stands there in stubborn picturesqueness, doggedly submitting to be pointed out and sketched. It is a wonderful image of the domiciliary conditions of the past—cruelly complete; with blended beams and joists, beneath the burden of gables, that seem to ache and groan with memories and regrets. The short low windows, where lead and glass combine equally to create an inward gloom, retain their opacity as a part of the primitive idea of defence. Such an old house provokes on the part of an American a luxury of respect. So propped and patched, so tinkered with clumsy tenderness, clustered so richly about its central English sturdiness, its oaken vertebrations, so humanized with ages of use and touches of beneficent affection, it seemed to offer to our grateful eyes a small rude symbol of the great English social order. Passing out upon the highroad, we came to the common browsing-patch, the 'village-green' of the tales of our youth. Nothing was absent: the shaggy mouse-coloured donkey, nosing the turf with his mild and huge proboscis, the geese, the old woman—*the* old woman, in person, with her red cloak and her black bonnet, frilled about the face and double-frilled beside her decent placid cheeks—the towering ploughman with his white smock-frock puckered on chest and back, his short corduroys, his mighty calves, his big red rural face. We greeted these things as children greet the loved pictures in a story-book lost and mourned and found again. We recognized them as one recognizes the handwriting on letter-backs. Beside the road we saw a ploughboy straddle whistling on a stile, and he had the merit of being not only a ploughboy but a Gainsborough. Beyond the stile, across the level velvet of a meadow, a footpath wandered like a streak drawn by a finger over a surface of fine plush. We followed it from field to field and from stile to stile; it was all adorably the way to church. At the church we finally arrived, lost in its rook-haunted church-yard, hidden from the workday world by the broad stillness of pastures—a grey, grey tower, a huge black yew, a cluster of village-graves with crooked headstones and protrusions that had settled and sunk. The place seemed so to ache with consecration that my sensitive companion gave way to the force of it.

'You must bury me here, you know'—he caught at my arm. 'It's the first place of worship I've seen in my life. How it makes a Sunday where it stands!'

It took the Church, we agreed, to make churches, but we had the sense the next day of seeing still better why. We walked over, some seven miles, to the nearer of the two neighbouring seats of that lesson; and all through such a mist of local colour that we felt ourselves a pair of Smollett's pedestrian heroes faring tavernward for a night of adventures. As we neared the provincial city we saw the steepled mass of the cathedral, long and high, rise far into the cloud-freckled blue; and as we got closer stopped on a bridge and looked down at the reflexion of the solid minster in a yellow stream. Going further yet we entered the russet town—where surely Miss Austen's heroines, in chariots and curricles, must often have come a-shopping for their sandals and mittens; we lounged in the grassed and gravelled precinct and gazed insatiably at that most soul-soothing sight, the waning wasting afternoon light, the visible ether that feels the voices of the chimes cling far aloft to the quiet sides of the cathedral-tower; saw it linger and nestle and abide, as it loves to do on all perpendicular spaces, converting them irresistibly into registers and dials; tasted too, as deeply, of the peculiar stillness of this place of priests; saw a rosy English lad come forth and lock the door of the old foundation-school that dovetailed with cloister and choir, and carry his big responsible key into one of the quiet canonical houses: and then stood musing together on the effect on one's mind of having in one's boyhood gone and come through cathedral-shades as a King's scholar, and yet kept ruddy with much cricket in misty river meadows. On the third morning we betook ourselves to Lackley, having learned that parts of the 'grounds' were open to visitors, and that indeed on application the house was sometimes shown.

Within the range of these numerous acres the declining spurs of the hills continued to undulate and subside. A long avenue wound and circled from the outermost gate through an untrimmed woodland, whence you glanced at further slopes and glades and copses and bosky recesses— at everything except the limits of the place. It was as free and untended as I had found a few of the large loose villas of old Italy, and I was still never to see the angular fact of English landlordism muffle itself in so many concessions. The weather had just become perfect; it was one of the dozen exquisite days of the English year—days stamped with a purity unknown in climates where fine weather is cheap. It was as if the mellow brightness, as tender as that of the primroses which starred the dark waysides like petals wind-scattered over beds of moss, had been meted out to us by the cubic foot—distilled from an alchemist's crucible. From this pastoral abundance we moved upon the more composed scene, the park proper—passed through a second lodge-gate, with weather-worn gilding on its twisted bars, to the smooth slopes where the great trees stood singly and the tame deer browsed along the bed of a woodland stream. Here before us rose the gabled grey front of the Tudor-time, developed and terraced and gardened to some later loss, as we were afterwards to know, of type.

'Here you can wander all day,' I said to Searle, 'like an exiled prince who has come back on tiptoe and hovers about the dominion of the usurper.'

'To think of "others" having hugged this all these years!' he answered. 'I know what I am, but what might I have been? What do such places make of a man?'

'I dare say he gets stupidly used to them,' I said. 'But I dare say too, even then, that when you scratch the mere owner you find the perfect lover.'

'What a perfect scene and background it forms!' my friend, however, had meanwhile gone on. 'What legends, what histories it knows! My heart really breaks with all I seem to guess. There's Tennyson's Talking Oak! What summer days one could spend here! How I could lounge the rest of my life away on this turf of the middle ages! Haven't I some maiden-cousin in that old hall, or grange, or court—what in the name of enchantment do you call the thing?—who would give me kind leave?' And then he turned almost fiercely upon me. 'Why did you bring me here? Why did you drag me into this distraction of vain regrets?'

At this moment there passed within call a decent lad who had emerged from the gardens and who might have been an underling in the stables. I hailed him and put the question of our possible admittance to the house. He answered that the master was away from home, but that he thought it probable the housekeeper would consent to do the honours. I passed my arm into Searle's. 'Come,' I said; 'drain the cup, bitter-sweet though it be. We must go in.' We hastened slowly and approached the fine front. The house was one of the happiest fruits of its freshly-feeling era, a multitudinous cluster of fair gables and intricate chimneys, brave projections and quiet recesses, brown old surfaces weathered to silver and mottled roofs that testified not to seasons but to centuries. Two broad terraces commanded the wooded horizon. Our appeal was answered by a butler who condescended to our weakness. He renewed the assertion that Mr. Searle was away from home, but he would himself lay our case before the housekeeper. We would be so good, however, as to give him our cards. This request, following so directly on the assertion that Mr. Searle was absent, was rather resented by my companion. 'Surely not for the housekeeper.'

The butler gave a diplomatic cough. 'Miss Searle is at home, sir.'

'Yours alone will have to serve,' said my friend. I took out a card and pencil and wrote beneath my name *New York*. As I stood with the pencil poised a temptation entered into it. Without in the least considering proprieties or results I let my implement yield—I added above my name that of Mr. Clement Searle. What would come of it?

Before many minutes the housekeeper waited upon us—a fresh rosy little old woman in a clean dowdy cap and a scanty sprigged gown; a quaint careful person, but accessible to the tribute of our pleasure, to say nothing of any other. She had the accent of the country, but the manners of the house. Under her guidance we passed through a dozen apartments, duly stocked with old pictures, old tapestry, old carvings, old armour, with a hundred ornaments and treasures. The pictures were especially valuable. The two Vandykes, the trio of rosy Rubenses, the sole and sombre Rembrandt, glowed with conscious authenticity. A Claude, a Murillo, a Greuze, a couple of Gainsboroughs, hung there with high complacency. Searle strolled about, scarcely speaking, pale and grave, with bloodshot eyes and lips compressed. He uttered no comment on what we saw—he asked but a question or two. Missing him at last from my side I retraced my steps and found him in a room we had just left, on a faded old ottoman and with his elbows on his knees and his face buried in his hands. Before him, ranged on a great *crédence*, was a magnificent collection of old Italian majolica; plates of every shape, with their glaze of happy colour, jugs and vases nobly bellied and embossed. There seemed to rise before me, as I looked, a sudden vision of the young English gentleman who, eighty years ago, had travelled by slow stages to Italy and been waited on at his inn by persuasive toymen. 'What is it, my dear man?' I asked. 'Are you unwell?'

He uncovered his haggard face and showed me the flush of a conscious-ness sharper, I think, to myself than to him. 'A memory of the past! There comes back to me a china vase that used to stand on the parlour mantel-shelf when I was a boy, with a portrait of General Jackson painted on one side and a bunch of flowers on the other. How long do you sup-pose that majolica has been in the family?'

'A long time probably. It was brought hither in the last century, into old, old England, out of old, old Italy, by some contemporary dandy with a taste for foreign gimcracks. Here it has stood for a hundred years, keep-ing its clear firm hues in this quiet light that has never sought to advertise it.'

Searle sprang to his feet. 'I say, for mercy's sake, take me away! I can't stand this sort of thing. Before I know it I shall do something scandalous. I shall steal some of their infernal crockery. I shall proclaim my identity and assert my rights. I shall go blubbering to Miss Searle and ask her in pity's name to "put me up".'

If he could ever have been said to threaten complications he rather visibly did so now. I began to regret my officious presentation of his name and prepared without delay to lead him out of the house. We overtook the housekeeper in the last room of the series, a small unused boudoir over whose chimney-piece hung a portrait of a young man in a powdered wig and a brocaded waistcoat. I was struck with his resemblance to my com-panion while our guide introduced him. 'This is Mr. Clement Searle, Mr. Searle's great-uncle, by Sir Joshua Reynolds. He died young, poor gentle-man; he perished at sea, going to America.'

'He was the young buck who brought the majolica out of Italy,' I supplemented.

'Indeed, sir, I believe he did,' said the housekeeper without wonder.

'He's the image of you, my dear Searle,' I further observed.

'He's remarkably like the gentleman, saving his presence,' said the housekeeper.

My friend stood staring. 'Clement Searle—at sea—going to America——?' he broke out. Then with some sharpness to our old woman: 'Why the devil did he go to America?'

'Why indeed, sir? You may well ask. I believe he had kinsfolk there. It was for them to come to him.'

Searle broke into a laugh. 'It was for them to come to him! Well, well,' he said, fixing his eyes on our guide, 'they've come to him at last!'

She blushed like a wrinkled rose-leaf. 'Indeed, sir, I verily believe you're one of *us!*'

'My name's the name of that beautiful youth,' Searle went on. 'Dear kinsman, I'm happy to meet you! And what do you think of this?' he pursued as he grasped me by the arm. 'I have an idea. He perished at sea. His spirit came ashore and wandered about in misery till it got another incarnation—in this poor trunk!' And he tapped his hollow chest. 'Here it has rattled about these forty years, beating its wings against its rickety cage, begging to be taken home again. And I never knew what was the matter with me! Now at last the bruised spirit can escape!'

Our old lady gaped at a breadth of appreciation—if not at the disclosure of a connection—beyond her. The scene was really embarrassing, and my confusion increased as we became aware of another presence. A lady had appeared in the doorway and the housekeeper dropped just audibly: 'Miss Searle!' My first impression of Miss Searle was that she was neither young nor beautiful. She stood without confidence on the threshold, pale, trying to smile and twirling my card in her fingers. I immediately bowed. Searle stared at her as if one of the pictures had stepped out of its frame.

'If I'm not mistaken one of you gentlemen is Mr. Clement Searle,' the lady adventured.

'My friend's Mr. Clement Searle,' I took upon myself to reply. 'Allow me to add that I alone am responsible for your having received his name.'

'I should have been sorry not to—not to see him,' said Miss Searle, beginning to blush. 'Your being from America has led me—perhaps to intrude!'

'The intrusion, madam, has been on our part. And with just that excuse—that we come from so far away.'

Miss Searle, while I spoke, had fixed her eyes on my friend as he stood silent beneath Sir Joshua's portrait. The housekeeper, agitated and mystified, fairly let herself go. 'Heaven preserve us, Miss! It's your great-uncle's picture come to life.'

'I'm not mistaken then,' said Miss Searle—'we must be distantly related.' She had the air of the shyest of women, for whom it was almost anguish to make an advance without help. Searle eyed her with gentle wonder from head to foot, and I could easily read his thoughts. This then was his maiden-cousin, prospective mistress of these hereditary treasures. She was of some thirty-five years of age, taller than was then common and perhaps stouter than is now enjoined. She had small kind grey eyes, a considerable quantity of very light-brown hair, and a smiling well-formed mouth. She was dressed in a lustreless black satin gown with a short train. Disposed about her neck was a blue handkerchief, and over this handkerchief, in many convolutions, a string of amber beads. Her appearance was singular; she was large yet somehow vague, mature yet undeveloped. Her manner of addressing us spoke of all sorts of deep diffidences. Searle, I think, had prefigured to himself some proud cold beauty of five-and-twenty; he was relieved at finding the lady timid and not obtrusively fair. He at once had an excellent tone.

'We're distant cousins, I believe. I'm happy to claim a relationship which you're so good as to remember. I hadn't counted on your knowing anything about me.'

'Perhaps I've done wrong.' And Miss Searle blushed and smiled anew. 'But I've always known of there being people of our blood in America, and have often wondered and asked about them—without ever learning much. Today, when this card was brought me and I understood a Clement Searle to be under our roof as a stranger, I felt I ought to do something. But, you know, I hardly knew what. My brother's in London. I've done what I think he would have done. Welcome as a cousin.' And with a resolution that ceased to be awkward she put out her hand.

'I'm welcome indeed if he would have done it half so graciously!' Again Searle, taking her hand, acquitted himself beautifully.

'You've seen what there is, I think,' Miss Searle went on. 'Perhaps now you'll have luncheon.' We followed her into a small breakfast-room where a deep bay window opened on the mossy flags of a terrace. Here, for some moments, she remained dumb and abashed, as if resting from a measurable effort. Searle too had ceased to overflow, so that I had to relieve the silence. It was of course easy to descant on the beauties of park and mansion, and as I did so I observed our hostess. She had no arts, no impulses nor graces—scarce even any manners; she was queerly, almost frowsily dressed; yet she pleased me well. She had an antique sweetness, a homely fragrance of old traditions. To be so simple, among those complicated treasures, so pampered and yet so fresh, so modest and yet so placid, told of just the spacious leisure in which Searle and I had imagined human life to be steeped in such places as that. This figure was to the Sleeping Beauty in the Wood what a fact is to a fairy-tale, an interpretation to a myth. We, on our side, were to our hostess subjects of a curiosity not cunningly veiled.

'I should like so to go abroad!' she exclaimed suddenly, as if she meant us to take the speech for an expression of interest in ourselves.

'Have you never been?' one of us asked.

'Only once. Three years ago my brother took me to Switzerland. We thought it extremely beautiful. Except for that journey I've always lived here. I was born in this house. It's a dear old place indeed, and I know it well. Sometimes one wants a change.' And on my asking her how she spent her time and what society she saw, 'Of course it's very quiet,' she went on, proceeding by short steps and simple statements, in the manner of a person called upon for the first time to analyse to that extent her situation. 'We see very few people. I don't think there are many nice ones hereabouts. At least we don't know them. Our own family's very small. My brother cares for nothing but riding and books. He had a great sorrow ten years ago. He lost his wife and his only son, a dear little boy, who of course would have had everything. Do you know that that makes me the heir, as they've done something—I don't quite know what—to the entail? Poor old me! Since his loss my brother has preferred to be quite alone.

I'm sorry he's away. But you must wait till he comes back. I expect him in a day or two.' She talked more and more, as if our very strangeness led her on, about her circumstances, her solitude, her bad eyes, so that she couldn't read, her flowers, her ferns, her dogs, and the vicar, recently presented to the living by her brother and warranted quite safe, who had lately begun to light his altar candles; pausing every now and then to gasp in self-surprise, yet, in the quaintest way in the world, keeping up her story as if it were a slow rather awkward old-time dance, a difficult *pas seul* in which she would have been better with more practice, but of which she must complete the figure. Of all the old things I had seen in England this exhibited mind of Miss Searle's seemed to me the oldest, the most handed down and taken for granted; fenced and protected as it was by convention and precedent and usage, thoroughly acquainted with its subordinate place. I felt as if I were talking with the heroine of a last-century novel. As she talked she rested her dull eyes on her kinsman with wondering kindness. At last she put it to him: 'Did you mean to go away without asking for us?'

'I had thought it over, Miss Searle, and had determined not to trouble you. You've shown me how unfriendly I should have been.'

'But you knew of the place being ours, and of our relationship?'

'Just so. It was because of these things that I came down here—because of them almost that I came to England. I've always liked to think of them,' said my companion.

'You merely wished to look then? We don't pretend to be much to look at.'

He waited; her words were too strange. 'You don't know what you are, Miss Searle.'

'You like the old place then?'

Searle looked at her again in silence. 'If I could only tell you!' he said at last.

'Do tell me. You must come and stay with us.'

It moved him to an oddity of mirth. 'Take care, take care—I should surprise you! I'm afraid I should bore you. I should never leave you.'

'Oh you'd get homesick—for your real home!'

At this he was still more amused. 'By the way, tell Miss Searle about our real home,' he said to me. And he stepped, through the window, out upon the terrace, followed by two beautiful dogs, a setter and a young stag-hound who from the moment we came in had established the fondest relation with him. Miss Searle looked at him, while he went, as if she vaguely yearned over him; it began to be plain that she was interested in her exotic cousin. I suddenly recalled the last words I had heard spoken by my friend's adviser in London and which, in a very crude form, had reference to his making a match with this lady. If only Miss Searle could be induced to think of that, and if one had but the tact to put it in a light to her! Something assured me that her heart was virgin-soil, that the flower of romantic affection had never bloomed there. If I might just sow the seed! There seemed to shape itself within her the perfect image of one of the patient wives of old.

'He has lost his heart to England,' I said. 'He ought to have been born here.'

'And yet he doesn't look in the least an Englishman,' she still rather guardedly prosed.

'Oh it isn't his looks, poor fellow.'

'Of course looks aren't everything. I never talked with a foreigner before; but he talks as I have fancied foreigners.'

'Yes, he's foreign enough.'

'Is he married?'

'His wife's dead and he's all alone in the world.'

'Has he much property?'

'None to speak of.'

'But he has means to travel.'

I meditated. 'He has not expected to travel far,' I said at last. 'You know, he's in very poor health.'

'Poor gentleman! So I supposed.'

'But there's more of him to go on with than he thinks. He came here because he wanted to see your place before he dies.'

'Dear me—kind man!' And I imagined in the quiet eyes the hint of a possible tear. 'And he was going away without my seeing him?'

'He's very modest, you see.'

'He's very much the gentleman.'

I couldn't but smile. 'He's *all*——!'

At this moment we heard on the terrace a loud harsh cry. 'It's the great peacock!' said Miss Searle, stepping to the window and passing out while I followed her. Below us, leaning on the parapet, stood our appreciative friend with his arm round the neck of the setter. Before him on the grand walk strutted the familiar fowl of gardens—a splendid specimen—with ruffled neck and expanded tail. The other dog had apparently indulged in a momentary attempt to abash the gorgeous biped, but at Searle's summons had bounded back to the terrace and leaped upon the ledge, where he now stood licking his new friend's face. The scene had a beautiful old-time air: the peacock flaunting in the foreground like the genius of stately places; the broad terrace, which flattered an innate taste of mine for all deserted walks where people may have sat after heavy dinners to drink coffee in old Sèvres and where the stiff brocade of women's dresses may have rustled over grass or gravel; and far around us, with one leafy circle melting into another, the timbered acres of the park. 'The very beasts have made him welcome,' I noted as we rejoined our companion.

'The peacock has done for you, Mr. Searle,' said his cousin, 'what he does only for very great people. A year ago there came here a great person—a grand old lady—to see my brother. I don't think that since then he has spread his tail as wide for anyone else—not by a dozen feathers.'

'It's not alone the peacock,' said Searle. 'Just now there came slipping across my path a little green lizard, the first I ever saw, the lizard of literature! And if you've a ghost, broad daylight though it be, I expect to see him here. Do you know the annals of your house, Miss Searle?'

'Oh dear, no! You must ask my brother for all those things.'

'You ought to have a collection of legends and traditions. You ought to have loves and murders and mysteries by the roomful. I shall be ashamed of you if you haven't.'

'Oh Mr. Searle! We've always been a very well-behaved family,' she quite seriously pleaded. 'Nothing out of the way has ever happened, I think.'

'Nothing out of the way? Oh that won't do! We've managed better than that in America. Why I myself!'—and he looked at her ruefully enough, but enjoying too his idea that he might embody the social scandal or point to the darkest drama of the Searles. 'Suppose I should turn out a better Searle than you—better than you nursed here in romance and extravagance? Come, don't disappoint me. You've some history among you all, you've some poetry, you've some accumulation of legend. I've been famished all my days for these things. Don't you understand? Ah you can't understand! Tell me,' he rambled on, 'something tremendous. When I think of what must have happened here; of the lovers who must have strolled on this terrace and wandered under the beeches, of all the figures and passions and purposes that must have haunted these walls! When I think of the births and deaths, the joys and sufferings, the young hopes and the old regrets, the rich experience of life——!' He faltered a moment with the increase of his agitation. His humour of dismay at a threat of the commonplace in the history he felt about him had turned to a deeper reaction. I began to fear however that he was really losing his head. He went on with a wilder play. 'To see it all called up there before me, if the Devil alone could do it I'd make a bargain with the Devil! Ah Miss Searle,' he cried, 'I'm a most unhappy man!'

'Oh dear, oh dear!' she almost wailed while I turned half away.

'Look at that window, that dear little window!' I turned back to see him point to a small protruding oriel, above us, relieved against the purple brickwork, framed in chiselled stone and curtained with ivy.

'It's my little room,' she said.

'Of course it's a woman's room. Think of all the dear faces—all of them so mild and yet so proud—that have looked out of that lattice, and of all the old-time women's lives whose principal view of the world has been this quiet park! Every one of them was a cousin of mine. And you, dear lady, you're one of them yet.' With which he marched towards her and took her large white hand. She surrendered it, blushing to her eyes and pressing her other hand to her breast. 'You're a woman of the past. You're nobly simple. It has been a romance to see you. It doesn't matter what I say to you. You didn't know me yesterday, you'll not know me tomorrow. Let me today do a mad sweet thing. Let me imagine in you the spirit of all the dead women who have trod the terrace-flags that lie here like sepulchral tablets in the pavement of a church. Let me say I delight in you!'—he raised her hand to his lips. She gently withdrew it and for a moment averted her face. Meeting her eyes the next instant I saw the tears had come. The Sleeping Beauty was awake.

There followed an embarrassed pause. An issue was suddenly presented by the appearance of the butler bearing a letter. 'A telegram, Miss,' he announced.

'Oh what shall I do?' cried Miss Searle. 'I can't open a telegram. Cousin, help me.'

Searle took the missive, opened it, and read aloud: *'I shall be home to dinner. Keep the American.'*

III

'Keep the American!' Miss Searle, in compliance with the injunction conveyed in her brother's telegram (with something certainly of telegraphic curtness), lost no time in expressing the pleasure it would give her that our friend should remain. 'Really you must,' she said; and forthwith repaired to the housekeeper to give orders for the preparation of a room.

'But how in the world did he know of my being here?' my companion put to me.

I answered that he had probably heard from his solicitor of the other's visit. 'Mr. Simmons and that gentleman must have had another interview since your arrival in England. Simmons, for reasons of his own, has made known to him your journey to this neighbourhood, and Mr. Searle, learning this, has immediately taken for granted that you've formally presented yourself to his sister. He's hospitably inclined and wishes her to do the proper thing by you. There may even,' I went on, 'be more in it than that. I've my little theory that he's the very phoenix of usurpers, that he has been very much struck with what the experts have had to say for you, and that he wishes to have the originality of making over to you your share—so limited after all—of the estate.'

'I give it up!' my friend mused. 'Come what come will!'

'You, of course,' said Miss Searle, reappearing and turning to me, 'are included in my brother's invitation. I've told them to see about a room for you. Your luggage shall immediately be sent for.'

It was arranged that I in person should be driven over to our little inn and that I should return with our effects in time to meet Mr. Searle at dinner. On my arrival several hours later I was immediately conducted to my room. The servant pointed out to me that it communicated by a door and a private passage with that of my fellow visitor. I made my way along this passage—a low narrow corridor with a broad latticed casement through which there streamed upon a series of grotesquely sculptured oaken closets and cupboards the vivid animating glow of the western sun—knocked at his door and, getting no answer, opened it. In an armchair by the open window sat my friend asleep, his arms and legs relaxed and head dropped on his breast. It was a great relief to see him rest thus from his rhapsodies, and I watched him for some moments before waking him. There was a faint glow of colour in his cheek and a light expressive parting of his lips, something nearer to ease and peace than I had yet seen in him. It was almost happiness, it was almost health. I laid my hand on his arm and gently shook it. He opened his eyes, gazed at me a moment, vaguely recognized me, then closed them again. 'Let me dream, let me dream!'

'What are you dreaming about?'

A moment passed before his answer came. 'About a tall woman in a quaint black dress, with yellow hair and a sweet, sweet smile, and a soft low delicious voice! I'm in love with her.'

'It's better to see her than to dream about her,' I said. 'Get up and dress; then we'll go down to dinner and meet her.'

'Dinner—dinner——?' And he gradually opened his eyes again. 'Yes, upon my word I shall dine!'

'Oh you're all right!' I declared for the twentieth time as he rose to his feet. 'You'll live to bury Mr. Simmons.' He told me he had spent the hours of my absence with Miss Searle—they had strolled together half over the place. 'You must be very intimate,' I smiled.

'She's intimate with *me*. Goodness knows what rigmarole I've treated her to!' They had parted an hour ago; since when, he believed, her brother had arrived.

The slow-fading twilight was still in the great drawing-room when we came down. The housekeeper had told us this apartment was rarely used, there being others, smaller and more convenient, for the same needs. It seemed now, however, to be occupied in my comrade's honour. At the furthest end, rising to the roof like a royal tomb in a cathedral, was a great chimney-piece of chiselled white marble, yellowed by time, in which a light fire was crackling. Before the fire stood a small short man, with his hands behind him; near him was Miss Searle, so transformed by her dress that at first I scarcely knew her. There was in our entrance and reception something remarkably chilling and solemn. We moved in silence up the long room; Mr. Searle advanced slowly, a dozen steps, to meet us; his sister stood motionless. I was conscious of her masking her visage with a large white tinselled fan, and that her eyes, grave and enlarged, watched us intently over the top of it. The master of Lackley grasped in silence the proffered hand of his kinsman and eyed him from head to foot, suppressing, I noted, a start of surprise at his resemblance to Sir Joshua's portrait. 'This is a happy day.' And then turning to me with an odd little sharp stare: 'My cousin's friend is my friend.' Miss Searle lowered her fan.

The first thing that struck me in Mr. Searle's appearance was his very limited stature, which was less by half a head than that of his sister. The second was the preternatural redness of his hair and beard. They intermingled over his ears and surrounded his head like a huge lurid nimbus. His face was pale and attenuated, the face of a scholar, a dilettante, a comparer of points and texts, a man who lives in a library bending over books and prints and medals. At a distance it might have passed for smooth and rather blankly composed; but on a nearer view it revealed a number of wrinkles, sharply etched and scratched, of a singularly aged and refined effect. It was the complexion of a man of sixty. His nose was arched and delicate, identical almost with the nose of my friend. His eyes, large and deep-set, had a kind of auburn glow, the suggestion of a keen metal red-hot—or, more plainly, were full of temper and spirit. Imagine this physiognomy—grave and solemn, grotesquely solemn, in spite of the bushy brightness which made a sort of frame for it—set in motion by a queer, quick, defiant, perfunctory, preoccupied smile, and you will have an imperfect notion of the remarkable presence of our host; something better worth seeing and knowing, I perceived as I quite breathlessly took him in, than anything we had yet encountered. How thoroughly I had entered into sympathy with my poor picked-up friend, and how effectually I had associated my sensibilities with his own, I had not suspected till, within the short five minutes before the signal for dinner, I became aware, without his giving me the least hint, of his placing himself on the defensive. To neither of us was Mr. Searle sympathetic. I might have guessed from her attitude that his sister entered into our thoughts. A marked change had been wrought in her since the morning; during the hour, indeed—as I read in the light of the wondering glance he cast at her—that had elapsed since her parting with her cousin. She had not yet recovered from some great agitation. Her face was pale and she had clearly been crying. These notes of trouble gave her a new and quite perverse dignity, which was further enhanced by something complimentary and commemorative in her dress.

Whether it was taste or whether it was accident I know not; but the amiable creature, as she stood there half in the cool twilight, half in the arrested glow of the fire as it spent itself in the vastness of its marble cave, was a figure for a painter. She was habited in some faded splendour of sea-green crape and silk, a piece of millinery which, though it must have witnessed a number of dull dinners, preserved still a festive air. Over her white shoulders she wore an ancient web of the most precious and venerable lace and about her rounded throat a single series of large pearls. I went in with her to dinner, and Mr. Searle, following with my friend, took his arm, as the latter afterwards told me, and pretended jocosely to conduct him. As dinner proceeded the feeling grew within me that a drama had begun to be played in which the three persons before me were actors—each of a really arduous part. The character allotted to my friend, however, was certainly the least easy to represent with effect, though I overflowed with the desire that he should acquit himself to his honour. I seemed to see him urge his faded faculties to take their cue and perform. The poor fellow tried to do himself credit more seriously than ever in his old best days. With Miss Searle, credulous passive and pitying, he had finally flung aside all vanity and propriety and shown the bottom of his fantastic heart. But with our host there might be no talking of nonsense nor taking of liberties; there and then, if ever, sat a consummate conservative, breathing the fumes of hereditary privilege and security. For an hour, accordingly, I saw my poor protégé attempt, all in pain, to meet a new decorum. He set himself the task of appearing very American, in order that his appreciation of everything Mr. Searle represented might seem purely disinterested. What his kinsman had expected him to be I know not; but I made Mr. Searle out as annoyed, in spite of his exaggerated urbanity, at finding him so harmless. Our host was not the man to show his hand, but I think his best card had been a certain implicit confidence that so provincial a parasite would hardly have good manners. He led the conversation to the country we had left; rather as if a leash had been attached to the collar of some lumpish and half-domesticated animal the tendency of whose movements had to be recognized. He spoke of it indeed as of some fabled planet, alien to the British orbit, lately proclaimed to have the admixture of atmospheric gases required to support animal life, but not, save under cover of a liberal afterthought, to be admitted into one's regular conception of things. I, for my part, felt nothing but regret that the spheric smoothness of his universe should be disfigured by the extrusion even of such inconsiderable particles as ourselves.

'I knew in a general way of our having somehow ramified over there,' Mr. Searle mentioned; 'but had scarcely followed it more than you pretend to pick up the fruit your long-armed pear tree may drop, on the other side of your wall, in your neighbour's garden. There was a man I knew at Cambridge, a very odd fellow, a decent fellow too; he and I were rather cronies; I think he afterwards went to the Middle States. They'll be, I suppose, about the Mississippi? At all events, there was that great-uncle of mine whom Sir Joshua painted. He went to America, but he never got there. He was lost at sea. You look enough like him to make one fancy he *did* get there and that you've kept him alive by one of those beastly processes—I think you have 'em over there: what do you call it, "putting up" things? If you're he you've not done a wise thing to show yourself here. He left a bad name behind him. There's a ghost who comes sobbing about the house every now and then, the ghost of one to whom he did a wrong.'

'Oh mercy *on* us!' cried Miss Searle in simple horror.

'Of course *you* know nothing of such things,' he rather dryly allowed. 'You're too sound a sleeper to hear the sobbing of ghosts.'

'I'm sure I should like immensely to hear the sobbing of a ghost,' said my friend, the light of his previous eagerness playing up into his eyes. 'Why does it sob? I feel as if that were what we've come above all to learn.'

Mr. Searle eyed his audience a moment gaugingly; he held the balance as to measure his resources. He wished to do justice to his theme. With the long finger-nails of his left hand nervously playing against the tinkling crystals of his wineglass and his conscious eyes betraying that, small and strange as he sat there, he knew himself, to his pleasure and advantage, remarkably impressive, he dropped into our untutored minds the sombre legend of his house. 'Mr. Clement Searle, from all I gather, was a young man of great talents but a weak disposition. His mother was left a widow early in life, with two sons, of whom he was the elder and the more promising. She educated him with the greatest affection and care. Of course when he came to manhood she wished him to marry well. His means were quite sufficient to enable him to overlook the want of money in his wife; and Mrs. Searle selected a young lady who possessed, as she conceived, every good gift save a fortune—a fine proud handsome girl, the daughter of an old friend, an old lover I suspect, of her own. Clement, however, as it appeared, had either chosen otherwise or was as yet unprepared to choose. The young lady opened upon him in vain the battery of her attractions; in vain his mother urged her cause. Clement remained cold, insensible, inflexible. Mrs. Searle had a character which appears to have gone out of fashion in my family nowadays; she was a great manager, a *maîtresse-femme*. A proud passionate imperious woman, she had had immense cares and ever so many law-suits; they had sharpened her temper and her will. She suspected that her son's affections had another object, and this object she began to hate. Irritated by his stubborn defiance of her wishes she persisted in her purpose. The more she watched him the more she was convinced he loved in secret. If he loved in secret of course he loved beneath him. He went about the place all sombre and sullen and brooding. At last, with the rashness of an angry woman, she threatened to bring the young lady of her choice—who, by the way, seems to have been no shrinking blossom—to stay in the house. A stormy scene was the result. He threatened that if she did so he would leave the country and sail for America. She probably disbelieved him; she knew him to be weak, but she overrated his weakness. At all events the rejected one arrived and Clement Searle departed. On a dark December day he took ship at Southampton. The two women, desperate with rage and sorrow, sat alone in this big house, mingling their tears and imprecations. A fortnight later, on Christmas Eve, in the midst of a great snowstorm long famous in the country, something happened that quickened their bitterness. A young woman, battered and chilled by the storm, gained entrance to the house and, making her way into the presence of the mistress and her guest, poured out her tale. She was a poor curate's daughter out of some little hole in Gloucestershire. Clement Searle had loved her—loved her all too well! She had been turned out in wrath from her father's house; his mother at least might pity her—if not for herself then for the child she was soon to bring forth. But the poor girl had been a second time too trustful. The women, in scorn, in horror, with blows possibly, drove her forth again into the storm. In the storm she wandered and in the deep snow she died. Her lover, as you know, perished in that hard winter weather at sea; the news came to his mother late, but soon enough. We're haunted by the curate's daughter!'

Mr. Searle retailed this anecdote with infinite taste and point, the happiest art; when he ceased there was a pause of some moments. 'Ah well we may be!' Miss Searle then mournfully murmured.

Searle blazed up into enthusiasm. 'Of course, you know'—with which he began to blush violently—'I should be sorry to claim any identity with the poor devil, my faithless namesake. But I should be immensely gratified if the young lady's spirit, deceived by my resemblance, were to mistake me for her cruel lover. She's welcome to the comfort of it. What one can do in the case I shall be glad to do. But can a ghost haunt a ghost? I *am* a ghost!'

Mr. Searle stared a moment and then had a subtle sneer. 'I could almost believe you are!'

'Oh brother—and cousin!' cried Miss Searle with the gentlest yet most appealing dignity. 'How can you talk so horribly?'

The horrible talk, however, evidently possessed a potent magic for my friend; and his imagination, checked a while by the influence of his kinsman, began again to lead him a dance. From this moment he ceased to steer his frail bark, to care what he said or how he said it, so long as he expressed his passionate appreciation of the scene around him. As he kept up this strain I ceased even secretly to wish he wouldn't. I have wondered since that I shouldn't have been annoyed by the way he reverted constantly to himself. But a great frankness, for the time, makes its own law and a great passion its own channel. There was moreover an irresponsible, indescribable effect of beauty in everything his lips uttered. Free alike from adulation and from envy, the essence of his discourse was a divine apprehension, a romantic vision free as the flight of Ariel, of the poetry of his companions' situation and their contrasted general irresponsiveness.

'How does the look of age come?' he suddenly broke out at dessert. 'Does it come of itself, unobserved, unrecorded, unmeasured? Or do you woo it and set baits and traps for it, and watch it like the dawning brownness of a meerschaum pipe, and make it fast, when it appears, just where it peeps out, and light a votive taper beneath it and give thanks to it daily? Or do you forbid it and fight it and resist it, and yet feel it settling and deepening about you as irresistible as fate?'

'What the deuce is the man talking about?' said the smile of our host.

'I found a little grey hair this morning,' Miss Searle incoherently prosed.

'Well then I hope you paid it every respect!' cried her visitor.

'I looked at it for a long time in my hand-glass,' she answered with more presence of mind.

'Miss Searle can for many years to come afford to be amused at grey hairs,' I interposed in the hope of some greater ease.

It had its effect. 'Ten years from last Thursday I shall be forty-four,' she almost comfortably smiled.

'Well, that's just what I am,' said Searle. 'If I had only come here ten years ago! I should have had more time to enjoy the feast, but I should have had less appetite. I needed first to get famished.'

'Oh why did you wait for that?' his entertainer asked. 'To think of these ten years that we might have been enjoying you!' At the vision of which waste and loss Mr. Searle had a fine shrill laugh.

'Well,' my friend explained, 'I always had a notion—a stupid vulgar notion if ever there was one—that to come abroad properly one had to have a pot of money. My pot was too nearly empty. At last I came with my empty pot!'

Mr. Searle had a wait for delicacy, but he proceeded. 'You're reduced, you're—a—straitened?'

Our companion's very breath blew away the veil. 'Reduced to nothing. Straitened to the clothes on my back!'

'You don't say so!' said Mr. Searle with a large vague gasp. 'Well—well—well!' he added in a voice which might have meant everything or nothing; and then, in his whimsical way, went on to finish a glass of wine. His searching eye, as he drank, met mine, and for a moment we each rather deeply sounded the other, to the effect no doubt of a slight embarrassment. 'And you,' he said by way of carrying this off—'how about *your* wardrobe?'

'Oh his!' cried my friend; 'his wardrobe's immense. He could dress up a regiment!' He had drunk more champagne—I admit that the champagne was good—than was from any point of view to have been desired. He was rapidly drifting beyond any tacit dissuasion of mine. He was feverish and rash, and all attempt to direct would now simply irritate him. As we rose from the table he caught my troubled look. Passing his arm for a moment into mine, 'This is the great night!' he strangely and softly said; 'the night and the crisis will settle me.'

Mr. Searle had caused the whole lower portion of the house to be thrown open and a multitude of lights to be placed in convenient and effective positions. Such a marshalled wealth of ancient candlesticks and flambeaux I had never beheld. Niched against the dusky wainscots, casting great luminous circles upon the pendent stiffness of sombre tapestries, enhancing and completing with admirable effect the variety and mystery of the great ancient house, they seemed to people the wide rooms, as our little group passed slowly from one to another, with a dim expectant presence. We had thus, in spite of everything, a wonderful hour of it. Mr. Searle at once assumed the part of cicerone, and—I had not hitherto done him justice—Mr. Searle became almost agreeable. While I lingered behind with his sister, he walked in advance with his kinsman. It was as if he had said: 'Well, if you want the old place you shall have it—so far as the impression goes!' He spared us no thrill—I had almost said no pang—of that experience. Carrying a tall silver candlestick in his left hand, he raised it and lowered it and cast the light hither and thither, upon pictures and hangings and carvings and cornices. He knew his house to perfection. He touched upon a hundred traditions and memories, he threw off a cloud of rich reference to its earlier occupants. He threw off again, in his easy elegant way, a dozen—happily lighter—anecdotes. His relative attended with a brooding deference. Miss Searle and I meanwhile were not wholly silent.

'I suppose that by this time you and your cousin are almost old friends,' I remarked.

She trifled a moment with her fan and then raised her kind small eyes. 'Old friends—yet at the same time strangely new! My cousin, my cousin' —and her voice lingered on the word—'it seems so strange to call him my cousin after thinking these many years that I've no one in the world but my brother. But he's really so very odd!'

'It's not so much he as—well, as his situation, that deserves that name,' I tried to reason.

'I'm sorry for his situation. I wish I could help it in some way. He interests me so much.' She gave a sweet-sounding sigh. 'I wish I could have known him sooner—and better. He tells me he's but the shadow of what he used to be.'

I wondered if he had been consciously practising on the sensibilities of this gentle creature. If he had I believed he had gained his point. But his position had in fact become to my sense so precarious that I hardly ventured to be glad. 'His better self just now seems again to be taking shape,' I said. 'It will have been a good deed on your part if you help to restore him to all he ought to be.'

She met my idea blankly. 'Dear me, what can I do?'

'Be a friend to him. Let him like you, let him love you. I dare say you see in him now much to pity and wonder at. But let him simply enjoy a while the grateful sense of your nearness and dearness. He'll be a better and stronger man for it, and then you can love him, you can esteem him, without restriction.'

She fairly frowned for helplessness. 'It's a hard part for poor stupid me to play!'

Her almost infantine innocence left me no choice but to be absolutely frank. 'Did you ever play any part at all?'

She blushed as if I had been reproaching her with her insignificance. 'Never! I think I've hardly lived.'

'You've begun to live now perhaps. You've begun to care for something else than your old-fashioned habits. Pardon me if I seem rather meddlesome; you know we Americans are very rough and ready. It's a great moment. I wish you joy!'

'I could almost believe you're laughing at me. I feel more trouble than joy.'

'Why do you feel trouble?'

She paused with her eyes fixed on our companions. 'My cousin's arrival's a great disturbance,' she said at last.

'You mean you did wrong in coming to meet him? In that case the fault's mine. He had no intention of giving you the opportunity.'

'I certainly took too much on myself. But I can't find it in my heart to regret it. I never shall regret it! I did the only thing I *could*, heaven forgive me!'

'Heaven bless you, Miss Searle! Is any harm to come of it? I did the evil; let me bear the brunt!'

She shook her head gravely. 'You don't know my brother!'

'The sooner I master the subject the better then,' I said. I couldn't help relieving myself—at least by the tone of my voice—of the antipathy with which, decidedly, this gentleman had inspired me. 'Not perhaps that we should get on so well together!' After which, as she turned away, 'Are you *very* much afraid of him?' I added.

She gave me a shuddering sidelong glance. 'He's looking at me!'

He was placed with his back to us, holding a large Venetian hand-mirror, framed in chiselled silver, which he had taken from a shelf of antiquities, just at such an angle that he caught the reflection of his sister's person. It was evident that I too was under his attention, and I was resolved I wouldn't be suspected for nothing. 'Miss Searle,' I said with urgency, 'promise me something.'

She turned upon me with a start and a look that seemed to beg me to spare her. 'Oh don't ask me—please don't!' It was as if she were standing on the edge of a place where the ground had suddenly fallen away, and had been called upon to make a leap. I felt retreat was impossible, however, and that it was the greater kindness to assist her to jump.

'Promise me,' I repeated.

Still with her eyes she protested. 'Oh what a dreadful day!' she cried at last.

'Promise me to let him speak to you alone if he should ask you—any wish you may suspect on your brother's part notwithstanding.'

She coloured deeply. 'You mean he has something so particular to say?'

'Something so particular!'

'Poor cousin!'

'Well, poor cousin! But promise me.'

'I promise,' she said, and moved away across the long room and out of the door.

'You're in time to hear the most delightful story,' Searle began to me as I rejoined him and his host. They were standing before an old sombre portrait of a lady in the dress of Queen Anne's time, whose ill-painted flesh-tints showed livid, in the candle-light, against her dark drapery and background. 'This is Mrs. Margaret Searle—a sort of Beatrix Esmond—*qui se passait ses fantaisies.* She married a paltry Frenchman, a penniless fiddler, in the teeth of her whole family. Pretty Mrs. Margaret, you must have been a woman of courage! Upon my word, she looks like Miss Searle! But pray go on. What came of it all?'

Our companion watched him with an air of distaste for his boisterous homage and of pity for his crude imagination. But he took up the tale with an effective dryness: 'I found a year ago, in a box of very old papers, a letter from the lady in question to a certain Cynthia Searle, her elder sister. It was dated from Paris and dreadfully ill-spelled. It contained a most passionate appeal for pecuniary assistance. She had just had a baby, she was starving and dreadfully neglected by her husband—she cursed the day she had left England. It was a most dismal production. I never heard she found means to return.'

'So much for marrying a Frenchman!' I said sententiously.

Our host had one of his waits. 'This is the only lady of the family who ever was taken in by an adventurer.'

'Does Miss Searle know her history?' asked my friend with a stare at the rounded whiteness of the heroine's cheek.

'Miss Searle knows nothing!' said our host with expression.

'She shall know at least the tale of Mrs. Margaret,' their guest returned; and he walked rapidly away in search of her.

Mr. Searle and I pursued our march through the lighted rooms. 'You've found a cousin with a vengeance,' I doubtless awkwardly enough laughed.

'Ah, a vengeance?' my entertainer stiffly repeated.

'I mean that he takes as keen an interest in your annals and possessions as yourself.'

'Oh exactly so! He tells me he's a bad invalid,' he added in a moment. 'I should never have supposed it.'

'Within the past few hours he's a changed man. Your beautiful house, your extreme kindness, have refreshed him immensely.'

Mr. Searle uttered the vague ejaculation with which self-conscious Britons so often betray the concussion of any especial courtesy of speech. But he followed this by a sudden odd glare and the sharp declaration: 'I'm an honest man!' I was quite prepared to assent; but he went on with a fury of frankness, as if it were the first time in his life he had opened himself to anyone, as if the process were highly disagreeable and he were hurrying through it as a task. 'An honest man, mind you! I know nothing about Mr. Clement Searle! I never expected to see him. He has been to me a—a——!' And here he paused to select a word which should vividly enough express what, for good or for ill, his kinsman represented. 'He has been to me an Amazement! I've no doubt he's a most amiable man. You'll not deny, however, that he's a very extraordinary sort of person. I'm sorry he's ill. I'm sorry he's poor. He's my fiftieth cousin. Well and good. I'm an honest man. He shall not have it to say that he wasn't received at my house.'

'He too, thank heaven, is an honest man!' I smiled.

'Why the devil then,' cried Mr. Searle, turning almost fiercely on me, 'has he put forward this underhand claim to my property?'

The question, quite ringing out, flashed backward a gleam of light upon the demeanour of our host and the suppressed agitation of his sister. In an instant the jealous soul of the unhappy gentleman revealed itself. For a moment I was so surprised and scandalized at the directness of his attack that I lacked words to reply. As soon as he had spoken indeed Mr. Searle appeared to feel he had been wanting in form. 'Pardon me,' he began afresh, 'if I speak of this matter with heat. But I've been more disgusted than I can say to hear, as I heard this morning from my solicitor, of the extraordinary proceedings of Mr. Clement Searle. Gracious goodness, sir, for what does the man take me? He pretends to the Lord knows what fantastic admiration for my place. Let him then show his respect for it by not taking too many liberties! Let him, with his high-flown parade of loyalty, imagine a tithe of what *I* feel! I love my estate; it's my passion, my conscience, my life! Am I to divide it up at this time of day with a beggarly foreigner—a man without means, without appearance, without proof, a pretender, an adventurer, a chattering mountebank? I thought America boasted having lands for all men! Upon my soul, sir, I've never been so shocked in my life.'

I paused for some moments before speaking, to allow his passion fully to expand itself and to flicker up again if it chose; for, so far as I was concerned in the whole awkward matter, I but wanted to deal with him discreetly. 'Your apprehensions, sir,' I said at last, 'your not unnatural surprise, perhaps, at the candour of our interest, have acted too much on your nerves. You're attacking a man of straw, a creature of unworthy illusion; though I'm sadly afraid you've wounded a man of spirit and conscience. Either my friend has no valid claim on your estate, in which case your agitation is superfluous; or he *has* a valid claim——'

Mr. Searle seized my arm and glared at me; his pale face paler still with the horror of my suggestion, his great eyes of alarm glowing and his strange red hair erect and quivering. 'A valid claim!' he shouted. 'Let him try it—let him bring it into court!'

We had emerged into the great hall and stood facing the main doorway. The door was open into the portico, through the stone archway of which I saw the garden glitter in the blue light of a full moon. As the master of the house uttered the words I have just repeated, my companion came slowly up into the porch from without, bareheaded, bright in the outer moonlight, dark in the shadow of the archway, and bright again in the lamplight at the entrance of the hall. As he crossed the threshold the butler made an appearance at the head of the staircase on our left, faltering visibly a moment at sight of Mr. Searle; after which, noting my friend, he gravely descended. He bore in his hand a small silver tray. On the tray, gleaming in the light of the suspended lamp, lay a folded note. Clement Searle came forward, staring a little and startled, I think, by some quick nervous prevision of a catastrophe. The butler applied the match to the train. He advanced to my fellow visitor, all solemnly, with the offer of his missive. Mr. Searle made a movement as if to spring forward, but controlled himself. 'Tottenham!' he called in a strident voice.

'Yes, sir!' said Tottenham, halting.

'Stand where you are. For whom is that note?'

'For Mr. Clement Searle,' said the butler, staring straight before him and dissociating himself from everything.

'Who gave it to you?'

'Mrs. Horridge, sir.' This personage, I afterwards learned, was our friend the housekeeper.

'Who gave it Mrs. Horridge?'

There was on Tottenham's part just an infinitesimal pause before replying.

'My dear sir,' broke in Searle, his equilibrium, his ancient ease, completely restored by the crisis, 'isn't that rather my business?'

'What happens in my house is my business, and detestable things seem to be happening.' Our host, it was clear, now so furiously detested them that I was afraid he would snatch the bone of contention without more ceremony. 'Bring me that thing!' he cried; on which Tottenham stiffly moved to obey.

'Really this is too much!' broke out my companion, affronted and helpless.

So indeed it struck me, and before Mr. Searle had time to take the note I possessed myself of it. 'If you've no consideration for your sister let a stranger at least act for her.' And I tore the disputed object into a dozen pieces.

'In the name of decency, what does this horrid business mean?' my companion quavered.

Mr. Searle was about to open fire on him, but at that moment our hostess appeared on the staircase, summoned evidently by our high-pitched contentious voices. She had exchanged her dinner-dress for a dark wrapper, removed her ornaments and begun to disarrange her hair, a thick tress of which escaped from the comb. She hurried down with a pale questioning face. Feeling distinctly that, for ourselves, immediate departure was in the air, and divining Mr. Tottenham to be a person of a few deep-seated instincts and of much latent energy, I seized the opportunity to request him, *sotto voce*, to send a carriage to the door without delay. 'And put up our things,' I added.

Our host rushed at his sister and grabbed the white wrist that escaped from the loose sleeve of her dress. 'What was in that note?' he quite hissed at her.

Miss Searle looked first at its scattered fragments and then at her cousin. 'Did you read it?'

'No, but I thank you for it!' said Searle.

Her eyes, for an instant, communicated with his own as I think they had never, never communicated with any other source of meaning; then she transferred them to her brother's face, where the sense went out of them, only to leave a dull sad patience. But there was something even in this flat humility that seemed to him to mock him, so that he flushed crimson with rage and spite and flung her away. 'You always were an idiot! Go to bed.'

In poor Searle's face as well the gathered serenity had been by this time all blighted and distorted and the reflected brightness of his happy day turned to blank confusion. 'Have I been dealing these three hours with a madman?' he woefully cried.

'A madman, yes, if you will! A man mad with the love of his home and the sense of its stability. I've held my tongue till now, but you've been too much for me. Who the devil are you, and what and why and whence?' the terrible little man continued. 'From what paradise of fools do you come that you fancy I shall make over to you, for the asking, a part of my property and my life? I'm forsooth, you ridiculous person, to go shares with you? Prove your preposterous claim! There isn't *that* in it!' And he kicked one of the bits of paper on the floor.

Searle received this broadside gaping. Then turning away he went and seated himself on a bench against the wall and rubbed his forehead amazedly. I looked at my watch and listened for the wheels of our carriage.

But his kinsman was too launched to pull himself up. 'Wasn't it enough that you should have plotted against my rights? Need you have come into my very house to intrigue with my sister?'

My friend put his two hands to his face. 'Oh, oh, oh!' he groaned while Miss Searle crossed rapidly and dropped on her knees at his side.

'Go to bed, you fool!' shrieked her brother.

'Dear cousin,' she said, 'it's cruel you're to have so to think of us!'

'Oh I shall think of *you* as you'd like!' He laid a hand on her head.

'I believe you've done nothing wrong,' she brought bravely out.

'I've done what I could,' Mr. Searle went on—'but it's arrant folly to pretend to friendship when this abomination lies between us. You were welcome to my meat and my wine, but I wonder you could swallow them. The sight spoiled *my* appetite!' cried the master of Lackley with a laugh. 'Proceed with your trumpery case! My people in London are instructed and prepared.'

'I shouldn't wonder if your case had improved a good deal since you gave it up,' I was moved to observe to Searle.

'Oho! you don't feign ignorance then?' and our insane entertainer shook his shining head at me. 'It's very kind of you to give it up! Perhaps you'll also give up my sister!'

Searle sat staring in distress at his adversary. 'Ah miserable man—I thought we had become such beautiful friends.'

'Boh, you hypocrite!' screamed our host.

Searle seemed not to hear him. 'Am I seriously expected,' he slowly and painfully pursued, 'to defend myself against the accusation of any real in-delicacy—to prove I've done nothing underhand or impudent? Think what you please!' And he rose, with an effort, to his feet. 'I know what *you* think!' he added to Miss Searle.

The wheels of the carriage resounded on the gravel, and at the same moment a footman descended with our two portmanteaux. Mr. Totten-ham followed him with our hats and coats.

'Good God,' our host broke out again, 'you're not going away?'—an ejaculation that, after all that had happened, had the grandest comicality. 'Bless my soul,' he then remarked as artlessly, 'of course you're going!'

'It's perhaps well,' said Miss Searle with a great effort, inexpressibly touching in one for whom great efforts were visibly new and strange, 'that I should tell you what my poor little note contained.'

'That matter of your note, madam,' her brother interrupted, 'you and I will settle together!'

'Let me imagine all sorts of kind things!' Searle beautifully pleaded.

'Ah too much has been imagined!' she answered simply. 'It was only a word of warning. It was to tell you to go. I knew something painful was coming.'

He took his hat. 'The pains and the pleasures of this day,' he said to his kinsman, 'I shall equally never forget. Knowing you,' and he offered his hand to Miss Searle, 'has been the pleasure of pleasures. I hoped something more might have come of it.'

'A monstrous deal too much has come of it!' Mr. Searle irrepressibly declared.

His departing guest looked at him mildly, almost benignantly, from head to foot, and then with closed eyes and some collapse of strength, 'I'm afraid so, I can't stand more,' he went on. I gave him my arm and we crossed the threshold. As we passed out I heard Miss Searle break into loud weeping.

'We shall hear from each other yet, I take it!' her brother pursued, harassing our retreat.

My friend stopped, turning round on him fiercely. 'You very impossible man!' he cried in his face.

'Do you mean to say you'll not prosecute?'—Mr. Searle kept it up. 'I shall force you to prosecute! I shall drag you into court, and you shall be beaten—beaten—beaten!' Which grim reiteration followed us on our course.

We drove of course to the little wayside inn from which we had departed in the morning so unencumbered, in all broad England, either with enemies or friends. My companion, as the carriage rolled along, seemed overwhelmed and exhausted. 'What a beautiful horrible dream!' he confusedly wailed. 'What a strange awakening! What a long day! What a hideous scene! Poor me! Poor woman!' When we had resumed possession of our two little neighbouring rooms I asked him whether Miss Searle's note had been the result of anything that had passed between them on his going to rejoin her. 'I found her on the terrace,' he said, 'walking restlessly up and down in the moonlight. I was greatly excited—I hardly know what I said. I asked her, I think, if she knew the story of Margaret Searle. She seemed frightened and troubled, and she used just the words her brother had used—"I know nothing." For the moment, somehow, I felt as a man drunk. I stood before her and told her, with great emphasis, how poor Margaret had married a beggarly foreigner—all in obedience to her heart and in defiance to her family. As I talked the sheeted moonlight seemed to close about us, so that we stood there in a dream, in a world quite detached. She grew younger, prettier, more attractive—I found myself talking all kinds of nonsense. Before I knew it I had gone very far. I was taking her hand and calling her "Margaret, dear Margaret!" She had said it was impossible, that she could do nothing, that she was a fool, a child, a slave. Then with a sudden sense—it was odd how it came over me there—of the reality of my connection with the place, I spoke of my claim against the estate. "It exists," I declared, "but I've given it up. Be generous! Pay me for my sacrifice." For an instant her face was radiant. "If I marry you," she asked, "will it make everything right?" Of that I at once assured her—in our marriage the whole difficulty would melt away like a rain-drop in the great sea. "Our marriage!" she repeated in wonder; and the deep ring of her voice seemed to wake us up and show us our folly. "I love you, but I shall never see you again," she cried; and she hurried away with her face in her hands. I walked up and down the terrace for some moments, and then came in and met you. That's the only witchcraft I've used!'

The poor man was at once so roused and so shaken by the day's events that I believed he would get little sleep. Conscious on my own part that I shouldn't close my eyes, I but partly undressed, stirred my fire, and sat down to do some writing. I heard the great clock in the little parlour below strike twelve, one, half-past one. Just as the vibration of this last stroke was dying on the air, the door of communication with Searle's room was flung open and my companion stood on the threshold, pale as a corpse, in his nightshirt, shining like a phantom against the darkness behind him. 'Look well at me!' he intensely gasped; 'touch me, embrace me, revere me! You see a man who has seen a ghost!'

'Gracious goodness, what do you mean?'

'Write it down!' he went on. 'There, take your pen. Put it into dreadful words. How do I look? Am I human? Am I pale? Am I red? Am I speaking English? A ghost, sir! Do you understand?'

I confess there came upon me by contact a kind of supernatural shock. I shall always feel by the whole communication of it that I too have seen a ghost. My first movement—I can smile at it now—was to spring to the door, close it quickly, and turn the key upon the gaping blackness from which Searle had emerged. I seized his two hands; they were wet with perspiration. I pushed my chair to the fire and forced him to sit down in it; then I got on my knees and held his hands as firmly as possible. They trembled and quivered; his eyes were fixed save that the pupil dilated and contracted with extraordinary force. I asked no questions, but waited there, very curious for what he would say. At last he spoke. 'I'm not frightened, but I'm—oh excited! This is life! This is living! My nerves— my heart—my brain! They're throbbing—don't you feel it? Do you tingle? Are you hot? Are you cold? Hold me tight—tight—tight! I shall tremble away into waves—into surges—and know all the secrets of things and all the reasons and all the mysteries!' He paused a moment and then went on: 'A woman—as clear as that candle: no, far clearer! In a blue dress, with a black mantle on her head and a little black muff. Young and wonderfully pretty, pale, and ill; with the sadness of all the women who ever loved and suffered, pleading and accusing in her wet-looking eyes. God knows I never did any such thing! But she took me for my elder, for the other Clement. She came to me here as she would have come to me there. She wrung her hands and she spoke to me. "Marry me!" she moaned; "marry me and put an end to my shame!" I sat up in bed, just as I sit here, looked at her, heard her—heard her voice melt away, watched her figure fade away. Bless us and save us! Here I be!'

I made no attempt either to explain or to criticize this extraordinary passage. It's enough that I yielded for the hour to the strange force of my friend's emotion. On the whole I think my own vision was the more interesting of the two. He beheld but the transient irresponsible spectre—

I beheld the human subject hot from the spectral presence. Yet I soon recovered my judgement sufficiently to be moved again to try to guard him
against the results of excitement and exposure. It was easily agreed that
he was not for the night to return to his room, and I made him fairly
comfortable in his place by my fire. Wishing above all to preserve him
from a chill I removed my bedding and wrapped him in the blankets and
counterpane. I had no nerves either for writing or for sleep; so I put out
my lights, renewed the fuel, and sat down on the opposite side of the
hearth. I found it a great and high solemnity just to watch my companion.
Silent, swathed and muffled to his chin, he sat rigid and erect with the
dignity of his adventure. For the most part his eyes were closed; though
from time to time he would open them with a steady expansion and stare,
never blinking, into the flame, as if he again beheld without terror the
image of the little woman with the muff. His cadaverous emaciated face,
his tragic wrinkles intensified by the upward glow from the hearth, his distorted moustache, his extraordinary gravity, and a certain fantastical air
as the red light flickered over him, all re-enforced his fine likeness to the
vision-haunted knight of La Mancha when laid up after some grand
exploit. The night passed wholly without speech. Towards its close I slept
for half an hour. When I awoke the awakened birds had begun to twitter
and Searle, unperturbed, sat staring at me. We exchanged a long look, and
I felt with a pang that his glittering eyes had tasted their last of natural
sleep. 'How is it? Are you comfortable?' I nevertheless asked.

He fixed me for a long time without replying and then spoke with a
weak extravagance and with such pauses between his words as might have
represented the slow prompting of inner voice. 'You asked me when you
first knew me what I was. "Nothing," I said, "nothing of any consequence." Nothing I've always supposed myself to be. But I've wronged
myself—I'm a great exception. I'm a haunted man!'

If sleep had passed out of his eyes I felt with even a deeper pang that
sanity had abandoned his spirit. From this moment I was prepared for the
worst. There were in my friend, however, such confirmed habits of mildness that I found myself not in the least fearing he would prove un-
manageable. As morning began fully to dawn upon us I brought our
curious vigil to a close. Searle was so enfeebled that I gave him my hands
to help him out of his chair, and he retained them for some moments
after rising to his feet, unable as he seemed to keep his balance. 'Well,' he
said, 'I've been once favoured, but don't think I shall be favoured again. I
shall soon be myself as fit to "appear" as any of them. I shall haunt the
master of Lackley! It can only mean one thing—that they're getting ready
for me on the other side of the grave.'

When I touched the question of breakfast he replied that he had his
breakfast in his pocket; and he drew from his travelling-bag a phial of
morphine. He took a strong dose and went to bed. At noon I found him
on foot again, dressed, shaved, much refreshed. 'Poor fellow,' he said,
'you've got more than you bargained for—not only a man with a grievance
but a man with a ghost. Well, it won't be for long!' It had of course

promptly become a question whither we should now direct our steps. 'As I've so little time,' he argued for this, 'I should like to see the best, the best alone.' I answered that either for time or eternity I had always supposed Oxford to represent the English maximum, and for Oxford in the course of an hour we accordingly departed.

IV

OF that extraordinary place I shall not attempt to speak with any order or indeed with any coherence. It must ever remain one of the supreme gratifications of travel for any American aware of the ancient pieties of race. The impression it produces, the emotions it kindles in the mind of such a visitor, are too rich and various to be expressed in the halting rhythm of prose. Passing through the small oblique streets in which the long grey battered public face of the colleges seems to watch jealously for sounds that may break upon the stillness of study, you feel it the most dignified and most educated of cities. Over and through it all the great corporate fact of the University slowly throbs after the fashion of some steady bass in a concerted piece or that of the mediaeval mystical presence of the Empire in the old States of Germany. The plain perpendicular of the so mildly conventual fronts, masking blest seraglios of culture and leisure, irritates the imagination scarce less than the harem-walls of Eastern towns. Within their arching portals, however, you discover more sacred and sunless courts, and the dark verdure soothing and cooling to bookish eyes. The grey-green quadrangles stand for ever open with a trustful hospitality. The seat of the humanities is stronger in her own good manners than in a marshalled host of wardens and beadles. Directly after our arrival my friend and I wandered forth in the luminous early dusk. We reached the bridge that under-spans the walls of Magdalen and saw the eight-spired tower, delicately fluted and embossed, rise in temperate beauty—the perfect prose of Gothic—wooing the eyes to the sky that was slowly drained of day. We entered the low monkish doorway and stood in the dim little court that nestles beneath the tower, where the swallows niche more lovingly in the tangled ivy than elsewhere in Oxford, and passed into the quiet cloister and studied the small sculptured monsters on the entablature of the arcade. I rejoiced in every one of my unhappy friend's responsive vibrations, even while feeling that they might as direfully multiply as those that had preceded them. I may say that from this time forward I found it difficult to distinguish in his company between the riot of fancy and the labour of thought, or to fix the balance between what he saw and what he imagined. He had already begun playfully to exchange his identity for that of the earlier Clement Searle, and he now delivered himself almost wholly in the character of his old-time kinsman.

'*This* was my college, you know,' he would almost anywhere break out, applying the words wherever we stood—'the sweetest and noblest in the whole place. How often have I strolled in this cloister with my intimates of the other world! They are all dead and buried, but many a young fellow as we meet him, dark or fair, tall or short, reminds me of the past age and the early attachment. Even as we stand here, they say, the whole thing feels about its massive base the murmurs of the tide of time; some of the foundation-stones are loosened, some of the breaches will have to be repaired. Mine was the old unregenerate Oxford, the home of rank abuses, of distinctions and privileges the most delicious and invidious. What cared I, who was a perfect gentleman and with my pockets full of money? I had an allowance of a thousand a year.'

It was at once plain to me that he had lost the little that remained of his direct grasp on life and was unequal to any effort of seeing things in their order. He read my apprehension in my eyes and took pains to assure me I was right. 'I'm going straight down hill. Thank heaven it's an easy slope, coated with English turf and with an English churchyard at the foot.' The hysterical emotion produced by our late dire misadventure had given place to an unruffled calm in which the scene about us was reflected as in an old-fashioned mirror. We took an afternoon walk through Christ-Church meadow and at the river-bank procured a boat which I pulled down the stream to Iffley and to the slanting woods of Nuneham—the sweetest flattest reediest stream-side landscape that could be desired. Here of course we encountered the scattered phalanx of the young, the happy generation, clad in white flannel and blue, muscular fair-haired magnificent fresh, whether floated down the current by idle punts and lounging in friendly couples when not in a singleness that nursed ambitions, or straining together in rhythmic crews and hoarsely exhorted from the near bank. When to the exhibition of so much of the clearest joy of wind and limb we added the great sense of perfumed protection shed by all the enclosed lawns and groves and bowers, we felt that to be young in such scholastic shades must be a double, an infinite blessing. As my companion found himself less and less able to walk we repaired in turn to a series of gardens and spent long hours sitting in their greenest places. They struck us as the fairest things in England and the ripest and sweetest fruit of the English system. Locked in their antique verdure, guarded, as in the case of New College, by gentle battlements of silver-grey, outshouldering the matted leafage of undisseverable plants, filled with nightingales and memories, a sort of chorus of tradition; with vaguely-generous youths sprawling bookishly on the turf as if to spare it the injury of their boot-heels, and with the great conservative college countenance appealing gravely from the restless outer world, they seem places to lie down on the grass in for ever, in the happy faith that life is all a green old English garden and time an endless summer afternoon. This charmed seclusion was especially grateful to my friend, and his sense of it reached its climax, I remember, on one of the last of such occasions and while we sat in fascinated *flânerie* over against the sturdy back of Saint John's. The wide discreetly-windowed wall here perhaps broods upon the lawn with a more effective air of property than elsewhere. Searle dropped into fitful talk and spun his humour into golden figures. Any passing undergraduate was a peg to hang a fable, every feature of the place a pretext for more embroidery.

'Isn't it all a delightful lie?' he wanted to know. 'Mightn't one fancy this the very central point of the world's heart, where all the echoes of the general life arrive but to falter and die? Doesn't one feel the air just thick with arrested voices? It's well there should be such places, shaped in the interest of factitious needs, invented to minister to the book-begotten longing for a medium in which one may dream unwaked and believe unconfuted; to foster the sweet illusion that all's well in a world where so much is so damnable, all night and rounded, smooth and fair, in this sphere of the rough and ragged, the pitiful unachieved especially, and the dreadful uncommenced. The world's made—work's over. Now for leisure! England's safe—now for Theocritus and Horace, for lawn and sky! What a sense it all gives one of the composite life of the country and of the essential furniture of its luckier minds! Thank heaven they had the wit to send me here in the other time. I'm not much visibly the braver perhaps, but think how I'm the happier! The misty spores and towers, seen far off on the level, have been all these years one of the constant things of memory. Seriously, what do the spires and towers do for these people? Are they wiser, gentler, finer, cleverer? My diminished dignity reverts in any case at moments to the naked background of our own education, the deadly dry air in which we grasp for impressions and comparisons. I assent to it all with a sort of desperate calmness; I accept it with a dogged pride. We're nursed at the opposite pole. Naked come we into a naked world. There's a certain grandeur in the lack of decorations, a certain heroic strain in that young imagination of ours which finds nothing made to its hands, which has to invent its own traditions and raise high into our morning-air, with a ringing hammer and nails, the castles in which we dwell. *Noblesse oblige* —Oxford must damnably do so. What a horrible thing not to rise to such examples! If you pay the pious debt to the last farthing of interest you may go through life with her blessing; but if you let it stand unhonoured you're a worse barbarian than we! But for the better or worse, in a myriad private hearts, think how she must be loved! How the youthful sentiment of mankind seems visibly to brood upon her! Think of the young lives now taking colour in her cloisters and halls. Think of the centuries' tale of dead lads—dead alike with the end of the young days to which these haunts were a present world, and the close of the larger lives which the general mother-scene has dropped into less bottomless traps. What are those two young fellows kicking their heels over on the grass there? One of them has the *Saturday Review*; the other—upon my soul—the other has Artemus Ward! Where do they live, how do they live, to what end do they live? Miserable boys! How can they read Artemus Ward under those windows of Elizabeth? What do you think loveliest in all Oxford? The poetry of certain windows. Do you see that one yonder, the second of those lesser bays, with the broken cornice and the lattice? That used to be the window of my bosom friend a hundred years ago. Remind me to tell you the story of that broken cornice. Don't pretend it's not a common thing to have one's bosom friend at another college. Pray was I committed to common things? He was a charming fellow. By the way, he was a good deal

like you. Of course his cocked hat, his long hair in a black ribbon, his cinnamon velvet suit and his flowered waistcoat made a difference. We gentlemen used to wear swords.'

There was really the touch of grace in my poor friend's divagations—
the disheartened dandy had so positively turned rhapsodist and seer. I was
particularly struck with his having laid aside the diffidence and self-
consciousness of the first days of our acquaintance. He had become by this
time a disembodied observer and critic; the shell of sense, growing daily
thinner and more transparent, transmitted the tremor of his quickened
spirit. He seemed to pick up acquaintances, in the course of our contem-
plations, merely by putting out his hand. If I left him for ten minutes I
was sure to find him on my return in earnest conversation with some
affable wandering scholar. Several young men with whom he had thus
established relations invited him to their rooms and entertained him, as I
gathered, with rather rash hospitality. For myself, I chose not to be present
at these symposia; I shrank partly from being held in any degree responsible for his extravagance, partly from the pang of seeing him yield to
champagne and an admiring circle. He reported such adventures with less
keen a complacency than I had supposed he might use, but a certain
method in his madness, a certain dignity in his desire to fraternize, appeared to save him from mischance. If they didn't think him a harmless
lunatic they certainly thought him a celebrity of the Occident. Two things,
however, grew evident—that he drank deeper than was good for him and
that the flagrant freshness of his young patrons rather interfered with his
predetermined sense of the element of finer romance. At the same time it
completed his knowledge of the place. Making the acquaintance of several
tutors and fellows, he dined in hall in half a dozen colleges, alluding afterwards to these banquets with religious unction. One evening after a par-
ticipation indiscreetly prolonged he came back to the hotel in a cab, accompanied by a friendly undergraduate and a physician and looking
deadly pale. He had swooned away on leaving table and remained so
rigidly unconscious as much to agitate his banqueters. The following
twenty-four hours he of course spent in bed, but on the third day declared
himself strong enough to begin afresh. On his reaching the street his
strength once more forsook him, so that I insisted on his returning to his
room. He besought me with tears in his eyes not to shut him up. 'It's my
last chance—I want to go back for an hour to that garden of Saint John's.
Let me eat and drink—tomorrow I die.' It seemed to me possible that with
a Bath-chair the expedition might be accomplished. The hotel, it appeared, possessed such a convenience, which was immediately produced. It
became necessary hereupon that we should have a person to propel the
chair. As there was no one on the spot at liberty I was about to perform
the office; but just as my patient had got seated and wrapped—he now had
a perpetual chill—an elderly man emerged from a lurking-place near the
door and, with a formal salute, offered to wait upon the gentleman. We
assented, and he proceeded solemnly to trundle the chair before him. I
recognized him as a vague personage whom I had observed to lounge

shyly about the doors of the hotels, at intervals during our stay, with a depressed air of wanting employment and a poor semblance of finding it. He had once indeed in a half-hearted way proposed himself as an amateur cicerone for a tour through the colleges; and I now, as I looked at him, remembered with a pang that I had too curtly declined his ministrations. Since then his shyness, apparently, had grown less or his misery greater, for it was with a strange grim avidity that he now attached himself to our service. He was a pitiful image of shabby gentility and the dinginess of 'reduced circumstances'. He would have been, I suppose, some fifty years of age; but his pale haggard unwholesome visage, his plaintive drooping carriage, and the irremediable disarray of his apparel seemed to add to the burden of his days and tribulations. His eyes were weak and bloodshot, his bold nose was sadly compromised, and his reddish beard, largely streaked with grey, bristled under a month's neglect of the razor. In all this rusty forlornness lurked a visible assurance of our friend's having known better days. Obviously he was the victim of some fatal depreciation in the market value of pure gentility. There had been something terribly affecting in the way he substituted for the attempt to touch the greasy rim of his antiquated hat some such bow as one man of the world might make another. Exchanging a few words with him as we went I was struck with the decorum of his accent. His fine whole voice should have been congruously cracked.

'Take me by some long roundabout way,' said Searle, 'so that I may see as many college-walls as possible.'

'You know,' I asked of our attendant, 'all these wonderful ins and outs?'

'I ought to, sir,' he said, after a moment, with pregnant gravity. And as we were passing one of the colleges, 'That used to be my place,' he added.

At these words Searle desired him to stop and come round within sight. 'You say that's *your* college?'

'The place might deny me, sir; but heaven forbid I should seem to take it ill of her. If you'll allow me to wheel you into the quad I'll show you the windows of thirty years ago.'

Searle sat staring, his huge pale eyes, which now left nothing else worth mentioning in his wasted face, filled with wonder and pity. 'If you'll be so kind,' he said with great deference. But just as this perverted product of a liberal education was about to propel him across the threshold of the court he turned about, disengaged the mercenary hands, with one of his own, from the back of the chair, drew their owner alongside, and turned to me. 'While we're here, my dear fellow,' he said, 'be so good as to perform this service. You understand?' I gave our companion a glance of intelligence and we resumed our way. The latter showed us his window of the better time, where a rosy youth in a scarlet smoking-fez now puffed a cigarette at the open casement. Thence we proceeded into the small garden, the smallest, I believe, and certainly the sweetest, of all the planted places of Oxford. I pushed the chair along to a bench on the lawn, turned it round towards the front of the college, and sat down by it on the grass. Our attendant shifted mournfully from one foot to the other, his patron eyeing him open-mouthed. At length Searle broke out: 'God bless my soul, sir, you don't suppose I expect you to stand! There's an empty bench.'

'Thank you,' said our friend, who bent his joints to sit.

'You English are really fabulous! I don't know whether I most admire or most abominate you! Now tell me: who are you? what are you? what brought you to this?'

The poor fellow blushed up to his eyes, took off his hat and wiped his forehead with an indescribable fabric drawn from his pocket. 'My name's Rawson, sir. Beyond that it's a long story.'

'I ask out of sympathy,' said Searle. 'I've a fellow-feeling. If you're a poor devil I'm a poor devil as well.'

'I'm the poorer devil of the two,' said the stranger with an assurance for once presumptuous.

'Possibly. I suppose an English poor devil's the poorest of all poor devils. And then you've fallen from a height. From a gentleman commoner—is that what they called you?—to a propeller of Bath-chair. Good heavens, man, the fall's enough to kill you!'

'I didn't take it all at once, sir. I dropped a bit one time and a bit another.'

'That's me, that's me!' cried Searle with all his seriousness.

'And now,' said our friend, 'I believe I can't drop any further.'

'My dear fellow'—and Searle clasped his hand and shook it—'I too am at the very bottom of the hole.'

Mr. Rawson lifted his eyebrows. 'Well, sir, there's a difference between sitting in such a pleasant convenience and just trudging behind it!'

'Yes—there's a shade. But I'm at my last gasp, Mr. Rawson.'

'I'm at my last penny, sir.'

'Literally, Mr. Rawson?'

Mr. Rawson shook his head with large loose bitterness. 'I've almost come to the point of drinking my beer and buttoning my coat figuratively; but I don't talk in figures.'

Fearing the conversation might appear to achieve something like gaiety at the expense of Mr. Rawson's troubles, I took the liberty of asking him, with all consideration, how he made a living.

'I don't make a living,' he answered with tearful eyes; 'I can't make a living. I've a wife and three children—and all starving, sir. You wouldn't believe what I've come to. I sent my wife to her mother's, who can ill afford to keep her, and came to Oxford a week ago, thinking I might pick up a few half-crowns by showing people about the colleges. But it's no use. I haven't the assurance. I don't look decent. They want a nice little old man with black gloves and a clean shirt and a silver-headed stick. What do I look as if I knew about Oxford, sir?'

'Mercy on us,' cried Searle, 'why didn't you speak to us before?'

'I wanted to; half a dozen times I've been on the point of it. I knew you were Americans.'

'And Americans are rich!' cried Searle, laughing. 'My dear Mr. Rawson,

American as I am I'm living on charity.'

'And I'm exactly not, sir! There it is. I'm dying for the lack of that same. You say you're a pauper, but it takes an American pauper to go bowling about in a Bath-chair. America's an easy country.'

'Ah me!' groaned Searle. 'Have I come to the most delicious corner of the ancient world to hear the praise of Yankeeland?'

'Delicious corners are very well, and so is the ancient world,' said Mr. Rawson; 'but one may sit here hungry and shabby, so long as one isn't too shabby, as well as elsewhere. You'll not persuade me that it's not an easier thing to keep afloat yonder than here. I wish *I* were in Yankeeland, that's all!' he added with feeble force. Then brooding for a moment on his wrongs: 'Have you a bloated brother? or you, sir? It matters little to you. But it has mattered to me with a vengeance! Shabby as I sit here I can boast that advantage—as he his five thousand a year. Being but a twelve-month my elder he swaggers while I go thus. There's old England for you! A very pretty place for *him*!'

'Poor old England!' said Searle softly.

'Has your brother never helped you?' I asked.

'A five-pound note now and then! Oh I don't say there haven't been times when I haven't inspired an irresistible sympathy. I've not been what I should. I married dreadfully out of the way. But the devil of it is that he started fair and I started foul; with the tastes, the desires, the needs, the sensibilities of a gentleman—and not another blessed "tip". I can't afford to live in England.'

'*This* poor gentleman fancied a couple of months ago that he couldn't afford to live in America,' I fondly explained.

'I'd "swap"—do you call it?—chances with him!' And Mr. Rawson looked quaintly rueful over his freedom of speech.

Searle sat supported there with his eyes closed and his face twitching for violent emotion, and then of a sudden had a glare of gravity. 'My friend, you're a dead failure! Be judged! Don't talk about "swapping". Don't talk about chances. Don't talk about fair starts and false starts. I'm at that point myself that I've got a right to speak. It lies neither in one's chance nor one's start to make one a success; nor in anything one's brother —however bloated—can do or can undo. It lies in one's character. You and I, sir, have *had* no character—that's very plain. We've been weak, sir; as weak as water. Here we are for it—sitting staring in each other's faces and reading our weakness in each other's eyes. We're of no importance whatever, Mr. Rawson!'

Mr. Rawson received this sally with a countenance in which abject sub-mission to the particular affirmed truth struggled with the comparative propriety of his general rebellion against fate. In the course of a minute a due self-respect yielded to the warm comfortable sense of his being re-lieved of the cares of an attitude. 'Go on, sir, go on,' he said. 'It's whole-some doctrine.' And he wiped his eyes with what seemed his sole remnant of linen.

'Dear, dear,' sighed Searle, 'I've made you cry! Well, we speak as from man to man. I should be glad to think you had felt for a moment the side-light of that great undarkening of the spirit which precedes—which precedes the grand illumination of death.'

Mr. Rawson sat silent a little, his eyes fixed on the ground and his well-cut nose but the more deeply dyed by his agitation. Then at last looking up: 'You're a good-natured man, sir, and you'll never persuade me you don't come of a kindly race. Say what you please about a chance; when a man's fifty—degraded, penniless, a husband and father—a chance to get on his legs again is not to be despised. Something tells me that my luck may be in your country—which has brought luck to so many. I can come on the parish here of course, but I don't want to come on the parish. Hang it, sir, I want to hold up my head. I see thirty years of life before me yet. If only by God's help I could have a real change of air! It's a fixed idea of mine. I've had it for the last ten years. It's not that I'm a low radical. Oh I've no vulgar opinions. Old England's good enough for me, but I'm not good enough for old England. I'm a shabby man that wants to get out of a room full of staring gentlefolk. I'm for ever put to the blush. It's a perfect agony of spirit; everything reminds me of my younger and better self. The thing for me would be a cooling cleansing plunge into the unknowing and the unknown! I lie awake thinking of it.'

Searle closed his eyes, shivering with a long-drawn tremor which I hardly knew whether to take for an expression of physical or of mental pain. In a moment I saw it was neither. 'Oh my country, my country, my country!' he murmured in a broken voice; and then sat for some time abstracted and lost. I signalled our companion that it was time we should bring our small session to a close, and he, without hesitating, possessed himself of the handle of the Bath-chair and pushed it before him. We had got halfway home before Searle spoke or moved. Suddenly in the High Street, as we passed a chop-house from whose open doors we caught a waft of old-fashioned cookery and other restorative elements, he motioned us to a halt. 'This is my last five pounds'—and he drew a note from his pocket. 'Do me the favour, Mr. Rawson, to accept it. Go in there and order the best dinner they can give you. Call for a bottle of Burgundy and drink it to my eternal rest!'

Mr. Rawson stiffened himself up and received the gift with fingers momentarily irresponsive. But Mr. Rawson had the nerves of a gentleman. I measured the spasm with which his poor dispossessed hand closed upon the crisp paper, I observed his empurpled nostril convulsive under the other solicitation. He crushed the crackling note in his palm with a passionate pressure and jerked a spasmodic bow. 'I shall not do you the wrong, sir, of anything but the best!' The next moment the door swung behind him.

Searle sank again into his apathy, and on reaching the hotel I helped him to get to bed. For the rest of the day he lay without motion or sound and beyond reach of any appeal. The doctor, whom I had constantly in attendance, was sure his end was near. He expressed great surprise that he should have lasted so long; he must have been living for a month on the very dregs of his strength. Towards evening, as I sat by his bedside in the deepening dusk, he roused himself with a purpose I had vaguely felt gathering beneath his stupor. 'My cousin, my cousin,' he said confusedly. 'Is she here?' It was the first time he had spoken of Miss Searle since our retreat from her brother's house, and he continued to ramble. 'I was to have married her. What a dream! That day was like a string of verses— rhymed hours. But the last verse is bad measure. What's the rhyme to "love"? *Above!* Was she a simple woman, a kind sweet woman? Or have I only dreamed it? She had the healing gift; her touch would have cured my madness. I want you to do something. Write three lines, three words: "Good-bye; remember me; be happy."' And then after a long pause: 'It's strange a person in my state should have a wish. Why should one eat one's breakfast the day one's hanged? What a creature is man! What a farce is life! Here I lie, worn down to a mere throbbing fever-point; I breathe and nothing more, and yet I *desire!* My desire lives. If I could see her! Help me out with it and let me die.'

Half an hour later, at a venture, I dispatched by post a note to Miss Searle: '*Your cousin is rapidly sinking. He asks to see you.*' I was conscious of a certain want of consideration in this act, since it would bring her great trouble and yet no power to face the trouble; but out of her distress I fondly hoped a sufficient force might be born. On the following day my friend's exhaustion had become so great that I began to fear his intelligence altogether broken up. But towards evening he briefly rallied, to maunder about many things, confounding in a sinister jumble the memories of the past weeks and those of bygone years. 'By the way,' he said suddenly, 'I've made no will. I haven't much to bequeath. Yet I have something.' He had been playing listlessly with a large signet-ring on his left hand, which he now tried to draw off. 'I leave you this'— working it round and round vainly—'if you can get it off. What enormous knuckles! There must be such knuckles in the mummies of the Pharaohs. Well, when I'm gone——! No, I leave you something more precious than gold—the sense of a great kindness. But I've a little gold left. Bring me those trinkets.' I placed on the bed before him several articles of jewellery, relics of early foppery: his watch and chain, of great value, a locket and seal, some odds and ends of goldsmith's work. He trifled with them feebly for some moments, murmuring various names and dates associated with them. At last, looking up with clearer interest, 'What has become,' he asked, 'of Mr. Rawson?'

'You want to see him?'

'How much are these things worth?' he went on without heeding me. 'How much would they bring?' And he weighed them in his weak hands. 'They're pretty heavy. Some hundred or so? Oh I'm richer than I thought! Rawson—Rawson—you want to get out of this awful England?'

I stepped to the door and requested the servant whom I kept in constant attendance in our adjacent sitting-room to send and ascertain if Mr. Rawson were on the premises. He returned in a few moments, introducing our dismal friend. Mr. Rawson was pale even to his nose and

derived from his unaffectedly concerned state an air of some distinction. I
led him up to the bed. In Searle's eyes, as they fell on him, there shone
for a moment the light of a human message.

'Lord have mercy!' gasped Mr. Rawson.

'My friend,' said Searle, 'there's to be one American the less—so let
there be at the same time one the more. At the worst you'll be as good a
one as I. Foolish me! Take these battered relics; you can sell them; let
them help you on your way. They're gifts and mementoes, but this is a
better use. Heaven speed you! May America be kind to you. Be kind, at
the last, to your own country!'

'Really this is too much; I can't,' the poor man protested, almost
scared and with tears in his eyes. 'Do come round and get well and I'll
stop here. I'll stay with you and wait on you.'

'No, I'm booked for my journey, you for yours. I hope you don't mind
the voyage.'

Mr. Rawson exhaled a groan of helpless gratitude, appealing piteously
from so strange a windfall. 'It's like the angel of the Lord who bids people
in the Bible to rise and flee!'

Searle had sunk back upon his pillow, quite used up; I led Mr. Rawson
back into the sitting-room, where in three words I proposed to him a
rough valuation of our friend's trinkets. He assented with perfect good-
breeding; they passed into my possession and a second bank-note into his.

From the collapse into which this wondrous exercise of his imagination
had plunged him my charge then gave few signs of being likely to
emerge. He breathed, as he had said, and nothing more. The twilight
deepened; I lighted the night-lamp. The doctor sat silent and official at
the foot of the bed; I resumed my constant place near the head. Suddenly
our patient opened his eyes wide. 'She'll not come,' he murmured. 'Amen!
she's an English sister.' Five minutes passed; he started forward. 'She's
come, she's here!' he confidently quavered. His words conveyed to my
mind so absolute an assurance that I lightly rose and passed into the
sitting-room. At the same moment, through the opposite door, the servant introduced a lady. A lady, I say; for an instant she was simply such
—tall pale dressed in deep mourning. The next instant I had uttered her
name—'Miss Searle!' She looked ten years older.

She met me with both hands extended and an immense question in
her face. 'He has just announced you,' I said. And then with a fuller consciousness of the change in her dress and countenance: 'What has happened?'

'Oh death, death!' she wailed. 'You and I are left.'

There came to me with her words a sickening shock, the sense of
poetic justice somehow cheated, defeated. 'Your brother?' I panted.

She laid her hand on my arm and I felt its pressure deepen as she spoke.
'He was thrown from his horse in the park. He died on the spot. Six days
have past. Six months!'

She accepted my support and a moment later we had entered the room
and approached the bedside, from which the doctor withdrew. Searle

opened his eyes and looked at her from head to foot. Suddenly he seemed to make out her mourning. 'Already!' he cried audibly and with a smile, as I felt, of pleasure.

She dropped on her knees and took his hand. 'Not for you, cousin,' she whispered. 'For my poor brother.'

He started, in all his deathly longitude, as with a galvanic shock. 'Dead! *He* dead! Life itself!' And then after a moment and with a slight rising inflexion: 'You're free?'

'Free, cousin. Too sadly free. And now—*now*—with what use for freedom?'

He looked steadily into her eyes, dark in the heavy shadow of her musty mourning-veil. 'For me wear colours!'

In a moment more death had come, the doctor had silently attested it, and she had burst into sobs.

We buried him in the little churchyard in which he had expressed the wish to lie; beneath one of the blackest and widest of English yews and the little tower than which none in all England has a softer and hoarier grey. A year has passed; Miss Searle, I believe, has begun to wear colours.

APPENDIX II

James's Preface to 'A Passionate Pilgrim', 'The Madonna of the Future', and 'Madame de Mauves'

[Nine of the eighteen Prefaces James wrote for the New York Edition of his novels and tales are to the volumes carrying the shorter things. While they follow no consistent design—some tales are discussed at length, others are dismissed with a brief mention—these intriguing exercises in critical recapitulation throw an interesting perspective on the works from the novelist's own point of view. The excerpt below is from the volume, *The Reverberator*, Etc., where the three tales are collected in their final form. It is worth adding here that, in this case, there is a gap of forty years between James's final account and the original appearance of the tales.]

'A Passionate Pilgrim', written in the year 1870, the earliest date to which anything in the whole present series refers itself, strikes me today, and by the same token indescribably touches me, with the two compositions that follow it, as sops instinctively thrown to the international Cerberus formidably posted where I doubtless then didn't quite make him out, yet from whose capacity to loom larger and larger with the years there must already have sprung some chilling portent. Cerberus would have been, thus, to one's younger artistic conscience, the keeper of the international 'books'; the hovering disembodied critical spirit with a disengaged eye upon sneaking attempts to substitute the American romantic for the American real. To that comparatively artless category the fiction I have just named, together with 'Madame de Mauves' and 'The Madonna of the Future', belong. As American as possible, and even to the pitch of fondly coaxing it, I then desired my ground-stuff to remain; so that such situations as are thus offered must have represented my prime view of the telling effect with which the business-man would be dodged. He *is* dodged, here, doubtless, to a charm—he is made to wait as in the furthest and coldest of an infinite perspective of more or less quaint antechambers; where my ingenuous theory of the matter must have been that, artfully trifled with from room to room and from pretext to pretext, he might be kept indefinitely at bay. Thus if a sufficient amount of golden dust were kicked up in the foreground—and I began to kick it, under all these other possible pretexts, as hard as I knew how, he would probably never be able, to my confusion, to break through at all. I had in the spring of 1869, and again in that of 1870, spent several weeks in England, renewing and extending, with infinite zest, an acquaintance with the country that had previously been but an uneffaced little chapter of boyish, or—putting it again far enough back for the dimmest dawn of sensibility—of infantine experience; and had, perceptively and aesthetically speaking, taken the adventure of my twenty-sixth year 'hard', as 'A Passionate Pilgrim' quite sufficiently attests.

A part of that adventure had been the never-to-be-forgotten thrill of a first sight of Italy, from late in the summer of 1869 on; so that a return to America at the beginning of the following year was to drag with it, as a lengthening chain, the torment of losses and regrets. The repatriated victim of that unrest was, beyond doubt, acutely conscious of his case: the fifteen months just spent in Europe had absolutely determined his situation. The nostalgic poison had been distilled for him, the future presented to him but as a single intense question: was he to spend it in brooding exile, or might he somehow come into his 'own'?—as I liked betimes to put it for a romantic analogy with the state of dispossessed princes and wandering heirs. The question was to answer itself promptly enough—yet after a delay sufficient to give me the measure of a whole previous relation to it. I had from as far back as I could remember carried in my side, buried and unextracted, the head of one of those well-directed shafts from the European quiver to which, of old, tender American flesh was more helplessly and bleedingly exposed, I think, than today: the nostalgic cup had been applied to my lips even before I was conscious of it—I had been hurried off to London and to Paris immediately after my birth, and then and there, I was ever afterwards strangely to feel, that poison had entered my veins. This was so much the case that when again, in my thirteenth year, re-exposure was decreed, and was made effective and prolonged, my inward sense of it was, in the oddest way, not of my finding myself in the vague and the uncharted, but much rather restored to air already breathed and to a harmony already disclosed. The unnatural precocity with which I had in fine 'taken' to Europe was to be revealed to me later on and during another quite languishing American interval; an interval during which I supposed my young life to have been made bitter, under whatever appearances of smug accommodation, by too prompt a mouthful—recklessly administered to one's helplessness by responsible hands—of the fruit of the tree of knowledge. Why otherwise so queer a taste, always, in so juvenile, so *generally* gaping, a mouth? Well, the queer taste doubtless had been there, but the point of my anecdote, with my brace of infatuated 'short stories' for its occasion, is in the infinitely greater queerness it was to take on between the summer of '70 and that of '72, when it set me again in motion.

As I read over 'A Passionate Pilgrim' and 'The Madonna of the Future' they become in the highest degree documentary for myself— from all measure of such interest as they may possibly have at this time of day for others I stand off; though I disengage from them but one thing, their betrayal of their consolatory use. The deep beguilement of the lost vision recovered, in comparative indigence, by a certain inexpert intensity of art—the service rendered by them at need, with whatever awkwardness and difficulty—sticks out of them for me to the exclusion of everything else and consecrates them, I freely admit, to memory. 'Madame de Mauves' ... is of the small group of my productions yielding to present research no dimmest responsive ghost of a traceable origin. These remarks have constituted to excess perhaps the record of what may have put this, that, and the other treated idea into my head; but I am quite unable to say what, in the summer of 1873, may have put 'Madame de Mauves'. Save for a single pleasant image, and for the fact that, dispatched to New York, the tale appeared, early in the following year, in the *Galaxy*, a periodical to which I find, with this, twenty other remembrances gratefully attached, not a glimmer of attendant reference survives. I recall the tolerably wide court of an old inn at Bad-Homburg in the Taunus hills— a dejected and forlorn little place (its *seconde jeunesse* not yet in sight) during the years immediately following the Franco-Prussian war, which had overturned, with that of Baden-Baden, its altar, the well-appointed worship of the great goddess Chance—a homely enclosure on the ground-level of which I occupied a dampish, dusky, unsunned room, cool, however, to the relief of the fevered muse, during some very hot weather. The place was so dark that I could see my way to and from my inkstand, I remember, but by keeping the door to the court open—thanks to which also the muse, witness of many mild domestic incidents, was distracted and beguiled. In this retreat I was visited by the gentle Euphemia; I sat in crepuscular comfort pouring forth again, and, no doubt, artfully editing, the confidences with which she honoured me. She again, after her fashion, was what I might have called experimentally international; she muffled her charming head in the lightest, finest, vaguest tissue of romance and put twenty questions by.

APPENDIX III

Some Contemporary Notices of the Tales.

[The *Nation* continued to comment on James's stories through its regular 'preview' of current periodical writing called 'Magazines for the Month' (see the first volume of this edition, p. 512). However, during the period in question, its notices became less frequent and the magazine tended to ignore the more important of James's stories; its critic, for instance, had little to say about such remarkable early successes as 'The Madonna of the Future' and 'Mme. De Mauves'. The three items in section A below are taken from this magazine. The first, a general estimate of young James's art, is from the *Nation*'s account of James's first novel, *Watch and Ward*; the other two deal directly with two tales.

Section B contains excerpts from the first ever, extended critique of James's fiction—a review of his first book of stories, *A Passionate Pilgrim*. It is, inevitably, by W. D. Howells, who was, for most of the stories gathered in the volume, their first publisher.]

(A) The *Nation* on James:

1. ... the story [*Watch and Ward*] takes the reader's attention less after the characters are fairly at work upon each other than while they are being presented to us. And this, we should say, may be set down as a principal mark of Mr. James's stories. The characters are usually touched —we do not say hit off—in a way that shows nice observation and refined sensibilities; and the situation or action is likely enough to be interesting, especially if the reader is an intending lover or is, for any reason, interested in the study of the relations in which somewhat sophisticated young men and young women frequently stand to each other; but we doubt if many even of the more interested readers find the people in his stories very recollectable, or if the views of life which the stories present appear to any readers very sufficing. If it is the business of the novelist to paint society and to moralize upon it, Mr. James will doubtless be thought to have less success in the latter part of the task than he has attained in the former, while in the former his success is not yet perfect. That it is considerable, none of his readers will deny; and the careful and conscientious use of the means by which he has attained it is full of promise, as it is of good example.

(Vol. xiii, 30 November 1871, p. 358.)

2. Mr. Henry James brings to an end his story, to call it so, of 'A Passionate Pilgrim'. Like everything else of his, it is done with care and pains, and with literary skill. Perhaps with a literary skill which is somewhat too obvious in some passages to suit some tastes; but to us enjoyable—and often very highly enjoyable. This of the outside merely. We cannot say that we think Mr. James has succeeded with the weightier

matters. Clearly it is not skilful in a novelist who would have us believe in the existence of his personages to draw characters as the characters of the three Searles are here drawn. The only person who gives the reader the impression of being a probable human being is the man who wheels the Bath-chair about. Searle, the passionate pilgrim, is a man with no root of will in him, who at first pursues pleasure with profuse carelessness, and then, having reduced himself to poverty or something near it, allows his later years to slip away, he drifting and dreaming and aimless, tired of himself, and taking a sort of sick satisfaction in confessing to himself that he is a failure, dying slowly frome mere inanition apparently, and having, at the time when we make his acquaintance, only this left of his old capacity for enjoyment—that he passionately feels the charm of the old, the settled, the calmly beautiful, that breathes repose into all his being. England, rural England, with nothing to remind one of that stir and stress of life which in new, busy, practical America constantly offends his sense of beauty, and tells him, too, of the failure he had made; England with her green lanes of immemorial age, with its abbeys, with its softer and more sheltering skies than ours, is what he craves. To England he has gone then, and is there resting his weary soul when the story-teller discovers him. Now in all this there seems to be nothing that does not well reflect a certain state of feeling with which the American, especially if he be of imaginative and artistic mind, is often apt to regard the old country. But Mr. Searle stands for this alone; except this there is nothing of him; he is the mere incarnation of this one human trait. The other Mr. Searle, too, taxes credulity. So, too, are the main incidents of the story improbable, and two or three of them needlessly clumsy in their improbability; as, for instance, the deaths of both the cousins; the fierceness and unreasonableness of the elder of them; the behaviour of Miss Searle.

Miss Searle, by the way, is, in this respect at least, like most of Mr. James's heroines, that the account given of her—we do not mean of her personal appearance, which is, as usual, done with skilful particularity—will not please his female readers. Why not, it would be difficult, but doubtless not impossible, to tell; as it would be difficult but not impossible to explain how it happens that Mr. James's heroines are more recollectable than his heroes. But we have not space to enter on a discussion of these matters here.

(Vol. xii, 6 April 1871, pp. 242–243.)

3. 'Guest's Confession', by Mr. Henry James Jr., is concluded in this number [November 1872] of the *Atlantic* ... 'Guest's Confession' is a study of character which no one could have written who had not habitually observed closely; who had not been on several sides open to impressions; who did not get great enjoyment from the analysis of motive and feeling. It is a sort of comment on character, or a dissection of human nature, which is pretty sure to be interesting; but a danger to the way of the analyst is that he may be tempted to make his personages

rather with a view to their cutting up interestingly and easily, than with a view to their being men and women capable of being alive, and to this danger Mr. James appears to us to have fallen a prey in this instance. We would not say, indeed, that we should be immensely pleased by a perfect success; but could we be so pleased, we think Mr. Guest's confession would not go very far towards pleasing us, acute and clever as it is.

(Vol. xiii, 31 October 1872, p. 284.)

(B) Howells's Review of *A Passionate Pilgrim*:

Mr. Henry James, Jr., has so long been a writer of magazine stories, that most readers will realize with surprise the fact that he now presents them for the first time in book form. He has already made his public. Since his earliest appearance in the *Atlantic* people have strongly liked and disliked his writing; but those who know his stories, whether they like them or not, have constantly increased in number, and it has there-fore been a winning game with him. He has not had to struggle with in-difference, that subtlest enemy of literary reputations. The strongly characteristic qualities of his work, and its instantly recognizable traits, made it at once a question for every one whether it was an offence or a pleasure. To ourselves it has been a very great pleasure, the highest pleasure that a new, decided, and earnest talent can give; and we have no complaint against this collection of stories graver than that it does not offer the author's whole range. We have read them all again and again. and they remain to us a marvel of delightful workmanship. In richness of expression and splendour of literary performance, we may compare him with the greatest, and find none greater than he; as a piece of mere diction, for example, 'The Romance of Certain Old Clothes' [in Vol. I of this edition] in this volume is unsurpassed. No writer has a style more distinctly his own than Mr. James, and few have the abundance and felicity of his vocabulary; the precision with which he fits the word to the thought is exquisite; his phrase is generous and ample. Something of an old-time stateliness distinguishes his style, and in a certain weight of manner he is like the writers of an age when literature was a far politer thing than it is now. In a reverent ideal of work, too, he is to be rated with the first. His aim is high; he respects his material; he is full of his theme; the latter-day sins of flippancy, slovenliness, and insincerity are im-measurably far from him.

In the present volume we have one class of his romances or novelettes: those in which American character is modified or interpreted by the conditions of European life, and contact with European personages. Not all the stories of this sort that Mr. James has written are included in this book, and one of the stories admitted—'The Romance of Certain Old Clothes'—belongs rather to another group, to the more strictly romantic tales, of which the author has printed several in these pages [of the *Atlantic*]; the scene is in America, and in this also it differs from its present neighbours. There is otherwise uncommon unity in the volume, though it has at first glance that desultory air which no collection of short stories can escape. The same purpose of contrast and suggestion runs through 'A Passionate Pilgrim', 'Eugene Pickering', 'The Madonna of the Future', 'Madame de Mauves', and they have all the same point of view. The American who has known Europe much can never again see his country with the single eye of his old ante-European days. For good or for evil, the light of the Old World is always on her face; and his fellow-countrymen have their shadows cast by it. This is inevitable; there may be an advantage in it, but if there is none, it is still inevitable. It may make a man think better or worse of America; it may be refinement or it may be anxiety; there may be no compensation in it for the loss of that tranquil indifference to Europe which untravelled Americans feel, or it may be the very mood in which an American may best understand his fellow-Americans. More and more, in any case, it pervades our literature, and it seems to us the mood in which Mr. James's work, more than that of any other American, is done. His attitude is not that of a mere admirer of Europe and contemner of America—our best suffers no disparagement in his stories; you perceive simply that he is most contented when he is able to confront his people with situations impossible here, and you fancy in him a mistrust of such mechanism as the cis-Atlantic world can offer the romancer.

However this may be, his book is well worth the carefullest study any of our critics can give it. The tales are all freshly and vigorously conceived, and each is very striking in a very different way, while undoubtedly 'A Passionate Pilgrim' is the best of all. In this Mr. James has seized upon what seems a very common motive in a hero with a claim to an English estate, but the character of the hero idealizes the situation: the sordid illusion of the ordinary American heir to English property becomes in him a poetic passion, and we are made to feel an instant tenderness for the gentle visionary who fancies himself to have been misborn in our hurried, eager world, but who owes to his American birth the very rapture he feels in grey England. The character is painted with the finest sense of its charm and its deficiency, and the story that grows out of it is very touching. Our readers will remember how, in the company of the supposed narrator, Clement Searle goes down from London to the lovely old country-place to which he has relinquished all notion of pretending, but which he fondly longs to see; and they will never have forgotten the tragedy of his reception and expulsion by his English cousin. The proprietary Searle stands for that intense English sense of property which the mere dream of the American has unpardonably outraged, and which in his case wreaks itself in an atrocious piece of savagery. He is imagined with an extraordinary sort of vividness which leaves the redness of his complexion a stain on the memory; and yet we believe we realize better the dullish kindness, the timid sweetness of the not-at-once handsome sister who falls in love with the poor American cousin. The atmosphere of the story, which is at first that of a novel, changes to the finer air of romance during the scenes at Lockley Park, and you gladly accede to all the romantic conditions, for the sake of otherwise unattainable effects. It is good and true that Searle should not be shocked out of his unrequited affection for England by his cousin's brutality, but should die at Oxford, as he does, in ardent loyalty to his ideal; and it is one of the fortunate inspirations of the tale to confront him there with that decayed and reprobate Englishman in whom abides a longing for the New World as hopeless as his own passion for the Old. The character of Miss Searle is drawn with peculiar sweetness and firmness; there is a strange charm in the generous devotion masked by her trepidations and proprieties, and the desired poignant touch is given when at the end she comes only in time to stand by Searle's death-bed. Throughout the story there are great breadths of deliciously sympathetic description. At Oxford the author lights his page with all the rich and mellow picturesqueness of the ancient university town, but we do not know that he is happier there than in his sketches of Lockley Park and Hampton Court, or his study of the old London inn. Everywhere he conveys to you the rapture of his own seeing....

Mr. James does not often suffer his sense of the ludicrous to relax the sometimes over-serious industry of his analysis, and when he has once done so, he seems to repent it. Yet we are sure that the poetic value of 'A Passionate Pilgrim' is enhanced by the unwonted interfusion of humour, albeit the humour is apt to be a little too scornful. The tale is in high degree imaginative, and its fascination grows upon you in the reading and the retrospect, exquisitely contenting you with it as a new, fine, and beautiful invention.

In imaginative strength it surpasses the other principal story of the book. In 'Madame de Mauves' the spring of the whole action is the idea of an American girl who will have none but a French nobleman for her husband. It is not a vulgar adoration of rank in her, but a young girl's belief that ancient lineage, circumstances of the highest civilization, and opportunities of the greatest refinement, must result in the noblest type of character. Grant the premises, and the effect of her emergence into the cruel daylight of facts is unquestionably tremendous: M. le Baron de Mauves is frankly unfaithful to his American wife, and, finding her too dismal in her despair, advises her to take a lover. A difficulty with so French a situation is that only a French writer can carry due conviction of it to the reader. M. de Mauves, indeed, justifies himself to the reader's sense of likelihood with great consistency, and he is an extremely suggestive conjecture....

The baron's sister, in her candid promotion of an intrigue between Madame de Mauves and Longmore, we cannot quite account for even by the fact that she hated them both. But Madame de Mauves is the strength of the story, and if Mr. James has not always painted the kind of women that women like to meet in fiction, he has richly atoned in her lovely nature for all default. She is the finally successful expression of an ideal of woman which has always been a homage, perhaps not to all kinds of women, but certainly to the sex. We are thinking of the heroine of 'Poor

Richard', of Miss Guest in 'Guest's Confession', of Gabrielle de Bergerac
in the story of that name, and other gravely sweet girls of this author's
imagining. Madame de Mauves is of the same race, and she is the finest
—as truly American as she is womanly; and in a peculiar fragrance of
character, in her purity, her courage, her inflexible high-mindedness,
wholly of our civilization and almost of our climate, so different are her
virtues from the virtues of the women of any other nation.

'The Madonna of the Future' is almost as perfect a piece of work,
in its way, as 'A Passionate Pilgrim'. It is a more romantic conception than
'Madame de Mauves', and yet more real. Like 'A Passionate Pilgrim', it
distinguishes itself among Mr. James's stories as something that not only
arrests the curiosity, stirs the fancy, and interests the artistic sense, but
deeply touches the heart. It is more than usually relieved, too, by the
author's humorous recognition of the pathetic absurdity of poor Theobald, and there is something unusually good in the patience with which
the handsome, common-minded Italian woman of his twenty years' adoration is set before us. Our pity that his life should have slipped away from
him in devout study of this vulgar beauty, and that she should grow old
and he should die before he has made a line to celebrate her perfection or
seize his ideal, is vastly heightened by the author's rigid justice to her;
she is not caricatured by a light or a shadow, and her dim sense of Theobald's goodness and purity is even flattered into prominence. In all essen-
tials one has from this story ... the conception is fine, and the expression
nowhere falls below it—if we except one point that seems to us rather
essential, in a thing so carefully tempered and closely wrought. The reiteration of the Italian figure-maker's philosophy, 'Cats and monkeys,
monkeys and cats; all human life is there', is apparently of but wandering purport, and to end the pensive strain of the romance with it is to
strike a jarring note that leaves the reader's mind out of tune. Sometimes even the ladies and gentlemen of Mr. James's stories are allowed a
certain excess or violence in which the end to be achieved is not distinctly
discernible, or the effect so reluctantly responds to the intention as to
leave merely the sense of the excess.

'Eugene Pickering' is, like 'Madame de Mauves', one of those realistic
subjects which we find less real than the author's romantic inspirations.
There is no fault with the treatment; that is thoroughly admirable, full
of spirit, wit, and strength; but there is a fancifulness in the outlines of
Pickering's history and the fact of his strange betrothal which seems to
belong to an old-fashioned stage-play method of fiction rather than to
such a modern affair as that between the unsophisticated American and
Madame Blumenthal; it did not need that machinery to produce that
effect, thanks to the common conditions of ours that often enough keep
young men as guileless as Pickering, and as fit for sacrifice at such shrines
as hers. However, something must always be granted to the story-teller by
way of premises; if we exacted from Mr. James only that he should make
his premises fascinating, we should have nothing to ask here. His start,
in fact, is always superb; he possesses himself of your interest at once,

APPENDIX III

and he never relinquishes it till the end; though there he may sometimes leave your curiosity not quite satisfied on points such as a story-
teller assumes to make clear. What, for example, were exactly the tortuous
workings of Madame Blumenthal's mind in her self-contradictory behaviour towards Pickering? These things must be at least unmistakably
suggested.

Since Hawthorne's Donatello, any attempt to touch what seems to be
the remaining paganism in Italian character must accuse itself a little,
but 'The Last of the Valerii' is a study of this sort that need really have
nothing on its conscience. It is an eminently poetic conceit, though it ap-
peals to a lighter sort of emotions than any other story in Mr. James's
book; it is an airy fabric woven from those bewitching glimpses of the
impossible which life in Italy affords, and which those who have enjoyed
them are perfectly right to overvalue. It has just the right tint of ideal
trouble in it which no living writer could have imparted more skilfully
than it is here done. If the story is of slighter material than the others, the
subtlety of its texture gives it a surpassing charm, and makes it worthy
to be named along with the only other purely romantic tale in the book.
[A lengthy discourse on 'The Romance of Certain Old Clothes' follows;
Howells finds the tale particularly weak in its 'patronizing' treatment of
the characters, but goes on to add:]

But this is a very little matter, and none of our discontents with Mr.
James bear any comparison to the pleasure we have had in here renewing our acquaintance with stories as distinctly characteristic as anything in
literature. It is indeed a marvellous first book in which the author can invite his critic to the same sort of reflection that criticism bestows upon
the claims of great reputations; but one cannot dismiss this volume with
less and not slight it. Like it or not, you must own that here is something
positive, original, individual, the result of long and studious effort in a
well-considered line, and mounting in its own way to great achievement.
We have a reproachful sense of leaving the immense suggestiveness of the
book scarcely touched, and we must ask the reader to supply our default
from the stories themselves. He may be assured that nothing more novel
in our literature has yet fallen his way; and we are certain that he will
not close the book without a lively sense of its force. We can promise him,
also, his own perplexities about it, among which may be a whimsical
doubt whether Mr. James has not too habitually addressed himself less to
men and women in their mere humanity, than to a certain kind of
cultivated people, who, well as they are in some ways, and indispensable
as their appreciation is, are often a little narrow in their sympathies and
poverty-stricken in the simple emotions; who are so, or try to be so, which
is quite as bad, or worse.

(*The Atlantic*, vol. xxxv, April 1875, pp. 490–495.)